D1256491

A
Commentary
on
Henrik Ibsen's Peer Gynt

A Commentary, critical and explanatory on the Norwegian text of

Henrik Ibsen's Peer Gynt

its language, literary associations and folklore

by H. LOGEMAN, Ph. D., Hon. L. L. D. (Glasg.),
PROFESSOR IN THE BELGIAN STATE UNIVERSITY OF GHENT.

GREENWOOD PRESS, PUBLISHERS
WESTPORT, CONNECTICUT

Originally published in 1917
by Martinus Nijhoff

Reprinted from a copy in the collections
of the Brooklyn Public Library

First Greenwood Reprinting 1970

SBN 8371-3027-1

TO BE OBSERVED.

1. The line-numbering in the following commentary is that of an edition at one time contemplated (cf. Textual Criticism, §§ 9 and 143) but now abandoned. They are kept here as an easy means of reference from one part of the commentary to another; it should be remembered that the play is not devided into scenes except in some translations. And as each page of this commentary will contain cross-references to nearly all the various editions, they will serve at the same time as a sort of index to these editions.

2. The text of Peer Gynt I quote here is that of the first edition, unless otherwise stated.

3. The translation given at the head of each note, although not always approved of in all details, is that by Messrs. Archer, unless otherwise indicated.

4. An index and a full list of abbreviations will be found at the end of the work.

5. The references at the foot of the pages of the commentary to the various editions quoted, are those to the text of the f i r s t note beginning on the page in question.

6. (Add.) refers to the Addenda at the end of the work.

* * *

The compiler of the present work will feel much obliged to Ibsen-students for calling his attention to any note or paper on the matter he may have overlooked and to reviewers of this work and other writers on the subject for a copy of their criticism.

CONTENTS.

Prefatory and Introductory .... p. VII
To be observed XVI
A Commentary on Henrik Ibsen's Peer Gynt I
Textual Criticism on Henrik Ibsen's Peer Gynt
    Preface 367
    Textual Criticism 373
Addenda and Corrigenda 465
Abbreviations and Bibliography 469
Index 477

PREFATORY AND INTRODUCTORY.

When a man like Georg Brandes, than whom few have better qualifications to understand Ibsen, writes that Peer Gynt is "difficult to understand i n i t s l a t e r p a r t s", the foreign student of the play is likely to read this with a sigh of relief. At the same time many a reader will have been inclined so far as he himself is concerned, to make the sentiment his, o m i t t i n g t h e f o u r l a s t w o r d s. For, if there is any play of the Master's that requires for its understanding a special knowledge of the milieu and the circumstances that gave rise to it, it is this child of the poet's most exuberant fancy, written at one of the rare periods of his life and practically the first when everything smiled upon him, when, owing to the success of "Brand", some dissonants notwithstanding (n. to l. 3179) he must have felt like the literary lion of the day, when his way seemed made and his life's dream to become a great poet was in a fair way to be realised. The allusions to contemporary events and currents, literary and ethic, certainly not less and perhaps much more frequent than even in Brand, the apparently inextricable interweaving of the play with the folklore of Norway, bewilder the student on first and no doubt even later readings and we do not wonder that, when the first translation of the drama was announced to Ibsen, he himself expressed a mild doubt as to whether it would be possible to bring that undertaking to the desired end. It was in the early part of 1880 that Ludvig Passarge had told the poet of his plan and in reply Ibsen (*Breve*, II, 79) wrote of his great surprise "when finding that you consider this work fit to be translated and published in German". He has his doubts whether this will in the end prove feasible. For, "among all my books, it is Peer Gynt that I look upon as least likely to be understood (der mindst egner sig) outside Scandinavia". For in order to understand it, the reader must possss, Ibsen adds: "a very intimate knowledge of Norwegian nature and the life of the Norwegian people (et meget nøjagtigt kendskab til den norske natur og det norske folkeliv), the student must be familiar with Norwegian literature and Norwegian mentality (vor folkelige tænkemåde) .. and "no doubt", you, Mr. Passarge, .. possess all this, but .. do your readers? And when a couple of years after this letter, he wrote once more to Passarge, who appears to have asked the poet to send him an explanation of all such passages as were likely to present difficulties to the foreign student of the play — surely, no little order! — Ibsen answers that this he cannot undertake: much as he should like it, he does not see his way to give an explanation of the many allusions that might require comment for German readers, — Passarge as a German must know better than he as a Norwegian what the German looks upon as a difficulty. Hence it is no use asking Prof. Dietrichson either, or any Norwegian for that matter; when in Norway, Passarge will be able to get all the information he wants. So Ibsen vouchsafes two explanations (to the adj. våset and the subst. pusselanker ; cf. notes to l.l. 4488 and 4016) and that is all!

Any one who has even tried to penetrate into the dramatic poem at all, will have found how very clearly Ibsen has here foreseen the difficulties that beset the unfortunate student that, without any special knowledge of all this and without a big library, tries to master its intricacies. There is the Norwegian folklore then in the first place, with which the play, more especially the earlier part of it, is soaked through if the expression may pass. And apart from the actual allusions to men and things that the play is full of, there is the much more subtle, much more elusive substratum of Ibsen's own ideas, conceptions, ideals, his longings and his disappointment that must be clear to the student in order to unable him to understand the play in all its bearings. "It is of no little moment to him that wishes to understand Ibsen and especially his relation to Norway, to try and get to the bottom of all his associations with Norwegian spiritual life", Eitrem has written (Maal og Minne,

1910 p. 37). And this is not only of s o m e moment, but absolutely necessary. On the whole, Ibsen shared with his brethern-authors an inclination towards a certain bewildering, mystic chiaroscuro and he seems even at times to have felt a mischievous sort of pleasure in leaving his utterances as obscure as they were. J. Paulsen in his Samliv med Ibsen (p. 74) tells us how Ibsen refused to explain a poem as he was asked to do. "A poem that is worth anything explains itself!" And, quoting Goethe, Ibsen is said to have added that "no doubt some day or other a commentator will come and tell me what I meant by it." And the cases where he tries to mystify his commentators or at least unintentionally does so, are legion. Think of his Strange Passenger being "only a caprice" and remember Eitrem's paper in the Samtiden of 1906 (n. to 1. 2995) where quite a number of what Eitrem looks upon as Ibsen's *conscious* mystifications of his public will be found discussed. And yet that same Ibsen at one time earnestly meditated a sort of running commentary on the "inner and outer history of his plays". "What if I were to write a little book", he writes in the May of that same year to Hegel the publisher, "on the outer and inner conditions under which my literary products saw the light" (om de ydre og indre forhold, hvorunder hvert enkelt af samtlige mine literære arbejder er blevet til), in which he would give a plain account of the genesis of his work, (at) fortælle jævnt om de omstændigheder og vilkar, hvorunder jeg har digtet" and what follows bears out in a remarkable way what was observed just now about his somewhat unfortunate propensities to the 'oscuro'. For not only does he add that he will not venture to give an i n t e r p r e t a t i o n of his works (på nogen fortolkning af mine bøger vil jeg naturligvis ikke indlade mig) because it is better that public and critics should be allowed to r i o t about according to their own sweet pleasure in this respect (får lov til at tumle sig efter eget behag på det felt) but he winds up openly by saying that he "wishes to leave open a wide range for all sort of guesses". (Breve II, 80, 81). Very much in the same way, Goethe wrote to Schiller that he was trying to re-write some tragical prose-scenes of his Faust in verse "da denn die Idee wie durch einen Flor erscheint, die unmittelbare Wirkung des.... Stoffes aber gedämpft wird" (Witkowski, Goethes Faust, II, p. 278). We can only regret that Ibsen admitted Hegel's scruples (ib. p. 84: betænkeligheder) and gave up the plan, for precisely this account of the "indre forhold" would have been of the utmost interest to the student, especially the foreign student who, not being to the manner born, must laboriously gather such knowledge in bits and scraps as his more fortunate Norwegian colleague has imbibed so to speak with the mother milk,—a consideration that holds of course of much more than of these "indre forhold" This explains not only satisfactorily why on the whole a commentary is necessary, but we have here reached the very point that accounts for the apparent foolhardiness of the present writer, a foreign student too, taking upon himself to write such a running commentary on this most Norwegian of Norwegian works. When, some little time after the idea of undertaking this work had taken a more definite shape in my mind, I heard that two accomplished Norwegian scholars each of them independently of the other, had been collecting materials for a commentary of this play, I must confess, apart from this impression of my extreme boldness in tackling the work at all, to a feeling of considerable disappointment at the idea that my labours might thus prove in vain. But reason soon asserted itself and gave me the hope that there might be room for my work by the side of the others , considering that the point of view, the starting point must needs be totally different in their case and mine. The present work, containing as it inevitably does, very little that your average Norwegian is not thoroughly conversant or at least acquainted with, may for all that supply the almost proverbial want for those students to whom it is in the first place if not exclusively designed, viz. the non-Scandinavian ones. And such a commentary I make bold to say, only a non-Scandinavian can write. This must have been at the bottom of Ibsen's mind when he wrote to Passarge (Breve II, 80) that no Norwegian could help him with any information which he, Passarge himself, had not expressly asked for, — indeed: no one but a foreigner can appreciate which difficulties your non-Scandinavian student meets with and will want explained. And as to the broader issues, the part of the commentary that will necessarily be touched on by my successors too, I can only say that my work may prove not wholly in vain for them either, when remembering that generally speaking, nothing is so useful as the making of a mistake, provided the master be there to point them out and correct them. It is therefore my earnest wish that Ibsenians will not have to wait too long for the works in question, which however, so far as I know, have not yet advanced beyond the stage of conception.

This commentary then is destined to incite and, it is hoped, enable foreign lovers of the drama to become students of it without the aid of a voluminous library which the fewest may be supposed to have at their disposal. The author does not wish to conceal from his readers as little as he does from himself, the grave defects his work must necessarily suffer from. For entirely apart from the question of his competency for the work, a consideration which it is not for him to enter upon, he should be allowed to explain the scrappiness of the material by the fact that no systematic study has been possible under the circumstances. A labour of love in the midst of the work of desolation in a world gone mad, composed under the frequent booming of the distant guns, it was entirely written under the enforced leisure from professorial work by the enervating circumstances of the hour, when for the most part correspondence was, when not absolutely impossible, at least extremely difficult, when books could only be procured very exceptionally, when reviews and periodicals were only accessible during a stay in my happily not very distant fatherland, and when the writer was dependent on the haphazard aid that devoted friends in Scandinavia continued, whenever possible, to encourage and cheer him up with. And when at last the work had to be written out for the press and corrected, the author was exiled from his adopted fatherland by the authority of the Occupant and thus cut off from his library and thereby from the means of verifying quotations and re-adjusting others. And it should in this connection be added that if the work will prove useful at all and not too ful of gaps, this is owing to a very great extent to these very collaborators who when helping in my need proved

friends indeed. I would mention in the first place Hr. Overlærer
Stavnem of Stavanger and Docent Brynildsen at Horten for
their never failing help and courtesy when applied to for information. This holds good to a much greater extent even of
Hr. Bibliotekar Anders Krogvig whose valuable help has had
to be acknowledged in many notes. More still perhaps I owe
to Hr. Cand. mag. C. L. Christensen of Copenhagen and certainly to my old and tried friend Dr. August Western of Fredrik-
stad who both of them have read through practically the whole
of the work and who as many a note will testify have enriched
the book with much useful information; that by Dr. Western
will prove especially copious, interesting and suggestive. It
should however be distinctly understood that no one but the
author is responsible for the text as it stands although he may
perhaps in justice to himself be allowed to add that the work
was given its final shape and that the proof-reading had to
be done under circumstances of extreme mental fatigue which
it is hoped will cause the Benevolus Lector to excuse not only
some of these little slips that he is usually asked to correct
himself but also more in general, to some extent at least, the
deficiency in form the work is likely to exhibit.

Although Ibsen has continually been the object of literary
investigation, not only in his own country, but also, perhaps
we should say: especially, at the hands of foreigners, the present writer's attempt would seem, curiously enough, to be the
first on any larger scale to study a play also from the non-liter-
ary point of view; Prof. Olsen's American ed. of Brand is the
nearest approach to it, although it is here left far behind in extent. The consequence of all this is the extreme dispropor-
tion in the notes, some running to a truly uncharitable length.
For, Norwegian Philology being little studied outside the Scandinavian countries except at some American Universities, it
follows that even if circumstances had allowed me to make use
of German and other periodicals, for the publication of some
of the larger notes, I should have found but little space in them
at my disposal. Hence an appalling number of notes had to
be inflicted on the student, that in the corresponding case of a
work on English, French or German philology would have been

thrashed out in some Zeitschrift, a Modern Language Review or similar periodicals. Moreover many notes would have been absolutely uncalled for (such as the one on *Bedemandsstil;* n. to l. 4491) if Norwegian lexicology had advanced beyond a petition to the Storting (Maal og Minne, 1915, p. 221) and could boast of a Littré, Grimm, a New Engl. Dict. or an Ordbok för Svenska Språket, — for Dahlerup has not got further than one specimen part and a paper in the Zeitschrift für Deutsche Wortforschung.

Whilst it was not always possible, nor even advisable, to hold back my own views of controversial points, it has never been my aim at all cost to decide them. On the contrary, on the plan of a Variorum edition, quotations are given from sometimes *inter se* contradictory views. If the reader will only hold himself prepared for such conflicting statements, the plan may be acceptable and even work well, he should look upon them only in the light of pabulum reflectionis and — "try his own conclusions." And seeing that of course N o r w e g i-a n books and especially papers in the various Scandinavian periodicals will be less accessible to foreign readers than those that have appeared outside Scandinavia, the former have been extracted to a larger extent than the latter.

The commentary is one on the N o r w e g i a n text of the play in the first place only; it is meant to do duty also for the student of the realia and to be helpful for the study of any text. Hence a translation had to be added at the head of each note and necessarily one in the language in which the commentary is written. The one chosen is that of the Archers, not only because it was the first in the field but because its aim is literalness of reproduction and consequently invited less criticism than the freer one of Mr. Ellis Roberts. Absence of criticism should however not be thought to imply approval of it in every detail.

With very few exceptions words and expressions have only been commented on when they or their application could not be found in the dictionaries, — Brynildsen's splendid second edition was here naturally the test.

There is one chapter that the present writer has purposely abstained from entering upon and that is the domain of rhythm. The student desirous of knowing more about it should look up the Archers' Introduction and a passage in that to the Efterl. Skr. (I. p. LV). Ibsen when he wrote the drama was as in the case of Brand "i en rim-og ritmerus (Eitrem, Samtiden, 1908 p. 577); yet — one might like to say: hence — as the student will have remarked, some lines do not scan (as Eitrem has truly remarked of Brand too) but in order to decide such questions the ear of one to the manner born is an absolute necessity and hence the foreign critic's patent duty here is abstention.

Some readers, it is to be feared, will think that a full commentary such as this, cannot but make the student overlook the beauties of the wood for the very number of trees he is made to study. The criticism would no doubt be damning if he should fall into the error of b e g i n n i n g with a study of the trees. The Archers give the readers of their translation the excellent bit of advice "to skip the introduction, to ignore the footnotes and heedless of the ethical and political intentions (of the poem), to take it as it comes, simply as a dramatic romance or phantasmagoria of purely human humour and pathos." Then when the pure poetry in it has been enjoyed in a general way, perhaps somewhat vaguely, "at a second reading, with the aid of such side-lights as we can afford him, he will probably find many of the obscurities vanish". And this is exactly the attitude I hope those will take up that should wish to use this book. If they would kindly not set to a minute study of my commentary until the beauties of the play have penetrated them as the spring atmosphere of his new-born happiness had dizzied the author of Peer Gynt, if they will postpone the details until a later reading of the text has excited enough of their interest to allow them to wade through some facts and some no doubt at first sight deterrent disquisitions, then it is the present writer's earnest belief, as it is his hope, that when thus "sent to (his) account.... with all (his) imperfections on his head", he will not meet with Hamlet's comment on this, but that his readers even if of this work with its many faults, they cannot say that they "love it still", — that they may yet find it contribute to some extent to a better understanding and a greater appreciation of Ibsen's "Central masterpiece".

„BERKENOORD", NIJMEGEN, April 1917.

FØRSTE HANDLING. ACT FIRST.

De handlende. Characters.

The editors of E. S. tell us (p. XXXI) how in many cases they have been able to prove that Ibsen made up for himself a complete list of dramatis personae before he had begun to write down any part of the drama itself. Among the cases quoted we do not find that of Peer Gynt and it is indeed not certain that it is in point. The list of the "Handlende" in R. differs considerably from that in U. The latter (E. S. II, p. 79) has Kurgjæster fra forskjellige Lande, which have either disappeared or been replaced by the Snyltegjæster, Master Cotton etc. The Brylupsgjæster and Flere Brylupsjæster of U. figure in R. as Bryllupsgjæster only. The Udenlandske Sjøfolk of U. have entirely disappeared. Changes of minor importance in the names themselves are those of Frasenfeldt into Begriffenfeldt (cf. n. to l. 3045) of Tuhu into Huhu, En levende Fellah into En fellah med en Kongemumie etc. But the most momentous difference is the absence on the list in U. of some of the most important characters, an investigatior of which additions (infra l. 4429) will cast a curious light on the growth of the play in the poet's mind. For all this, the very careful handwriting in which the list of the Handlende is written in U., as well as the greater part of the first act, at any rate of the first scene, makes it certain that we have not got a first draft here.

For the notes on the various items of this list, compare besides the §§ of T. C. quoted ib. § 10, the notes lower down in this commentary on the lines where they occur for the first time.

1, —; 3, 4;. F, 265; M, 165; 14, 4; J, 171; 16, 4.

57.   Peer, du lyver! Peer, you're lying!

The first words spoken give us the l e i t m o t i v of the whole, like the first scene of Macbeth which in the same way strikes the key-note of the play. Although Ibsen has certainly known this drama (cf. n. to l. 2444) and might consequently be supposed to be indebted to Shakespeare here too, it is of course not necessary to think of Shakespearean influence in this case.

As to the "lies" he is telling, in Makreldorg (H. Ev, p. 286), Ibsen had read of a certain story of three witches that it was "of that sort which are called skipper–lies now-adays, but in old days people believed in them as in the Lord's Prayer, "—av det slaget som kaldes skipperløgner nu til dags, men i gamle dager trodde de paa det som paa fadervor" (cf. his Stormsvalen, Digte, F, IV, 280, where he uses the same word) and in En Sommernat paa Krok-skogen he may have come across the following passage (ib. p. 214:) the deuce take me if I understand how you can sit here and say that you have seen such a thing yourself,-you are s'posed to be a clever fellow, but 'deil take me if you don't run ahead quicker nor that black mare of mine lies .. je kan for faen itte skjønne paa d e t, at du kan sitta her aa seia, atte du har sett slikt sjøl, — du ska' jo væra en vettu' mann, men jagu traaver du fortere enn den svarte mærra mi ljuger", and still more appositely, Pær Fugleskjæillé introduces the story of Peer Gynt in Asbjørnsen's collection (H. Ev. p. 154) by saying that it is "a story which we don't believe in either". Now, all this is very characteristic of Peer. When in the fifth act he offers for sale his own Grane in what is perhaps the most intensely tragic scene of the play (l. 3850), Peer says of himself, (with a possible but vague reminiscence of the words quoted above) that Grane "was as quick at flying, as Peer Gynt was at lying". His mother too knows (l. 68) that he is always ready with his "hunter's lies" — mener du at faa mig bildt ind de værste Skytterløgne!—

1, 1; 3, 5; F, 267; M, 167; 14, 5; J, 173; 16, 5.

never with any d e e d; so much so that when he actually d o e s do something, be it only to carry off a girl,
her astonishment knows no bounds: What, h e could do
such a thing,..he who went always with romances and
lies .. han, som stødt foer med Løgn og Digt (782)—this
is simply incomprehensible! His immense capacity for
lies is intimately akin to his continual dreaming and to
his fancy or rather his phantasy, i. e. precisely that
quality in your average Norwegian that Ibsen wished to
chastise in Peer Gynt; cf. a paper by Collin, Samtiden,
1913, p. 595, 602. .. And again: fantasy is very much
the same as the poetic faculty itself. Peer goes even so far
as to upbraid himself again and again with this fantasy
of his: Over the Gendin-edge flying. Stuff and accursed
lies!.... sporting with crazy girls;.. lies and accursed
stuff (Flugt over Gjendin-Eggen. Digt og forbandet Løgn
.... turet med galne Jenter;.. Løgn og forbandet
Digt! (l. 900 seq.) and cf. the beginning of the third act.
And as to his dreams, as he says in the fourth act: Ev'n
as a boy, in visions sunny, on clouds far o'er the sea I
flew,.. "Som Gut jeg har i Drømme rullet, vidt over Havet paa en Sky." (l. 2075) and when Peer, holding forth
in the same scene to his parasite friends on losing one's
self (l. 2086) says: Thus it says — or something like it,
and this is no "Digt" (Saa staar der,—eller noget Sligt;
og dette Ord er intet Digt), it is tempting to interpret
this word as: this is no l i e, just as later on, the bailiff
calls Peer Gynt en vederstyggelig Digter (l. 3867) i. e. a.
fantastic, visionary dreamer. Compare also Ibsen's: det
var kun et Digt, Det var kun en flygtig, poetisk Drøm,
En bristende Boble paa Livets Strøm. (Norma, E. S., I.
81) An amusing specimen of such lying-stories may be
found in Ivar Kleiven's Segner fraa Vaagaa, 1894, p. 82:
Kaas'n å 'n Endre Aaseng (not reprinted in the second
ed. "I gamle daagaa").

1, 1; 3, 5; F, 267; M. 167; 14, 5; J. 173; 16, 5.

59.   Det er sandt — hvert evigt Ord!
                     It is true — every blessed word.

Professor Storm writes (S. M p. 9): "this should have
been: hvert evige Ord; but this does not fit in quite so
well in the metre; I have therefore allowed Ibsen's word
to stand as a poetic licence." "Therefore" is interesting
as it tells the sorry tale of the unwarrantable changes the
Editor has introduced but too many of into this first
Norwegian reprint; cf. T. C. § 103. In this particular
case it means that if the metre had not fortunately indeed held Prof. Storm's hand back, the poetic licence —
if any; see below — would have been levelled away.

Moreover the poetic licence would seem to be far from
certain. For, as Dr. Western writes: "Hvert evigt ord is
grammatically correct; cp. hvert ubesindigt ord, hvert
godt menneske, hvert frit folk etc. After hver the adj. is
put in the strong form. But we generally say hver evige
dag, hvert evige ord, which I take to be formed in analogy
with hver tredje dag, etc. From Lie, Western quotes hver
evig Mand (Familje Paa Gilje, IX) by the side of: hver
evige Dag (Naar Sol gaar ned, II) and from Ibsen's Folkefiende, II: hver evig eneste Dag.

62.   maanedsvis i travle Aannen.
                     for months together in the busy season.

For the omission of the article before the substantive
whilst the latter retains the postpositive one, compare
Western, Skriv Norsk p. 9: midt i travleste onnen, midt
paa lyse dagen.

66.   med aabne Øjne. With round and innocent eyes.

This is Ellis Roberts' translation, who seems to think
that the open eyes are Peer's. But are they not rather
Aase's, who evidently thinks she is quite "wide awake"?
This would appear from the stage-direction later on
(l. 168) where she looks at him "with open mouth and
big eyes" (in U. only: with big eyes) just before she sees
through his lies, and even more clearly from the fact that

Ibsen had first spoken of h e r open eyes: Opp i h e n d e s aabne Øjne kommer du med Skytter Løgne U, I. 3, v°. But for these reasons however, the words i n t h e m - s e l v e s might very well mean: mener du at lyve mig fuldt uten at blunke?

69. Naa, hvor traf du saa den Bukken?

Well, where did you find the buck, then?

The story bears such a very great verisimilitude that this very reindeer's head is supposed to be sold at the auction in Act V (cf. n. to l.l. 57 and 3835).

73. Skaresneen. Snow-crust.

This typically Norwegian word does not mean, as Mr. Ellis Roberts translates: in the mess of the slush, which suggests dirty melting snow, but quite on the contrary: recent hard frozen snow.

75. Pusten.

Observe this remarkable word of Ibsen's: "p u s t e n har han her dannet for at gengi stakåndethed efter et anstrængende løb." (C. L. Christensen).

80. Gjemt i Røsen opp jeg glytted;

Hidden in a cairn I peeped forth.

Røsen is a specifically Norwegian word: glytted the specifically Norwegian form for the more usual gløttede. cf. S. M. p. 26 and S. I. S. p. 190.

83. Nej, bevares vel! No, of course not!

The exact shade of meaning of the Scandinavian bevares (= [gud] bevare os) is very difficult to render once for all, if not impossible. Here it is ironically meant, Aase is still incredulous, and whereas Mr. Ellis Roberts' Oh, I know, much, much larger, hardly hits it quite off, the Archers' No of course not, if pronounced with the proper intonation, will do very well. See the n. to l. 3172.

89. bagom Skolten, behind the head.

Skolten is specifically Norwegian; cf. S. I. S. p. 191 and Petter Dass "Det gik i hans Skolt" (Nordahl Rolfsen, No. Digtere, p. 10).

90.   den Styggen. The brute.

The substantivation of the adjective as well as the use of the article are specifically Norwegian; cf. the note to l. 99 and Poestion, No. Gr.³, § 87, 4, and id. Dan. Gr. § 76; compare infra n. to l. 3819.

93.   Kniv og Slire. Knife and sheath.

Slire is an obsolete word although it fits in well into "Peer's eventyrlige fortællestil". — Ibsen, especially in his earlier works, was very fond of using two words to render the same meaning, e. g. Skam og Skændsel (Chr.)

99.   Har du set den Gjendin-Eggen nogen Gang?

Have you ever chanced to see the Gendin-Edge?

This Gjendin is a mountain-edge between lake Byg-din and lake Gjendin in Jotunheimen, but the description is not very exact; see Jæger, 1888 p. 206. I have no means of determining whether Ibsen himself had seen it before 1867, but it is of course not impossible that he should have put the incorrect description into Peer's mouth on purpose, thus giving a hint as to the latter's unrelia-bleness (about which see the n. to ll. 2208, 2371, 2586).

A much-esteemed correspondent suggests that pos-sibly den Gjendineggen does not here present a case of "dobbelt bestemmelse" (both post-and prepositive arti-cle) because such expressions as den gutten etc. "utpeker jo en enkelt av flere, men nu findes der bare én Gjendin-egg, saa det er unødvendig at utpeke den særskilt! Desu-ten er jo Gjendin-eggen et egennavn, som er bestemt nok i sig selv. — Nu er det vistnok saa at dette slags egennavn kan faa dobbelt bestemmelse naar de nævnes som almin-delig bekjendte. Saaledes.... om der er tale om en lang, støvet vei, kan det hete: Ja, den x-veien er frygtelig trættende". Men da maa vedkommende sted være vel kjendt netop for den nævnte egenskap." He suggests that Ibsen may have meant to use Gjendin-eggen as a sort of apposition to den, .. Har du set den, Gjendin-eggen nogen Gang".... Denne opfatning stemmer ogsaa

---

1, 3; 3, 7; F, 269; M, 168; 14, 6; J, 174; 16, 7.

bedre med verset: set den [set: n] danner da et fuldkomment rim med tretten, men opfattes den som artikkel (resp. paapekende pronomen), maa vi læse: "Har du set— den Gjendin-eggen, og der blir intet rim.

The remarks are so interesting in themselves that I do not feel justified in withholding them from my readers, although I do not share my correspondent's views. In view of the n. to l. 218, the objection from the point of view of the rhyme will hardly carry weight, and if Ibsen had meant it thus, a comma would certainly have been added,—it is neither in R., nor in U. Moreover, as Gjendin eggen has been mentioned t w i c e before, without any qualification, all the required conditions are there to justify the dobbelt bestemmelse: Did you ever see that edge, the one I spoke of, before?

102. seqq. Ljaa, Bræer, Skred, Lider, rakt, Urder, lukt, svarte, are all specifically Norwegian words; cf. S. I. S. p.p. 190, 191.

106.   lukt i Vandene, straight into the waters.

See the n. to l. 102 and Folkefienden: lukt ind i fordærvelsen, M, IV, 204). Andersen, Thomsen, Festskr. gives an account of lukt differing from that found in the dictionaries. He looks upon it as "an adverbial form of Lowgerman *lucht* = air, and hence it would originally be properly used only in such cases as lukt i vejret. Its transfer into such a combination as the above would then be owing to the influence of lukke = to close.

The Vandene are the very Gjendin and Bygdin lakes already mentioned. Hence some would prefer: straight into the lakes.

107. tretten..hundred alen, divided over two lines, cf. n. to l. 218.

111, 113. fole rhyming on sole sounds incorrect to the modern Norwegian ear [fåle]: [sole] but the rhyme is perfect in Danish (Christensen) and Ibsen may well be supposed to have had this in his ear.

1, 4; 3, 8; F. 269; M, 168; 14, 7; J, 174; 16, 7.

113, 118.   fram, Isflak
are Norwegian, un-Danish; cf. S. I. S. p. p. 190, 191.
Fram was introduced by Ibsen first when copying
out U. where we read: Bølger brød sig gult. It may be
especially interesting as pointing to Wergeland's Maalstræv (Eitrem, M. og M. 1910, p. 39). Frithjof Nansen
called his famous ship: Fram, .. not Frem.

115.   i det vide svimle Slug. ın the wide and dizzy void.
This wide void over which Peer jumps on his reindeer,
reminds us vaguely of the imagery that Ibsen had already made use of in his Kjærlighedens Komedie (first
act, F, II, p. 142) where in reply to Lind's high-falutin':
jeg kender mig saa stærk: lå der et slug for min fod —
hvor gabende. ... jeg over sprang, Falk observes coolly:
Det sige vil i simpelt prosasprog, Din kjærlighed har
gjort dig til et rensdyr.

120.   Hvirvlens Vætter. Sprites of dizziness.
Ibsen himself has explained the expression hvirvlens
vætter as equivalent to Svimmelhedens ånder,...giddy
sprites (that danced around) as Mr. Ellis Roberts translates it. Dr. August Western writes: I should translate
"whirling sprites" (instead of the Archers' sprites of
dizziness) and he adds: "Svimmelhedens aander" sounds
very tame; they produce giddiness by dancing or whirling round you, but this is a secondary effect, not their
intention—," so Dr. Western's translation comes close to
that of Mr. Ellis Roberts — and "they may of course be
compared to the dancing elves, but are of a much wilder
nature." In U., Ibsen had written Svimlens Hvirvel.
On the natural phenomena underlying this imagery
(taakernes hvirvel) and their interpretation, cf. Just
Bing, Elverskud og Elverhöi in M. og M., 1913, p.p. 27
and 31.

124.   paa en raadløs braabratt Plett.
                    at a desperate, breakneck spot.
The use of raadløs here: a spot that makes the wander-

er desperate, should be compared to maalløs skrækk, l. 186, n.

130.   Himmelspring. leapt sky-high.

A correspondent thinks this word = a very great leap, should be commented upon; from himmelhøi, himmel seems to have been deduced in an intensifying sense. "Thus we have himmelhund, generally used as a word of contempt" (to which another appends a query, adding: very seldom so used! cf. the translation of Arnold Bennett's The Card as "En Himmelhund") and "han er himlende gal: completely mad".

151.   Ja, der laa vi nu og plasked., *etc.*
There we lay, floating, plashing.

The whole of this passage is very characteristic of the way Ibsen makes Peer's fancy lead astray not only mother Aase but himself too. And when he is ready with his story he cannot find the way out of it in the same gradual manner from the height of fancy he has succeeded in working himself up to. So down he falls and lies grovelling on his stomach before Aase and Ibsen's readers, — his fancy a bankrupt, so beautifully pictured by

Langt om længe, du, vi naade
nordre Landet p a a e n M a a de.

All he can do in the presence of Aase's breathless interest in the buck is to put her off with the characteristic Kan du finde ham, saa tag ham! (C. L. Christensen).

There is a delicious if indistinct flavour of the fairy tale about this, vaguely reminding us of the wellknown tag: 'and if he is not run away, you may find him there still' of our early youth. Compare such passages in the H. Ev. as the following: And if he has not died, he is alive yet (Men æ a iιι dau, saa leve a fell ennaa, p. 57, Lunde-ætten), and: (she came to) the hill-folk.... at Lesja, and she is no doubt there still if she has not been bored to death (mæ haugfolkom.... paa Lesja, og der æ 'o fell øinnaa, dæssom ho ikkje ha sy'rt ihæl se; ib. p. 134,

---

1, 5; 3, 9; F, 270; M, 169; 14, 8; J, 175; 16, 8.

En Søndagskvæld til sæters).

169.   Rægglesmed. A story..teller.

See lower down: den Rægglen er god (650); de Fandens Ræggler (800) and especially the line (1639) where Peer himself has got sick of this very story, whereas his mother who has quite forgotten it was a lie reminds him of it: and then you'd been riding a reindeer, no wonder your head was turned: og saa havde du redet paa Bukken; det var rimeligt nok, du var yr! In the first scene of the second act, she tells Solveig's father that Peer can ride through the air on a buck (l. 814) as though it were gospel-truth. As to Peer himself, when he is in distress in the lunatic-asylum, a reminiscence of this crops up in his words to Hussejn: just think! to be a reindeer; to jump from on high, to fall, — never feel the ground under one's hoof!: Tænk Dem: være Renbukk; springe fra oven; — altid stupe,—aldrig kjende Grund under Hoven!

As to the w o r d rægglesmed, it is found in Asbjørnsen's story: That Peer Gynt was a peculiar fellow, he was truly a storyteller and adventure-monger,..he would have been fun for you, he used to pretend that he had been concerned in all these yarns that people said had happened in the old days: Dæin Pær'n Gynt va ein for se sjøl, hæin va rigtogt ein æventy-Kræmar og røgel-sme du skult havt moro di taa; hæin fortæilde støtt at 'n ha voré mæ ti æille di historiom folk sa ha hænda i gamle daagaa", which hint as we see, Ibsen has acted upon here as well as lower down (l. 652) where somebody else recognises Peer's story about the Devil in a Nut-shell (cf. F. Ev., p. 112: Gutten og Fanden; n. to l. 629) that Peer had just "appropriated", as being known to him from the days of his grandfather. And like their colleagues the skippers, the hunters were equally famous for their yarns, so that the proverb went: No hunter ever gets rich: De bli ingen skjyttar rik (Kleiven, I gamle daagaa²,

---

p. 158) for .. they spent all they got in standing a treat!

173. En Jente paa de tyve.

A girl about twenty.

This peculiar use, as Mikkelsen calls it (Dansk Sprog-lære, 1894, p. 307: "paa en særegen Maade") of the definite article is proper to both Danish and Norwegian, but is little noticed by grammarians. I subjoin therefore the following instances supplied by Dr. Western:

Nu var han vel de fyrretyve aar (Aanrud, Fortællinger II, 183), En Mand paa de firti (Stein Riverton, Skjulte Spor, p. 4); hun var mellem de tredive og firti, (Aanrud, *ib.* II, 223), in all of which cases it is used when speaking of people's age; and it should be noticed that being used with round figures only, it expresses a sort of indefiniteness; an expression like: paa de to og tyve is unthinkable, and paa de tyve should not therefore be rendered: a girl *of* twenty, as the Archers have it; compare Dutch: in de twintig, where the idea of rather more than twenty is put slightly more on the foreground than in the corresponding Norwegian.

It is also used in other expressions:

Det var mindst de fyrretyve aar (again: a b o u t forty years) siden Peer havde været der (Aanrud, Fortællinger, II, 85), Du har selv set det de hundre ganger (Bjørnson, En Hanske, II, 1), supplied with others by Western. Add: De 7 Eventyr av Asta Graa Bolander; av disse forsøk, i alt 50, mislykkedes de 6 (Samtiden, 1915, p. 174) etc.

In U., Ibsen had first written: har jeg hørt før jeg var tyve, but it was changed already in U. into the present reading.

174. Gudbrand Glesne er det hændt.

Gudbrand Glesne it befell.

The story is found in the Huldre Eventyr (p. 142) and may be rendered thus: There was a hunter once in the mountains to the west of the Gudbrandsdal, called Gud-

---

1, 6; 3, 10; F, 272; M, 170; 14, 10; J, 176; 16, 10.

brand Glesne. He.... is said to have been an excellent
huntsman. Once, in the autumm, he came across a splendid reindeer; he shot it and it lay quiet for some time, so
he thought of course that it was stone-dead! So he went
and sat down across its back as they are in the habit of
doing and was about to cut the skull from the neck-bone.
But just as he had sat down, the buck jumped up, threw
its horns back and squeezed him so hard between them
that he sat as in an arm-chair and thus they rushed on
for the bullet had just grazed the animal's head and had
caused it to swoon. And a ride such as Gudbrand then
had, surely no one has ever got. Wind and weather notwithstanding they went on over the most dangerous gla-
ciers and moraines. He made straight for the Bess-edge,
and then Gudbrand commended his soul to the Lord for
he did not think he should ever see sun or moon again.
But after all the buck swam right across the lake with
the hunter on his back. In the mean time Gudbrand had
been able to get at his knife and just as the reindeer put
its foot on land, he plunged his knife into the animal's neck
and it fell down dead. But Gudbrand Glesne said he
would never do this journey over again for all the riches
in the world. (Asbjørnsen, H. Ev. p. 142, Rendyrsjagt
ved Rondane; a Dutch translation may be found in the
Tijdspiegel, 1915: Peer Gynt vóór Ibsen, and an English
one in the Archers' Peer Gynt, p. 286).

186.   maalløs Skrækk. speechless dread.
    The boldness of such images as: s p e e c h l e s s d r e a d
for the fear that renders one speechless, will be found explained in Jespersen's Mod. Engl. Gr. vol. II. ch. 12. 4
and 12. 5 and his Større Engl. Gram. II. p. 184 ff. Compare n. to l. 124 and: halsløs Daad. l. 757.

201.   en stakkars magtløs Enke. a poor defenceless widow.
    It may be worth noticing that Ibsen by writing stakkars
and in U. stakkels (? stakkers; U reads stakkels as we have
it, but with *is* corrected from one or two other letters,

probably—r s), as he does, without a capital, shows that he did not feel it as a substantive; cf. n. to l. 336, 4077.

206.   Skjæpperne med Mynt. The bushels of coin.

En Skjæppe is about half a bushel, a little over 17 litres; so here: a bag full.

208.   Faer din gav dem Fødder, han.
                      your father lent them wings.

There is some autobiography here; see Ibsen's letter to Georg Brandes of the 21st of Sept. 1882 (Breve, II, 112, 113) where he thanks his Danish helpful friend (støtten-de ven) who had just published his second "portræt" [1]) and where he speaks of his quondam rich father's hospitality regardless of cost, the subsequent bankruptcy in 1836 and how he has used this as a sort of model for his pictures in Peer Gynt of the house of "the rich Peer Gynt". See also lower down: Just think, a son of Jon Gynt! (l. 516: Tænk, Søn til Jon Gynt) and hence also Peer's allusion at the end of the dream-scene in Act II, when addressing himself, he says: Peer Gynt, thou art come of great things and great things shall come of thee; Peer Gynt, af stort est du kommen, og till stort skalst du vorde en Gang (l. 952). Aase herself tells us later in the 3d scene of the 3d act: God pardon him: Jon; he was drunk you see, and then he cared neither for tin nor for gold (l. 1405) to which compare Aase's description early in the second scene of the 2nd act (l. 787). And in the fifth act, the Button-moulder too knows about Jon's little habits who had the reputation to squander everything (han havde Ord for at sløse) and compare for this theory of heredity where Ibsen to a very slight extent anticipates his "Ghosts", Aase's just quoted attempt

---

[1]) A literary biography: Henrik Ibsen, af Georg Brandes, 1898, Forord and p. p. 55—122; andet Indtryk, 1882; the first dates from 1867 and the third the Danish critic wrote in 1898, when Ibsen celebrated his 70th anniversary: Min far sad som Købmand i en mangeartet og vidtløftig virksomhed og ynded en hensynsløs gæstfri-hed i sit hus. I 1836 måtte han indstille sine betalinger.... I Peer Gynt har jeg be-nyttet mine egne barndomsforhold og erindringer som et slags model ved skildrin-gen af livet i „den rige Jon Gynts" hus (l. 944).

1, 8; 3, 12; F, 273; M, 171; 14, 11; J, 177; 16, 11.

to excuse Peer by her account of his youth (l. 786 seqq.). See H. Jæger, '88, l. l. p. 18 on this period and the influence this catastrophe had on his character.

As to the expression gav dem Fødder, it occurs in Ibsen's source: H. Ev. (p. 18) vi fik slike føtter under os, at vi itte stane' før vi var.... and cf. Aasen, No. Ordspr. p. 223: Dat fekk Føter til aa gonga paa. i. e. get the opportunity of going away. Instead of fødder til at gaa paa, we find: ben, gode ben; cf. Mau, Ordsprogsskat, II, p. 125. Compare to some extent: jemand Beine machen and Dutch: iemand voeten maken; Stoett, n°. 2033.

214. da hver Gjæst lod Glas.... klaske.

when each guest sent glass and bottle shivering all.

Compare lower down, Aase's next speech but one and Peer's references to this in II, 4 (l. 940).

216. Hvor er Sneen fra ifjor?

Where's the snow of yester-year?

This expression, although originating in Villon's "où sont les neiges d'antan?" (Ballade des Dames du Temps jadis) has become common property in Norwegian and Danish (cf. Aasen, No. Ordspr. p. 8: Dan Snjoen som fall i Fjor er longo gløymd; eller: Kvar vardt av dan Snjoen som fall i Fjor; and Mau, II, 317: Hvor blev den Sne som faldt i Fjor?) as well as e. g. in England (where are the snows of yesteryear, Brynildsen) so the reminiscence is as little to be put down to Peer's credit-side as his use of the Molièrean: Hvad vilde jeg ogsaa paa den Gallej? (cf. n. to l. 2500). On Peer's (French) debit-side cf. n. to l. 2208.

218. Hvert andet Rude-
Hul er fyldt med gamle Klude.

Every second
window-pane is stopped with clouts.

The breaking off in the middle of a word at the end of a line in order to form a rhyme, or at least actually forming one, whether with the intention of doing so or no,

is a device that will shock many an ear. English readers
will have been reminded of the witty, it is true, but not
exactly poetic Ingoldsby Legends and may be tempted
to conclude that Ibsen has here descended to the lower
depths. However, it is dangerous to let one's judgment be
guided here by the ear of a foreigner. The following quotations will suffice to show that in itself the proceeding is
quite admissible.

When we find that Wergeland writes:

> et dræbe-
> lystent Syn
> "Ha", Epilogus, S. S. VI p. 29

and

> en Naphta-
> kildes Luefraade
> ib. p. 37

(etc. etc. passim; e. g. p. 113)

> men
> sjælen sig vikler, som sommer-
> fuglen, af svøbet, og aande-
> kraften forøger....

(Gran, Nordm. i. d. 19e Aarh., I, p. 256)
and Oehlenschläger:

> "Ja-
> mænd vil han saa".   and:
> I Badet bølger Rosen-
> og klart Lavendel-vand

(both from Aladdin),
the evidence is sufficient to prove that to a Norwegian
ear it is not unworthy of serious poetry.

And from Ibsen himself we may quote as absolute cases in point not only the early (1859) and comic:

> Heller end at hyle Rama-
> skriget mod vor unge Stat.

(Hastværkslinjer til H. Ø. Blom, Samtiden. 1911, p.
366)

1, 8; 3, 12; F, 274; M, 171; 14, 12; J, 177; 16, 12.

but later on the quite serious:

paa de isom-

spændte vidder

(from Paa Vidderne, F, IV, 349, rhyming with visdom)

and:

barne-

glade flok! Hin uerfarne

strudseseer var, (etc)

(from Ballonbrev, ib. p. 379).

Compare further:

tretten

hundred alen (l. 107).... where tretten rhymes on *set den* of l. 99. Related are in the first place such groupings as: det rygger længer og længere bort (l. 882) for: længere og længere (cf. German: mein Blick wird trüb–und trüber) and, much more distantly of course, the principle of overflow in verse [1]).

220. Skigard. fences;

On the spelling of this word, cf. S. M. p. 29. § 25. Norwegian only.

227. Der er saltstrød, hvor den grode.

Salt-strewn is the soil it grew from.

Salt was traditionally known to chase evil spirits away; see on this lustral power of salt: Eitrem, Saltet i Tro og Overtro, Feilberg, Festskr. p. 176 seqq. Compare also Feilberg's own Jydsk Ordb. in v. *salt* and his paper Dania II, 81—127 (esp. p. p. 95 seqq.) à propos of Judges, 9, 45.

Aase does not of course equate luck with the evil spirits, she means on the contrary: as evil spirits are chased by salt, so here luck has long since abandoned us as if that too had been chased away [2]).

---

[1]) At least that sort of enjambment illustrated by such rhymes as:

would stagger a

Bard for a simile short of Niagara,

which is of course from the Ingoldsby Legends.

[2]) A correspondent writes: „In my opinion saltstrøn here has nothing to do with

Other passages illustrative of the use of salt in Folk-lore are found in Feilberg, Ordb. (I, 654, b) in v. hoved: the strewing of salt p r e v e n t s the head of the troll from growing on again. When the cruel king in "Gjæte Kongens harer" has slices cut out of poor Peer's and Paul's backs, one is apt to think that it was only a refine-ment of his cruelty that he has salt thrown into the wounds; in view of the above it would almost seem as if he had added insult to injury by preventing it from grow-ing to again. — See also Dania, II, 225 a paper on Nord-fynsk Overtro: When salt was put into the milk, it be-came at once useless when it was to serve in a bad cause; ib. 228. Hence too, exorcisms are read over a cup of salt: "but they had need of some incantations from the book of necromancy. They read them over a cup of salt and sunday-grinded meal which they stirred with a steel-knife (berr-stæld kniv, so a knife of steel only?) and a knife was either driven into the wall over the animals or fastened between the horns (de var naa-gaa Bønne utu Svart-Boken som vilde te. Di Bønninn las døm ivi ein Kopp me Salt og sondagsmale Mjøl som døm rørde i me einn berr-stæld kniv og ein kniv vart an-tell drivi inni Fjøsveggen upp-ivi Krytyre, hell lagt imil-lom Hønnom; Kleiven, I gamle daagaa, s. 37).

But it is not always that the salt is efficacious; re-member Asbjørnsen's story of the Tiurleik i Holleia [1] H. Ev. p. 179) where Gamle Peer had shot at an enor-mous specimen of these birds "with salt as well as with

---

the use of salt in sorcery. Salt is commonly used to kill weeds in gardens. By strew-ing salt in the places that you wish to keep free from weeds, you make it easier to keep off the weeds. So here luck will not grow again because the soil in which it should have grown has been made sterile". This is no doubt in itself not impossible and my readers must decide for themselves. Perhaps they may agree with an other correspon-dent who thinks my explanation fits in better with Aase's course of thought. He adds: down to this very day in Jutland people say to a little fellow he must eat a bush-el of salt to grow up, „a very clear expression of the belief in salt and its wondrous working".

[1] *Tiurleik* is the play of the woodcock when wooing the hen. He works himself up to a sort of ecstacy in which he neither sees nor hears anything, a sort of love-rage.

silver" but the gamle Suggen [1]) did not seem to take any notice of it.

228.   du er Storkarl. you are a rare one.

See T. C. §§ 117, 135.

229,30. kaut (bumptious) kry (proud) are specifically Norwegian words; cf. S. I. S. p. 191, in shrill contrast to knøv (smart) in the next line which is so little Norwegian that Brynildsen does not even give it; cf. Storm l. l. p. 196: "new-Danish, unknown to us"!

233.   sligt et Nemme. such a headpiece.

The Archers' headpiece is a somewhat free rendering for wit, apprehension; the Dutch translation renders it boldly by: name!

234. sakned mangen Prins. many a prince might envy.

Sakned is the specifically Norwegian form of savned: S. I. S. p. 191.

As to the Prince, attention may be called to the gradual preparation of the reader (if not of Peer himself) for the development of Peer's princely, indeed imperial aspirations; here Aase as in passing compares her son's position to that of a prince, lower down she likens Peer to Askeladd, the Norwegian Ashiepattle (cf. n. to l. 255) and so almost quite naturally Peer is led to reason: well, like Askeladd I may have luck with me, ascend the social ladder and sit "høit paa Straa"; cf. l. 434. See also l. 312, n.

240.   dagstødt. daily.

Specifically Norwegian; S. I. S. p. 191; cf. n. to l. 318.

242.   Men i Nød skal kjendes Næsten.

But it's need that tests one's neighbour.

Various other forms of this proverb may be found in the Scandinavian languages: I Trang skal man Venner prøve, i Nød skal man Venner kjende, I Naudi skal ein

---

[1]) *Sugg,* „old fellow", — a term of more or less goodhearted contempt; there is a „by-tone" of something peculiar in the word; as shown by this very passage, it is also said of animals.

Vinerne røyne, etc. etc.; cf. Mau, I, 419; II, 535; Aasen, Ordspr. p. p. 156, 168.

Moltke Moe, Episke Grundlove, Edda 1915 p. 103 quotes stories from the Middle-Ages that teach this lesson e. g. from the Disciplina Clericalis. The best known in English is of course that of Everyman, translated from the Dutch of Petrus Diesthemius.

245.   skræppe. a bag.

The word skræppe or more usually perhaps skreppe is specifically Norwegian in this sense. It occurs in literature already in Bjerregaard; cf. Seip's Wergeland p. 25. A contribution to the history of numerous Ibsenian words and forms being found in this book, a list of the principal ones is subjoined here: those that occur in Peer Gynt. See Seip, W. p. 150 seqq.

aann	no.	halling	no.
barskog	da. barskov	hei	no.
blygsel	da. blusel	helg	Danish (also norw; W.)
briske sig	no.	hestehov	Danish (also norw; W.)
dumbjelde	no.	hop = ihop	no.
elv	also Danish	hubro	no.
esle	no.	huldre	no.
fant	no.	hvælv	da.
fell	no.	ihop	no.
fillet	no.	jøkel	no.
fort = hurtig;	also Danish	kall	no.
fram	no.	kar	no.
fugleskræmme [1])		kaut	no.
fyld [2])		kjærring	no.
gamlen	no.	lensmand	no.
grisk [3])	Danish gridsk	-let cf. enlet	no.
gubbe	in Danish felt as a	fiinlet	
	loan word from Nor-	handlet	
	wegian or Swedish.	langlet	
hakkespet	cf. ib. p. 144.	rødlet	

---

[1]) Ibsen uses the Danish skræmsel in l. 343: det kvindfolk-skræmsel. norsk et (fugle) skræmsel.

[2]) In Danish = stuffing; no. = drunkenness.

[3]) cf. n. to l. 2436.

I, 9; 3, 13; F, 275; M, 172; 14; 13, J, 173; 16, 13.

lie	no.	snau	no.
likt	no.?	snev	no.
lue luve	no.	sprute	da.
lux	no.	spræk	adj. no.
løsunge	no.	stabur	no.
niste	no.	stry	no.
nøre op (p. 146)	no.	stubbe	da.
nøste	no.	svart	also da.
plent	no.	sæter	no.
rev i seil	da.-rev (reb? W.)	tilgagns	no.
ryddig	no.	tilgars	no.
sexti	no.	tusse	(p. 194: thusse)
ski	no.	ving	da. vinge
skigard	da. -gaard	yr	no.
smidje	no.	øx	da. øxe.

254. Skarv. a scamp; cf. S. I. S. p. 191, in the sense of a crow it is both Norwegian and Danish.

255. Hjemme ligger du i Gruen.

Lounging by the hearth at home.

In the note to. l. 234 the reader has already had his attention called to this description by Aase of her son as an Askeladd [1]). But in order to see to the full the irony of the description that Aase, unconsciously of course, here gives, it is necessary to recall the position that, in sharp contradiction to Peer, this Norwegian hero of folktales occupies in the mind of his countrymen and in the literature of Norway, as indeed under various names in that of most other countries [2]).

---

[1]) The utterly incomprehensible notion (cf. the Publ. Soc. Adv. Sc. Study I.) that Per, Paal og Espen are "sons of the poor peasant Askeladd", needs no further refutation beyond the note published ib. p. 216; cf. infra n. to l.l. 4421,2.

[2]) In English we find: ashcat, ashchat, axencat (Wright, E. D. D. in v. ash); ashiepattle, ashiepeet (ib.); and of course Cinderella on whom Miss Cox has written a monograph which I have unfortunately not seen, possibly the same as the "extensive paper" on the subject that the Folklore Society was to publish (c. 1892) according to Dania, I, 258.

in French: Cendrillon;

in German: Aschenbrödel, (ein schmutziger Küchenjunge der in der "Asche brodelt", d. i. herumstäubt, "auch von Küchenmädchen" (Heine) and as the heroine of the fairy tale: d a s Aschenbrödel; Aschenhans and Aschenputtel.

1, 10; 3, 14; F, 275; M, 172; 14, 13; J, 178; 16, 13.

I borrow a description from Henrik Jæger's Illustreret
No. Lit. hist., I, p. 143: "As a rule he is the youngest of
three brothers [1]) and he occupies a very modest place;
he is supposed to be lazy, stupid as well as incapable"
— and here we certainly have the only real tertium
comparationis between Peer and Askeladd, for, in the
words coming immediately after, we do not recognise
our Peer any more: "and he has very often in the beginning appearances against him, but as soon as he comes
away from the narrow conditions at home, he shows
what stuff he is made of. He has both heart and head in
their proper place, and he is the genius born under the
lucky star, executing without any difficulty the task that
neither his clever brothers nor any one else has been able
to manage". Quantum mutatus....! How far are we not
here from Peer Hamlet's pretexts (cf. n. to l. 1228) for
not doing anything and from his Macbeth-like abstention

in Dutch: Asschepoester, now usually feminine because the word, derived by the
masculine ending -er from poesten = to blow, was erroneously taken to contain the
now feminine ending -ster; it is moreover popularly supposed to be the one "die
poetst", i. e. who polishes, cleans and is consequently sometimes written: -poetster.
As one of the rare cases where it is still used for a masculine person, I quote Pol De
Mont and Alfons De Cock, Vlaamsche Vertelsels, p. 442: "De (zoon) groeide op als
een kool, maar doordat hij gaarne in assche en modder wroette en er altijd vuil en
zwart uitzag, noemde zijn vader hem Asschepoester." He is also called Asschevijster.
   in Swedish: Askepjäsk (cf. H. E., Folkminnen, 1907 p. 519; on pjäsk, see Rietz, p.p.
504b and 513b), Askfis and Pintel, cf. Lill-Pintel ock Stalogubben, in Lapska sagor, Bergström ock Nordlander, Sagor, Sägner ock Visor, Svenska Landsmålen, 1885,
p.p. 37, 41, 43; ib. p. 37 n: Askepotten.
   in Icelandic: Amlodi-Uffi; cf. Jørgen Moe, quoted by Jæger, l. l. p. 143 and Olrik,
Nordisches Geistesleben, p. 51; and last not least:
   in Dano-Norwegian: Askefis (cf. on -fis, Feilberg, Skældsordenes lyrik, Da. Studier,
1905, p. 29), Askelad, Askepot ,Esben (= Asbjørn), cf. Feilberg in v.; Halvor (cf. No.
Folkeev. p. 97 in Soria Moria Slottet) who "bare sat og rakte i asken". Hans in Or-
nen min Stallbror: "Per, Paal og Hans skulde ut og skjota"; Jesper, cf. Feilberg in v.
and in v. Peder: Jesper Nåsfis, ib. Per, Povl og bitte Lars Pind, and: Lille Jes, Os-
kefot, Oskeguva, Oskunge, cf. Ross in v.; Peik in the well-known tale of this name:
Asbjørnsen, No. Folkeev.³, 1914 p. 185 and ib. p. 242; Pinken, in "Per, Paal og Pinken", Knutsen, Bentsen og Johnsson, Udv. Eventyr for Børn, quoted by Moltke Moe
(p. 56) in his introduction to the collection of Kr. Janson, Folke-Eventyr fra Sandeherad, 1878; Pøne, cf. p. 25 of this collection of Janson's; Terkel, cf. Feilberg, III,
783 in v. and Tyrihans, cf. Asbjørnsen, No. Folkeev. ed. 1914 p. 23 (Tre Citroner).
   [1]) The example of Peik (cf. the preceding note) shows that Jæger is right in admitting exceptions and allows us to compare the case of Peer who is quite alone, although Ibsen had first in U. given him an elder brother.

from wetting his feet, although he would so like to catch fish! And yet.... his mother's comparison, intuitive as it is of course, hits him off well-enough if we only remember that he still has his life before him, that Aase does not therefore, cannot judge him as we do, and that he *is* an Askeladd — in his dreams!

From an abridged Danish rendering of Sainéau's paper on Folk-tales (Dania, X, 99 seqq.), I quote the following: Always and everywhere, the people have shown a true predilection for the little, for the weak and the frail, for those, whose crippled, pitiful, nay even dirty exterior usually brings them into disdain, but whom the folk-tales now seek to make up for, by endowing them with supernatural power.... it is in consequence of this tendency to counter-balance this inequality of nature, that the youngest of the children outdoes the elder ones either by his wit or his courage; the youngest is always the most fortunate, the most courageous; corporal weakness aided by intellect, continually vanquishes raw strength." It should be added that this explanation, drawn from literary history, would not suffice if such a custom as Borough-English, the "tenure in some parts of England by which the youngest son inherits all the land and tenements" (N. E. D. *in voce*) and the corresponding *Jüngste Recht* in Germany, did not supply the historical underground for this reason. (See Feilberg *in v.* Esben, ung, yngst; Grimm as quoted *ib.* Littré *in v.* juveigneur and Ducange in v. Junior, Junioratus, p. 450 a). The above will show how absurdly far off the mark is J. Collin who tells us (Henrik Ibsen, p. 293) that in Asbjørnsen's Askelad "alle Niedrichkeit und alle Verachtung des gemeinen Volkes zusammen gefasst ist."

Bergsgaard in a paper "Kring Solveig og Peer Gynt" (Syn og Segn, 1915, p. 51) thinks that we here have a picture of your "national mynsterman", the truly national example Ibsen has had for his Peer, who, Bergsgaard

---

1, 10; 3, 14; F, 275; M, 172; 14, 13; J, 178; 16, 13.

supposes, is not only "your Norwegian", but more particularly "the Norwegian hero Ashiepattle".

259.   gjør mig Spe. shaming me.

Compare in Asbjørnsen's Folkeev. (p. 15): til spot og spe, and such proverbial expressions as Spe og Spott gjør ingen godt, Mau, II. 345; Aasen, No. Ordspr. p. 35.

264.   paa Lunde. at Lunde.

It is of course likely to prove nothing but a coincidence but there can be no harm in adding that Lunde (in a place of which name Ibsen also locates the coward-incident in the fifth act; cf. n. to l. 3670) is mentioned in two of Ibsen's sources, not only in the Huldre-ev. (cf. p. 54: Lundeætten, where "ein gong.... va ei kjærring.... som heitte Aase) but also in Faye's No. Sagn (p. 161) where we also read of a smith that lived at Lunde.

267.   Knækte Armen paa han Aslak Smed.
broke Blacksmith Aslak's arm for him.

Han = acc. instead of ham as we should expect in Norwegian riksmaal, is a characteristically popular turn, proper to Landsmaal; cf. Aasen, Det Norske Folkesprogs Gramm². p. 177 and esp. Hægstad, Maallæra⁷, § 55, note: honom is used only "when the word has especial stress", and "before a proper name han may be used always". As a few cases in point I quote: Gamle Knut Vinje spurde eingong han Aanund, and: Dette var et Sneidord til han Knut, Dølen, l. c. I, 457; Rolv dreiv han Asgeir, Bugge-Berge, Folkesagn, II, 54; han Anders Fange, Landstad, Folkeviser, p. 716; paa'n Per Haagaa (as in the genetive hass Per Gynt) Syn og Segn, 1903, p.p. 121, 125). That *han* is not used with a proper name o n l y appears from Moltke Moe og Liestøl's No. Folkeviser, p. 85: her spyrst alli so raske drengjir som 'n Herre Jon Remarsson (cf. han vant ham herr' Jon, quoted by Paasche, Gildet paa Solhaug, p. 33 from Landstad p. 660). It is interesting to find that whereas one text of the Peer Gynt tale has: mæ'n Per (No. Sagn, p. 33), another reads:

I, 10; 3, 14; F, 275; M. 172; 14, 13; J, 178; 16, 13.

mæ 'om Pær (Huldreev. p. 156). If (Landstad, Folkeviser p. 5), raaihæst is rightly explained as meaning: den
överste Raadgiver, we have there a very rare case of
han before an adjective used as a substantive.

cf. Feilberg, Jul, I, 147: slå han Tor drukken and Gadesproget p. 193.

286.   Om jeg hamrer eller hamres.
                        Though I hammer or am hammered.
Compare the almost proverbial: Amboss oder Hammer
sein.

>   Du musst herrschen und gewinnen
>   Oder dienen und verlieren,
>   Leiden oder triumphieren,
>   Amboss oder Hammer sein.

Goethe, Gesellige Lieder, quoted in Zeuthner, p. 19.

308.   Jeg skal blive Konge, Kejser!
                     I will be a King, a Kaiser.

This is like Ashiepattle's dream in the nursery-tale;
cf. the n. to l. 255. But as Ibsen has more than once told
us (cf. e. g. Breve, II, 82) that a poet cannot write about
what he has not himself "gone through" (*gjennemlevet*
if not necessarily *oplevet*), the student may here be reminded of Ibsen's immense confidence in his own life's mission; his letter to King Charles will be in everybody's
thoughts, cf. Breve I, p. 84. In this connection the abstract of a conversation which his friend Vilhelm Bergsøe
had with him at Ischia may be welcome: "I won 't go
back to Norway before Norway calls me back", the poet
had said and Bergsøe adds: "On the whole Ibsen was not
without a great deal of self-consciousness and he often
asserted that he did not work for time but for eternity,
and when I answered that no poet could reach so far, that
even the greatest genius would be forgotten after thous-
ands of years were gone, he got into a rage and said:
Get along with your metaphysics! If you take Eternity

1, 12; 3, 16; F, 277; M, 173; 14, 15; J, 179; 16, 15.

from me, you take all". — After this, it sounds almost like an anticlimax when Bergsøe tamely adds that Ibsen "at that time f e l t f u l l y — i øvrigt hadde (han) den gang fuldt ud den Tanke — that he would die as a very great poet"; cf. Bergsøe's chapter: Erindringer fra Aarene 1863—69, in Henrik Ibsen paa Ischia p. 163.

Since the above note was written, three papers have appeared that may with advantage be referred to.

In "Edda", Sigurd Høst has recently published a paper (1915, p. 328 seqq.) in which he writes of the contrast between Ibsen's "proud, heaven-storming dream and reality in Grimstad" and how the cowardly and lazy dreamer is chastised in Peer Gynt. Rector H. Eitrem (Edda, 1915, p. 74, "Stellanea") has pointed out an early reference to Ibsen's life's dream in one of his youthful poems, where he writes of two purposes in life, a big one to become "an immortal man" and a little one "to own a delightful Lily":

> Jeg satte mig to Formaal, et lidet og et stort
> Det store var at blive en udødelig mand,
> Det Lille var at eie en deilig Liljevand,

where the "deilig Liljevand" must refer to a certain Clara E.

And lastly, Henning Kehler, (Edda, 1916 p. 56) calls attention to the difference between Brand's phantasy and Peer Gynt's dreams: "Brand is a fantast of the will .... a much greater one than Peer Gynt, who, all dreams notwithstanding, has practical sense enough to work himself up to the position of a great ship-owner at Capetown". (Add.)

313.   Ja, giv Tid, saa blir du Prins, siges der.

Give you time, you'll be a prince, so the saying goes.

You'll be a prince is meant rather more in a general way (such as *e. g.* if you can only learn to wait, you'll become King of Spain: "Har du lært at vente skal du bli konge i Spanien" which A. Krogvig quotes), than addressed to Peer only. — cf. all comes round to him who will but wait; *du* is therefore practically as indefinite a pronoun as *you* in the famous: "to lay is a transitive verb, Sir, because y o u can lay an egg".

318.   dagstødt. daily.

See the n. to l. 240. Here Ibsen had first written (in U): selvmant; a word that is not found in Aasen nor Ross nor in any dict. at my disposal and unknown to my correspondents. The context seems to lead us to such a word as sjølvmint, which I find glossed as beredvillig, som gjør noget uden nogen Opfordring, and which, as one of my correspondents writes, might at a pinch be supposed to have been "translated or rendered by a made-up selvmant" by Ibsen [1]). That it does not seem to fit in quite with Aase's words, may be the very reason why the poet changed it when copying out U.

328.   stavrer.... efter, stumps.... after.

Prof. Storm, S. I. S. p. 179, compares: kommer stavrende in Borkmann, and remarks that the word "sounds quite Danish, although it is used by some Norwegian writers, but the Norwegian form is stabbe [2]). Typically enough stavre is found in the Danish Ordb. over Gadesproget, but it is used very seldom (C. L. Chr.)

331.   Odelsjente. land entailed on her.

This translation by the Archers, followed by Ellis Roberts, is not quite up to the mark, Odel (cf. Eng. Udal = allodium) being on the contrary = fee simple.

336.   Stakkars dig. Poor you.

Here as in the case of l. 201 (cf. n. ib.) Ibsen had written stakkels in U.

---

[1]) An other correspondent writes later on: "it is very intelligible: it means manet av sig selv": encouraged by oneself, spontaneously. The word is not common," which seems to bear out the above. But as he admits: "it does not fit in with the context", the explanation of the word does not seem quite so much above suspicion as one would like.

[2]) Dr. Western writes: *stavre* (lit. to walk by the help of a staff) is properly used of old people who lean upon a stick. The Norw. *stabbe* does not necessarily mean this, but to walk with short strides and therefore slowly; it may be used of a little child who has just learnt to walk. Of old people we say: *humpe*.

---

353. Hejsan, Moer! Vi sparer Kjærren.
      Mother, jump! We'll spare the cart.
      Hejsan is hardly *jump* here (Ellis Roberts too uses it),
      but an exclamation of joy: Cheer up! Come on!
      Very carelessly Count Prozor renders the latter part of
      the phrase by "Nous attelons. Ja vais chercher la ju-
      ment" which is practically the reverse of the original.

356. Slipp mig.
      Here as in l. 369, Ibsen wrote slip in R., which the
      corrector of the first ed. in accordance with the ortho-
      graphy of R. changed into slipp in the present line, but
      he left it in l. 369.

357. bær jeg.
      This is metrically preferable to the bærer jeg of U. On
      the contracted bær, cf. T. C. § 23 and the n. to l. 724.

360. Jeg er baaren till en gjildere Død.
      I was born for a braver death.
      Compare Hamlet who was "born to set (the world)
      right", i. e. destined, predestined for. — Gjildere takes
      the place in U. of bedre which Ibsen had written first.

362. du blir sagtens hængt tillsidst!
      sure enough, you'll hang at last!
      "Den drukner ej, som hænges skal" as the saying is!
      In her momentary wrath Aase predicts this direful end
      for her son, but when Aslak the Smith threatens to do
      so, she sings an other tune: What! hang m y Peer! Just
      you try l. 716 ¹). And compare later on in the auction
      scene (act V; l. 3875) when some one in Peer's presence
      says that no doubt this "remarkable man" has been
      hanged long ago, Peer devotely adds: "Hanged? Dear
      me! Of course he must have been! Bless the man. He
      has all the time been himself!"

---

¹) Compare Chr. Collin, Die neue Rundschau, 1907, S. 1281: "in einer Reihe von
Meisterwerken.... stellt (Ibsen) Norwegen.... an den Pranger. Aber er meint
es gut; er schimpft auf Norwegen wie Mutter Aase auf Peer Gynt, ihr Schmerzens-
kind. Ich glaube nicht, dass er irgend einem Andern erlaubt hätte, vom Lande Norwegen Schlechtes zu reden".

1, 16; 3, 20; F, 280; M, 175; 14, 18; J, 181; 16, 18.

363.   dit Ubæst! you brute.

The particle *u-*, strengthening the word it is composed with as it does, makes ubæst much stronger than bæst which Ibsen uses in l. l. 416 and 481. Ubeist will be found in Asbjørnsen's Norske Folkeeventyr (ed. '14, p. 188): For et ubeist du er, Peik! sa kongen. Compare on the particle u-, the note to l. 1100. In U., Ibsen uses similarly udød (fo. 1, 6, v°).

374. nu er Evjen rukken. now we've reached the shallows.

For Evjen, still part of a river (not necessarily s h a l l- o w), U. had: Bredden. Brons (mis)translates: 't word al vloter, — nog eyn ruk; where somehow rukken = reached has reminded him of Low-German ruk = a jerk, a wrench — "one more effort" and we're there.

"The form *rukken* for *rukket* is of course used to get a rhyme for *bukken ;* it is bad enough as the latter word is pronounced [bokken], while rukket always had [u]." (W.)

377.   Takk for skyds — to thank you for the ride.
See l. 1795, n.

387.   Du skal vakkert Skudsmaal faa.
       Fine's the character I'll give you.

A great improvement on the much more general, watery: Han skal hele Leksen faa of U; lekse, lektie = lesson, task, here: the whole story; he shall hear the whole rigmarole.

394. Hm; saa faar jeg gaa alene. Hm; then I must go alone.

There is a very delicately shaded difference between this final reading, and that of U all in favour of the former: Godt; saa faar jeg etc. It has become a more reflective: Well.... if you really do not promise to be good....

404.   Aldrig! Jeg vil med i Laget! To the feast I'm coming.

Compare: Kan du nægte du var første Mand i Laget (l. 262) and l.l. 535 (542):
Piskende død, jeg maa med i Laget.
So: at være med i Laget = to j o i n in the fun, the game

---

etc. "Ibsen was very fond of certain words and turnings which he used quite regularly sometimes". (C. L. Christensen)

408.   jeg beer.

On the spelling with double e, afterwards abandoned, cf. S. M. p. 22, § 3; Storm, No. Sprog, 1896, p. 12 and T. C. § 111.

409.   Græstørv. a sod of grass.

The roof of the little mill on which Peer had hoisted his mother, is grown over with grass, as Count Prozor truly remarks on p. 17 of his translation. Hence too the stones of l. 414 (ikke riv og rusk i Stenene) are not the shingles as the Archers translate nor the tiles (Ellis Roberts) but more likely the (boulder-) stones that are found on many a thatched cottage roof to hold, by means of wooden laths or otherwise, the grass-sods that otherwise might be blown away.

413. seqq. Ikke spark.... ikke riv.... ikke spræl.

Putting the negation before the imperative is peculiar to the colloquial language; cf. Poestion³, § 168. Compare: Ikke passiar, Dukkehjem, F, VI, 224 (as in the first draft: Eft. Skr., II, 349) and: ikke forstyr: ib. p. 334.

416.   dratte. to fall.

Specifically Danish, Norw. dette; S. M. p. 179; cf. l 4314: Saa dratted da Haabet af Pinden igjen.

418.   Gid du var blæst som en Bytting ud af Verden!

I'd have you blown, like a changeling into space!

Stavnem (Symb. Væsener, p. 98) remarks in connection with the "fairy-tale mood" (eventyrstemning) he is speaking of, that Mother Aase too partakes of it, — "ogsaa Mor Aase har en rem av huden" as he expresses it. For it is amusing to see that when she gets angry, she scolds and storms in the very expressions taken from the troll-stories". I can but suppose it is a scene like the present he is thinking of, — or Stavnem was thinking of, for it is perhaps only fair to add, that in the copy "with corrections and additions" that the author honoured me with, the present passage is crossed out. It is interesting to notice that these words that recall the "eventyrstemning" here som en bytting (as a changeling) were only introduced in R., and are not found in U, where the line runs:

Gid du var blæst væk fra Jorden, ud af Verden.

As to the word bytting, now a very common nickname, used as if = a fool, or an idiot, by people without any thought of changelings, the belief in those unfortunate creatures, supposed to be children of supernatural beings or evil spirits and substituted — byttet — for the children of men, seems to have been alive as recently as 1884 according to Mr. Hartland's (misnomered!) Science of Fairy Tales. Some were supposed to be children of Old Harry and a human being whom even in Martin Luther's belief (Meyer, p. 63), Old Nick was in the habit of "knowing" in the water. Idiots were often said to be changelings, thus guarding the unfortunate parents from self-reproach that the theory of heredity otherwise might expose them to. They are also called skiftinger, Feilberg III, 251, in v., in Swedish also Bortbytingar, Wigström, Folktro, p. 77 or Mördingar, H. and E., Folkminnen, p. 393 (cf. an interesting description in Norwegia, I, 256), they were recognised by their voraciousness, and go also by the mysterious name of kill-crops, germ. kiel-kropf. When a human mother wished to get rid of them and recover her own child, an efficient means was to drown them or give the substituted brat a sound thrashing, when hey, presto! the changeling would disappear through the air — be "blown out of the world" — and the mother's darling be thrown into the cradle, or on to the hearth; a beautiful trait amidst of all this nastiness, and one that makes all the world akin! Of course, the clergy had its remedy too: take the changeling to the church and it will die!

Compare Meyer, p.p. 63 and 181; Herrmann, Nord. Myth. p.p. 68 and 109, Norwegia, l.l. and p. 265, and Baring Gould's Folklore p. 247: If you are in doubt as to whether your child is a changeling or not, cram a red-hot poker down its throat; if it be a fairy brat, the mother will come and snatch it away. The test is ingenious to say the least of it, but — query to a mother: if it should be your own?

Mr. Fred. Grøn in his Folke-medicin i Sætersdalen explains that a mother who tries to prevent her child from being "changed" is bitten by the tusse (goblin) and hence any incurable ulcer or sore is called a "tusse-bit". (Maal og Minne, 1909, p. 75).

421.   dænge.

Specifically Norwegian, cf. S. M. p. 191, although at Molbech's time it seems to have been in use. ("i daglig Tale", Molbech, Ordb.)

434.   saa højt paa Straa? Well, you *are* exalted!

An almost untranslatable pun, — the expression being current in the metaphorical sense of to occupy a high position, to be in an exalted position, which the Archers': you *are* exalted reflects right enough. Only, she is also l i t e r a l l y sitting "high upon straw" i. e. on the thatched roof cf. n. to l. 409. Passarge's Auf so hohem Tron, Morgenstern's so hoch gestiegen, Mrs. Clant van der Mijll's wat zit je hoog, and Ellis Roberts' you are on high, where I suppose a r e should be stressed, are more or less correct renderings (Prozor's que faites-vous donc sur le toit? is very poor) but the one happy rendering actually wanted, has not yet been forthcoming. If Aase were simply sitting high and no stress had been laid on the fact of her sitting on the roof of the water-mill, a pun like: hallo! you *are* on the top of the tree, which Brynildsen gives (in v. top) as the equivalent of høit paa straa, would render the joke right enough. Perhaps only: well, I do declare, "you have reached the

1, 21; 3, 25; F, 285; M, 177; 14, 23; J, 183; 16, 23.

top". Or, as Dr. Western proposes: Well, you have risen high to-day —" which undoubtedly as he says, gives a better connection with what follows.

The expression is of course Danish too (Gadesproget, p. 489) and also known in Jutland (Feilberg): howt po stro = i en fornem stilling). Instead of være h. p. s., we also find standa højt p. S., which Aasen, No. Ordspr., p. 230 renders: være af høj Stand, and højt paa Brættet, paa Spillet; Mau I, p. 471.

436.   jeg himler. I'll be heaven-high!

The verb at himle "bruges ikke i alvor", says Feilberg and according to Prof. Kristopher Nyrop too, (Dania, VI, 203) "tilhører mærkelig nok også at himle udelukkende det humoristiske sprog"; hence we are not astonished to find that it has found a place in "V. Kristiansen's" (Prof. Fausbøll's) Ordbog over Gadesproget; cf. ed.[2] in voce. Nor is this humorous meaning confined to Danish seeing that Brynildsen[2] renders it by "to pop off". But surely, Aase is not in a mood to joke, so it is here used more likely in a more serious application, as in Fru Inger til Østråt, (F, I. 305): "Nils Sture er himlet"; as Kalkar does not give the word in the sense, Ibsen is not likely to be under the influence of the older language. On the other hand, when in the fifth act, Peer asks of the Lean one whether there is one that must die — "der er en som skal himle" — (both the Archers and Ellis Roberts translate: there's someone bound heavenwards), we seem to see a little twinkle in Peer's eye and feel inclined to render it here by a more popular expression too. In the two following cases, the humorous element although not certain, is not excluded: "Jeg vil ikke à la Carolus Magnus forsøge himle mig for at faae det at høre (Jørgen Moes breve, ed. Krogvig, p. 122) and: Naar det regner og soien skinner, saa himler der en Skrædder, Mau, II, 159.

437.   Signe Rejsen. Bless your passing.

The infinitive signe here must be dependent on some

1, 21; 3, 25; F, 286; M, 177; 14, 24; J, 184; 16, 24.

auxiliary understood. Mr. C. L. Christensen calls attention to a use of the expression "in folkloristic Danish" — signe for folks døre (on the whole almost everything may be "blessed") in the sense of to damage or to protect an other person's property, by the use of certain signs or mysterious formulas." Compare to this the title of Bertha Tuppenhaug's Fortællinger who in the older editions was called a Signekjærring.

439.   Sønnen jers?

The post-position of the possessive pronoun is specifically Norwegian as against Danish riksmaal; Poestion, No. Gr.², § 142,2. Jers is obsolescent if not obsolete; cf. ib.² § 141, to be compared to the corresponding passage in his third ed. Jers, as here used in singular to Aase only, is becoming more and more unusual; again a comparison of Poestion's 2nd and 3d editions (§ 136) is instructive. ¹)

Compare 1. 1380: faar I sidde till jer Død; as in the nominative I in 1. 815: Er I gal and from Fru Inger (F, I, 257:) I kunde blive den udkårne, but it should be remarked that here it is Olav Skaktavl that is speaking to Fru Inger, so the case is not illustrative of modern usage, as in Gildet på Solhaug (ib. p. 142, three times). From the No. Sagn, I quote only one instance which will suffice: "jeg synes ogsaa jeg skulde kjende jer" etc., spoken to a person who turns out to be the 'King' of the Ekeberg. (No. Sagn,² 1902, p. 94). See also Huldre Ev. p.p. 24 and 186, where the editors note: i høflig tiltale til en enkelt, nu forældet, and Falk and Torp, Da. no. Syntax, § 74, p. 115: I is now found in the historical.... speech; at Bergen and in the Nordland it is yet conversational. On the use of I to one person in Denmark, cf. H. F. Feilberg, Navneskik, Dania III, p.p. 290 and 296; (at) itte =

¹) Dr. Western writes that he does not know Jers or jeres as Norsk Riksmaal; for all that it may be found in Norwegian b o o k s, cf. Hamsun V, 154: I foretrækker at henflagre Jærs Dage i Basaren, as well as jer which is slightly less unusual; cf. Bjørnson II, Over ævne, II, 2: Tør I sige jer aldeles uskyldige?

to say "I" to a person (cf. dutte, jatte, to say du, ja; Feilberg, II, 33) does not seem to be Norwegian.

452.   En Mandsstemme. A man's voice.

This man's voice is not found in De handlende. One would therefore be inclined to think that this was one of the cases Ibsen had in view when he wrote (Eft. Skr. III, 414; cf. T. C. § 15) to the publishers that he holds the list of the dramatis personae back "as I possibly may have to enter an additional figure or two, — et par biti-gurer". Only he does not mention the various voices of the Furumo-scene either (l. 3995 seqq.). Moreover: is it not too unimportant a "voice" to be anything but Ejvind's or Anders'? (Dr. Western).

460.   Sendingsfolk. The farm guests.

As the Archers explain (p. 24): "When the Norwegian peasants are bidden to a wedding-feast, they bring with them presents of eatables." These presents are called "send" in Jutland (in Jutland: fon, in norw. dialects: Fonn or Fønn as Mr. Christensen and Dr. Western write respectively; cf. Aasen in v. Forn). Ibsen himself speaks (l. 470) of sendingskost. A sendpige is a girl that brings such gifts (Feilberg in v.v. send, sendpige). Should the wedding not take place, the "send" is returned. In the case of a wedding among the Fairy-folks, one of the things that was brought in a basket, a "sending korg" was the bridal dress, crown and all: Da detta Folke ha gaatt der og vimsa um ein-ann ei Stonn, va de eitt 'taa Kvinnfolkom som bar te aa finne fram Brurstas utu ei Sendings-korg, ho gjekk me paa Arme" (Kleiven, I gamle daagaa², p. 7; cf. also Aasen Ordb.² p. 644.

461.   det er kanske rettest jeg vender.

To turn back now perhaps would be wisest.

J. Collin, Henrik Ibsen p. 296 thinks that here Peer's better self makes him hesitate and is about to cause him to turn back. It is very dubious to say the least of it. Many will look upon it as merely showing, what we find

---

— 35 —

all along to be the case, that there is not the necessary
go in him.

463.   Stødt saa flirer de bag ens Rygg.
           Still they must titter behind your back.

In U, Ibsen had here written of the un-uttered, the
"wordless" thoughts (ordløse tanker) in a passage that he
omitted when copying U out as R. (Eft. Skr. II, 83, 84;
ib. III, 416). They seem to return in R. as the Nissebuktanker of l. 1424.

J. Collin (l.l. p. 297) here quotes an appropriate passage
from Ibsen's letter to his mother-in-law, (3/12/'65; cf.
Breve, II, 103): "hjemme var jeg ræd, når jeg stod inde
i den klamme flok og havde følelsen af deres stygge smil
bagved mig." Dietrichson, Svundne Tider, I, 366 quotes
Ibsen to the effect that whenever any one walked behind him, Ibsen thought he would put a knife into his
back: "Jeg (Ibsen) troede altid, naar der gik et Menneske bag mig at han vilde stikke mig en Kniv i Ryggen."
See Eitrem, Samtiden 1908, p. 570 (Ibsens Gjennembrud)
on this mood of the poet and compare lower down, n.
to l. 572.

466.   Den, som havde noget stærkt at drikke.
           If I'd only a good strong dram now.

Compare later on: Manden min drakk (l. 787) and En
bruger Brændevin, etc. (l. 796). The motif of Gjengangere!, — as I now find noticed by Henning Kehler, Edda
1916, p. 78 who remarks: I ,Peer Gynt' er Heltens Ka-
rakter arvelig forklaret baade fra den fordrukne Svire-
broder Jon Gynt og den sentimentale Mor Aase," and
later on: Ved siden af denne nøgterne Anvendelse af Ar-
velighedsmotivet, er det spillevende i Forholdet mellem
Peer og hans vanskabte Tankebarn."

471.   laak. weak.

Specifically Norwegian; cf. S. I. S. p. 191. The same
meaning apparently in l. 1748: Den Farten, den gjør mig
saa laak og træt. Laak = miserable, shabby; but here it

1, 23; 3, 27; F, 288; M, 178; 14, 25; J, 184; 16, 25.

must be = weak of character; han er et laak: he is no
better than he should be (Brynildsen), would contain an
unmerited insinuation about Aase's honour that might
well render Peer furious of course, but would not in any
way explain why the boy should have become a good-for-
nothing (drog).

479.   paa en Lime; on a broomstick.
See the n. to l. 1005.

484.   Sølvtopp. crested with silver.
Top = en pynt paa Hestens Hovedtøj, made of silver.

492.   Kvinderne nejer sig. Women are curtseying.

As to the reflexive use of neje, which may strike many
a reader as unusual, Brynildsen, who gave this very
passage as an illustration of it, omits it in his second ed.,
where the use is quoted however as familiar. In Kjærl.
Kom. (F, II, 270) Frøken Skære "nejer", not "nejer sig".
The reflexive use may be illustrated already from Old-
Norsk; cf. Fritzner in v. hneigja, where hneigja sik may
be found in this signification; not, it would seem, the corresponding hneigjast. Compare for the later stages of the
language, the Danish folk-song: Jeg har været saa søn-
derlig, alt som den sol hun nejer sig (Hævnersværdet),
where however it simply means: gaa ned; Oehlenschläger
still writes: Den Bonde sig monne neie Med Qvinden drø-
velig and Han sig til Jorden neied, (Nordens Guder).
Sig is here as superfluous as in the oldfashioned gaa sig =
(Landstad, Folkeviser, p. 18; still in Ibsen's Et puds,
Eft. Skr. I, 114: jeg gik mig i Graneskoven; være sig =
være, cf. Eg va meg ut paa Glateimsbergje; M. Moe and
Liestøl, No. Folkeviser, p. 4; er jeg mig et slegtfred Barn,
Danish folksong: Liden Engel and Oehlenschläger in
Nordens Guder: Det var sig Jetten Svare; se sig, ride sig
etc. which all smack of the old ballad style and are quo-
ted here as possible [1]) parallels of this occasional, if per-

---

[1]) To which Dr. Western rightly remarks that there is an essential difference between være sig, ride sig etc. on the one hand and neje sig on the other, viz. that in the
first group sig cannot have been originally felt as an object.

1, 24; 3, 28; F, 289; M, 179; 14, 26; J, 185; 16, 26.

haps colloquial construction. In Gunnar Heiberg's Paradesengen we find still, ser sig trist i speilet, where, as the
context shows (p. 34) sig is not the object but practically, logically, an appositional subject.

As to this vision of Peer's, one is reminded of it
when reading Olaf Liljekrans (S. V. X, 98); cf. infra
note to l. 544. Compare T. C. § 22 for the reading
nejer — neje.

498.   Engelland.

This reading of the old texts, M was the first to change
into the modern Engeland; T. C. § 115. Even if perhaps
Mr. Archer (in a private letter to Mr. Ellis Roberts; see
the latter's Peer Gynt-translation, p. 245) seems to go too
far when he says that Engelland bears the same relation
to Engeland, as does "Norroway of the ballad to our
Norway", there is a good deal in the remark that Mr.
Ellis Roberts adds: "The reader must understand that it
is a dim country of romance that Peer is dreaming of".
Think of Vesle Aase Gaasepike (No. Folkeev. p. 110) who
was waiting for "Kongssønnen fra Engeland; ib. p. 204;
Kongen av Engeland; Landstad, Folkeviser p. 347 and
of the "Kongens folk i England" in the children's game
Bro-bro-brille (Dr. H. F. Feilberg, Bro-bro-brille legen,
Sv. Landsmålen, 1905, p. 18) So we certainly obscure the
case by simplifying the consonant and the Archers, followed by Mr. Ellis Roberts very appropriately use the
form Engelland too. It is even far from unlikely that, as
in, say the 16th Cent. for many a German, so for many a
Norwegian the form Engel-land may have vaguely suggested the country of angels, — think of the classical non
Angli sed Angeli, attributed to Gregory, from which association Moltke Moe, (Episke Grundlove, Edda 1914, p.
247) concludes that it supported the conception of Ire-
land and England as the "land of souls". Hartland,
Science p. 279 tells of a poor mortal who married a "night-
mare" from Engel-land, evidently only on the strength

1, 25; 3, 29; F, 289; M, 179; 14, 27; J, 185; 16, 27.

of the "bitone" (V. Andersen, Festskrift V. Thomsen p. 303) that suggested aṇ "angelic" origin.

In Adam Homo I find once Engellænder with two l's (II, 181); Landsmaal knows the form Engelland as well as England; cf. Dølen, Vinje's Skrifter i Utval, I, 391, 467. Mr. C. L. Christensen reminds me of the Danish Nursery-rhyme: Jeg er født i Engelland og du er født i Skaane, vil du vær min lille mand, saa vil jeg vær din kone. A correspondent thinks that Ibsen has given the word three syllables only on account of the metre. Only: Engeland would have three syllables too; the English England two.

502.　　　Kejseren letter paa Kronen.
　　　Raising his crown the Kaiser.

A delightful instance of the results of Peer-Ibsen's eventyr-mood. We remember the story of han Herreper: King Asbjørnsen (for as the reader may remember, Werenskjold, painter and illustrator by divine inspiration of folk-tales, has immortalised the great story-teller as one of the Kings in the Fairy-Tales) — the King coming into the royal kitchen with his long pipe in his hand and the crown on his head and we need no very great imagination to see him just raise the crown a little to show his innate politeness to Herreper's ambassador.

508.　　　　　　Karl.

This Dano-norwegian word takes the place of the much more characteristically norwegian Gut of U.

509.　　　　　bergtagen. troll-taken,

as the Archers translate it, i. e. kidnapped by the fairies or mountain sprites. This is what actually happens to Peer, when later on he meets his fate in the person of the "Lady dressed in Green", l.l. 956 seqq., see a monograph by Feilberg: Bjærgtagen, Studie over en gruppe træk fra Nordisk Alfetro, København, 1910 and lower down the note to l.l. 1000 seqq. An interpretation of this motif that suggests itself at once is the being "taken in" not so much literally into a mountain but metaphorically by a person's charms, in other words by love that takes one's reason prisoner. This has been elaborated very beautifully it would seem by a Danish classic, M. A. Goldschmidt in his story, precisely called Bjergtagen, on which see a study by Prof. Vilhelm Andersen, Edda, I, p.p. 75 seqq.

514.   Korp, raven.

Specifically Norwegian; S. I. S. p. 191.

523.   Jeg er lige sæl. It's all one to me.

This expression sounds strange in Danish ears, where sæl = happy, pleased is obsolete and sounds Norwegian.

529.   Ringagten. scorn. See T. C. § 99.

535.   piskende Død. Galloping death.

The expression used by the Archers and Mr. Ellis Roberts to translate this is utterly unsatisfactory and shows that they have not understood its force and meaning. The error is no doubt primarily owing to the very common misbelief that piskende must be a real present participle simply because it has its form. As a matter of fact, just as we have e. g. pinende gal and ravende gal by the side of pinegal and ravgal out of which the former have developed (Ordb. over Gadesproget; cf. ib. p. 402: ravruskende gal) and even such forms as kullende sort and gullende ren for kulsort and ren som guld, where the possibility of real present participles is absolutely excluded[1]) (cf. a paper by the present writer on these — ende-forms in the Arkiv f. n. filol, XXX, p. 35), so piskende død may

---

[1]) Dr. Western quotes quite a number of such "present participles" as he too calls them (cf. his "Skriv Norsk, p. 60:" I talesproget har denne form av nutidsparticip visst praktisk mistet sin verbale natur og brukes.... som adj. eller gradsadverbium: bekende mørkt) which I copy here as they each and all serve to bear out my point that semasiologically there can be no question of a present participle: Hamsun, Ny Jord, 64: Stjærnende gal, id. V, 220: klinkende stille. Kinck, Emigranten, 185: strupende tunge og tause. Hamsun, V, 220: dørgende stille. Elster, Mester 25: livende ræd. id. ib. 137: svidende godt. Ring, Den kjærligheten, 130: murende stille. Scott, Kari Kveldsmat, 86: knaldende blaa. Kinck, Naar kjærlighet dør, 224: knakende morsomt. J. Lie, III, 152: himlende nok at gjøre. Gran, Hvor Sydlyset flammer, 84: stummende mørkt. Bennecke, Sjørøverskuben: huggende stilt. Egge, Trøndere, 108: knaldende hvit og blaa. Lie, V, 538: blottende Ungdommen and cf. rivende gal, P. G. l. 662.

go back to a simpler form without any such — ende-ter-mination. And just as in English we have the well-known 's Death, standing for God's death [1]), so in the Scandinavian languages we find not only Guds dø(d), but also Guds død og pine, as well as pine død [2]) and even Guds bittre død (cf. Norvegia, I, 62: æ du sjuk? — nei guss bitter dö æ eg ei, and Brand: Bonden skriger: Stands mand! Guds bitre—! Her er bræen; F, III, p. 4) or more simply: bitter død (Ja, saafort som denne skulde, Bitter-dø, eg klive upp Kampen, ou', sa Budeia; Kleiven, I gamle daagaa, p. 93 and Jeg skal bætter dø karnøfle jer!; Huldreev. p. 254, En aften i Nabogaarden). Now, "besk er døden" (we have Peer's word for it, l. 1922: "som man siger") and den beske død is a s t a n d i n g expression (cf. han holdt fast som den beske død, Feilberg, Bjærgtagen, p. 20) of which such a form as bekkede (Huldreev. p. 138, explained simply as "an oath", may be a further corruption.

So far, it will be clear that we need not have recourse to the verb piske, to whip, to pelt, in order to explain our expression; indeed, its own semasiology and if it had any connection with piske, that into galloping would be difficult to explain. And we are prepared for the suggestion that this piskedød may have developed out of this (Guds) beske død, — perhaps by a cross with this very pinedød, just as we find piskegal and piskende gal by the side of pinegal. Brynildsen who does not give piskende død, on being asked whether he knew the expression, quoted from Caspari's Højfjeld an expression" piskadausen '-which to some extent supplies the missing link in the present chain of arguments [3]) — and remarks that as

[1]) See an interesting paper on the various imprecations in English by Professor Swaen in the Engl. Studien, XXIV, p.p. 16 seqq.

[2]) In l. 718 (end of first act) we have Guds død og plage. As to død og pine and pinedød, see Professor Jespersen's paper in the Festskrift to Dr. Feilberg, p. 38.

[3]) Dr. Western supplies another by telling me that he seems to have heard "jo, piskadau". I add that Johan Bojer uses: bitterdausen in Den Store Hunger and that I have a distinct recollection of having at one time found piskende død in print as well as a short note on the expression; I regret to say that no trace of it can be found in my notes. Compare also "piskede" which may be found in Arne Garborg's little sketch, Han Lars i Lia: Ja, so piskede fær eg til Amerika!

"piske is found in similar imprecations (Fanden piske mig om. . . . ; det er faen piske mig sandt) it might be a (much obscured) reference to the passion of the Christ, in casu the flagellation. And it is interesting to read in his communication that although he does not know himself, colloquially, this piskedød, — he is quite familiar with "pisketre, hvor tre er maskert for død." This finds a remarkable parallel in Swedish pinade, pinatre, which I find passim in Wigström's Folktro (cf. ib. p.p. 27, 44, 142, 218, 221, for these and other mutilations such as piratre, pirodal, etc.) The German Tod und Teufel, zum Henker is therefore much better if not the nearest approach imaginable and the English should run: God's death or some such phrase.

538. Hallingen "a somewhat violent peasant dance" (Archer, p. 29) traakken, the green; glup (excellent).

The Archers' green is not quite beyond criticism, — it is the well-t r o d d e n place, as a rule a courtyard, — the dance is supposed to take place outside the house or Peer would not be able to see it from where he now stands, but green would suggest too much. All these words are specifically Norwegian; cf. S. I. S. p. 191. On the Halling, cf. n. to. 1. 551; U had Springeren which is perhaps slightly less characteristically Norwegian. According to Seip, Wergeland, p. 165, the word Halling occurs also in the sense of a dancing-t u n e.

544.   Kjögemesteren. The master-Cook.

The Kjøgemester (sometimes contracted into Kjømester; cf. Kjømeister, Syn og Segn, 1896, p. 72) is a sort of master of ceremonies at the Norwegian peasants' wedding-feast, who does not only see to it that people get enough to eat and (see l.l. 548 and 580) to drink (cf. Syn og Segn, 1902, p. 102: Kjære Kjøgemeister, skjænk i Bollen din), but who is supposed to come out once and again with a poem or a song composed for the occasion (Aa, altidt so hè kjøkemeisterinn ei Vis, Norvegia, I, 283) and to make a speech "i det Øieblik da Brudegrøden er baaren paa Bordet", Aasen, Prøver af Landsmaalet i Norge², p. 53, where one of these kitchenmaster's speeches may be found printed. The Danish corresponding term is skaffer, cf. Feilberg in v. skaffer and køks. He had a place of honour in the bridal procession, — cf. Olaf Liljekrans, S, V, (F) X, p. 98, a truly Ibsenian passage, strongly reminding one of Peer Gynt's Imperial vision, l.l. 493 seqq.

The bridal custom here referred to may be found reflected both in the world of the animals and of the Underjordiske: cf. Landstad, Folkeviser, s. 626, etc.: Bjønnen skal vera kjøkemeister i skóginn (Ravna-bryllaup uti Krakalund) and Norske Sagn², p. 95 where we read of a magic castle where there was "et stort følge med trold.... Der var Kjøgemester og Spillemand akkurat som det er skik i store brylluper paa landet". (Kaproning med Nøkken i Kristianiafjord.)

Peer Gynt was written at Ischia in 1867. Jæger, Henrik Ibsen og hans Værker, 1892, p. 67 thinks it possible that the splendid surroundings there have contributed largely to give the sketch of Norwegian folk-life a somewhat brighter and lighter tone (en noget lysere og lettere tone) and he compares especially the present scene which in this respect is characteristic of the whole of Peer Gynt.

547   Nu faar I, Godtfolk, paa Dunken lænse.

Now then, good folk, you must empty the barrel.

Mr. C. L. Christensen has been good enough to favour me with the following note: "This dunk" — which should be rendered by "stone-bottle" or (stone) - j a r rather than by "barrel", — "has always been a beloved companion among the peasantry. It is still known, people bring it with them into the fields at harvest-time, when all drink of it together. It has a form like a Dutch ginflask, only much larger and of stone; its popular names are many, in Jutland it is often called æ skegmand = the bearded man. As a proof of its popularity it may be said that in Denmark a "work-soldier" (arbejdssoldat) i. e. one that does not belong to any special arm or corps but that does some odd jobs here and there is commonly called a "dunk".

548.   Takk, som byder. Thanks to you, friend.

The comma behind Takk is in R and subsequent editions. But the reading of U = Takk som, without the comma is much more in accordance with the way in which the words are colloquially pronounced; some will regret therefore, that Ibsen added it in R.

551,2. Gjildt Kast.... højt till Loftet og vidt till Væggen! The roof here is high and the walls wide asunder.

To this the Archers append the useful note (p. 30): "To kick the rafters is considered a great feat in the Halling-dance. The boy (read the young fellow) means that in the open air, his leaps are not limited even to the rafters." In l. 973, the Green Lady boasts of a similar feat that her father, King Brosë, can perform. To get an idea of what such a dance means, the student should read accounts of it, such as the one found in Norske Sagn², p. 126 seqq., about Store-Hans, "efter Olav Aasmundstad i Sveinn Urædd". The men in Valdres are famous for their litheness and vigour when dancing the Halling.... they danced it on their heels and their hams (he dansede paa hæl og haser), jumped and kicked, whizzed round on the floor and managed sometimes to soar in the air and "take the crown" i. e. "touch the rafters" ¹) so that it

---

¹) "Det er et Beviis paa Hallingdandserens Flinkhed, naar han i sine Rundkast kan "tage Bjelken", som det heder; "Landstad No. Folkeviser, p. 223. It would appear from the ballad that L. there prints, that even girls when dancing the Halling tried to kick the rafters: Myllars dottri dansar og kveð og slær imót remi med fóte, — at least if Landstad's interpretation of remi = "beam-pole", bjelkestangen, is right. But as Dr. Western remarks, it would be considered very indecent for a girl to kick the rafters, and as he has never heard of a girl dancing the Halling, he doubts Landstad's explanation of remi.

---

rang in the room, — saa det skraldede i stuen". And then comes the description of Store Hans' feats on the table that had been laid: "Nu skal jeg røre op i svinehaugene deres", — I'll just kick up a little in that pig-sty of theirs! And so the little game began. Cups and mugs and dishes hailed down upon the dancers, boiling soup and other victuals trickled down upon their faces and on to their bodies.... Then.... he began even to kick the table and benches to pieces." At a certain moment he has kicked the whole room empty and finds himself quite alone. "He had been in such a berserker's fury — run amuck! — that he scarcely knew where he was". Well, blood is thicker than water and when at one time a certain Salve Kvaas went up to Holy Communion, he could not contain himself and kicked up a Halling round the altar, — this happened nearly two centuries ago! (cf. Maal og Minne, 1915, p. 182). Quite recently on the contrary, Selma Lagerlöf has given a description (Gammal Fäbodsägn, Troll ock Människor, p. 73), of the robber that comes to the lonely girl in a sæterhut, that might well stand for one of a berserker. All this testifies eloquently to the popularity of the t h i n g, — that of the expression as imagery becomes picturesquely clear from the fact that Jørgen Moe in a poem of 1834 (Anders Krogvig, Fra det nationale Gjennembruds Tid, p. 304) makes the stars dance one and kick at the moon! "Hvad toner gjennem Sangen? Sphærers Laat, Naar alle Himlens Stjærner dandse Halling Og spænder efter Maanens Hat." We almost feel it as a shame that not one of them as yet has reached it! (Den endnu ingen af dem dog har naaet!)

550.   Jenten.

As the girl is introduced for the first time, we should expect: en Jente, like En Kone, En Mand, En Gut, etc. But U too has Jenten.

553, 557. Kaut (proud) and naut (lit. cattle, here an ass, a

1, 28; 3, 32; F, 292; M, 181; 14, 30; J, 187; 16, 30.

blockhead) are specifically Norwegian, S. I. S. p. 191.—
559. Peer Gynt er paa Gaarden? Here comes Peer Gynt.
On the point of interrogation, utterly uncalled for, in
the first ed., see T. C. § 17 and compare n. to l. 567.
567. Ikveld? Er du rent fra Sans og Samling?
To-night? are you utterly out of your senses?
Here, the point of exclamation — Samling! — is
actually found in R too, whereas U has: Samling. See
T. C., n°. 53, § 128; Professor Storm, S. M. p. 24 (4. d.)
explains it as a case of "spørgende udråb" and the number of analogous cases adduced looks imposing enough,
only we never know if his references do not reproduce the
printed texts which are not to be trusted and in how far
they agree with the unsophisticated Ibsenian Manuscripts. As to "Ikveld?", as Mr. Archer remarks (p. 32),
the wedding-festivities often last several days.
572. Øjekast; sylhvasse Tanker og Smil.
Mocking looks; needle-keen thoughts and smiles.
Here, U read: Bare Tanker, — ordløse Tanker og
Smil, — Bare Tanker was changed later by Ibsen into:
Latter bag en! The first U-reading was transferred by
Ibsen to this place in U from a preceding scene; cf. Eft.
Skr. II, 84.
Where Ibsen found the imagery appears clearly from
his own youthful reminiscences (H. Jæger, H. I. '88, p. 7),
where he speaks of the noise that filled the air in Skien
all day long "af dæmpet drønnende sus fra Langefos og
.... andre faldende vande, og gennem fosseduren skar
fra morgen til kveld noget, der lignet hvasse, snart hvi-
nende, snart stønnende kvindeskrig. Det var de hundrede sagblade som arbejdede ude ved fossene." And
he adds that when later on he read about the guillotine,
he must always think of these saws.
And the sentiment itself is supposed to be a reminiscence of his youth too, — at least Professor Gran (Nordm.
i det 19de Aarh. III, 187) writes of Ibsen's feelings when

his father became a bankrupt that the latter unhappy man must have been the object of a good deal of impudent pity. "Henrik som havde de indesluttede naturers hele saarbarhed, følte smertelig svien ved at være en deklasseret borgers søn; endnu tredve aar efter dirrer det efter krænkelserne han har maattet udstaa i sin opvekst" and then Gran quotes these lines as well as l.l. 463, 4; 526,7. Compare also the n. to l. 463.

576. Hedalen.

There is a Hedal near the Spirillen lake in Valdres and one in Gudbrandsdal. But as they come "from the West", the former is the more likely one for Ibsen to have thought of. It may be merely a reminiscence of the (Smaagguttene som traf trollene paa) Hedalskogen that the poet had read of in Asbjørnsen's Folkeeventyr. (ed. 1914 p. 132). That this Hedalen should be strongly under the influence of the "stille" (n. to l. 689) as the context might seem to suggest, is not known to my correspondents.

580. Er du kommen, saa skal du vel stikke paa Kruset?

Since you *are* here, you'd best take a pull at the liquor.

On the point of interrogation and its peculiar force, see T. C. § 61. All the translations, the Archers' among the number, have suffered somewhat under the substitution by the 6th ed. of a point of exclamation which obscures a delicate shade of meaning: the kitchenmaster's r e l u c t a n t invitation, to some extent. Koht, Eft. Skr. III, 416 gives the reading of U merely: Velkommen till Peer Gynt, du faar stikke paa Kruset., but it is interesting to know that already in U Ibsen had changed this into: Er du kommen saa faar du stikke paa Kruset; it was therefore not until in R that Ibsen added the here so important point of interrogation.

For stikke paa, cf. Ordb. over Gadesproget[2], p. 486: tage for sig af, næsten udelukkende i Forb.: stikke paa Varerne, ɔ: Mad-og Drikkevarerne; and cf. Vildanden: stik paa glassene, F. VII, 208.

_____

1, 31; 3, 35; F, 295; M, 182; 14, 32; J, 189; 16, 32.

581.   Jeg har ingen Tørst. I am not athirst.

Ibsen here uses the common Dano-Norwegian expression, as against lower down l.l. 1509 and 1668: han er tørst; er du tørst, Danish: han er tørstig. Tørst for tørstig here is one of the Norwegianisms that Lyder Sagen, the famous teacher of Dansk-Norsk — for whom every Norwegian form was bad because "only dialect"—, thought it his duty to protest against; cf. S. I. S. p. 148.

584.   Skotted ned paa.... det hvide sprede!

looked down at her.... snow-white apron!

Here U has: Saa ned paa det hvide Spredet, rhyming on Klædet instead of as in R, on Klæde. The substitution of the more "grammatical" Dano-norwegian det hvide Sprede, for the popular Norwegian double expression of the definite article is worth paying attention to. Immediately lower down however, paa den Jenten remains. Dr Western writes moreover that he thinks det hvide sprede better than det hvide spredet. "The latter expression (which is however pronounced exactly as the former) presupposes that this *sprede* had either been mentioned before or is known, or that he was pointing to it." Compare "Skriv Norsk", § 5.

As will have occurred to any reader of Goethe's Faust, there is a clear reminiscence to be seen in Solveig of Margaret, — "wie sie die Augen niederschlägt"! Margaret comes "von ihrem Pfaffen" too as Solveig "gik ivaares till Presten." On further influence of the Faust on Peer Gynt, see Index in v. Ibsen's Paa Vidderne which in a way may be called a first study of Peer Gynt (cf. Sturtevant l.l.) presents a point of resemblance too: Hun saa, jeg tror, paa Skoen sin (F, IV, 338). On Solvejg cf. Ellis Roberts, p. p. IX, XXII. As to the name of the Norwegian Margaret, Wörner makes a rather bad mistake when he volunteers the information (I, 411) that it means Sonnenmauer, — sunwall! Veig occurring in other female names (Gudveig, Oddveig) cannot of course

---

1, 32; 3, 36; F, 296; M, 182; 14, 33; J, 189; 16, 33.

be connected with væg = wall, but may be related to O. N. veig = woman, which Aasen however only quotes (p. 914) from Egillson; it is not found in Fritzner. (Add.)

586.   Salmebog, psalm-book.

The book meant, as Dr. Western tells me, is likely to be a hymn-book rather than a psalm-book and this the word salmebog in the text notwithstanding, which Dr. Western thinks is "hardly correct". The psalter was often used as a defence against evil powers; cf. the n. to l. 1263 and l.l. 745, 3320, 4644. As to the use here, Dr. Western writes: "It is the custom in the country (or was at least) for women (especially old ones) going to church to carry their hymn-books enveloped in their handkerchiefs. Now these people who were pietists, evidently thought that this would be a religious wedding, that consequently they would want their hymnbook there"

602.   Aa, Kors da! Oh heaven!

The fact that Ibsen writes Kors with a capital shows clearly that he still felt it as a substantive, although it has practically changed function and has become a mere exclamation. As such it is very common (ja kors, nei kors) expressing wonder, sympathy, fear or as here, painful surprise. Cf. (older) English (by the) mass! This picturesque expression takes the place of a tame: "Peer Gynt?" in U, to which Peer's answer is: Naa, hvad er det nu? See the n. to l. 1741.

608.   du var værd at bindes i Baasen!
             you're only fit to be tied in a stall!

This bind e s was changed by the 9th ed. into the (perhaps "slightly more common", Dr. Western) active construction binde i baasen; cf. T. C. § 75. There is no actual difference in meaning. (W.) For you are *fit*, you deserved would be preferable.

614.   Aah!

This now unusual spelling of the earlier editions (1,2) is also in U as well as R, but was changed later on into Ah.

1, 32; 3, 36; F, 296; M, 182; 14, 33; J, 189; 16, 33.

(found in 6, 8, F, 14; the others could not be collated any more when the deviation was observed.

622.   Konster.

See on this form T. C. § 114. Professor Storm who admits and respects Ibsen's Sveacisms and of course his Norwegian dialect forms, does not even give the question a thought if the o could possibly be owing to either influence. But if these Sveacisms are left alone, it is not easy to see why the Danisms which are both more common and more natural, should be ruled out of court. P r e c i s e l y because konst is older Danish, i. e. because Ibsen must have been familiar with it (it is common in Ibsen's source Adam Homo; and even quite recently Lynner, Hærmændene paa Helgeland, p. 55 still writes: Skaldekonsten), the word should have been kept.

As kunst in the sense not of art, but in that of (difficult) f e a t, is colloquially pronounced kånst, Dr. Western thinks of the possibility that this is what Ibsen meant, but concludes that "it is quite as likely that it is a Danism."

626.   mane Fanden. call up the devil!

Like all Peer's feats that he boasts of, he has heard this too as told about others, if he has not got it from his grandam who could do that before he was born (før jeg blev født; observe the interesting mistake in U: *fra hun* blev født). See e.g. the Huldreev. 1912, p. p. 173 and 174, the very amusing story of a priest that called the Evil one into a bottle. (Plankekjørerne) It is not very difficult to manage either, *teste* Johnsson's Sägner fra Östre Göinge, Svenska Landsmaalen 1904, p. 114): "That happened in this way that he that wanted to do it put a bit of paper into the keyhole of the church (door) and on it he wrote that if on such and such a day (the evil one) would come, they would enter into a compact". And the price is not prohibitive either! "Holy-Mary, a widely famous fortuneteller (klogkone, Hellig Mari) had

offered a boy to call up the devil for 25 øre", we read in
Dania, III, 14: Studier fra Læsø; he did not accept the
offer however but ran away. He evidently thought the
thing suspiciously cheap.

629.   Jeg har en Gang manet ham ind i en Nødd.
        I one day conjured him into a nut.

This and the next lines are practically a reproduction
of the story of "the Boy and the Devil" (Gutten og Fanden, Folkeev. 1912 p. 112) a translation of which may
therefore find a place here:

"There was once a young fellow that was walking
about and cracking nuts. He found a worm-eaten one and
just then met the Devil.

Is it true, said the boy, what people say, that you can
make yourself as little as you like and squeeze yourself
into a pin-hole?

Yes, said the devil.

O, I say, do let me see that and creep into the nut said
the fellow, and the Devil did so.

When the devil had squeezed himself through the
worm-hole, the young fellow put a pin into the hole. Now,
I've got ye, said the boy and put the nut into his pocket.

After having gone a little way, he came to a smithy.
He went in and asked the smith to crack the nut for him.

Well, yes, said the smith, that's easy enough and took
his smallest hammer, lay the nut on to the anvil and hit
it, but the nut did not go in pieces. He took a bigger one
but that was not heavy enough either, a still bigger one
would not do it any better. So the smith got angry and
took his sledgehammer. "I'll get it all right this time! he
said and hammered away as much as he could and then
the nut d i d go in pieces, but half of the roof flew away
too and there was a noise as if the whole house should
tumble down.

I do believe that the D e v i l was in that nut, said
the smith.

1, 37; 3, 41; F, 301; M, 184; 14, 37; J, 191; 16, 37.

Well yes, — he w a s, said the boy."

On the story itself, its origin and its congeners, see Moltke Moe, Eventyr og eventyrforvandling, Samtiden, 1908, p. p. 34 seqq. Further: Feilberg, II, 719, b.; Dania, X, 192; Clouston, Popular Tales and Fiction I, 385; Edda, 1915, p. 93 and infra n. to l. 692 on Loki in a nut. On the very distantly related story of the smith whom they did not dare to let into hell, see infra the n. to the Button Moulder, l. 4096.

635.   plent. just.

Norwegian and familiar, colloquial only, cf. Storm I. S. p. 192, who gives it even as vulgar, which view Dr. Western (in a private communication) endorses.

639.   Smidje, a smithy.

Norwegian (cf. the form smie in the text just quoted of Gutten og Fanden) for Danish smedje, cf. S. I. S. p. 190 — which curiously enough is in U. (Smedjen).

643.   stødt. ever.

Specifically Norwegian, S. I. S. p. 191; cf. l.l. 1703, 3660.

645.   for som en Brand, — cf. Addenda.

651.   digter ihob. making it up.

Compare l. 3869, where det digted han ihob is rendered by he made believe; perhaps slightly less felicitously for make up a story. The expression is not exclusively in popular use as Brynildsen[2] seems to hint; cf. e. g. Kejser og Galilæer S. V. V., p. 338 where the Emperor Julian is made to use it.

659.   at tryggle saa tyndt. of begging so hard.

Compare jeg beer saa tyndt, l. 3866 and No. Folkeev. p. 79: Fanden bad saa tyndt som en toskilling (Smeden som de ikke turde slippe ind i helvede).

668.   jeg er Kar', jeg. I'm a rare one.

Literally of course: I am (the) fellow, I, (to do such a thing); as in han er Kar for sin hat: he holds his own. See T. C. § 117, 135 on the spelling of kar.

The repetition of this pronoun is no doubt felt as spec-

1, 38; 3, 42; F, 301; M, 184; 14, 37; J, 191; 16, 37.

ifically Norwegian, cf. Poestion, Norw. Gr.³ § 140, anm.
p. 108. Its use in Danish authors is rare; cf. for once: jeg
ogsaa gaaer paa Heden, jeg. Oehlenschläger's Amleth;
ed. 1843, p. 44. An imitation of this is frequent in Elizabe-
than English; such as in Romeo and Juliet, III, 1, 56: I
will not budge for no man's pleasure, I; cf. Herrig's
Archiv, CXVII, 283 (Some cases of Scandinavian influence in English).

669.   Usynligheds–Kuften, — Hatten? —
         The Invisible Cloak? — Hat?

This means of rendering a person invisible, of frequent
occurrence in the fairy tales, is also called gjemsels-
hatten or Dværgehatten, cf. Brand (F, III, 244): brødre
ser sig sidde spage, krøbne under gemselshatten; cf. Eitrem, Samtiden, 1908, p. 626, 7: At folk vender sig bort
fra sine pligter, falder det naturligt for folkloristen (Ibsen) at udtrykke ved: de kryber under gemselshatten".
See: Feilberg in v. v. hat, I, 562, kappe (II, 89) dvær-
gehat (I, 230) and ib. Tillæg p.p. 115, 202, 253. In Folge-
svenden, (Asbjørnsen's No. Folkeev., ed. 1914, p. 178)
that mysterious personage is invisible "for han hadde
tresøsterhatten paa". Readers of Ibsen's Doll's House
will remember Dr. Rank's doleful joking about it (F. VI,
315) when he gives a hint about his plan to commit suicide by saying that at the next masquerade he will bear
the "hat that makes invisible". The origin of the notion
is by some supposed to be owing to dreams, — for that
is no doubt what Prof. Anathon Aall means when in his
Eventyr og Drøm (Maal og Minne, 1914, p. 61) he speaks
of the Usynlighets-r i n g e n and says: I drømme er
subjektet tilstede uten at være synlig. Usynlighetsrin-
gen i eventyret har sit psykologiske forbillede i drøm-
men." Others think of mist around the mountains; which
teste the well-known case of (Mons) Pil(e)atus has at
least endowed one mountain with a hat! cf. Paul's
Grundriss, I¹, p. 1031 (omitted however in the corres-

ponding passage in III[3]) and Meyer, Mythologie der Germanen (p. p. 156, 170). We may no doubt also think of the earth that hides the "huldre" — the hidden people. — It will be remembered that later on in the play it is this very hat that is supposed to be sold at the auction, cf. l. 3839.

The references to this hat in Scandinavian folklore are numerous; see, besides those given: Löland, Norsk Eventyrbok, Norske Samlaget, Oslo, 1915, p. 182; Olsen, No. Folkeev. og Sagn, p. 1; Faye, p. 29; En Aftenstund i et Proprietærkjøkken. Huldreev. 1912, p. 37; ib. p. 265 (Fra Sognefjorden); ib. p. 83 (En aften ved Andelven); Feilberg, Jul. II, 133; id. Sjæletro, 1914, p. 161; Hermelin, Sägner ock Folktro, p. 22; H. ock E. Folkminnen, 1907, p. 409.

It would seem that it is not at all difficult to get hold of one, you have only to take good care to call for one at the very moment that you see the Underjordiske put them on, —then a hat will be slung out of the mountain to you, perhaps a very old and dirty one, but that you must not mind, — put it on and it will serve its purpose; cf. Thiele, Danske Folkesagn, II, 211, Weis, Sägner på Aspelandsmål, Sv. Landsm. 1906, p. 97; Wigström, Folktro, p. 65. In my Faustus-Notes (p. 80, 81) other instances will be found enumerated.

Usynligheds-k u f t e n has at least one parallel as will be remembered in Jack the Giantkiller.

675.   Vær ikke tvær. do not be wayward.

In U, Ibsen had first written Vær ikke sen, do not be slow, which is much less expressive. In consequence of this, the original hver og en, was changed into: en og hver.

684.   Du skjæms, fordi jeg ser ud som en Fant.
       You're ashamed to, because I've the look of a tramp.

On Du skjæms, see S. M. p. 35 § 41; on Fant which is specifically Norwegian, Seip's Wergeland p. 25.

1, 41; 3, 45; F, 305; M, 186; 14, 40; J, 192; 16, 40.

686.   paa en Kant. taken a drop.

On this Norwegianism, = slightly fuddled, half seas over, so perhaps slightly stronger than the Archers' take a drop, see Seip, l. l. p. 169.

687.   men det var paa Trods, for du havde krænkt mig.

but that was to spite you, because you had hurt me.

The reading of U here was: men det er fordi de andre har krænkt mig. Vil du? (for: Kom saa, of R.) Ibsen seems to have felt that it would render Peer's excuse more plausible if it was Solveig herself that caused him pain.

689, seqq. han er af de stille! Hælder han med Øret?....Er Faer din Læser? he is one of the quiet ones! One of the godly, eh?.... Is your father a psalmsinger?

"To read with a Clergyman" — at læse med Præsten — is the almost technical expression for attending a confirmation-class, what Solveig has before (l. 599) expressed by saying: Jeg gik i vaares till Presten; cf. Feilberg, II, 502,6. Here Læser is the name for a sect of pietists, such as crop up at all times and in any country, that look upon most pleasures if not all, as inspired by the evil one and hence to be avoided. What this meant at the time precisely for the folktales (eventyr, etc.) is clear from a letter of Jørgen Moe (cf. A. Krogvig, Fra det Nationale Gjennembruds Tid, p. 266) where he speaks of the difficulties that these pietists caused him: Many look upon these ,Viser og Eventyr' as the doings of Satan", — and see the editor's comment, p. 62. — In Norway, the great movement in that direction was started early in the 19th century by H.N. Hauge; his followers were called the Haugianer or the "awakened ones" — "de vakte". In Ibsen's own time, a clergyman of the (Lutheran) State-church of Norway, called Lammers started a similar movement at Skien, Ibsen's birth-place, such as Wales has known not so very long ago and it was no doubt this Lammers that may be looked upon in many respects as

the model of Ibsen's Brand; cf. Karl Larsen's ed. of the
"Episke Brand" (p.p. 244 seqq.) and Eitrem, Samtiden, 1908, p.p. 633 seqq. It should not however be imagined that this aversion from pleasure was the sum and
substance of Haugianism. It was in reality essentially
an almost necessary reaction by the force of circumstances against the realism and rationalism of the 18th century. Whatever objection to it later times concentred
or condensed in such nick-names as "de stille" and especially "at hælde med Øret" was directed against the parallel movement of the sixties, changed as it was from
the early days. Far from attributing to him the attitude
of mind that such expressions as hældøre, hængehoder,
indicate, Hauge's biographers on the contrary lay stress
on the energy he showed in his life and the fact that
everywhere he combated all despondency ("modløshed");
cf. e. g. Ullmann's sketch in Nordmænd i det 19de Aarh.
I, p.p. 2, 3, 22, etc.

"De Stille", i. e. "de stille i landet" suggests Ps. 35,20:
(them) that are quiet in the land" and cf. the Lamenta-
tions of Jeremiah where the Danish text runs: Det er
godt at man haaber og er stille til Herrens Frelse ("quietly wait' in the A. V.; Lam. 3, 26). For: hælder han med
øret? Ibsen had written in U: hænger med Hodet; and indeed, "helde med hovedet" was looked upon as a sign of
piety", as Brynildsen (in v. hælde) will tell you. Hence in
a(very unsympathetic) description of a pietist to be found
in Asbjørnsen's and Moe's Huldreev. (Fra Sognefjorden,
p. 267) we read about a certain Læsar-Per, that he "tok paa
i en sangrende og suttrende præketone at utbrede sig
om drikkens og brændevinets fordærvelighet.... han
hadde h æ n g e h o d e n e s vanlige væsen og fakter",
etc. But why does Ibsen substitute øret for hovedet?

Hældøre (which, teste the Ordb. over Gadesproget is
known in Denmark too) is explained by Mau (II, 617) as
blive forsagt, tabe Modet, whereas ib. p. 548 we find:

1, 43; 3, 47; F, 306; M, 187; 14, 42; J, 193; 16, 42.

Verden er skuløret = skuler og hælder med Øret, in the
slightly different sense of: to be cunning; but of course
the accusation of wiliness against the Puritans was but
one of the many launched against them; cf. my Faustus-Notes p. 49 for a choice collection. In Dutch a corresponding, 'de ooren laten hangen' occurs = to lose
courage (Stoett, n°. 1467) just like "at hænge med Hovedet" also occurs in Danish "om den skinhellige saa
vel som om den bedrøvede" (Mau, I, 467). The Archers'
"one of the godly" is hardly quite satisfactory, but an
exact equivalent has not been suggested.

692.   Jeg kan skabe mig om till et Trold.
              I can turn myself into a troll!

The faculty of taking the shape of an animal that Peer
more suo attributes to himself here, is again one that is
quite common in the great source for Ibsen's reading and
Peer's boasting: the popular tales and stories as well
as in the older histories such as Saxo, Snorre and the
Edda itself. It is intimately connected as a doctrine with
its more spiritual counterpart if it may thus be expressed
of the transmigration of souls of the Indian religions, the
metempsychosis of Pythagoras and a characteristic feature of Manichæism. The essential thing in this transformation must be supposed to be the transplanting of
one's own fylgja i. e. one's soul, into another's body; cf.
the note on the Fremmede, who is nothing but Peer
Gynt's spiritus familiaris. — See e. g. on this "Fähig-
keit des Gestaltenwechsels", Herrmann, Nordische Mythologie, p. 68, ib. 71, on the change of sex; 454 and 553;
masquerading may be a reminiscence of this; Paul's
Grundriss I¹, 1009 = 3², 262. On the werewolf more especially: ib. I¹, 1017 = 3², 272, v. d. Leyen, Herrig's Archiv, CXIII, 268, Tylor, Primitive Culture, I, 308, on Vam-
pires ib. II, 193. On this motiv in the older Folkeviser,
I refer to Olrik's and Ida Falbe Hansen's useful little
edition (extract) of the Danske Folkeviser, 1899, intro-

1, 43; 3, 47; F, 307; M, 187; 14, 42; J, 193; 16, 42.

duction p. 70. Belief in the werewolf lies at the bottom of an other famous creation of Ibsen's: "Pappa, Lille Eyolf asks of his father, about Rottejomfruen who in the first version of the play is actually called Frøken Varg. —: "Så kanske det kan være sandt alligevel, at hun er varulv om natten? (S. V. IX, 191 = Eft. Skr. III, 277).

For the Edda it will suffice to refer to Loki's frequent transformations e. g. into a fly, a flea to steal the Brisingamen (Meyer p. 419) and into a nut which reminds us of the Devil in the nut ante n. to l. 629.

In Saxo we have Bjarki as a bear (ed. Jantzen, p. 101); with regard to Snorre I refer inter alia to Olav Trygveson's Saga: Kong Harald bød en tryllekyndig mand at fare i hamfærd til Island og friste hvad han kunde fortælle ham; han fór i hvals ham; Snorre, ed. G. Storm p. 161; cf. ib. p. 201: Jeg (Øivind) er en aand, skabt i menneskeham ved Finnens Trolddom. It appears from this that also the reverse can take place, cf. Molke Moe og Liestøl, Norske Folkeviser p. 71: a water sprite "skapte seg i ein kristen-mann" and cf. ib. p. 40: En trollmand... kan ogsaa kaste ham (helst dyreham) paa andre and then the authors remind the reader of the frequent tricks that for exemple a wicked step-mother plays upon her victims in the fairy tales.

These fairy tales are full of such transformations of which I quote a few; the reference is here to the Fællessamlingen ed. by Moltke Moe in 1899. A prince is found transformed into a dog (1,11) a horse (1,83; 2,172,3) a foal (1,189,90) a wild duck (1,200) a white bear (2,50) a duck (2,29) a loaf (2,29) a gadfly (2,30) and a clod of earth (2,30). In the Huldreeventyr (ed. 1912, p. 12) we have even the remarkable case of the Ekebergkongen (the mountain-spirit of Ekeberg, just outside Kristiania) who takes upon himself the likeness of Bernt Anker, a well-known patrician of the metropolis at the time. In Bertha Tuppenhaug's Fortællinger (ib. p. 27) a girl has

---

1, 43; 3, 47; F, 307; M, 187; 14, 42; J, 193; 16, 42.

received the visit as she thinks of her betrothed who has been talking all the time of the wedding, — after a time the real man turns up and hearing her account concludes: "det maa vel ha vöri enhaarr (nogen) som har tii (tat) paa sig min lignels."

According to a Swedish tradition, a suicide too possesses this faculty: en självspilling.... kan.... ta på sig vems skepnad han vil, Wigström, Folktro, p. 213; n° 651.

In "Makreldorg" three witches that wish to get rid of their husbands turn themselves even into breakers (braadsjø) to drown them in. In Skarvene fra Utröst, three men are changed into cormorants. Olsen l. l. p. 141 tells a story "Lapkjærringen bankes til bjørn" where the theory of the transformation very tragically threatens to become miserable reality, where Laps dress a poor woman in bearskin and hammer away at her, so much so that under the terrible suggestion of the possibility of the thing her nature changes actually and in a real berserkerfury (cf. n. to l. 4141) she kills a couple of men until at last she is overcome and killed herself. Compare Tylor, Primitive Culture I, 414: Gautama, during his 550 jatakas or births took the form of a frog, a fish, a crow (cf. ib. II, 11: four times the Maha Brahma.... a hermit, a king, a slave, a potter, a curer of snakebites, an ape, etc.) and so far were the legends of these transformations from mere myths to his followers that there have been preserved as relics in Buddhist temples the hair and feathers and bones of the creatures whose bodies the great teacher inhabited.

The acme of such transformations is presented by such stories as Bonde Veirskjeg (No. Folkeev. 1912, p. 241) Runekallen aa Drengjen hans (Aasen, Prøver af Landsmaalet i Norge, p. 14) and cf. Svein i Hei og Jomfru Agnusmøy in Norske Eventyr og Sagn by Bugge-Berge, II, 1913 where on p. 45 an illustration will be found of

---

Agnusmøy that "transmuted the boy to a pond and herself to a duck that swam on the pond!"

On the substitution in later editions of Danish *en* (trold) for *et*, see T. C. § 53.

697. Vesle. little.

Specifically Norwegian, cf. S. I. S. p. 191; cf. ll. 790, 1539.

An other form is vetle, veltle (Aasen², p. 925).

701. Nu var du stygg. Then you were grim.

The idiom seems curiously enough to have caused nearly all the translators a little difficulty. Neither Mr. Ellis Roberts': You were horrible then, nor Messrs Archers' Then you were grim (in the note: literally: now you were ugly) hits off entirely the v a r and the s t y g of the original. "Then" almost seems to show that the translators (cf. g r i m and h o r r i b l e too) thought of Peer as he must have looked in the imaginative little transformation-scene if enacted. To render var by were is tempting and not absolutely wrong but if we think of this idiomatic use of the past tense instead of the present: det var mærkelig i. e. that i s remarkable and e. g. when giving change: det var altsaa syv kroner: that m a k e s just seven kroner etc. (cf. e. g. Poestion², § 210 p. 149) it will be clear that Solveig means: how u n k i n d you a r e, and although in this particular case English idiom would also admit of: This w a s unkindly said, the present tense would seem to render the Norwegian shade of meaning intended slightly better.

Prozor: Tu as été méchant, Mrs. Clant v. d. Mijll: Hè, dat was slecht; Brons: Dat was gemijn; Passarge: Nun warst du recht hässlich; Morgenstern: Jetzt warst du arg; Wörner (I¹, 223) Nun warst du hässlich, — each and all are rather unsatisfactory.

cf. l. 1351: det var Fanden till Kropp.

702. Kommer drivende.

That drivende is as little a real present participle here

---

as the corresponding English: he comes sauntering along, will be clear from a study of the note on l. 535 and the paper there quoted.

704. Peer Gynt eller jeg skal i Bakken bændes.

Peer Gynt or I must be bent to the hillside or "made to bite the dust", be taught a lesson; the three alternatives given by the Archers. On this specifically Norwegian expression see S. I. S. p. 191 and on its meaning T. C. § 58, lower down n. to l. 896. To such "brydekamper" or "basketag" it is that Aase refers in l. 263 (in the mighty battle royal.... when you raged like mongrels mad; det store Basketag som for nylig stod paa Lunde, hvor I slogs som olme Hunde). Brons (p. 261) compares the modern German students' "mensur" which he thinks may be a survival of this and refers to a paper on Knud Sellestad, the same presumably that will be found quoted *ante* n. to l. 551.

705. nappes. fight.

Det skal der nappes om (have a scrummage, a bit of a dust about) is the very expression to be found *passim* in the fairy tales.

708. Lad os heller gjøgle med alle hans Løgne!

Let us rather tease him with all his lies!

To tease, to make fun of is no doubt meant. Only literally at gjøgle is to juggle but the subst. gjøgl = buffoonery shows the shade of meaning in which the verb is here used, corresponding quite closely to the gjøne of U.

709. Sparke ham of Laget! Kick him out of the company!

U reads here less delicately: for Bagen, where "back" stands of course for its "unmentionable" part!

710. Stikker du opp, du? You're not backing out, Smith?

In U, it is the smith that says: jeg stikker ikke opp, før jeg faar ham slagtet (but it was changed into the reading of R already in U) i. e. I do not give it up, give in, = jeg gir ikke tapt, which is the very equivalent that the Danish Ordb. over gadesproget gives for stikke op.

Øget skal slagtes. The jade shall be slaughtered.

Of course by Øg, Peer is meant. Mr. Ellis Roberts' the a s s must to the slaughter is not a very happy rendering for øg: en udslidt hest, to which the Archers' jade comes much closer; cf. han er et stakkels Øg; dit sølle Øg! (Da. ordb. f. F.).

711.   Tomsing. windbag,

as both the Archers and Ellis Roberts render it; literally: an empty head, a fool, is a specifically Norwegian word; cf. S. I. S. p. 191.

715.   spytter i Hænderne. spits on his hands.

The action is so common and so perfectly in keeping with what we may suppose our friend the smith's little habits to be, that we are apt to pass it by as merely one more of those little traits true to life that the master gives us so many of. Again in the "session at Lunde" (l. 3694) the Captain "spytted, pegte ud og sagde gaa!" and Peer Gynt in approaching the Norwegian coast "spytter og stirrer mod Kysten" and at first blush these words seem to mean exactly what they say and nothing more (In the last case, Wörner incidentally remarks (I^1, p. 255) that Peer spits like a sailor: I am afraid that it is not only the sailors that are guilty of what many people not to the manner born would look upon as breach of decorum, but that is neither here nor there.) But if not in all, at least in our case there is "more than meets the eye". The fact of spitting and its "incorporation" if I may say so, in the simple interjection "tvi", point nearly always where found in the eventyr, to a very interesting survival. I may refer to an excellent paper on the subject by Flentzberg (in "Fataburen" 1908, p. 105): Spott ook Spottning, from which it will appear that as Feilberg (III, 512; see also ib. in v. måle²) puts it: spitting brings luck and is in fact a preventive against all evil. Compare also Herrmann, Nordische Mythologie p. 197: der Speichel, Mittel der Seelenvereinigung beim feierlichen Bunde: if

---

1, 45; 3, 49; F, 308; M, 187; 14, 44; J, 194; 16, 44.

anyone were to spit in your face, it is doubtful whether you would feel honoured; yet this is the feeling the action would evoke among some tribes in Africa.

For some cases in point from Scandinavian folklore, cf. Huldreev., p. 24: A wise woman's invocation ends invariably by "et gjentat *tvi !* mot alle verdens fire hjørner" It is of course even more effective to spit "i guds nabn" (ib. p. 264). If you wish to get rid of your warts, look up Dania, II, 217 and you will find the recipe there that folk observe with success in East-Jutland, — I only betray here so much of the secret that you must spit at a certain moment as many times as there w e r e warts. And you see now why the magician that wishes to ride up a steep rock as easily as if the country were the proverbial Cheshire cheese, s p i t s upon the hoofs of his steed. (Feilberg in v. hest). See further Feilberg in v. dørhug; Wickström, Folktro p. 115; Weis, Sägner på Aspelandsmål, Sv. L., 1906, p. 106, H. and E., Folkminnen, 1907, p. 375, nos 294, 295; ib. p. 419 and Hermelin, Sägner ock Folktro, p. p. 20 and 27 who gives the safe advice that there is no harm in it: spotta kan man ju altid göra", and cf. Brand's Popular Antiquities, III. 259 for some other illustrations of this point from classical lore and older English writers.

716.   prøv om I tør. Just try if you dare.

This seems to be if not of course exactly a proverb, nor even a proverbial expression, one of those familiar turns of phrase that one pronounces "in inverted commas" — i Gaaseøine — i. e. with a slight raising of the voice: "as who should say" etc. At least it is found thus in Danish, cf. Mau, II, 139.

717.   Aase og jeg.

These words as spoken by Aase who therefore speaks of herself in the third person adding: and I, are called by the Archers a peasant idiom. It is slightly more common perhaps; we may call it a colloquialism that boarders upon

---

1, 45; 3, 49; F, 309; M, 188; 14, 44; J, 194; 16, 44.

the vulgar. Hence it is in perfect keeping with Jacob Engstrand's education (or absence of same!) that Ibsen lets him make use of it: "Aa ja, saamæn gjør det saa; for her staar Jacob Engstrand og jeg" (Gjengjangere, F, VI, 458; M. IV, p. 127) and in Holberg's Ellevte Junii, a certain Niels Studenstrup says (II, 4): Det maa jeg og Niels Studenstrup forstaae, just as in Jacob von Tyboe, the hero says of himself: "men det veed jeg at Jacob von Tyboe og jeg maatte tage den hele Armee paa sin Samvittighed". Overlærer Stavnem of Stavanger supplied the two following references: "Jo min Siæl er hun virkelig gift med Leander, nu svor Magdelone og jeg", (Holberg's Henrik og Pernille, III, 2) where Magdelone herself is the speaker (cf. Bjørnson's Paa Storhove, where Knut Ura says: Her svor Knut Ura); and: "Jeg vil have hende til Kone" — "Du skal Fanden, skal du, nu svor Petter Jensen og jeg" (H. Schultze, Petter og Inger, 21de scene). So the idiom does not "remain strange" as I at one time thought (Publ. Soc. Adv. Scand. Study, I, 220).

723. paa Gjetens Vis. like a goat.
See T. C. §§ 33 and 118.

724. Han bær' hende, Moer, som en bærer en Gris.
Will it be believed that a translator of Ibsen has managed to misunderstand this passage so as to translate it: hij draagt haar als een b e e r een zwijn, — where, however incredible it may seem, b æ r must have been looked upon as Norwegian for a bear? This may be found in Mrs. Clant v. d. Mijll's Dutch translation, issued by Messrs. Meulenhoff & Co., at Amsterdam. And the translation into Platt-Deutsch too (by Bernard Brons, Emden 1889), prints on p. 47: As 'n bare varken dragt hy höör, where we do not know what to admire most, the translators' imagination of a bear carrying a pig or their knowledge of the language out of which they ventured to translate this masterpiece. That ei Bera = hunbjørn

still exists in the Norwegian dialects (Skard) as bär in the Swedish ones (cf. e. g. Hjelmström, från Delsbo; Sv. Landsm. (1897) XI, 4 p.p. 33, 34, 39, 47, etc.; I have not got Rietz at hand) as *teste* the "Latin" Bero, it must have existed in Old Norse, does not save the situation of course.

Bær for bærer like skjær for skjærer (l.l. 892, 3809), ær for ærer (Mau, II, 206) and destiller'r (quoted in Ordb. over gadespr. p. 152, a form that presents the missing link!) are merely cases of haplology.

See T. C. § 23.

725. Træd varsomt i Hældet. Take care of your footing.

In this translation Hældet (usually heldet) = slope is not taken into account. In the first draft of Når vi døde vågner (Eft. Skr. III, 325) the same expression is used by Ulfhejm under precisely the same circumstances: Træd varsomt. Det er dødsens vej vi går.

726. Bruderov. Bride-rape.

Colloquia prava as we used to be taught at school, corrumpunt bonos mores! — as Peer has found to his detriment; see l. 799 where Aase tells us that she used to tell Peer stories about such bride-rapes: "Vi brugte Eventyr — om Bruderov med". It is not quite impossible that Ibsen has read the story in Asbjørnsen (En Søndagskveld til sæters; ed. 1912, p. 123) that presents some little analogy to this one. And it looks like ringing the changes on the same motif (what Ibsen is exceedingly fond of) when later on Peer is made to commit another rape, where he carries off Anitra.

727. Aase.

In Aase, we have according to Mr. Ellis Roberts (p. p. XX, XXI) "portrayed for the first time in literature the love of a mother and son without any sentiment and without any falsehood"; see the rest of his characterisation. The name is common enough, if not very much so at present in real life, at least in literature, e. g. as that of

1, 47; 3, 51; F, 310; M, 188; 14, 45; J, 195; 16, 45.

Halvdan Svarte's mother and in Harald Haarfagres saga. It is also the name of a bride of the Hill-folk — Tussebruden; cf. Norske Sagn ²p. 78. With regard to this portrait as such, Ibsen has written himself that in a way his own mother was the model: til Aase har med fornødne overdrivelser, min egen moder afgivet modellen" (letter to Peter Hansen; Breve I. 215).

ANDEN HANDLING. ACT SECOND.

728.   uvillig. sullenly.

The form used by Ibsen both in U and R, is found changed into uvilligt already by F; cf. T. C. § 4 and ib. § 123 on similar cases.

729.   Gaa ifra mig! Get you from me!

How absolutely necessary it is to know Norwegian life and manners for him who sets about this play, is shown by Count Prozor who actually does not hesitate to call Ingrid "une jeune fille dévergondée" (p. 18). Must a girl necessarily be lost to shame when the custom of the time and the milieu allow her liberties that at present we allow men only? For it should be remembered that Ingrid could reasonably—see the note to l. 870 on the customs of the Saturday night and that to l. 3702 — take Peer's visit with its consequences as a promise of marriage.

As to the whole of the scene, see Christen Collin's comparison between this passage and one in Bjørnstjerne Bjørnson's Halte Hulda, (Collin, Bjørnson, II, p.p. 221, 222): An involuntary change is prepared in his mind — essentially the same as that which Ibsen has painted in Peer Gynt where the hero turns away from the bride, from the woman that was so willing to elope and through whom he has diminished as a man, —gjennem hvem han har minket som menneske. As Peer turns away from the bride at Hægstad to the pure and innocent Solveig, who

---

1, 48; 3, 52; F, 311; M, 189; 14, 46; J, 196; 16, 46.

appeals as it were to the best elements in his nature, so Eyolf Finnson turns almost imperceptibly away from Halting Hulda who has made him a murderer, to Svanhilde, the bright playfellow of his youth."

733.   Brott — og Brott igjen os binder!
                Sin — and sin again unites us.

One of Ibsen's Sveacisms which occur mostly only as "Pikanterier"; S. I. S. p. 197. The compound Forbrot = brøde, crime, is pure Norwegian, cf. Aasen, p. 177 and even Brot is there recognised (p. 82) as occurring figuratively = Krænkelse, Overtrædelse, Brøde.

737.   Ikke dig. 'T is not you.

On this accusative, see Poestion, Norw. Gramm.², 140, 1.

757.   halsløs Daad. it will cost your neck.

For the concentration, the conciseness of the adj.: a deed where one's neck is at stake, a capital affair — compare such an expression as Hovedkuls raad er tidt halsløs gjerning (Mau, II, 146) and the notes to l.l. 124, 186.

761.   brister i Taarer. bursting into tears.

Changed by the 6th ed. into brister i graad, T. C. § 63, which will be looked upon as more "correct" by those who consider the original expression "sprogurigtig", as a correspondent expressed himself; cf. Edda II, p. 139, a note in my paper: Tilbake til Ibsen. Apart from the consideration that it is à priori inadmissible even on apparently weighty grounds to "correct" an author's expression, it should be noticed that as Ibsen had actually written "brister i Graad" in U, his change in R of this into brister i Taarer, has all the looks of a well meditated change which we should respect, not an unconscious one.

As could be expected, other correspondents defend it and think it quite admissible, as why should it not be when we think of such equivalents as the above: burst into tears, never *into weeping*, in tranen uitbarsten, not *in geween* etc. And Overlærer Stavnem quotes: Og Murillo

---

1, 48; 3, 52; F, 311; M, 189; 14, 46; J, 196; 16, 46.

brast i Taarer, slutted' Drengen i sin Favn, from H. C. Andersen's Det har Zombien gjort. But Morgiana in Oehlenschläger's Aladdin "brister i Graad" and Ibsen himself in the first draft to Dukkehjem (E. S. II, 352) as well as in that to Vildanden (ib. III, 63) uses this expression: brister i hulkende gråd, and it may be said to be more common perhaps. It is remarkable that in a passage of U, Ibsen having written: Tør du Taarene af Øjet, changes Taarene into Graaden! (l. 290). In Swedish too I find: "brister i tåror"; Anders Eje, Georg Kessers General-kupp, p. 216.

762.   yr. frantic.

yr is Swedish in form and meaning; cf. S. I. S. p. 195; No.-Da. would be ør. Professor Storm shows l.c. that the word occurs often enough in Norwegian, partly in dialect with a different signification but "it is after all Swedish and not Norwegian". To which Dr. Western remarks that it "may be Swedish in form (though Ibsen has no doubt used it so as to get a rhyme to dyr) but not in meaning. It is prose ør and means giddy esp. from drink. Compare farther down (in the death-scene): det var rimeligt nok du var yr, where it rhymes on gjør". (l. 1638).

776.   Rap. rift.

See l. 973: Fjeldene raper.

779.   Den Bytting. the oaf.

Bytting, literally changeling, oaf, here however only used in the general non-complimentary sense of wretch; cf. n. to l. 418.

781.   Er det ikke rent utænkeligt, sligt?
                             Is not it clean unbelievable this?

Aase's astonishment that Peer actually has gone and d o n e something is great and prepares us for Peer's own, l. 1359 that the young man, coward as he was in a way, as at least w e make him out to be, did not only t h i n k of hewing off his finger to escape donning the King's uniform, but d i d it, and this contains the key to Peer's character: a blending of Hamlet's: don't do to-day what you can possibly put off till to morrow and Macbeth's "letting I dare not wait upon I would"; n. to l.l. 1228, 1359.

Cf. T. C. §65 on the comma behind utænkeligt, which has also escaped the Archers' attention.

793. Det er saa fælt at se Skjæbnen under Øjne;
It's a terrible thing to look fate in the eyes.

Compare (l. 1641): Hvad tungt er, det vil vi spare till siden — en anden Dag. All that's heavy we'll let stand over till after — some other day.

796. En bruger Brændevin, en anden bruger Løgne;
aa, ja! saa brugte vi Eventyr *etc.*

Some take to brandy, and others to lies;
and we — why we took to fairy tales *etc.*

In Camilla Collett's I de lange Nætter (at the end of the 16th night, p. 157 of the 3d ed. 1906) a work that appeared before Peer Gynt, the authoress tells of an old woman whose talent of telling fairy tales was so great that Sara, her daughter, used to forget her hunger over them. The late Professor Kahle (Henrik Ibsen, Bjørnstjerne Bjørnson und ihre Zeitgenossen, 1908, p. 20) thinks that this may be the origin of the present passage. The student should compare the passage in question and decide for himself, — one thing is quite certain, viz. that Ibsen's reputation for a d a p t i n g would grow enormously by it for the substance of (l. 793:) –Det er saa fælt at se Skjæbnen under Øjne" is not in Camilla Collett. But surely we need not look for "originals" in such cases as this? (n. to l. 466).

799. Om Bruderov med.

On "Bruderov" see the n. to l. 762, "Om", the reading of U, R, and the earlier editions (T. C. § 4, n) is changed as early as in F, into: Og (bruderov med) which is found even in the latest editions.

801. Det er Nøkken eller Draugen!
It's the nixie or droug!

The stories about the Nøk, Draug or as they were also called Fossegrimen, Fossekallen etc., abound in Scandinavian tales as those about the corresponding nickers and nixies or kelpies, banshees etc. do in English folklore. In the collection of Asbjørnsen, the nøk will e. g. be found in "Paa Højden af Alexandria", (ed. 1912, p. 292); in the often quoted No. Sagn² p. p. 89, 91, 95, etc.; cf. ib. 84 on the Fossegrimen whose speciality curiously enough was the giving of violin lessons; visitors of what alas w a s the central part of Bergen will remember the celebrated violonist Ole Bull's monument. In the same collection (p. 97) and in Asbjørnsen's Huldreev., Tuftefolk paa Sandflæsen (also in No. Sagn² p. 57) we find a description of the draug (which differs from the two others mentioned in that it is always found in the sea,) — instead of a head they sometimes had a tangled mass of seaweed; he who sees one at sea is supposed to be lost! In some of its forms the draug reminds us vaguely of the Bøyg, as when in Olsen (l.l. p. 14) he is found described as a "stor slejp aal"; cf Danske Studier, 1916. p. 184. — Ibsen's strange draug in Hærmændene paa Helgeland about which see Lynner's monograph p. 29, may be distantly related to our Strange Passenger; infra n. to l. 3499 (draugen as a gjenganger, cf. Feilberg, I, 443 seqq, in voce). See further: Paul's Grundriss, I¹, 1009, 1011, ib.³ 262, 265; Herrmann, Nordische Mythologie p.p. 41, 59 seqq; 64, 101, 128.

805. Ikke Spor at se. Not a sign to be seen.

This is not here the colloquial ikke spor, keine Spur = nothing at all, as it is tempting to take it (and as some apparently h a v e done; cf. Mrs. Clant v. d. Mijll p. 332: volstrekt niets te zien) but: no t r a c e of him! cf. l. 832: Spor af Mandefod.

819. Mestermands Hænder, — the hangman's hands.

On this euphemism for the executioner, cf. Feilberg in v., Tillæg, p. 305 and Kr. Nyrop, Dania, VI, 206. Later on

Peer comes under *Mesters* hænder = the hand of God; curiously enough, Mester (Hans) is also used = hangman cf. Feilberg ib. in v. mester.

842. Fremst kan en høre Hæggstadgubben tude.

Foremost I hear the old Hegstad-churl howling.

On *en*, cf. S. M. p. 33, § 36, f. and n. to l. 3390. Hægstad-gubben is perhaps literally = the master, the Lord of Hægstad, but here = that Hægstad-f e l l o w, rather than the stronger: churl. In U, this line ran: Over Vidden kan en høre Mandgaren tude, where "Mandgaren" as it is now usually spelt = (a heap of) people, a (large) c i r c l e or (long) c h a i n of men, to e n c i r c l e e. g. a runaway criminal.

845. Det er Liv! En blir Bjørn i hvert et Led.

This is life! Every limb grows as strong as a bear's.

This is a Peer Gynt such as we see very little of in the play (notes to l. l. 781, 1228, 1806 etc.), — a man that really w i l l s something, before his better self has been vanquished by his worser one and been "bereft of the power to will" — han har mig røvet selve evnen til at ville!" as Ibsen had written in 1859 of Peer's proto-type in Paa Vidderne (F, IV, 345). And is it a mere coin-cidence, something that merely "looks like a thought — et tilfælde der kun ser ut som en tanke" — that here his not very reputable adventure with the three girls at the same time marks the end of his energy? cf. n. to l. 1029.

The bear is clearly used here to symbolise strength, — a strong man is made out to be the son of a bear (Da. Studier, 1910, p. 162) for, Romeo notwithstanding, there is a good deal in a name, as those who gave the name to B j ø r n stjerne Bjørnson could tell us. In a different, considerably weakened sense, we read in the story of Røderev og Askeladden that a young peasant says to the king: "Ja, staa du der og strø korn og kagl hønemaal, til det blir en bjønn av dig" i. e. till you show you are worth something, that you are worth your salt. Similarly,

1, 57; 3, 61; F, 320; M, 193; 14, 53; J, 200; 16, 53.

Ibsen wrote himself in a letter (published by Chr. Collin in the Samtiden for 1913): Jeg har en arbeidsstyrke og en kraft saa jeg kunde slaa bjørne ihjel", which indirectly it is true, but still to some extent bears on the word in question.

850.   vassne. savourless.

The word vassen = watery, is specifically Norwegian, cf. S. I. S. p. 190.

851.   Trond.

The mistake Trold, introduced by the 10th ed. (T. C. § 79) and not corrected until the Mindeudgave, has misled Mr. Ellis Roberts not only into translating Trolls h e r e, but also in the case of l. 865 where his original must have duly had Trond; in l. 875 he has the correct Trond.

This, "denne vildskapens høisang", as Stavnem (Bugge Album, p. 98) quotes from Wörner, prepares us for the scene in the Dovrëking's palace as Wörner remarks (H. Ibsen, I¹, 235); of course, your average Norwegian does not need such a preparation at all; his case is that of Peer Gynt and Camilla Collett's Sara (cf. n. to l. 796) whose youthful daily food was fairy tales instead of porridge.

Here Ibsen has but three trolls although the version of the Peer Gynt tale that he used knew four; cf. Archers' translation p. 284. But in the same Asbjørnsen's collection, there occurs another version of the Peer Gynt tale much shorter (it does not contain the Boyg-episode) and here the classic number of t h r e e is found, Trond, Christopher and Tjøstol (Huldreev. p.p. 135—137) mountaintrolls, called respectively Valfjæille (after the Valfjeldet i. e. Wal-mountains) Aeillførpongje, 1. ∽. Eldførpungen, tinderbox ("Likheten med en slik pose har git fjeldknuten navn"; ib. p. 136 n) and Aabakken i. e. Rivulet; cf. l. 875 where they "make a nose" at the m o u n t a i n s! The names Baard and Kare that Ibsen substitutes are very common.

1, 57; 3, 61; F, 320; M, 193; 14, 54; J, 200; 16, 54.

854. Trond! Far med Lempe! Baard! Far med Vold!
Trond, come with kindness! Bård, come with force!
Instead of this Ibsen had written in U: Trond, Tag
mig med Lempe, Baard, Tag mig med Vold. At first sight
the change may appear insignificant or even a doubtful
correction. But we must remember that here the girls
are shouting at the top of their voice to the far-off mountains and from this point of view the substitution of the
short Far for the dissyllabic Tag mig is a very happy one.
See the note to l. 856.

855. Sælet. The sæter.
Sæl (or sel; cf. T. C. § 111; in R the æ is corrected
from some other letter, probably e) = a Sæter-hut, the
out-farm of a Norwegian "gaard" — usually far away
from the inhabited world so that the sæter-girl can allow
her often not over-nice morality free play as we are
inclined to call it, her instincts as we should perhaps say
from the Norwegian point of view; see the notes to l.l.
729 and 870. Compare: One day when she was alone at
the sæter and was pottering about in the hut (stuslede
inde i sælet), lo and behold who should she see but the
"tusse ', a goblin who was after her, so that it is not
only the attempts at her purity from earthly lovers that
the poor girl must have the force to resist. (Tussebruden;
No. Sagn², p. 80).
That the word s æ l e t is comparatively rare results
from the fact that A. O. Vinje in his Dølen (Skrifter i
Utval, I, p. 294) when using the word, adds in parenthes-
is: sæterbudi, so he thinks it as necessary to explain as
e. g. Sjauleik which he uses for skuespil (ib. IV, 5).

856. Vold er Lempe! Og Lempe er Vold.
Force is kindness! And kindness is force!
A correspondent sends me an interpretation which is
not only interesting in itself but that puts another construction on the change noted in l. 854 and which I will
therefore not keep back:

1, 58; 3, 62; F, 320; M, 193; 14, 54; J, 200; 16, 54.

"The line may be interpreted in two ways: In connection with the preceding exclamation (l. 854: Far med Lempe, etc.) it may be explained as indicating that it is the most brutal form of carnal pleasure the girls desire. For them there is voluptuousness in a vehement harsh treatment, whereas kindness would give them no contentment and would be felt as an injury. On the other hand, considered by itself, the exclamation may mean that in their orgiastic mood force and kindness after all are but one". The former alternative would seem to suggest that Ibsen's substitution in l. 854 of Far (med Lempe) instead of Tag mig was meant as a softening down in the brutality of the expression used; but see the n. to l. 576. What may be attained of "force" by an action of "kindness" will be seen by ˅ ˙:at may amount to a repetition of this motive in the Boygscene: the Boyg wins everything with "Lempe" (l. 1255).

867. Jeg er tre Hoders Trold og tre Jenters Gut!
I'm a three-headed troll and the boy for three girls!

No doubt it is the parallelism between tre Jenters Gut and tre Hoders Trold that has influenced the spelling of the latter expression in three words instead of Jeg er (et) Trehoderstrold for he means of course that he is a three-headed troll as the Archers rightly translate and not a troll f o r three heads like a fellow f o r three girls (the Archers' boy is too tame an expression here, chosen, no doubt with a view to the metre for which they often sacrifice a shade of meaning) = tre Jenters Gut; cf. the reading of U: tre Kræfters Gut. Compare l.l. 1015, 16: Tre Hoders Trolde gaar rent af Mode, selv Tvehoder faar en knappt Øje paa.

On the form hode by the side of hoved which is recognised by the Danish dictionaries too (cf. e. g. Ordb. over gadespr. and Da. ordb. f. Folket), compare Storm, No. Sprog, 1896, p. 12 and S. I. S. p. p. 189, 190: "uegentlig" hovedsag and hovedstad but: ondt i hodet. If Professor

Storm's rule holds, l. 1541: Aa nej! for et H o v e d der
sidder paa den Kropp! requires an explanation, for in
accordance with it we should expect: for et Hode. And
here an inspection of U is interesting: Ibsen had first
written Hove; as the d was not added, it is clear that
the subsequent correction into Hode was made whilst
writing the word; this Hode is again crossed out and
Hoved written next to it, b e h i n d it, not over the line.
So the form Hoved is the result of wavering and deliberate choice, not one written down in a moment of irre-
flection.

The explanation is supplied by Dr. Western who remarks that hoved(e) was used in both senses at the time
when Peer Gynt was written, and 'that *hode* is a much
more modern "radical innovation".

With regard to the number of heads itself, the gen-
tlemen in question could boast not only of 2 and 3 heads
but of 4, 5, 6, 8, 9, and 12 too; cf. Feilberg in v. hoved,
I, 654, b. Curiously enough no trace of 10 and 11-headed
ones seems to be found. But all this is mere child's play
in comparison with the Devil's grandmother who was
adorned with 300 of these sometimes useful implements.
(P. Herrmann, Nord. Myth. p. 380) and Hymirs mother
who must have been rather bothered by having 900 of them
(Hymis Kviđa, 8). Compare further Norwegia, I, 228,
9 (Konkel i Kungsgaarden by Ivar Aasen), P. Herrmann,
l. l. p. p. 149, 190, 455, Paul's Grundriss, I¹ 1041, 2 = 3²,
300 and Løland, l. l. p. 182: ett troll med sju hovud, etc.
etc. According to Meyer, l. l. p. 229, the rational explanation is that these trolls represent or are reminiscences of
the "grummelköpfe der gewitterwölken."

870.   Denne Lørdagsnatt skal ingen Kover staa tomme!
No cot shall stand empty this Saturday night.

That of all the evenings in the week, Peer Gynt should
come to these girls a Saturday night! Or did he choose it
on purpose, k n o w i n g what hospitality he might expect

then, more than on any other day? The fact is that on
Saturday evening when the week's work in the out-farm
was done, and in view, one cannot but suppose, of the
next day being given to as much rest as circumstances
allowed (Brand, Popular Antiquities, ed. Ellis, II, 37),
custom willed it that the youths of both sexes met in conditions of peculiar intimacy: in bed, although decorum
would have it that neither party should undress and oft-
en that the young man should even content himself to
sit on the bed-s i d e (paa senge s t o k k e n); whether
Peer Gynt and especially his free-spoken new friends
intended to o b s e r v e this part of the silent compact
is another question. This way to make acquaintance
in is as good as an other, — nay better perhaps and it
should be excused when thus explained not only in general
by the time-honoured "honi" be he that thinks ill of it,
but more especially by the fact that hardly any other
opportunity was given the youths in some countries at
least, to make acquaintance with one another, as marriage
with relations was not allowed and it was considered
a proof of effeminacy for a young man when seen to seek
a girl's society. (Troels Lund, Dagligt Liv i Norden, IX,
p. 14). Hence the very probable interpretation that the
German fenster(l)n should be ultimately connected with
finster = dark (ib. p. 21) and only later on supposed
to mean the courting of a girl at the window — fenster
(Paul; cf. also gässlein gehen, Grimm in v. kilt). In a
Middle Dutch poem (Niederl. Geistliche Lieder, Horae
Belgicae, X, n° 99, quoted by Wirth, Der Untergang des
Niederländischen Volksliedes) it is actually said of Jesus
that he "is een avontgangher, Tot eenre Jonferen was
alle sijn gang"; this recalls the German kiltgänger, i. e.
"evening-goers" in which kilt we recognise the Scandinavian kveld, evening. The more usual term in Dutch
was kweesten, which van Dale expressly defines as being
the custom of the young man of sitting or lying o n the

sheets, whereas the young lady has her place u n d e r them; the door and windows remain open [1]!

The English technical term is "to bundle"; cf. the N. E. D. in v. v. bundle and bundling, where the oldest instance quoted is from 1781 but it is already used in Webster's Duchess of Malfi, (1623); cf. also Notes and Queries 1892, I. p. 175. The fullest account of the Scandinavian custom (at gaa paa Natte-frieri) is found in Troels Lund, l. l. p. p. 13—28 (at ligge paa Tro og Love) and see A. Sandvig, De Sandvigske Samlinger, p. 110 (at gaa udpaa); the custom died out very early among the nobility but is even yet perhaps not quite extinct among the peasantry; of course it could not but degenerate into less innocent practices as in Peer Gynt's case of which Troels Lund gives both instances and explanation. References to it in Scandinavian literature are of course legion, I quote but a few: Søndagskveld til Sæters, Huldreev., ed 1912, p. 128; cf. Jæger, Norske Forfattere, p. 71: Asbjørnsen's picture is a little too idyllic); En Aftenstund i et Proprietærkjøkken (ib. p. 34); Ibsen's Rypen i Justedal (Eft. Skr. I, 342) etc. etc.

871.   som glohede Jernet. like white-heated iron.

This construction with the postpositive article instead of the more usual det glohede jern is already very common (cf. l. 872: svarteste Tjernet and l. 1739: salig Provstinden and as Dr. Western writes: "seems to gain ground even alarmingly. In some authors it has become quite a mannerism"; cf. his recent "Skriv Norsk", § 8: hele dagen, halve riket (the hallowed phrase from the fairy tales where Ashiepattle gains "prindsessen og halve riket"

---

[1] Van Wijk-Frank does not give the word; Vercouillie says it is quite unknown elsewhere but does not venture upon an etymology. Holthausen (Herrig's Archiv, CXXI, p. 294) thinks of quester, to quest, to ask, to seek. See also: Vragen en Mededeelingen op het gebied der Geschiedenis, Taal en Letteren, I p. p. 245, 264, where Dr. Prick van Wely in an interesting paper quotes a modern German sketch: "Die Probier" in L. Thoma's "Assessor Karlchen."

---

as in l. 1020 of our text as it originally stood in U: Din Datter og h a l v e Riget, ja); often after a superlative: midt i travleste onnen; cf. l. 62: maanedsvis i travle onnen, n. ib.), ældste gutten vor, etc. etc.

872.   svart, black.

Looked upon as especially Norwegian ,cf. S. I. S. p. 191, for Dano-norwegian *sort* ; cf. Svartekjolen, l. 1215. But svart is common enough in Danish dialects and even in some strata of the Danish rigsmaal; Larsen quotes it as poetic and a young friend of mine is continually endearingly called: "svarten" by his (Danish) wife. Instead of svarteste Tjernet, U read: fra Bunden af Tjernet.

876.   Fik I sove i Armene vore?
                Will you sleep in our arms?

Some translators such as Mrs. Clant van der Mijll and the Archers, not observing the difference between this *Fik* I and the preceding Vil I (l.l. 852 and 866) miss the point here: Well, — whilst they pull them a long nose — well now, d i d you (after all) sleep in our arms? So, not: Zou je willen here and will you sleep, but: heb jelui geslapen and d i d you sleep? See the n. to l. 856.

878.   Mellem Ronderne. Among the Ronde mountains.

From a certain point of view this scene is one of the most remarkable of the poem for the understanding of Peer's character and hence for that of the play. Many commentators such as Passarge in earlier days and J. Collin (who gives perhaps the fullest account; cf. his Henrik Ibsen, 1910 p.p. 267 seqq.) and A. Dresdner only quite recently, have laid stress on the importance of Peer's hypertrophical imagination. It is his "Uebermass der Phantasie" as Passarge says, that Ibsen is at in the drama. Dresdner (Ibsen als Norweger und, Europæer, 1907, p. 19) had even accounted for Peer's inactivity by suggesting that there was no r e a s o n why Peer with his mentality s h o u l d act. "Wozu auch, da er doch schon in seiner Phantasie[1] alle Freude des Schaffens, allen Reiz des Erlebens durchkostet?"

Indeed, Ibsen gives us the clearest of indications possible as to what is the matter with Peer. When we are told in the first stage-direction that he sees nothing but "Shining snow-peaks all around" at sunset, we do not need the second one to make us understand that he must be "dizzy and bewildered", his immense, truly Scandinavian imagination is at work. If there is one thing the non-scandinavian reader must try to understand when setting about the study of northern literatures on the pain of not understanding them, it is the endless power of this imaginative faculty. Selma Lagerlöf is an extreme case. But even the products of the dii minores yield most interesting examples. In a little book by Gabriel Scott, Far sjøl i stua, we make the acquaintance of a little boy who sees the trunks of trees in the twilight. And as the merest matter of course, the boy takes them to be his opponents and challenges them to fight. There is no nonsense about it, and when the reader is in the right disposition of mind, he ceases even to wonder at it. At any rate he should not. The author at least takes the thing for granted like the boy himself and consequently calls the sketch: the Duel, Tvekampen, without more ado and does not condescend to explain as a non-Scandinavian author would have done. And another of Gabriel Scott's little boys has a hoop which is of course his horse. Well, that is nothing more than what the most sober-minded little boy might be capable of anywhere. But a horse wants food! Klaus gives him hay and "at times Klaus c o u l d c l e a r l y s e e that Rulle (the hoop-horse) had been eating heartily of it during the night!" And just you try

---

[1] Mr. Ellis Roberts in his introduction (p. XVI) will have it that Peer is the slave not of imagination but of fancy. If we may trust Mr. Ruskin and take it that "Fancy sees the outside and imagination the heart and inner nature and makes them felt", the opinion is open to question.

---

and convince Klaus that the hay had not diminished. And this is what any chance visitor to Peer's country may at any time meet with the most amusing outcome of. In my mind's eye I see them still, my two little girl-friends down in the Hardanger on a country road. A third comes up and squeezing herself between the two, exclaims: now I am the King and I am walking with two princesses! And spying an odd-fashioned tree whose fantastic forms d i d suggest something creepy in the twilight [1]), she adds: "But what is this troll there! Never mind, I shall defend you against any monster". Truly, these high-strung nerves create a turn of mind of their own! And this free play given to the imagination *teste* already the were-wolf-scene (l.l. 692), Peer's boasting to his mother and later on to the boys at Hægstad as well as his Imperial dreams about Engelands Stormænd (500) are very closely akin to downright lies, — the whole of the play is there to bear this out. And especially this scene where, in contradistinction to the former version (which is to be noticed especially!), his former phantasies are r e c o g-n i s e d as digt og forbandet løgn so that poetry and dreams are expressly put on a level with lies (l.l. 901,907). And when in his delight that he will become something great — til stort skalst du vorde engang, — he s p r i n g s f o r w a r d, he is given the lie in the most tangible way by hurting his nose against a piece of rock!

And this imagination with the fancy that gives rise to it is indeed most characteristically Norwegian. Why, Ibsen himself is not free from it as might perhaps be expected or he would not have been able to reproduce the feeling, — he has "en rem av huden" too as the phrase goes. Vilhelm Bergsøe tells us in his reminiscences of the poet (Henrik Ibsen paa Ischia, 1907, p. 167 seqq.) that

---

[1]) See some interesting remarks about this "wood terror" in Paul Herrmann, Nordische Mythologie, p. p. 138, 579.

1, 60; 3, 64; F, 322; M, 194; 14, 56; J, 201; 16, 56.

they were one day walking together in a very wild gorge and so narrow that they could hardly get on. Suddenly Ibsen exclaimed: Where do you bring me? Will you have me "taken into the mountain? — ind i Bjerget — I won't go further! The mountain will close itself over our heads!" And that this was not merely a way to express things but sheer reality, results clearly from the fact that Bergsøe tells us Ibsen said so "terror-struck — rædselsslagen."

881.　　　　　　　Det rygger bort. it's drifting away.

Compare uryggelig, l. 3764 and the note ib.

892.　　　　　　　　　skjær.

"Ibsen is fond of the old forms: bær, skær, in verse as well as in prose", Professor Storm writes, S. M. p. 33, § 37. See on this case of haplology, *ante* n. to l. 724: bær; l. 3802: Tiden tærer og Elven skjær, but: en dyb vig som skærer ind (F, X, 485).

896, 898.　　　　　En bændende glohed·Ring —!

　　　　　　hvem.... bændte mig den omkring!

a tightening red-hot-ring-! who.... has bound it around.

See, T. C. § 58, where the lines will be found treated at length.

897.　　　　　　　hvem Fanden. Who the Devil.

Compare l. 1503: Hvad Fanden. The same mysterious collocation of words whose grammatical relation is not very clear (see Jespersen in the Festskrift to H. F. Feilberg, p. p. 34, 39: Om Banden og Sværgen, who openly recognises that he cannot explain it [1])) occurs in other modern languages: Que diable y allait-il faire? Qui, diable, êtes vous? Wat duivel is dat? Who the devil (dickens, deuce) is this? Wer (zum) Teufel (Henker) hat das gesagt? Compare such loose constructions as: ‚gu' min

---

[1]) In the following instance it is quite clear that the apparently isolated fanden there is owing to the elision of the verb gaa: Tör nogen af Jer gaa frem?.... Nej!.... Fanden frem. (Phantasmer, Wergeland's S. S. VI, 130.)

A similar explanation for other cases is not excluded.

salighed er vi nervöse'. (Drachmann *apud* Jespersen, l. l.)

911, 912.   traske og tørne.... i Mudder og Søl.

splash and stumble.... quagmire and filth.

Mr. Christensen observes that this is one of the cases where Ibsen uses doublets, sometimes making the style more powerful and to "stiffen it up" — for at udfylde og gøre stilen kraftigere — and more picturesque (a circumstance on the other hand that makes Ibsen's style usually so concise, somewhat overloaded) — at other times to give a fuller image, as here. Just so in the case of mudder og søl." ..

On this latter expression, Dr. Western writes that Ibsen seems to have used the less common søl instead of søle on account of the metre; søl meaning usually carelessness or dirty w o r k. However, Brynildsen recognises søl in the sense of dirt too.

914.   Jeg vil vaske mig ren i de hvasseste Vindes Bad!

I will wash myself clean in the bath of the keenest winds!

Eitrem, Gads danske Magasin, 1913, p. 459, writing about Peer Gynt and Paludan Müller's Adam Homo, compares the hero's "unequalled desire" — uforlignelige længting — here to wash himself clean, to Adam's religious period after his crisis. Paludan Müller's Adam Homo is in more than one respect to be looked upon as one of the prototypes of Peer Gynt; on the Danish poet's influence on another of Ibsen's works: Kjærlighedens Komedie, cf. Ording's study of this drama, Cappelens Forlag, Kristiania, 1914, p. 46.

925.   Jo, kanske jeg svipper derned.

Yet, may-be I'll swoop down too.

Ibsen's Paa Vidderne (1859) contains so much that reminds us of Peer Gynt that it may perhaps be looked upon as a "study" for it; this has been remarked more than once, most recently by Professor Sturtevant; cf. infra n. to the Strange Passenger. Peer's aspiring dreams here may contain a reminiscence of the poem too. Peer tells us that he will perhaps just look down there — svippe ned is hardly rendered correctly by to s w o o p down; "en avstikker" is what Peer is evidently thinking of. As in l. 1611: jeg maatte nu se herned, refers to such a short flying visit paid to his mother, so here he seems to be thinking of Solveig; cf. Paa Vidderne (F, IV, p. 349, VII): (jeg) kan ej ensomheden bære.... nedad må jeg til de kære", but alas! "nu er alle stier stængte". The imagery he uses before when he says that "længslen er et tvætningsbad" p. 341, reminds us of our l. 914. See the notes to l.l. 1424 and 3013 for other points of resemblance with Paa Vidderne.

952. est du. thou art.

Du est is of course entirely uncolloquial language, used as in l. 1081: du est en medgjørlig Fyr (cf. l. 953: till stort skalst du vorde) and l. 3924: af Jord est du kommen to characterise the speaker or the situation. It reminds us of the more or less screwed up language that Oehlenschläger lays everywhere in the mouths of his "heroes" and is therefore found passim e. g. in Aladdin [1]. When used in more modern speech or letters (such as Jørgen Moe's: Ved du at du est en Smörpave; du est Manden, etc.: Krogvig, Fra det nationale Gjennembrud, p. 254), it is a conscious archaism or bible reminiscence, very often with a savour of the comic showing the speaker to be momentarily soaring in higher spheres. Hence: Nora, du est en Kvinde, Dukkehjem (F, VI, 190). In Helge Hundingsbane (Eft. Skr. I. 95) Ibsen used on one page in exactly the same circumstances est du and skal (not: skalst; originally: skalt) du.

955. En Lid med store susende Lövtræer, etc.

A hillside, wooded with great soughing trees, etc.

---

[1]) Jespersen in his recent Nutidssprog hos voksne og børn, tells an amusing story of the poet, who, when he was a little boy, had so often heard his father say by way of a joke: Est du en Carnaille? that the youngster repeated this to some horrorstricken guests!

According to Mr. Eitrem, Samtiden, 1908 p. 619, who quotes the whole of this stage direction, this is a parody by Ibsen of a scene in Welhaven's Eivind Bolt, who "like Peer Gynt sees people pass before him on a Whitsuntide feast. There he must submit to his ordeal of fire" — da maa han undergaa sin ildprøve, *etc*. The author does not tell us what this parody consists in and his meaning is not very clear; cf. however n. to l. 994.

En grøndklædt Kvinde. A Green-clad woman.

As will presently appear, she is the daughter of the "King of the Dovrë-mountains, — perhaps, to make the gentleman's position quite clear, we should say: the King i n the Dovrë-mountains, as the n. to. l. 1000 will show, in one word: the Dovrë-troll. The reason why Ibsen dresses her Royal Highness in g r e e n is quite obvious for him who has read the whole of the Eventyr from which Ibsen borrowed the story of Peer Gynt and the Boyg (Rensdyrjagt ved Rondane; Huldreev. 72. p. 139) For there, immediately after Peer Fugleskjæille has told h i s story (the one about Peer Gynt) another hunter comes out with a yarn about a certain Klomsrud who had a little tussle with no less than f o u r t e e n green-clad ladies — fjorten grønklædde jomfrugo (ib. p. 159) who turn out to belong to the race of the "underjordiske" — the gnomes or pygmies. So this is the origin of I b s e n's lady dressed in green. The question as to why the old stories fix upon that colour is perhaps not quite so easy to answer. Most people will probably think (with Mannhardt in his Baumkultus der Germanen) of the natural colour of the wood and conclude that these gnomes must originally have been sylvan spirits. But such a "conclusion" may on investigation turn out to be nothing more than a "deduction" from the very colour it is meant to explain. According to a hypothesis that the present writer has advanced elsewhere (in the Dutch periodical Groot-Nederland March, 1916) the reason is to be

---

1, 63; 3, 67; F, 325; M, 196; 14, 58; J, 203; 16, 58.

found in the fact that this pygmy race was precisely supposed to dwell in the earth, under the "green" (sods) — in more than one acceptation of the word, for their origin is no doubt to be sought in the re-incorporation of the souls of the dead — and that hence they are popularly clad in the colour of those sods. Possibly connected is the expression: the Devil believes a monk when he is dressed in green (Fanden tror Munken naar han bliver grönklædt; Mau, II, 45) and undoubtedly: Stepmothers look best in green clothes, i. e. under the black earth, Stifmödre se bedst ud i grönne Klæder ib. 358. For more details I must refer to the essay.

As to the meaning of the Green Lady in the economy of the drama, she takes the place of Lotte in Paludan Müller's Adam Homo, the Danish epic that our poet adapted — Ibsenised if you like — in his Peer Gynt; cf. n. to l. 914, and like this young lady whom the hero had seduced and abandoned, represents the hero's youthful sins that stand in the way of his happiness in later life; see the note to l. 1228.

957.   skjærer med Fingren over Struben.
    drawing his fingers across his throat.

The jest might have been accompanied by some such explanation as Polonius' when he points to his head and shoulders: Take this from this if it be otherwise (II, 2, 156).

962.   Aldrig skal jeg dig i Haaret trække —
    I will never drag you about by the hair.

To the uninitiated it may seem nothing more than a rather peculiar expression of a lover's regard for the object of his passion that Peer here makes this promise, a peculiarity culminating in the Green Lady's evident fear lest he should possibly beat her. A beating, matrimonial or otherwise is alas, not entirely unknown in the history of mankind, but it is certainly not the thing your average human beauty is in the habit of guarding against

---

1, 63; 3, 67; F, 325; M, 196; 14, 58; J, 203; 16, 58.

as here by a sort of *viva-voce* marriage contract! But Peer Gynt has not been formed for nothing by Aase in the school of fairy-tales, he knows his huldre when he sees one and there is a special reason for this apparently so uncalled-for declaration. As coming events cast their shadows before, so Peer would seem to have a notion of the true nature of the lady who is not one to be made small beer of if she should get it into her head to set hard against hard. It is dangerous to treat these creatures unkindly for their superhuman force may disappear t e m-p o r a r i l y when she is humanised by her marriage with one of the earth earthly, but her dormant faculties are apt to break out at a most inopportune moment foi her "Lord and Master" if he should forget his position. Asbjørnsen's collection contains again some very instructive items in this respect.

See one of Bertha Tuppenhaug's Stories (ed. '12, p. 42, also in No. Sagn² p. 66) of a huldre who married a soldier and just to show the metal she was made of, bent straight a horse-shoe with her fingers. No wonder if we read that the husband henceforth was quite an "aparte" man to her! See also and more especially the story (ib. p. 43 seqq.) called: The race of the Hill-folk — Huldreæt.

Hence, there is a peculiar force in the "suggestion" we often read of in the folk-tales, when a huldre is married to a human being (l.l. p. 46; Kleiven, I gamle daagaa, p. 15, Feilberg, Bjærgtagen, p. 86, *etc*) that the man should be kind to his bride, and then they will not want wedding presents or anything they might need for the farm, "saa skal det ikke vante Dere paa himagift. Di skal faa alt det Di trænger til gaardsens drift og mere til." But if not...!

Mr. E. S. Hartland, (The Science *etc*. p.p. 311 and 340) quoting a couple of cases in point from English and Welsh folklore, discusses the theory of Liebrecht as to the origin of this trait "assault and battery must strike the elf" (no pun intended!) "still more strongly than re-

---

1, 63; 3, 67; F, 325; M, 196; 14, 59; J, 203; 16, 59.

proaches.... and remind her still more importunately
of her earlier home...."

But alas for the frailty of — a m a n's promise! Here
for once Peer has not profited sufficiently by the lessons
his youthful Eventyr-reading should have taught him.
The promise given so freely here is going to be broken in
the very same act and again when he meets the "troldhex" (l. 1527) he threatens hér: I'll split your skull open
— Jeg skal slaa dig i Skallen", just like a vulgar little
member of the brotherhood of man!

963.   Ikke slaa mig heller? Nor beat me?

The point of interrogation of R, 1, was changed as early
as in the 7th ed. into a point of exclamation: cf. T. C. § 4.

             var det ligt? can you think I would?

Specifically Norwegian, S. I. S. p. 191. Compare l.l.
2311, 3361, etc. And Asbjørnsen, No. Folkeev. 1914, p.
13: Nei, han skulde ikke se paa det, var det likt sig. Also:
var det sig likt, Kleiven, I gamle daagaa, p. 26: Raakaa
eg deg? Nei, va-de-se-likt!

965.   Jeg er Dovregubbens Datter.
             I am the Dovrë-King's daughter.

Mr. Ellis Roberts has managed to misunderstand the
nature of the Dovrë-gubben, looking (p.p. X, XIV, 247,
8) for a symbolic signification which is far to seek, reject-
ing, as if it were a scientific hypothesis of Peer's the
latter's "identification" with Memnon (l. 3019) and
comparing this gubbe (see *infra ;* and l. 1000) to Niet-
sche's Superman; all this presumably by "thinking too
precisely on the event"! The discussion, below, on the
origin of the scene in the Dovrehall, will show that Dovrë who according to Halvdan Svarte's sagn had actually given his name to the Dovrë-mountains (Paul's Grundriss, I¹, 1050, III³, 309; Moltke Moe, Eventyrlige Sagn,
Helland, Norges Land og Folk, Finmarkens amt, p. 582)
as well as the "King of the Ekeberg" (Huldreev, '12, p,
9), the Heiberg-gubben (Bugge-Berge, II, 58) and so many

---

other gubber (and perhaps even the Haugbønder) are nothing else but troll-incarnations and even to some extent "humanifications" of the old mountain-spirits.

The word gubbe, originally simply a stoutish figure (Noreen, Sv. Etymologier, Upsala, 1897 p. 33) and quite common in the sense of old man (cf. Digtergubben Moe's breve, ed. Krogvig, p. 95) even more colloquially: old fellow, indicates the familiar character of the apparently not very "royal" Dovrë k i n g better than long dissertations.

969.   Kong Brose. King Brosë.

The only one to my knowledge that has tried to explain the name is Stavnem who in his paper on the "Symboliske Væsener" in Peer Gynt (p. 97 seqq.) suggests that the word may be connected with "brosa, stormbyge", and he quotes Aasen's first ed. where indeed this brosa is found; Aasen there refers to Rosa, rosever, also = a strong gust of wind. In Aasen's second ed. we are referred to Brysja, et Uveir, som snart gaar over; cf. also Ross in v.

The reference to this word seems to suggest that Stavnem looks upon Brose as the existing name of such a troll-king; he compares such names as Blæstr and Gust i Være, one of the trolls in the Peer Gynt-tale (cf. Archer, p. 284 who does not translate it). But no trace of Brose as the name of a troll is found outside Ibsen's drama.

Instinctively one thinks of the bucks Bruse (Bruse means buck it would seem; cf. Fritzner and Moltke Moe's Ep. Grundlove, Edda, 1915, p. 113) and I seem to remember having been told by Liestøl that Moe used to speak of a possible connection between the two names, but the difference between those bucks (Folkeev ed. '12 p. 168) and a giant is enormous! Still the suggestion leads us in a direction that may prove worth investigating, that of, if not an animal as a person, of a real personage bearing that name and then the Brusajökilskvæđi at once

---

suggests itself. But this it is far from certain that Ibsen should have heard of; only as the name Bruse occurs more than once in the old tales (Fritzner I², p. 200 and compare the "Unhold und Menschenfresser Brusi", that Hermann, Nord. Myth. p. 146 quotes from the Fornmanna sögur) both as a personal name and as a nickname (in Danish even under the form Brose: cf. Feilberg, Tillæg, in v. brase) as well as in Snorre as a jarl's name (Olav den helliges saga) and of a peasant (ib.), we may very well suppose Ibsen to have been familiar with the form Bruse. ¹).

Now, if Ibsen had either made up the name Brose himself or adapted it in the way suggested from this Bruse, we cannot imagine why he should have written it Brose, instead of as rhyming with Aase: Braase; the Archers rightly indicate the pronunciation with the vowel of such a word as broad in their note (on p. 69): "Pronounce Broasë." The reason, unconscious or conscious, for his fixing upon Brose with an *o*, can only have been that he had this Brose-form, and as a proper name, in his mind's eye too. I do not know whether Brose is or ever was common as a proper name, I can only adduce a Sognepræst Anders Jensen Brose from Olafsen's I gamle dage and there is a lieutenant K. Bruse mentioned in Moe's Breve (p. 160, n). But it is certainly worth remarking that Ross quotes Brose as an appellativum in the sense of en stor kraftig og statelig kar. This word too may have been present in Ibsen's mind if we imagine him to be acquainted with the word, which is quoted from Dalane between Lister and Jæderen. Brøseleg and brøsen are connected words quoted respectively from Sogn and Nordfjord, where for that matter Brose too may be known even if not quoted in the Dictionaries. These considerations lead to the suggestion that (Kong) Brose is owing to a sort of contamination (see index in v.); Ibsen

---

¹) On Brusi as a proper name, cf. Gamle Personnavne; Norske Stedsnavne, by Olav Rygh, 1901, p. 53.

1, 64; 3, 68; F, 326; M, 196; 14, 59; J, 204; 16, 59.

when fixing upon Brose as the name of a Troll-king had the Jötul Bruse in his mind for the matter and the form Brose either as a proper name or an appellative: a fine strong fellow. And the result was the cross between the two.

972.   De raper. They reel.

As l. 776 "med Skred og Rap" shows, rape would have been better rendered by to glide, to slip, for Rap is a landslip. So here the mountains "cave in" at her father's thundering voice! Rap (as well as Skred) is specifically Norwegian; cf. S. I. S. p. 191.

973.   Faer min kan spænde under højeste Hvælven.
My father can kick e'en the loftiest roof-tree.
See the n. to l. 552.

974.   Moer min kan ride gjennem strideste Elven.
My mother can ride through the rapidest river.

A correspondent thinks that Peer here refers to the old story about the reindeer-buck, his mother being substituted for himself.

978.   Det tykkes dog ligere Stry og Stilke.
It looks to me liker tow and straws.

Peer does not yet "see" things with the eye of the trolls. So he sees that what she pretends to be gold and silk is in reality but tow and straws; cf. the Princess' explanation about the two-fold form of all they possess, — which distinction with a difference Peer is so quick to see that he catches at the joke at once and says it is just the same with them. But alas, he forgets all about her teachings at the supreme moment when his lady-love dances before him with her little sister and when he pronounces the performance to be "supermonstrously monstrous", cf. n. to l. 1100. Compare Aasen's Ordsprog, p. 249: Det vardt upp i Stry, *i. e.* that came to nothing and the locution: at narre en op i stry = to deceive one completely (W.). See the next note.

986.   Rusk og Boss. litter and trash.
The two words are specifically Norwegian; cf. S. I. S.

p. 191. Rusk, rubbish is again found in l. 1334. Compare Skuler og rask og ligge i boss; Grisen og Levemaaten hans, Moltke Moe, Barneeventyr, p. 106; han lid inkje Bos i Maten; Aasen, Ordsprog, p. 217.

987.   og kanske vil du tro, hver glittrende Rude
er en Bylt af gamle Hoser og Klude.

And you'll think, mayhap, every glittering pane
is nought but a bunch of old stockings and clouts.

Of course Peer here thinks of the realities of his "Palace", cf. l. 218: hver andet Rude hul er fyldt med gamle Klude[1]) but when the Green-clad woman seems to fear that Peer, on coming to her father's abode, may think he stands in "a dismal moraine", (l. 984: i den styggeste Stenrøsen), there is here perhaps a little more than meets the eye. For a very usual trait in the folk-tales is precisely that the hill-folk are able by their supernatural power to make the lowly and the plain, nay the ugly and even the downright disgusting a p p e a r as aristocratic and fine and quite delicious; see the note to l. 978. To quote one case in point from the Huldreeventyr, I may once more refer to Bertha Tuppenhaugs Fortællinger (ed. 1912, p.p. 26, 27, 28): A pail with splendid food in it turned out to be filled with nothing but cow-dung as soon as the hill-folk had disappeared; cf. Feilberg, Bjærgtagen, p.p. 41, 47, 48, 101, 102. The operation is very simple: just one little cut in the eye and hey, presto, there you are. See the n. to l. 1125 and l. 1216.

990.   Stort tykkes lidt. Big it seems little.

lidt in this sense is only Danish; norw. lidet (litet).

992.   Som Benet og Brogen. Like the leg and the trouser.

Compare: det passer som fod i hose, — which Ibsen seems to have "beautified" into the above. A correspondent thinks Ibsen has himself hit upon som Haaret og Kammen, an expression that seems forced.

---

[1]) Brandes, Henrik Ibsen, p. 131, compares the following passage from Olaf Liljekrans: Har du aldrig hört om Haugkongens Skat, Der lyser som röden Guld hver Nat, Men vil du med Hænder tage derpaa, Intet du finder uden Grus og Straa, *etc. etc.*

994. En kjæmpestor Gris. A gigantic pig.

It may be entirely Ibsen's own imagination that this remarkable fantasy is owing to; at least there is nothing in any of the fairy tales that corresponds very closely to it; it has "scarcely any support, næppe nogen støtte" in tradition, as Anders Krogvig writes.

We find, of course references enough in these stories to the hog being used as a means of conveyance, — even old Harry does not disdain to sit on one (cf. Thiele, Danske Folkesagn, II, 98) as in the well known bible story he condescended to enter one and compare Wigström, Folktro, p. 178, n° 561, where the sugga is undoubtly Old Nick himself [1]). And in the nature of these very mountain-folk we have to do with, there is just enough suggestion of the Evil one to pay attention to such little items which may lead to a discovery of further connections. In order to facilitate researches for others, I mention the references in Feilberg, III, 450 to riding on a sow, which I cannot investigate further. I doubt whether the tailor riding on one to church (Tilmed bruger han soen som ridehest: Hvis der er nogen der har noget derimod, han sige til i tide og tie siden stille, "sagde Skrædderen, han red ad kirken til på en so, Dania, I, 186) can cast any light on the subject in hand; compare besides p e r- h a p s the Swedish gloso that Hermann, Nord. Mythologie, p. 142 gives on account of.

That the huldre people on the other hand, did make use of a "bridal-steed" (brudehest), appears from an amusing story given by Kleiven, I gamle daagaa, p. 7, — the bride is being dressed and adorned with her bridal wreath and every thing glittered in the sun; even "the bridal steed stood at the door with a saddle so bright that it shone a long way"

And the bride is just about to be lifted on to the horse

---

[1]) In H. ock E., Folkminnen, Sv. Landsmålen, 1907, p. 385 we seem to have a sow incarnating the soul of a newly deceased person.

1, 65; 3, 69; F, 327; M, 197; 14, 61; J, 204; 16, 61.

when — alas! for the vanity of infra-human wishes, — a gun is shot off over the fairies' heads and the whole swag disappears.

In a paper, printed in Samtiden for 1908 (p. 619) Mr. Eitrem mentions this passage as one of the parodies that Ibsen according to him is guilty of, comparing it to Welhaven's Eivind Bolt where "the huldre rides into the mountain on a snow-white reindeer with a motley wreath on its horns whilst Eivind accompanies her on a silvershod, coal-black horse". See the n. to l. 996 and compare that to l. 955.

I find a very interesting suggestion in a paper by Mr. A. Leroy Andrews, Journal of Engl. and Germanic Philology, 13, p. 241, to the effect that it may have been suggested by the steed of Baubo "die unflätige Amme der Demeter" (Witkowski, Faust, II p. 268) in the Walpurgisnacht; the passage runs: Die alte Baubo kommt allein, sie reitet auf einem Mutterschwein.

See the index in v. for other cases of Faust-influence. The suggestion is possibly due to J. Collin who speaks (p. 302) of this *gris*, "die auf Anruf der nordischen Baubo erschienen (ist)", but may have been made independently. It will be noticed that Eivind Bolt's coalblack horse now appears much more distantly related, if at all.

996.   Rapp dig, rapp dig, min Ganger god!
     Gee-up, gee-up, my courser fine!

Peer's joyous mood finds utterance in the use of such fine classic expressions as "min Ganger god!" (I wonder whether gee-up is a fully adequate rendering of the finer: rap dig) and it may not be quite a stranger either to his more or less pompous: Paa Ridestellet skal Storfolk kjendes! Both expressions are used later on once more when Peer is about to meet Anitra, cf. l. l. 2456 where the Ganger has received a name from northern mythology: Grane, min Ganger god, and, when galopping into the desert on a r e a l horse: Raa Ridestellet, etc.: you may know the great by their riding-gear; see also Aase's death-scene. As to the "solution" (Lösung) that this line brings with it, lovers of The Profound may be referred to Weininger's book, p. 17.

There are several of these correspondences, some, as Ellis Roberts remarks (p. X) mere parallelisms, some with a deeper meaning: "These hints as it were of a dream-life, help the unity of the play tremendously". J. Collin (Henrik Ibsen p. 321) comparing in the same way the gigantic pig with the horse of l. 2459 that is to carry him to Anitra remarks that both lead Peer Gynt "in ein Abenteuer hinein das.... mit seiner tiefsten Entwürdigung und Beschämung endet." (cf. n. to l. 994).

1000. Dovregubbens Kongshal. Stor Forsamling af Hoftrolde, Tomtegubber og Hougmænd. Dovregubben i Højsædet med Krone og Spir.

The Royal Hall of the King of the Dovrë-Trolls. A great assembly of Troll-courtiers, Gnomes and Brownies. The old man of the Dovrë sits on his throne, crowned and with his sceptre in his hand.

From the point of view of folklore this is perhaps the most important scene in the play. Peer Gynt has met his fate in the shape of the green-clad lady and has been kidnapped, i. e. she has "mountain-taken" him (see n. to l. 509).

The scene has apparently not always been understood in all its niceties by the translators as perhaps not by readers either, but of that there is no trace. And this should be excused here if anywhere because Ibsen has here blended two different sorts of supernatural beings in such a way that the reader not to the manner born is apt to lose his bearings and to confound what the poet, not writing a scientific treatise on the subject, necessarily does not keep quite distinct. And only such a very full treatise concerning the origin, fictitious and real of the various beings, their peculiarities and life would enable the non-initiated fully to grasp the subject and such a treatise in its most concise form would far exceed the limits of even the longest note of this commentary. Such an account is ready and will be published in due time; here a few indications will have to suffice: There are then in the first place the old giants, beings that in the olden times were fabled to be inimical to man and gods, — a real supernatural species, of course enormous in size, but looked upon often as inferior in wit and wisdom. And then the gnomes, dwarfs, nickers, elves and goblins as you like to call these mountain-, earth- and water-spirits that as a rule in contradistinction to the former class are said to be small in stature, — malignant at times and full of pranks but often quite friendly disposed towards mankind. They are after all the re-incarnation to a great extent of man's soul not only, but also a resurrection of the body and amusingly ape mankind in its manners, its habits and even in its institutions. How far this troll-world is in fact nothing but a reflex of our own, quite mirroring ours, appears pleasantly from a story that Hermelin tells of (p. 27). The trolls in the Røgavels grotto were going to give a party in honour of the eldest daughter's wedding and all the troll-families of the neighbourhood were invited. But one had been left out. Why? Well, you see they were not 'chic' enough. Truly Peer knew what is what when, in answer to the Dovrë-king's question about the difference between trolls and men, he said that there was *none*!

The mistake made but too often in connection with this scene, — but one which you may be cured of by witnessing one representation of the play if the mise-en-scène is only properly managed, — is that the personages here are invariably treated of as belonging to the second category, that of the "under-earthlings" and that the giant-element is overlooked. And curiously enough,

1, 66; 3, 70; F, 328; M, 198; 14, 61; J, 205; 16, 61.

the study of Ibsen's sources for this scene reflects the same duality in the origin as in the outcome. For the scene is said to be inspired by Botten-Hansen's Huldre-bryllupp where the second act has a "Hal i Jutulbjer-get" (see a note, Eft. Skr., vol. I, p. LXVIII) which has not been without influence. Here we are in the midst of the Huldre, i. e. the fairy-world. And it may be mentioned that the first draft of this scene (cf. lower down) contained a passage which points to its being meant as a satire on P. A. Jensen's Huldren's Hjem, which Ibsen had criticised sharply in Andhrimner (cf. S. V. F. X. p. 326 seqq.); it ends with the singing by all the actors of a skit [1]) on Johan Nordahl Brun's national hymn: For Norge, Kjæmpers Fødeland vi denne skaal vil tømme, which Ibsen makes into: For Dovre, Trol-des Fødeland, etc. So here also the giant- and the fairy world are blended.

So far for the huldre-origin of our scene. Nor is "giant-influence" wanting for those at least who have read Over-lærer Stavnem's convincing remarks in the Bugge-Al-bum about the debt Ibsen here owes to H. C. Ander-sen's amusing "Elverhøj", which cannot but be sup-posed to have been drawn upon by our poet, and which, as its readers will remember, reflects the g i a n t-world, Norge (for these youngsters come from Norway!) K j æ m p e r s land, all this its t i t l e n o t w i t h-s t a n d i n g: the 'elve-hill' receives the visit from the Norwegian cousins who are assuredly no dwarfs! We must therefore in our mind's eye see before us men-actors of colossal size rather (at least in the majority of cases) than miniature creatures incarnating the smal-ler inhabitants of the fairy-world.

---

[1]) Curiously enough the hit on Brun was, to some extent at least, one on his own former self, for Ibsen had been one of the bards that had received "an order for a song" which he sneers at in the Epic Brand where he calls Norway: "et Folk af Kæm-per og Kæmpinder naar Skalden har Bestilling paa en Sang" for he had more than once written such a song by order with the selfsame theme (we might almost say: to the selfsame tune!) of Brun's celebrated outburst (Eft. Skr. I, p. LXVII).

A study of the origin of this scene or rather its growth is interesting and can be made by the help of U. — We have three versions of this scene, or even four. Ibsen began to write it in verse on fo. 9, 2, v° (of U) directly after the end of the scene where Peer enters the Ronde-porten on a sow with his bride, the Princess in Green; just like in the present text. This scene will be found printed by Koht in the Eft. Skr. II, p. p. 94—97. It begins with a stagedirection (ib.). and then the parody on Johan Nordahl Brun s "Norges skaal ', — mentioned before. This version contains four trolls omitted in the later version, — the Professortrold (or Visdomstrold), Bispetrold, Digtertrold and Folketrold whose words are nearly all preserved in the definite version (although changed here and there) and given to the Hoftrold or the Dovrëgubben himself with the exception of one speech by the Professor-trold, where he recognises that he probably pronounced this speech before, but that is no doubt forgotten; this looks suspiciously much like a pointed reference to a contemporary: If Lieblein whom Ibsen owed a good turn for his scathing criticism of Brand had been a professor we might perhaps think of him, — I am moreover not in a position to state whether he was in the habit of pronouncing his professorial harangues over and over again. At the same time that there was a special person Ibsen had in his mind would seem to follow from the fact that although he omitted the sneer (as too personal or pointed if given to a p r o f e s s o r-trold?) in the later version, the skit itself makes its appearance again in a milder form in de Unges Forbund where gamle Lundestad is highly applauded for his speech on the national day, the 17th of May, although he had held the same speech every year as some of his audience remember. (Add.)

On f° 9, 4, v°, when Peer Gynt has said "for sig selv"; En Hale gjør jo ingen Mand till et Dyr, Ibsen writes:

1, 66; 3, 70; F, 328; M, 198; 14, 61; J, 205; 16, 61.

Dovregubben, evidently intending to continue the scene (it is even possible that a word or two of this speech was written down, some scribblings are crossed out) when he must have thought better of it, for he then crossed out the whole of the preceding scene and began again on the same page: Dovregubbens Kongshal. Stor Forsamling af Trolde .Dovregubben i Höjsædet med Krone og Spir. Peer Gynt staar for ham. Stor Allarm mellem Hougmænd, Tomtegubber og Hoftrolde.

But he did not get any farther! The rest of the page is filled up with curves such as he used to cross out words or scenes with, — he evidently had another idea in his head. And it is not difficult to see which. After this f° 9, 4, v°, there follows a Tillæg as Ibsen writes himself in the left hand corner at the bottom: N. B. Hertill Tillægsbladene: a, b, c, d and e.

Of this Tillæg, he evidently began to write on what is now p. 4 of Tillægsblad *b*. This contains the fragmentary prose-version of this scene which Koht, Eft. Skr. II, printed at the bottom of his p. 94 (U²). — It will be seen on comparison that the stage-direction there is but slightly different from the one I printed here for the first time; supra. That this prose version is a n t e-r i o r to the one to be mentioned presently is clear.

For we should otherwise have to suppose that this page 4 of tillægsblad *b*, now "standing on its head" had been squeezed in the middle of the scene. It can therefore only have been a f t e r he had again crossed out this scene that Ibsen after all decided to write the scene in verse, and it is t h i s version (the third) which now follows directly after f° 9, 4, v° in the present form of the U-manuscript.

This third version was not printed in full by Koht in the Eft. Skr. for the very simple reason that it differs so little from the one of R, that the variant readings could be communicated as such, — cf. vol. III p. p. 415 seqq.

— And the fourth version, if we like to call it a fourth, is that in R. itself.

1001.   Kristenmands Søn, a Christian-man's son.

Compare a similar construction without the article later on (l. 4335): Men Dattersøns Afkom.... har faaet, *etc.* In S. M. p. 11 we read that "it has been proposed" (flere har foreslået) to read: Min dattersøns afkom, which Prof. Storm thinks unjustified, for: "dattersøn er efter norsk sprogbrug at opfatte bestemt". There can be no doubt of course that Prof. Storm is right in pooh-poohing any change, — if "mellem Kristenmand og Troll (U; Eft. Skr. II, 94), is perhaps not a perfect parallel, "at riste remmer av andenmands hud (Brynildsen in v. rem) would seem to be one. (In l. 1739: Salig Provstinden, the definiteness is of course expressed by the postpositive article as in the case of glohede jernet; l. 871).

But a reference to S. M. p. 40 will show that by the many that have p r o p o s e d to read m i n are meant the printers of some editions (9—13, inclusive of F, the edition of the Samlede Værker that Prof. Storm had been called upon to bring up to date) where in l. 4267 for Men dattersøn er bleven baade fed og stor, they had: M i n dattersøn *etc.*, a simple misprint therefore and nothing more, which no one would be more astonished than those very printers to see raised to the dignity of a reading.

Dr. Western writes that Kristenmands søn is different from dattersøns afkom, in so far as the former stands for e n K—s søn; the latter for m i n d—, which should of course be borne in mind. And I reproduce the rest of his useful note: The indefinite article is often left out when the substantive mand is in the gen. case and has an adjective before it. Thus: dette er ikke dannetmands optræden; dette er jo drukkenmands tale; gal mands snak (or: galmands). Therefore andenmands hud

---

is a perfect parallel. On the other hand dattersøns afkom
is curious. When Prof. Storm says that dattersøn er efter norsk sprogbruk at opfatte bestemt, he is no doubt
thinking of such expressions as: søn din, for sønnen din
where søn stands for søn'n. (We also say far din, datter
di, so søn in søn din may be explained in the same way).
But we do not leave out din or another pass. pron.
except after far and mor. We may ask: Er far hjemme?
(= er *din* f. hj.), Hvor er mor? But we could not say:
Hvordan lever søn? When the Dovrëking says: Men
dattersøns afkom and Men dattersøn er bleven baade
fed og stor, he treats dattersøn as a proper name; it is
as much as to say: Peersøn.

1005.   Troldhex. Skal han lages till Sodd og Sø?
A Troll-witch. Shall he be boiled into broth and bree?
As the very compound troldhex shows we have the
witch here in a variety that points to her close relation-
ship with the inhabitants of the inner-mountain, she
is in other words nothing but a female troll, a trold-
kjærring. But the word witch itself suggests also if not
in the first place a human being, better: a superhuman
one in that she was supposed to be endowed with extraordinary magic powers, "a revival from the remote stages of primeval history" when "witchcraft was part and
parcel of savage life" (Tylor, Primitive Culture, I, 137).
They share with devils and other abhorrent creatures
the reputation of having the most fantastically-repel-
lent formation of body (cf. e. g. legs like those of an
ostrich, a body like a frog's, the neck of a goose, the head
of an eagle; Wigström, Sagor från Skåne, '84 p. 57) and
appear most usually in the form of a black cat (cf. e. g.
Kleiven, I gamle daagaa, p.p. 33, 39), sometimes if
rarely a white one (cf. Dania, II, 227: Nordfynsk Overtro). They come "riding on broomsticks ("riandes paa
limer", cf. l. 479) and rakes and dungforks and bucks
and goats" (Huldreev., 1912 p. 92, Graverens Fortælling-

er) and meet periodically at orgiastic festivals, especially at Midsummer (Feilberg, Ordb. III, 161, Tillæg, 205; Troels Lund, Dagligt Liv i Norden, VII, 229, seqq.) at Dovrefjeld (Aften i Nabogaarden, Huldreev p. 248) and Bloksbjerg (n. to l. 4315).

Sodd, Sø, are both specifically norwegian, (S. I. S. p. 191) although the former is also found in Juttish (Feilberg, Ordb. III, 451. b., sub sod $= (s \circ d)$ not $=$ sod 2 $= (s o^u d)$.

1012.   Stærkbygget. strongly-built.

On this reading of U. and R. $=$ strong-built, changed in later editions into stærktbygget $=$ strongly-built (and the reading therefore that the Archers are likely to have had before them), cf. T. C. § 99.

1020.   Din Datter og Riget i Medgift, ja.

Your daughter and the realm to her dowry, yes

Like the Ashiepattle of the fairy tales, Prince Peter gets the hand of the princess and h a l f the kingdom, — as the reading of U ran: Din Datter og halve Riget, ja. Compare Ibsen's Olaf Liljekrans (F. X. 187): In the old chronicles ($=$ fairy tales; infra) we read that when a good king lost his daughter, he promised her hand and half of the kingdom to him who finds her. The motive is of course found *passim* in the folktales; cf. Folkeev. ed. 1899, I. p. p. 7, 16, 22, 82, 149, 184; II, 22. 43. 44. 109; 111, 123. See l.1. 308 : I will become King, Emperor; 2070: his aim in life is to become emperor; cf. l. 3855: My empire *etc. etc.* On the word chronicles as used here $=$ fables, eventyr, cf. n. to l. 2905.

1023.   Det er jeg nøjd med. Ja, stopp min Gut.

I'm content with that. Ay, but stop, my lad;

Prof. Storm, S. I. S. p. 198 remarks that nøjd is not Swedish as one might think but East-Norwegian; Brynildsen gives it as popular; cf. l. 1764: ligenøjd. In U, Ibsen had first written: Saa er det godt. On the change in punctuation in this line, see T. C. § 65.

1029. Dag skal du sky, og Daad. day you must shun and deeds.
Or, as U had it: sky Dagen og Daad (with the *en* of
Dagen crossed out). Compare l. 845: Det er Liv! En
blir Björn i hvert et Led. There Peer seemed really a
man of action — for once! Henceforth his actions will
be — well, look at l. 2028: the whole art of living one's
life consists in possessing the courage of d o i n g a certain thing — den Kunst at eje D a a d e n s Mod —
which sounds quite manly and courageous, until we find
that his conception of d o i n g something here is:....
to remain free to do it! See the notes to l. l. 1579, 80 and
2026. And it is quite clear (cf. the n. to l. 845) that, if
his spree with the sæter-girls marks the end of his energy, it is the troll-doctrine that bears the responsibility.

1035,36. Hvad er Forskjellen mellem Trold og Mand?
Der er ingen.
What difference is there twixt trolls and men?
No difference at all.

Peer is not the only one to think that the trolls are
not w o r s e than men! Compare a passage from the
German Ruodlieb (which I happen to find quoted in
Chantepie de la Saussaye's Religion of the Teutons,
p. 319) of a dwarf that is taunted with deceitfulness
and who retorts: "Far from it that such deceit ever obtained among us; we should not else be either so long-
lived or so healthy. Among you one opes (one's) lips
only when deceit is in (one's) heart; hence you will
never reach maturer old age.... We speak nought else
than what lies in our hearts. Nor do we eat various kinds
of food that give rise to maladies.... "etc.

In U, in the corresponding passage, Ibsen has used
the word Skillnad for Forskjel; cf. Eft. Skr. II, p. 94:
Der er ikke nær saa stor Skillnad mellem Kristenmand
og Troll nu som før." The word looks Swedish but
is common enough in Norwegian dialect; cf. Skard,
Nynorsk Ordbok. I find it even used in Dr. Western's

purest Riksmaal: Den Skilnad som gjøres neden for, Skriv Norsk, p. 14. It was introduced into no. riksmaal by Knudsen as Dr. Western tells me.

1040.   Men Morgen er Morgen, og Kveld er Kveld,
           saa Forskjell blir der nu lige vel.
           Yet morning is morning, and even is even,
           and there *is* a difference all the same.

Later on (l. 2269) we find the "scripture reference" that the morning is not always like the evening: "Morgen er ikke Kvelden lig" (cf. n. *ib.*) and it is just possible that the remark about this truth having been "discussed" often enough, should contain a covert reference to the present passage. But there is much difference (with all the resemblance) between the two passages for our lines simply come to this: "that there are eternal differences at the bottom (evige til grund liggende forskjelligheter) that can neither be changed nor explained". (Krogvig).

1044.   Mand, vær dig selv!.... Trold, vær dig selv — nok.
           Man, be thyself! .... Troll, to thyself be — enough!

This, a central motif of the play as it is that in a way of Brand, whose "all or nothing" it underlies, is one that finds its source of course in life itself. It is therefore not as a likely original, but as interesting prototypes that it may seem worth while to point to some passages in Wergeland's farces that seem to make fun of the desire that some people have to be themselves. In the second scene of Wergeland's Harlekin Virtuos we have Alvilde who wishes to "remain herself" (S. S. VI. p. 149). And in "Om Smag og Behag man ikke disputere" (ib. p. p. 188, 189) we have "a voice from the public" telling "a fool" that he must begin i f r a sig selv, and end with himself. In "Lyv ikke eller Dompapen" (ib. p. 519) we have a man even called Moi-même. And cf. Seip's paper in the Samtiden (1913, p. 572) who shows that the motif as well as Brand's Intet eller alt had been ridi-

culed among others in Wergeland's "De sidste Kloge".
See the n. to l. 1221.

1053.   Sætte Pris paa vor jævne hjemlige Levevis
to appreciate our homely, everyday way of life.
"Under the figure of the *Trolds*, Mr. Gosse has written
(Northern Studies, 1897, p. 54) the party in Norway
which demands commercial isolation and monopoly for
home products, is most acutely satirised."

And this is quite true. As Jæger has told us in an ex-
cursus quite worth studying in its context (Illustreret
Norsk Lit. hist., II, 99), "A real Norwegian patriot
should vindicate Norwegian independence also with
respect to food, drink and clothes", and he proceeds to
quote from "Folkebladet", a Norwegian paper of the
pre-Ibsen period (a periodical whose characteristic
"norskhet" had even called forth a new adj. folke-
bladisk = Wergelandsk Nationalnorsk) the following
passage: Hvis et Folk vil være selvstændig maa (det
ikke være) afhængig i Anskaffelsen af Föde og Klæder,
og i Henseende til sidste skamme sig ved Landets egne
Frembringelser," — which must be quoted in the original to show how utterly un-Norwegian, how un-
original! — the style is; especially the next high falu-
tin' passage: "Landsmænd af den hæderlige Bondestand!
Lader Eder — biblical; — nøie med de Klædingsstyk-
ker, Eders Jordbund giver Materialier til, og Eders
Kvinder virker!" And the ideal picture of a Bonde that
the paper proceeds to give is one "dressed in trousers of
blue frieze" (Vadmelsbuxer; wadmal as those from
across Gretna-bridge would have it) grey frieze coat,
red-chequered woolsey waistcoat and a strong cap of
Norwegian leather." Well, this was in the times before
Ibsen, but it was just as bad later on. On the 15th of
April 1866, Vinje's "Dølen" contained a paper "Om det
Nationale i Storthinget" in which the author, complain-
ing that the last "white-coat" (Kvitkufta) had, alas!

1, 69; 3, 73; F, 331; M. 199; 14, 64; J, 207; 16, 64.

been seen in the Parliament (the man that wore it bore the predestinate name of Grave!) remarks that, true enough, d r e s s is but "something exterior", so it is not so v e r y bad to exchange individual dress for uniform ("Sambunad) but adds: "otherwise" — you see he has thought better of it — "otherwise it would have shown the love for the people as well as a desire for economy (det vilde ellers vera likso folkelegt som sparsamt) and recall as it were old methods of domestic management (vitna om gamalt Husstell) if Members would always go about in home-made clothes." Ibsen, who at an early period had felt a good deal for Wergeland and his Norsedom (cf. on this the n. to l. 3179) and who had even worked in the direction of the "Hjemmevirket" (Eft. Skr. I, p. LXVI. and Samtiden, 1911, p. 361), had turned away from it pretty soon; see e. g. his Sendebrev til H. Ø. Blom, where in his first draft he compliments the author of the above extract (Vinje, the "Dølen" himself) by saying that "the Danish way of thinking was a "drag" even for Vinje" — Dansk Tankesæt er Hemsko selv for Vinje, [1]) just as in one of his letters he had written "Hils Vinje hin Nationale"; n. to l. 3179.

A little lower down in the play, we find in the same way the Old man say: "here all things are mountainmade, nought's from the dale" (l 1069) and there is possibly an other skit on it when we read (l. 3328; cf. n. ib.) of the world that "like other self-made things", was reckoned by our Lord to have been managed so well. But the severest hit of all was undoubtedly the passage in the fourth act when Ibsen sneers at the "languagereformers", — see that same note to l. 3179 and the quotation from Sanct Hans Aften given in T. C. § 26, n.

Of course, Ibsen was not the only one to attack this

---

[1]) In reality, Vinje was not so exclusive as his opponents tried to make out; cf. Vetle Vislie, A. O. Vinje, p. 323.

---

party, nor the first to do so. In "Harlekin Virtuos",
Wergeland makes Alvilde complain of a curious contradiction in her father: "he will put himself at the
head of a limited liability company — but his daughter
is not allowed to go in a house-made dress" etc. (Saml.
Skrifter, VI, 152) and in his "Papegøien", Siful Sifadda
is thus made fun of by Aesthetikkel: "He walks about
in a dress of frieze, which proves his vulgarity" (pøbel-
agtighed, ib. VI, 237) which will be savoured more especially by those who remember that Siful Sifadda was
the name by which Wergeland introduced himself!

And in Welhaven's "Norges Dæmring", the outcry of
Wergeland's chief opponent against this Ultra-Nation-
alism of these "home-knit politicians, hjemmestrik-
kede Politikere" as Henning Kehler aptly calls them;
Edda, 1916, p. 268, Wergeland has to put up with
many a sneer, of which I quote only one as a parallel
to Ibsen's:

Her kommer en af Norskhedens Forfegtere
og raaber: Holdt! Hvo taler om Fortabelse?
Just nu arbeide vi paa Norges Skabelse,
jèg og de andere Folkesagens Vægtere;

Den sande Kraft bor kun i Norges Klipper;
Selvstændighed skal være al vor Tragten, —
en Bom for tydske, danske Discipliner!

Kun norske Meninger og norske Miner,
og Stoffet norsk i Sjelen og i Dragten,
og norske Nymfer i de norske Kipper!"

But this battle between the "Norwegians" and the
"Europeans" was more than one of dress and food and
language! "From the literary point of view", Professor
Gran has remarked (Nordahl Rolfsen, No.-digtere, p.
227) "it was a fight between the influence of Anglo-

1, 69; 3, 73; F, 331; M, 199; 14, 64; J, 206; 16, 64.

french naturalism on the one hand and Dano-german
aesthetical romanticism on the other; politically it was
the opposition between democracy and red-tapism, and
only s o c i a l l y speaking a battle between the "fine"
and the "simple" ones, between homespun Norsedom
and Danish civilisation".

1054.   Mad og Drikke. Food and drink.

Even the consideration that the proffered food and
drink is home-made (cf. the preceding note) does not
help Peer over its bitter taste, — what an apparent bible reminiscence (l. 1063: It is written: thou shalt bridle
thy nature) does. We may choose between two possible
grounds, which is it, the golden bowl or the daughter?
However this be, he does taste of it, the old man afterwards (l. 4293) reproaches him with it: "You pulled
on the troll-breeches, don 't you remember, and tasted
the mead" and this may have sealed his doom. For, as
Mr. Hartland has remarked (Science of Folk-tales, p.
47) "to join in a common meal has often been held to
symbolize if not to constitute, union of a very sacred
kind" (of which the holy communion is of course the
one we think of first). And classic mythology has taught
some of us a similar lesson too! So, if you should chance
to find yourself one day in Hades, do not taste of what
is offered you or you must remain there (cf. Feilberg,
Sjæletro, p. 17) and this classic trait is quite current in
Scandinavian folklore too; cf. e. g. Thiele, Da. Folkesagn, II, 200; Bugge-Berge, II, 45; Ingemann, De fire
Rubiner and of course, Feilberg: Ordb, III. 495 in voce
spise. And it is the same with drink; cf. e. g. Herrmann,
Nord. Mythologie, p. p. 106, 107; Maal og Minne, 1913,
p. p. 32, 34; ib. '14, p. 47; Landstad, Folkeviser, p. 721:
den drykkin eg drakk, han var inki stor, da glöymde
eg burt báðe himmel og jord; and Feilberg, Tillæg p.p.
83, 106. A realistic trait is sometimes added such as for
example the one in Hermelin, Sägner ock folktro, p. 10,

that the drink is so burning-sharp that the hair of a horse on which a drop falls is singed off.

Peer does not seem to attach very much importance to his having tasted it, for later on, in reply to his "father-in-law's" reproach (see *supra*) he admits that he took it, but adds that he flatly declined the decisive test, and as a matter of fact, although on the Old Man's showing Peer had remained a troll, he has been allowed to leave the mountain!

And for this too there is authority in the old tales; cf. for example the story of one Isak in Asbjørnsen's Skarvene fra Utrøst (ed. '12 p. 275) who eats away "like hell" (to keep to the proper sphere of ideas) and yet is nothing the worse; cf. Feilberg, Bjærgtagen, p. 102 seqq. Sometimes even it actually causes illness or brings other misfortunes when it is refused; cf. Feilberg, Ordb. II, 525, a. in v. mad.

1059.   Fanden med eders hjemlige Drikk!
        The devil fly off with your home-brewed drinks!

Or, as Mr. Ellis Roberts puts it: May your home-brewed drink help hell to blaze! The latter paraphrase may be owing to the exigencies of the rhyme, the former points clearly to a non-understanding of the colourless use as we may call it (and one difficult to explain in the context) of "fanden!" to which attention has been called in the n. to l. 897. A simple: 'the deuce with' or 'bother your home-brewed ale', or 'your homebrewed ale be blown" would have done quite as well.

The expression may be a contamination of: fanden ta eders hjemlige drik and: til helvede med eders hjemlige drik as Dr. Western suggests.

1063.   Der staar jo skrevet: Du skal tvinge din Natur.
        It is written: Thou shalt bridle the natural man.

Mr. Christensen calls my attention to Holberg's Jeppe paa Bjerget, I, 5: Tving din Natur, Jeppe! and quotes Jæger to the effect that Ibsen knew his Holberg well.

1070.   Halen. your tail.

The trolls are most easily recognised by their tails which shows them to be of the family of Old Nick himself (cf. the illustrations of Troels Lund, Dagligt Liv i Norden, VII, 30, for the huldre and *ib.* p. 150 seqq. for Satan) who is of course also adorned with this post-corporal appendix; simple but neat, as the devil said, and he painted his tail a pea-green! Mau, I, 199. References to this ornament in the case of under-earthlings are simply legion. As a rule the possessors are not very proud of it. Hence, if you should ever discover one and have reason to court the young beauty's favour, do as Peer Gynt is reported to have done (Syn og Segn, 1903, p. 129) when at a country-feast at Skoë. "At one time Peer had been invited to a little party. There came a tip-top girl. She was a stranger. She was dancing. It must have been a huldre. All of a sudden Peer went up to her and whispered something in her ear; what he said was this: "do take in that little silk thingumajig of yours" he said and that was of course the tail that was hanging out of the posteriors, don't you see!" Nepp inn att silkje-vippa di", where I have ventured to translate the silkje-vippa thus although it may also mean: a bow of silk, — the very "silkesløjfe" of our line! Then we have the case of a young man that delicately warned a huldre of danger by speaking of the protruding tail as her "garter" — honi soit qui mal y pense! (No. Sagn², p. 61) and compare some most amusing stories from Swedish folklore in: Wigström, Folktro, p. p. 99, 263; Hjelmström, från Delsbo, Sv. Landsmålen, IX, 4 p. p. 35, 47; Storckenfeldt, Västgötasägner, 1907, p. 9; compare further: Feilberg, Bjærgtagen, p. 86, n; and Wörner I¹, 391, ²413, who quotes Holberg's Niels Klim, ch. X, ed. Elberling, p. p. 153, 157, which I cannot now verify. He who helps the poor things thus is rewarded roundly for his delicacy but — woe upon him who "calls a tail a tail!" Then she is apt to vent her wrath by giving the delinquent something "on his tail" (Tijdspiegel, Okt. 1915. p. 141).

This excrescence is to such an extent the symbol, the outward sign of certain inward qualities that it falls off of itself when the huldre by a marriage with a human being is consecrated by the priest and is hence out of the reach of Satan. Compare the story of the Dragoon that was married to one of the hill-folk in No. Sagn (⁸ p. 64) and in Bertha Tuppenhaugs Fortællinger (Huldreev. '12 p. 41). One of the bridesmaids is requested to stand behind the bride so that no one shall see the tail, when at the nuptial blessing that symbol of Satan falls to the ground; cf. the n. to l. 1523. Readers of Ibsen's Sanct Hansnatten will remember Julian Paulsen and his horror when he discovers that his beloved had.... a tail and his disgust at Asbjørnsen in whose eventyr he made the discovery! (Eft. Skr. I, p. p. 398, 418 and p. LXIV of the Introduction). Later on (p. 406) Paulsen calls the tail: the abnormal excrescences, here present, that are at variance with every idea of beauty: "de her forhaandenværende, abnormale, med Skjønhedsideen stridende Udvæxter!"

As to the origin of the notion, for those who look for "natur motive" in all that concerns the troll-world, the tail is of course "dem lang nachschleppenden Gewölk entsprechend" (E. H. Meyer, Mythologie der Germanen, p. 168); others think more rationalistically of a confusion with the tails of cows and horses, cf. Feilberg, Bjærgtagen, p. 112: "it is conspicious that loose cows and horses have oftenest given rise to the huldre's tail". Those who have observed what in some cases may well be called abnormally long tresses your Norwegian country lass exhibits, will be inclined to think that these ornaments at the back should at any rate not be left out of account altogether. And when we read in one

---

1, 70; 3, 74; F, 332; M, 200; 14, 65; J, 207; 16, 65.

of the stories that Ibsen himself collected (Lars Medlid,
No. Sagn² p. 69 and. F. X, p. 477) that the "mountain-
taken" man describes the huldre as having hair that
"hung down on the back very long and like silk", we
surmise that the only reason why the young man does
not call this a tail, lies in the fact that his eye had not
been "turned" (cf. n. to l. 1125) because he had not yet
eaten of the food the beauty tries to press upon him.

1076.   høvelig. mannerly.

The Archers seem to have confounded høvelig and
høvisk, the latter of which means mannerly, the former: fitting. Prof. Storm quotes høvelig here (S. I. S. p.
191) as specifically Norwegian.

1082.   svanse, waggle.

The verb is here used no doubt in connection with
the actual tail that Peer has just had bound to his
hind-parts. But there may be an association (a "bitone")
of another meaning of the word. It is used too of the
movement that some ladies, innocently or designedly,
make with their bodies. As an amusing story of 1711
(Syn og Segn, 1899, p. 122) has it: Knaparne kom op aa
dantze, Moyanne kunne bra svantze.

1086.   Troen gaar frit. Doctrine goes free.

Compare Tanker ride toldfri; Mau, II, 413 and: D'er
Band fyre Talen men inkje fyre Tanken; Tankar ganga
tollfrie; Aasen, Ordsprog, p.p. 1. 2.

1092.   Vi trolde. We troll-folk.

In l. 857: Fattes der Gutter, en leger med Trold! (where
U has: Troll), we find the plural form used which is now
the only current one in Norwegian, whilst formerly trolde was more common; Wergeland uses it rarely, cf. Seip
Wergeland, p. 210. Ibsen uses trolde himself elsewhere,
cf. at digte er kamp med trolde and I Billedgalleriet,
XIV, where trolde rhymes on kolde; Publ. Society
Scand. Study, II, 133. — On the gender, see the n. to l.
2859.

1100. Noget ustyggelig styggt. Something unspeakably grim.

The Archers append a note in which ustyggelig is called a portmanteau-word, i. e. a contamination, compounded of usigelig and styg and they give as an alternative rendering: beyond grimness grim.

As the present writer has shown in a paper on this passage in the Dutch periodical: Neophilologus (I, p. 225 seq.), this view is untenable.

This becomes clear from the fact that by the side of u-styggelig we find styggelig (kaangsdottri klaga o va' saa steggleg solti, Bugge-Berge, Norske Eventyr og Sagn, II, p. 61), as well as avstyggelig (Kongespegelen, transl. into Landsmaal by Möller, p. 52; Aasen gives only ovstygg = yderst hæslig on p. 564 but "corrects" ustyggjeleg (p. 883) into ovstyggjeleg(!) and hence it is clear that our ustyggelig is composed, not at all "paa Trods af al Fornuft" as Vilh. Andersen says of an apparently similar case (Vilh. Thomsen-Album, p. 276; his example uvorn is not at all beyond suspicion), but on the contrary quite "purely" if I may say so, without any contamination at all, of styggelig = styg, ugly and the particle u — which has here an *intensive* force. When in the first act Aase calls her scapegrace of a son an Ubæst, as she does repeatedly with great gusto, she does not take away the force of the simplex bæst by the u —, on the contrary she strengthens it. In the same way we have utal, not = no number, but: a great number (although it is possible to explain it as "hvad der ikke kan tælles", Falk og Torp in v.) Lower down in the play, we have ustyrtelig (and it is not without interest to note that in this passage, Ibsen in the first draft had written ustyggelig too) = overmaade, which Falk and Torp compare to m. low germ. unstormelik. Again norw. ustøyteleg and utyske = monster contain the same intensifying prefix; just like Swedish opyske, which we have by the side of pyske (Rietz, p. 513). And if we did not know better, an explanation of the quite recent U-baat = U(ntersee) boot as a very bad sort of a boat would seem to fit in splendidly: only in the case of ubaat the accent would be different: enkelt tonelag ('ubaat) as against `ubæst, *etc.* (W.) See the n. to l. 363, Ubæst.

Hence such an expression like something supermonstrously monstrous would be the nearest equivalent, however strange it may appear.

As to the expression noget ustyggelig styggt itself, it is interesting to find that it was not made up by Ibsen, as some might imagine. Ustyggelig alone (in the sense of course of "very much", cf. the use of awful(ly), is found several times in the collection of fairy tales of Asbjørnsen that Ibsen has drawn upon so often both for the tales themselves, consciously and, no doubt unconsciously for some words; here again he may be supposed to be indebted to it for this exquisite expression, for not only does it occur there twice by itself: det er ein ostyggele ovane (Huldre-Eventyr, 1912, p. 127; En Søndagskveld til sæters) and Den andre böia.... var saa vild og ustyggelig at, etc. (ib. p. 280: Makreldorg) but in En Sommernat paa Krogsskogen we find the actual typically Norwegian expression that roused Prof. Storm's enthusiasm: Haare' det sto som grisebust, og skjegge'var itte likere det heller, saa je rekti syntes det var en ustyggeli stygg fant". Possibly as a reminiscence from the Ibsen-passage, it is used by Ragnhild Jolsen, in her sketch Ormen (Samtiden, 1906, p. 498): Og saa syntes Hilma Sofie den (ormen) vokste op fra sengestolpen indtil den blev til noget ustyggeligt styggt noget.

1102.   Stutthoser. In socklets.

The word seems rare as it is not in Brynildsen, nor even in Aasen or in the more recent Nynorsk Ordbog of Matias Skard. But Ross gives it = kortlægget strømpe. However, Skard has the evidently connected stubbho-

---

1, 72; 3, 76; F, 334; M, 201; 14, 67; J, 208; 16, 67.

sa = halvstrømpe which is quoted by Aasen in his Ordsprog (p. 192): "D'er leidt aa stiga upp i Smöret med Stubbesokkar. Hos Wilse: Stubhoser."

Ross explains Stubhose along with Stubbesokk as a stocking just covering the ankle; cf. ib. stubba = strømpelæg uden Fod. Feilberg, Jysk ordb. III, p. 627 gives another related word: Stunthose (cf. another instance ib. in v. damask), explained as footless stockings (so = Ross' stubba) and he quotes from Blichers noveller: Mett Kölvro war en kön stonthos tös." If Peer had only been in the right disposition of mind, he might have thought her a beauty too.

A Norwegian correspondent writes that these "short stockings" are certainly nothing but socks, — which remark a Danish one calls wrong — "at least so far as Danish is concerned"; he compares them to Feilberg's stunthoser and describes them as a l o n g stocking, of which the inner part of the foot is cut away; thus a sort of flap is formed covering the surface of the foot with a strap sewed on in front, that is put on the second toe. This flap is often beautifully embroidered and is especially in favour with shepherd's boys in the country". Where doctors disagree...., the present writer will not attempt to decide between the two views.

1110.   Katten klore mig. The cat claw me else.

In reply to a question whence the poet had taken the expression, Ibsen wrote to Rector Munthe (Stockholm; Katt-eder p. 75): "I fancy the expression is my own (hidrörer fra mig) I think, I chose the word klore for the sake of the alliteration". But this does not set the question as to the origin quite at rest, for if Ibsen c h o s e the word klore for the sake of alliteration, a similar phrase with a word with which klore was to alliterate must have been in existence and then of course "ta mig Katten", "Katten rive mig" or a similar expression may be thought of. As Ibsen expresses himself with the necessa-

ry prudence, he "thinks" it was his own, we have a right
to look upon another origin as possible too, viz. that
"klore mig" was the older part of the expression (cf. Nej,
klör mig om jeg gjör, Barderudsgutten, Norwegia, I,
257) and that Katten klore mig must be supposed to be
owing either to a filling-up of this klore mig with the
cat that suggests itself at once as the clawing animal
par excellence, or, if we look upon klore mig as abbreviated from a longer expression w i t h a subject [1]
(and this view seems the more likely one) owing to a
substitution of Katten for the subject in the fuller expression, such as fanden; faen klore mig is actually found
in Ibsen's source, the Huldreeventyr (Plankekjörerne,
ed. '12, p. 168). It will be remembered that the devil
was popularly supposed to be in possession of claws (cf.
the n. on the well-developed nail-system, l. 4449).

The translation, in the present expression, of Katten
by the cat may seem above reproach, but one thing
should not be overlooked or rather overheard, *viz.* that
the cat does not call up the same association in English
as Katten does in Norwegian. For, unlike the former, I
imagine, the latter suggests not only fanden in connection with the numerous other cases where His Satanic
Majesty occurs in similar imprecations (cf. former note)
whilst Katten is found in perhaps as many that yield a
close parallel [2]), but as handen and danden are found

[1]) By the side of the fuller expressions: faen salte mig, faen plugge mig (Huldreeventyr p. 165); Faen æte mig (Gjengangere, F, VI, 353), fanden gale mig, fanden
rive mig (Samfundets Støtter, first draft, Eft. Skr. II, 280, 303) and cf. Wergeland,
S. S. VI, 449: dat skal F—hakke mig bli Lögn, det! ib. jeg er F—dands' i mig ingen
Nar, jeg, etc., we find similar imprecations: tordne mig, klinke mig (Huldreev, p. p.
292, 296) etc., where the subject omitted may be either Katten or fanden.

[2]) Remember the modern Norw. han bryr sig katten om, han gir katten i, which
Brynildsen² compares to Eng. a deal he cares about, where deal stands of course for
devil; further: Feilberg, II, 105a: det må æ kat ved; ib. 106a: fy for katten = fy for
fanden; det var katens = det var som pokker, Feilberg, Tillæg, p. 255; För ta mig
katten, da jag var i gästabud för några dar, Sv. Landsm., 1904, p. 128; en så beslut-
sam min som om han gav sig Katten på at.... (Eje, George Kessers Generalkupp, p.
52; A Katten! = oh the deuce! ib. p. 187 and besides heaps of instances in Rector
Munthe's paper.

(Feilberg, Tillæg p. 134) as what one might call rhyming substitutes for fanden, so Katten may very well
be one for Satan (Ordbog over Gadesproget², p. 265 ¹)),
a substitution which may have been promoted by the
fact that the cat has always been connected with the
Devil and the witches; see Asbjørnsen, Preface to the
2ⁿᵈ ed. of the Folkeev., p. XXIV: That the cat is a
witch-animal and why the witches can transmute themselves into one, is explained most easily by the fact
that the cat was sacred to Freya", which even if it
should turn out to be questionable as an e x p l a n a-
t i o n — for w h y was the cat sacred to Freya? —
establishes the connection as a very old one — which is
what we want. And the suggestion of this connection,
as Nyrop has remarked (Sprogets vilde Skud, p. 94),
sufficiently explains its use in oaths and asseverations.
So some such expressions as the deuce take me else
would have been more adequate perhaps as coming
closer to the original in "devilry", — although it should
be admitted that the pun, slight as it is, of the original
is thus lost too.

And there is another circumstance that seems to
point in the direction of klore not having been chosen
for the sake of the alliteration with Katten. There are so
many clear references to the clawing out of eyes by cats
in the old tales (cf. Herreper, ed. '12 p. 106; ib. p. 109;
and p a s s i m as in the story of Peer Gynt itself,
Huldreev. p. 158, where we have the word klore used
of the clawing by a bear) that the whole expression may
be supposed to have been suggested ²) by these tales.
On the other hand the fact remains so far as I can

---

¹) For satan is often popularly pronounced with a second syllable as stressless as
that in Katten ['satən, 'satn̩: 'katən, 'katn̩] which strong stress on the first syllable helps to explain the colloquial: det var sytten = det var faen.

²) As they had possibly influenced the poet's son of whom the story goes that he
said when a little boy of the Swedish "whom father does not like" that he would
scratch their eyes out, "for I have something of a troll in me too — thi der er ogsaa
trold i mig, du!" Vilhelm Bergsøe, Henrik Ibsen paa Ischia, p. 238.

see that katten klore mig is not found before the appearance of Peer Gynt. And when we read in Munthe's essay (p. 80) that according to Ross, Ibsen must have borrowed it from Denmark it should be remarked that the nearest approach to it pointed out (by Feilberg) is: "Katen klo dæ" and that no other Katten klore mig has as yet made an appearance that may not (like Johan Bojer's *apud* Munthe) be owing to Ibsen himself [1]).

1120.   den gamle Adam. the old Adam.

As in Dutch: den ouden Adam afleggen (Stoett, n 49) or, closer to the original bible texts: the old man (Rom. 6, 6; Eph. 4, 22; Col. 3, 9): den ouden mensch afleggen". As Mephisto puts it: Der kleine Gott der Welt bleibt stets von gleichem Schlag Und ist so wunderlich als wie am ersten Tag (Prolog in Himmel), — which sentiment receives a probably unexpected application in: Vi ere alle Adams börn og vil gjærne have Pandekager! (Mau, II, 68) And a little less trivially in our own play: Bærmen, siger Ordsproget, hænger længst i. (l. 3369)

1124.   denne hersens Menneskenatur.
            this pestilent human nature.

It must be the colloquial nature of the word hersens that has so sorely puzzled the Archers and the other translators, although if they had looked for it, they could have found it in more than one dictionary, such as Brynildsen, Ordbog over Gadesproget, Ordbog for Folket, *etc*. Denne hersens mand is merely a colloquial extension of denne her mand, cf. this 'ere man, standing for denne her som er Mand, old Danish: denne hersom(s); Falk og Torp in voce. It will necessarily be found mo e especially in lighter literature, such as farces; compare Wergeland, S. S. VI p. p. 313 and 442:

---

[1]) Dr. Western, approving of the above explanation, adds that he looks upon it as simply a sort of euphemism for: fanden klore mig and adds Søren to the names for the devil that I have mentioned: Det var da Søren, and: Søren snuse mig, fanden ta mig.

1, 73; 3, 77; F, 335; M, 201; 14, 68; J, 208; 16, 68.

denne hersens Pram som tror, *etc.*; Oplysning paa dette
hersens Ugesbladet, *etc.*

As to the translations, we must be glad if it is not
translated at all, as in Ellis Roberts who simply gives:
For your human nature; perhaps he did not venture
upon the exact equivalent: for this 'ere human nature!
But is it not a delightful trait to have the k i n g of the
Dovrë lapse into such a colloquialism? Others have
evidently thought they recognised a word in it qualify-
ing and apparently depreciating the following menneskenatur; such as the Archers and Count Prozor who
translates: cette maudite nature humaine. What shall
we say of Passarge's die störrische (obstinate) Men-
schennatur (echoed it would seem in Mrs. Clant van
der Mijll's: die hardnekkige menschennatuur? The answer will probably be that all these, nothing but bold
shots after all, are simply excellent in comparison to
Morgenstern's: diese d i c k s c h ä d e l i g e Menschen-
natur. And as my readers after this are likely to ask for
the explanation of this pink of translations, they shall
have it; it is worth giving. Let them look up Brons'
low-german version and the riddle will be solved. Brons
has evidently recognised the word hersens = brain in
it and hence translates: Tegen disse harsens minske
natur (whatever this may mean!) accompanying the
translation by a delightful note: harsens, plur. Gehirn,
harsenschaal, Schädel, out of which Morgenstern seems
to have gloriously evolved his dickschädelig! [1]

125.   I venstre Øjet jeg risper dig lidt, saa ser du
skjævt.

---

[1] A correspondent explains the s of hersens as owing to analogy with (denne) fan-
ens (Peer), (denne) Pokkers (fyr), hersen having been felt as an equivalent of these
words. He remarks that it is of course only used in a degrading sense and that it
would e. g. never do to p r a i s e a man by such a collocation as: denne hersens
Frithjof Nansen! Hence ,pestilent' and ,maudite' are "not far from the mark",
which opinion I would query thus: are these expressions not far too s t r o n g for
the Norwegian word which after all is but the exact equivalent of: this 'ere fellow,
– which no one would equate with: that pestilent fellow.

In your left eye, first, I'll scratch you a bit, till you
see awry.

As the Archers have shown (Introd. p VI) one of
Bertha Tuppenhaug's stories is the source of this incident. There (Huldreev. p. 28) we find the story of
"King" Haaken who was about to wed the dairy-maid,
— all that remained to be done was to "change her eyesight" — Jaa, naa veit itte je det er anna att enn at
vrænge aua paa a", one of the bridesmaids had said,
— when a shot brought the whole most unexpectedly
and from the troll point of view, most unfortunately to
an end; exactly the same incident may be found in No.
Sagn², 1902 p. 81, quoted from a story called Tussebruden, told by Tormod Knudsen in Vinje's Dölen. But
there is another reference in point in Bertha's story:
when Asbjørnsen asks Bertha if a certain person has
been bewitched, she answers: no! not quite that, but
something had happened to him and since then he was
exactly "as if he had been spat upon", — sea va'n rekti
som 'n var spytta paa; and she adds another equivalent: you see, he remained "huldrin" a long time after;
"huldrin" is the word that expresses a state of being bewitched very mysteriously, and hence: strange, —
"overlooked". As Peer expresses it later on (l. 4283)
when he refers to the incident by saying his eyesight had
been "cast a glamour over' , — I vilde k v e r v e mit
Syn; literally to change, to turn ¹).

Ibsen changes it slightly by substituting the cutting
in the eye for the "turning" it. Another way of causing
a man to "see" things in the troll-way, to make him
"synsk" as the term goes, is to smear a certain salve

¹) One is reminded of Maeterlinck's delicious Blue Bird, where the poet has however substituted the turning of a diamond for the cut in the eye to produce the radical changes. As to the expression itself, an example of modern application may be
welcome: see Professor Gran's Norsk Aandsliv i hundrede Aar, where, speaking (p. 30)
of the hatred Ibsen often felt for his fatherland, the author writ s: Norge — det var
Dovregubbens hal, — der skulde et snit i øiet til for at bli blind for dets hæslighet
og jammerlighet."

upon the eye; this is done even to troll-children directly after their birth, — cf. Huldreev. ed. '12 p. 11 (Eke-
berg-Kongen): when the child had been washed and
dressed the (mountain-) queen sent (the midwife) to the
kitchen to get a jar with a salve to smear upon its
eyes". See ib. p. 13 for the dangers attending disobe-
dience: when you smear this on your own eyes, you get
it is true second sight but woe upon you if you are
found out (as you are almost sure to be!) for then "the
underearthlings spit in (your) eye" and so you remain blind. And this is nothing in comparison to what
Thiele tells of (in his Danske Folkesagn, II p. 202): one
who had got the salve on her fingers without knowing it
and so rubbed her eye by mistake, became "synsk"
which sounds like an encouragement, only when she was
discovered, she had her eyes put out. [1]

---

[1] Hartland in his Science of Fairy Tales gives similar stories concerning the remarkable working of the magic ointment; cf. e. g. p. p. 60, 216 and his Fairy Tales,
p. 92, the result we might express in the well-known words: "Fair is foul and foul is
fair" for, as in the case of Peer Gynt (n. to l.l. 987 seqq.) o, ye powers of Fairy land,
what a change was there! The neat but homely cottage.... seemed to undergo a
mighty transformation. The mother and one babe were remarkably beautified (if no
modern Hamlet thinks the word vile!) whilst on the other hand two children looked
a couple of flat-nosed imps with long ears and hairy paws.
About Ibsen's own treatment of a similar motif in his Gildet paa Solhoug, see Frederik Paasche's monograph on that drama, p. p. 72, 73, 95, 96, 97. An amusing story
of one's eyesight being corrupted, the well-known tale bears witness to of a girl who
is seen to lift up her dress exceedingly high, because she "sees" the water rising so
much that she can only wade through it in this way. Of many versions I quote one in
H. and E. Folkminnen, 1907 p. 409.
As to the closely related motif of becoming "synsk", the getting of second sight
already mentioned in the text, is "as easy as lying". You have only to look through
something round, — "when you look through a keyring, you can see all you like" (Asbjørnsen, No. Folkeev. ed. 1914, p. 62, Røderev og Askeladden, and see Prof. Nyrop
excellent paper "Kludetræet" in Dania, I, l, seqq. as well as a paper in the Dutch periodical Groot-Nederland (1916, March) Or if you are born on a Sunday or have found
a four-leaved clover, you can see hidden persons though they cannot see you (Huldreev. 1912 p. 287, Makreldorg). And of course, if you are so clever as to get hold of
the troll-monster's only eye (Trollene i Hedalsskogen, Udv. Æventyr, I. p. 22; Kleiven, I gamle daagaa, p. 18) you can see everything too. Compare further Feilberg,
Ordb. in v. v. angermus, dø, hoved, hulaget, se, synsk; id., Dania, II, 108; Sjæletro,
p. 66; Jul, II, 51; Olafsen, I gamle dage, Bergen, Floor, 1908, p. 151: a sketch, called
den Fremsynte and of course Jonas Lie's book of that name.

1128.   den højre Ruden. your right window-pane.

Of course the eye is meant; cf. windows = eyes, peep-ers, Slang Dict.; Farmer.

1130.   Spjeld skal du faa, som den olme Studen.

Blinkers you will wear like the raging bull.

As in the No. Folkev. (ed. '12 p. 253): de kom buren-de (lowing) som mandolme stuter. Morgenstern, evident-ly thinking of the German Stute, translates the word by Gaul which Mrs. Clant van der Mijll's "old jade" (oude knol) seems to echo. Count Prozor is sorely puz-zled: Je te ferai un grand œil de bœuf ou plutôt un œil de taureau!

Dr. Western remarks: "It is quite curious that he promises him Spjeld. He says he will cut his left eye to make him see things as the trolls see them. — We might suppose that the meaning of spjeld has not been quite clear to Ibsen. Or perhaps we are to suppose that after the operation it would be necessary to put a bandage on his eye and that this is meant by spjeld."

1135.   han er den vise og du den gale.

it 's he that is wise and it 's you that are crazy.

Here we have a foretaste of the Lunatic Asylum: cf. l. 3124.

1141.   forarger dig Øjet, saa slaa det ud.

if thine eye offend you, then pluck it out.

Compare Matthew, 5, 29. See Wörner I, p. 237: Ueber die verlangte Operation sucht er sich hinweg zu helfen mit der Stelle: Ärgert dich dein Auge, so reiss es aus. Psychologisch ein feiner Zug und zugleich der beis-sendste Hohn auf das frömmelnde Norwegen, wie sie sich mit den Worten des Heils abfinden zu ihrem Heile

1146.   Nej, stopp! Det er lettvindt at slippe herind;

men udad gaar ikke Dovregubbens Grind.

No, stop! It 's easy to slip in here

but the Dovrë-King's gate does not open outwards

Compare what Mephistopheles says in J. L. Heiberg's

En Sjæl efter Døden:
Man kun ind her, men ud ikke gaaer.

1151.   troldeligt. troll-like.

An unusual form, going back to O. N. trollsligr, but Ibsen wanted, metri causa, a trisyllabic word. Cf. 1. 4320: det troldelig nationale, which Brynildsen², explains rather than translates by: nationalism to the bitter end.

1160.   Og sagtens kan jeg ogsaa faa losset Baaden
        for denne Dovriske Levemaaden.
        And lightly enough I can slip my cable
        from these your Dovrëfied ways of life.

The translation "slip my cable" points to a misunderstanding of the expression which seems to have puzzled more than one of the translators. What does it mean: to loosen a boat f r o m something here? "Fra" should have shown the way; losse is not to loosen but to discharge, so the meaning is that he thinks he can easily get rid (literally to empty himself with regard to; by vomiting? as a correspondent suggests) of these Dovrëfied ways of life.

1163.   en Ed kan en jo altid æde i sig.
        an oath one can always eat op again.

An English ear might seem to scent a pun here, the slight difference in the vowel notwithstanding. But I have Norwegian authority for saying that a play upon the two words is out of the question.

1167.   træde tillbage, to beat a retreat.

On this, Peer Gynt's supreme life's wisdom, see n. to l. 1029 ante and infra l. l. 1579, 2027.

1170.   Sandt for Udyden, sure as I live.

The nicest of shades of difference that distinguishes this Dovrëfied (in Dovre "foul is fair and fair is foul!) Sandt for Dyden from the original expression: true by my virtue! escapes us in the translations, for the English sure as I live and by my royal life are at least as little satisfactory as Morgenstern's bald wild and Passarge's

---

1, 75; 3, 79; F, 336; M, 202; 14, 68; J, 209; 16, 68.

wirklich zornich, whilst the Dutch: waarachtig toch is more watered out than any. "Ibsen turns the whole of the romantic huldre-apparatus inside out" (paa vrangen), as Krogvig wrote to the present writer and the expression under discussion is a splendid proof how Ibsen pursues this in the minutest of details; cf. n. to l. 4315.

Of course there is this to be said, that an exact equivalent does not exist, — so the translators should make one up, just as Ibsen himself made up the expression he used. Sandt for Dyden itself may also be rendered by: forsooth, by the powers, as sure as I am a sinner (Brynildsen).

The last expression might of course be used here and not without effect, only the obvious point would be missing. Nor is such a thing as: by my infernal powers, nor even: by my vice, more satisfactory. This latter may be said to be putting it on too thick with its downright negation of virtue, whereas Ibsen's use of the negative particle is a stroke of genius.

Paulsen in Sct. Hansnatten has an equally unusual but not so picturesque: sandt for Herren (E. Skr. I, 391).

1171.　　　　　at gantes med. to be trifled with.

According to Professor Storm, (S. I. S. p. 179), at gantes "sounds quite Danish". The word is also found in Swedish dialects; cf. Rietz in v. and as an instance: Pintel (= Ashiepattle) han tog på att gantes med dem, Bergström ock Nordlander, Sagor, Sägner ock Visor, p. 39. And Aasen quotes it from the Northern country (Nordlandet) and eastern dialect, adding however that it is not very common. Still, Skard gives gantest = fjase in his Nynorsk Ordbok. Rietz quotes Engl. dial. gant, jolly, jocose, for which see the E. D. D. in v. ganty and ganse.

1172.　　　　　Du dagblakke Pilt! you pasty-faced loon!

Literally, if we may use the word in its old and dia-

lect senses: you dayb l e a k fellow. Mr. Ellis Roberts'
thou treacherous hound is much less satisfactory than
the Archers' translation. But in either the contempt for
the day has disappeared, so characteristic in the mouth
of the Lord of the Underground Realms where light is
far to seek; cf. l. 1029: dag skal du sky.

1176.   hun var i din Attraa og i din Begjær.
          you lusted for her in heart and eye.

"If a man's inner life shall be put to his credit-side,
he must answer for his wishes and desires, even if by
chance they should not be converted into action", we
read in a paper (by S. Høst, Edda, 1915 p. 330) on Henrik Ibsen's " Dream and Deed" and we are quite prepared for the author quoting Peer's case here and that
of the Dovrëking's daughter as in point.

There is indeed a clear reference in this passage to
Matthew, 5, 28: "But I say unto you that, whosoever
looketh on a woman to lust after her, hath committed
adultery with her already in his heart" although the
spiritual interpretation of the gospel has been changed
enormously by its combination with the more physical
one of the fairy tales and which l. 1182: you shall soon
have ocular proof of it, clearly foreshadows [1]). For similar, if not identical stories, I refer to that of the King
that sent the boy off in a glas-barrel (Kaangjen som
sende guten av i glastonna, Bugge-Berge, II, 60): a
young peasant comes to the king's palace; his presence
causes a great stir among the princesses and one of them
is so much impressed by him that her mere desire has
the most remarkable consequences: The young man
addressed the youngest, who was the most beautiful
of all and said: "You think you are pregnant" and true

[1]) J. Collin speaks curiously enough (p. 305) of "die nie zur Tat gewordenen Aus-
geburten seiner sündigen Gedanken", but then, for J. Collin, all this is but a dream;
p. p. 306, 307, 313: "alles nur Hexentrug!" Just like he thinks the Boyg-scene a
dream too, probably through a wrong interpretation of l. 3029: I lay in a fever! See
the n. to l. 1217.

enough "in no time she was great with child"! See further Feilberg, I, 376, b, about another princess who was got with child simply by a young fellow's desire and the reference to a similar case where this result is obtained through a young man's d r e a m; cf. Feilberg, Bjærgtagen, p. 125. Compare the n. to l. 1509.

1182.   Syn for Sagn. Ocular proof.

This is the original, current form of the expression, lit. sight for, i.e. proof of, the saying, which is however often changed into: syn for sagen, i. e. for the thing. The latter is rare in print, — cf. e. g. Mau, II, 391 and Gran, Nordmænd i det 19de Aarh., I, p. 321, in a letter from Goldschmidt to Wergeland, and twice in the 6th vol. of Wergeland's works, once in his "Kringla", once in the editor's comment; p. p. 439 and 596.

1185.   I et Bukkeskind. in a he-goat's skin.

Why in a goat's skin? One Norwegian correspondent answers this question by saying that it may be because a buck is usually supposed to be a symbol of sexual desire; cf. horebuk = adulter. Another, after apparently giving vent to an inaudible sigh writes: "I really do not know", but offers a suggestion all the same. "Perhaps it may be a reminiscence of the skins of Thor's two rams (Gylfaginning) which could be eaten and yet would be called back to life next day"

1187. Skal han skikkes till Kongsgaarden? Skikk ham paa Sognet!
Shall we send him to the palace? You can send him to the parish!

With regard to the King's Palace, it should be remembered that Peer is still supposed to be the son of "Queen" Aase. The expression paa Sognet, to the Parish, almost necessarily makes us think at present of a more or less comfortable home for the youngster in an orphanage or so. And if as is likely such an institution did not exist, the poor brat was simply sent from farm

1, 76; 3, 80; F, 338; M, 203; 14, 71; J, 210; 16, 71.

to farm, where the treatment must have left a good
deal to be desired; compare an account, very much in
point, in the Svenska Landsmålen, XI, 4, 1879, p. 56:
Hjelmström, Från Delsbo.

1191.   sligt Blandingskræ voxer urimelig fort —
          such mongrels shoot up amazingly fast.

See the n. to l. 1515. The Blandingskræ is referred to
afterwards as Krydsningsdyr (l. 3023).

1198.   Hiv ham i Knas. Dash him to shards.

Iknas or ikras (Aasen, Prøver af Landsmaalet* p. 58)
= to shivers, "to crash", in a thousand pieces.

1200.   Ulvelegen! Graamus og gloøjet Katt!
          The wolf-game! Greymouse and glow-eyed cat!

No such games are known to any of my correspondents, — they must have been invented — or rather: the
names must have been made up by Ibsen as those of
games, fit for the little ogres. "Rent dovrehalsk", as
one expresses it.

1202.   gjennem Skorstenspiben. up the chimney.

Peer's effort to escape thus may be a reminiscence
of Aeilførpongje's flight from Peer in Asbjørnsen's two
stories: Huldreev. '12 p.p. 137 and 157. Compare a
similar story in Kleiven, Segner traa Vaagaa, p. 45.

On the parallelism between this scene and one in the
fourth act (l.l. 2285 seqq.) see Ellis Roberts, Introduction p. X., and the notes to l.l. 1209 and 2324.

1203.   Tomtegubber! Nisser! Brownies! Nixies!

There is very little difference between these goblins
brownies and pucks. Other names are: tusse(n), ga(a)rd-
vor(d)en, tunvor(d), tunkall, tuftekall etc. Asbjørnsen
thus describes a man he once met than whom he had
never seen anyone that came closer to the idea he had
formed of the nisse (originally: little Nils, Nicholas):
He was a dry little man with his head awry (paa skakke)
red eyes and a nose that was very much like a big parrot's
beak", and he looked "as if he wanted to spit people in

their eyes" (En Sommernat paa Krogskogen; Huldreev.
ed. '12 p. 214; cf. ib. p. 298: Paa højden af Alexandrien;
Feilberg in v. and a paper by Haakon Schetelig, Fol-
ketro om gravhauger, Festskrift til H. F. Feilberg, p.
211). This seems to have been a malicious one; like the
one Asbjørnsen tells of (ib. p. 61: En gammeldags
Juleaften) who had got hold of seven souls and was
then and there trying to get number eight into his power.
But they are often really very sweet or as Faye amusingly expresses it (No. Sagn² p. 83) they are as a rule
"af en honnet tænkemaade", — really "decent" chaps!
These Robin Goodfellows are as a matter of fact the
guardian spirits of the place, which the name gaards-
vord points to, lit. farm-guard, and tun-kall, lit. the
man of the (farm-)yard, and they usually teach the
inhabitants of the place the wisdom of doing as they
would be done by, sometimes in a very hard-handed
manner. Treat them well and put out porridge (especially rømmegrøt) for them and if then you only do not
disturb them before two o'clock in the night (Asbjørnsen, Huldreev, 1912 p. 61) you will be all right. They are
often recognised by their having but four fingers and
having shaghaired hands (Asbjørnsen, Huldreev. p. 35:
En aftenstund i et Proprietærkjøkken).

1209.   Den gamle var fæl; men de unge er værre!
The old one was bad, but the youngsters are worse!
See the notes to l. l. 1202 and 2324.

1211.   Ak; var jeg en Lus! Would that I were a louse!
As in 'Marlowe's Faust Pride wished herself like to
Ovid's flea (to) creepe into every corner of a wench (i.
e. Ofilii Sergiani Carmen de Pulice; cf. Faustus Notes
p. 68) so Peer does not hesitate to wish for a change
into "das verächtlichste Tier" (see J. Collin's comment, Henrik Ibsen, p. 330, comparing the last lines
of the fourth act) in order to escape from his enemies.

1, 79; 3, 83; F, 340; M, 204; 14, 73; J, 211; 16, 73.

1213. Kirkeklokker ringer langt borte. Church-bells sound far away.

For the effect that the ringing of the church-bells has, Aase had already prepared us when she said (l. 824): that if Peer should be "taken into the mountain", we must ring the bells for him. For the hill-folk cannot abide the sound of the church-bells, which even when it does not as in the case of Faust forebode the resurrection of Christ, always recalls the Saviour and his passion. One of the trolls was so disturbed by the ringing of them in his peaceful dwelling at Svintru that he decided to change house! — like your poor little nervous mortal of the present time: "Jeg boede saa lunt i Svintru men da Rygjg-saata (kirken) blev reist og de fille Kubjællerne (these disgusting cowbells i. e. churchbells; remember the little imps speak of "black-coat's kine" [1]) ringede, kunde jeg ikke faa fred og maatte flytte" (No. Sagn[2], p. 29: Troldet og Hitterdals Kirke). The references to this ringing of bells and the flight of trolls in consequence are exceedingly numerous in the literature of folklore and elsewhere; cf. e. g. Welhaven's Eyvind Bolt and Jørgen Moe's Helgenotra, as well as the prose source of this story, in No. Sagn[2] 1902, p. 40: Helge had already come into the outer hall (svalen) and was just about to raise the latch when the rope burst that was attached to the bells".... and poor Helge disappeared for ever! A girl hears the church-bells and then suddenly remembers that she has been fourteen years "in the mountain" (Landstad, Folkeviser p. 453: Margit Hjuxe som vert inkvervd). Compare Meyer l. l. p. 142 (ib. p. 170), Kleiven, I gamle daagaa, p. 11 and many other references about which see Feilberg, Bjærgtagen, p. p 58, 60, 122, 123; i d., Dania, II, 106 (klokkeringning

---

[1] For the priest's cow-bells, compare a quotation from Djurklou, which I cannot now verify, in Mannhardt, Baumkultus der Germanen[2], p. 130 n.

1, 79; 3, 83; F, 340; M, 204; 14, 73; J, 212; 16, 73.

har vist de levende vej!) and his Jysk Ordb. in v. Kir-
keklokkerne and in v. ding-dong; ib. Tillæg p, 260.

It is like a far-off echo of this notion that we may have
to interpret Svanhild's words to Falk in the Kjærlighedens Komedie (F, II, 226): jeg var død og hørte
klokken kime som kaldte mig til lys fra livets tant, — a
case by the way, of "when the dead awaken" before Rosmersholm and the poets' "Epilogue" of the name; cf. n.
to l. 1234.

1215   Svartekjolen. The Black-Frock.

As in German (Schwarzrock) and in Dutch (zwartrok)
Svartekjolen (U: Svartkjolen) is here used as a not
over-flattering denomination for the priest whose dress
is black [1]). The semasiology of the case is illustrated
by black-cap in English (indicating as it does not only
the article that the judge puts on when passing sentence of death but also the judge himself) and in a different sphere of thought: petticoat; fr. calotte (la calotte
= the clergy) flemish kulder (a sort of cape, worn at
Ghent by the orphans, hence the orphans themselves);
engl. blue-coats = bluecoat boys, as it may be the key
to the enigma of girl = a. s. gyrele, a sort of (female)
dress; cf. the case of Swed. flicka as explained by Flom,
Journ. Engl. and Germ. Philology, XII, 1.

In Brand we have similarly Svartemanden (F, III,
168) = the minister. See lower down: svart kan ligne
baade Prest og Neger, (l. 3959) and compare: Ja, er du
ikke andet, saa er du svart nok til prest, du og, sa gran-
nene til kulbrænderen (Asbjørnsen, No. Folkeev. 1914,
p. 91); cf. ib. p. p. 125 and 129 and Aasen, Ordsprog, p.
233: Han var inkje kvit, som skulde gjera dat = det
maatte den slemme gjøre. In Asbjørnsen's Huldreev.
we find the corresponding svartsærk (ed. 1912, p. 173):
Tænker du aa faa mig ut, Krestjan Svartsærk? sa faen;

---

[1]) In the language of the sea-laps, a priest 's name was "sidkofte", on the principle of t a b o o; cf. n. to l. 2310; M. og M. 1909, p. 89.

---

ib. p. 234: Søren Svartsærk. An amusing interpretation
of this "black-coat" is found in Kamp's Danish folk-
lore-collections, quoted apud Feilberg III, 469 (in v.
sorteskole): all priests must go through the black school
(of necromancy) and only those that have done so, may
wear the black-coat! So the black-frock is ipso facto
made into a magician! On Svartekjolens k j ø r, see n.
to l. 1213. Svart is of course the dialect form (both Norwegian and Danish) of the literary s o r t; n. to l. 872.

1216.   alt forsvinder. everything disappears.

A reminiscence of the frequently recurring motif in
the fairy-tales that when the hill-folk are frightened
e. g. by the name of the Saviour being used or by a shot
fired over their heads, they disappear suddenly, leaving silver implements behind, which are sometimes
though rarely discovered in their pristine glory by the
human beings that have chased the trolls, — they are
usually found to be changed into the most disgusting
substance; cf. Bertha Tuppenhaugs fortællinger (Huldreev. 1912, p. p. 26, 27, 28): a woman sees a suspicious
tail (cf. n. to l. 1070) and by way of preventing which is
better than cure, writes the name of Jesus on the pail
that the person suspected is sitting on: the huldre rush-
es away, the tail is wrenched off, but the pail and the
food appear like an old tanned jar with cow-dung. Another time, the trolls are seen to fly away in the shape of
thread-balls (n. to l. 4011) on the firing of a shot and the
silver is left standing on the table, but all the "food of
the dinner-party" — gjestbus-kosten — had turned to
cow-dung, fleas, worms, witches' vomit and similar
delicacies. See further Aasen, Prøver af Landsmaalet[1]
p. 9 (a fisherman who sees the man disappear to whom
he has just sold his fish along with the house and all) and
Feilberg, Bjærgtagen, p. p. 41, 47, 48, 101 and 112.

1217.   The Boyg-scene.

Peer afterwards refers to this scene as if it was a fever-

1, 79; 3, 83; F, 341; M, 204; 14, 73; J, 212; 16, 73.

dream (jeg laa i Feber, l. 3029) which e. g. Count
Prozor seems to take literally: j'étais au lit avec une
fièvre. Lest others should be tempted to do so too and
think that Peer does but dream his encounter with the
Boyg, I add the interpretation that Overlærer Stavnem gave me: Peer's later remark shows his scepticism,
— he is of course supposed to be a rationalist.

1219.   Stemmen. Voice.

Here Ibsen uses the Dano-Norwegian word; cf. S. I.
S.p. 185. In the second ed. of Catilina he had substituted
røst, more usual in Norwegian, for stemme, which he
also uses in the speech at the grave, l. 3652.

1220.   udenom. Roundabout.

The Boyg's "central word": cf. n. to l. 1228 and the
fifth act, where Peer Gynt, at last, sees his way by the
the aid of or rather by his love for Solveig, "to go right
through" — at gaa tvers igjennem! (l. 4642).

1221.   Hvem er d u? Mig selv. Who are y o u ? Myself.

Compare T. C. § 53 on the non-spacing of the pronoun
in some later editions. Some of the translators have
been victimised by this: thus Mrs. Clant v. d. Mijll
should have translated: Wie ben jij, seeing that we
d o boast an emphatic pronoun in Dutch and not: Wie
ben je ?

Myself. The Boyg here plays with the motiv that
some will look upon as the central idea of the work: Mand
vær dig selv as against the vær dig selv n o k of the
Trolls, on which see the n. to l. 1044.

1228. H v a d er du? Den store Bøjgen. *What* are you? The
                    great Boyg.

What are you?

In l.l. 1221 and 1226, the answer that the Boyg is "himself", is given to the question *who* he is, but in l. l. 1228
and 1243, we hear that he is the (great) Boyg in reply
to the question *what* he is; in l. 3056 on the contrary in
answer to a similar question, Peer-Boyg is "himself". This

1, 80; 3, 84; F, 341; M, 204; 14, 74; J, 212; 16, 74.

slight discrepancy it is of course a commentator's duty to call attention to, though I for one am not inclined to attach any great importance to it.

An exhaustive treatment of the meaning of this strange being, both in Norwegian folklore and in Ibsen, its origin and name would far exceed the limits of even the longest note in this commentary. The present writer's views of these matters will be stated briefly and the student must be referred to a couple of papers where what is looked upon as the proofs of these views may be found as well as a full discussion of the views of others. In chronological order these papers are: "De Buig in Ibsen's Peer Gynt" for the readers of Dutch in "De Tijdspiegel" (1915) and, later and more complete: one on "Den Store Bøjgen" in "Edda" (1916 p. 356), and one on Bøjgens Oprindelse in "Danske Studier". (1916, Sept.)

The Boyg was taken by Ibsen from Asbjørnsen's version of Peer Gynt (given in English by the Archers at the end of their translation of the drama). There the Boyg is an invisible but apparently enormous troll, related it would seem to the Giants of ancient and old Norse mythology. In the papers referred to, the hypothesis will be found worked out that the Boyg goes back directly to, or at least is intimately connected with the Midgardsorm of Edda-fame: the world-serpent which like Okeanos was supposed to be coiled round the world and that hence our Boyg is related not only to the famous sea-serpent "this famous nonentity, The wondrous worm that won the height of fame by keeping out of sight", as a modern bard has sung [1] but also to "that seabeast Leviathan which God of all his works created h u g e s t" (Milton), the Jasconicus (Brandaen), Fastitocalon (= Aspidochelo; Codex Exoniensis), and not to mention other possible analogues: Beowulf's formidable antagonist, Grendel and his mother,

[1] Oliver Herford, the Mythological Zoo.

1, 80; 3, 84; F, 342; M, 205; 14, 74; J, 212; 16, 74.

all of which are usually interpreted as being incarnations of the spirit of evil, Antichrist.

The name Boyg is transparent enough for those who recognise Dutch buigen, German beugen in it and consequently means originally curve, meandering, bend, — I have followed the example of Messrs Archer and left it untranslated.

As to the meaning oi I b s e n's Boyg, it cannot, as some have imagined, be meant to symbolize Peer Gynt's p a s t, — this is done in the Green-clad Lady; cf. n. to l. 955. Ibsen's idea must have been to make this unstable, form-shifting, form-less something the incarnation of Peer's characteristic absence of will, of firmness. Peer is like Macbeth, letting I dare not wait upon I would in that he too like the cat in the adage would catch fish, but would not wet his feet. But he is also like Hamlet and more so, in that he would like no doubt to have certain things done if only he must not do them himself. And the voice that speaks here out of the darkness, is not that oi a man, of a (more or less human) being, — compare a little lower down: not so much as a shape; ingen Skikkelse heller and observe that the Boyg is mentioned in the list of the dramatis personae, not as such but only as "a voice in the dark"! — it is Peer's voice of his own irresoluteness, of his vacillating, wavering personality (if he have any!), like Macbeth he is "infirm oi purpose." It is clear that these views so far as they will be seen to deviate from those of others, cannot be supposed to be proved here where no evidence of any kind could be adduced but it is hoped that a perusal of the papers quoted may convince the students of their plausibility.

There is reason to think that the Boyg, central and consequently necessary to the play as it no doubt appears at the first blush, was as a matter of fact an episode, in so far that the Boyg does not seem to have been in cluded from the first in the conception of the play. This

---

1, 80; 3, 84; F, 342; M, 205; 14, 74; J, 212; 16, 74.

conclusion, revolutionary as some may think it, is forced upon the investigator by a concurrence of circumstances that can here only be indicated, a full inquiry will be found in a paper on the "Caprices" in Peer Gynt (Edda 1917, probably March). The whole of the Boyg-scene is written in the first draft (U) not on the quarto-pages on which Ibsen began, continued and finished U, but on a series of Tillægsbladene (stamped as a whole by a remark of Ibsen's on one of them) on which also the third version of the Dovrëhall-scene is found; cf. n. to l. 1000. Now, it will be clear, I hope, from the investigation of this Dovrëhall-scene conducted in that paper, that Ibsen was there composing the Dovrë-hall-scene over again. And in support of our conclusion, I wish to urge, although an argument ex nihilo is never quite without danger, but it is remarkable, that the Boyg is not mentioned at all, not even, as in the later version as a Voice only, in the list of the dramatis personae of this first draft (U) and this circumstance may be taken to bear out in a way the conclusion that this apparently central figure did not form part of Ibsen's original scheme.

On the non-spacing in some texts of H v a d and its consequences, cf. T. C. § 53 and the n. to l. 1221. — In U, Hvad was corrected from Hvem.

As to den store Bøjgen, Western in his "Skriv Norsk" arranges the cases of a substantive with the postpositive article as well as the definite art. before the preceding adjective, under two headings of which the first contains this very example. It will appear from this exposition that Norwegian "sprogfølelse" makes use of this arrangement when "the thing is looked upon as so well known that a further definition is unnecessary" (gjenstanden anses for saa kjent at nogen nærmere bestemmelse er unødvendig). That Ibsen has not here written den store Bøjg must be in accordance with this linguistic instinct (see the note to l. 1229). Only, the metre would have been improved by the suffixless substantive.

1229.   Før var Gaaden svart; nu tykkes den graa.

The riddle was black; now I'd call it grey.

Peer was a great reader of fairy-tales, his mother used to while away the time and forget her misfortunes: a drunken husband, etc. by telling them to her son; cf. "we, why we took to fairy-tales of princes and trolls (n. to l. 796). So, the Boyg may be supposed to be an old acquaintance of his, but the enigma has not by any means been solved quite!

1232—'34.   Bøjgen, Peer Gynt! En eneste en.

The Boyg, Peer Gynt! the one only one.

Bøjgen to be pronounced with emphasis on the second syllabe as The Boyg with stress on the article. We must h e a r him think: no! not more than one: [b œ i ' g ɛ r] but only o n e: [b œ i ' g ɛ n]: en eneste en!

On the mutilations that the text has undergone, død substituted for saarløs, cf. S. M. p. 9; T. C. § 53.

1234.   Bøjgen som er død, og Bøjgen som lever.

the Boyg that is dead, and the Boyg that's alive.

The Boyg is dead but lives up again, a feat not without precedent; cf. the performance by Thor on his goats in the prose-Edda (Gylfaginning, ch. 43).

It would be quite in keeping with a very usual spiritual interpretation of such passages, if we were to explain this line as foreshadowing the wakening up of the dead. In the n. to l. 1213, attention has been called to a passage in Kjærlighedens Komedie and we may add that Ibsen had written already in 1857 a propos of the old Norwegian ballad-poetry: As everything that bears a germ of spiritual life (et åndeligt Livsmoment) in itself, so the old ballad-poetry (Kjæmpevisen) does not die at its death" (S. V., 354). And of how many heroes of ancient fiction, King Arthur, Barbarossa *etc.*, does not (pseudo-) history tell us that they are not dead but like the Great Hero of the Bible, will be resuscitated when the fullness of their time has come?

But there can hardly be any doubt that the explanation of this line is not quite so profound; if my readers will think of the explanation hinted at in the n. to l. 1228, the Boyg clearly simply says: you may momentarily kill me, i. e. rouse yourself to an action, — it won 't last long, a moment only and I am alive again, I have vanquished you and you have fallen back once more into your apathy.

1235.   Værget er troldsmurt; men jeg har Næver!
         The weapon is troll-smeared; but I have my fists.

In a note to his translation of this line, Brons (on. p. 80) gives us the benefit of his ignorance by the following remark: "Die trolde ummauern Einen im Kreise mit Nebel". The reader may think that he is in the same plight, the mist before his mind's eye preventing him from seeing what all this has to do with our line. Until the light suddenly begins to shine again on his finding out that troldsmurt was taken by Brons to be: trolds-murt as if it possibly could be: provided with a wall, instead of trold-smurt i. e. smeared, rubbed in, (magically) anointed, i. e. charmed by a troll. There is something truly "charming" about this translation: Wat mi hinderd is 'n troldmüür, what bothers me is a troll's wall!

1239.   Atter og fram, det er lige langt; —
         ud og ind, det er lige trangt!
         Forward or back, and it's just as far; —
         out or in, and it's just as strait.

Here the words simply indicate that there is no change in the position of the Boyg, and so it takes Peer as long to go there as to come back from the monster, — and everywhere outside or inside there is as little room, — where Ellis Roberts has for once sacrificed sense to rhyme by changing the Archers' "and it's just as strait" into: and it's strait as strong.

But Peer in his mania of quoting and making fun of himself where no one else is at hand, quotes this later on (l. 2894) by way of illustration of his remark that he is not minded to go backwards like the lobster and gives as his source: a witty pamphlet (hardly a s p i r i t- u a l or luminous work as the Archers render "et aan- drigt Skrift"); again (l. 3800) on coming back to Hægstad when all his relics are about to be sold by auction and lastly, when (l. 4636) he is about to find Solveig, i. e. to find himself in her sweet remembrance. There is something terribly affecting if the contradic- tion perhaps apparent only may be allowed, in the antithesis between the "alvor" of the circumstances in which he pronounces this "deadly chant" as Ellis Rob- erts calls it, in the last two cases and the lightheart- edness with which he has quoted these "witty" words before.

As to the words of the chant (on Norwegian *fram* see n. to l. 113) its form will remind some of one Ibsen may have found in Kari Træstakk:

"Lyst fore og mørkt bag
saa prinsen ikke ser hvor jeg ri'r hen i dag!"
(Folkeev. 1912, p. 73; cf. Feilberg, II, 489 in v. lyst and compare Asbjørnsen's No. Folkeev. 1914 p. 68: Stutt foran og langt bak! Stutt foran og langt bak! in Gutten som vilde fri til datter til mor i kroken.) But the expres- sion as such is proverbial; cf. Mau II, 523: Frem og til- bage er lige langt, who compares the jocose: "Der er langt frem, sagde Kærlingen, hun saa sig tilbage" and explains: om den som gaar en Vej forgjæves.... ogsaa om den der tager en anden Beslutning i timelige Anlig- gender. Aasen p. 186: Fram og Tilbake er like langt. By the side of atter (= tilbage) og fram, we find: at og fram; cf. Seip, Wergeland, p. 151.

1, 81; 3, 85; F, 343; M, 205; 14, 75; J, 213; 16, 75.

1245.   Ingen Skikkelse ·heller! Det er som at tørne
        i en Dynge af knurrende halvvaagne Bjørne!
        Not so much as a shape! It 's as bad as to battle
        in a cluster of snarling, half-wakened bears.

Here as well as later on: Were there only as much as a year-old troll! — var her bare saa meget som et aarsgammelt Trold, Peer Gynt knows what he is about, for there can hardly be any doubt that this contains a reminiscence of the trolls he has just had to cope with. (l. 1213). So, when as in the performance of the play e. g. at Kristiania, the trolls take the shape of bears, there is full authority for this in Scandinavian folklore.

On ingen Skikkelse, see the n. to. l. 1228.

1258. Vingeslag af store Fugle. The wing-strokes of great birds.

As to the meaning of these big birds we read in J. Collin's study (p. 309): Es sind gleichsam die Aasgeier die das Opfer wittern das im Kampfe mit seinem Ich zu erliegen droht." This is not very satisfactory. Much more in keeping with the magic character of the scene is Stavnem's explanation (Overnaturlige Væsener, p. 102) who reminds us first once more of Asbjørnsen as Ibsen's probable source: In many of his tales, such as Grimsborken, Bonde Vejrskjeg, Makreldorg and Graverens Fortællinger, Ibsen may have read of such birds, hostile to men; especially the last one is interesting: Some hunters were one easter-night out on a trip. As they were sitting in the sæter-hut, about dawn, they suddenly heard a terrible roaring and soughing in the air; it was as if a heap of big birds came to alight on the ground. Now, these birds turn out to be witches that had been out on a spree. In Grimsborken the evil powers sent out these birds to stay the hero and in Makreldorg three witches turn themselves into three ravens that bring misery wherever they come [1]). And Stav-

---

[1]) In many stories (such as in Gullslottet i havet apud Løland p. 157, from Vang, Gamla reglo aa rispo fra Valdres) there is one of the three sisters "that rule over all the birds that fly in the air" but it is doubtful whether this lady is related to ours.

1, 82; 3, 86; F, 343; M, 205; 14, 75; J, 213; 16, 75.

nem (whose words I have rendered freely, in accordance with private communication and corrections to his paper) explains these "troll-birds as the brood of the night into whose power he falls that gives up his life's struggle and forgets his mission". And this is exactly the case with Peer. In connection with the notion that these birds should be able to talk, I quote (at second hand, from Dania, II, 180) an investigation by Schirmer on the legend of S. Brandanus, who meets in his travels with birds that have a human voice, being originally some of the Angels that did not side with Lucifer but were all the same hurried along in the Fall and consequently not allowed to appear before the face of the Lord. In the case of this originally Irish mythology, the faculty of speech of these creatures, is supposed to be due to the myriads of sea-birds on the Irish coast whose cries at a distance resemble human voices. The spirits of the dead too are often found re-incarnated in birds.

1259.   Kommer han? Is he coming?

Why should these birds ask whether Peer is coming? As a correspondent writes (who frankly avows that he cannot explain this), it may mean: Is he coming to us, in our power? *i. e.* faar vi ham? It is hardly possible that kommer han should stand for: Kommer han sig i. e. is he gaining. To this the next line would otherwise seem to lend some countenance where the birds seem to be calling up their reserves.

1263.   Spændebogen. Your clasp-book.

This "clasp-book" is of course a prayer-book here or that very psalmbook we have heard of before (cf. lower down) but certainly not as it was rendered by a Dutch translator (Gids, 1893 p. 88) who apparently confounded it with Du. boog: the bow, as if it were the cross-bow Solveig was to fling in the monster's eyes! Now I am locked like a clasp-book, "lukket som en spænde-

---

bog", the klokker says in Brand (F. III, 190; in the first draft, less clearly: Now I am like a spændebog) but in his early sketch En brudevielse (F., vol. X, p. 410) Ibsen has an idyl about the light-haired lasses with their spændebøger that go to church. Just like Solveig who (l. 586) "carried a psalm-book" and looked down upon her shoes, so here he tells her as a reminiscence no doubt of that very passage: Gaze not adown so, lowly and bending: glan ikke ned for dig, lud og bøjet (where lud stands for luded, luden [1]) = stooping so that the Archers' lowly is rather free); cf. n. to l. 584 for the Faust-Gretchen reminiscence. To throw such a book at the head of a troll is of course a very excellent means of getting rid of it, — when Odin tempted Olav den Hellige, the latter flung his prayer-book into the former's face, saying: you I would not be for the world, you wicked Odin! (Feilberg, Sjæletro, 1914, p. 119 and cf. id. Ordb. III, 146 in v. salmebog). And compare Landstad, Folkeviser, 16: Dei slog meg med skrá i skallen, they threw a bible (skrá, lit. "book of law", bible or missal) at my head. Similarly, Hjelmström tells among his stories from Delsbo (Sv. Landsmålen, XI, 4, 39) about one who, becoming afraid, "reov upp e salmbok.... o kastara mitt i trollhopen." Mau gives an amusing proverbial expression: "I punish my wife with good words, said the man, (and) he threw a bible at her head." (II, 372).

The Spændebog makes a great impression on Peer, cf. l. 3320, where he says of himself to Hussejn that he was "in a woman's keeping a silver-clasped book, Jeg var i en kvindes eje en sølvspændt bog" and in the terrible auction-scene in the fifth act, he offers for sale: "a dream of a silver-clasped book".

---

[1] To this form supplied by a Norwegian correspondent, Dr. Western appends the remark that he does not know any such forms, adding: "Lud is often used: han var litt lut = he was a little crooked, stooping; the verb is lute = to stoop.... So, instead of lud we might say ludende.

1269.   svinder ind till intet. shrinks up to nothing.

Wörner who has explained the Boyg to mean (far too generally, see the papers quoted in the n. to l. 1228): Peer's battle with his own character, says (I¹ p. 240): "Darum endlich schrumpft er machtlos zusammen, sobald Peer an Solveig denkt, der das Bessere in ihm, allein zu schwach im Streite, hilfesuchend zustrebt".

The closest parallel to this shrinking up to nothing that I know of, is that of a troll who having been wounded by Goffar (Tor) and having asked in vain to be brought home to Puckabärget, was d i s s o l v e d into slime: sedan hon legat en god stund upplöstes hon och där syntes endast något slem efter hänne (Hermelin, Sägner ock Folktro, p. 49).

1273.   et tungt Øjekast. heavy eyes.

ramsaltet Sild. a pickled herring.

On tungt, cf. T. C. § 56.

Instead of ramsaltet, very salt, U. had: en lagebrændt sild, i. e. "at den har faat usmaken av at ligge i laken", too much tasting of the brine (lage), rancid, salt-burnt", Brynildsen.

1274.   Nistebomme. basket of food.

Niste is specifically Norwegian; cf. Seip, Wergeland, p. 25.

1278.   ta dig i Fang. take you in my arms.

As later on the Green-clad Lady is said to desire "at krystes i fang" lit. to be pressed in (his) arms". Some of the translators would seem not to have understood this, at least it is hardly imaginable that e. g. Count Prozor should not have dared, verecundiae causa, to use a more drastic expression than: que je t'enlève!

1281.   Da var det vel, der blev ringet med Klokker.

Then it was well that the bells were set ringing.

The bells were set ringing to frighten the trolls; see n. to l. 1213, hence da var det *vel*, with stress on this word.

1, 84; 3, 88; F, 345; M, 206; 14, 77; J, 214; 16, 77.

1283. Aa, hun taer Benene fatt! Oh, she's running away!

Of course Solveig flees from Peer Gynt who has frightened her by his words and whom she now — hvad siger *du ?* — sees coming towards her. J. Collin finds a deeper meaning in it: "Als er aber gar von seinem Erlebniss im Berge zu prahlen beginnt, und, selbstgefällig, als bedeuteten sie für ihn nichts, über die Glocken a b s p r i c h t die dem Verzweifelnden aus der Not geholfen, scheucht der so jäh wieder in 's Kraut geschossene Dünkel des Unverbesserlichen.... sein besseres Selbst sofort wieder weg!"

1289. Gud naade dig, hvis du ej —! God pity you if you don 't!

The semasiologically remarkable development from God be good to you, to: God punish thee (which is of course not the actual *meaning* here, but practically, in the context, the sense in which it is *applied*) is well hit off by V. Andersen in the Festskrift to V. Thomson, p. 308, who observes that it is now usually pronounced "with an intonation that fits the pious words as such as a clenched fist does a pair of folded hands and which gives expression to something that is not essentially different from: The devil shall take you!"

What should we say of Count Prozor's: "Que Dieu te r é c o m p e n s e"?

TREDJE HANDLING. ACT THIRD.

1293. du gamle Kall. you ancient churl.

Kall is originally the same word as Karl (churl), fellow, man, but with the meaning differentiated along with or at least as well as the form; cf. Torp, Nynorsk Etym. Ordb. in v. As to the semasiology of the case, compare the use that Aladdin makes of the word knark, old fellow in Oehlenschläger's play of that name, which he applies to a spinning-wheel: man vænner sig til slig en gammel Knark (fourth act; Morgiane's Stue) but a little lower down where he adresses an imaginary lamp: Ha, bi du kun, god' Karl!

1302.   Løgn! Lies!

The leitmotiv of the first act once more; practically that of the whole play, cf. n. to l. 57.

1305.   tungvindt. heavy.

This word Ibsen had already used in U, but crossed it out and changed it into trættsomt over the line. We have an interesting example here of the pains the poet took to find the right word. It was once more changed to tungvindt when he copied out U as R. He may have cancelled it because it sounded like a Sveacism, trøttsam, indicating just that "fatiguing, wearisome" that the context demands. But as the Norwegian dialects know a word trættesam (= quarrelsome; Aasen and Skard), it is just possible that Ibsen was not guilty so much of a Sveacism here as of confounding Norw. trættesam with trættende.

1315—16. spike Tyri, nøre (Ild), stulle, stelle, lage.

split fir-roots, light fire, bustle around and prepare.

These words not all recognised as belonging to Riksmaal are Norw. dialect forms; cf. S. I. S. p. 191. See Asbjørnsen, No. Folkeev. 1914 p. 44; han lærte snart at stulle og stelle (hesterne).

1337.   grøsser. shudders.

A specifically Norwegian word, cf. S. I. S. p. 191, which was not found originally in U., where the text read: nedover Ungskogens, but nedover was crossed out by Ibsen and changed already in U. into the present reading.

1342.   En Gut! Bare en. Han tykkes skræmt.

A lad. Only one. He seems afraid.

This, the so-called coward-episode ("poltron-episoden") was taken bodily by Ibsen from the first (epic) draft of his Brand (here referred to as E. B.); see the ed. by Karl Larsen p. p. 136, 137 for the two versions and

1, 87; 3, 91; F, 348; M, 208; 14, 80; J, 215; 16, 80.

ib. p. 226 for the editor's comment on it. Karl Larsen, after having shown that Ibsen may have known of an actual case in point (a young soldier had hewn off his finger in June 1864 for fear of being sent off to the war that then threatened with Germany if Norway had come to the assistance of the "brother-people", Denmark) comments on this as follows: A nobler more scorpion-poisonous find Ibsen could not have made in the mood he then was in: a Norwegian boy, that shows his courage by mutilating himself of cowardice". And Larsen in view of the funeral oration that Ibsen causes to be held over him in the fifth act (l. l. 3646 seqq.), concludes that all this was "with a view to expressing the poem's deepest irony".

Professor Chr. Collin in a remarkable paper in the Samtiden (Nov. 1913; reprinted in his "Det geniale Menneske", 1914) calls attention to the funeral oration, compared to the Epic Brand episode. In the poem, the soldier that refused to go to the war, represented according to Collin, the coward Norway who refused to go to war to save the Danish brethren. But in Peer Gynt, — quantum mutatus ab illo! "The poet's disposition towards him has apparently softened down. From a satirical popular type he has become an individual, a human being too (et medmenneske) regarded with human eyes, a man who has to fight his own battle and who, his sad limitations notwithstanding, (med al sin sørgelige begrænsning) fights it valorously. The poet has put himself in the other's place in life, visited him in his own parish, lived his life with him. And the same severe satirist that in the E. B. showed him to us as a despicable coward, now holds a touching funeral oration over this man" — and that there is but an apparent contradiction between the two views quoted is shown clearly by Collin's last words that Ibsen uses him "to put Peer Gynt to shame. And so little

Peer Gynt will feel at times, that he admires the coward's courage!" For Sigurd Høst too (Henrik Ibsen's Drøm og Daad, Edda, 1915, p. 332) the coward is superior to Peer Gynt. "He (the coward) is more of a man (mere til kar) than the phantast Peer; in his way he can "do a deed" whilst Peer Gynt's life is an empty string of beads" (why p e r l e s n o r, one is inclined to ask?) "with actions undone or at most half-done!"

Larsen's suggestion that the story of 1864 may have reached Ibsen just in time to be used by him in his epic Brand is very plausible. But it is worth pointing out that the incident of the hewn-off finger does not stand alone and that the thing is known to have occurred before. However, there is nothing that points to this being Ibsen's source so that it is quoted as an illustration only.

In and about 1831 at any rate, when a man did not want to go into the King's service, it appears to have been the usual thing, if he had not got money enough to bribe his captain (about which a word anon!) to make himself unfit for service by various sorts of self-mutilations. This results very clearly from a rather remarkable series of documents (if the word may be used of this controversial matter) published in 1902 in the pages of "Syn og Segn" by Overlærer J. A. Schneider: Gamall Bygdemaals Diktning. Incidentally we hear there a good deal about those bribes — "løysning" — that some "butter-captings" (smørkaftener) did not think beneath themselves to put into their pockets. And the writer very naively asks, why, you who object to this system of bribery, where is the wrong, when the captains help a man out of the King's service, that they get something for their trouble? And what would you have a poor fellow do? If he must not bribe his man, would you have him cut himself in his leg? Must he throw tobacco into his own eyes? M u s t h e hew off h i s f i n g e r s? Do you think the lasses will take them

---

1, 89; 3, 93; F, 350; M, 209; 14, 81; J, 216; 16, 81.

with their mutilated bodies?" So here the coward's little remedy is spoken of as the commonest thing in the world and his action is raised to a higher dignity, in fact it seems t h e thing to do if you don 't want to lose your sweetheart, — as who would if he can help it?

But there was a very much easier way out of the difficulty! Just as even now those in holy orders are exempted everywhere, so then you had only to become a schoolmaster! Compare Vetle Vislie's biography of A. O. Vinje, p. p. 22, 23: His father wanted him to become a schoolmaster, so that he need not enter the King's service — "so kunde han sleppa (den fæle) Kongens Tenesta" — Feilberg (Ordb. III, 10) quotes still another way out of it: many simply joined the gypsies —- mange gav sig i rakkerselskab for at bli fri for Kongens tjeneste![1]) And that Ibsen knew at any rate of more than this one means to the desired end, appears from a passage in the first draft, 1868, of De Unges Forbund (Eft. Skr., II, p. 127; cf. ib. I, p. LXXII): "gamle Lundestad.... han hugg da vel ikke en Finger af ham?", referring to his son whom L. wished to secure against the "chances of war" — mod Krigsm o l e s t — and the other answers: "Bosh! that happened only in the days of yore." "Well, perhaps he made him shortsighted or gave him a squint?".... And it ends with the most unkindest cut of all: in order to be quite sure that he will not be wounded, the father makes him.... a soldier!

In the first draft, U (1, 6, v°; E. Skr. II, 82), Ibsen accentuates Peer-Poltronens cowardice by making Aase oppose to him his brother Nils who did accept the King's shilling and, what is more, earned it!

---

[1]) Dr. Western tells me of an other means: that of becoming a bailiff's servant (lensmands dreng). This means was utilised by the bailiffs in this way: when such a post was vacant, they advertised it like another post: a rich young man then might present himself as an applicant and paid the bailiff a certain sum (say 500 kroner) to get the post. He then gave it up paying a poor young fellow to do the work for him. Dr. Western has often seen these advertisements in the newspapers and thinks the trick may still be practised.

1, 89; 3, 93; F, 350; M, 209; 14, 81; J, 216; 16, 81.

1348.   Han bløder, som en Stud. He bleeds like an ox.

As it is not clear that a bull bleeds more than any other animal, there may seem little force in the expression (for the very Norwegian expressions under discussion here are sufficient to disprove Stoett's view, that the Dutch: het land hebben als een stier must mean originally: like a bull fastened to his tether"), until we remember that it may be transferred from another context, where the comparison "like a bull", implying strength, does intensify the expression, e. g. as strong as a bull i. e. very strong. So here: he bleeds very much. Compare sterk som en stut, Johan Bojer, Den store Hunger and the n. to l.l. 1130, 1518.

1351.   Det var Fanden till Kropp. What a devil of a lad!

Kropp, literally body, here colloquially: (the body of) a person, fellow, chap, takes the place of Fant in U. On the substitution of er for var of both the oldest texts, see T. C. § 49. The difference in meaning between det er and det var it is easier to feel than to explain. "Det *er* fan til" something, may however be said to refer, as a friend formulated it, to a general characteristic, — "det var" to a special case. This, if not very precise, shows at any rate how a casually substituted reading may make hash of a thing, for thus Peer is made to say: a person is a devil of a thing. See the n. to l. 701.

1359.   gjøre det.... *do* it!

The key to Peer Hamlet's character; cf. the n. to l.l. 781, 1228 and 1342. Observe the apparent irony of l. 3771 where Peer is made to speak of this same fellow as his "Aandsfrænde"; cf. n. ib.

1367.   Hvad er det, som rumler? What is that rumbling?

Rumler was changed in the second ed. into ramler, about which see T. C. § 24. Both verbs mean practically the same thing, ramle meaning however also to break, to tumble. For ramle = rasle, larme, cf. Feilberg, III, 12 b. and Lappiske Eventyr, p. 92: kjærringen hørte igjen

---

1, 89; 3, 93; F, 350; M, 209; 14, 82; J, 216; 16, 82.

rammel fra Stalden.... det kan aldrig være ret med
hesten siden den ramler så. This change into ramler is explained by the fact that some look upon this as decidedly
the better word to express the meaning. Dr. Western
writes: As far as I know rumle would not be used of
the noise made by a heavy waggon. He knows rumle in
two senses only: the noise made by the stomach, and
in that of to make a night of it = at rangle. This is interesting as it shows this to be the leading sense for
the scholar in question. Only, it should not be supposed to mean that Ibsen was wrong in using r u m l e,
cf. the fact that e. g. in Brynildsen², to rattle, to rumble
is the leading meaning given, whereas to go on the spree
comes in the last place only.

1382.   han, Peer, blev jer dyr. your Peer's cost you dear.

To the discussion of this passage in T. C. § 129, it
should be added that according to Dr. Western in the
mouth of the woman han Peer fits better than: han,
Peer and that the reading in U of which it takes the
place is: Ja Gud bedre jer Moer, den Gutten blev jer
dyr? The proper name behind han (without the comma)
is also found in the genetive: han Henriks Kjæreste;
Seip, Wergeland, p. 174. It is interesting to read (Paulsen, Nye Erindringer p. 148) that Ibsen, formal as he
was, felt hurt at Mrs. Wergeland always calling her
husband h a n Henrik, — but then of course she was
only "a simple woman, without any culture."

1388.   Bud efter Presten. word to the parson.

Prest designates both the Roman Catholic and the
Protestant man of God, here of course the latter; so that
it should not be translated as has been done by a word
merely used of the former.

1400.   har han leget Knappestøber.
         he would play buttonmoulder.

Peer playing "at buttonmoulder" in his baby-days
was destined to meet a formidable one in later-life; see
the n. to l. 4095.

1, 91; 3, 95; F, 351; M, 210; 14, 83; J, 217; 16, 83.

1403.   Kong Kristians Mynt. King Christian's coin.

According to the stage-direction at the bottom of the list of Dramatis Personae, the drama begins early in the 19th century, so Peer was a little boy at the end of the 18th. Hence, Ibsen was quite justified in making Aase speak here of King Christian, — Christian the Seventh we may take it, who reigned from 1766—1808.

1420.   Rensdyrhorn over Dören
A reindeer's horn over the door.

We still find skulls and antlers nailed up in the halls of sportsman's houses and even elsewhere, in the former case as a sort of trophy of more or less daring acts, in the second simply because the thing looks decorative. In former less civilised times, as still among the anthropophagi, it was the heads of the enemy that the victor exhibited in or outside his lodge, in both cases not only as a symbol of his courage in the past and hence a guarantee of happiness to come, but more especially as a preventive against the evil powers. Horse's heads were used in this way more than those of other animals perhaps [1]), — they were nailed up with gaping mouths. Hence in the Peer Gynt story, where Peer has shot a fox, he skins it and coming to the sæter he "puts the heads (of this and other animals) on the wall outside, with their jaws gaping!" (Archer p. 283; ed. 1912. p. 156) For a note on this "uraltes germanisches Abwehrmittel gegen böse Geister", Brons, in his translation of the Peer Gynt (p. 257), refers to a paper I have no access to, but at any rate worth indicating here: in the Weser-Zeitung (18/1/'99) on "Die Eiszeit des Nordens." See also Herrmann, Nordische Mythologie p. 275 and especially p. 461 seqq. (Tieropfer); Thyregod, Et afsnit af Folkets besværgelsestro, Dania, IV, 195, 197, 198 and

---

[1]) "When the Stiéns of Kambodja asked pardon of the beast they killed and offered sacrifice as expiation, they expressly did so through fear lest the creatures' disembodied souls should come and torment them". (Tylor, Primitive Culture).

1, 92; 3, 96; F, 352; M, 211; 14, 84; J, 218; 16, 84.

213. A more than usually effective means against witchcraft is the so-called "Trums-hest", the Trums or Frums-horse being the first-born of its mother; cf. Aasen, Prøver af Landsmaalet i Norge², p. 10: Trumskaren: no witchcraft has power over such a horse when it draws the plough, — dæ æ ingjen trollskap so har Magt mæ haano; for d'æ Trumshest, so dræg Plogjen.

1424.   (lukke) for alle de arrige Nissebukke.
    (shut out) all the cantankerous little hobgoblins.

And a little lower down: de arrige nissebuk t a n-k e r, the hobgoblin-t h o u g h t s or "black thoughts" (zwarte gedachten, as Prof. Boer, Gids, 1893, p.p. 62, 64, renders it).

See the n. to l. 463; — the ordløse tanker which return here as nissebuktanker is an expression that Ibsen had already used in a very much similar meaning in Paa Vidderne, which is to some extent a Peer Gynt drama in posse, han havde mine ordløse tanker hørt. (F, IV, 351). In l. 1570 we have the "smygende tanker". With regard to the expression used, it is just possible that such a collocation as that found in Ibsen's source: nisser og haugbukke (En Sommernat paa Krogskogen, ed. 1912, p, 214) has contributed to Ibsen's nissebuktanker. On the other hand, as a correspondent remarks, it is not necessary to suppose any such contamination. For just as saubuk = a he-sheep, gjetebuk = a he-goat, so nissebuk may be a (he)-nisse.

1431.   Skier. Snow-shoes.
Less usual plural form as in l. 1463 for ski, — see n. ib.

1433.   Budsendt jeg kommer. You sent for me hither.
Solvejg's words nothwithstanding: One message you sent me by little Helga. — Bud har du skikket med Helga lille, Peer had not in reality sent any message, literally interpreted therefore, the reading of U: Ubedt jeg kommer, is truer to fact. But the substitution is an improvement when one comes to think of it, — sweet

---

maidenly reserve being shown by this very pardonable untruth. — Ubedt was not changed into Budsendt until in R.

1444.   hvad Sind du aatte; how you might be minded.

aatte is specifically Norwegian; cf. S. I. S. p. 191.

Mr. Christensen thinks the use ot aatte may be owing to Ibsen's study of the Folkeviser.

1461.   Og ved du Forliget? And know you the compact?

Wörner's Bannspruch (for Forlig; I¹, p. 238) is not quite correct, nor is the Archers' compact very satis-factory. Forlig, an arrangement, agreement, compro-mise, here evidently refers to the c o n s e q u e n c e of the doom, whether we must think of the result of any compromise or no.

1463.   Skier. snow-shoes.

Many a countryman of the poet's, I presume, will feel this plural as Danish rather than Norwegian. As Dr. Western writes, it is right enough, but obsolescent and replaced by ski. Here the bisylllabic skier may be sup-posed to be owing to the metre, this cannot however be the case in the preceding stage direction. Wergeland too used skier; cf. Seip, Wergeland p. 185.

1466.   Nu trænges ingen Stængsel mod Nissebukktanker.

No need now for bars against hobgoblin-thoughts.

Alas for the vanity of human hopes and thoughts! See lower down:

Smygende Tanker vil følge mig ind.

Ingrid! Og de tre som paa Hougene sprang.

Thoughts will sneak stealthily in at my heel.

Ingrid! And the three, they that danced on the heights.

1473.   Jeg skal ikke smudse dig. Med strake arme...

I will not soil you. With outstretched arms...

See the different attitude he had assumed towards the Lady in Green; l.l. 960 seqq., and also his rude remark to Solveig herself as to whether she is afraid he will "take her in his arms" (l. 1278). On strake see T. C. § 44.

1489. bjart, bright.

Specifically Norwegian as Storm has remarked, S. I. S. p. 191. It is certainly not Dano-norwegian riksmaal, but it is also found in the Jutlandish dialect; cf. Feilberg in v.

1493. Hej! Nu skal, etc. Hei! Now etc.

This Hej (U: Hejsan) found in the first and second editions, was changed as early as the 6th into Nej! cf. T. C. § 4.

1494. En gammelagtig Kvinde.... En stygg Unge.... halter efter.... an old-looking woman.... an ugly brat.... limps after....

In U., it is the mother that is represented as limping instead of the ugly little son: han griber Øxen og gaar bortover; idetsamme træder en halt gammelagtig Kvinde i en fillet grøn Stakk ud af Holtet; en stygg Unge holder hende i Skjørtet.

On the following passage J. Collin enlarges (H. Ibsen, p. p. 311 and 312) in the way your German philosopher is but too apt to do: Dieses "draussen", dieses "Ausser sich sein", wird ihm zum Verhängniss, — the sober-minded student looking it up in the context will probably conclude that J. Collin has gone too far in his symbolic interpretation of the scene.

1495. Godkveld, Peer Rappfod!

Good evening, Peer Lightfoot!

If the Green-clad Lady could have read a paper "On Salutations" (Um Helsing) in Aasen's Prøver af Landsmaalet² (p. 28), she would have seen that she does not here conform to usage as there prescribed: gin a body meet a body, he says: Well met! — " Naar du møte einkvann paa Vei' a sa seia du Godtmot."

Rappfod; cf. lower down: din fodlette Fant, you light-footed scamp. For the following Hvem der?, U. has: hver der, where hver is of course nothing but a lapsus calami influenced by the following der.

1498. Alt som Hytten din byggtes, byggte min sig med.
Even as your hut was builded, mine built itself too.

Byggtes was changed in M. by a simple misprint,
(if not before; the divergency was discovered only
when some editions had been sent back) into bygges; cf.
T. C. § 4.

The symbolism of the hut that is built unseen by him
along with his own is on a par with that of a dozen lines
lower down, where the son proves lame in his leg like
the father in his soul, and again lower down (n. to l.
1523) where the Green one says she will miss her
"snout" if Peer will but send Solveig away, not to
mention the hobgoblin-thoughts, the Strange Passenger, the Green Lady herself, and so much else.

1500.   jeg trasker nu efter og raaker dig tillslut.
I'll trudge behind you and catch you at last.
Instead of trasker, U. had: hinker, limping.

Raaker sounds Swedish but is less strange, it occurs
also in Norwegian dialects; compare S. I. S. p. 198. I
quote: No raakast Grisen og Næpesaekken, and: Dat
raakade dan Rette, — Aasen, Ordsprog, p.p. 213, 240
and of course Aasen's dict. in voce.

1503.   Hvad Fanden, — what Devil.
See the n. to l. 897.

1506. Hvad rører du om? What's this that you prate of?

Passarge translates røre = to twaddle by rühren =
to touch, instead of by something like quatschen!
If Ibsen, when Passarge's translation appeared, has
given himself the trouble to go through it a little carefully, it will have become clear to him that he had expressed himself somewhat too hastily in 1880 (Breve,
II, 99 and cf. our preface) when he called Passarge a
translator "who with complete discernment has penetrated into the deepest meanings of the poem: som med
fuld klarhed har trængt ind i digtningens inderste opgave". And for us who have before us the many blund-

ers [1]) and insipidities his German text contains — what
to think for example of Passarge's introducing the word
(der) eiserne (Schädel) about a troll! into the comparison of the Boyg in the Sphinx's scene, — we are not
astonished to find that Ibsen had noticed some mistakes in Passarge's translation of the poems: And in the
same way I found in your translation of the poems,
some passages here and there, that seemed to me not
quite to render the spirit of the original or its fundamental idea (grundstemning). Breve, II, p. 160; cf. n. to
l. l. 1515, 3702.

1509.   Byd Faer din Drikke; Give your father a drink.

Ibsen had first written: Giv Faer din Drikke (U) but
Giv was there changed into Byd, the very word as we
shall see used in Ibsen's source.

If the student will refer to the n. on l. 1176 he will be
prepared for the present one. Here a brief reference to
some stories where similar incidents are related will have
to suffice. See first of all in Kleiven, I gamle daagaa, (p.
4) the story of a man who, when out in the woods, receives
the visit of a comely person whom in the dark he takes
to be his wife. She complains of his having taken the
house-key with him, so of course she must pass the night
with him. About nine months after a 'hill-lady' comes
and presenting him a new-born baby she requires him
to dress the child: Du maa klæ'e Baane ditt, Mann, she
said. And then he saw through the joke of the latch-key.
Similarly Peer Paulsen in Asbjørnsen's En Nat i Nord-
marken (Huldreev. p. 77) had been away from home
and lay down quite alone as he thought in the woods to
sleep. But when a year and a half afterwards a woman
with a baby in her arms approaches him, he may have
had a presentiment of what would happen. Here you

---

[1]) Passarge introduces words foreign alike to the letter and to the spirit of the original, such as dräng and faùx pas into his text (Reclam ed. p. 80) which he has no
right to do, omits lines and adds others (cf. p. p. 81, 83 and 87) and omits expressions
that puzzle him (p. 85); cf. n. to l.l. 1515 and 1541.

---

have your baby, Peer, she said. My baby, says Peer, that looks very strange! How on earth did I get that baby? Well, you have not forgotten, I suppose, said the huldre, that you have been here before? See also in Moltke Moe's Eventyrlige Sagn, p. 592, a quotation from the Kjalnesinga saga. For a similar motif in Swedish, I refer to Ahlström, Om Folksagorna p. p. 71 and 117, the story of store Cnees where the father recognised the son by his axe that the huldre has taken with her. See also Meyer's Mythologie der Germanen, p. 189. But the closest parallel to our version is found in another of Asbjørnsen's tales, viz. in Berta Tuppenhaugs Fortællinger (ed. '12 p. 16). A man has evidently forgotten all about a little adventure he has had with an unknown beauty and comes back to a wood in her neighbourhood some four or five years after. All of a sudden he finds himself somehow in a hut where he sees an ugly old woman (these women grow very soon old; perhaps the n. to l. 1515 should be compared) and in a corner a four year old boy. The old woman takes a beercan and goes up to the child saying: Get thee gone and give your father a drop of ale: Gaa sta og by far din en øldraapa, — which words the reader will recognise. The poor father is so frightened at this discovery that he runs off as fast as his legs will carry him, and, more fortunate than Peer Gynt, he never hears of them again. But he remains "strange" ever after. The same motif: a father discovering a daughter by the fact that the mother tells her to get "father" a drop of something is quoted by Feilberg, Bjærgtagen p. 125 and explained rationally and not without a touch of the hyper-idyllic, as the result of dreams about the absent wife!

1515.   Han er voxet fort. He's shot up apace.

A reminiscence no doubt of a trait in ancient mythology according to which all that is prominent in any way, but especially evil grows up quickly, — in fact the philosophy that if the small h e r b s have grace, great w e e d s do grow apace; cf. Onde urter voxe mest, Mau, II, 98). And even so in the modern fairy tales, like the Fenris-wolf that grew visibly daily, so Eva Wigström tells us (Folktro, p. 126) of a seamonster that grew whilst some one stood and looked at it: "sjørå.... det vexte medan han stod ock tittade på det". And I have a quotation from Færøisk in Landstad's Folkeviser about another that also "grew very quickly in a short time": Vox skjott a skamri stund. And Peer's little darling has at a later time (act V. l. 4266) not only become "big and fat" (baade fed og stor, what Passarge translates by: ist frisch und lacht!) but has of course in his turn got "fine" children, and has through his grandson's progeny become quite a power in the land! Men Dattersøns Afkom har faaet her i Landet slig svare Magt, cf. n. to l. 4435. See Meyer, p. p. 288, 352, Herrmann, Nord. Mythologie p. 396 and for more or less distantly related traits: Feilberg, Bjærgtagen p. 48; i d. Jydsk. ordb. III, 790 in v. tid and Eva Wigström, Folktro, p. 79.

1517.   grov, som en Stud! rude as an ox.

Compare the n. to l. 1349: you are rude as a bull (stud) = you are very rude.

1521.   I Høst, da jeg fødte, holdt Fanden om min Rygg.
Last fall in my labour, the Fiend held my back.

Compare Asbjørnsen's Huldreev. 1912 p. 96, and p.p. 170, 171. The Evil one has been cheated of a soul and thus gives vent to his disappointment: "drat the fellow! (tvi være dig!).... when you called me I was twenty mile north of Trondhjem and held the back of a girl who was about to wring the neck of her brat: Da du rofte paa mig, var je tjue mil nordafor Trondhjem og heldt over ryggen paa e jente, som var i lag med aa vrie om hælsen paa ungen sin." (Graverens Fortællinger) and once more, his Satanic Majesty "had to go to the neighbouring farmhouse and hold a girl's back". And just then some one comes and tells of a poor girl in that farm who had that very night got a child which she had killed with an axe and given to the hogs to eat! Of course we draw our own conclusions as to Old Nick's little ways to get at souls! As to the Green one's giving this as the r e a s o n why she is so ugly, that, it should be admitted, is not explained in the passage quoted, but she means of course very much in general: it's no wonder I am so ugly when the Devil has helped me.

1523.　　　　dersom du vil se mig saa ven, som før

　　　　skal du bare vise Jenten derinde paa dør.

　　　　if you would see me as fair as before,

　　　　you have only to turn yonder girl out of doors.

The symbolism of this is clear: it is simply because you love h e r more now, that you do not care for me and think me ugly. An amusing story with the same point may be found from the Irish in Hartland's Science of Fairy Tales, p. 198: The King changes his daughter by magic into an ugly pig-headed monster, confident that thus no one will wed her and that hence he is safe for the son-in-law who according to the Druid was to take the crown from him. But alas, — young Oivin has heard of the story, weds her and.... "that same moment her deformity was gone — "misted hun trynet". See the notes to l. l. 1070 and 1498 and Feilberg, Bjærgtagen, p. 91.

1538.　　　　　　fodlett. light-footed.

See the n. to l. 1495 and on (fod) l e t, supra p. 19.

1541.　　　　　　for et Hoved. what a head.

Count Prozor's Mauvaise petite tête! shows that he has not seen how on the contrary the woman p r a i s e s the son for his headstrongness. Passarge's "lieb Peterchen" is a very clever rhyme to "Schwerenöterchen" but of either it should be said that "it is not in the bond!"

See T. C. § 56 on the omision of et, n. to l. 867 on hode

as against hoved and observe with regard to these forms that in U Ibsen had first written Hove, then, not finishing the word, changes it into Hode by the correction of the v, — finally crossed it out and writes Hoved as he evidently had intended to do from the first.

1542.	Du blir Faer din opp af Dage.
	You'll be father's living image.

The a f of opp af Dage was changed by Professor Storm (S. M. p. 36, § 47) as a w r o n g form into (op) ad (Dage); see T. C. § 126. To the references there given to justify the retention of Ibsen's form of R, I wish to add Adam Homo I, 412: Hvad gaar der ad Dem, and Dania, V, 111, where the following little jingle is quoted: i Stat-af bliver jeg glad, i Kryb-i-ly bliver jeg kry, from which it is clear that af and glad must rhyme: (a') and (gla). Of course in Danish, such an expression as Staa af is colloquially always: (stɔ: a'). Conversely, in Holberg, Den Politiske Kandestøber, V, 6, we read: jeg blæser af dem and: da han steg op av toget, Joh. Bojer, Den store Hunger, p. 191. Cf. Hvad gaar der a' dig (U, for l. 710) and Falk og Torp, Da. No. Syntax p.p. 194, 218. Vilh. Andersen thinks or at one time thought (p. 272) that op ad Dage may contain (indeholder maaske) the Low-german up und daal, up and down.

1557.	Der staar noget om Anger.... Jeg har ikke Bogen.
	There's a text on repentance.... I haven 't the book.

No doubt, by t h e book (? Book) Scripture is meant. Ellis Roberts' No book to remind me! seems to point to his recognising this as little as the Archers. The exact reference it will be vain to look for as "repentance and remission of sins" (Luke, 24, 47) is to be met with everywhere.

1561.	Anger? Repentance?

In the first draft, Solveig's father had proposed that Peer should p r o v e his remorse by going for seven years into prison! Eft. Skr. II, p. 91.

1, 100; 3, 104; F, 360; M, 215; 14, 91; J, 222; 16, 91.

1570. Smygende Tanker. Thoughts (that) sneak stealthily.
See the notes to l.l. 1424 and 1466.

1579, 80. Jeg faar udenom dette paa Sætt og Vis,
saa det hverken blir Vinding, eller Forlis.
I must roundabout, then, as best I may,
and see that it brings me nor gain nor loss.

In this paa Sætt og Vis, "in a way" rather than: as
b e s t I may, we easily recognise the Peer Gyntian
essence of "træde tilbage", cf. notes to l. l. 151, 1029,
(1167) and 2027.

1583. Saa stygg og skjæmt. So befouled and disgraced.

An inspection of the manuscripts is of some interest
here. In U. we read Saa sky og skræmt, so shy and
frightened, which, especially skræmt, would constitute
such a weak anti-climax that we should be inclined to
look upon it as a mere slip of the pen. In R, it was copied
out as: Saa stygg og skjæmt but both the t of stygg and
the j of skjæmt are on erasure; so it is clear that Ibsen
was on the point of writing sky and skræmt again.

1587. Kirkebrøde. Sacrilege.

In U. this word is corrected from an other word, so
far as I can make it out: Helligbrøde, which, curiously
enough, is the much more common word, whilst Kirkebrøde is not in Brynildsen, nor does a man like Dr.
Western know it. J. Collin, Henrik Ibsen, p. 349 seems
to think this a mere pretext; at least he speaks of the
"selbstbetrügerische(n) Sorge die Geliebte zu entwei-
hen". In the same way, Bergsgaard looks upon this as
one more proof of Peer's "flugt fraa alvoret" (Syn og
Segn, 1915: Kring Solveig og Peer Gynt.)

If true, this would be on a par with the pretexts that
Peer's a a n d s f r æ n d e Hamlet always has ready
to hand whenever he wishes not to do a certain thing.
But cf. on the other hand Ellis Roberts (p. XXI) who
speaks of Peer's "evasion.... that has cost him r e a l
a g o n y".

1596.   Aases Stue. Aase's room.

Aase's hut would probably be more correct.

This scene has been translated by the late Mr. Garrett, see his Lyrics and Poems from Ibsen, p. p. 49 seqq.

1599.   dryger. drags.

Specifically Norwegian for the more common drøie; S. I. S. p. 191. In Riksmaalsbladet for March, 7, 1914, the word is quoted as not even belonging to "Rixen" (Med Nordland og Finmarken drygde det endda længere).

1603. Hvem skulde det tænkt. Who could have foreseen?

This construction where the auxiliary is omitted (it is the rule now in Norwegian, but only after the past tense: kunde, skulde, vilde, maatte; W.), occurs again and again in Ibsen, cf. e. g. De skulde tiet; haand.... De vilde rakt mig (Kjærlighedens Komedie, F. II, p. p. 171, 174) skulde man troet, Ibsen's paper in the Morgenbladet 11/9/'62, reproduced Morgenbladet August 1916. etc. Compare Seip, Wergeland, p. 130. Although much less common, it also occurred in older Danish (it is obsolete now): Gudmund vilde tabt Ligevægten (Ingemann, De fire Rubiner, p. 76) as it is of course quite common in Swedish. Compare Dania, III, p. p. 166, seq., 239 seqq. and Falk og Torp, Da.-norskens Syntax, § § 94, anm. and 136.

1604.   Aa, dersom bare jeg vidste
                      jeg ikke har holdt ham for strængt!
                      Oh me, if I only were certain
                      I'd not been too strict with him.

The change of Aa (by 3; cf. T. C. § 45) into Aase has led many a commentator into the wrong direction. But it is going too far to say with Prof. Storm (S. M. p. 10) that Aase does not yield any meaning. Readers of the late Mr. Garrett's excellent translation of Aase's death-scene will hardly fail to be convinced that in itself it is right enough, nay that it yields very excellent sense:

If you could but be sure, Aase woman,
You were not too hard on the lad!

about which translation a reviewer (Times Lit. Suppl 14, 2, 1913) remarks that these lines "render with delightful audacity the old woman's address to herself". (See Garrett's translation in his "Lyrics and Poems from Ibsen", London, Dent, 1912) This passage may be found considered more in detail in the American "Publications of the Society for the Advancement of Scandinavian Study" vol. I, p. 217 (unfortunately full of misprints through my not having read any proof). Other translators that have been misled by the introduction of Aase into the text are Count Prozor: Aase, si tu l'avais su, tu aurais été moins sévère (p. 105; the translation is of course incorrect); Christian Morgenstern (Aase, wenn ich nur wüsste Ob du's nicht zu schwer ihm gemacht; read: dass du's nicht etc.); and Brons: Aase, O, kun 'k man bloot gissen Of 'k hum nijt tau streng heb upbrogt!", p. 101, where o f should certainly be d a t and gissen can hardly be right; it should be denken. Only — the rhyme-word is missen! And of: man-bloot, one is superfluous!

1606. (Peer Gynt) kommer. Peer comes.

Aase wishes for her son's presence when — lo and behold! there he is, like the devil sirreverence, that always crops up when spoken of. See on a possible influence of Shakespeare for a similar motif, although of course not necessary here, the n. to l. l. 2238, 2446, 2945.

1611. Jeg maatte nu se herned. I felt that I must look in.

In Paa Vidderne too, the Peer of the poem "must down to his dear ones" but finds "all the paths barred" — nedad maa.... til de kjære — alle stier (er) stængte; F, IV, 349). Here they are "opened up" by the Lady in Green! Fortunately for her, Aase cannot smell Peer's fib.

1618. Fra det tunge jeg render. I'm fleeing from trouble.

Peer's words on discovering that here too he is not

I, 103; 3, 107; F, 363; M, 217; 14, 94; J, 224; 16, 94.

"free" — viz. from misery — are usually interpreted as showing very little to his advantage. Compare, to quote the last-comer, J. Collin, Henrik Ibsen, p. 314, who speaks of Peer's cowardice and phantasy running riot here at Aasen's death-bed. "Nur von nichts Schweren gesprochen.... alles Schlimme und Schmerzliche ver-vergessen! Wie könnte er da so etwas Ernstem wie dem Tode in's Auge blicken!" And then we get of course the almost obligatory confrontation if I may call it so with Brand.

"Yet, is this quite fair?" we may well ask with Ellis Roberts (p. XXI) who continues: Peer has just gone through, by evasion — but by an evasion that has cost him real agony — the greatest torture of his life and can we expect that he, or any other human being, should not look around for an anodyne against the over-whelming pain?" .... (What he does) "is not heroic: and yet would any other behaviour have been half as adequate, half as real, and essentially true, with such a case as Åse?"

And when Professor Chr. Collin (Samtiden 1913, p. 609 and now also: Det geniale Menneske, 1914) asks if there is not here a charmingly fine mixture of a weak character dreaming itself away from reality and filial tenderness and goodness of heart?", I think the answer must be heartily in the affirmative and exonerate Peer from the unjust charge of being here too exclusively self-centred.

1625.   lad den bli gjild. be sure it's a fine one.
When we read in Wörner (I¹ p. 221) that Aase would like to have "einen goldbeschlagenen Sarg", we wonder at the author's exaggeration for nowhere does Aase express such a wish. Can it be that gjild was confound-ed with the German vergüldet?

1638.   det var rimeligt nok, du var yr!
              no wonder your head was turned.

The Dutch translation points to a misunderstanding: dat je dol was is duidelijk genoeg, for which the student should be warned. Yr is not dol = excited, crazy, but more like the Archers translate = dizzy, nor is rimeligt = duidelik, clear, apparent, but reasonable.

On yr, see n. to l. 762. Here Ibsen had just written ør in U. but it was there already changed into yr.

1651.   du ved, hvad det varsler, du!
        you know what that bodes, my boy.

Mr. Garrett's translation: The rogue! and goes courtin' nightly, Ah, *you* know all about that! is rather unfortunate as the italics of *you* might mislead the reader into thinking that according to Aase, Peer knows all about nightly courting, instead of about what it bodes. — cf. next note.

1653, 4.   De siger, her findes etsteds en Jente, etc.
        There's somewhere about, they say, a girl.

Here Mr. Garrett's translation is wrong: "they say there's a lassie that's bent on somebody gone into hiding" and not to be excused by the necessity of finding a rhyme-word on betiding. Of course, Solveig is meant.

1669.   stutt, short.

A "popular" (folkeligt) Norwegian word, S. I. S. p. 191.

1675. sang baade Stev og Lokk? Sang many a lill and lay?

Stev, originally a dance melody and comparable to the German Schnadahüpfrl (Dr. R. Steffen, Enstrofig no. folkelyrik, Sv. Landsm. 1898), is in reality a refrain, a reply-stanza in the capping of verses and lokk a song to the tune of which the cattle is called back by the outfarm girl. Here as the Archers clearly indicate by their translation, the musical element is more to the fore than some of the translators seem to have thought, Mr. Garrett's "many a charm and rhyme" being e. g. rather far off the mark.

Lokk will be found passim in the Folkeeventyr and Huldreeventyr by Asbjørnsen, e. g. in Fra fjeldet og

---

1, 105; 3, 109; F, 365; M. 218; 14, 97; J, 225; 16, 97.

sæteren and En Søndagskveld til Sæters, and see Folkeev. 1912 p. 76: Reven som gjæter. See especially
Landstads Folkeviser, p. p. 794—803: Hjuraingvisur
og Huldrelok.

For some S t e v, compare not only Landstad l. l.
p.p. 365 and 735 but more especially Dr. R. Steffen's collection of nearly 1200 Norwegian stev in Sv. Landsmaal-
en, XV, 1899 and for some more modernised ones Syn
og Segn, 1896, p. p. 346, seqq. Lastly: Norske Folkeviser
fra Middelalderen ved Knud Liestøl og Moltke Moe,
Notes p. 1. for further indications.

1678.   Karmesprede. sledge-apron.

Karm is a poetic word (Brynildsen) for a sort of carriage, cf. Aasen in v. Karm (Rygstød i en Slæde); Karm-
slede and Karr (ophøiet Kant, Tværkant, som i en
Slæde) and Alf Torp, Nynorsk Etym. Ordbok in v. v.
Karm and Karr, p. 259.

1680.   Ja, men det allerbedste. Ah, but the best of all.

The exigencies of rhyme no doubt excuse many a
little inaccuracy but when they force the translating
"poet" to say exactly the r e v e r s e of what there is in
his original, it becomes time to draw the line. Passarge
translates this by: Doch Mütterchen, das allerb ä n g-'
s t e, (i, e. practically: the w o r s t!) Wie rieselt's durch
Mark und Bein (!sic!), simply because for Heste he has
got it into his head to translate: (Wär doch die Fart
mit den) H e n g s t e n!

1686—8. Slottet vestenfor Maane og Slottet østenfor Sol, till
Soria-Moria-Slottet. The castle west of the moon and
the castle east of the sun, to Soria-Moria castle.

Ibsen had first written (in U): Till Slottet østenfor
Maane og Slottet vestenfor Sol. The confusion is perhaps owing to the fact that the title runs: Østenfor sol
og vestenfor maane, so here the east comes first. Both
stories are found in Asbjørnsen's collection of Folkeeventyr (ed. 1912 p. p. 169 and 97). The former was versi-

---

1, 107; 3, 111; F, 366; M, 219; 14, 98; J, 226; 16, 98.

fied by William Morris in his Earthly Paradise. Even the thorough German investigation into the sources of this work (Julius Riegel, Die Quellen von W. Morris' The Earthly Paradise, 1890, p. 41) cannot find an e x a c t equivalent, which is not to be wondered at since the poet told the present writer that nothing but "vague reminiscences" of his earlier reading had been woven into his work.

The name Soria-Moria Castle comes from Arabic; it is that of a group of little islands outside the Red-Sea, which the Arabians believed to be the islands of the Blessed, the "insulae fortunatae". Moltke Moe, Episke Grundlove, Edda, 1914, II, p. 246.

1696.   gamle Styggen. Ugly old mother.

Even the Archers' old i. e. dear does not save their rendering, for ugly is far too literal and causes their translation not to do justice to the original. For Styggen is used hypocoristically here and has become practically a pet name (on the form, cf. n. to. l. 3819). Mr. Ellis Roberts' old mother mine comes very much closer if not to the letter, at least to the spirit of the original, which m e a n s: however nasty (ugly) your behaviour might seem, — I know you are a dear old darling.

1708.   Postillen. The prayer-book.

See the n. to l. 2371. It is rather a collection of sermons usually called Huspostillen.

1720.   Grane. Granĕ.

The famous horse belonging to Sigurd Fafnir-slayer of old Norse Mythology; cf. e. g. Vølundarkviđa, 14 etc. Here as so often used simply = a horse, but always felt as a proper name; e n Grane = a horse would be impossible. See the Archers' n. p. 118. Possessors of works on Norwegian art will find a picture of this celebrated horse in the so-called Hyllestad-reliefer; cf. e. g. Dietrichson, Norges Kunst i Middelalderen p. 248, whence it was reproduced in a paper on Norway in the Dutch periodical "Op de Hoogte", March 1914.

In I (T. C. § 26) Ibsen had crossed out the G by mistake when changing all the capitals into small letters but restored it again in the margin.

Instead of Grane, U read first: (at) Traveren (lægger ivej); cf. l. 1753 n.

1726. (og sukker saa) underlig (vildt).
and sighing so strange and wild.

In U. Ibsen had written (Saa tungt og saa) underligt (vildt). On the difference in the adverbial forms, see T. C. § 123.

1730. Hvor kommer den Lysningen fra.
Whence comes all this blaze of light?

The characteristically Norwegian den Lysningen takes the place in R. of den Lysning in U. It is however clear from an inspection of that m. s. that Ibsen had felt the reading not to be quite satisfactory. For he crosses out the n of den and the word Lysning (Hvor kommer den Lysning fra?) is crossed out and Lysene is written over the line, but the letters crossed out are again dotted under so that he evidently at one time again wishes them to stand. The first ed. wrongly omits the point of interrogation which is restored in the later edd. (7th ed.) See T. C. § 4, n.

1733. Sankt Peter. Saint Peter.

The Porter of Heaven is a common enough figure in the Norwegian Folktales; cf. l. 1757 and n. to l. 1773. The nearest approach however to the way in which he is introduced here by Ibsen is the part he plays in Heibergs En Sjæl efter Døden, — where Sanct Peder is made to use such familiar expressions as: that's stupid nonsense, det er tosset snak, etc.

1739. salig Provstinden. the Dean's wife.

Or, as the Archers add in a note: literally, the late Mrs. Provost. The words salig Provstinden were substituted already above the line in U. for: Jomfru Maria as Ibsen had written first. Ibsen had plenty of authority in the old tales for the introduction of the holy Virgin into his matter. See e. g. n. to l. 1753, then: Jomfru Maria som Gudmor, Folkeev. 1912 p. 29; Jomfru Maria og Svalen, Asbjørnsen's collection ed. 1914 p. 222 and Feilberg in v., II, 555, n° 2. But he evidently did not wish to risk the somewhat daring experiment of making her treat a mortal to coffee and cakes.

See the n. to l. 1773 and that to l. 1001 (Kristenmands søn), for the omission of the article.

1741.   Aa, Kors; kommer vi to sammen?

Oh, Christ; shall we two come together?

It is true that John Gynt in his halcyon days had often received the provost (cf. l.l. 239 and 949) so that Aase may no doubt mean, as Count Prozor translates; Nous allons donc nous retrouver, but the more likely interpretation is the one that presumes some glad surprise on Aase's part on the honour on being received in paradise by the person in question. It is especially to be borne in mind that this line must have been written before Ibsen had changed Jomfru Maria into salig Provstinden, so Peer Gynt's: saa tidt og saa jævnt du vil, means, by the most probable of subauditions: Yes is not it an honour? Just think: as often and as much as you like!

On Kors, see n. to l. 602.

1753.   Grane, min Traver! Granë, my trotter.

Count Prozor whose translation is in prose, every now and then and for no apparent reason, breaks out as here into verse. It should be said that the poetic rendering is as good as it could be. See the n. to l. 1720.

1756.   Peer.

There was o n e single point or rather one single case, in which Ibsen did not conform to the decision of the Stockholm-meeting (cf. T. C. § 26) in the matter of orthography and that was the spelling of the name Peer,

---

1, 110; 3, 114; F, 370; M, 220; 14, 101; J, 228; 16, 101.

which in all consistency should have lost one e (T. C. § 111), but which m u s t retàin them both. But here in U, Ibsen had actually for once written Per!

1757, 8. ...Herr Sankt Peder? Faar ikke Moer slippe ind?
...Master Saint Peter? Shall mother not enter in?

Feilberg, in his Sjæletro (p. 58) quotes (from Arnasson and Kamp's Aeventyr) the following story from Icelandic and Danish sources: A certain man was very ill and as his life had not been spotless, his wife was thinking how she should get his soul into paradise. When he had given up his ghost, she caught the soul in a leathern bag and went to the door of Paradise. On her knocking Saint Peter was the first to open it, then Saint Paul and at last the holy Virgin herself, but they all knew too much of her poor John and would not admit his soul. When she knocks for the fourth time, Christ himself answers the door and asks what she wants. But the Saviour too, on hearing her message, says: no, my good woman! he did not believe in me, and unceremoniously slams the door in her face. However, the woman had succeeded in flinging the bag into paradise just before the door is banged to and her goodman's soul is saved! Surely a remarkable parallel to Aase being "lyved ind i himlen".

1762. jeg kan vende ved Slottets Port. I can turn at the gate.

Count Prozor (Le Peer Gynt d'Ibsen, 1897 p. 43) remarks that to run away from his duty has always been Peer's strong point, which in a general way is true. But the remark does not seem very apposite with regard to this line: Je tourne bride et je détale.

1772. fra Byggderne. from the parishes.

The translation is far too literal. Better: from the country. Brons: van na un van veeren (p. 110).

1773. Gud Fader. God the Father.

See the n. to l. 1739. "Vorherre" occurs often enough in the folk-tales, but then as a rule, God the son seems to be meant; cf. e. g. Gertrudsfuglen, Vorherre og S. Peder paa Vandring (Folkeev. p. 4; ed. 1914, p. 220, etc.)

1776. Hold opp med de Kjøgemester-Lader.

Have done with these Jack-in-office airs, Sir.

Mr. Ellis Roberts': Stop these airs, this official ha'-humming, is perhaps a little more in tone and certainly preferable to Mr. Garrett's: Have done with this highty-tighty". "Tu parles en portier" (Count Prozor who, on p. 42 of his study has paraphrased it much better by saying that Peer "en appellera au bon Dieu qui r a-b a t t r a l e c a q u e t à son portier") and Morgenstern's Hör auf mit dem Pförtner-getue! are not very expressive either, a Kjøgemester is moreover in reality something quite different from a porter; cf. n. to l. 544. Mrs. Clant van der Mijll evades the difficulty as if she were a very Peer Gynt herself by giving no equivalent for the expression at all: houd op met al dat gezeur daar (p. 371). As the kjøgemester is a sort of master of ceremonies, some such play upon words as: do stop that ceremonial nonsense, or: do let that ceremoniousness stop now, may be deemed to render the spirit of Ibsen's words better, as it certainly comes nearer to the letter.

1792. for Bank og for Barne-Byss! for beatings and lullabys!

In U. Ibsen had first written: For Hugg og for Barnebyss! then changed Hugg into Bank, afterwards this into Sang. In R., he returned to the second suggestion.

Bysse et barn = to lull asleep; a rather rare form seems to be: at bye et barn, which I find in Krogh's Isl. Folkesagn, p. p. 175 and 204, but not in the dictionaries. (In the nursery language bye may mean the bed or the cradle. W.)

1795. Se saa; det var Takk for Skyds.

There; that was the driver's fare.

Literally, as the Archers add: "thanks for the driver", a reminiscence no doubt of the boxing of his ears,

---

I, 112; 3, 116; F, 371; M, 221; 14, 103; J, 229; 16, 103.

Peer had got by way of thanks, when fording Aase across
the river; cf. 1. 378. Here he makes of course his dead
mother kiss him by putting his cheek to her lips and
so thank him for the last "skyds".

1802.   Jeg faar friste at fare herfra.
I must try to fare forth from here.

"Auch Peer überwindet rasch den Tod der Mutter,
auch ihm geht alles nur *skindeep*", Wörner has said (I¹,
p. 260; I², 267), where many a reader will be inclined
to ask how Wörner knows.

But if true, one is led to think of Ibsen's own feelings
for his home and his mother which do not seem to have
been very much more than "skindeep" (Gran, Henrik
Ibsen; Nordmænd i det 19de aarh., p 180).

FJERDE HANDLING. ACT FOURTH.

1806.   Wörner has asked for the bridge that leads from the
third to this fourth act. (I¹, 241, ²247). There is no
dramatic sequence in these scenes he thinks, which
come after each other instead of next to each other.
"Der unverbesserliche Tagdieb und Träumer den wir
aus den ersten drei Aufzügen so gut kennen, soll es
durch eigene Thatkraft zum reichen Schiffsrheder
gebracht haben". Which Wörner thinks impossible
and a huge mistake in the drama. But does not Peer
himself give us the solution? He says later on: "I had to
battle sore for bread; trust me, I often found it hard" (l.l.
1919 seqq.) and after all, one loves life and as the phrase
goes: death is bitter and a s I m y s e l f w a s e l a s t i c
— the Archers' versatility: da jeg selv var tøjelig; Wörner himself compares Peer Gynt on the same page to
caoutchouc!— all went well. To deny, in the face of this
excellent self-characterisation, the possibility of a lazy-
bones making his way to wealth through mere stress

1, 113; 3, 117; F, 372; M, 222; 14, 104; J, 230; 16, 104.

of circumstances is not only to forget that Ibsen himself has shown us that in Peer too a latent energy did exist (cf. n. to l. 845: This is life! Every limb grows as strong as a bear's) but is especially to ignore what so many Norwegians to this very day give an example of, who exile themselves or are exiled by force of circumstances to the ever-sweetly-winking terra promissa "across the herring-pond". In Heiberg's En Sjæl efter Døden, one of Ibsen's sources, the soul itself actually asks Sankt Peder to be allowed to go to America! — lad mig (o jeg beder!) Helst reise til America, Herr Peder! — and the soul which had always "longed for that country which has such big possibilities" (kræfter), hopes to come back "more civilised"! And as a matter of fact, how many Norsk-Amerikaner do not come back well-to-do nowadays and more in the luxus-cabin of the "Kristiania-fjord" that have gone thither perhaps as steerage-passengers, like Peer, "a poor fellow, empty handed" (l. 1917)? Bold is he who would maintain that it is only the energetic to whom this happens; see moreover the n. to l. 308 (end). Mr. Ellis Roberts (Introd. p. XIX) thinks that this change, though abrupt, is artistically sound. "Nothing less sudden and startling would have given us a true idea of the degree and nature of Peer's (later) downward course".

On Peer as the typical representative in this scene of Norway, or rather of your average Norwegian, of "Peer Normand" to express it more concisely, see Jæger, Illustreret No. Lit. hist. III, p. 662 — "the whole of this scene is a strongly-masked attack on the pitiful political attitude of 1864" when Norway and Sweden left poor Denmark to her fate; cf. also Jæger's Henrik Ibsen, 1892 p. 72. As Jæger appears to base his explanation of this scene in general as well as that of the Fellah and Hussejn, on authentic information from Ibsen himself, it is worth paying especial attention to. —

1807.   Master Cotton.

It is curious that in U, both in the first and second
version of this scene, Ibsen had actually written Mr:
Cotton, just as in U¹ he had first written a little lower
down Mr: Gynt, where only the colon instead of full
stop betrays the unpractised hand. But not only did
he write Master Cotton, ib. lower down, but used this
form throughout in R.

Ibsen himself has recognised that he was not very
well "at home" in English — which he had "taught
himself without the help of others" (Breve II,. 11 in
a letter dated 15/11/'74 to Edmund Gosse). Which does
not prevent him from judging and calling Gosse's translation (part of Peer Gynt) "masterly" and saying that
he knows of nothing in it that he could wish different.
There are various little things that point to Ibsen not
having underrated himself. Lower down he writes both
in U² and R: stewart, (S. M. p. 10; U¹: Hovmester)
possibly under the influence of Norwegian stuert, and
he presents us with a Sam Wellerian Werry Well (corrected however, it should be said, later on by himself;
cf. T. C. § 34). Our Master Cotton is paralleled by a
passage in the first draft of Samfundets Støtter (Eft.
Skr. II, 289) where Grosserer Bernick says: "Good
Morning, master Rawlinson" (who is a captain) "This
way, if you please Sir! I am Master Bernick!" This
same Captain Rawlinson has a visiting card on which
we are supposed to read: "John Rawlinson, Esqr: (ib.
p. 287; but compare p. 309: Capt$_=^n$ John Tennyson)
just as in one of Asbjørnsen's stories (Huldreev. 1912
p. 151) a certain Mr. Bilton had written his name: "Bilton Esq"! And lastly, Sir Gynt (l. 2109) should be.
quoted here, — a mistake that is alas but too common
everywhere on the continent. Even Sir Peter Gynt
(l. 2168) however correct of course from a formal point
of view, would hardly have been used here if Ibsen

1, 114; 3, 118; F, 374; M, 223; 14, 105; J, 231; 16, 105.

had remembered that Peer cannot be imagined to have got that title in America.

That Cotton is a speaking name "whereby there hangs a tail" is clear from the poem on Abraham Lincoln's Mord (F, IV, p. 360) where John Bull is called the Cotton-magnate — "Bomuldsmagnaten". Still more eloquent is a passage from Ibsens's review of a drama to which Mr. Eitrem has called attention (Samtiden 1908, cf. p. 633) where Ibsen speaks of "a complete Englishman, who is willing enough to help his friend, but by no means loses sight of cotton-interests — "bomuldsinteresserne". (S. V., F, X, 323).

That Ibsen was particularly struck by John Bull's materialism appears not only from the well-known passage in Brand where among the sad visions of the future, he sees the "Britons" stuffy coal-clouds lie black over the land (S. V. F., III, 245) as Paludan Müller [1]) had complained before him, but from many a passage lower down, e. g. that where he recognises to have received from England not only "an industrious hand" but also "a keen sense for my own advantage" (l.l. 2046,7). Compare also: No sense of honour, Monsieur Ballon had said — Ej Sans for Ære — and Mr. Cotton answers: Bah! Honour! that's neither here nor there! — Aa, Æren, den fik endda være, — but think of the profit! And see Mr. Cotton's complaints of the lost chances of Mount Olympus and the river Castale (l. 2180 seqq.). But what was perhaps the most unkindest cut of all is shown by a change lower down in the present scene. In U, Peer had been vaunting of his supplying the missionaries with "all they wanted as stockings, bibles, rum and rice, at a profit of course", — and it prospered. Just so in Goethe's Faust the Marshall had said of the

---

[1]) See his Adam Homo, 9 Sang, II p. 181: den Røg, den Dampmaskine-Stöi, Der producerer mig det Jern — og Bomuldstöi, Hvormed til Lands og Vands, jeg oversvömmer Verden. Vinje had followed and afterwards Bjørnson; cf. Chr. Collin, Bjørnstjerne Bjørnson, I, 272, II, 372, 3.

---

paper currency (Faust, II, Lustgarten): Die Wechsler-Bänke stehen sperrig auf, Man honorirt daselbst ein jedes Blatt Durch Gold und Silber, f r e i l i c h m i t R a b a t t. But Ibsen makes it into a pungent satire on the English by one little trait of genius: he makes Mr. Cotton i n t e r r u p t Peer's flow of eloquence by those very words: Yes, at a profit? — Ja, mod Profit?
Trumpeterstraale.

This is the spelling of R. and the two first editions, until it was changed by Ibsen himself (in I) into — stråle, not because this is the only proper Swedish spelling as we might expect for this typical Swede, but because it was thus brought into accordance with the orthography adopted by the Stockholm meeting (T. C. § 26). It deserves notice that in U Ibsen had begun to write it Trumpeterstråle, throughout, until the end of sheet 14. Sheet 15 is lost, in sheet 16 we find the spelling with aa; cf. the parallel change of Eberkopf (T. C. § 13) into v: Eberkopf, also first found in sheet 16. —

Ibsen did not love the Swedish very much, — quite the contrary if we may trust an account by V. Bergsøe, Henrik Ibsen paa Ischia, p. 236, so that, even if we take this as well as what the author adds about "little Sigurd" (n. l. 1110) with the necessary proverbial grain of salt, we can imagine how little harmonious this Trumpet-blast was meant to sound in our ears. It may not be amiss to add that a Swedish Baron in "Stockholmsfareren" (one of Wergeland's farces that Ibsen is known to have read) was called Bombenundgranatenstråle. — (Wergeland, S. S. VI, p. 376).

Professor Storm has discussed the Sveacisms that occur in Ibsen's works; cf. S. M. p. p. 153, 195, 197 etc. and add now the word skillnad, in U., quoted in the n. to l. 1035. Some of these seem to have been used quite unconsciously by the poet, others no doubt contain a slight sneer, such as bror Gynt, because the Swedish are known for "drinking brotherhood" on a very slight provocation; cf. Faye, p. 301: Sover du, bror, *etc*. Others are used consciously, without the slightest malevolent intention, merely to give some local colour. Just as e.g. Dickens in his Tale of Two Cities makes his French speak a sort of French-English like: But what will you, my friend? (n. to l. 1819) so tusen and forlad in l.l. 1934 and 2137 (see the notes *ib.*) are only Swedish in Norwegian spelling. See also the notes on traakig and bra litet rolig (3641, 4519).

The question of Sveacisms in Danish and Norwegian is a ticklish one. Seip (Wergeland, p.p. 18, 19) rightly remarks that some may be Norwegian — we have found a possible case in point in skillnad (ante n. to l. 1035). On the reason why and the question whence Sveacisms at that time were likely to be introduced, Krogvig sends a remark or two worth reproducing: "Ibsen's many Swedish words and phrases in the sixties may be due partly to his Scandinavianism, although it should be remarked that the fifties, at the time of the Vice-regal troubles, are the only period when Sveacisms had any influence worth speaking of on the spoken language. The upper ten in Kristiania at that time showed a sort of Sveacising snobbism (snobbet sig i denne tid med at "svenske"). Vice-royalty had introduced for the first time something like a court in Kristiania, — these people were mostly Swedes and so it became "the" thing to patter as they did. And some of these expressions have probably found their way into the parlance of the unsnobbish, so that Ibsen may have got a touch of the ague too, — however, his Scandinavianism is likely to have been the principal cause." —

1817.   skjelden. seldom.

This form qualified as an "impossible" one in T. C. (§ 34) is however a mistake that as a correspondent

---

tells me is often met with and is moreover not entirely without analogues. When in a Norwegian dialect we find the word itself written skiølla (Syn og Segn, 1902, p. 6), when Jørgen Moe in his letters writes skjudskede by the side of the "correct" sjuskede (p. 225) and when in Danish we find spellings as skeni and skersant for geni [sjeni] and sergeant [sjersant] [1]); cf. Ordb. over Gadesproget, p. 430, then we should pause before we rule that "skjelden" as only a peculiarity of the author, should be relegated to the limbo of unbaptised i. e. of unrecognised words. The spelling is of course owing to the fact that *skj* — being always pronounced sj, sj has gradually become looked upon as the proper rendering of the sound.

1819. et visst, jeg ved ej hvad — a certain, — what's the word.

The comma behind visst is really in R; that it is ñot found in U might of course in itself be due to the hurry with which in the matter of punctuation especially, that first draft is often (but not here) composed. At any rate, it *should* not be there. It is quite evident that Ibsen here wishes to give Monsieur Ballon the Frenchman's speech a tinge — a dash, et skjær — of the French idiom as in the note to l. 1807 we found Dickens doing and that he meant: et visst jeg ved ej hvad: "un certain je ne sais quoi". The translations have suffered under this comma.

1821. Verdensborgerdomsforpagtning. Cosmopolitanisation.

See the Archers' explanation of this "burlesque", — if we remember that "the exact sense of nonsense is naturally elusive", the rendering, — think of the absolutely concordant rhythm — seems perfect. Of course the long compound in itself is a skit on German word-formation. —

---

[1]) For the sj(ɛrfant) due to what has been called phonetic anticipation, compare the spelling sjersanten: "Farvel i Huus! Sjersanten staaer og raaber: Kom!" Claus Frimann, No. Digtere by Nordahl Rolfsen.

1829.   ikke ganske saa smukt det klinger i det franske.

not quite so loftily it sounds in French.

I det franske for paa fransk is not very common, at least not in the colloquial language [1]). But compare: Med Færdigheid han tale kan det Spanske, Det Italienske, Polske, Tydske, Franske, Paludan Müller's Luftskipperen og Atheisten, p. 5; and in Mau, I find: I skulde nylig ej saa meget talt det Franske, saa havde kanske nu I bedre vidst det Danske! (I, 121), which Dr. Western tells me is taken from Wessel's "Gaffelen".

1830.   Ej wass!

See T. C. § 38. Morgenstern actually adopted *was* in his German text; compare Ej hopp in Peer's lyrical outbreak to Anitra (l. 2818) and Ej or Eja, passim in Wergeland's farces, as it is in Rypen i Justedal, Eft. Skr. I, 341. This half-germaniseḍ Ach wass occurs in a more fully Norwegian form in Kejser og Galilæer, Eft. Skr., II, 200: Ej hvad, nu føres de til badstuen (ib. 202: Ej hvad gælder det should on the contrary be: Ej, hvad gælder det) and still more so in Svanhild: Aa hvad. (Eft. Skr. I, 458; cf. S. I. S. p. 201).—

1837.   Om s i g og s i t han skal sig kære.

He should regard *himself* and *his*.

Kære sig = sich kehren, a germanism and now nearly obsolete (S. I, S. p. 180). In U Ibsen had written it kjære (which is the spelling in which even Brynildsen still gives it!) but had crossed out the j; the explanation of this j-spelling, wrong from a certain point of view, because the word seems of recent German origin (cf. however Falk-Torp in voce), is like the skj- of skjelden, that kj represents the sound k in Danonorwegian. The fact that Ibsen crossed out the j seems to point to his hearing it with the so-called ‚hard' k, and may mean that he more or less instinctively felt it as a German word.

---

[1]) Dr. Western doubts if it was ever used in Norwegian.

1, 115; 3, 119; F, 375; M, 224; 14, 106; J, 232; 16, 106.

1849.   henkastende. carelessly.

To the note T. C. § 63, add that henkastet is actually found used in exactly the same way, — cf. e. g. Heiberg's Paradesengen, p. 28.—

1850.   Adelstroll! Noble-trolls.

Mr. Ellis Roberts omits the hyphen which scarcely seems an improvement. Perhaps troll-nobles may come closer to the original? Bogus-noblemen? A correspondent thinks that Adelstroll stands for "cursed noblemen" i e. these nobles whom we, non-nobles, despise deeply.

Dr. Western writes: this "troll" has of course nothing to do with the trolls of the fairy tales. It simply means a bad fellow, a shrew. Grammatically we should translate noble shrews, noble beasts, but logically beastly nobles would be better. —

1851.   Forlagte Højheder. Old fossil Highnesses.

The reason of this translation does not seem quite clear. What is there fossil about these princelings that hold aloof from the plebeians? But when highnesses dó show that sort of pride, it is often because their circumstances would render some sort of condescension necessary. Hence the context may seem to demand something like royalty in reduced circumstances.

But a correspondent offers two other suggestions. Forlagte højheder, he writes substantially, may mean "removed highnesses" The reference would then be to natural children of royal persons who have been removed to a lower sphere. What follows about their pride "to keep plebeian blots excluded from their line's escutcheon — sin stolthed i, Plebejerpletter at holde væk fra Stammens Skjold" — would then have to be understood ironically. Or the word may mean "hidden highnesses". Peer is thinking of the daughter of the Dovregubben, — formerly people believed in them, but now they are not believed-in any more, they are "hidden away".

As to the form of the word here with two ll's, Professor Storm (S. M. p. 29 § 21) keeps — troll, as Swedish; it's Trumpeterstraale who uses it. If Ibsen has really written it thus for that reason (— ll is also in U) it is one that only his readers can have appreciated, for no one could hear it.

1872.   der raader dog et Fatum! there is a ruling fate.

Compare what we read later on (l. 1886) on the wise control of Fate and (l. 2247) about the safe feeling of knowing oneself specially protected, — and Fate will help me away from the land.

Fatum is of course neuter, but in l. 1924 we have the personified gamle Fatum, h a n var bøjelig.

1893.   Med samme Norm De alting maaler.
     One norm to all things you apply.

See T. C. § 52, 60, etc. The mistake there pointed out of non-capitalising De, when meaning y o u, is one that may be observed in every other letter one gets from not over-accurate correspondents, especially ladies. In U, we find plenty of instances of it too. See e. g. Eft. Skr. I, p. 322: De vilde fremdeles blive i Majoriteten, m. h., d e behøver ikke at ængste dem (in a speech: till: Mine herrer, members of the Scandinavian association).

1898.   Jeg er, som jeg Dem før har sagt.
     I am as I have already said.

In U, the line ran: Jeg er, som jeg saa tidt har sagt, — as I have said so often. The removal of this so often will seem a very happy change to him who shares the impression that saa tidt points to a rising temper, or rather an outburst of temper, which we have no reason to assume in Peer Gynt a s y e t, for he is very calm here and has not yet been drinking freely (stukket paa Flaskerne; l. 2017).

1931.   gjøre i. to trade in.

Gjøre i noget is the characteristic "trade"-expres-

sion for to "deal" in ,— "to trade" is a shade too formal.
See Ordb. over Gadesproget, in v.

1934.　　　　　　For tusend, Farbroer Gynt!
　　　　　　　　The devil, Uncle Gynt.

　　In the n. to l. 1812 it has been suggested that Ibsen
used bror, like farbror here, in imitation of the Swedish. This suggestion is perhaps borne out by the fact
that in each case U has bror, spelt with an *o* and not
as he would have done in the case of the Norwegian
word: broer, with *oe*. However in each case too in *R. o*
was changed into *oe*. — It is a ticklish thing therefore
to render farbroer by uncle (or its equivalents) as the
translators generally do; Mrs. Clant van der Mijll even
descends so low as to use the utterly uncalled-for vulgar-
ism: oom*e*! Count Prozor's: Peste, l'ami Gynt seems a
very excellent shot, nay almost a hit. For this Swedish
use, cf. e. g. Weis, Sägner på Aspelandsmål, p. p. 109,
127. It should be added that bror and farbror thus used
are not entirely un-Danish (i. e. in this case un-Norwegian). See Feilberg in v. v. bror: "... a mode of adres-
sing one's equals; in v. farbror: "petname for old men
of some position, — a man may be the farbror of the
whole parish", — which to those versed in recent South-
African history will recall Oom Paul. In Dania V, 43,
in a paper by Feilberg on Fattigmands snaps, I find
it used even as an address to the Devil! But this case
where for once contempt has bred familiarity, seems
translated from the Swedish.

　　The Swedish tusan, here turned into tusend as if it
were the numeral and as such expressive of a larger
quantity, i. e. something great, important, is of course
originally an exclamation of agreeable or disagreeable
surprise, and like its German counterpart, Der Tausend
(Passarge and Morgenstern) "verhüllt für Teufel". Very
properly therefore, Schulthess renders it by Diantre and
Messrs Harlock and Wenström by: the dickens, deuce,

which first two expressions admittedly stand for diable and deuce i. e. ultimately for devil too.

By the side of the various names of the horn-footed one, which will be found enumerated elsewhere (n. to l. 1110 and see l. 2843) there are some formed by the process exemplified here i. e. by a filling up with sounds meaningless in themselves, of a pause caused by an aposiopesis verecundiae causa, after the first sound(s) only of the obnoxious term has been uttered. Thus: God when puritanically felt as hurting the speaker's (or hearer's) feelings would be abbreviated "g—" first and then "filled up" as golly-, good (in good bye) or goodness (in goodness knows) etc. etc. Similarly in Norwegian: "aa gid" for "aa gud", well-known in the mouth of (very young) ladies and in Danish: gumi (Feilberg, Tillæg, p. 193) need not stand for gud min as the compiler suggests, but may be a simple s u b s t i t u t e for gud. Instead of for fanden, your Swede will say för fämten (Wigström, Folktro, p. 263) just as det var sytten is quite common for det var s—atan! Thus in Karl Erik Forlslund's novels we find his characters colloquially ringing the changes on djäfvel by such forms as djäker (quite common elsewhere) and tjäder and even tjäderanitta! There we also find the picturesque: det var då självaste sexagesima till Karl!: he was a devil of a fellow, to which add: järnvägar (railways!) which according to Nyrop, Ordenes Liv (p. 9) also stands for (d)jävlar! Thus we may explain: pigen ta' mig (Feilberg II, 814) as standing for pokker, puki and possibly even herren ta' mig (ib. Tillæg, p. 210) for *handen* ta mig, which itself is no doubt a rhyme-substitute for fanden; cf. n. to l. 1110. Other English equivalents are Crikey (Cracky) for Christ, Gis (by Gis and S. Charity, Hamlet), George and perhaps Jingo for Jesus; Goldam, Gorram, Gosh, Gum, Gummy etc. for God (cf. Farmer), Dutch ones: gommies, gorrekies, gossie myne (aided on by god zie mijner?)

goddorie and even goddomenezel for god (ver) domme mij, jessus for Jesus; verd-ikkie for verdomme, etc. etc. See the n. to l.l. 2310, 4314—16.

1935,6.   Bedriften svævende paa det tilladeliges Pynt.
business hovered on the outer verge of the allowable.
If Mr. Brynildsen's instance: svæve paa det *anstændiges* pynt (in v. pynt) does not represent a vague reminiscence of this very passage, then the expression: "svæve paa — pynt" would seem to be a standing one that Ibsen here has used or adapted, and anstændiges pynt would then be an interesting analogue to the above. Mr. Carl Nærup in an account of Peter Nansen's latest says of some of its characters that "de har det allesammen rigtig godt i sin svævende.... stilling "paa det tilladeliges pynt" where it will be observed that the words are marked as a quotation (from Ibsen no doubt) by the inverted commas.

Pynt (cf. landpynt = landhuk where both the second parts of the compound are borrowed from a Low-german dialect) is the land-point, i. e. the point, end of something. Dr. Western quotes by way of Norwegian analogues: paa kanten av loven: just within the law; and debattere paa kanten av klubben, i. e. "on the point of (having the speaker's) club (raised) to stop one's (unparliamentary) eloquence". Cf. n. to l. 3472.

1945.   Det "overtvert" jeg kan ej lide.
That "once for all" I can't abide.

That our prudent friend cannot stand this 'breaking off at once' is in perfect keeping with his never burning his ships; cf. n. to l.l. 1029, 2027.

1958.   og skille Bukkene fra Faarene.
that parts the sheep and goats asunder.

The reference is of course to the well-known biblical comparison, e. g. Matth. 25,33, but a similar one is already found in one of Ibsen's immediate sources, Heiberg's En Sjæl efter Døden, p. 223: Jeg bringer de Døde

---

1, 120; 3, 124; F, 380; M, 226; 14, 111; J, 235; 16, 111.

til Himlens Port, Der pleier man Buk fra Faar at skille
Og de, som ikke for gode tages Maae drage til Helved
hvor de aldrig vrages.

In Professor Lorenz Dietrichson's Svundne Tider, we
find (I, p. 346) what looks like an interesting reminiscence of this passage. An eccentric, crotchety Dane,
the painter Lars Hansen is reported to have made the
great discovery that mankind is to be divided in sheep
and goats. He himself belonged of course to the category
of the innocent sheep, his enemies on the contrary (e.g.
all the shoemakers because they invariably caused his
shoes to pinch him!) being of the goats. Now, "Ibsen
was one of the prominent goats", and he told Mrs. Ibsen
some years later in all confidence that the goats had
their own manuals in goat-lore (sine egne Lærebøger i
Bukkevidenskab) and that she ought not to be ignorant
of the fact that one of the most recent of those manuals
was "Peer Gynt". Of course the amiable maniac need
not necessarily have thought of this passage, but there
is hardly any more appropriate place to insert this
"judgment" on our drama.

1966.   Ja, mod Profit? Yes, at a profit?
See the n. to l. 1807.

1970.   en Kulier. a coolie.

Professor Storm changed this into en Kuli; see T. C.
§ 70, n (and §§ 108, 109). As has there already been briefly hinted, the form Kulier which Ibsen is "guilty of"
according to Prof. Storm and Mr. Eitrem (cf. S. M. p.
10) is not by any means without analogues. Not now
taking into account the origin of the following words
from which point of view they would have to be treated
in more than one group, I here quote them merely as
parallels, in so far as in each case we have two word-
forms, one terminating in -er and one without that ending, but both felt as a singular: rabbi(n) — rabbiner;
beduin — beduiner (both mentioned in T. C, § 70, n);

and besides: Student — studenter; bekendt — bekendter; musikant — musikanter; spillekant — spillekanter; fejl — fejler, and cf. such apparent nonce-
words as gentiler, publikummer = gentil, et gentilt
menneske and an individual. [1])

Studenter as a singular occurs e. g. passim in Bertha
Tuppenhaugs Fortællinger (Huldreev., p.p. 23, 24, 25,
etc., nót if my memory may be trusted in the older editions, for example the one Ibsen used, but only in that
of 1912, here always quoted and the one where dialect
was substituted for the literary language of the previous editions). But we actually also find it in Adam Homo, one of Ibsen's sources: Du er jo en Studenter (I,
211); cf. also Feilberg III, 621 and Landstad, Folkeviser, p. 825: Sa kom der ein Studentar, sa kom der ut
ein Prest. All the other forms may be found in the Ordbog over Gadesproget (p.p. 26, 116, 167, 391 and 472).
Spillekanter is most likely formed on the pattern of
musikanter (possibly a cross between this and spillemand) which I can only quote from Danish sources, —
Feilberg, Jul, II, 239 and id. Jy. ordb, in v. and ib. II,
850 in v. plovgang.

The question of principle involved in Professor
Storm's correction of the author — and such an author!
— has been discussed already in the T. C. § 108, 109, as
quoted. It must be clear from these paragraphs if not
from what precedes here, that there are mistakes and
mistakes and that it will not do to try and justify the
change by simply saying as the Editor of M. does that
we *must* read kuli, because "det heder en Kuli, flere Kulier". — "Det heder", we might reply (see n. to l. 59)
'hvert evige ord', yet Professor Storm there established

---

[1]) Bekendter (perhaps nothing but a nonce-word and a slavish imitation of German: ein Bekannter) and fejler are so rare that Dr. Western does not remember ever
hearing them.

And Publikummer, also used jokingly only, seems to belong to quite a different
category as it seems formed (in the sense of: a person b e l o n g i n g to, forming
part of, the public) on the pattern of en bergenser, en drammenser etc.

1, 121; 3, 125; F, 381; M, 227; 14, 112; J, 235; 16, 112.

(vi coactus it is true but that is not to the point) a new norm, — why not do so here?

For what does it come to, that crime of writing en kulier? Simply this that a plural form having been felt as a singular is used as such, [1]), and this phenomenon is far from being without parallels. The word Rabbin may be a case in point (cf. the N. E. D. in voce; T. C. § 70), — then the singular Rabbiner would actually contain two plural endings. Here of course the *n* was never felt as a plural sign by the speakers of the language into which it was adopted as little as in the case of assassin and beduin or *m* in that of seraphim and cherubim, all of which are now used as singulars although originally plurals. But that consideration does not do away with the force of the analogy, for just because and only if kulier was not felt as a plural by Ibsen, could it be used as a singular. In his paper on grammatical substraction (V. Thomsen-Festskrift, 1894; cf. p. 10) Professor Jespersen quotes un fait-divers, a remarkable form, halfway I am afraid, in the opinion of some on the royal road to perdition — for think of the horrible possibility (which only the strait-waistcoat of orthography can prevent) that the *s* too should be "looked upon as a sign of plurality, and a naked "fait-diver" the criminal result?

---

[1]) I leave this as it stands and give my readers the benefit of a marginal note by a correspondent whose explanation some may prefer to the above suggestion: „I do not think that the form Kulier, beduiner are originally plurals used as singulars. They are ethnological names formed on the pattern of en russer, en tysker, en perser etc. and have been felt as a singular". (Note the important concession that en Kulier is an ethnological name, so the singular is recognised implicitly here just as explicitly in what follows:) „From a Norwegian point of view en kulier, en beduiner may be said to be as good as en kuli, en beduin etc. The latter forms are due not to any better conception of the difference between singular and plural, but to a better knowledge of foreign languages". (We may here ask: a better knowledge of the language from which kuli is taken? Does the form occur outside Ibsen's works?) "Mark that we still say en beduinerhøvding where the first part of the compound is singular since we don't have compounds with the first part in the plural (except blomsterhandel, -pike, etc.) Compare also the still common form soldaterhjem, for which soldathjem is now getting into use". As to my conclusion it is comfortable to find that my opponent reaches it too if by an other road for he ends his communication by saying that of course Kulier should have been left alone. — Q. E. D. —

But to come to actual English analogues, the student will at once have thought of *news* where the *s* is more likely to be originally a plural one (on the pattern of French des nouvelles) than a genitival one as in the corresponding Dutch (iets) nieuws, and compare the more unusual a tidings; see the N. E. D. in voce, where the quotation from Shakespeare constitutes a doubtful case as comes — the tidings comes; John, IV, 2, 115— *may* be a plural form (Abbott, Sh, Gr. § 333; Anglia, Beiblatt, VII, 342 and Mod. Language Notes, XX, 54), but there are other sure cases to be found in Schmidt's Sh. Lex., and such a phrase as Carlyle's The tidings was world old, speaks volumes. And with regard to Norwegian itself, en Østers, en Kjæks, et slips (German schlips) representing originally the plurals oesters, cakes and slips are sufficient to show that the thing is not unknown there either. Ross, p. 83, in v. Bøys quotes besides et Drops, en Roks, en turnips and cf. moreover Bøys itself, which in the sense of a big woman (f.) and an unruly boy (m.) he derives from Eng. *boys*.

1981-3. Og dertill kom de tusend Snarer fra vore Filantropers Lejr, for ej at nævne Kapringsfarer.

And then there were the thousand pitfalls laid by the philanthropic camp; besides, ... the hostile cruisers.

In the first draft, Ibsen had first written that the play began in the 18th and ended in the 19th century; cf. T. C. § 94 n. 2. The antislavery movement to which Peer here refers is possibly an echo of this, for in the sixties — slutter henimod vore Dage — Peer need not have feared these philanthropists any more. As to the privateers, which may seem a better rendering of kapringsfarer than the Archers', they too would seem to fit better into the original plan. The dangers that Norwegian ships were exposed to in those days, if they did not fly the Swedish flag, may be read of in Toralf Greni's paper in Prof. Gran's Bjørnson-Studier.

1, 122; 3, 126; F, 381; M, 227; 14, 112; J, 236; 16, 112.

2013.   (holde) med Dyder mine Synder Stangen.

(hold) my misdeeds balanced by my virtues.

Peer is very proud of himself, cf. the passage later on at the end of his monologue after the burial scene, where he boasts of being poor but virtuous (l. 3796). The button-moulder's rebuke: to call you virtuous would be going too far (at kalde dig dydig, vilde gaa for vidt) must therefore have come as a shock to poor Peer who shows a great deal of self-command when he answers that he did not lay claim to that himself.

2021.   at holde Øret tætt igjen

to keep one's ear close shut against.

Mr. Christensen writes: "igjen is here used in its old Norse signification of "imod".

2027, seq. Hvad hele Vove-Kunsten gjælder, den Kunst, at eje Daadens Mod, — det er: at staa.... imellem Livets lumske Fælder,.... at vide, dig staar aaben bag en Bro, som bære kan tillbage.

The essence of the art of daring, the art of bravery in act is this: to stand amid the treacherous snares of life.... to know that ever in the rear a bridge for your retreat stands open.

A comparison with the first draft is instructive here:

Hvad altsaa hele Kunsten gjælder, den store Kunst at eje Mod, det er at staa.... imellem alle Livets Fælder.

"Altsaa", a reference to what Ibsen had written first in U, — 23 lines, crossed out afterwards and certainly not up to his usual standard; cf. Eft. Skr. II, 99-100 — is of course left out. The addition of lumske before Livets is in itself important and makes the line gain enormously in rhythm and gravity. But a most momentous change is that of the addition of the word Daadens (Mod).

We must admire Peer 's self-knowledge here, for it is perfectly true what he says about the great art of living, or rather about h i s great art of living — an art

preached by Peer but put into practise later on by Stens-
gaard. And it is not difficult to see where they have
learned their art of never burning their ships behind
them. It is the thing that bishop Nicholas in Kongsemnerne warned Duke Skule against. Skule's curse was
(F, II, 319): "you want to know every way open in
case of need — you do not dare to break off all bridges
behind you and defend but one, — and conquer there or
die" (cf. ib. p. 419). According to Messrs. Koht and
Elias (Breve, I, 20) it is likely that Peer Gynt was mod-
elled partly on Vinje "as he who always wants to hold a
back-door open". It may be so, but we do not need poor
Vinje's faults of character to explain Peer's principal
one for, apart from the very important fact that it is
alas a very common trait of the human mind, it should
be observed that a similar fault is one that Ibsen had
read of in Heiberg's En Sjæl efter Døden, where we read
of the souls in purgatory that their only consolation is
as they say the certain hope that an exit remains possible: "Den eneste Trøst for de arme Stakler For hvilke
man Livet her forqvakler.... Er som de sige, den visse
Haaben At for dem en Udgang tilsidst er aaben." And
just like Peer is frightened at the idea of not being able
to "turn back", so in Heiberg, as soon as the soul
hears Mephistopheles say (p. 197) that in *his* dwelling
"no one ever turns back, he must remain here perpet-
ually — ei nogen tilbage skrider: man maa blive her
til evige Tider" — she exclaims: I see! that's an other
thing. And if this example should not be admitted as a
perfect parallel, because it is Mephisto who speaks the
words, I may refer to Adam Homo (I, 82) where the
hero tells us quite plainly: to stick to an opinion is what
I could never get into my head — "at slaae en Mening
fast, ei ind mig faldt." To call this "nordische art" as J.
Collin does (p. 287) is at once too much and too little.
For if we do not recognise it to be a general human

trait, characteristic of Adam *Homo*, i. e. the man Adam, and so of Peer Homo, then surely we must restrict it to the Norwegians for Ibsen wrote this play ‚at' m a n to a certain extent if you like, but much more ‚at' his countrymen; there is nothing to show that he wrote it at the Scandinavian as such.

We can hardly imagine a more daring exposition of the foible than here, where to do nothing is boldly called to possess the courage of action. Pretty close to it comes however a famous expression by a Dutch writer who, when making fun of the lachrymose Wertherians, hit upon the splendid: the deed is prose, but the complaint, the tear is poetry"; — Piet Paaltjens: "de daad is proza, maar de klacht, de traan is poezij!"

See the notes to l.l. 1029, 1167, 1359 and 1945. And see l. 2524: I can always turn back, jeg kan jo altid træde tillbage; l. 2889: many a way is open to me, mangen Vej staar mig aaben; and l. 4478: Even the warmed room he asks of the Lean One, he should like to have the permission to leave after convenience, — where by the way Peer's words: as it is said, som man siger (recalling the som de sige of Heiberg's Sjæl) may show that he is, more suo, enjoying a hit at himself.

The art of turning back in time is not inappropriately called in Jutlandish to be "see-sawing", — at gøre svikmøller; cf. Feilberg, Jydsk ordb. III, 674.

2040.   Gemyt. Spirit.

A German word of course but quite naturalised, used passim in Vildanden (e. g. F, VII, 326) and not even mentioned in S. I. S. p. 199 among the words pointing to German influence.

2069.   ingen hejser sit Sejl for blot og bart at sejle.

no one hoists his sails for nothing but the sailing.

Mr. Cotton does not think apparently of what Ibsen had written in the Comedy of Love about the mere delight of sailing even if you should "sail your ship aground":

1, 124; 3, 128; F, 383; M, 229; 14, 114; J, 237; 16, 114.

Kan hænde du sejler din skude paa grund;
men så e r det dog dejligt at fare.

2081, (skrevet) — jeg mindes ikke hvor — s e l v d i g t a b t e.
(a text) — I don 't remember where — l o s t y o u r s e l f.

J. Collin remarks (p. 317) that Peer here refers to S.
Luke. See ib. 9, 25 but compare also the corresponding
passages in S. Matth. 16, 26 and S. Marc 8, 36 (lost his
own soul instead of "lose himself").

2093. Det gyntske s e l v. The Gyntish S e l f.

J. Collin (p. 328) recognises Hegel in what follows.

2099. Men som Vorherre trænger Muldet,
skal han bestaa som Verdens Gud.
But as our Lord requires the clay
to constitute him God o' the world.

The meaning seems quite clearly: as God the Father
must necessarily be incarnated (Muldet; in God the
Son) if he is really to be Lord of our world, etc. and I am
not sure that this is rendered very adequately in Messrs.
Archers' translation. Other translations are even less
satisfactory; Mr. Ellis Roberts seems quite at sea: But
as the Lord requires the Clay f o r w o r l d s which
him as God obey.

Dr. Western writes that he is not quite sure that this
explanation is correct. "Muldet is to God what guldet is
to Peer. Now guldet is the means by which Peer will be
able to maintain himself as an emperor, it is his instrument. In the same way muldet i. e. mankind is the instrument by which God vindicates his position as the
God of the world. In other words: God rules the world
through men, just as Peer hopes to be emperor through
the gold."

2108. Sir Gynt.

The mistake has of course been noticed before. See
S. M. p. 10 (Compare T. C. § 110 and n. to l. 1815). The
correct Sir Peter Gynt occurs lower down, l. 2168. The
same mistake without the Christian name occurs in a

1, 126; 3, 130; F, 385; M, 230; 14, 117; J, 239; 16, 117.

paper by Ibsen, printed S. V. (F. X, p. 323): Sir Hotham.

2111. Og alle Karl den tolvtes Værger!

And all the blades of Charles the Twelfth.

Of the four utterances here that are meant to be characteristic of the respective speakers, only the present one requires a note. The Swedish hero, King Charles XII, 1682 (reigned 1697)—1718 had warred a great deal against Poland, Norway, Russia and Turkey. My English readers will remember Byron's: "by moving Christians down on every side as obstinate as Swedish Charles at Bender"; cf. the n. to l. 2129.

2114. og dertill var vor Ankring Grunden.

our anchoring here supplied me with it.

There would appear to be some little confusion here in this passage. When a little later on, after the scene with his golden calf-adoring friends, they have left him, the picture of our hero in despair and afraid to die *in the desert* certainly does not recall a great amount of civilisation. Then what can Peer have anchored for here? To get some papers? — the same that happen to bring the news that causes all the hubbub? Aviserne jeg f i k ombord, the papers I r e c e i v e d on board, can only mean: those that I f o u n d here, not: those I got (some days ago) and h a v e on board for then there would be no "ground to anchor here" — observe that Messrs. Archers' translation omits the very word — grunden — that puzzles us most. Since when are newspapers a produce of the desert? Moreover: where does the "superb host" get his dinner, his awning and his matting from, not to speak of the hammocks? If from the ship, then where are the future Robinson Crusoe's Fridays?

2129. Jeg finde skal i Bender
de verdenskjendte Sporespænder.

I'll find again in Bender
the world-renowned spur-snap-buckles!

Compare: Grasped in my Swedish hands
I saw the great, heroic spur-snap-buckles! —
Jeg saa i mine Svenske Hænder
de heltestore Sporespænder (l.l. 2176, 7).

The Archers have given the required elucidation: an
allusion to the spurs ("heltestore" simply because they
belonged to a great hero) with which Charles XII (n. to
l. 2111) is said to have torn the caftan of the Turkish
Vizier [1]. Vilhelm Bergsøe tells us (Ibsen paa Ischia,
p. 237) that the poet became quite vehement when the
Swedes were praised. Once when his wife imprudently
began about the laurels of Gustavus Adolphus and
Charles the Twelfth, Ibsen burst out: All this is nonsense, for what are these fellows now? — thi hvad er de
karle nu? Even now they, the Swedish, trot about in
Charles the Twelfth's boots, but when all comes to all
they have not got a shoe to step in — "de trasker endnu
den Dag i Dag omkring i Karl den Tolvtes Støvler men
har ikke de Sko, de kan rende i, naar det kommer til
Stykket." The present writer ignores if the allusion here
to the great King's boots is anything but a poetic licence,
dictated it may be by the poet's antipathy to the
Swedes, as well as to his countrymen who had not
helped Denmark (n. to l. 1807). Moreover, as Eva Wigström reports some one to have expressed it (Vandrin-
gar i Skåne ock Blecking, 1888): nej! det där sludder
med detta usla Tørkeriet (!sic = Turkey). Det var a n-
d r a Tørkeriet, som Karl den Tolfte kom till. Där ska
vara långt dit....! — it's s u c h a long way off!

English students may remember both Bender and the
hero-king from the interest that Addison's Political
Upholsterer professed for him (Tatler, 155). — Ibsen

---

[1] Passarge makes it into the spurs that he had l o s t at Bender, simply because
verloren is such a convenient word when one has to rhyme on *sporen*. — He is
followed by Mrs. Clant van der Mijll who, as her translation was not meant to be
rhymed, had not even this excuse.

---

has another allusion to the king in his Ballonbrev (Digte F, IV, 378): remember the prisoner at Bender, — "husk den fangne mand i Bender."

2137.   Forlad. Forgive.

Although norw. forlade = to forgive is of course common enough and even the one word to use in some cases such as ,forlad os vor skyld' where tilgive would hardly be used, the Swedish förlåt is likely to have been the word Ibsen thought of here where it is Trumpeter-stråle that uses it; cf. n. to l. 1807.

2156.   man till Kanonmad er som skabt.

one's born to serve as food for powder.

Ellis Roberts too has (He's) food for powder (from his birth) where a more literal translation might have been preferred if this were not the very expression (often I think attributed to Napoleon) that Shake-speare uses (I, Henry IV, 4, 2, 72). — The more usual word is kanonføde.

2181.   God dam!

Professor Storm has left this "old-fashioned form of the oath" untouched, he tells us (S. M. p. 11) although he contracts Ibsen's two words into one. His reason is that it is also kept in other, older authors such as Beau-marchais(!), —- according to whom "God-dam is the foundation of the English Language"! Messrs. Archer fortunately keep it, but it is too much for Mr. Ellis Roberts' feelings who changes it into Damn it.

2182, 2186.   Olympen, Kastale.

Messrs. Archer remark here (p. 144) that Mr. Cotton seems to have confounded Olympus with Parnassus. For the Kastale is of course the celebrated f o u n t a i n, not a river, on Mount P a r n a s s u s, — sacred to Apollo and the Muses, — Castalidæ.

Overlærer Stavnem in a private letter suggests that there might be a reminiscence here of Tieck's Verkehrte Welt, which Ibsen may have known in Oehlenschläger's

---

translation (as well as in the original) and he compares that scene in the play, where the representative of utilitarianism Bajas (nyttemoralens representant) asks Apollo how much profit the Parnassus yields yearly and is told in reply that the fountain Kastale is the only source of revenue. Bajas asks among other things if the water is not used for manufacturies and if there are no water-mills? For: revenues one must have, etc. The parallelism with our passage (as to a much lesser extent with l. 2421) is of course striking. If any one should look upon it as m o r e than a parallel and suppose that Ibsen may have used this passage, the circumstances will require an explanation that Tieck rightly speaks of a source and Parnassus, Ibsen wrongly of a river and Olympus.

2199.   En Kongetanke! A royal notion.

This rendering, adopted by Mr. Ellis Roberts does not seem a very happy one, if at least we may take it for granted that there is just the slightest perhaps, but still a very distinct reminiscence present here in the word, of that certain "King's Thought" that Ibsen knew all about viz. that of gathering the Norwegian peoples into one, the 'Kongstanke' that lies at the bottom of Haakon's success and Skule's defeat in Ibsen's Kongsemnerne (cf. ib. F, II, p. p. 409: Norway was one realm — it shall become one people.... That, Duke, (you) cannot bring about), that same Kongstanke which was the rallying point of Scandinavianism at the time when Ibsen wrote his Peer Gynt, as well as long before and after [1]) and which was crowned finally by the separation from Sweden in 1905; cf. Gerhard Gran, Norsk aandsliv i hundrede Aar, p. 34. (Add.)

In the play itself the expression is of course used in the much more general and in a way weakened sense

---

[1]) According to Vesle Vislie (A. O. Vinje, p. 204 seqq.), Vinje wrote his „Olaf Digre" a t and a g a i n s t Kongsemnerne and its teaching.

---

of: a happy thought that will bring success with it.

In Kongsemnerne, Ibsen uses the form kongstanke (p. p. 409, 430) by the side of other compounds with kongs- (instead of: konge-) such as kongsfiender, kongsbarnet, kongsnavn, kongsretten, kongsgerning, kongskaabe, etc. etc. (p. p. 398, 399, 405, 408 etc.) In l. 1492 of the Peer Gynt, Ibsen had used the s-form too: Min Kongsdatter! cf. T. C. § 93. All these may be added to the comparatively few "kongs-"compounds that the dictionaries give, — Brynildsen has but three. On the forms with — s, instead of — e (or no connecting letter at all) cf. Seip, Wergeland p. 132; Wergeland was inclined to reject such a form as Kongegaard for kongsgaard. Mr. Alfred Eriksen's study on the compounds in Ibsen (Nyt Tidskrift, IV, 1885, p. 371: Sammensatte ord hos Ibsen) does not in any way elucidate this point. Not a single word from "Peer Gynt" is treated of.

2208.   enfin as a rhyme word to iflæng.

The rhyme does not seem very perfect "after the scole of Paris atte Seine", but it is unfortunately quite common in countries where the language of Molière is not cultivated sufficiently. The self-satisfied German's "Ich habe jetzt den richtigen Pariser a g z a n g" is a well-enough known joke; the like may constantly be heard, and it is to similar contorsions of untrained Danish or Norwegian mouths that we owe such forms as sjangen (= gen(r)e; Feilberg in v.); fjong adj., french (donner le coup de) fion; and even a verb: fjongse op = pynte op; Ordbog over Gadesproget, p.p. 129 and 287) commang = comment; and sjangtil = gentil which Ibsen in his Wild Duck, puts in the mouth of Pettersen, a Norwegian James Plush. (F, VII, 194; M. IV, 230) In Adam Homo, Paludan Müller makes bassin rhyme on stræng and eng. But the most amusing illustration of this was once found in a very unexpected

---

1, 134; 3, 137; F, 393; M, 234; 14, 124; J, 242; 16, 124.

place, when at a little Norwegian country hotel, one day the "menu" bore the mysterious word "chreteng", which when the course came up proved to be fish "(au) gratin"!

The "gammelvise" from which Feilberg (Sjæletro, 1914, p. 165) quotes: den havmand ind ad døren tren, og alle de små billeder, de vendte sig omkr*ing*", may be thought to prove either that as in cockney, — ing is often pronounced — *in*, or that the change exemplified above occurs in native words too, — if it is not merely a case of assonance and nothing more !

There are one or two more French expressions that might seem open to criticism. When we hear Peer flirt with Anitra about the "tetatet'en" in which he is himself only (l. 2666) we smile and not only at the foolishness that made him look for cherries in November. And to a purist it may seem suspicious to hear Peer say to the Lean One that he has abstained from sins "en gros" (l. 4445). The context shows that he means 'great sins' not "wholesale", as Mr. Ellis Roberts has it: from sins in excess. But it is after all an extension of the original meaning that a Frenchman himself might very well use.

We shall hear a great deal about Peer's "half culture" — see especially the n. to l. 2371 and that to l. 2586 — and I foresee a possible suggestion that besides these "sins en gros" ,the "tetateten" should be placed on this debit-conto. When we remember however, how thick Ibsen is in the habit of putting it on when he characterises such persons as Jacob Engstrand or Gina — whose "galne folk (der) pressenterer den intrikate (for ideale; F, VII, 359) fordring" is almost too much of a good thing — we must bethink ourselves twice before we admit it here, where the mistake (if mistake there be) would be imperceptible for the greater part of his public.

1, 134; 3, 137; F, 393; M, 234; 14, 124; J, 242; 16, 124.

2211.   (jeg)... protesterer for Alverden —!
          I protest for all the world.

Messrs. Archer find an allusion here (see their note, p. 145) to the Swedish Count Manderström. He is generally considered to be aimed at not here, but o n l y in the character of Hussejn; cf. the Archers, ib., the n. to l. 3308 and especially Jæger, as quoted in the note to l. 1806.

2215.   Mareridt. A night-mare.

The belief in night-mares forms part and parcel of ancient popular tradition — a common story being that of a man who finds out that she comes through a little hole in the wall and when a plug is put into it, she is usually discovered as a beautiful naked girl whom the man marries and gets children with. When a long time after perhaps he shows her the hole through which she came, the woman disappears and is never heard of afterwards; H. and E. Folkminnen, 1907, p. 401; the same story in Kviteseid, cf. Muro, Syn og Segn, 1903, p. 31; Wickström, Folktro, p. p. 260; Feilberg in v., II, 550 where as usual an immense amount of material is collected; cf. further: Maal og Minne, 1914, p. 44, 61 (Anathon Aall); Meyer, p. p. 130, 137; Dania, II, 215 (she cannot mention three, the holy number of the trinity, so if you lay a sieve over your face, you are quite safe as she must count the holes first and cannot get beyond two!), a story in the Ynglinga Saga and Paul, Grundriss, I¹, 1013, III³, 267, 269.

2232.   Nej-Gud om han hører! I'm blessed if he hears me!

There is just enough of the original sense left in Nej-Gud to make us regret that no corresponding idiom allowed the Archers to render it more literally. Perhaps something like: God bless me if he heard me would come nearer to it.

The whole passage: Peer's addressing God with the vulgar Pst! (a substitute for Hør, later Men, in U) is a daring piece of work on the part of the very author who

---

I, 134; 3, 137; F, 393; M, 234; 14, 124; J, 242; 16, 124.

substitutes med sin Overmand for med Vorherre in
l. 2260, and who omitted the sub=title "eller Vorherre
og Comp." from "The League of Youth"; n. to l. 2247.
Compare to some extent The Wild Duck where Hjalmar
in a moment of despair addresses God; Å, du der
oppe—!— Hvis du er da! (F, VII, 394: O you up
there! — i f you exist, that is!). Peer's attitude is that
of the drowning man Feilberg, (Tillæg, p. 109 in v.
drukne) tells a good story of. When his prayer had been
heard and he had got hold of a saving plank, he exclaimed: all right Lord Jesus, I can help myself now. And
it is that, to come to the graver side of the question, of
so many of Ibsen's creations, that throw the blame of
their own sins on God; see J. Collin, l.l. p. 25 (who by the
way, seems to misinterpret Allmers's "meningsløst") and
about the present passage ib. p. 288 where he speaks of
Peer's attitude — "kindisch mutet (sie) an" — "in der
sich lächerliche Anmassung mit kriechender Demut
wunderlich genug mischt." However this be, Ibsen's
personages are here but too true to life. Some people
make it quite a regular little habit to throw the blame
of their own faults on to others, it's "human nater"
as Peggotty tells us and if Peer had only thought
of this he might not have refused to marry, for then
his wife would have been the "Pakk-kamel" (l. 1838)
for his own W o e if not his W e a l.

2238.   Aa, hjælp mig ombord —! help me on board.
See the discussion of a Shakespearean motif, infra,
ad l. 2444 (1604, 2945).

2247.   at vide sig selv separat beskyttet.
      to know oneself specially shielded.
Peer's childish belief in the special protection that
he thinks his virtues demand is far from being peculiar
to him; see the note to l. 2232 and that to l. 1872. Ibsen
has chastised it again later on in Steensgaard. This is
not quite so clear from the final version of De Unges

Forbund as from the first draft, (Eft. Skr. II, 113) whose
very sub-title speaks volumes; it was omitted at the
suggestion of Fr. Hegel, Ibsen's Copenhagen publisher
(Eft. Skr. III, 422; cf. Vorherre er med os, II, p.p. 120,
121: Hurra for Vorherre og Compe, Vorherre junior,
Samfundets Vorherre, etc.). Steensgaard is confess-
edly supposed to be a skit, if only to some extent on
Bjørnson (Eft., Skr. III, 421) whose "trust in his own
good fortune and a strong belief that God rules everything for our best" — "lykketro og den sterke tro paa
at Gud styrer alt til det bedste" caused a recent writer
(Seip, Bjørnson-Studier, p. 89), to compare this very
passage from Peer Gynt as related, however distantly.

An echo of this sentiment, very faint it is true, but
clearly enough distinguishable, we come across, whenever a man thanks God for some special favour shown
or benefit received, as when Falk in the Comedy of
Love, on learning that his beloved Svanhilde is yet free,
bursts out: O, praised be the Lord! O, how good and
friendly the Lord is!

2254.   Lade Herren raade; ikke hænge med Ørene —
Leave it all in the Lord's hands; and don't be cast down.

The text reflected in this translation as well as in
that of others is the imperative: "*Lad* Herren raade
on which see T. C. § 93. The difference is a very
slight one in form but the change in style will be felt
to be great.

2260.   Med sin Overmand er det ikke grejdt at bides.
They know it's no joke to fall foul of their betters.

Overmand is the substitution for Vorherre of the
first draft (n. to l. 2232), a substitution possibly not
of a word or an expression only, but of the thought,
the things expressed, in other words, by Overmand
Peer does not mean Vorherre here, but with his habitual, delicious conceit: h i m s e l f! Later on again,
he compares himself to an elephant: De bæster skulde

hytte sig, tænke som sandt er, det er vogsomt at lege
med elefanter; l.l. 3469,70. The expression seems
proverbial; cf. Mau, II, 114: Det hjælper dig ej, hvo
du est, med din Overmand at fægte, etc.

2268,9. Morgenen er ikke Kvelden lig;
    det Skriftsted er ofte nok vejet og drøftet.
    Morning and evening are not alike
    that text has been often enough weighed and pondered.

One of the places where this has been discussed by
Ibsen (as pointed out by Boer, Gids, 1893, 4, p. 81) is
in his Brand. After a stormy scene that ends calm
enough Brand has sent his mother away (F, III, 73)
promising to come to her in the hour of her remorse
and turning to Agnes, Brand says: "Kvelden blev ej
morgnen lig. "Then" — in the morning — "I was minded to war", but what he wants now in the evening
is not some thing exterior — udad — but it 's the w i l l:
— det er viljen som det gjælder. Agnes has taken the
expression up and replied: Yes, the morning was pale
as compared with the evening. — But, besides of this
passage in Brand, Ibsen may have been thinking of
one in our play where we have heard the profound wisdom from the Old Man in Dovrë that "Morning is morning and evening is evening" (cf. n. to l. 1040); here
we have a discussion (drøftet; if we do not strain the
word) of what ne calls a "skriftsted".

An actual bible reference that Ibsen could have had
in his mind I have been unable fo find, nor did any correspondent point one out, but one of them, Mr. Anders
Krogvig gave himself the trouble to send me a few
remarks which may seem worth reproducing: If no
such thing is actually found in scripture, the psalmist
has sung of the grass that "in the morning it flourish-
eth, and groweth up; in the evening it is cut down
and withereth", (Psalm 90,6) where we have the same
idea: the uncertainty of life and the fickleness of for-

1, 136; 3, 140; F, 395; M, 235; 14, 126; J, 244; 16, 126.

tune, and he continues: a good many of the "scripture references" and quotations Peer comes out with are in reality nothing of the kind. The words of wisdom that flow from his lips he calls bible-references either because he thus invests them with greater authority or because with his restricted book-knowledge he could not possibly think of another source. Practically the bible was the only book the country-people read at the time.

What Peer wishes to say has found proverbial expression in many languages. Compare Aasen, Ordspr.: Ein skal ikkje rosa Dagen, fyr kvelden er komen. And Krogvig quotes "Ingen kjender dagen før solen gaar ned" from Ingemann's "Guds Fred". I add a reference to Mau: Morgenvejr er bedst at prise om Aften (II, 38, 39) and to: Aften er ikke altid Morgen lig, (ib. I, 9; cf. p. p. 113, 173, 366) which comes much closer. Very distantly related is father Cats': Een ei dat is nog ongeleijd, daarvan en dient niet veel gezeijd".

2278.   Natt. Marokkansk Lejr.

Night. An encampment of Moroccan troops.

This little scene is slightly different from the one in the first draft, cf. Eft. Skr. II, 102, 103, the main point of difference being that the Sheikh was replaced by the Keiser, — with great effect as thus Peer might actually be said to have become an Emperor! The two last lines: "Hundred Rørslag under Saalen, hvis I flux ej Tyven fanger!" are corrected over line into the present, so much more severe and hence so much more witty reading.

2285.   Abekatte. Monkeys.

As a possible analogon of this monkey-scene, Mr. A. Leroy Andrews quotes the one with the Meerkatze in the Hexenküche; Journal of Germanic and English Philology, XIII, 243.

2299.   Kun et Fnug. Motes, no more.

Compare what Peer says in the Dovrëhall-scene to

---

the Old man: Der siges jo, Mennesket er kun et Fnug. (l. 1079).

2301.   De... kryr. They swarm.

Compare S. I. S. p. 191: specifically Norwegian.

2303.   en forloren Hale. a false tail.

The ‚forloren' — cf. forloren Skildpadde, mock-turtle, — bogus, dummy was too much for one of the translators who rendered it by a lost tail ¹)!

2309.   Buss. Bus.

Mrs. Clant van der Mijll's Sim (= monkey) and Passarge's amusing Peterchen (to rhyme on an equally uncalled-for: Schwerenötherchen = a "sad little dog"!) are wild shots at a translation that like the Archers' undoubtedly more simple Bus point to the idea that Buss was meant as a proper name. And the fact that even in the third ed. where Ibsen replaced the capitals in substantives by small letters (T. C. § 26) and after, the word continued to be written with a capital certainly seems to bear this out. Only, although Ibsen may have u s e d it as a proper name, Bus (or busse, the more usual form) is in reality nothing but a colloquial word for good friend: de er gode busser = they are excellent "chums" — which is the very word that might have been used. Or: my dear old fellow.

2310. Han er skikkelig, han! Han kan tages med det gode! He's a good beast, he is! He will listen to reason!

Like the German *er*, the pronoun for the 3d person singular is sometimes used for that of the second person in Norwegian too (as in l.l. 4087 and 4246); cf. Falk og Torp, Dansk-Norskens Syntax, §74, p. 116: in Norwegian "han" and "he" are used to this day in some places

---

¹) Dr. Western suggests that it „may not be amiss to point out that forloren in the sense of „false" has been developed out of the literal sense in this way: it was first used in the phrase „forlorent haar", hair that has been lost in combing; this „lost hair" was used to make false curls and buckles of and so came to mean false hair. Then it was also used of false teeth: forlorne tænder and so the sense false, mock was established. We have not only forloren skildpadde but also forloren venlighet, forloren sorg, forloren ydmyghet, and the like". Cf. forloren høitidelighet, Gran, Bjørnstjerne Bjørnson, p. 56.

1, 138; 3, 142; F, 397; M, 236; 14, 127; J, 245; 16, 127.

as an address to strangers and people of standing as
it was the ordinary mode of address in Holberg's com-
edies. In modern Dano-norwegian it may only be used
in a scornful way (som en haanlig tiltale) to inferiors
and younger people" [1]. If Peer's use of it belongs to
the former category, 'Buss' as a person of consequence
has been proof even against this flattery. As the
use of he for you is also known in English dialects (E.
D. D.: "used when the speaker wishes to be particularly polite and recognises your superior position, Suf-
folk") the Archers may be justified (if it was done purposely) in translating han by he, but the subtlety will
be lost upon most readers. The Germans might have
used *er* but a Dutch translation should fight shy of
‚hy'. — Compare also the German plural Sie.

At the bottom of this substitution of the third for the
second person there is of course a certain feeling of reverence; the person addressed stands so high that the
speaker was not "worthy" to pronounce his name. We
may here compare what with a name borrowed from
primitive culture is called t a b o o, what is sacred,
forbidden and therefore unmentionable; the devil can-
n o t pronounce the name Gud and h e n c e says:
Garun for Gudrun and see the n. to d e n o g d e n
for the devil (l. 4526; cf. Maal og Minne, 1909, p. 89 for
an interesting form of name-taboo among the Sea-
Laps). In a more general sense taboo is anything forbidden, cf. Feilberg, Tillæg, p. 354 and Hartland,
Science of Fairy Tales, p. 270, seqq.

Related perhaps, but then certainly much more distantly still, is the feeling of awe and reverence that we
have already referred to, that makes some of us sub-

---

[1] A similar explanation to be found in Poestion[2], § 136 has been mysteriously
omitted in the 3d edition. Dr. Western observing that this use of han is quite obsolete
in spoken Norwegian, suggests that the sentences may be „asides" that Peer speaks
to himself. I must leave the decision to others but would urge that the point, at least
a point — Peer's obsequiousness when in a fix! — is thus lost.

---

stitute "unmeaning" words or parts of words (but with a good deal of meaning in them after all!) for the names connected with our religion, such as gosh for God, or crikey for Christ (n. to l. 1934). —

2319. Hvad er det for en Tænker....? What thinker is it...?

The thinker who had pronounced the profound words in question was the great philosopher Peer Gynt who in the Dovrëhall-scene had said: One must trust to the force of habit. (l. 1066)

So here Peer makes fun of himself as he has done before and as Ibsen does too; cf. n. to l. 2833. Wörner (I¹. p. 244) àpropos of this scene condemns this, quoting Stendhal's judgment on Voltaire: "C'est qu'il est par trop contre nature qu'un homme se moque si clairement de soi-même". The argument seems certainly too sweeping. Did not Bjørnson admittedly make fun of himself in the professorial hero of "Geography and Love" and possibly of his own extreme love of horses in the person of lieutenant Hamar in "A bankruptcy"? (Seip, Da Bjørnson kjøpte Aulestad", Bjørnson-Studier, p. 92). And, what is much more to the point, did not Ibsen admit at one time that he had represented h i ms e l f in one of his poems as "a bear from the farthest Thule"? (som en Bjørn fra det yderste Thule; cf. his defence against the accusation of "Tyske-had", Eft. Skr. I. 298; n. to l. 3045).

2323.   Gevalt! Gevalt! Murder, murder!

Gevalt which the Archers have hit off very happily is of course a German word like so many others both in Danish (cf. Ordb. over Gadesproget) and in Norwegian. It is very rare — "hardly ever heard nowadays", S. I. S. — Brynildsen gives only the corresponding adjective gevaltig. Observe that though German, it is written with a v, cf. the n. to l. 2586.

2324.   Den gamle var fæl, men de unge er værre!

The old one was bad, but the youngsters are worse.

See the same line at the end of the scene in the Dovrëhall, l. 1209 and the n. to l. 1202. Weininger translates it (l. c. p. 22): Der alte war schlimm, die jungen sind
B e s t i e n! with which we may compare his peculiar
notion (to say the least of it!) that "So sehen wir ihn
denn im vierten Akte am tiefsten gesunken. Der
Mensch lebt nun in völliger Gemeinschaft mit den Affen,
a l s w e l c h e s i c h d a s T r o l l p a c k d e s
z w e i t e n A k t e s e n t g ü l t i g e n t p u p p t"!!

2326.   En Tyv og en Hæler. A thief and a receiver.

That the list of the Handlende still gives to Tyve is
explained by the fact that in U there really were two
thieves, Hestetyven and Klædningstyven (Eft. Skr.
II, 103); the receiver was only substituted for one in R,
and Ibsen forgot to have it changed in the Dramatis
Personae; cf. T. C. § 15.

2330.   Knappen. my head.

U had Hodet, so that Ibsen's slangy Knap (cf. Ordb.
over Gadesproget) is but a substitution of word, not of
meaning. Ellis Roberts' limbs is a very bad shot.

2333.   Min Fader var Tyv; hans Søn maa stjæle.

My father he thieved; his son must be thieving.

See the Archers' note of warning, p. 152 to the effect
that this is not to be taken as a pre-Ghosts-ian dealing
with the problems of heredity (on which see the index in
v. Gjenganger) but simply "an allusion to the fact that
in the East thieving and receiving are" (I add: supposed
to be) "regular and hereditary professions"

2345.   sin Kugle. his ball.

On this dung-beetle (Skarnbasse), Ateuchus sacer,
the Illustreret Norsk Konversationsleksikon (in v.) gives
the following information to which Mr. Anders Krogvig
was good enough to call my attention: The he-beetle and
the she-beetle form together a dung-ball, about 5 cM.
in size. This they roll away, one goes before and pulls at
it with his crooked back-legs, the other pushes it with

1, 139; 3, 143; F, 398; M, 237; 14, 128; J, 246; 16, 128.

the forelegs".... then ....they "dig the ball in the earth after the she-beetle has laid an egg in it. For every egg they form a separate ball". So it is not strictly correct to make the beetle roll her eggs, as Count Prozor does.

2347.   Morgenen; ja, den har Guld i Mund. —
The morning; ay, it has gold in its mouth.

In its usual form in Norwegian the proverb runs of course: Morgenstund har Guld i Mund, Mau, p. 38 where some amusing applications of the proverb may be found. As to the still mysterious origin (it will not do here to discuss the various explanations, for which see the dictionaries), independently of each other it would seem, two scholars have hit upon the idea that it may be owing to a mediaeval etymological guess: Aurora habet aurum in ora (sic!); cf. Dr. E. Slijper, German. Rom. Forschungen, IV, 607, who seems to be unaware that he has been preceded by Brunner, Deutsche Rechtsgeschichte (aurum in ore, p. 71) which I quote from Taal en Letteren, XIII, p. 370; cf. however ib. p. 575.

2351.   om saa var. at need.

On the omission of the subject here or perhaps: on the substitution of saa for the subject (cf. her er deilig, Western); cf. Poestion, § 153.

2356.   Firbenen. Lizard.

This firben*en* was changed by Professor Storm into firben*et* ; cf. T. C. § 125, a change all the more uncalled-for as the dictionaries recognise both the common and the neuter genders of the word; cf. e. g. Brynildsen, (both the 1st and 2nd editions) and Feilberg in voce. Wergeland in "De sidste Kloge" (n. to l. 2406) had also used Fiirbenen. Compare tusenben e n as well as tusenben e t (Western).

2359.   efterretteligt. fulfil.

Compare: Lovene kan man jo nok holde sig efterrettelig (F, IV, 99: De Unges Forbund) and: vi har nu sat

Termin til kl. 10¼ men desværre ikke endnu holdt os den efterrettelige; Jørgen Moes Breve, ed. Krogvig, p. 197, where, as will be observed, the first instance does not as in our case and that of Moe give us the inflected form.

2362.   paa hans første Bliv. at his primal: Be!

The Archers seem to be the only translators to see, as they certainly are to show, that Bliv is the imperative used as a substantive. Some other cases and a couple of parallels may be given here: Du intet Creatur formeener At see effecten af Dit Bliv! (Kr. B. Tullin; Nordahl Rolfsen, Norske Digtere, p. 73); Da vaktes Liv, da spirede Kjærnen ved Herrens Bliv, i Dage og Nætter vilde. (ib. p. 413). In a private letter Brynildsen quotes: ved aandens tryllende Bliv = skaper-ord; from Welhaven (III, 7) and compares German: das Werde. And compare the use of "Vil" and "bliv" in the two following quotations given at second hand from Samtiden, 1904, p. 97 and Gran's Norsk aandsliv i hundrede Aar, p. 49 respectively): O, hvor ophøiet er ei støvet dog der ved en himmel ligger foldet sammen, og folder ud sig i dit eget "Vil"! (Wergeland) and: han vil og med et sympathetisk: bliv! opvække Norges kunst til Aand og Liv; A. S. Olsen, 1814.

2364.   En Padde. Midt i en Sandstensblokk.

Forstening omkring. etc.

A toad. In the middle of a sandstoneblock.

Petrification all round him, etc.

Compare one of "Alma's posthumous poems" in Adam Homo (II, p. 416). When she has asked herself once more if there is no salvation from the "second death" — Er ei der Frelse meer fra denne Død?" — she goes on: When the stones are shattered, a living toad has often been found, which, jammed in for centuries perhaps, sat there and waited, forgotten by all the world —

Naar Stene sprængtes, stundom man der inde
En levende Tudse jo har kunnet finde,
Som, maaskee hele Sekler indeklemt,
Der sad og vented, for Alverden glemt —

so it is her hope that God one day will free her soul from
its prison, — "that lost soul, whose life ended in impot-
ence and like the toad could only w a i t!" —

Den tabte Sjæl, hvis Liv i Afmagt endte
Og som, lig Tudsen, mægted kun at v e n te.

That the toad represents the soul of the dead is a
piece of Scandinavian folklore that is but distantly
connected if at all with Alma's utterances, — as it may
possibly be with Peer's. (Compare e. g. Feilberg, Jul, I,
43 and his Jydsk ordb. in voce) Toads were even actual
persons before the deluge; Wickström, Folktro, p. 93. —
Craigie, Scandinavian folklore (p. 426) suggests that
"the toad as a common feature may be explained by a
confusion of Tudse (toad) and Tusse, = ðurs = giant.

2370.   en saakaldt Storbog. a so-called classic.

The Archers' c l a s s i c is undoubtedly too general a term. A storbog is evidently here t h e one
book of all, the bible. See Aasen, p. 756: Storbok, især
om bibelen. Som det stend i Storboki. Compare Feilberg,
Tillæg in v. bog, p. 53, b. So translate: in what may be
called t h e Book. Or at most as Dr. Western suggests:
"a religious book", — Peer does not remember which.

2371.   Salomons Ordbog. Solomon's proverbs.

This passage has been dealt with at length in a paper
in the Dutch Tijdspiegel, Febr. 1915 and in T. C. § 102,
the result of this investigation being that Ibsen would
seem to have used ordbog as a j o k e for ordsprog, to
characterise Peer's half-culture. For him who accepts
this the translators have each and all missed a point
here, some gravely translating it as Proverbs, words of
truth, sprüche, spreuken and .... la clavicule de Salo-

mon! [1]) Others, such as Passarge, leave it out all together, which is the safest way not to give a wrong rendering.

2380, 81.   Hovmod maa bøjes.
Og hvo sig fornedrer, han skal opphøjes.
The proud shall be humbled,
and whoso abaseth himself, exalted.

See the Proverbs of Solomon, 16, 18; 29, 23; James 4, 6 and Mau I, 436, 438.

2406.   Et Gjennembrudd blot, en Kanal.
It wants but a gap, — a canal.

This mere "breach" in the barrow as Mr. Ellis Roberts has it, certainly more correctly, was actually proposed in 1874 by Rodaire and in 1877 by Mackenzie. And later on we had of course the Frenchman Jacques Lebaudy who was going to be Emperor of the Sahara.

But all this Ibsen could not be thinking of in 1867. A passage that to some may recall the present one is found in Wergeland's farce De sidste Kloge. "Prokurator" Zobolan gets an idea (Wergeland, VI, p. 278): Da glimrer Gadekjær og Ocean eens, eller hiin Mudderkanal og — Ha, *det* var en Tanke! Hiin Mudderkanal! Tys, jeg tør endnu ikke sige det til mig selv. Men er det ikke Murene af Pugerens Magaziner, der stejlt styrte sig ned.... ikke ladende Fiirbenen en Revne?.... Both the puger and the firbenen occur in the very passage of our text.

"As Faust finally found eager occupation in the restor-

---

[1]) This work, Clavicula Salomonis, treating of the „halbe Höllenbrut" that the poodle makes Faust think of (Studierzimmer; Faust ed. Witkowski, l. 1258, ib. II, p. 222), raises the king to the dignity of a first-class sorcerer; cf. Feilberg III, p. 146 in v. Salomon. Professor H. Gollancz (after a short newspaper notice) in his edition (1903) would seem to attribute the authorship to the king himself which undoubtedly seems surprising in view of the piety that characterises this „godly" book (Witkowski). This is the „trolldoms-bok" of Solomon that Moltke Moe speaks of in the Samtiden for 1908 p. 34. It is sad to think that the royal sorcerer is thought to have fallen so low as to become a — freemason, — the world's f i r s t freemason it is true, (See Eva Wickström, Folktro, p. 363: Kung Salemo.... var världens förste frimurare.) but still....! For when a man is once called a „frimurare" he is lost.

---

ation of land from the sea by means of dikes and drainage", Mr. A. Leroy Andrews writes in his essay comparing the two dramas, so Peer conceives the idea of the Sahara (l. c. p.p. 243, 244) and in support of this the writer quotes the expression of the first draft,.... "et Dødens Holland" (Eft. Skr. II, 104).

2421—24.   Tombuktu, Bornu, Habes.

Tombuktu is the capital of French Sudan, on the Niger to the south of the Sahara, Bornu (U: Burnu) a part of the Sudan, also to the south of the desert. Habes or Habesch is the Arabic name for Abyssinia.

Brons, in order to get a rhyme-word to Kultur, unblushingly changes Bornu into Sur, the Semitic name for Tyrus.

2427.   det dølske Blod. the Dalesman's blood.

It is an open question whether Ibsen did or did not think of any special one of the Norwegian "dales" here, but if so, it must almost certainly be the Gudbrandsdal as Morgenstern has it and not the Hallingdal which Count Prozor thinks of. It is well known that the people from Gudbrandsdalen are particularly proud of their ancestors, but I cannot actually quote any reference for dølsk referring to Gudbrandsdalen to the exclusion of the other valleys.

2429.   Rundt om en Vik paa en stigende Strand.
    Skirting a bay, on a shelving strand.

This situation of the future capital reminds one of Bergen and perhaps a little more of Kristiania.

2432.   Gyntiana.

Ole Bull, the celebrated violonist (see the n. to l. 801) had founded a Norwegian colony in America in 1852 on the pattern of those of the French socialists, which he called Oleana. With his "restless phantasy" which Ibsen got to know better than others, (J. Paulsen, Samliv med Ibsen) Ole Bull has undoubtedly been one of the prototypes of Peer Gynt, — and here Gyntiana (cf. later on: paa Gyntianas Banker, l. 2727) is nothing but a skit on the name Oleana. See on these attempts of colonisation, on which the Norwegian Paganini lost quite a fortune, the Eft. Skrifter I, p. LXXII (= the Nachgelassene Schriften, IV, 274) and Catharinus Ellings' scrappy sketch of Ole Bull in "Nordmænd i det 19de Aarh." p. 474.

2436.   Den griske Puger. The close-fisted old churl.

Here perhaps better: the grasping miser. Aasen assigns also the meaning splendid, first-rate, to it, in which it was used by Wergeland; cf. Seip, Wergeland, p. 164.

2439.   Asnet i Arken. like the ass in the ark.

See the Addenda.

2444.   Mit Rige, — mit halve Rige for en Hest!

My kingdom, — well, half of it, say — for a horse! The substitution of mit halve Rige is an amusing reminiscence of that h a l f of his Kingdom that at one time he was master of when he had conquered the ,princess'. Considering that halve riket is a standing expression (cf. n. to l. 1020) the Archers' translation does not do justice to the original.

The line contains of course a clear reference to King Richard's: A horse! a horse! my kingdom for a horse! (Rich. III, V, 4, 1.), and this is not the only point of contact with Shakespeare.

When in Macbeth the king receives the new-made thane of Cawdor, nothing doubting of the treason that the latter is meditating, he has just said of the late Cawdor and in spite of a later time's teaching: There's no art to find the Mindes construction in the Face: He was a Gentleman on whom I built an absolute Trust" — and at this very moment the man enters upon whom the king had relied as absolutely and who was to betray him much more perfidiously than Cawdor had done. This is indeed as the critics have called it "an admirable stroke of dramatic art". Nor does it stand alone in Shakespeare's works, cf. Macb. I, 4, 14; I, 7, 28; V, 5, 28 ("signifying nothing" and what follows signifies a good deal); Hamlet III, 4, 102; Romeo and Juliet, II, 5, 16 etc. but nowhere does it seem so striking as in Macbeth. That Ibsen had read his Shakespeare may be taken for granted, take for example the Sanct Hans Natten which shows undoubted influence of the Midsummer-night's Dream; compare in the Kongsemnerne (F, II, 365) the Bishop's dying remarks with the "Galgenhumor" of Shakespeare's Gravediggers in Hamlet, and Wörner assumes influence (I[1] 191) of Antonius' famous piece of irony on Julian's address to the soldiers. [1]) That Macbeth was among those dramas of Shakespeare's he must have known and known well and that the resemblance between Macbeth and Ibsen was therefore not owing to the indirect influence of the Faust, replete with Macbeth reminiscences (Faust, ed. Witkowski, II, p. 280) may appear from two passages in the Kejser og Galilæer (Fyrstinden dør, kort og afværgende, F. V, 174 and Macbeth, V, 5, 7; and Kald mig en ildsindet mand, høje Caesar, etc. (ib. p. 175) with Macbeth, II, 3, 90: Who can be wise, amazed, temperate and furious, loyal and neutral in a moment? Moreover Furia's characteristic of Catilina (Catilina F,

---

[1]) The influence of Shakespeare on Ibsen I find touched upon in Professor Chr. Collin's paper: „Shakespeare and the Norwegian drama" in „A book of homage to Shakespeare" that the Clarendon Press has just issued. Of Ibsen's plays Collin mentions (cf. p. 499) in passing: the Pretenders, Fru Inger af Østråt, Emperor and Galilæan; it is only apropos of one play or even one character that he enters somewhat in to details: „it is indubitable that Hamlet, the enigmatic, the inscrutable, from the very outset has exerted the greatest fascination on Henrik Ibsen's subtle mind. A reflection of his early vision of Hamlet I seem to see in the whole series of Ibsen's most self-revealing studies of character from Skule and Julian the Apostate to Solness, Borkmann and Rubeck. Shakespeare's Hamlet, viewed in a somewhat incomplete light, seems to have helped Ibsen to read the riddle of his own soul". On the influence of Hamlet on Ibsen v i a Goethe's Faust, see a note in Chr. Collin's Bjørnstjerne Bjørnson II, 91.

Henning Kehler (Edda, 1916, p. 290) finds influence of Gengangere, Fruen fra Havet, Rosmersholm *etc.* and sees in this trick a "kontrastvirkning" which Ibsen makes use of "instead of real action which the dramas of fate are so deficient in and by which he replaces the psychic action" (sjælelig handling).

I, 143; 3, 147; F, 401; M, 240; 14, 132; J, 248, 249; 16, 132, 133.

I, p. 54) is almost literally Lady Macbeth's opinion of
her husband: Du higer mod et højt, forvovent mål; vil
gerne nå det; og du skrækkes dog af hver en hindring
(Macbeth I, scene 5 and 6). And Stavnem even thinks
that the Boyg-scene has "a certain resemblance with
Macbeth, where the troll-sisters dazzle the hero's eyes
and empoison his mind" (ll. p. 101). The analogy, it will
be seen, is at least striking, although of course, Ibsen
need not have gone to Shakespeare for the traits! And
see Ibsen's criticism of "Lord William Russell" (S. V.
X, p. 381) where Macbeth is mentioned. A similar trick
may be found in Oehlenschläger's Aladdin where the
hero comes in just when Gulnare has called upon her lover (whom she does not know to be Aladdin) to appear
to her; Oehlenschläger's Aladdin is full of reminiscences
of Shakespeare's Romeo and Juliet. And there is something approaching the motif in the first draft of Rosmersholm when Fru Rosmer as she is there already,
symbolically asks for 'lys' when just at the moment
Madame Helseth comes in with a lamp: Her er Lam-
pen, Frue!" But of course, especially the well-known
motif in Bygmester Solness where "youth knocks at the
door" (F, IX, 35, 36) is to be viewed in this light.

Passages to a certain extent similar to this are the one
on the coast of Morocco where Peer asks to be helped on
board his yacht just when a column of fire shows it to
have perished (l. 2238, n), Peer's coming to his mother's sickbed (l.l. 1604) and especially the repetition
of this same trick a little later on where we shall find
that the passage (l. 2945) cannot be properly understood if we do not consider it in this connection.

Finally, when lower down, in the lunatic asylum the
Fellah offers his l i f e for a halter (l. 3292) the reading
of U helps us to another parallel, for there we read: Mit
Land for en Strikke!

2452. ab esse ad posse.

1, 143; 3, 147; F, 402; M, 240; 14, 133; J, 249; 16, 133.

Peer's study of Latin appears to have borne better fruit than that of French and English (n. to l.l. 216, 2208 and 1807) although the latter would have been much more useful to him and he could have studied it practically in America. His latin is absolutely faultless for which he had no doubt to thank a certain young apothecary-apprentice at Grimstad (n. to l. 2461); cf. not only (l.l. 2760 and 2938): status quo and facit where the expressions may almost be said to be common property as in the case of ad undas (l. 4388) but also Petrus Gyntus Caesar fecit (l. 4007) and: Sic transit gloria mundi, l. 4361.

2459.   Paa Ridestellet etc. by their riding-gear.
See the n. to l. 996.

2461.   The scene in the tent of an Arab chief.

Here Peer's oriental adventures remind one irresistibly of Oehlenschläger's Aladdin. That Ibsen had read the play is a priori likely; influence of this play is already quite visible in a poem by Ibsen, reprinted in the Samtiden of 1909 (cf. p. 339) by C. J. Hambro where the words about the "Eier af Lampens Skat" and its "gode Aander" tell a very plain tale. But it becomes a quasi-certainty for him who reads the play through with a view to this comparison (see n. to l. 2444). And it may just be worth remarking that Ibsen must have had a copy of the Danish poet's works at his disposal at Grimstad (cf. n. to l. 3615) already in his youthful days when one's reading-appetite is most insatiable and one's impressions stick fast; see Maal og Minne, 1910 p. 47.

Compare J. Collin, l.l. p. 283, and my n. to the Button-moulder, and to the Lean one. Mr. A. Leroy Andrews (J. Engl. and Germ. Philology, XIII, 243) thinks that Peer's "amour" with Anitra may possibly be a "whimsical counterpart of Faust's Union with the restored Helen", which, to some, may seem a rather "whimsical" notion.

1, 144; 3, 148; F, 402; M, 240; 14, 133; J, 249; 16, 133.

2463. seqq.   Pigernes Kor. Chorus of girls.

This passage has been translated excellently by Mr. Edmund Gosse, Studies in the Literature of Northern Europe, 1879, p. 55.

On the wrong repetition of the first line in some editions, cf. T. C. § 107.

2478.   Glansens Glans af de Stjerners Straaler!

the rays of those stars in their blinding splendour!

After this line there is an open space in R (of one line), which did not appear in the first edition as it happened to be the last line of the page. Hence it was not reproduced in any subsequent edition.

2483.   Samum. simoom.

This passage about the simoom's blast — a wind that is uncommon hot, as Mr. Barham sung, may have been suggested by the terrible scirrocco heat that Ibsen suffered from at Ischia just when he was composing the Peer Gynt in 1867. Compare Vilhelm Bergsøe, Henrik Ibsen paa Ischia, p. 212, to which the editors of the Eft. Skr. (I p. XXVIII) assent. See my paper on Henrik Ibsen's Caprices in Peer Gynt, Edda, April, 1917.

2487.   Kaba.

When this Kaba (Kaaba) is said to be empty, Anitra lays herself open to the charge of wrongly imagining this holy building at Mekka to be i n h a b i t e d by the prophet. The reading of U gives us perhaps a solution: Graven i Medina, — and the prophet's g r a v e may of course be supposed to be "tom" when the prophet comes riding here like a mortal o'er the sand-ocean.

2491.   Pigerne danser under dæmpet Musik. They continue to dance, to soft music.

This is the passage to which Edvard Grieg composed his "Anitra's dans". In the first draft to the Doll's House, Ibsen makes Nora sit down to the play a n d s i n g Anitra's s o n g! (Eft. Skr. II, 381) This amusing mistake of the author's, the editors of the Eft. Skr.

1, 144; 3, 148; F, 402; M, 240; 14, 133; J, 249; 16, 133.

(I, p. LXXXVIII) improve into her "singing and dancing Anitra's dance".

2493.   Ingen blir profet i sit eget Land.

no one's a prophet in his native land.

Compare S. Luke, 4, 24; S. Matthew, 13, 57; S. Mark 6, 4 and S. John 4, 44. Mau, II, 332.

2500.   Hvad vilde jeg ogsaa paa den Gallej?

What tempted me into that galley at all?

The word is of course Molière's famous: Que diable allait-il faire dans cette galère? (Fourberies de Scapin, II, 11; cf. infra l. 2850 and on French quotations, supra, n. to l. 216), but it is no doubt common property in Norway as it is in Dutch (although we usually quote it in French). See Brynildsen: paa galei = on the spree (also in Jutlandish, cf. Feilberg in v.; Ordbog over Gadesproget, etc.) Oehlenschläger uses it in his Aladdin: Hvad vilde du min Søn! paa den Galei! Bagefter kommer tyndt Øl! (III act, Sultanens Divan). Compare Styver's amusing misunderstanding of this in the Comedy of Love, (F, II, 151; T. C., § 102).

2520.   træffe Naturens Børn paa min Vej.

meeting these children of nature e n   r o u t e.

After this line in U, Ibsen added afterwards (perpendicularly, in the margin) these two lines:

> Det var jo den skjære Dumhed at nægte,
> naar Majoriteten svær man er ægte.

Var was changed over line into er; they were both omitted in R.

Was it not one of Dickens' creations that gave the advice always to shout with the mob, and when there are two, to shout with the l a r g e s t? This is the teaching at any rate of the two lines which we find already indicated clearly enough in Brand (F, III, p. 139) where the Bailiff does not "shout black but grey" when he thinks something is as "white as glacier-ice", but when the multitude thinks it's "black as snow", and

1, 145; 3, 149; F, 403; M, 241; 14, 134; J, 250; 16, 134.

which Ibsen afterwards worked out so brilliantly in The enemy of the people where Dr. Stockmann recalls Schiller's "Der Starke ist am mächtigsten allein" (W. Tell, 1, 3) and many utterances of his in Demetrius (Zeuthner p.p. 28 and 94). See also Eft. Skr. I, p. XCIV and the Add., n. to l. 3213.

2524.   træde tillbage. withdraw again.
See the n. to l. 2027.

2525.   det er ikke værre. it's a simple matter.
More literally: that isn't so bad. For this use of the comparative instead of the positive, compare: en ældre dame, a lady of a certain age, — i bedre kaar = in pretty good conditions; Germ. ein besseres Mädchen, etc.

Dr. Western adds: In this particular case the comparative is easily explained. The expression is of course elliptic for: det er ikke værre end som saa, det er ikke værre end at jeg naarsomhelst kan træ tilbake (Dr. W.'s words should not of course be taken to mean that Ibsen himself must be supposed to have felt the expression as an ellipsis for the fuller one given; det er ikke værre is a standing expression and the explanation given is one that might illustrate the semasiology if it were original here!) "The idiomatic Norwegian use of the comparison begun with the attributive use: en ældre dame etc. Here too I suppose we have originally an ellipsis: en bedre middag—a dinner better than.... (e.g.: I am used to)"

2533.   de kan i Afstand troppe opp.
in the distance I'd have them assemble.
What to say of a rendering like: "er maar even gauw van door gaan" (= just cut their sticks quickly) which the Dutch translation treats us to?

2535.   Mændene... er en skrøbelig Slægt.
Men are a worthless crew.
See the n. to l. 2945.

2545.   som Trommestikker raske. nimble as drumsticks.

In Adam Home (II, 62), Ibsen may have read: Milles
Been der gaar som Trommestikker, but of course the
idea of expressing quick movement by a comparison
with drumsticks seems common enough. In Kleiven's I
gamle daagaa, I find (p.p. 30, 31): Staven gjekk saa tidt
sum ei Trumstikke, and in Barbra Ring's Lille Fru Ter-
tit (p. 5): Jo, det klask-plask regner, saa det smelder
som trommestikker paa vinduerne, — here the idea of
quickness has given place, I presume, to that of force.

2556. det middels gjør vammel. — the medium is mawkish.

Aurea mediocritas! Afterwards he comes to a different
conclusion: dette middels er i Grunden bedst (l. 2885)
and later on when Peer hears from the Button-moulder
that he is 'scarcely a middling sinner' (l. 4131: knapt en
middels Synder) he is quite elated.

2567.   Men jeg har ingen Sjæl. — Saa kanst du faa!

But I haven't a soul. — Then of course you must get
one!

Note the parallelism with the scene in the Dovrëhall;
l. 1071, n. Cf. Stavnem, l.l. p. 101, n.

Prof. Seip, Samtiden, 1913, p. 573 thinks that Ibsen
has borrowed the notion of the soul-less woman from
one of Wergeland's farces (Harlekin Virtuos, 1830)
where Pappa says to his daughter Alvilde: for Sjel er du,
som Kvinde, fri. And not only that we have another reference to this on the very next page in the same farce
(S. S. VI, p.p. 151, 152) but in another, "Lyv ikke, eller
Dompapen" (1840) there is an account of Aristophanes
who had caught a couple of birds that had soiled his
bust, and put them into a couple of boys' heads that
had chanced (and it is not so rare either!) to be borne
without a soul (ib. VI, 512).

2577.   Skidt. Never you mind.

Of course originally the exclamation skidt was a substantive = dirt. In U and R, Ibsen still writes it with a
capital S. Here it has dwindled down into a mere

1, 148; 3, 152; F, 405; M, 242; 14, 137; J, 251; 16, 137.

enfin!; as Brynildsen (quoting l. 1051 of our play in the Dovrëhall-scene), renders it: Here goes! Who cares. — The expression is not of the finest and little heard in the mouth of ladies.

2579.   Profeten er god — The Prophet is gracious.

The Archers' translation obscures the fact that in Norwegian the nominative (Profeten) is used as so often as a vocative, — i. e. the prophet, you the prophet.

2583—6. Peer Gynt (henrykkt, idet han rækker hende Smykket).

> Anitra! Evas naturlige Datter!
> Magnetisk jeg drages; thi jeg er Mand,
> og, som der staar hos en agtet Forfatter:
> "das ewig weibliche ziehet uns an!"
> Peer (enchanted, handing her the jewel).
> Anitra! Anitra! true daughter of Eve!
> I feel thee magnetic; for I am a man.
> And, as a much-esteemed author has phrased it:
> "Das Ewig-Weibliche zieht uns hinan!"

The corresponding passage in U contains some of the most important lines in the drama and has yet, remarkably enough not been reproduced in the Efterladte Skrifter:

> Peer Gynt
> (rækker hende Smykket og favner hende)
> Kvinde; Evas naive Datter;
> magnetisk du drager mig; thi jeg er Mand,
> og som der staar hos en agtet Forfatter:
> "Das evig weibliche ziet uns herann!"

As the facsimile will show, though not always with the same clearness as the original, the following changes were made: Kvinde is crossed out and replaced by Anitra; naive by naturlige, a comma is added after drager; and mig is crossed out as the semi-colon after it was evidently meant to be. — The very important changes

---

1, 149; 3, 153; F, 407; M, 243; 14, 138; J, 252; 16, 138.

Anitra.

Profeten er god —

Peer Gynt:

Du noer? Tal!

~~Men jeg ønsker heller~~

Anitra.

Men jeg ønsker heller —

Peer Gynt.

~~Bekymret~~ Fuldt af ved om Sjælen

Anitra.

Jeg bryder mig ikke om meget om Sjælen;
giv mig heller —

Peer Gynt.

Hvilket?

Anitra

(peger på hans Turban)

Hun sljernen Opal

Peer Gynt

(vælter hende ~~lmykhed~~ og femme hud)
~~Hund~~; Evas naturligvis datter;
magnetisk du drager, mig; th. jeg er Mand,
og som der står hos en ægte Forfatter:
- Das ewig weibliche ziehet uns hinan! .

---

in the fourth line will be found detailed in § 38 of the Textual Criticism.

The final form of the passage in U was as that of R given above, except that in U ewig remained written evig (as in l. 2331 we have gevalt for the German gewalt), but thus it will be found in the first and second editions only, for in I, Ibsen himself changed ziehet into zieht, — which was reproduced by all the subsequent editions, so that not one of them reproduces the "agtet forfatter's" words exactly which ran: "Das Ewig-Weibliche Zieht uns hinan". When Messrs. Archer "venture to restore" this reading (p. 162; Brons had done this silently! p. 147) they are wrong simply because we should not change a great poet's "mistakes" at all (T. C. § 38) but their text does not constitute a crimen læsæ (poetæ) majestatis as will soon appear.

In my Edda-paper and in the T. C. the passage has been discussed at length and the conclusion there arrived at is that so far from Ibsen having introduced the mistakes into the quotation to characterise Peer's half-culture as has been suggested, the wavering in spelling points to it being nothing but a slip of the memory. The student is requested to read this account before proceeding with the present note.

The only objection to this interpretation that has reached me is one which to my knowledge has never appeared in print; it was contained in a private letter from the poet's son, Hr. Statsminister Dr. Sigurd Ibsen who did not agree with the above explanation. Coming from that quarter it is of course but meet that his arguments should be laid before a larger public than the one to be expected for another paper where I have already met them, viz. the readers of the Dutch periodical Tijdspiegel (Febr. 1915).

Dr. Ibsen thinks it quite improbable that the poet "should not have remembered the exact wording of the two last lines of "Faust". Especially because these lines must "strike a cognate chord" (måtte anslå en beslægtet streng) in himself, what many of his works and especially "Peer Gynt" bear witness to. Not to mention that "Das Ewig-Weibliche zieht uns *an*" as a final-chord of Faust, would mean a platitude which a Peer Gynt no doubt could attribute to Goethe, but not Henrik Ibsen". — No, the wrong form was given on purpose, Dr. Ibsen continues and the changes in the first draft on which I have laid so much weight, only show according to him "that the poet hesitated a moment as to the form of the vitiation" (at digteren et øieblik famlede med hensyn til forvanskningens f o r m"). Of course the substitution of "herann" for "hinan" was an obvious means (lå snublende nær) but directly after it dawned upon him (gik det op for ham) that "zieh(e)t uns an" answered his needs in a way at once simpler and clearer" So far Dr. Ibsen.

With regard to the apparently most formidable argument, *viz.* that the final chord struck would thus turn out a terrible platitude, I should like to ask if Goethe's e x a c t words: Das Ewig-Weibliche zieht uns hinan" would not have produced precisely the same impression of a platitude a s s p o k e n b y P e e r G y n t under the circumstances assumed? For the platitude lies in the quotation i t s e l f, and surely not in the form. For what makes the whole thing repugnant is the fact that the "Eternally womanly" here does not as in the Chorus Mysticus lead us to the Higher Spheres of "Das Unzulängliche (das) Ereigniss (wird)" but that it is here used as in a conversation of certain adolescents, to characterise the speaker's not over-pure feelings for a hardly purer daughter of Eve. So whether Ibsen makes Peer Gynt say that the "Womanly" zieht" (him) an" or "heran" or even "hinan", the form there does not add to or detract from, the impression the quotation a s s u c h

1, 149 ; 3, 153; F, 407; M, 243; 14, 138; J, 252; 16, 138.

produces when it drags us down from the higher spheres of thought to the lower depths of earthliness.

And again: as to the related chord that the words must have struck in Ibsen's heart, I do not see any reason to deny this. But here too it seems we may reply that this chord will be struck by the quotation i t s e l f and not by its form. And although no doubt this fact, as Dr. Ibsen urges, would make us expect the poet to remember the words absolutely correctly, such spellings (in the first draft) as zie*t* and e*v*ig, which as remarked could not possibly be supposed to serve Ibsen's purpose of indicating Peer's half-culture, show clearly that in the hurry of scribbling down the passage (see the facsimile and compare the fact that in R too we find "das ewig weibliche" without the hyphen and capitals of the original) he had not got the German text before him and did not pay the necessary attention to the form of what he wrote, precisely because he was lost in the spirit of it.

* *. *

It is almost incredible but nevertheless true that a recent writer has actually attributed the condescending "esteemed author" to Ibsen himself (A. Leroy Andrews, l. c. 239). And this although he recognises that "these profound words being quoted by the worthless Peer under such peculiarly vulgar circumstances might almost seem an affront offered the great German poet" Now, if, as I venture to think, few of his readers will agree with Mr. Andrews that the Faust is satirised here (! p. 245), I believe that no one after reading his paper will demur to another conclusion of his, *viz.* that Ibsen in writing Peer Gynt, had Goethe's Faust "very vividly before his mind". As a matter of fact, when reading the Faust over again, he who remembers the Peer Gynt in all its details, cannot help being struck not only by the many points of actual resemblance such as those that Mr. Andrews has very diligently pointed out, but more especially and much more forcibly by that indefinable

1, 149; 3, 153; F, 407; M, 243; 14, 138; J, 252; 16, 138.

something, — a general atmosphere and, as here, a great resemblance in form (irregular metre, no division in scenes, etc.) that we feel rather than can bring under words [1]), even if it should be admitted that from this latter point of view, J, L. Heiberg's Sjæl efter Døden may have to be taken into consideration too.

The word naturlig (Datter) takes the place in R of Evas naive Datter in U, and this shows clearly enough that Ibsen here uses naturlige in a somewhat unusual sense, a true daughter of Eve, as the Archers very properly render it. Otherwise, en naturlig søn or datter as the corresponding English: a natural son or daughter suggests a child in accordance with the natural process only, and implicitly: born out of wedlock which meaning is here of course excluded.

2599, 600.　　　Ombord jeg steg paa Slettens Skib,
　　　　　　　et Skib paa fire Ben.
　　　　　　　I climbed on board the desert ship,
　　　　　　　a ship on four stout legs.

Compare Ballonbrev, F, IV, 376: "Beduinen og hans Mage, båren højt paa dromedaren, så vi gennem Ørknen drage". U read: Ørknens (Skib) instead of Slettens. The effect that these dromedaries had on an 'unexperienced North-man' (the first letters of whose name may have been Henrik Ibsen; see the n. to l. 3045) will hardly be guessed: "første gang en uerfaren Nordbo så det, skreg han studsende: mine Herrer, ser De Strudsene?"

2601.　　　　　Piskens Hieb. the lashing whip.

Ibsen now and again uses German words, which is not to be looked upon as a proof of his special admiration either of the people (n. to l. 3045) or of the language;

---

[1]) See the notes to l.l. 584 (Solveig and Margaret); 994 (riding on a hog and Baubo); 1967 (the tone of a joke, cf. also n. to l. 1807 and that to l. 4526) 2995 (the big birds and the klassische Walpurgisnacht); 3328 (a skit on the delight in what is „selvgjort") 3499 (the Strange Passenger and Mephisto); 3995 (the Furumo-scene); 4037 (the Susning i Luften and the Irrlichter); 4139 (the Button-moulder and Mephisto); 4429, 4572 (the Lean one and Mephisto) and lastly l. 4684 (the salvation by Solveig and that by Margaret: gerichtet!).

---

it is simply because German was and is to a certain extent supposed to be as stylish in Norway as French or English is in Holland. See Storm S. I. S. p. 153 on German in the works of Ibsen's predecessors and ib. p. 195 on Ibsen's own German words. From Ibsen's own works outside Peer Gynt I quote Geschichter (Eft. Skr. I, 417), jeg er rent Sterbens (ib. 430), and Ulrik Hetman's (Brendel's) Donnerwetter, nach Belieben, unter uns, Bauerne (sic)! and Geduld (ib. III, p. p. 121—123) which with the exeption of Bauerne have passed into the final text, where we also find: en Feinschmecker (F, VIII, 34), common enough elsewhere too. But the most remarkable specimen of Ibsen's germano-Norwegian comes from his Ballonbrev where we read of "et entrüstungsfæigt Skovdyr!" (F. IV, 379). And I quote a couple of cases from non-Ibsenian sources: "Ak, hvor blev Geisten af, one finds in Aladdin; in Jørgen Moe's letters I note: brevlein, Allenfals, daraussen i (sic) das grosse Vaterland and even: daraussenfra (p. p. 180, 279, 280, 281; and cf. Mau, I, 291: Ens Bir, sa Gassen, han drak af syv Rendestene; German Kinder simply = my friends, is or was so common that it has found a place in the Ordbog over Gadesproget, where we can find not only the very word of our text (spelt: Hib) but also: heran, herut, cf. Heraus, læg an, of our text, n. to l. 4438. Gestalt and gevalt (2323; S. I. S. p. 180) and see further in the Peer Gynt: gemyt (ib. n. 2040), de flestes sehen ins blaue (4496,7). Not only does Dr. Begriffenfeldt burst out into German as well as Schaffmann whose "Es lebe hoch der grosse Peer" closes the fourth act (the remarkable thing about it is of course that he does not either speak it always or not at all; cf. l. 3039: Ach Sfinks, wer bist du?) but the Fellah too speaks of rechts and links (l. 3251). Begriffenfeldt even gives us the hybrid: Famost (3053) and "en Lebensfrage" where the Norwegian form of the

---

1, 150; 3, 154; F, 408; M, 244; 14, 139; J, 253; 16, 139.

article makes us feel the expression as very homely.

2609. Anitra, ak, som du. Anitra, ah, as thou.

There is something peculiarly high-falutin' about this ak (as well as perhaps in l.2625) which suggests the possibility of its having been introduced on purpose into this not over-poetic poetry to characterise these "ha-stemt" literary products of Ibsen's earlier days. Compare Maal og Minne, 1910, p. 38. (Add.)

2636, 7. minsæl! I declare!

The form minsæl for min Sjæl may be compared with dævel for djævel (F. X, 298: Kleiven, Segner fraa Vaagaa, p. p. 82, 84; dævelungerne, F, IX, 48; dævel-skab, Eft. Skr. III, 265; saa dævelen rive mig, F, VI, 173) and perhaps the Danish development of the kj before palatal vowels into k, such as kære, at one time written and pronounced kjære. See the written form: min s'æl (F, IX, 56) and min sæl og salighed, Folkef. (M. IV, 171, 190; cf. n. to l. 4168 and T. C. § 126.).

2645. kanske. mayhap.

Here no doubt meant to be pronounced ['kanskə] as still occasionally, especially on the west-coast and as a correspondent tells me even now elsewhere with people of a certain age, especially ladies and the clergy, instead of the more and more usual: ['kansjə] or(the rarer) [kan'sje]. See the n. to l. 1829 for another case of ['kanskə]

2648, 9. Ligne dig, o Verdens Skatt, med en ækkel gammel Katt!

Liken thee, o world's great treasure, to a horrible old cat!

Bernhard Shaw, The Quintessence of Ibsenism, in the last paragraph of his account of Rosmersholm, discusses (apropos of Peer comparing himself to a Tom-cat) the problem of the lower and higher love as exemplified in Peer and Rebecca. I must rest content with referring the curious student to it (ed.[2], p. 106) as the context of nearly the whole book alone would allow of an appreciation.

2657, seqq.   Jeg er spøgefuld i Grunden, etc.
                 I am full of jest at bottom, etc.

It has been suggested that Ibsen should here have been thinking of himself (exact reference inaccessible) but it may well be asked if in 1867 his position could force him into "assuming a solemn mask" (l. 2660: bunden till en Maskes Alvorsskjær).

2680.   Kan din Datter.... Sjælen fange?
                 can thy daughter.... catch a soul?

To catch is of course wrong here for to get; the verb fange is the obsolete and poetic form of faa (du. vangen, germ. fangen).

2709.   Hvis jeg blot min Turban svinger,
                 Verdenshavets Flod jeg tvinger *etc.*
                 Were I but to swing my turban,
                 I could force the ocean-flood, *etc.*

Peer more suo represents here the dreams of a possibility (l. 2406, seqq.) as a certainty: The ridge is narrow.... it wants but ... a canal, — like a flood of life would the waters rush, etc.

2714. Ved du, hvad det er at leve? Know you what it is to live?

Involuntarily one thinks of the answer the poet himself gave at one time to the question: Leben, das heisst bekriegen In Herz und Hirn die Gewalten — as the German original runs and: At leve er — krig med trolde i hjertets og i hjærnens hvælv, according to his later much more powerful, Norwegian translation. (F, IV, p. p. XVIII and 433). The difference between this and Peer's philosophy, to come "dry-shod down the river of years" is that between Ibsen himself and his indolent, apathic hero.

2721.   Støder. fogey.

Professor Storm is surprised (S. I. S. p. 196) to find such a modern Danish word as Støder here, instead of the Norwegian stabeis. This latter word is however known in Danish too; also in the form staabi, cf. Ordb.

over Gadesproget in v. — The appropriate beauty of
Mrs. Clant van der Mijll's: "'t oude ram krijgt zwakke
pooten!" should not be spoilt by any commentary.

2727.   Gyntiana.

See the n. to l. 2432.

2758, 9.   jeg taer Plads i Sjælestedet,
                     og forøvrigt — status quo.
                     I will be your soul by proxy;
                     for the rest why, *status quo.*

Jæger ('88 p. 261) thinks that these lines contain not
only the germ of Helmer's character, but that they
point also indirectly to the claim of a Doll's house for
personality in woman too — "Umiddelbart indeholder
jo disse linjer skitsen til Helmers portræt; mere middel-
bart — som forudsætning for deres satire — indeholder
de allerede det standpunkt der i "Et dukkehjem" bringer
Ibsen til at gjennemføre personlighedskravet ogsaa for
kvindernes vedkommende."

2779. Profeten er ikke gammel. The prophet's not old at all.

Ibsen evidently first intended to write "Profeter
blir ikke gamle" but when, in U, he had written Profeter blir, he changed this into Profeten er, a remarkable
stroke of genius, this materialisation, if it may thus
be called, of a doubtful general statement into a special
case that Peer was the one person to judge of.

2797.   det hele Pøjt! the whole of the trash.

The word is not really Norwegian, rather Danish;
cf. Ordb. over Gadesproget, 397: sure eller kraftløse
Drikkevarer; intetsigende Tale, Snak, Vaas. Hence,
more generally: things of no value, trifles, trash. Compare Kalkar, III, p. 498 in v. Pøjt(e): vin du Poitou;
Feilberg, II, 906.

2798.   Lifligt. Dulcet.

A somewhat old-fashioned word or like dulcet, somewhat literary, characteristic of the bible (Ordsprog,
XVI, 24: Liflige Taler ere Honningkage) and of the

---

older period of language in general (except when applied to "Good things to eat or drink": en liflig vin, det smaker liflig; Western). It is thus found e. g. in Aladdin (Folkeudg. p. p. 87, 130, etc.), Paludan Müllers' Luftskipperen og Atheisten (e. g. p. 53), in Adam Homo (passim) as well as in Ibsen's own works if more especially in his earlier ones (F, X, p. p. 17, 87, 98, 114, 130, 159 etc. etc.)

2807.   Spilopper. high-jinks.

For the formation of this word as a subst. from the imperative spil op, cf. such compositions as rykind, svingom, skrabud, farimag(sgade) etc.

2809.   Nerium. oleander.

It is the french nérie, laurette; and not a "jewel" as one translator guesses.

2813.   Vinløv. Vine-leaves.

Compare Hedda Gabler F, VIII, 474: Eft. Skr. III, 232: "Havde han Vinløv i Haaret?" Hedda asks, a question suggested by the preceding Bacchanal and one which Tesman does not understand a word of.

2817.   Tippe. pullet.

Tippe, a West-norwegian dialectform as Brynildsen informs me for the East-norwegian and more common tuppe, toppe. So: biddy, chucky.

2825.   en Galfrands. the maddest wag.

Strictly speaking a madcap would perhaps be better or a boon companion. The second part seems to correspond to Dutch "een vroolijk Fransje", which is explained (Stoett, n° 152) as a Dutch rendering of ("La Vraye Histoire comique de) Francion (... par Nicolas de Moulinet, Sieur du Parc). The author's real name seems to have been Charles Sorel de Sauvigny. In answer to my inquiry, Anders Krogvig writes to say that to his knowledge this work has not been translated into Norwegian or Danish as it has been done into Dutch. This circumstance would seem to make for Falk and

---

1, 159; 3, 163; F, 416; M, 249; 14, 147; J, 259; 16, 147.

Torp's suggestion that the word, contrary to the above view, does not contain the proper name Frans, but older Danish frans = franskmand (= tysk Franz, which is there called a scornful denomination for a frenchman, but cf. Goethe's : den Franzen liebt der Deutsche nicht, nur ihre Weine trinkt er gerne, where there is hardly any disdain noticeable); which Krogvig quotes from Hj. Falks' "Kulturminder i Ord" (1900) and which is found reproduced literally in their Etymological Dict. — For the other alternative would be that the Norwegian word has been borrowed from Dutch. This is not of course inherently impossible but there does not seem to be much that speaks in favour of it.

2827.   Pytt, sa'e Peer. Pooh, says Peer.

Krogvig writes that this is "possibly an allusion to a very common, popular : Pyt, sa'n Peer til Kongen, an expression of presumptuous recklessness — "overmodig likegladhet".

2833.   gjør mig en hæftig Sorg; —
                  vouchsafe me a vehement sorrow.

In the epic version of Brand, the hero asks the Lord to make him "rich in sorrow", — Herre, gjør mig paa Smerte rig — where the impression is very strong that this was written by Ibsen as something he had "lived through — gjennemlevet". And this is borne out by a passage in one of his letters. As early as 1853 he had written (Breve, I, 73) to a friend with whom he had been for a tour in Hardanger : "believe me, it is not very pleasant to see the world from its October-side, and yet, ridiculous as it may appear, there has been a time when I desired nothing more" — da jeg intet ønsked heller! I have had a b u r n i n g desire for a great sorrow, nay, almost p r a y e d for one to fill up my existence completely and give life some contents. It was silly, it has cost me much to get out of this, however, its recollection remains. — Jeg har brændende længtes

---

1, 159; 3, 163; F, 417; M, 250; 14, 148; J, 259; 16, 148.

efter, ja næsten b e d t om en stor Sorg, som ret kunde udfylde tilværelsen, give livet indhold. Det var tåbeligt, jeg har kæmpet mig ud at dette stadium, dog bliver der altid en mindelse tilbage."

One thinks of a German Poet who "out of his greatest sorrows made his smallest songs" (Freiligrath) or one for whom "Der Schmerz ist die Geburt der höheren Naturen" (Tieck) or of Bjørnson's manly: be glad when danger equals your strength — vær g l a d naar faren veier hver evne som du eier (I en tung Stund) — where a weaker nature would be glad if his strength on the contrary could only meet the danger, i. e. have as little of it as possible and may be inclined to doubt whether it was really so very "silly" as Ibsen thought. The sentiment of the Certaminis gaudia is after all so intensely human in s t r o n g characters that we may well ask if by it Ibsen did not prove what metal he was made of. However this be, — the "recollection of it remained" as he said and it was destined to play a very important part in his work. "Give me an agony, a gigantic crushing sorrow", Falk exclaims in the Comedy of Love (F, II, 129: Skaf mig en kval, en knusende, en kæmpesorg); it is interesting to compare this final passage to the first working out (Svanhild, Eft. Skr. I; cf. p. p. 453 and 454) where Falk does not yet know what he wants: happiness or sorrow. And just like Falk asks for the anguish because he feels that this will make him a poet, so Jatgejr in Ibsen's next play: "got the gift of sorrow and then he was a poet "(Kongsemnerne, F, II, p. p. 410, 411 etc.: fik sorgens gave og da var han skald). And ever so much later he makes Fru Linde complain that her husband left her nothing "not even a great sorrow or a big want to think of" (Dukkehjem, F, VI, 199: ikke en gang en sorg eller et savn at bære paa). Mr. Henning Kehler explaining how as he expresses it, "Sorrow is paradoxically attached to a feeling of happi-

---

1, 160; 3, 164; F, 417; M, 250; 14, 149; J, 259; 16, 149.

ness", compares Brand's more serious: Sejrens sejr er alt at miste, Tabets *alt* din Vinding skabte, Evigt ejes kun det tabte! [1])

But when here we see Peer Gynt ask for this great sorrow under súch circumstances of súch a species of Eve-hood, it does not require a very lively imagination to see in our minds's eye, a smile play round a usually very severe mouth.

2842.   gjennem Ørken. across the desert.

Dr. Western observes that Ibsen here uses, perhaps as a mere slip only, Ørken as the definite form of Ørk whereas the only current form is of course (en) Ørkèn, def. Ørkenen, which Ibsen of course knows too; cf. n. to l.l. 2599, 600.

2843.   Naa, saa skulde da ogsaa— — —!

Well, now, may I be— — —!

We must supply some such words as: fanden ta dig! The aposiopesis, often as here a sort of euphemism (Nyrop, Dania, VI, 199), may be compared to one like: så gid da også... (ib.).

2846.   Der ligger Tyrken, og her staar jeg! —

There lies the Turk, then, and here stand I!

Compare En gammeldags Juleaften (ed. '12 p. 66): Presten stod paa prækestolen;... som han var bedst inde i præken, gjorde han et rundkast midt ned i Kirken — han var bekjendt som en rask kar — saa samarien for paa én kant og kraven paa en anden. "Der ligger presten og her er jeg" sa han m e d e t m u n d h e l d (so the saying is expressly recognised to be proverbial) han hadde og la os nu faa en springdans"! And Mr. Krogvig adds: Lignende historier og dette samme ordtaket er meget utbredt og henføres paa forskjellige steder til forskjellige navngivne præster, f. eks. paa Frederikshaldskanten til præsten Aschehoug som skal

---

[1]) See Karl Larsen, Episke Brand, l. 672 and p.p. 228, 233; Fr. Ording, Henrik Ibsens Kærlighedens Kom., J. W. Cappelens Forlag, Kristiania, (1914), p. 61; J. Collin, l.l. p. 150; Eft. Skr. I. p.p. LXXVII; III, p. 300; H. Kehler, Edda, 1915, IV, p. 211.

1, 161; 3, 165; F, 418; M, 250; 14, 149; J, 260; 16, 149.

ha været officer før han blev præst og som var en ivrig kortspiller, " — the latter reminds one of a clergyman somewhere across the herring-pond, who asked his audience to sing of psalm 55, verses 8, 9, 10, jack queen ... etc!

2848, 49.   i Klæderne baaret,
og ej, som man siger, i Kjødet skaaret. —
                     a matter of clothes
and not as the saying goes, bred in the bone.

Compare Mau, I, 541: Det er ham i Kjødet baaret og ej i Klæder skaaret, with variant readings: i Benene baaret, etc. The inversion is of course Peer's!

2853.   støtte sin Færd til Lov og Moral.
to base all one's dealing on law and morality.

The study of U often reveals an interesting search for the right word. Here Ibsen had written first: Støtte sin Færd till Lov og Moral. He first added men before støtte, but crossed it out again afterwards. Færd was crossed out, sin changed into sit and Levnet written above Færd; Levnet was then changed into Liv, so that the final version of U runs: Støtte sit Liv til Lov og Moral. But in R, he returned to the first reading of U.

2855.   Tale ved Graven. A speech at one's grave-side.
Compare l.l. 3774 seqq. about this "beautiful christian custom".

2857.   paa et hængende Haar. on the very verge of.
Compare: Det var jo på et hængende hår at han havde trukket mig med i undergangen (First draft of the Wild Duck; Eft. Skr. III, 466).

2859.   Jeg vil være et Trold ifald, etc.
            May I be a troll if, etc.

Peer is so much under the influence of his life's experience with the hill-monsters, one might suppose, that he thinks of nothing else and instead of some such imprecation as I may be hanged, jeg lar mig hænge, det

var da fan, he uses the present one. But there is a special
flavour in the word that should not be lost upon the
student. "Det var troll" means: that is very remarkable, the devil is in it; cf. det var troll, det da! sa haug-
kjærringen (No. Folkeev. ed. 1912, p. 222); den her
Sjødalselven er no e troll te Elv de = en fandens en;
Aasen, Prøver af Landsmaalet², p. 17; but the proof
that trold is often used as here = the devil or a similar
word in imprecations is furnished by the expression "der
er trold i nogen (or: noget)"; cf. Feilberg, den fattige
mands Snaps, Dania, VI, 31: at der bogstavelig er trold
i øllet; det løyp ofta troll i ord, Aasen, No. ordspr., p. p.
12, 27. And in Bygmester Solness, Hilda uses an expression (S. V. IX, 97) which is very suggestive in this
respect: Så er der vel — så'n lidt trold i Dem også da ?
(in Dutch: iets van den du(i)vel in je hebben) and which
reminds us of the story concerning the little boy (supra
note to l. 1110, p. 115), who said: "Jeg vil kradse deres
Øjne ud, thi der er ogsaa trold i mig, du!" We see the
troll-cat in our mind's eye.

On the gender of the word trold, neuter in Norwegian,
communis generis in Danish, see T. C. §53; S. I. S. p. 156,
195 and Seip, Wergeland p. 115 where several other
cases will be found mentioned.

As any student of folklore will know, the word is used
quite generally in connection with almost any sort of
supernatural being of Scandinavian mythology; cf.
Paul's Grundries, I¹, p. 1020 = III³, p. 274. Sievers (ib.
p. 300) connects it with the verb trudan, to tread,
which little detail might not have been mentioned here
if it was not deemed necessary to sound a note of warning in connection with the words by which the etymological indication is followed up: c o n s e q u e n t-
l y an incubus — "also ein Druckgeist"! Here things
are turned topsy-turvy. The form-connection of a word
can only be determined when the study of realities in-

1, 161; 3, 165; F, 419; M, 251; 14, 150; J, 260; 16, 150.

volved has shown the way. And a casual resemblance should not be made to force the folklorist to interpret it in any special way.

2861. det fik Slut! that's done.

Compare Seip, Wergeland, p. 52 on Slut for slutning.

2871. man flux er Bét. you throw up the game.

The Low-german translator misunderstands the word when he explains it as beet hebben (to get hold of), an der Angel haben, bét (as well as labet, where the article is also incorporated; cf. Feilberg in v.) is from French bête and Spanish puesta (cf. Falk og Torp in v. and Ordbog over gadesproget, p. 32) and taken from L'hombrespillets Terminologi, Dania III, 27; cf. Wergeland's Kringla, cf. Efterspil: Nu kan jeg sige Pas: jeg vandt jo min Misère.... Du burde været b ê t e. (S. S. VI, 482); and figuratively: I Kirkehistorie satte jeg.... Dietrichson Beet (J. Moes Breve, ed. Krogvig, p. 172. Compare Dutch beest zijn; Stoett, n° 164.

2877. ved at svinge og svanse! by capering and prancing.

No doubt a reminiscence of the Dovrëhall-scene: Prøv nu, hvor fint du kan svanse og svinge! (l.1082).

2887. ingen Besvær. no difficulty.

Compare T. C. § 125.

2896. der staar i et aandrigt Skrift. in some luminous work.

Aandrigt which the Archers translate by luminous, is not literally spiritual (as they note on p. 176) so much as clever, brilliant, spirit*ed*. This 'brilliant pamphlet' is of course Peer's own utterance, *ante* l. 1239.

2898. Pengene.

Changed in some editions into Pungen! cf. T. C. § 102.

2900. (Om jeg skrev mit Levnet).... till.... Efterfølgelse? (Shall I write my life) for imitation?

These two lines are not in U, whose next line begins: Lad se, jeg har Tiden, etc. So the delightful idea of making Peer set up his life for imitation was one of these happy afterthoughts a close study of the Ibsen-text reveals so many of; compare Koht's remarks in the Eft. Skr. I, p.p. LI,LII [1]).

2904.   I Sandhed, ja; det er noget for mig!

Aye, sure enough, *that* is the thing for me!

Compare J. Collin's Henrik Ibsen, p. 323: Vom ruhigen Port aus als Zuschauer die Grossthaten der Vorzeit an sich voi überziehen zu lassen, das behagt dem Schwächling besser als sich selbst im Streit der eignen Zeit einzusetzen", *etc.* See also ib. p. 329.

2905.   Krøniker læste jeg. Legends I read.

Messrs Archers' translation is technically correct, but the point is lost, Peer's words that he reads "chronicles" being the very expression he wants to make believe (himself in the first place)! that he was keeping up that "branch of science" — the fact is that the word means not only "gests" (as Brynildsen translates it) but also = fairy tales = eventyr! Compare Olaf Liljekrans (S. V. F. X. p. 187) as quoted in the note to l. 1020 supra.

2914,15. se Verdensepoker slaa ud af det smaa;....

jeg vil skumme Historiens Fløde.

see world-epochs grow from their trifling seeds....

I will skim off the cream of history.

In Adam Homo, we find practically the same expression used when his father asks the hero (i spøg!): "om du, som Doctor, medens andre lide, vil skumme Livets Fløde først og sidst" (end of 3d Song) and in another of Ibsen's sources we read: Ufortrøden i Historien jeg var Og har altid Skummet Fløden af Begivenhedens Kar, which comes even closer to our expression (En Sjæl efter Døden, p. 183), — cf. Mau, I, 39: han skummede Fløden, ɔ: tog det bedste. Besides English to take

---

[1]) Jørgen Tesman's silly: Tænk det, mentioned there as one of the cases is not quite in point, as the words are mentioned if not quite so often in the first draft too; cf. Eft. Skr. III, 233, which Henning Kehler, Edda 1916, p. 89 has also overlooked.

---

the cream off a thing, or skim off as the Archers have it, we may compare German: den Rahm abschöpfen, Dutch: 't potje is geschuimd, cf. Stoett, n° 1975.

2916.   Jeg faar se at faa Tag i et Bind af Becker.
          I must try to get hold of a volume of Becker.

U read first: Jeg faar skaffe mig et Exemplar af Becker, which is certainly rhytmically far from ideal! Ibsen changed it into: Jeg faar se at faa Tag i et Exemplar af Becker, — hardly superior. Then, evidently thinking this line too long, Ibsen wrote: i et Bind a (this a — for af? — crossed out) over et Exemplar (these two words crossed out too). The word fik written (later on, as evidenced by the ink) over the line too as well as the fact that "se at faa Tag i" are placed between brackets, shows that Ibsen thought of an other form, perhaps: at jeg fik Tag i, which would not be open to the objection that faar se at faa is a not over-harmonious jingle.

A correspondent, when discussing Peer's want of culture (cf. T. C. § 38) quoted as another case in point the present line: Peer's wish to get hold of Becker, which my Homeric friend thought was characteristic of Peer Gynt, "who of course meant a volume of Bæde-ker"! As others may conceivably fall into the same error, it is perhaps as well to add that Becker's Weltgeschich-te (K. F. Becker, 1777—1806; the work published for the first time from 1801—1809) had been translated in-to Danish repeatedly, e. g. 1851 and following years; so Ibsen may have had either one of the numerous German editions or one of the Danish ones in his mind. Truly, Peer's methods are not yet perfect!

2921.   After this line U had the following three, crossed out:
          Og desforuden, al positiv Viden
              blir mer eller mindre aflæggs med Tiden —
          Og alle de andre Betingelser har jeg,
and then follows Hvor løftende dog as in R., l.2922. It will be noticed that the last line ends in a comma and

---

1, 163; 3, 167; F, 420; M. 252; 14, 152; J, 262; 16, 152.

as the next line in this Ms. has a capital H in Hvor, it is clear that the three lines were crossed out by Ibsen directly after writing them and that Hvor løftende etc. is meant to follow line 2922 immediately. Hence it is not certain that the two lines written perpendicularly in the margin to this passage:

og det som jeg har at bringe for Dagen
er jo nettopp det gyntske Syn paa Sagen.,

belong here, what the printing them after the three preceding ones in Eft. Skr. II, p. 107 seems to indicate, for if the poet had meant them to come instead of those, crossed out as we had to conclude b e f o r e he wrote Hvor *etc.*, he would have written them u n d e r the three crossed out. But as they certainly fit very well there (although he crossed them out too), we may perhaps assume that he substituted them later on and forgot to change the full stop behind originalest into a comma. —

2924.   stille bevæget. with quiet emotion.

This stage direction is not in U; so this bit of fun that Peer pokes at himself Ibsen added afterwards. This Ibsen's creations often do (cf. e. g. Wörner, II, 323, supra n. to l. 2319) just as their creator more than once makes fun of others. When e.g. Kystron in Emperor and Galilæan (S. V. V., p. 449) in the midst of a battle gives expression to his regret that his paper on "Quietness of Mind in circumstances of difficulty" is not yet ready, we cannot help thinking that this little trait was meant to show how ridiculous Julian himself was, who was always flourishing *his* papers in the face of friend and enemy, cf. the play passim; e.g. F. p. 458. And Ibsen does not stop at this, he often makes fun of himself, sometimes quite openly; han skjemtar med sig sjølv likesom, as Dølen (Skrifter i Utval, I, 413) admits in his own case. See Wörner, II, 8 (Ibsen and Dr. Stockman) and Georg Brandes (l.l. p.p. 145, 146) who speaks of den cynisk-godmodige Relling, 'another (viz. Gregers) humoristic incarnation of Ibsen himself". And see a passage in S. V. Vol X, where Ibsen adduces the fact of having made fun of himself as an attenuating circumstance *in re* his jokes at the Germans; cf. n. to l. 3045.

2940.   Samtiden er ej en Skosaale værd.

The present is not worth so much as a shoe-sole.

In the tale of Prindsessen som ingen kunde maalbinde (cf. n. to l.4422), this very symbol of worthlessness comes to the fore, instrumental as it is in gaining the Princess for the Ashiepattle-hero of the story!

2945.   og Kvinderne, — det er en skrøbelig Slægt!

And women, — ah! they are a worthless crew!

In the scene with Anitra, Peer the prophet had given utterance to a similar sentiment concerning man: men, my child are a worthless crew (l. 2535: Mændene, Barn, er en skrøbelig Slægt), a splendid example of Peer's self-knowledge and self-irony. But here the words, if rightly understood in their context, are pathetic in the extreme! For at the moment that Peer has thus judged, or shall we say: spoken of her who was to save him, Ibsen opens a side-window as it were of his stage, shows us Solveig and makes us see how little truth there was in Peer's words.

The 'trick' is that of Macbeth to some extent, see the n. to l.2445 which, if the commentators had but understood it, would have saved them many a misunderstanding. Compare e.g. Count Prozor (p. 49) and especially Wörner who actually goes so far as to say that this constitutes ein dramatisch unfruchtbarer Gegensatz (I, p. 244), simply because the little intermezzo is one for the public and not for Peer Gynt himself. If J. Collin does not seem to see the (s.v.v.) Shakespearean connection of Solveig and the skrøbelig Slægt he fortunately sees at any rate an "ergreifendes Wirklich-

---

1, 164; 3, 168; F, 421; M, 253; 14, 153; J, 262; 16, 153.

keitsbild" in it. (l.l. p.p. 323, 4). Mr. Leroy Andrews (l.l. p. 234) compares this to the vision of Gretchen, — at the same time contrasting the two episodes: happy Solveig and guilty Gretchen.

2948. Solveig's song.

The germ of this song is perhaps to be found in a Swedish folksong; see Dr. Frederik Paasche, Gildet paa Solhaug, Kristiania, 1908, p. 15, as well as a paper by the same in Samtiden 1909, p. 651. —

2957. Ægypten. In Egypt.

An association of ideas between Norway that oldest of saga-lands living only on its recollection of a glorious past and Aegypt must have caused Ibsen, Stavnem thinks, to bring Peer to that latter country where so many memorials of the past make one dream of greatness gone: Naar Ibsen fører Peer Gynt til Aegypten kan dette skyldes en ideassociation mellem det gamle sagaland Norge som slaar sig til ro med en glansfuld fortidshistorie og Aegypten, ogsaa et gammelt rike, hvor hvert fortidsmindesmerke synes at drømme om svunden storhet. Der kan til en tid være tilfredsstillelse i drømme og digtende længsel; men der kræves dog altid en omsætning i daadkraftig handling. Men herhjemme var det likesom nationen — endog dens førere — trivedes bedst i fortidsmørket — "saganatten" (Think of Bjørnson's "Saganat som sænker drømme paa vor jord", who was however in full earnest when he wrote the line). And Professor Christen Collin has expressed a similar opinion in two remarkable papers (Samtiden Nov. 1913, p. 604 and Morgenbladet for 13 Nov. 1913; now both reprinted in his "Det geniale Menneske"); cf. n. to l.2995. He reminds us moreover of the fact that just before Peer Gynt was written, the University of Kristiania had received a valuable collection of Aegyptian antiquities as well as an Aegyptolog*ist* in the person of a young scholar who was afterwards to accompany Ibsen on his grand tour to that very country, Prof. Lieblein (Breve, I, 240, 330).

And the voices to praise the past were not few. Maurits Hansen had called out: Op! sværger: Norges Søn skal ei vanslægte! And the following commentary on the motif from one of Jørgen Moes letters (Krogvig, Fra det nationale Gjennembruds Tid, 1915, p. 83) is eloquently illustrative of the feelings that may have led to Ibsen's equation. It is not quoted here by any means as being unique, on the contrary Ibsen himself (think of Brand, De Medskyldige!) and contemporary literature are full of such utterances, but merely because it is perhaps less known and certainly typical in this respect.

End staar Dovre, end hæver det kneisende sin snebedækkede Spidse mod Skyerne; med uforandret Kraft, med Oldtidens Vælde styrter end Sarpen ned ad Norges Klipper;.... kun Sagnet have vi tilbage af Norges fordums Frihed, Hæder og Held; kun et svagt Billede have Skjaldene levnet os af vore Fædres Kjækhed, af deres saa glimrende Bedrifter: O! gid dog Saga ogsaa udslettet disse sidste Træk, disse svage Levninger af Oldtidens tappre Asaæt, paa det at sildigere Slægter ikke med Afskye skulle fremsætte Nordmændene som et afskrækkende Exempel paa i hvor høi Grad Efterkommere kunne udarte fra deres Forfædres Kjækhed!"

For Ibsen however, the past promises an equally glorious future: "Normændene er jo desuden et Fremtidsfolk, det vil sige et Folk, som af to Grunde trøstigt kan sove i Nuet og ligesaa trøstigt vil kunne sove i ethvert kommende Nutidsmoment; for det Første fordi vi har den historiske Visshed for at vore Forfædre har gjort et forsvarligt Dagværk, og for det Andet fordi vi er saa inderligt forvissede om, at vore Efterkommere engang vil vaagne til en stor Fremtidsmission...." Nyfundne

---

I, 165; 3, 169; F, 422; M, 253; 14, 154; J, 263; 16, 154.

Teaterartikler av Henrik Ibsen (1862), Morgenbladet, Aug. 1916.

2970.   ihærdig. patiently.

Compare S. I. S. p. 198: originally Swedish but now quite common and even v i a Ibsen now used in Danish.

Some such translation as energetically, doggedly would be better than the Archers' patiently.

2971.   sin vanlige Morgensang. its habitual dawn-song.

There would seem to be a contradiction between this line according to which Peer clearly e x p e c t s to hear a song and the words lower down (l.l. 2993, 3003) where he is quite astonished when it does come.

It may be as a correspondent suggests, that Peer's words about the "usual" morning song are merely a joke or a piece of irony: he does not really believe the truth of the story he has been told about the vocal capacities of the statue. So when he does hear a sound he naturally feels some astonishment; he continues to look upon it as a hallucination — "sansebedrag". —

This so-called Memnonstøtte as the name indicates was formerly connected with Memnon, the son of the Dawn, when the metallic sound produced in a way not fully explained, was interpreted to be the voice of Memnon hailing his mother Eos, but more recently the pillar has been connected with King Amenoph III of Egypt.

That is at least what Ibsen's friend and (in a way) biographer, J. Paulsen, tells us about it (Samtiden, 1909 p.p. 624 seqq.):

"I aaret 27 før Kristus faldt ved et jordskjælv den øverste del af denne Kolos til Jorden og fra da af og indtil Septimius' Severus' tid er det at støtten om morgenen kort efter solopgang skal ha givet en klang om hvis art det er vanskeligt at faa et rigtigt begreb, da selv besindige reisende som Strabo, der endog taler om at her mulig forelaa et bedrag, betegner lyden som en

---

1, 165; 3, 169; F, 422; M, 254; 14, 154; J, 263; 16, 154.

raslen eller susen, mens andre kalder den en tone, og
de mest modtagelige endog har troet at høre sang.

Da de misforstod det ægyptiske ord mennu (Paulsen
does not tell us what this word means), antog de den
klingende støtte for et billed af den homeriske helt
Memnon, en søn af Tithonos og Eos som ved Troja
faldt for Achilleus' haand. Siden dengang siger sagnet,
hilser hans billedstøtte hende med sagte klagesang hver
morgen, naar hun viser sig i østen og i sorgen over den
elskte søns tidlige heltedød væder hun statuens sten-
kinder med sine duggtaarer.

Moderne videnskabsmænd mener at de hemmelig-
hedsfulde toner, som enkelte har hørt, har en ganske
naturlig aarsag. Det er morgenvinden, i forening med
morgensolens brænden paa den om natten afkølede
meget porøse stenkolos som frembringer dem."

As early as 1855 (Eft. Skr. I, p. LXVIII) Ibsen had
made the statue's song give us an image of those "frase-
helte hvis frihedstale bare var læbeklang", when in a
17th of May prologue for his theatre at Bergen, he wrote
of how "selv den stirred, kold som Vintrens Fjælde
Med sjælløst Blik mod Østens Himmelrand. Saa stod
den Aar for Aar i sløve Drømme Thi kun fra Læben
monne Klange strømme. (ib. I, 135). Later on he mentioned "gubben Memnons brustne toner" once more (Ballonbrev, F, IV, 377) when Memnon accords an audience
to "norske normænd, som min ringhed og Peer Gynt",
and still later (p. 389) where in his antipathy to the
German régime he speaks of "Bismarck og de andre
gubber" (who) "vil, som Memnons søjlestubber sidde
sprød paa Sagastolen u d e n sang mod Morgensolen"
for the old man has his whims (et skaldenykke) and
holds his tongue. (See further the n. to l. 2995). Finally, although the passage is but distantly related to
our subject at most, I may mention that Bergsøe tells
us of a conversation he had with Ibsen at Ischia (l.l. p.

1, 165; 3, 169; F, 422; M, 254; 14, 154; J, 263; 16, 154.

162) and adds: Saaledes gik vi som to Memnonstøtter = silently. There can be little doubt that the image comes from Ibsen.

2977.   hængende Haver og Skjøger.

harlots and hanging gardens.

Some of the translators (Morgenstern, Mrs. Clant van der Mijll) draw the line at "skjøger" which they blushingly omit, thereby rendering the witticism in the next line pointless. To be sure, when Ibsen uses such a word — Ibsen who with a "bashfulness of the soul" turned away from every thing sexually repulsive [1] —, the translators need not have tried to out-Herod Herod and omit it!

2995. Memnonstøttens sang. The Memnon-statue's song.

This passage has of late been commented on more than once. In a paper on Ibsen's Fremtidsdrøm, Prof. Christen Collin had given it as his opinion (Samtiden, 1906) that in this song we may look for Ibsen's innermost secret (inderste hemmelighed). The poet felt already he was to be the singer of a new "third empire", the theme later on of "Emperor and Galilæan", and in this song "som en ny tids morgenrøde hilsede han udsigten til en vældig social omvæltning". He thought that the state as such had had its time: "staten maa væk" and "der vil falde større hug end den: al religion vil falde. Hverken moralbegrebene eller kunstbegrebene har nogen evighed for sig." Collin thinks it certain (p. 487) that Ibsen was full of such a big romantic dream of a world-catastrophe "hvori gamle institutioner og ideer vilde ramle", all the time from 1862 till 1887 at least.

For this view Collin has been attacked, or at least met, first of all by Mr. Eitrem who (Samtiden, 1906, p.

---

[1] „Ibsen gik med en sjælelig blufærdighed.... afveien for alle seksuelle emner. Det erotiske element, der spiller en saa liden rolle i hans digtning traadte heller ikke frem i hans tale...." John Paulsen, Mine Erindringer, p. 19 and see a couple of remarks in Henning Kehler's study, Edda, 1916, p. 43. See the n. to l. 4504.

1, 166; 3, 170; F, 422; M, 254; 14, 154; J, 263; 16, 154.

591) points out in the first place that Ibsen knew not only of the usual interpretation of Memnon's song (n. to l. 2971) but that he had read the 13th book of Ovid's Metamorphoses, where Jove is represented as granting Memnon's mother's request to honour her fallen son and where the god changes the ashes of the dead Hero into birds that utter wild cries and fight each other. But — Ibsen does not really know the saga well, — the question: my birds, where do they slumber? is really a ridiculous question and Eitrem concludes that this "riddle" is not really one, that it is nothing but a satire against "turistmæssig overfladiskhed og videnskabeligt pedanteri" — and the "solution" of the riddle turns out to be that.... there is none! All this was but one of Ibsen's little jokes — a mystification of the public! [1])

This latter view does not seem likely to carry conviction. Is it not altogether too improbable that Ibsen really intended to 'do' ("at lure", the word is by Eitrem) his readers? No importance can be attached to the fact that the very words which Eitrem lays so much stress on (Hvor sover mine Fugle) did not come into the text until later on [2]) for the other commentators too make them the central point of their interpretation.

Chr. Collin came back to the question in his Morgen-

---

[1]) Det problem som denne mærkelige oldtidslevning stiller er altsaa alt andet end betydningsfuldt; det er *futilt* og *latterligt* som saa mange af de spørgsmaal der optog oldtidsforskernes opmerksomhed.... Spørgsmaalet er som sagt futilt og ikke værd en tanke. Det er altsaa bare vaas naar der tilføies:

Du maa dø eller raade.
Sangens gaade!

Det gjælder livet at faa dette ligegyldige spørgsmaal løst — det er en lebensfrage, som Begriffenfeldt vilde have udtrykt sig.

Mere var der altsaa ikke i skrinet med det rare i! Indfaldet er yderst originalt — om ikke netop blændende.... Gaaden er hverken dyb eller god — men god nok til at opfylde sin hensigt: at mystificere os og harcellere pedanteriet og løsningen er altsaa den, at — gaaden ingen sindrighed gjemmer"....

[2]) In U Ibsen had first written fang de Fugle; prøv at rade (sic) Sangens Gaade, but changed it there already into the present reading. Compare Ballonbrev, F, IV, 389: „Sfinxen på sin visdoms (Eft. Skr. I, 497: Stumheds) vagt, dødes af sin egen gåde."

1, 166; 3, 170; F, 423; M, 254; 14, 155; J, 264; 16, 155.

blad-paper (reprinted in "Det Geniale Menneske"). Casting his former interpretation overboard and silently passing by Eitrem's, he writes as follows: [1]

De foryngende Fugle som stiger syngende og stridende frem av Halvgudens Aske (inde i Gravhaugen) er Memnoniderne, antagelig opfattet som hans Aetlinger og Efterkommere. Hvor sover mine Fugle? Det vil si: hvor er nu de Aetlinger av en Kjæmpeslægt, som fornyer og forynger en stor Fortids Bedrifter med Heltedaad og Sang? Hvor er nutidens Memnonider? Sover de eller er de vaakne og rede til ny Kamp?

Memnonstøtten spør Peer Gynt, Repræsentanten for det norske Folks Undladelsessynder, Personifikationen av det Norge, som efter Ibsen's Mening i k k e hadde vist sig som Memnonider i 1864." Then comes the remark (cf. n. to l. 2957) why Ibsen sends Peer Gynt to Egypt, the analogy between the two countries and Collin continues:

Men av Gjenopvækkelsen av Fortidens Helteaand avhænger Folkets Skjæbne. Dets Visdom eller Videnskab er Dødsens, hvis den ikke kan tyde den Gaade.... Hvad hjælper al vor antikvariske Videnskab, hvis den ikke kan vise os, hvor Nutidens Kjæmper er at finde." And there is perhaps more in this than appears at first sight. Lieblein (cf. n. to l. 2957) had just reviewed Ibsen's Brand and called him a madman. And Collin shows how very probable it is that Ibsen "i dette Digt paa en maate avlægger Lieblein en kontravisit — i Aegypten! Memnonstøttens Sang er sandsynligvis et Led i Ibsens Svar.... til Lieblein med at la Støtten gjennem Peer Gynt spørge Minervas ugle (det norske Universitet med dets Arkeologer?) hvor Heltesønner nu er at finde i Norge? Kan Uglen ikke tyde den Gaade da fortjener dens Visdom ikke at leve.... Hvor sover mine Fugle?

---

[1] That Collin's interpretation clearly stands under the influence of the politics of the day need not necessarily speak against the correctness of his views but should here be recorded.

1, 166; 3, 170; F, 423; M, 254; 14, 155; J, 264; 16, 155.

Hvor er de Aetlinger av store Fædre.... hvor slumrer
nu Morgenrød-Gudindens Aet, Skaperne av en ny
Tids Morgenrøde?" [1])

Overlærer Stavnem agreeing with Chr. Collin who already in the Samtiden-paper had looked upon these
birds as being meant for the "foryngende fugle som en ny
tids daadkraftige, sangbare handlinger", adds that Ibsen seems to have thought of the bird Phoenix too, that
symbol of renovation of the old saga and quoting many
analogues in thought and expression from the poet's
own works, so full of "fugle-symbolik", Stavnem gives
it as his opinion that what must have attracted Ibsen
most in the Greek story was its account of the b a t-
t l i n g of the birds. For in the battle of the birds he
sees "en analogi til Menneskelivets Strid"; compare
the Boygscene, l.l. p. 105 seqq; the remarks should
be read in their entirety.

Finally, I quote from a private letter of Overlærer
Stavnem the following passage which gives an interesting supplement and may even to some seem to clinch
the argument by the parallels quoted: I Memnonsangen
er der mindelser fra Welhavens "Norges Dæmring". I
Memnonsangen uttaler digteren at hjemme i Norge
svang ingen fugl sig syngende mot himlen, naar solen
randt. Naar Ibsen sammenligner sine landsmænd med
sovende fugle kan han ha tænkt paa det sted i Norges
Dæmring hvor Welhaven utbryter: "Var her — mellem
Fuglene, hvis Vinger hænge, lidt Glæde ved et Vingepar,
der fløi!" Ibid. heter det at i Norge er der "intet Vingeslag, naar solen rinder". Hans landsmænd er en jord-
bunden, søvnig slægt mener digteren. Sml. Welhaven,
Samlede Skrifter, I s. 180 og s. 234.

And it may, to conclude this long note, just be worth
while to call attention (in addition to Mr. Leroy Andrews'

---

[1]) It should be recorded as the acme of the translator's art that Mr. Brons coolly
renders mine Fugle by mijn vule: dirty, lazy, here: 'schlau, gerieben' as he adds in
a note!

1, 166; 3, 170; F, 423; M, 254; 14, 155; J, 264; 16, 155.

parallels between Peer Gynt and the Faust) to the fact
that not only the sphinx but also the Stymphalidae,
the big birds killed by Hercules are in the Faust too; cf.
Faust II, the Classic Walpurgis-night.

3004.   Fortidsmusik. Music of the Past.

An allusion to Wagner's Zukunftsmusik? Already in
1864 Wagner was sufficiently "en évidence" to allow of
this interpretation for he had visited King Lewis of Bav-
aria and what is more to the point, his book on Music
and the Future had appeared as early as 1848 so that
Ibsen's public may be supposed to understand the joke.

3014.   snart gjennem Lorgnetten, snart gjennem den hule
Haand.

now through his eyeglass, now through his hollowed
hand.

In U, Peer looks at the sphinx through the eye-glass
only, so that the ,hollow hand' is an afterthought; it
may be a reminiscence of Paa Vidderne (S. V. F, IV,
352, 354). In Fruen fra Havet (Eft. Skr. III, 152) Bal-
lesen (this time l i t e r a l l y "til vinding for perspek-
tivet") looks at a picture "gennem den hule haand" too
(Cf. Wörner, II, 22).

The great sphinx is of course in Faust too (II, Classic
Walpurgis-night) where she says to Mephistopheles:
Sprich nur dich selbst aus, wird schon Räthsel sein.
Gran (No. Aandsliv), aptly calls Ibsen himself den store
sfinks, and that notwithstanding the fact that he had
been called Gert Westfaler in his youthful days on
which see the n. to l. 4415.

3016.   Skabilken. hobgoblin.

This translation is not without danger just here,
where the monstrous Memnon can hardly be thought to
resemble a tiny goblin; fright, monster may seem
more in keeping with the gentleman's dimensions, —
we must not forget that he reminded Peer of the Dovre-
gubbe, who surely cannot be supposed to be so little

(cf. n. to l. 1000) as to give Mrs. Clant van der Mijll the right to translate it here by Kabouterkoning. When in Lille Eyolf, the Rottejomfruen says: Å, allersødeste frue, vær da aldrig ræd for så 'nt et lidet skabilken, the 'sweetest of ladies' may t h i n k it a little monster, — the speaker's meaning would be best rendered by: the darling!

3019, 20. Han, Memnon, faldt det mig bagefter ind,
        ligned de saakaldte Dovregubber.
        That Memnon, it afterwards crossed my mind,
        was like the Old Men of the Dovrë, so called.

In U, Ibsen had first written: Memnonstøtten minded om Dovregubben, but he must have crossed this out at once before he even wrote the next line which first ran: minded mærkværdigt om Dovregubben, for this line in this form can only be the sequel of the preceding line as changed into: Han, Memnon, faldt det mig bagefter ind (minder mærkværdigt om Dovregubben) and then after this change giving us the line ending in i n d, Ibsen could write on: slig som den sad der stiv og stind med Enden planted paa Søjlestubben; for this (-stubben) the plural will be found substituted (cf. Ballonbrev, F, IV, 389: som Memnons Søjlestubber) and in connection with this: Dovregubber for the singular became necessary too; this it is that seems to have necessitated the change of: minder mærkværdigt om into ligned de saakaldte, as minder m. o. Dovregubber would of course have been too general a statement. The words "faldt det mig bagefter ind" show that a certain time is supposed to have elapsed between these two scenes.

As to the comparison itself, the Danish critic Clemens Petersen for whom Ibsen had such a respect and who revealed things in the Peer Gynt that Ibsen had not dreamt of (cf. n. to Den Fremmede Passager, l. 3499) had written as early as 1867: "Combinationer som den mellem Dovregubben og Memnonstøtten, eller den mel-

---

I, 167; 3, 171; F, 424; M, 255; 14, 156; J, 265; 16, 156.

lem Bøjgen og Sphinx, ere som Gaader. Det er ganske
sandt, at en Skikkelse som Bøjgen er kommen frem ved
den samme Proces i Folkelivet som Sphinxen men at
gjøre dem begge til blot forskjellige Udtryk for det
samme, at ville finde det samme Stof, de samme Natur-
indtryk og de samme Instincter i dem begge, lader sig
ikke gjøre uden ved vilkaarlig Omdannelse. Det er
Tankesvindel." This expression and other similar ones [1]
are pretty sharp and many a reader will think that Petersen was too severe for the young writer but he seems
to have written in unconscious prevision of a criticism
such as that by Mr. Ellis Roberts who goes in for
something too much akin to a scientific "equation" of
the Boyg and the Sphinx (cf. his Introduction, p. X).

3021.   stind. stiff.

Characteristically Norwegian (now used only of that
stiffness which is the result of too much eating; W.) in
Danish only literary and obsolete; compare: Soffi var i
hænderne saa stind, Da. Folkeviser, p. 60.

3023.   Men dette underlige Krydsningsdyr, etc.

But this most curious mongrel here, etc.

This and the following lines are full of reminiscences
of earlier passages in the play, Krydsningsdyr recalls of
course the Blandingskræ of l. 1191, the bytting we have
had in l. 418 and of course more especially Peer's recollection of his meeting with the Boyg, which rationalistic
as Peer prides himself upon being (Stavnem), he now
tries to explain away as a dream in high fever (n. to
l. 3029) — Count Prozor even goes so far as to make him
lie in bed (ib. p. 166: j'étais au lit!) and it is difficult to
understand how the Archers can make this utterance
the key to the Boyg's primary significance; Introd.
p. XIV, n.

---

[1] Such as when Petersen speaks of Ibsen's ,overgreb': „Derimod gjør han et
Overgreb og flytter paa flere Punkter fra det symbolske ud i det blot eventyrlige
naar han lader Dovregubbens datter føde Peer Gynt et Barn og siden gifter hende
med Thrond i Valfjeldet" and then follows the passage quoted.

1, 167; 3, 171, F, 424; M, 255; 14, 156; J, 265; 16, 156.

3028.   i Skallen. the skull.

As a matter of fact, Peer does not smite the Bøyg on the skull at all, neither here in the play where it is Solveig who overcomes him, nor in the story where Peer shoots him, but that is one of Peer's amiable failings of memory.

How far the exigencies of the rhyme can bring a translator at bay is instanced by Passarge, who here introduces the adjective ("mit) e i s e r n e m (Schädel")!

3029.   jeg laa i Feber. I lay in fever.

This is of course the easiest way out of the difficulty of accounting for incomprehensible experiences, — oh, well it was a dream, — with which a rationalistic mind brushes them all aside. Thus in Aladdin, when Gulnare misses her beloved, she concludes (III, Sultanens Harem): var ei det hele Syn en Feberdrøm?, — and it is not always possible to show by tangible arguments that there was some reality behind it as when "somliga inbilla sig, att gubben har drømt, allt, det där, m e n d e n   s ø n d e r r i v n a   t r ø j a n   v i t t n a d e att han varit ilag med gastarne", of which Hermelin (Sägner ock Folktro p. 71) tells. Here (see n. to l.l. 1176, 1217 and 3023) Peer's utterances may be supposed to show that he was of this rationalistic turn of mind.

3034.   Ja saa da, Bøjg. Ay, so that's it, Boyg.

Typically colloquial Norwegian, which it is a delight to find in this play otherwise too much imbued with stiff Dano-Norwegian.

3040.   Ekkoet bryder paa Tydsk! Echo answers in German!

U had first: Et eccho som svarer paa Tydsk! which Ibsen changed into: Hvad! Ecchoet svarer paa Tydsk! And of t h i s the Archers' 'answers' would of course be the correct translation. But not of the characteristic "bryder paa" which it is interesting to observe did not make its appearance until Ibsen rewrote U in R. And 'bryte paa' is really a splendid find! For, don 't you

---

1, 167; 3, 171; F, 424; M, 255; 14, 156; J, 265; 16, 156.

see, Peer, who thinks he knows his modern languages, condescends to remark that although there is an accent of course, the unknown person's German is "not at all bad" for a foreigner; and then when it turns out to b e German: Hullo! it (! the echo) it actually speaks the language very well indeed; Peer can even recognise the Berlin dialect in the three words: "Wer bist du?" For "bryte paa Tydsk" means first of all, more generally: to mix up the language in question with German and secondly, simply: to speak with a German accent.

3045.   Begriffenfeldt.

That this is a speaking name cannot be doubted. For, although in the text of the first draft itself, he bears the same name, in the elaborately written list of dramatis personae of U, he is curiously enough called Frasenfelt and that has no doubt its reason! When we come to think of it, it must strike one that, whereas Begriffen-f e l d t necessarily points to p l e n t y of c o n-c e p t s — Count Prozor thinks the word might with advantage be replaced on the French Stage by Conception-arius [1]), — Frasenfelt on the contrary suggests in the bearer quite a *field* full of the flowers of rhetoric, a superfluity of good worts, good cabbage! Students of Ibsen's first drafts will have noticed how very often Ibsen changes the name of his personages — in the midst of a dialogue sometimes, cf. Eft. Skr. I, p. XXXII seqq., often clearly because the name would be too transparent, too cruel for the victims aimed at. The supposition will therefore not appear too bold that Ibsen, when writing Frasenfelt, in reality may have had in mind certain Fra-senhelte, just as in Begriffenfeldt there may have been the least little by-tone of the man who w a n t s con-cepts, for "eben wo B e g r i f f e f e h l e n, da stellt

---

[1]) Compare his translation, p. 166. In his monograph (p. 44) he tells us that if Ibsen had written his Peer Gynt in our days, he might have been supposed to have a bout in Begriffenfeldt with his own commentators, — of which I suppose Prozor is one!

---

zur rechten Zeit ein Wort sich ein" as Goethe had told him, and such a word would needs be a 'phrase'. Compare Ibsen's sermon on the t h i n g freedom as distinct from the w o r d in 1855: Og vi — begeistres af det smukke Ord, som Øiet sløver og som Tanken matter; Vi prise O r d e t høit og tusindmundet, men har dets rette Mening vi udgrundet?

And who w a s the victim of this attack? If we remember that a year or two after Peer Gynt, in his famous Ballonbrev (about which more anon), he spoke of the "heavy phrase-heroes" (svære.... Floskelhelte) that he seems to have met too many of in Dresden, we have no difficulty in seeing that the adjective omitted must refer to the nation whose "Sieges-Rausch" Ibsen with his strong Danish sympathies could ill digest, and in the Floskelhelte of 1870, we find a pretty clear echo of the Frasenfelte of 1867. And we are not astonished therefore to be told that "man so a l l g e m e i n (in Dr. v. Begriffenfeldt) eine Verspottung des Deutschen Gelehrten erblickt hat", Dr. Weininger, 1.1. p. 9 n. [1]. Surely, when we remember that in Abraham Lincolns Mord (1865), Ibsen had amiably spoken of Germany as "the land of a thousand lies" (F, IV, 360) as he was later on (in the Ballonbrev of 1870) to give vent to quite a little collection of anti-German sentiments [2]), we cannot wonder at the fact that the Germans recognised them-

---

[1]) Weininger thinks that Begriffenfeldt „übrigens mehr ist als eine blosse Karikatur. Denn er erkennt sehr wohl die ganze Hohlheit des Gyntschen selbst und weiss wo Peer's Kaisertum einzig Geltung hat.... im Irrenhause". Did Dr. Weininger really not see that Begriffenfeldt is himself as mad as a march-hare, seeing that he takes him so seriously?

[2]) jeg *vil*, men på anti-preussisk måde; ej i kraft af ret for nåde; tyske floskelhelte, Wacht am Rhein som kaldes Sang, denne klamme grav; en skok olden — eller militære rovdyr, and see ib. his contempt for dagens mænd, disse Fritzer, Blumenthaler, *etc.* His antipathy to the Germans was one of the tributary streams to his attitude in the question of Norwegian *versus* Danish (n. to l. 3179) Danish was too full of German; cf. Edda, I, 153: Du danske mand.... du kvad om dine sønners død, men tysk var kvadets gang, og tysk var dine døttres graad som dine skaldes sang...."

---

selves here and that one of them took him to task in the in the columns of a German weekly "Im neuen Reich"; cf. F, IV, p. XVI and Karl Larsen, Den Episke Brand, p. 230 seqq. It is as Larsen puts it (l.l.) "advokatorisk holdt"; like a certain famous heroine of Shakespeare's he protests slightly too much perhaps and for the un-biassed reader it does not take away the impression that at that moment, Ibsen's feelings were anti-German. Vilhelm Bergsøe tells us more than once in so many words (H. Ibsen paa Ischia, p.p. 236 and 306) that Ibsen h a t e d the Germans, so much so that he at one time cut the Scandinavian club in Rome because, his pro-test notwithstanding, they had accepted an invitation by the German club. But if we cannot but conclude from Bergsøe's words that Ibsen did harbour such a feeling of hatred, it should be added what all points to, that he did not hate a l l the Germans, not the Ger-ma*n*s, but the German, i. e. the then so typical victory-blatant phrase-monger as he considered it. If with all their faults he had not also loved them still a little, he would not have remained there "within daily earshot of sentiments inexpressibly repugnant to him" (Gosse, Northern Studies, 1879), the air around him would have been too thick for him to breathe and he would not have given his only son a thorough German education. He would have left "the land of lies" and returned home or gone on to his beloved Italy. Moreover in a letter to the German Sieboldt (his Brand-translator) Ibsen says (Samtiden, 1908, p. 94) that "striden er ført på en meget ridderlig måde, den forklaring jeg har givet af mit Standpunkt har man fundet tilfredsstillende" and he recognises how he has changed his mind a good deal during his long stay in Germany.

Anders Krogvig, although admitting (in a private letter) that Begriffenfeldt is here the representative of "abstract German science" seems to think that Ibsen's

---

1, 168; 3, 172; F, 425; M, 255; 14, 157; J, 265; 16, 157.

attack is directed more at its Kristiania epigones than at the Germans themselves. "Tysk aandsliv slik som det den gang (i 1850 og 60-aarene) gik igjen hos epigonerne ved Kristiania-Universitetet gjorde at det for de unge dengang stod som det uttrykte billede paa pedanteri og gold snusfornuft. Dette indtryk har Ibsen søkt at gi ut-tryk for i navnet Begriffenfeldt, som, især for den tids norske læsere har været meget talende." And, objecting that Begriffenfeldt "is no phrase-hero at all" rejects my suggestion that the name should "smack" of Begriffen-'fehlt'. Of course, Begriffenfeldt as we know him, has nothing essential of the phrasemonger in him but that may have been the very reason why Ibsen substituted another word, even if any one should take it that Be-griffen f e l d t expresses better what he must be sup-posed to be (and I for one do not think so) I submit that at any rate Begriffen*fehlt* would have expressed his es-sential quality as well if not better.

As to the name Frasenfelt, was the name perhaps suggested by Wergelands "Blasenfeldt, en afsindig Re-daktør af et stort Blad"? (Vinægers Fjeldæventyr; cf. S. S. Wergeland, vol. VI, p. 578: Udenfor en Daare-kiste, Blasenfeldt med en Papirkrands om Hovedet; infra n. to l. 3345; the editor in question must have been Stabell of the Morgenblad). This question suggested itself to my mind when reading Herman Jæger's Werge-landiana (Edda, I, p. 139) but as this story of the "Asin-æum" dates from 1841 I did not consider it further, — only when in D. A. Seip's paper ib. p. 154 I read of the various circumstances that point to Ibsen's s t u d y of Wergeland and especially the farces (cf. Samtiden, 1913, p. 572) the supposition gained in likelihood. Surely when in Chr. Collin's paper Det geniale Menneske (Edda p. 102 and his book p. 131) we read that "rig-dommen paa hjemførte og fra hjemlandet hentede liter-ære og andre værdier i Peer Gynt er langt lettere at faa

---

1, 168; 3, 172; F, 425; M, 255; 14, 157; J, 265; 16, 157.

øie paa" than the "Kulturværdier" in such an apparently simple little sketch as Bjørnstjerne Bjørnson's Synnøve Solbakken, we can only conclude that these latter ones must be hidden away very carefully indeed and that it is therefore from the remotest little corners they may have to be brought to light. (Add.)

3063. Peer Gynt! Allegorisk! Det var at vente. —
Peer Gynt? Det vil sige: det ubekjendte, —
Peer Gynt! Allegoric! I might have foreseen it....
That must clearly imply: The unknown.

To us, who are not of the learned "Academy" Peer is to become a member of, there is nothing allegoric in the name. So we can only conclude that it is Begriffenfeldt's want of the very concepts his name is so full of, that causes him to see things of which the soberminded man does not know. A colleague of the German savant Dr. Phil. von Begriffenfeldt, Dr. v. Weininger has imagined that he found there was so little "gravitation" in the n a m e Gynt. (Ueber die letzten Dinge, p. 10, n.). "Hat man wohl beachtet was für einen Namen Ibsen für seinen Helden gewählt hat? Peer Gynt! Wie wenig Gravitation liegt doch darin! Dieser Name ist wie ein Gummibal der immer wieder von der Erde aufspringt". As if Ibsen had made up the name! Still, phonetically the observation is very interesting, especially if we remember that in Norwegian the word is pronounced [jynt] not [gynt] which, however infinitesimal the difference, is slightly more substantial. [1] As to what Gynt, as a surname, better: a nickname, means or meant, we have not got further than what Ross tells us (p. 286) who connects it with gynta, furte, be sour and sulky, easily hurt *etc*. This does not throw a very favourable light on the young man who if we may trust tradition (cf. Sandvig's account in his book on his Sam-

---

[1] Although at present under literary influence, Danish or possibly even German as Prof. Storm once suggested, the name of the drama is often pronounced with a hard g.

1, 170; 3, 174; F, 426; M, 256; 14, 158; J, 266; 16, 158.

linger at Lillehammer) did not marry or as he expresses
it, has become in real life as little as in the play "a pack-
camel for others' woe and others' weal".

3088. de halvfjerdsindstyve Fortolkeres Kreds;
den er nylig forøget med hundred og treds —
the group of Interpreters three score and ten;
it's been lately increased by a hundred and sixty.

This as the Archers note (p. 185) is "understood to
refer to the authors of the Greek version of the Old Tes-
tament, known as the Septuagint". But what about the
hundred and sixty new interpreters? The Archers hon-
estly admit that they cannot account for it. Mr. Eitrem (Samtiden, 1906, p. 596 asks: Det skulde vel ikke
være et eller andet nystiftet videnskabsselskab som her
er pegt fingre ad?, as if this were the only conclusion
from the Archers' suggestion. Mr. Ellis Roberts (p. 250)
thinks that they are "merely a round number for the
languages into which the bible has been translated since
the Greek version", but would in that case Ibsen have
written that their number had l a t e l y been increased
in this way? (nylig; curiously enough, U has actually
s i d e n, since, which would fit Mr. Ellis Roberts' theory!) Passarge does not translate it at all which is an
easy way of the difficulty and preferable to the crime
of Count Prozor and Mrs. Clant van der Mijll who, confounding treds with tre, lead the investigator astray
by calmly rendering it: cent trois (p. 170) and honderd
en drie (p. 413)! Mr. Eitrem (l.l.) has his panacea at
hand: he explains this too (n. to l. 2995) as one of Ibsen's mystifications of his readers and enjoys a hearty
laugh at Messrs. Archers' expense, — whose "honest
doubt" I fancy, many will continue to share.

I cannot solve the riddle myself but wish to point
out that "for de 70 fortolkeres Skyld" almost seems to
have been, if not proverbial, at least a standing expression. Compare what Hartvig Lassen, the editor of Werge-

land's Samlede Skrifter (vol. VI, p. 133; 1853) remarks: Den Mand hvis Navn jeg her har udeladt opfordrede i "nyeste Skilderi af Kristiania og Stockholm" for 24 Aug. 1829 Wergeland til "for de 70 fortolkeres Skyld" at forklare hvad der mentes med dette sidehug til hans Forfattervirksomhed," — a hint which absence of books prevents me from following up. Perhaps the person meant is the Dahl Gjessing, Prof. Seip speaks of in a paper, Samtiden, 1913, p. 574. At any rate Seip there explains de "hundred og treds" as referring to the numerous attacks that Ibsen's Brand had called forth in 1866 and whose absurdity (of which he gives splendid examples; we shall see one lower down in the n. to l. 3179) seems fully to justify Ibsen when in his turn, he gives these "interpreters" a place in a lunatic-asylum.

As for the form tre(d)s instead of sexti, it was a matter of course that Ibsen used the Danish form (S. I. S. p. 179, 180); "det er jo først i den sidste Mandsalder at de norske (former) er blevne almindelige i det sydlige og østlige Norge", and cf. Seip, Wergeland, p. 148. To a Norwegian, Danish halvfems = 90, might suggest: femti = 50. It may be interesting to add not only that sexti also occurs in Danish (I have seen a receipt from a Copenhagen firm for "sexti Kroner"; and the word is found e. g. in the Danish ordb. f. Folket without any note restricting its use) but that traces of this use of counting by scores (originally Celtic? cf. Dania, II, 185; Feilberg III, p. 432: snes; 916: tyve) are also met with in Norwegian; cf. Kleiven, I gamle daagaa, p. 118: ho va sotten aar paa fjorde Tjuge = 77, and cf. Aasen in v. Tjug.

3091.   Mikkel, Schlingelberg, Schafmann, Fuchs.

When one has to choose a name of fiction, even under circumstances of apparently the greatest liberty of choice imaginable, one is apt to be guided, consciously

---

or unconsciously by reminiscences, sometimes very vague and remote, of names one has recently had to do with; in other words: there is a *reason* for the choice of the apparently most *un*reasonable, impossible names. So here one is led to ask if Ibsen had perhaps among his circle of acquaintance in München some whose names may have suggested the ones used. A Norwegian correspondent gives it as his opinion that these names which he thinks have been made up by Ibsen, "sound in a Norwegian ear as giving expression to all that is less sympathetic in the German. German names on the whole often make a comic impression on Scandinavians."

It should be added that the-*berg* of Schlingelberg seems to be corrected in U from some other ending. It almost reads like "Schlingeln"!

3107.   Daarekiste. A madhouse.

The word recalls some incidents of Ibsen's youthful days; cf. Jæger's biography of 1888 (p.p. 7, 13 and 34) reprinted in the Efterladte Skrifter (cf. I, p. 305). At Skien, there was a room in the Town Hall where the local Bedlamites seem to have been occasionally locked up in what was there known as "the Madhouse: Daarekisten".

J. Collin, Henrik Ibsen, sees a symbolic meaning in the fact that Peer lands against his will in such an asylum and compares his adventures there to Brand's visit to that creation of a lunatic: Gerd's ice church. (l.l. 255).

3109.   Stedet, —ved det.

Such pretty bold rhymes occur passim in Paludan-Müller's Adam Homo.

3115.   Münchhausen.

An allusion most likely to one of the adventurous Baron's stories: how he put his hand into the fox's mouth, groped further and further until he caught the

---

1, 173; 3, 177; F, 429; M, 257; 14, 161; J, 267; 16, 161.

tail and then, pulling it, turned the fox — skin and
all — inside out. The e e l is no doubt but an instance
of Begriffenfeldt's peculiar memory.

3121. seqq.   Nu er det klart, etc. Now it is patent, *etc.*·

Compare Byron, Don Juan XIV, 84: "Shut up the
world at large, let Bedlam out, And you will be perhaps
surprised to find All things pursue exactly the same
rout, As now with those of *soi-disant* sound mind".

3148.   Her er man sig selv aldeles forbandet.

It's here, Sir, that one is oneself with a vengeance.

Compare J. L. Heiberg's En Sjæl efter Døden (IIIe
Akt) where Mephistopheles recommends hell as the
proper place for the Soul: Her er Alt kun sig selv og
diskret (p. 195).

3166.   Huhu.

In the text of U, the name is Huhu too, but in the
list of De handlende there copied out calligraphically
apparently b e f o r e he had written more than part
of the poem, the form is Tuhu; it is a case of these
"møjsommelige eksperimenter" to find a proper name-
form that Henning Kehler, Edda 1916, p. 95 speaks
of. — It can be nothing but a misprint when, in Chr. Collin's Bjørnstjerne Bjørnson, we find the form Uhu. —
See the n. to l. 3179 as to who is caricatured here. —
min Dreng, my boy.

Dreng, although specifically Danish in the general
sense of a young boy, is found in Norwegian (as well as
Swedish) in the sense of a male servant, a farm-labourer;
cf. Aasen in v. and his Ordsprog, p. 69: Sjølv er
beste Drengen; Mau I, 129: Selv er en god Dreng = help
yourself.

3169.   ufortolket. untranslated.

The Archers' rendering uninterpreted in their note is
much to be preferred, if not the only correct one. —

3172.   Gudbevar's! Oh, by all means!

The semasiology of this somewhat puzzling idiom

1, 174; 3, 178; F, 430; M, 258; 14, 162; J, 268; 16, 162.

which stands of course contracted for: Gud bevare os, is very possibly as follows: Heaven protect me if I should nót do a certain thing — if I should not allow it to be done, — why should I not allow it? — oh, by all means — please do. Curiously enough, a German translator (Morgenstern, p. 535) who had his own bewahre close at hand, actually manages to misunderstand it as: Gott erbarme sich! Mrs. Clant van der Mijll's: 't Zal mij een eer zijn is somewhat free, but in perfect spirit.

A curious use of this, nothing but a substitution in fact for a word or expression one does not wish to give utterance to, may be quoted from Swedish: Wickström, Folktro, p. 90) Innan de gå därifrån, skulle bevars, Lina.... viz. Lina must like King Apis "gaa afsides"; (Compare: paa noksagt, paa das, paa do).

3174.   malebarske Strande. Malebarish seaboards.

On the form Malebarsk instead of Malebarisk, see S. M. p. 37, but Ibsen uses the longer form too a little lower down, l. 3220.

3179.   Disse Folk har Sproget blandet.

These have muddled up the language.

The whole of this passage is admittedly nothing but a violent attack on the Maalstrævere, the ultra-nationalistic group of Language-reformers [1]. In consequence of Aasen's discovery in 1849 of the continuity of the then Norwegian dialects with Old Norse and headed by him and Ibsen's quondam friend, the poet A. O. Vinje, the maalstrævere's aim was to throw Danish overboard: fremmedåget, the Portugiser and Hollændere of the allegory and to return to the old language called "New-

---

[1] There is a something in this word that does not admit of translation, a "by-tone" that it is even difficult to render by anything short of an elaborate paraphrase. It should not be forgotten that the name maalstrævere was originally given them by their opponents, even now they would rather call themselves: maalmænd or maalvenlige. And like the German *Streber*, the second composing element of the word hints very clearly if distantly at the (non-justified) accusation of being pushing busybodies that try to get at their aim at whatever cost (to their opponents!), by fair means or, if necessary, foul.

Norwegian" in order to give it a modern tinge, a modern aspect in its slightly rejuvenated inter-dialectal form, — to the "Urskogssprog" as Ibsen called it. [1]) Ibsen who himself at one time had exhibited a tendency to go in this direction (cf. Eft. Skr. I, p. LXVIII [2]) and Eitrem, Maal og Minne, 1910, p. 43, under Wergeland's influence) had entirely changed his standpoint [3]). If there could be any doubt about the question and as to the vehemence of Ibsen's sentiments here, two passages in his letters, one of Dec. '67 to Bjørnson and another of February '68 to Hegel the publisher, would make the thing clear. I shall become a photographer, he wrote, if I cannot be a poet, and all my contemporaries piece for piece, the one after the other I shall take up "as I have done with the Maalstrævere" (Breve, I, 160). And when some of that camp had complained that the Peer Gynt had not arrived in proper time at Bergen, Ibsen writes that as it seems to him, "these fellows" will soon find they got it soon enough: Efter hvad der senere er passert, synes det som om de Karle har fået den tids nok! (Breve I, 167, 168).

Vinje the poet who called himself the Dalesman (Dølen) because he came from one of the most "national"' and characteristically Norwegian "dales", Telemarken, Vinje had more than once before the publication of Peer Gynt been the object of sneers or attacks by Ibsen, friendly and harmless as when Ibsen wrote: hils Vinje

---

[1]) An attempt to characterise this movement in anything like detail would swell this note to inadmissible dimensions. A full account of its history and a review of its modern features by the present writer may be found in the Dutch periodical Groot-Nederland (1908) and the Norwegian Samtiden (1909).

[2]) Endog når han angreb Vinje og Målstræverne i Hu-hus skikkelse, havde han egne anfægtelser at gøre bod for; „Fjeldfuglen" viser at også han fra sit romantiske standpunkt havde været inde på målstræverske veje".

[3]) Yet, if we may trust one of Ibsen's younger contemporaries who has had special occasion to hear it from Ibsen's own mouth (although it is not certain that this is h e r e the case!), Ibsen owed a great deal to Vinje from the point of view of language: „Ibsens sprog som det særlig træder frem i „Peer Gynt", denne lykkelige blanding af folkeord, af daglig tale, af maalstræv, maa for en stor del tilskrives Vinjes inflydelse". J. Paulsen, Mine Erindringer, 1900 p. 21.

1, 177; 3, 181; F, 433; M, 260; 14, 165; J, 270; 16, 165.

hin Nationale (Breve I, 66; 1853), or in the first draft of his Sendebrev til H. Ø. Blom (Eft. Skr. I, 485 [1]): Dansk Tankesæt er Hemsko s e l v paa Vinje; cf. my n. to l. 1053; of a much graver character (apart from the fact that the preceding two sneers had of course not been published) when in the Kjærlighedens Komedie Ibsen wrote: Ej hver som ynder at håndtere Sølen, må derfor tro sig ligemand med Dølen"! ,which is certainly putting it on thick and even caused the Morgenblad of the time to speak of "a piece of dirty wit". (Fr. Ording, H. Ibsens Kjærlighedens Komedie, 1914, p. 43 [2]).

But all this was nothing in comparison to the attack upon Vinje in the present passage which Ibsen was goaded into by the former's criticism on Brand whom Vinje had declared a madman and nothing but a huge joke. "Good gracious", Vinje had written (cf. the full criticism which is worth reading, in Vinje's Skrifter i Utval, 1897, I, p.p. 86—102), "what a fuss about this.... Firebrand! Brand — Brandior — Brandissimus. What càn be the reason of all this.... fire-alarm? Nothing but that the author wanted money and hence all this beating of the big drum! Well, — Ibsen has got his subvention", (he received a state-pension to which Bjørnson helped him) so now we shall be quiet for he will himself calm down". Vinje actually goes so far as to say that the only way to understand Brand is to look upon it as a parody and he compares the play to Pope's Dunciad. The attack coming from an old friend, many will look upon as not excusable; it is at least explicable to some

---

[1]) For the poet's second attack on Blom, see „Et utrykt Polemisk digt av Henrik Ibsen, meddelt av Halvdan Koht, Samtiden, 1911 p. 361.

[2]) There is a curious hit at a „society for the restitution of the Old Norse tongue" and its originator Julian Paulsen in Sanct Hans Natten (1852, cf. Eft, Skr. I p.p. 380 seqq. which to some might seem to be written 'at' Vinje. Prof. D. A. Seip (Edda, I, 145 n. 2) tells of a Sprogforening and K. Knudsen and thinks that this is what Ibsen may have thought of, „although there are no further points of resemblance between Knudsen and Julian Paulsen". Anders Krogvig (in a private letter) thinks there is no allusion to any special person, but that Julian Paulsen is a hit at "datidens gjennemsnitstype paa en norsk kritiker."

---

extent when we remember that, as Chr. Collin tells us
(Bj. Bj. II, 452) Vinje considered Ibsen (like Bjørnson) as an impediment in the way of what seemed to
him the holiest of the holy: the very maalbevægelse, so
that Ibsen here attacks him in his weakest point: "for
Vinje stod baade Ibsens og Bjørnsons voksende forfat-
terry som en hindring for den norske Maalsag."

No wonder then that Ibsen could not digest all this
and that his latent anger against "these fellows" broke
out in the most patent of flames. And it is after all nothing but a very pardonable application of the principle about the biter bit, when Ibsen, remembering
that two could play at that game, makes Huhu land
in a lunatic asylum too. [1])

For Huhu is of course Vinje. [2]) The foreign yoke is
that of the Danes who indeed had been masters of the
land from the end of the 14th century to the beginning
of the 19th, when however briefly (May—Aug. 1814)
Norway had been itself! The Orang-utang is the
speaker of the old language whose "maal lød malebarisk". And here it is interesting to note that Bjørnson's
language in Synnøve Solbakken and Halte-Hulda had
been called not only a "ravnorsk lavet Idiom" but "en
malebarisk Dialekt" (Danish Dagblad, 18/8/'58) quoted Edda, I, p. 152 and Chr. Collin, Bjørnstjerne Bjørnson, II, 451) As to the Urskogssproget, it will appear
from the n. to l. 3190 that it had first been called Ursprungssproget (as in what is now l. 3204 U read: Ur-

---

[1]) The views here condensed are those of Chr. Collin in the two papers mentioned,
Morgenbladet and Samtiden, 1913 (now two chapters in „Det geniale Menneske").
The tone of the attack is that characterised by Gran (l.l. p. 182) as „Hollandsk"
which is of course to be taken „in a Pickwickian sense", a rough way peculiar to the
circle of Botten Hansen and others, cf. the n. to l. 4415, to which Ibsen belonged in
his early days. Gran (No. Aandsliv p. 172) thus characterises these „Dutchmen" that
they "saa intet andet (i bøndernes selvbevissthet) end ildelugtende plebeiervæsen, i
sprogbevægelsen og det nationale opkomme intet andet end sjølvgod seminarisme."

[2]) Which does not mean that Ibsen may not have thought here of all maalrefor-
mers in general or other individuals in particular. In a paper (Edda I, p. 156, n) by
Seip I find that Kristofer Janson e. g. vindicates the "honour" of standing for Huhu.

1, 177; 3, 181; F, 433; M, 260; 14, 165; J, 270; 16, 165.

tidsmaal) a splendid substitution: it was the Orang-
utang that spoke it! And now: "grunts and growls
are heard no longer — ikke længer blir der brummet".
These last words may perhaps receive an illustration
from a passage in Faye's Norske Sagn (which Ibsen has
certainly known as it gave him the matter for his Rypen i Justedal; Eft. Skr. I, p. 339) where the author
quotes (p. XVII) the old Chronicler Adam v. Bremen:
"i Norge har jeg hört at der findes Quinder og Mænd
som bor i Skovene og sjelden vise sig: de bruge de
vilde Dyrs Hude til Klæder og deres Sprog ligner mere
Dyrenes Brummen end Menneskers Tale, saa de næppe
kunde forstaaes af Naboerne...." where it is possible
to think of some confusion with the Berserker (n. to l.
4141).

3190.   Urskogs-Sproget. forest-tongue primeval.
The study of U is interesting here, — it is true that
we there now read Urskogssproget too, but k o is corrected from other letters, the original reading being very
likely: ursprungssproget; what a truly brilliant, "pal-
pable hit" when he made this into urskogs-sproget!

3203. seqq. Jeg har prøvet paa at fægte for vort urskogs-maal.
I have tried to fight the battle of our primal wood
speech.
Fred. Paasche, in a paper on Ibsen's National-roman-
tik, Samtiden, 1909, p. 652 writes: "Dette er Ibsen selv.
H a n hadde ogsaa paavist folkets trang til National
kost. Vi har nok av avisartikler fra hans haand som
vidner om at en fuldt utdannet teori støttet hans dig-
teriske maalstræv" etc.
skreget selv. shrieked myself.
The above view need not necessarily be in contradiction with the fact that in the whole of the passage and
e. g. these words in particular Ibsen undoubtedly
thought of Vinje, — Paasche's hypothesis comes to this
that Ibsen here spoke of what he had gjennemlevet

---

himself. And surely, Vinje had often enough "shown the need of shrieks in poems for the people". Landstad's Folkeviser ready in print ab. 1847 and published in 1853, as well as Lindemann's Ældre og nyere fjeldmelodier, which some might think of are not likely to be alluded to here. (Krogvig).

3227.   Østen har forstødt sin Sanger!
          East, thou hast disowned thy singer.

Fred. Paasche (see the preceding note) thinks these lines remind one of a passage from 1851:

Men Heltetiden sank i Dvale hen,
Og Skjaldens Røst forstummed i det samme;
Og Folkets Aand var kuet ret som hans,
Det havde ei som før en Egekrans
At slynge taksomt om sin Digters Tinding. —
Ei kviddred nogen Fuglerøst i Skoven;
Thi Folkets Aand sov Vintersøvn derinde.

See Paasche, l.c. p. 519. —

3237.   En Fellah som bærer en Mumie.
          A fellah with a mummy.

"This is a satire on the Swedes, always holding forth on their "royal mummy" the heroic Charles the Twelfth (hjeltakonungen Karl den Tolvte) with whom in 1864 they had not shown to possess any other points of resemblance than the negative one that they were as dead as the King himself". Thus Jæger writes (Ill. No. Lit. historie III, 662; cf. also his Henrik Ibsen 1892, p. 72) and this is the usual interpretation. But compare Chr. Collin (Morgenblad-paper) who thinks that this Fellah cannot be a personification of the Swedes, carrying Charles the twelfth's body on their back. It must be the Norwegian "Udaller" (Odelsbonden) who in certain "clans" were supposed to descend from the Kings and who carry about the recollection of the Great Saga-times, — a dead Greatness".... but this same Fellah,

i. e. the Norwegian Peasant who is proud of his ancestors is in Ibsen's eyes a very modest man, where there
are claims on him and his own contemporaries. He says
he is "only a Fellah, a hungry louse" that cannot do
any great work. The dead past is all his riches."

Arguments why the Fellah cannot have been meant
for the Swedes would no doubt have been very welcome
to some of Prof. Collin's more sceptic readers as they
may be supposed not to be quite convinced, perhaps
rather the contrary, by the hair-splitting interpretation
of the hungry louse where the author may seem to be
straining his point.

A correspondent sends me the following considerations which are certainly worth reproducing, although
I personally do not think I can subscribe to all the
details either:

"I do not think Collin's explanation of the Fellah
as the Norwegian odelsbonde a very happy one. — First
the Norw. "Apis" can hardly be said to have "kriget
med Tyrken baade rechts og links". Of course, it might
be said that this is a reference to the old Vikings. But
no one has "priset ham som en gud" or "stillet ham op
i templer" etc. And what is meant by his going "avsides
ind paa min oldefars grund", and how has this "grund"
afterwards "næret ham med sit korn? — All this does
not fit in with the Norwegian peasants of to-day.

On the other hand there are several things pointing
to the Swedes (esp. "Storsvensken", "Norskätaren")
and Charles XII. First the allusion to his great works
and his wars. Then the praising of him as a god: a
very great man; then his going "avsides ind paa min
oldefars grund", which may refer to Charles' war with
Russia. The latter is called "min oldefars grund", perhaps, because the Russian empire was originally founded by Swedes; and possibly, as Sweden gets a good deal
of corn from Russia, it may be said that "marken kong

Apis gøded hàr næret mig med sit korn". De "usynlige horn" that the fellah has, may be the horns Swedes have so often pointed against Norway; — when the Fellah says "Men jeg er denne kong Apis", he probably means that he (Storsvensken) is the right heir to King Charles' glory, and his real representative in our time. —

But again there are things that are difficult to explain. Why does he call himself "en sulten lus". It may either be irony, meaning how can you who consider me as a hungry louse, advise me to do great things like King Apis, or it may be an allusion to the many impoverished noble families in Sweden, who have nothing left of their pristine glory but their names and their memory. "At holde min hytte ryddelig for rotter og mus" would then mean: keep the wolf away from the door, or rather my creditors. —"

3247.   og er derhos aldeles død.
             and withal he's completely dead.

The subtle joke of a mummy that is "moreover" quite dead, suggestive of Mark Twain or Edgar Allen Poe is ignored or rendered not quite adequately by most translators.

3267. saa har jeg usynlige Horn. I have invisible horns.

The Apis of legendary history was King of Argos but his "descendant" seems to be mixing him up with the sacred Bull of the Aegyptians: Apis with the golden front — "Apis med den gyldne Pande" of Ibsen's Ballonbrev (F, IV, 382) and hence the Fellah's talk of the horns.

3283.   ryddig. clear.

Ryddig is the more specifically Norwegian form which Ibsen uses regularly as well as uryddigt (Vildanden, F, VII, 280) and which is also used in the Folkeeventyr (cf. ed. 1912, p. 99, Soria Moria Slot); ryddelig, more Danish, was substituted by the fifth ed. (T. C. § 56).

3292.   Mit Liv for en Strikke! My life for a halter!

Already as we have it here, the expression will remind

some readers of the motif, discussed supra, n. to l. 2444 "my kingdom for a horse". This suggestion is curiously borne out by the reading of U: Mit Land for en Strikke and we can even imagine that Ibsen changed Land into Liv because he remembered that he had made use of it before.

3301.   Overgangstillstand. A state of transition. See the n. to l. 4190.

3308.   Her er Noter, som skal besvares?

"Hussejn the Minister.... means a laugh at all the humbug with notes and adresses behind which the Norwegians as well as the Swedes tried to hide themselves in 1864" when Denmark was going to war with Germany "and more especially at the Norwegian-Swedish Foreign Secretary, count Manderström who thought he could impose on the powers with his Notes." (H. Jæger, H. Ibsen, 1892, p. 73; cf. id. Ill. No. Lit. Hist. p. 667). See L. Dietrichson, Svundne Tider 1896, I, p. 342 on a little tussle between Ibsen and Count Snoilsky, Manderström's nephew because Ibsen had drawn Manderström with a rope round his neck, and cf. esp. Eft. Skr. I, p. LXXI where a passage will be found reprinted from the (Danish) Dagblad (Dec. 1863) where the writer asks whether Manderström will turn out an "able pen" only or a real statesman: Det skal endnu først vise sig om han kun er en habil pen eller en virkelig Statsmand" which passage Koht thinks Ibsen is sure to have read.

3312.   plent. quite clearly.

Compare l.l. 635 and 3975 and S. I. S. p. 192.

3317;3320, 1. jeg er et Papirblad, etc.....

            i en Kvindes Eje en sølvspændt Bog, etc.

            I am a blank sheet of paper, etc.....

            in woman's keeping a silverclasped book.

In Gads Danske Magasin (1913, p. 459) Eitrem writes: At the decisive moment, when Peer did not dare to receive Solveig, the best in him showed itself; a shy admiration for the purity and the dignity (høihet) that had come to him. Nor does he ever forget Solveig. This Ibsen has made clear by a word that escapes Peer in a moment of despair, — and then these passages are quoted.

The sølvspændt bog that made such an impression on him is of course the salmebog of l.l. 586 and 745; it is the spændebog that he wants to kill the Boyg with (1263) the dream of which he sells at the auction (3853) and which Solveig symbolically still has with her at their last meeting (4644). Compare the n. to l. 3321.

3318.   jeg duer. I am good for.

This duer was changed by Prof. Storm into duger; cf. T. C. § 121. It is true that Ibsen himself wrote duge-ligt (l. 4160; rhyme brugeligt) but this is assuredly no reason to change the verb. Remarkably enough, "Vi avisskrivere d u e r ikke stort" (Folkefienden) is kept by the editor of M, cf. ib. vol. IV, p.p. 181 and 328.

3321. det er en og samme Trykkfejl at være gal og klog! it's one and the same misprint to be either mad or sane!

To talk of a misprint here is not such absolute mad-man's rant as one might be inclined to think at first sight. Recollections of Solveig's book of psalms (cf. n. to l. 3317) have made him compare himself to a book, led to this by Hussejn's being a pen and — hence — to a piece of paper and when consequently Ibsen read over what he had first written in U that it was all the same if one was mad as his interlocutor or sane as he himself, for both had landed in a lunatic-asylum: Jeg var i en Unges Eje som en sølvspaendt Bog; det er et og det samme at være gal og klog!, it must have struck the poet that this might be expressed by a term more in keeping with the "fact" of his b e i n g a book ('som' was omitted in R!), — hence: whether one is mad or sane, we are some of us "misprints" all the same!

3328, 9. Det var Synd for den Verden, der, lig andet selvgjort,

---

1, 183; 3, 187; F, 439; M, 263; 14, 170; J, 273; 16, 170.

af Vorherre blev funden saa inderlig velgjort.

A pity for the world which, like other self-made things
was reckoned by the Lord to be so excellently good.

The hint about other self-made things looks suspiciously much like a sneer at the 'home-made' nationalism for which Ibsen had taken some of his countrymen
severely to task; cf. n. to l. 1053. However the expression itself seems proverbial: Selvgjort er velgjort, Mau,
II, 236; Aasen, 147. That the world was looked upon as
so very well done by the Lord reminds us of Faust
(Hexenküche): Natürlich, wenn ein Gott sich erst sechs
Tage plagt und selbst am Ende Bravo sagt, da muss es
was gescheidtes werden" (cf. Witkowski, II, 240); the
source of both is of course Genesis I, 31, but the sneering
tone is common to Goethe and Ibsen. What would
happen when the world is out of joint, Ibsen has told
us in the first draft to Rosmersholm in Hetman-Brendel's
delightful skit and to some extent in the Button-moulder (cf. Eft. Skr., III, 136, ib. I, p. CIV).

3332.   Der er Ordet. That is the word.

Compare T. C. § 63: As the original reading is Der er
Ordet, the translation should run: There is the word.
But "det er Ordet would be better Norwegian." (Dr.W.)

3336.   han leved og han døde som en paaholden Pen!

He lived and died as a fate-guided pen!

To this the Archers append a note: "Underskrive
med paaholden pen" to sign by touching a pen which is
guided by another. — In this sense the expression is
quite common; cf. Hm! Vidner? Kan I ikke skrive Jesper Hansen og Jens Kristansen med og uden paaholden
pen, saa kan jeg mener jeg som Prokurator; Wergeland,
VI, p. 265 and: Med denne Raslen og Vinden af Bjørnson og hans Livnadslaup med "paaholden Pen" af Clemens Petersen, maatte dette kjærlege Kjøbenhavn
stupa Hovudkraaka", etc, Vinje (Utval, I, 250) where
Vinje therefore insinuates that Bjørnson himself made

---

all this bother about his own name and that Cl. Petersen (Ibsen's Peer Gynt-critic) was Bjørnson's "obedient
tool" just like Hussejn says that he has been 'et
viljeløst redskap' for others.

3341, 2. Jeg kan ikke hitte dit Navn i en Hast; —
    hjælp mig, du — alle Daarers Formynder!
    I cannot just hit on thy name at the moment; —
    oh, come to my aid, thou — all madmen's protector!
    "Au milieu de sa détresse, dans la sinistre cour de
l'hospice et dans les griffes de Begriffenfeldt, ce n'est
plus Solveig qu'il invoque, Count Prozor writes (Le
Peer Gynt d'Ibsen, p. 49 and compare p. 50), c'est le
dieu qu'il s'est créé à son image, un dieu dont il ne sait
plus le nom, tant il a changé comme lui et avec lui." To
think that Peer should not remember the name of God
anymore is surely going too far. But there is of course
undoubtedly an allusion to God: "hvorledes dog Vorherre er Daarernes Formynder", Kammerherre Brats-
berg had exclaimed in "De Unges Forbund" (F, IV,
55) and with this proverb [1]), in his mind of course, Ibsen
made Peer in his terrible agony address Begriffenfeldt
whose name he could not remember in words which to
all of us s u g g e s t God, but that do not m e a n God
as a caricature after Peer's own image as Prozor thinks.

3343.   med en Straakrans. with a wreath of straw.
    As observed before (n. to l. 3045) in one of Werge-
land's farces, Vinægers Fjeldeventyr, Blasenfeldt wears
"a crown of paper" and Prof. Seip (Samtiden 1913)
thinks that here too Ibsen may have been influenced by
Wergeland. See also the n. to l. 3857. (Add.)

3345.   Hans Kroning sker! To crown him now!
    As in the next line Han leve! etc., the subjunctive is
used, so here we might well expect: Hans Kroning s k e

---

[1]) As a proverb in Aasen: Vaar Herre er Lagverja fyre Daararne, efter Wilse; in
Mau (I, 211, II, 428)I find the following variants: Gud, (and even) Lykken er alle
Daarers Formynder, Vorherre er Fattigfolks Formynder; Tilfældet er alle Daar-
ers Formynder.

---

and it will be noticed that the Archers intuitively translate it as a wish; any possibility of this reading is however excluded of course by the exigencies of the rhyme
with Peer. Now, U has a reading which has hitherto
been overlooked: Hans Kroning s e r, which plural imperative smacks it is true of the bible (ser at Herren er
god, Ps. 34, 9) but that does not in itself make it impossible that it should have been used here; see what Seip
says (W. p.p. 85, 89) of Wergeland's language: that W.
uses the form "hardly ever" in ordinary language
(hverdagsstil) but pretty often in the higher prose. So
one is tempted to suggest that ser was changed by Ibsen
into sker in R. by a mere slip. I must not omit to add however that Norwegian correspondents think this unlikely
and that it would be a somewhat forced construction.

3348.
The end of the Scene.

The sudden disappearance of evil as if by enchant-
ment is certainly common enough if not in our experience, yet in Peer-Ibsen's folklore world; as Aladdin
exclaims when Hindbad, one of the evil elements, has
made away with himself: "Det har tilfælles du med alt
det Onde: dets hele Kraft, et øieblikkeligt Spil, Bort-
svinder i sit eget Giøglelys!" This is a fine phrase — wo
Begriffe fehlen! — to "explain" how Peer gets out of all
this, a question which one cannot help putting, but an
event we had perhaps better not enquire too curiously
into. Remembering however the obvious parallelism
between this scene and that in the Dovrëhall (cf. J.
Collin, p. 331) we may expect a similar ending here as
there and we may perhaps conclude that, although
Peer in intention invokes the madmen's earthly tutor,
God himself hears him and must be supposed to save
him here as the symbols of his power had done in former cases, the Church-bells in the Dovrëhall scene, and
Solveig's love in the case of the Boyg, — foreshadowing
the touching end of the play.

1, 185; 3, 189; F, 441; M, 264; 14, 172; J, 274; 16, 172.

FEMTE HANDLING. ACT FIFTH.

3350 seqq. The Shipwreck.

The exact spot where this shipwreck must be supposed to take place it is of course impossible to point out but from the fact that Peer can even imagine that he could see the various mountain-tops mentioned, we naturally think of some place on the way from Stavanger to Bergen, the so-called "inner-way: indre Leden", but in that case they could hardly have been in such peril of the sea. So it must be to the west not only of the Norwegian continent but of the islands. And from these the Galdhøpiggen and Ronden etc. cannot possibly be seen.

The Hallingskarven (locally: Hallingskarvet; W.) is a famous mountain in the Hardanger district along which they pass in any case; the Folgefond (cf. T. C. § 114 on the spelling) is the renowned immense glacier there; the Rondë-mountains are part of the Dovrefjeld and Galdhøpiggen is the highest top but one of Jotunheim; until lately thought to be the highest in Norway (± 2560 Meter).

Haartejgen is a mountaintop to the east of Odda in Hardanger. Blaahø(where hø is Norw. dialect for a mountain top and Blaa means black) is the name of various tops in Jotunheim and it may well be idle to enquire minutely into the various possibilities as to which particular one Ibsen had in mind, which consideration holds to some extent of the whole question of the localisation of the shipwreck-scene.

A writer in the Publications of the Society for the Advancement of Scandinavian Study (II, p.p. 127 seqq.), Mr. A. R. Andersen suggests (p. 147) that in this description of the shipwreck Ibsen was carrying out his promise implied in his words from Billedgalledgalleriet XVII:

Jeg ridser med blyant et vrag i storm
mellem rullende havsens vover;
i faldt jeg var digter, jeg ridsed med pen
en lyrisk skitse derover. —

3355. Folgefaannen, hun er nu saa fin.
The Folgefån, now, she is mighty fine.

Hun as referring to a mountain reflects the popular
language as it does in English. Moreover — fonn is
feminine in Norwegian dialects. —

3368. Bærmen, siger Ordsproget, hænger længst i.
and the dregs, says the proverb, hang in to the last. —

Compare the n. to l. 1120 where the same sentiment
is expressed by the well-known biblical reference to
Old Adam. —

3390. saa slipper en ogsaa for Krus paa Bryggen!
that saves you, at least, any scenes on the pier!

On slipper e n as against slipper j e g of the later
editions, cf. T. C. § 56. This substitution is explained
to some extent by the fact that e n as an indefinite pronoun "can only be used when *I* or *we* is comprised" (W),
as in English, it may be added. Hence, Madame Rundholmen's: Kunde en ikke gjerne kysse ham, is impersonal, as remarked T. C. § 56 in a way of course, but also
more personal in an other respect, for she means: Would
not *I* like to kiss the darling? But it would not
do to say: I det gamle Rom pleide *en* at gjøre dit eller
dat, — here *man* must be used. Krus = fuss, scenes as
the Archers rightly translate. The Dutch translation
confounds it with the homonym: krus = jug, mug!

3402. den svarte Hunger. black famine.

Compare Dutch: zwart van den honger (Stoett[2], n°
2209).

3407. Og Lys i Pladen? a light in the sconce?

The word used by the Archers is ambiguous; sconce
meaning a candlestick hung or attached to the wall as
well as the socket of a candlestick, and either sense would

fit in here: it may therefore be as well to add that, as a Norwegian correspondent tells me, the latter must be meant. —

3409. Og saa sidder de lunt? *etc.* And there they sit snug!
In U this passage read first:

Og saa sidder de lunt; har det varmt og godt;
har Ungerne om sig; den minste paa Fanget;
der er ingen som hører den andre tillende —
slig Glæde er der paa dem —

In U itself, Ibsen changed these four lines into the present reading, so far as the words are concerned, but not a single point of interrogation was added. It will be seen what an enormous difference the passage makes when addressed as questions to the captain or as mere reflections by Peer to — Peer! The Archers wrongly give us points of exclamation. —

3414. Nej, om jeg gjør! I'll be damned if I do!
We may well ask what makes him suddenly so hard-hearted again. The clue to this return to hardness is no doubt found in the line: If I've had to howl neath the lashes of fate, trust me to find folks I can lash in turn. Maatte jeg under Skjæbnens Piskeslag hyle, saa findes vel dem jeg igjen kan prygle, 3497, 8. And compare Adam Homo, 10ᵉ Sang, ed. 1879, II, p. 282: han loved alt da kan i klemme var. — The Archers' translation is pretty strong. His being hardened reminds us of the influence of the Fremmede Skytte in Paa Vidderne.

3428. ustyrtelig. enormous.
The word is composed with the intensive u —; cf. n. to l. 1100. — Here as well as in l. 3535 (where Ibsen had actually first written ustyggelig) later editions change it into ustyrlig, unmanageable (cf. så ustyrlig som han var, Hedda Gabler, Eft. Skr III, 236; Hilde, voldsom, ustyrlig, F, IX, 154); den ustyrlige kraft og livsfylde, F, VI, 463) cf. T. C. §§ 62, 130. For ustyrtelig, cf. Aasen in v. usturteleg, p. 883; en rent ustyrtelig mæng-

de (infusionsdyr), Folkefiende, M, IV, 157 and ustyrtelige penge, De Unges Forbund; F, IV, 10. —

3462.   nybagte enker. new-baked widows.

There is a flavour of the comic in this word nybagt
in Dutch and other languages (cf. een half-bakken ge-
leerde; Stoett, n° 664) and what is more, as Dr. Western tells me, in Norwegian too. No serious man would
speak of en nybakt enke, except perhaps if the widow
must be supposed to be glad of the riddance. Here it may
of course be a piece of sailor's wit. — Compare Mau, II,
77: et nybagt barn: nyfødt.

3464.   Der er ingen Tro mellem Menneskene mere.

There is no faith left among men any more.

Without any apparent reason Count Prozor omits
the whole of this passage is his prose-translation. —

3467.   Agt. respect.

In ordinary prose, agt means attention, (gi agt) care (ta
sig i agt) etc.; here it is used (cf. ring(e)agt, T. C. § 99.) =
esteem, respect; cf. Dr. Western's Skriv Norsk, § 47. —

3470.   vogsomt. dangerous.

Hazardous would perhaps be slighly preferable. On
the form vågsomt substituted in later editions, cf. T. C.
§ 114. —

3472.   paa .Offerpynten. for the sacrifice.

The word Offerpynt seems to have puzzled the translators: Ellis Roberts throws the Archers' sacrifice over
board and renders it: for the oblation; we have: der
Opferteller (Morgenstern), offerschaal (Clant van der
Mijll), offeraltaar (Brons) etc. As may be seen in the
notes to l. 1936, paa Pynten (cf. pynt = land's end) may
mean simply on the "point" of, about to. So here it
might be: at the moment of sacrifice, to which both the
Archers and Ellis Roberts come very close. A correspondent however explains it = the point of time, the
critical moment when one has to choose between sacri-
ficing or saving oneself.

1, 193; 3, 197; F, 449; M, 268; 14, 179; J, 278; 16, 179.

3475.   Samvittighedsfred er en dejlig Pude.
A conscience at ease is a pillow of down.
Compare Aasen, No. Ordsprog² (1881) p. 124: Godt
Samvitende er godt aa sova med. Anders Krogvig
tells me that it is usually quoted in German: Ein gutes
Gewissen, ein sanftes Kissen, and he thinks that this it
was that Ibsen must have thought of.

3477.   duer s'gu ikke for en snus ombord.
(does not) matter a snuff on board ship.
The construction due for en snus, unusual as Docent
Brynildsen tells me, if at all known = gjælde for, be
worth, stands for ikke due en snus = nothing at all,
and may be owing to a cross between this and such
an expression as gaa for, etc.

3482.   saa stryger jeg sagtens i Vasken med Flokken.
I shall no doubt be swept to the deuce with the rest.
Here U had some lines where the idea of responsi-
bility is worked out somewhat longer; they are printed
Eft. Skr. II, p. 109. See on the sentiment itself, ib. I, p.
LXXX.

3484.   man gjælder som en Pølse i Slagtetiden.
One counts but as a sausage in slaughtering-time.
This is proverbial, cf. Mau, II, 141: det kommer ikke
an paa en Pølse i Slagtetiden; i Aasen² p. 115: D'er
ikkje so vandt um ei Pylse i Slagtartidi; or: det er
ikkje so grant med etc. = one little bit of sausage does
not count etc. Anders Krogvig quotes from Hallingdal:
D'æ 'kje so vandt mæ ei kloter (blodklubb) i slagteti'en.

3491.   Gaarden vil jeg vinde med ondt eller godt, etc.
I'll get back the farmstead by fair means or foul.
Brons notes (p. 190): Nach dem Odelsrecht kann
jedes Familienglied den verkauften Odelshof inner-
halb einer gewissen Reihe von Jahren vom Käufer
gegen Taxe zurückfördern. I cannot control the statement. It does not appear from the context that Ibsen
thought of this; moreover we must suppose a long

number of years to have elapsed; so did it still hold
good?

The answer to this question, negative it would seem,
is supplied by the following quotation that Dr. Western kindly sends me from Illustreret Norsk Konversationsleksikon:

"Odelsret kan kun erhverves over jord paa landet.
Der kræves hertil 20-aarig uavbrutt eiendomsbesiddelse
av samme person eller hans ættæg (de som i ret nedsti-
gende linje nedstammer fra ham) eller hans egtefælle
..... Odelsmandens ret kan i korthet siges at gaa ut
paa at han i tilfælde av eiendommens salg til utenfor-
staaende kan indløse eiendommen efter takst av uvil-
lige mænd (impartial men).... Odelsret kan fraskrives,
dog kun for vedkommendes egen person og senere
fødte børn, men ikke for børn født før fraskrivelsen.
Videre kan den præskriberes; har eiendommen i *tre*
aar været ute av slegten, er hele slegtens odelsret her-
ved tapt, og enhver nærmere odelsberettiget taper sin
ret ved at eiendommen i tre aar indehaves av en fjernere
berettiget". —

3499. Den Fremmede Passager The Strange Passenger.
Stavnem compares this truly 'strange' figure to
those beings not rare in 19th century romanticism which
bring a message from the sphere of the supernatural
at a critical moment of the hero's life. But these figures
such as the Black Knight in Schiller's Jungfrau von
Orleans and Auden in Oehlenschläger's Hakon Jarl, differ in a very important point from Peer's mystical Fel-
low-passenger, for this Strange Passenger does not
like the others try to bring about the loss of a soul but
endeavours to rouse his conscience — "at ruske op i
Heltens samvittighed". For all that the dominating note
in the man's character is Mefistofelian and there is no
doubt about the literary connection with such truly
diabolical figures as Montechristo in Paludan-Müller's

Luftskipperen og Ateisten, and especially Ibsen's "Strange Hunter" — Den fremmede Skytte in "Paa Vidderne". The cynicism that characterises both is quite sufficient to establish the connection. So here, Peer's fellow-traveller who wishes to examine him critically "in his seams" — gaa Dem Kritisk efter i Sømmene (n. to l. 3531) represents to come extent Peer's better self, like his counterpart in Paa Vidderne represented the evil spirit of Peer's prototype and the way in which he tries to rouse Peer's conscience is indicated by Ibsen in a manner not to be mistaken:

> Ven, — har De e n Gang blot hvert Halvaar
> tillbunds fornummet Angstens Alvor?

and later on:

> Ja, har De blot e n Gang i Livet
> havt Sejren, som i Angst er givet?

No wonder that in view of this express s t a t e m e n t (one is almost inclined to say), critics have recognised "Angst' — fear, anxiety, (See the notes to l.l. 3611 etc.) as the moving force that was brought to bear on Peer, as had already been said by the first critic of the play, the Dane Clemens Petersen who in the winter of 1867 had written: Passageren er Begrebet Angst. Ibsen it is true had protested in a letter to Bjørnson (Breve, I, 150) and protested very strongly: but in words that are liable to be easily misunderstood: "If I stood on the scaffold and could save my life with this explanation, it would never have occurred to me, I have never thought of it, I added the scene as a caprice: jeg smurte scenen ind som en Kaprice!" But it should be noticed that Ibsen does not after all say more than that the e x p l a n a t i o n had not occurred to him, — d e n var ikke faldet mig ind. And Petersen had only said: the passenger i s the idea: fear, — so there is when all comes to all no difficulty in reconciling the two views when one only remembers that unconscious

---

1, 195; 3, 199; F, 450; M, 269; 14, 180; J, 279; 16, 180.

conceptions in a poet cannot be denied existence, — as Ibsen himself found unconscious symbolism in the Folkedigtning (F, X, p. 379). And as to the "caprice" which he "smurte ind" we are but too apt to take this as meaning that this was just a freak, a mere nothing, without any deeper meaning. But what it evidently means was that the figure of which he had not r e a l i s e d that it incorporated Terror was added later on a s a n a f t e r t h o u g h t. And if then we observe that the Fremmede Passager does not figure on the list of the Dramatis Personae as written out for U, we find that these two circumstances tally so completely that the plausibility of the conclusion is thereby very strongly enhaunced.

What precedes is nothing but an abstract from a longer paper where the various points touched on here may be found further developed and where the hint given by the omission on that list of personages is followed up. The student is requested not to judge the views here set forth before having read that paper — see Edda, April, 1917.

But one thing being independent of the above considerations would seem to be beyond reasonable doubt, viz. that the Strange Passenger did not form part of the original plan of the play, — as little as such other important 'personages' as the Bøyg (l. 1228), the Button-Moulder (l. 4095) and the Lean one (l. 4429).

3500.   Jeg er Deres Medpassager.
              Your fellow-passenger.

Like the Lady in Green whose hut was built symbolically along with that of Peer Gynt, unknown to Peer himself, so here Peer is unaware that it's the voice of his own conscience that accosts him. —

3514.   Ligene ler. The corpses all laugh.

The incident, reminding one vaguely of Coleridge's Ancient Mariner, may be found illustrated in Feilberg's Sjæletro, 1914, p. 122. —

1, 195; 3, 199; F, 450; M, 269; 14, 181; J, 280; 16, 181.

3521.

kuns. only.

This is Danish only, just like the more current kun.
Dr. Western writes:

I cannot explain the ending — s; it seems to be a
sort of adverbial ending as in medens, mens; compare
the English whiles, against (ayeines). It is a curious
fact that Molbech does not register the form kuns;
probably he did not recognise it as good Danish. The
form is sometimes heard by elderly people, though it
seems to be quite extinct in the younger generation,
and even in the generation I belong to.

3524.

griber i Lommen. puts his hand in his pocket.

By way of commentary I quote from Mau, II, 89:
Necessity opens the purse, Nød oplader vel Pungen.

3531.

gaa Dem kritisk efter i Sømmene —
with critical care I'llook into your seams —

Compare Paludan-Müller's Adam Homo:

Heraf sit Horoscop kan Homo stille,
Mens jeg, som nu mit Modbeviis har fört
Ham lidt i Sömmene vil efter-pille,

expressed as will be observed a little more drastically:
efterpille, as if to p i c k out his faults. (12th Song, II,
p. 461)

So: what if I were to d i s s e c t you, Peer's companion has asked which is here expressed upsey Ib-
senish by asking for his c o r p s e!

3533.

Bespottelige Mand! Blasphemer!

Not like the Dutch corresponding word: bespottelijk
= ridiculous (Brons, p. 193, has fallen into the trap!)
but blasphemous as the Archers rightly take it; cf.
Det er en bespottelig sammenligning, Folkefienden, M,
IV, 205 and Kejser og Galilæer, F, V, 104, 105, Da blev
jeg sint og begyndte at tale bespottelig om maalet
(Riksmaalsbladet, 1913, 6, 12, p. 8) where a translation
ridiculous would produce that effect with a vengeance!

3535.

en ustyrtelig Sjøgang. a terrible sea on.
cf. n. to. l. 3428 and T. C. §§ 62, 130. —

3550. Skibshunden. The ship's dog.

References in Scandinavian folklore to the devil making his appearance in the shape of a dog are legion; cf. e. g. Feilberg, Ordb. in v. v. bjærgmand, djævel, hund (where he refers to Asbjørnsen's 3d. ed. 1870 III, 213 = ed. '12, p. 173) puddel, puss and ib. Tillæg: djævel, hund, ringhalset, etc. and here where the Strange Passenger is taken bij the commentators to be a Messenger of Death, I may refer to Wackernagel, Kl. Schriften, I, 424, on the dog = death. For all that there is this indefinable something about the whole situation which involuntarily reminds us of what in the case of Faust proved to be "des Pudels Kern" (Studirzimmer), like later on, (Trüber Tag, Feld) Faust prays the endless spirit again to change "the worm into a dog's shape". As a matter of fact the appearance of the dog here (very much like what in England is called the "know" of the dog; E. M. Wright, Rustic speech and Folklore p. 191, E. D. Dict. in v.) may be a reminiscence of either scene or of both.

3552. Min Kuffert! Min Kasse! my box, my trunk.

Peer is like the coward whose ill-gotten gains do not remain with him, — cf. lower down the clergyman's speech at the grave.

3563. klamrer sig fast til Baadkjölen.
Clutches hold of the boat's keel.

Is it mere chance that it was precisely this cook here treated so harshly by Peer Gynt whom the skipper had recommended so warmly to him before: den som er trangest stillet, er Kokken?

3571. Kokken lamslaar sin ene Haand.
One of the Cook's hands is disabled.

In U Peer Gynt is responsible for it: Peer Gynt lamslaar kokkens ene Haand.

jeg er ungeløs endnu. I am childless still.

Dr. Western writes: I wonder if this does not count

1, 198; 3, 202; F, 454; M, 271; 14, 184; J, 281; 16, 184.

for something, when we try to explain the sudden change in Peer's behaviour after he had promised to do something for the sailors (l. 3381). It is when he hears that most of the sailors, esp. the cook, have wives and children at home, that he says: Nei, om jeg gjør...... Mener De jeg punger ud til fromme for andres *unger*? (l. 3415) — Peer begins to see in a vague way he has lived in vain. What he has gained he has lost, he is comparatively speaking a poor man, he cannot even leave a child behind him, and so he envies those who can. —

3582.   læs dit Fadervor! say your Lord's prayer.

In J. L. Heiberg's En Sjæl efter Døden, Death bids the actor say his Pater Noster before he dies and the actor answers: I can't, I have not got a prompter! Truly, he too: was "to the last grasp himself", var og blev sig selv til slutt; l. 3591, which is as humorously characteristic of the speaker as in the case of the 'Lean One' for whom even a soul is a "fat joint", l. 4530.

3598.   Jeg svømmer med det venste Ben.
        I'm striking out with my left leg.

Why with the left leg? — I have a misgiving that Ibsen here confuses the Strange Passenger with the Devil who is always represented with a horse's hoof instead of the right foot. — (W.)

3608. seqq. Hvad tror De? Ved De ingen anden, som er mig lig? Aa, jeg ved Fanden —! What think you? Do you know none other that's like me? — Do I know the devil —?

In U, the Passenger first only spoke the words: Hvad tror De? to which Peer replied: Kanske De er Fanden —. The words: Ved De ingen anden som er mig lig? are added afterwards and in connection with this addition, Ibsen crossed out Kanske De er, replacing this first by: Jeg ved kun (Fanden) then, having crossed out this too, by: Jo jeg ved (Fanden), Aa was substituted for Jo only in R. So we see that the exquisite: The devil if I do (= Aa jeg ved Fanden) is not the direct inspiration of the moment, but the result of a laborious, deliberate working up!

"Peer does not mean to say that the Strange Passenger reminds him of the devil, he only means to say that he does not know anybody who is like him, but the Passenger catches his answer and makes as if he meant to compare him to the devil." (W.).

3611.   Frygten. Fear.

Compare the note on the Strange Passenger, ante. Bjørnstjerne Bjørnson is his review of the poem in 1867 connects this with the story of the "boy that became anxious: Gutten som blev ræd."

From this passage it appears clearly that Ibsen was under the influence of Paludan-Müller's Luftskipperen og Ateisten whose Montechristo as has already been briefly noted (n. to l. 3499) may be one of the prototypes of the Strange Passenger who does not object any more than Montechristo to be looked upon as a devil. In the same way, just like Peer's better nature asserts itself when compelled by fear, so the hero in Paludan-Müller's poem "har lært af al den Angst og Möie" and it is this that helps him over.

3613.   Lysets Bud. a messenger of light.

Compare 2 Cor. 11, 13, 14: For such are false apostles, deceitful workers, transforming themselves into the apostles of Christ. And no marvel for Satan himself is transformed into an angel of light.

3615.   Angst. Dread.

Messrs. Archer note (p. 219) that Angst here probably means something like "conviction of sins" and that the influence of Sören Kierkegaard may be traced in this passage. Ibsen may be indebted to Paludan-Müller more than to Kierkegaard here too, on the whole the

---

1, 204; 3, 208; F, 459; M, 273; 14, 188; J, 283; 16, 188.

latter's influence should not be exaggerated [1]). As to
Angst, although no doubt the feeling in question con-
tributes largely to convict him of his sins, the meaning
of the word can only be anxiety, fear, alarm. Compare l. 3992: O, Angst, her var mit Kejserdom".

3629 seqq.   Hvor jeg er fra, der gjælder Smil
i Højde med pathetisk Stil......
Den Sværm, som sov i Askens Urner,
gaar ej till Hverdags paa Kothurner.
Where I come from, there smiles are prized
as highly as pathetic style......
The host whose dust inurned has slumbered
treads not on week-days the cothurnus.

I quote here from a private letter of Overlærer Stavnem, who writes:

Peer's mystiske medreisende optrær ikke som bods-
prædikant med "skjældende torden og flæbevorrent
ordgyderi" (som man i sin tid sa om en pietistisk prædikant i Kjøbenhavn). Ibsen vil indskjærpe at jevn og
likefrem tale, skjemt og ironi kan ofte virke kraftigere
end hul pathos og buldrende deklamation (Ridendo
dicere verum!)".... Stavnem compares Søren Kierke-
gaards "Stadier paa Livets Vei, — uvidenskabelig
Efterskrift: Humoren indeslutter Vemod ved og Sym-
pathi med Smerten i Livet og dens Smil og Spøg rum-
mer en dyb Alvor". And after having recalled that in
Paludan-Müller's Luftskipperen og Ateisten there is
a remarkable apparent mixing up of the serious and
the ludicrous, he calls special attention to Heiberg's
Skuespillekunst, (Blandede Digtninger) "hvor Publi-
kum bebreider Thalia at hun taler ikke ophøiet og
poetisk nok, men altfor hverdagslig". The Public says:

---

[1]) It can do no harm, however, to note for later investigators that Ibsen had read
Kierkegaard's Enten-Eller already in his Grimstad days (cf. n. to l. 2461) together
with his friend Due; cf. the latter's Erindringer, p. 38. Cf. the next note. See on
Ibsen at Grimstad some valuable remarks in Bergwitz's book on this 'Smaaby'.

1, 205; 3, 209; F, 460; M, 274; 14, 189; J, 284; 16, 189.

Er det en Muse der saadan snakker?
En pæn Gudinde!

And Thalia answers:

Du fordrer at alt skal være saa fiint.
Men dermed kommer du ingen Vei,
Comediens Muse......
...... hilser dig i et andet Sprog,
End det som vanker i en Epilog, etc.

In the same way, when Peer has reproached the
Strange Passenger that his "talk was droll; how could
you think 't would stir the soul" (Ellis Roberts), the
Strange Passenger answers: "All has his time, — what
suits the taxman, would damn the bishop" i.e. what
fits the one, does not fit in the mouth of the other."

The passage: den Sværm, etc. is rendered somewhat
freely by Mr. Ellis Roberts thus:

They who've gone thro' incineration
On week-days must have relaxation,

who adds a note (p. 251) to explain and excuse the
freedom with which the translator has rendered the
general sense that the Strange Passenger is protesting
against the idea that religious sincerity must always be
coupled with a repellent severity of aspect. Anyway, he
says: "Where I live" — i.e. in some spirit world — we do
take week days off. We allow ourselves to smile then."
And Mr. Stavnem reminds us in this connection of the
fact that in the Bible too, God is said to laugh; cf. Ps.
2, 4; 59, 9 and 37, 13.

So the passage means: Man behøver ikke at gaa paa
Kothurnen naar man har et Alvorsord at si! Man kan
ogsaa smilende indprente en et Varselsord! — Naar
Passageren sier: Hvor jeg er fra, der gjælder Smil, etc.,
saa kan jo digteren ha tænkt paa den *aande*verden som
dødsbudet (for det er jo passageren) tilhører — just
as Ibsen may have done when writing about the multitude whose dust inurned has slept, Stavnem adds. I would

---

1, 205; 3, 209; F, 460; M, 274; 14, 189; J, 284; 16, 189.

here refer to the n. to l. 3632 from which it will appear
that Ibsen at one time had written of the B i s h o p
sleeping in "Askens Urner", and ask if this multitude, if
a multitude of spirits — aandeverdenen, de overjordiske
regioner han tilhører — can be said to have slept (sov,
past-tense) in the ash-urns.

The question of literary influence on Ibsen here is
thus summed up by Stavnem: tænker man paa de
literære paavirkninger Ibsen har mottat, kan man
gjerne si: fra en "metafysisk", Heibergsk verden! sml.
den apokalyptiske komedie "En Sjæl efter Døden".
And as to the expression used, Stavnem aptly reminds
us of Welhaven's lines to Wergeland (1830):

> Og ei fordi man støier paa Kothurner,
> man vækker Asken i de Skaldes Urner, —

i.e. dine hastemte (high-falutin) digte vækker ikke poe-
sien herhjemme til nyt liv![1]

3632. for Tolder sømmeligt...... for Bisp fordømmeligt.
what fits the taxman... would damn the bishop.

Instead of Bisp, U had first Prest, then Bisp. And the
next two lines ran first in U:

> Den Sværm som sov i Askens Urner
> gaar ej og kror sig paa Kothurner —

but Sværm was changed into Bisp, — in R, Ibsen re-

---

[1] The image in itself is of course common enough: at gaa paa Kothurner = at
sætte noget paa Skruer (Mau, II, 290), — in Adam Homo the man that at the
masked ball comes forth „with his mask in his hand" tells us too that art does
reside in cothurns as little as in masks:

> Om Sokken og Cothurnen vel man vrövler
> Ret som om Konsten deri skulde boe;
> Men min Cothurne som du seer, er Stövler,
> Og jeg for Sokker foretrækker Skoe.
> Bort med Cothurne! Bort med Maske, Sokke!
> I vor Tid er Personen Eet og Alt;
> I denne Tro, mit Folk, lad ei dig rokke,
> Og Konsten elsk i Konstnerens Gestalt! (9e Sang, II, 166)

And Mephistopheles (Studirzimmer, Faust I) had said practically the same
thing:

> Setz deinen Fuss auf ellenhohe Socken,
> Du bleibst doch immer, was du bist.

The Strange Passenger narrows it down to every-day circumstances. —

1, 205; 3, 209; F, 460; M, 274; 14, 189; J, 284; 16, 189.

turned to Sværm. The next line was changed already in U into the present reading. See the n. to l. 3629.

3635.   Vig fra mig, Skræmsel. Avaunt thee, bugbear.

Of course, a skræmsel is a bugbear, something that frightens one. But as a translation bugbear is all the same less satisfactory since Ibsen may well be supposed to have been thinking of the well-known Apage Satanas (Matth. 4, 10) cf. n. to l. 4122. —

3637, 8.   For den Sags Skyld vær uforsagt; —
             man dør ej midt i femte Akt.
             Oh, as for that, be reassured; —
             one dies not midmost of Act Five.

The utterance will remind English readers of Byron's Don Juan — "an instant more had stopped this Canto and Don Juan's breath (IV, 42) and: "we'll try......another track With Juan, left half-killed some Stanza's back". (IV, 14) but the difference between the general tone and "atmosphere" of the English poem and the Norwegian one is great and hence many will share Wörner's feeling who calls this "ein dürftiges Witzwort im Stile der Verkehrten Welt von Tieck" with which the Strange Passenger 'aus dem Tone fällt' (Wörner[1], p. 251, [2]p. 257) and it should be added that Ibsen may have known this play in Oehlenschläger's translation: den bagvendte Verden; cf. n. to l. 2182. "It is perhaps the well-known romantic irony that crops up — Stavnem writes — when the poet looks smiling down upon all human battles". The present writer for one must confess to the same feeling of unpleasant surprise, the passage looks at first sight like bathos, unworthy of the poët. Count Prozor too seems to have been struck by it: le poète, sur de son œuvre (maintenant) ne craint plus rien. Il ose tout. Il nous dira à un moment donné (toujours par la bouche du démon, devenu son porte-parole): "On ne meurt pas au milieu d'un cinquième acte". Et malgré cela, l'œuvre continue

---

1, 205; 3, 209; F, 460; M, 274; 14, 189; J, 284; 16, 189.

à nous émouvoir!" You smell the delicate reproach: All this n o t h w i t h s t a n d i n g!

But Mr. Stavnem thinks the passage fits very well in the mouth of a dæmonic passenger "som med al sin kynisme og bedske ironi dog saa at si repræsenterer Peers bedre jeg og gjennem angst vil drive den gamle synder til selverkjendelse og omvendelse før det er for sent...... Efter min mening ligger der ogsaa et memento mori i hans sidste ord, som betyr saa meget som "Enden er ikke endda" Matth. 24, 6, men er umiddelbar forestaaende. Mærk at næste optrin skildrer en *begravelse*! —, ogsaa et memento mori men Peer kjender endnu ikke sin besøgelses tid". I reproduce these interesting remarks although I cannot suppress all doubt as to whether the considerations meet the case fully.

As to the use of a jest to express something serious, see the n. to l.l. 3629 seqq. — Only the cook h a s just died — "midmost of Act Five." —

"Concerning the appropriateness of these words, it must be borne in mind, I think ,that though the Strange Passenger is "Fear", yet at the same time he is also Ibsen himself. He is, so to speak, Ibsen's speaking-trumpet, but in these lines Ibsen reveals himself and speaks as the poet, not as the messenger of Death. "— (Dr. W.).

3641. han var en traakig Moralist. he was a sorry moralist.

Traakig is a Swedish word, — used occasionally in Norwegian as Anders Krogvig writes, 'with humorous effect'. Professor Storm, S.I.S. p. 197 thinks it is here used as "en ren pikanteri", which Ibsen might have written in inverted comma's like "bra litet rolig" (l. 4519). The curious thing is that although Ibsen wrote (in U) Trumpeterstråle, with the Swedish å (cf. the n. to l. 1807 on Ibsen's Swedish words) he wrote, both in U and, R, not tråkig, but traakig, thereby giving it the look of a Norwegian word. But although both Aasen (p. 830) and Ross (p. 835) give etymologically related words, traakall and trok, troken (cf. N. E. D. in v. traik) the actual word traakig does not seem to occur in Norwegian dialects, unless indeed Noreen's identification (in Språk ock Stil, 1902, p. 123) with Norwegian trokug be accepted. This latter word is given by Ross in the sense of fyldig og kraftig, før og trivelig, which does not seem to fit very well semasiologically, but as he compares the adj. troken = modstræbende, etc. the connection does not seem quite so impossible. However this be, we are not likely to be far out of the way when concluding that for Ibsen the word was Swedish. —

3645.   Gud ske Lov, at det ikke er mig.
                 God be thanked that it isn't me.
In exactly the same way, in Adam Homo (II, 353):
    Til Kisten med den Tanke ned man kigger:
    Aa gudskelov, at jeg der ikke ligger!

3647.   The Clergyman's speech at the grave.
In this "poetisk Perle af høj Rang" (Brandes, Henrik Ibsen, p. 51) Ibsen gives expression to "hele hans opfatning af forholdet mellem Stat og individ" (Koht og Elias, Ibsen's Breve, I, p. 35), where his sympathy is absolutely on the side of the latter.

3653.   vegt. abashed.
By the side of this form with the Danish g, (found passim e.g. in Hærmændene paa Helgeland, F, II, 41) Ibsen also uses vek, cf. T. C. § 121. —

3669.   for mange Herrens Aar.
Usually: for m. H. A. siden. "I can hardly believe that Ibsen was here influenced by vor vielen Jahren. It must be a case of "licentia poetica". (W). —

3670.   Session. sessions.
Here = a sitting of conscription-commissioners as in the Epic Brand, (l. 1136) from which this was trans-

---

1, 206; 3, 210; F, 461; M, 274; 14, 190; J, 284; 16, 190.

ferred to Peer Gynt. So Ellis Roberts' assizes is not correct. For a description of such a meeting, see Leirdølerne, efter Ludvig Daae, Norske Sagn, 1902, p. 178.

The whole of this passage should be compared to the correspondi g lines in the Episke Brand (ed. Karl Larsen, p.p. 138 seqq.) of which I quote some of the more instructive parallels:

Tillslutt kom en, som bar sin Haand i Klæde.
Hvor Dødens bleg han over Gulvet gik! (1145,6).

. . . .

han stammed noget om en Sigd, som foer
Han nævnte noget, som var hændt i Vaade (1151, seq.).

. . . .

de glode, glante, glemte rent at snakke,
og hvert et Blik traff Gutten som et Sting.
Stillt raadslog de en Stund, som sad om Bordet.
Da stod Kaptejnen opp, den gamle, graa; —
han vilde tale men han svælgte Ordet; —
han spytted, pegte ud og sagde "gaa!" etc.

. . . .

Han gik fragaarde, længere, højt tillfjells;
man saa fra Tunet efter ham fortællende;
han steg og steg till ikke mer han skjells; —
han hørte hjemme indimellem Fjellene. —

It will be seen from this how closely with all difference of language Ibsen has followed the text of his Epic Brand in this episode which he had no use for in the dramatic version. See the n. to. l. 1342.

3702. Spædebarn.... Fæstekvinde, betrothed... little child.

That Passarge could translate this by: "mit 'ner Dirne" shows how very little he was in touch with Norwegian life and manners, which is so necessary to do justice to the original; see the Introductory matter to this commentary. He should have known how common it is there that young people living high up in the mountains and far from the nearest village, simply cànnot get at a priest to marry them and they would be highly astonished and from their point of view j u s t l y indignant to hear that for this reason the betrothed was looked upon as a "wench"! Compare the case of Ingrid; n. to. l. 729.

Spædebarn, for the sake of the metre. The usual form is spædbarn. (W.)

3720.   førsled. carted.

Docent J. Brynildsen writes: this verb is not found elsewhere. He thinks of Swedish førsla, to carry, convey. Professor Storm on the other hand, (S. I. S. p. 194) speaks of "det folkelige førsled", without mentioning Swedish at all and as if it were quite beyond doubt — it is however not in the dictionaries. Remembering that the sb. førsel = carriage, transit is quite common, we may perhaps conclude that in form as well as in signification, a Norwegian førsle is the exact counterpart of English to cart, by which the Archers render it right enough if we do not press the meaning too much. For strictly speaking, the man is not likely to have used a cart (nor a horse for that matter) there where he had to toil. —

3736. af dem, ham nærmest stod. Of those most near to him.

Dr. Western writes: Happily there can be no doubt that ham is the correct reading. Of course han would be grammatically correct, but for all that it is a poor shift. Remember, he is represented as standing in a ring of his family: "dem han nærmest stod" could then only mean that he stood nearer one side of the circle than the other, which gives no sense at all. What is meant is of course the ring that stood nearest to him, i.e. his own family, opposed e.g. to his friends and acquaintances, if he had any. So, from a logical point of view ham is the only word possible here. — And the expression is not forced at all. Of course, in ordinary prose it would run: av dem som stod ham nærmest, but in poetry the present form is quite correct. —

See also T. C. § 135.

3745. Brottsling. offender. —

Mr. Anders Krogvig writes: et rent svensk ord; ubrukelig i norsk" after which he quotes the passage reproduced supra n. to l. 1807. —

3754. Hans Færd var Langspil under Spaanens Dæmper.
His days were as a lute with muted strings.

The general sense of this line that his life was that of a quiet man is of course clear enough and well rendered by the Archers, although the Norwegian langelek (-eik = langspiel) and lute are not quite identical. But the image as such is not at all clear. I must confess to not having seen the difficulty to which Anders Krogvig called my attention, — I had, wrongly as would now seem to be the case, explained it as: under Spaanen som Dæmper, where I seemed to have felt Spaan (Spon) = the 'trækasse' made of spaaner = chips by a figure of speech which the learned in language-lore speak of as "pars pro toto". My friend writes: "I have asked many versed in the lore of musical instruments but did not get any satisfactory explanation out of them. The Langleik, it is true, is "played or touched" (spilles eller slaaes) with a little bit of wood that is called spån, here and there, but then it is the other flat hand that is used as a sordine — Dæmper. And Mr. Krogvig quoting H. J. Wille's description of Sillefjord in Telemarken to the above effect, adds: Of course the Langspiel is a relatively quiet instrument, but howsoever you take it, the "spon" cannot be a 'Dæmper' and concludes that there must be some confusion in the mind of Ibsen as to how the langeleik was worked.

3764. uryggeligt. immovably.

See Maal og Minne, 1915, p. 170 where the word is explained and a preceding passage compared: det ryg-

— 294 —

ger længer og længere bort. (l. 881). The word is practically the same as urokkelig = unshaken, cf. however Kalkar in v. p. 690, who gives two words. Mr. Ellis Roberts translates: stand firm on a self-foundation which is perhaps rather free and not strong enough. The word may be said to form the leading motive of the Kongsemnerne, cf. F. II, 291; 367; 404, 427, etc. and it is the very term by which Ibsen himself might best be characterised if we had to do so in one adjective. In his earlier days he wrote (Breve, I, 114) to King Charles of Norway and Sweden about "den livsgerning som jeg uryggelig tror og ved at Gud har lagt paa mig", and he has since remained "uryggelig" throughout life, unshaken in the pursuing of his path as he was in his convictions; cf. the n. to. l. 4139. —

3771.　　　　　Aandsfrænde. Kinsman in spirit.

Peer's calling himself the kinsman in spirit of this quiet worker before the Lord is perhaps not quite so absurd as it appears at first sight. For with all the difference possible, there is some resemblance in that they have both been themselves "nok" — only, Peer fondly imagines that like the other man he has all the time been "himself". Of an entirely different opinion is Mr. Ellis Roberts for whom (cf. his Introduction, p. XIII) "this unnamed lad who suffered scorn and self-mutilation rather than desert his betrothed, his unborn child and his old mother.... stand(s) definitely for a keen, dogged faithfulness to others, in which alone self-realisation may be found." Has Ibsen pored out the vials of his ironical wrath in vain?

It is interesting to note that the sneer was a sort of afterthought. In U Ibsen had written: "paa Randen af denne Firfingrens Grav".

3780.　　før Graveren kommer. ere the grave-digger comes.

The Gravedigger shows himself soon enough even though Peer Gynt should not recognise the Messenger;

compare the Button-moulder-scene and the n. to l. 3629.

3796.   fattig men dydig. poor but virtuous ever.

To be compared to Peer's delightful modest declaration when later on the Button-Moulder has said: to call thee virtuous would be going too far, Peer answers: "that I do not lay any claim to"

3798.   The auction-scene at Hægstad-farm.

The desolation described in the stage-direction prepares us for the fact that Hægstad has not exactly flourished! The scene is perhaps as obscure as it is sordid, — Mr. Ellis Roberts' word which is surely not too strong; p. p. XVI, 252. Aslak seems to have married Ingrid. His love for her was no deeper than his fear is great that she might "take death by the nose", make fun of death i.e. come back to life! It is for her that he is now in mourning. The man in grey must be Mads Moen. The boy who calls after Aslak: Mother that's dead will be after you, Aslak (Salig Mor kommer efter dig, Aslak) is generally I think supposed to be the son of Ingrid and A s - l a k. As it is this remark that causes Peer the greatest disgust, Mr. Ellis Roberts thinks we must assume that the lad is the son of Peer and Ingrid, — in a note he speaks of a "bare possibility" that he should be the son of Mads and Ingrid. Neither supposition seems very likely considering that Peer must have been absent very long: he has come back with ice-grey hair and he finds Solveig an old woman — to the parasites in the fourth act he speaks of the time when he approached the age of fifty as long, long ago: jeg nærmed mig mod femtiaarene; l. 1952 — so his child cannot have been a boy anymore. And if Mads has had any marital relations with Ingrid (for which as Mr. Ellis Roberts aptly remarks with a reference to the fæstekvinde of l. 3702, the betrothal was frequently the legitimate beginning), this must have been before Ingrid's elopement with Peer. And as to Mr. Ellis Robert's objection that Peer Gynt's reply shows his special disgust at the lad's words, — these are very indelicate in a n y case. Now if the boy is Aslak's son, we are confronted with the undoubtedly curious case of a son calling his father by his Christian name, but as a correspondent writes: things are so topsy-turvy in this family (forholdene er noksaa opløste) that it is quite imaginable. But it is also possible that the gut should be a servant there, which would make any discussion as to whose son he is, quite superfluous and the 'matmor', the mistress of a farm, would of course, be called 'mor' by all the servants.

3800.   Atter og fram, etc. Forward and back, etc.
Compare the n. to l. 1239.

3802.   skjær = skjærer.
Compare the n. to l. 892.

3809, 10.   Jeg vil heller kalde det Hjemkommerøl; —
            Bruden ligger i et Ormebøl,
            I'd rather call it a house-warming treat; —
            the bride is laid in a wormy bed.

The grim humour of this passage is equalled and perhaps to some extent explained by a line in the Button-moulder scene: (l. 4099) where he delicately hints to Peer that in his body the worms will live at their ease, — i Skrotten skal Ormene leve gjildt". So: she who would be the bride if your suggestion were right is like Polonius "at supper", not where she eats but where she is eaten i.e. is with the worms, is dead and as "dust thou art, to dust returnest" (l. 3924: af jord est du kommen), — I propose to call it hjemkommerøl = a feast given on coming home!

The word Hjemkommerøl (cf. Maal og Minne, 1913, p. 129: the f o r m is Danish but the notion is Norwegian) occurs a couple of times in the Huldreeventyr; cf. ed. '12 p.p. 184 and 210; cf. Aasen and Ross; heimkome-øl, heimkomarøl, which forms suggest, that the original composition expressed, not: the feast of the home-com e r s, as the modern form would make us believe, but that of the home-com i n g.

3813.   en Stöbeske. a casting-ladle.

Compare the notes to l.l. 1399 and the Button-moulder.

3816.   En Skilling. A half-penny.

Thus Messrs. Archer and Ellis Roberts properly translate it, for a skilling is a doit, a very s m a l l value whereas the Schilling of Morgenstern and Brons wrongly suggests a comparatively high price. —

3819.   han var Svoger till Døden, etc.

he was kinsman to Death, etc.

Compare l. 3824: Kom, Svoger! Come kinsman. — As Svoger suggests a brother-in-law in the first place of course, one is likely to fall into the trap that un-like some other translators, the English ones have avoided, to render the word thus. Svoger is however quite common in the general sense of relative (den som ved ægteskab er anrørende, etc. Feilberg III, 686 ¹) like svogerskab actually and even in the first place means affinity, relation by marriage (Ibsen og Bjørnson kom i svogerskab da Ibsens eneste søn ægted en av Bjørn-søns døttre) and besides, svoger is used more definitely for other relations; cf. e. g. = svigersøn: du skal ikke ha to svogre til en Datter, Mau, p. 121. And cf. Ibsen's Ballonbrev (F. IV, 377): kun så meget får man ud.... dengang Farao var Gud og herr Potifar minister, samt at herr ministrens svoger Josef Jacobsen har bygt dem".

On Døden, cf. a note in T. C. § 31. — As we say of a pale looking man that he is en bror til døden, so svoger til Døden = a near kinsman of death, and of Aslak the

---

¹) And passim in Holberg, e. g. the relation of father-in-law to son-in-law (Gert Westphaler), Polit. Kandestøber, etc. In the Ellevte Junii simply = related (how-ever distantly) etc. —

Smith whereby the latter is put as far out of the pales of sympathy as the former.

3821. Du glemmer, paa Hæggstad var en Stabburdør.

You forget that at Hegstad was a storehouse door.

This is the door of the storehouse (Mr. Ellis Roberts' stable-door is an almost unpardonable slip!) and in which the unmarried daughters often slept (especially of a saturday night; cf. n. to l. 870) and through which Peer Gynt had been allowed to slip. And hence Peer was "related" to Ingrid. To which in reply there falls the well-deserved taunt; you were never dainty, for the fact and its consequences nothwithstanding, you married her!

3830　　　　　Aslak, hvis du Svælget fugter.

　　　　　Aslak, if you wet your whistle.

That the smith should be given to drink is in the nature of things, —: it's easier to find bread in a dog's kennel than any brandy left in a smithy, as the saying is: man finder lettere brød i hundehus end udrukken brændevin i smedje; Feilberg, Fattigmands Snaps, Dania, V, 117. —

3833.　　　　Se Katten paa Dovre!

　　　　　Look, the cat of the Dovrë!

The reference is to a tale "Kjætten paa Dovre", of which there exist several versions; see e.g. Folkeev. 1912, p. 240): a man from Finmarken on his way to the King of Denmark comes to Dovrëfield where he was allowed to sleep of a night in a house the inhabitants had had to flee from on account of the trolls that were expected there that Xmas evening. The man frightens the trolls away by calling his bear a "pussy". Another version is found as a motif in the very tale of Peer Gynt of which it forms the final incident; cf. Huldreev. 1912, p. 157 seqq. and Archers' translation p. 286. For other variants cf. Feilberg, Jul, II, p. 323. We have a reference here not to the drama but to a source. —

3835.   Her er den gjilde Renbukk.
              Here is the wonderful reindeer.

Peer's story has been told so often that we may perhaps suppose people ended by believing it; cf. the n. to l. 69. Or is it merely an ironical reference as in the case of the other objects sold?

3839.   Usynlighedskuften. The invisible cloak.
              See the n. to l. 669. —

3853.   En Drøm om en Spændebog.
              A dream of a silverclasped book.

On the Spændebog cf. n. to l. 1263. Mr. Ellis Roberts wrongly thinks the prayer-book itself is put up for auction (p. XVI).

3854.   en Hægtekrog. a hook and an eye.

A hægte or hægtekrog = a thing of no value, a mere nothing; cf. jeg giver ham en Hægte. det skal ikke fejle for en Hægte, Mau, I, p. p. 321, 487. — The translation should run: a hook, not: hook and eye.

3857. Kronen.... Af det dejligste Straa.... Et vindlagt Aegg!
a crown.... of the loveliest straw.... an addled egg.

All that Peer puts up for auction has a clear reference to his history — but what does the crown of straw mean that fits the first who puts it on and the vindlagt ægg? As to the former, if there were not this restriction about whom it fits, we should of course think of the crown that Peer is honoured with in the lunatic asylum, and although nothing is said there about it being one of straw, it will be remembered that Blasenfelt was crowned with one; n. to l. 3343. And this is perhaps the explanation i.e. the references would then all the same be to Begriffenfeldt's crown, for all I find besides about a crown of straw is that it's for a fallen woman (Feilberg, III, 616 b.). — As to the vindlagt æg, Brynildsen translates it with express reference to this passage by addled and is followed by the Archers and Mr. Ellis Roberts. Else we might think of a vindel-æg,

---

1, 214; 3, 218; F, 468; M, 279; 14, 197; J, 290; 16, 197.

vind-æg: egg without shell, cf. Feilberg, III, 1061, 1065.
Wind-eggs, — "de vana et frivola molientibus. Ab avi-
bus translatum quae Veneris imaginatione concipiunt
ova, sed inania, etc. Stoett, n° 2141 (Sartorius). Peer
would thus be supposed to say: An egg like my dream
of life which promises much but proved to be nothing!
As Mr. Anders Krogvig informs me that et vindlagt æg
is generally known as another term for et vindæg =
et tomt ufrugtbart æg, the difficulty disappears and
the reference becomes clear. —

3867   en vederstyggelig Digter — an abominable liar —
There is here a slight pun on the word digter which
means not only a poet but also one that "digter ihob"
that "gives to airy nothing a local habitation and a
name" i. e. who gives his imagination free play. Such
a "digter" is akin to a dreamer; cf. Sigurd Høst, Edda,
1915 p.p. 334, 336, where "Så gå da sigret frem
fra digt til dåd" will be found quoted from the Comedy
of Love. Mr. Ellis Roberts' romancer seems therefore
more adequate than the Archers' liar. cf. n. to l. 4341.

3875.   nu er han for mange Aar siden hængt.
it's many a year now since he was hanged.
Compare Aase's prediction: "Du blir sagtens hængt
tillsidst' (l. 363) and her disgust when the Smith
threatens to do so: Hvad, hænge min Peer! Ja Prøv
om I tør! (l. 715). —

3884.   der glider ligesom en fremmed Mine over ham.
a look of strangeness (as it were) comes over him.
Well yes, — "The devil in that witty yet serious San
Francisco episode is.... nothing but Peer at the auction. What his public looked upon as nonsense and a
brandy-inspired bit of a joke, was a desperate cry from
a soul that begins to see its emptiness but no one di-
vined how incisively-natural (skjærende naturligt) the
cry was" [1] (Eitrem, Samtiden, 1906). Compare also

---

[1] Wörner remarks (I[1] p. 253, [2] 260) quite rightly that the story was meant for
the public before the stage rather than on it. —

1, 216; 3, 220; F, 470; M, 280; 14, 199; J, 291; 16, 199.

J. Collin, Henrik Ibsen, p. 335 who quotes Thorbjørns
words in Synnøve Solbakken: "Other people have part
in what one has become oneself" and calls this apo-
logue "eine Selbstverteidigung Peer Gynts". Wörner
seems to think Ibsen's prophetic soul may here predict
what the criticism of Peer Gynt will be: "Wass sich der
Verfasser des Peer Gynt hier sarkastisch weissagt ist
ihm alsbald wiederfahren. Seine Landsleute haben
diese Leistung (P.G.) obwohl er einen leibhaften Norweger unter dem Mantel seiner Dichtung birgt, aüsserst
outriert gefunden".

That it was meant to apply to Peer Gynt is so patent
that in view of the line: "whereupon the performer
bowed low and retired" — hvorpaa Kunstneren bukked
ærbødigst og gik", (l. 3906) we involuntarily look for
a Stagedirection at the end: han bukker ærbødigst og
gaar. But as to the e x a c t bearing of it on Peer Gynt
and possibly on Ibsen, many of us will feel like the multitude there a p u z z l e d silence: en u s i k k e r
Stilhed.

Professor Sturtevant goes even a little further and
thinks there is a covert reference here to the response
which Ibsen's works had hitherto been given at the
hand of public and critics: "What could be more Ibsen-
esque than to affirm in this indirect fashion charged
with sarcasms and ridiculous caricature that his critics
had discovered everything but the truth." (Publications
of the Society for the Advancement of Scandinavian
Study, I p. 29). The story is at any rate not, as the professor thinks "a pure fabrication for the purpose of
bewildering these simple-minded peasants" (p. 37) but
a direct borrowing from Phædrus (Fabulæ, V, 5: Scurra
et Rusticus); as pointed out by Collin, Samtiden 1913,
p. 599, Wörner, l.c. etc. —

As to the form San Franzesco which Prof. Storm S.M.
p. 30 changed into San Francisco, cf. T. C. § 120. —

3898.   man muss sich drappieren" —
"en caprice som Ibsen smurte ind" — as we should be allowed to call it in the poet's own words; cf. the n. to l. 3499, a r e a l caprice this time!

3917.   Jordlög. Wild onions.
The word is not in the dictionaries. Mr. Brynildsen writes: Is not found anywhere. But as Rams (garlic, ramsons), ramsløk is called Allium ursinum and as the bear is mentioned just after this, jordløk may be a provincial expression for ramsløk, which is one with few swathings and so fits the context well — som er en i tankegangen passende, virkelig løk med faa svøp".

3924. af Jord est du kommen. of the earth art thou come.
Compare Genesis 3, 19; Eccles, 12, 7; the n. to l. 3809. For est, see the n. to l. 952. —

3936.   Du gamle Spaamands-Gjøg!
You old soothsayer-humbug!
In gjøg, literally cuckoo, there is indeed some element that recalls the humbug, the "vigtig-Peer" for, when in the Ordbog over Gadesproget (²p. 188) we find: Gøg, ungt menneske uden videre Erfaring eller Dygtighed med et ubehageligt, vigtigt Væsen", what must be looked upon as the essential point here is precisely the giving oneself the air of knowing and this is exactly what Peer now finds out he should nót do. —
As to the imagery, see the use Professor Gran makes of it in his Norsk Aandsliv i det 19de Aarh. (p. 162): Hvem av os har ikke hat øieblikke hvor han som Peer Gynt sat og pillet paa sit livs løk, skrællende lag efter lag, angstfuld speidende efter kernen som ikke kom, aldrig kom. Og kanske var netop saadanne øieblikke de kjernedannende i vort liv."

3939.   Det hjælper ikke enten du tuder eller beer.
You won 't escape either by begging or howling.
In U we read: enten du græder eller ler, and when we come to think of it, the 'either or' requires words more

---

1, 218; 3, 222; F, 471; M, 281; 14, 201; J, 292; 16, 201.

strongly opposed to each other than weep and pray, — and this condition is filled admirably by: to weep or laugh. Some will therefore feel inclined to look upon ber as a slip. But it is of course not entirely without meaning.

3971.   Livet... har en Ræv bag Øre.

              Life... plays with cards up its sleeve.

But as the Archers add in a note: "to have a fox behind the ear" is a proverbial expression for double-dealing, insincerity. The explanation is found in Falk og Torp: "dannet efter at ha en Skjælm bag øret med tanken paa rævens list!" By the side of the usual form here given, we also find: Han har Mikkel bag øret (Mau, II, p. 202) Mikkel (cf. the next line: sætter Mikkel paa Spring) = the German equivalent for Reynard. — In bag øre we have the popular form of the more literary: bag øret, the t not being pronounced; cf. the proper name in one of Bjørnson's later dramas: 'Daglanne' — for Dag-landet. —

3981.   Nissebukk-tanker. hobgoblin thoughts.

              See the n. to l. 1424. —

3992.   (Peer) löber ind over Skogstien.

              Hurries off along the wood path. —

Mr. Bernard Shaw tells us (The Quintessence of Ibsenism, p. 52, n) of a remarkable interpretation of Peer Gynt by a Miss Pagan according to whom Peer here goes away.... to die! Nature is ironical, says Peer bitterly (l. 3965) and that discovery of his own nothingness is taken by Miss Pagan as his death, the subsequent adventures being those of the soul". And Mr. Shaw adds: "It is impossible to demur to so poetic an interpretation" — but, not unlike Lord Byron's young lady who whispering she would n e v e r consent, consented, — he proceeds: though it assumes.... that Peer had not wholly destroyed his soul". See for further considerations ib. —

3995.   Furumo. A heath with fir-trees.

When soon after its publication the Peer Gynt was reviewed by Bjørnstjerne Bjørnson (in the Norsk Folkeblad, 23 Nov. '67) he called this scene the best of the book: "dette er det Bedste i hele Bogen". And the admiration of later critics is not less intense. John Paulsen (Nye Erindringer, 1901: Sidste møde med Ibsen, p. 129) speaks of this "marvellous scene" where Peer Gynt walks about on the heath, and where all nature seems to have become Peer Gynt's roused conscience, where all in the withered leaves, the broken straws, the falling dew-drops and the sighing in the air reproaches him with his useless good-for-nothing life (for hans gagnløse, forfeilede liv). He told Ibsen once how great the impression was that this scene never failed to make on him and that he had known the whole by heart, — at which Ibsen confided to him that he had originally meant to make Peer also hear at this supreme moment of reckoning, the voice of a hen — "a hen's cackling voice" to remind him of his old mother Aase, whom he had so often given pain, dear old Mother Aase, who was so fond of her sonnie, but whom she was always forced to scold, cackling like an old hen". This bit of information is very interesting from various points of view, among others because it suggests that an earlier "utkast" may have existed of the play, at least of this scene, and that Ibsen at all stages of his work unflinchingly rejected if necessary even the most picturesque passages. But I wonder if many of my readers will agree with John Paulsen where he adds his regret that Ibsen had not kept "this characteristic feature". Apart from the fact that a hen can hardly be supposed to be at home on this blasted heath, more redolent of witches than fowls, we can hardly imagine the comparison to be flattering to the dear old soul. And as Paulsen himself adds in a note: Now the image is more

---

1, 221; 3, 225; F, 475; M, 284; 14, 204; J, 294; 16, 204.

direct and more explicit, — we hear Aase's own voice"
(l. 4068). This is Aase's voice indeed! For even if the
references in her first words about the post-boy were
not so clear, we should have recognised her in the truly
touching last lines where the voice attributes all her
darling son's failings to the devil as in her life she had
excused him by drink. And Peer of course gladly seizes
the opportunity to escape. —

"The nearest approach to a justification of the moral
or problem purpose, which Ibsen's graver prophets
attribute to him is... (this)... scene, where quite in
the manner of Goethe, thoughts and watchwords and
songs and tears take corporeal form and assail the aged
Peer Gynt with their reproaches", Mr. Edmund Gosse
writes (H. Ibsen, p. 118). And it is certainly not excluded that here as in the case of the dog (cf. n. to l. 3550)
Ibsen was under the influence of the "esteemed author",
en agtet Forfatter (l. 2585), "whom he owed so much"
as has been remarked inter alios by J. Paulsen, Samliv
med Ibsen p. 72: It is especially in Peer Gynt that
traces of Goethe's influence will be found, not only in
the choice of the form, the nonchalant rhymed prose,
that comes so close to the colloquial language (interrup-
ted by some inserted lyrical poems) but also in the
composition itself" [1]; see ante p. 223.

"In der "Komödie der Liebe" vergleicht Falk das
verfehlte, von dem Ideal abgefallene Dasein des Men-
schen einem von Brand zerstörtem Walde", J. Collin
writes, l.l. p. 336. "Was dort nur bild ist, ist hier Szene-
rie und Symbol zugleich". What Collin does not seem

---

[1] Others who have observed the resemblance of Peer Gynt and Faust are Schirmer (Syn og Segn, 1915, p. 97 seqq.) and quite lately Henning Kehler, Edda, 1916,
who remarks: P. G. slutter sig i Formen til Værker som „Faust", Kaiser Octavianus
(Tieck), Aladdin, En Sjæl efter Døden, Ahasverus og Fibiger's Johannes den Døber",
— all on account of their form, i. e. rather formlessness. He also observes that the
division into scenes which is here wanting, "kan bruges til at markere en Handling
som bevæger sig frem i sæt, men ikke en fremadskridende „insinuant" eksposition."
— (p. p. 269, 281). —

---

to have noticed in his excellent paraphrase, there is even
to be found the very comparison, essential I should
almost say, where in the language of the Evangelist
(S. Matthew, 23, 27) Falk says: der lugter lig hvor to
gaar dig forbi paa gadehjørnet, smilende med læben,
med løgnens klumre kalkgrav indeni
(F, II, 242) juist as here Peer smells "Stank og Raaden-
skab forinden, alt ihob en kalket Grav."

Then there is the question of the origin of these
"accusing voices" that he hears in the thread-balls,
the troll-representatives of his past [1]) and which he
roughly kicks out of the way, and the others some of
which are voices of surrounding nature such as the
withered leaves, the sighing in the air, the dew
drops [2]) and the broken straws. Here it would seem we
are again on Norwegian soil. For these echoing voices
of nature are to be compared however distantly I think
in this case, to the voices out of the mountains as in
the Peer Gynt tale (Huldreev. p. 155); Archers' translation p. p. 283, 4; those of birds as in Manddatteren og
Kjærringdatteren (Folkeev. ed. '12 p. 53 seqq.) or by
other animals and by the trolls; cf. Feilberg III, p. p.

---

[1]) Thread-balls as the incorporations of trolls are legion in Norwegian, Danish
and Swedish folklore, as they are found in German too. The Archers have quoted
(p. VI) a passage from Bertha Tuppenhaugs Fortællinger which Ibsen is sure to have
read (ed. 1912. p 25; compare ib. p. 296). Further: Asbjørnsen, Udv. Folkeev. 1907,
I, 59 (Guldslottet som hang i Luften); Lappiske Eventyr ed. Qvigstad og Sandberg,
p. 102, 3; Kleiven, I gamle daagaa, p. 34; Olsen, No. Folkeev. og Sagn 1912, p. p.
34, 198, 235 (Kjerle = nøste?), 236. — See Feilberg in v. ild (II, 10, a), ib. III, 520,
b, Spøgelse som garnnøgle eller hestepære; and ib. III, 959 in v. udøbt: udøbt myrdet
barn ses som trillende garnnøgler. See also Feilberg, Bjærgtagen, p. p. 33, 48 (cf.
Mau, II, 94: Der er et Nøgle under ham = han kan ikke sidde stille. For Swedish
Folklore, see Wigström, Folktro, p. p. 85, 175 (trollan förskara sig till svarta Kattor
eller till store nystan, etc.); H. and E. Folkminnen, 1907 p. 374; Hermelin, Sägner
ock Folktro, p. p. 48, 60; Weis, Sägner pa Aspelandsmål, p. 116. — See R. Köhler,
Kl. Schriften, I, 407. —
The central idea underlying all this is of course the theory that not only animals
but p a c e the word, all inaminate objects have souls too; for which belief I refer
but to a couple of works: Meyer's chapter on the Seelenglauben p. p. 90 seqq. of
his Myth. der Germanen; Feilberg's book on Sjæletro, 1914 and of course the
chapters on Animism in Tylor's Primitive Culture.

[2]) As here the dew-drops, so elsewhere we have blood-drops which are introduced speaking; Asbjørnsen quoted by Feilberg, Tillæg p. 47. b.

127, 134 and Tillæg p. p. 115 and 162 (in v. v. røst,
dyrerøster, råbe, fugl)¹). It is in fact the motif that we
are almost daily reminded of when "a little birdie"
comes to tell us a secret. The origin may in some cases
be the echo, — called in Old Norse dvergamål, = the
language of dwarfs; cf. Paul's Grundriss, I¹ 1032 = III³,
290. The nøster (or nyster; Danish nøgle, Feilberg p.
723) may be explained as gusts of wind; cf. Feilberg,
Tillæg p. 314; Olrik, Nordisches Geistesleben, p. 26;
Mannhardt, Baumkultur, p. p. 76 seqq., on the contrary thinks of moss. —

By the side of the commentary of J. Collin mentioned, we have a very useful one in Count Prozor's
little book on the Peer Gynt (1907, p. 53, seqq.) Ce-
pendant, Peer est plus paysan et plus avocat que jamais. A chaque reproche il répond par un argument
spécieux, à chaque cri de sa conscience il oppose un
audacieux sophisme. Jamais il n'a si bien manié l'art
des détours inspiré par le Grand Tordu."

Georg Brandes had written of these "anklagende
ord med hvilken man kan tænke sig at Digteren i
slappe timer har sporet sig selv.... men som det er
umuligt at forestille sig under Form af en Peer Gyntsk
Selvanklage. Hvor skulde den elendige Peer nogensinde
har kunnet stille sig et Løsen, hvor kan han bebrejde sig

¹) When in the Merchant of Venice, Bassanio is commenting on the caskets to
himself, a song is heard which undoubtedly directs the suitor's choice, — „So may
the outward shows be least themselves", he exclaims, clearly showing that the teaching of the poem: fancy is but engendered i n t h e e y e s has not been vouchsafed
in vain. There is nothing whatever in the scene to indicate that the song was
sung at the order or the instigation of Portia of which the sly little wench was
otherwise quite capable. So the possibility remains that it was meant by the poet
as an interpretation of this motif of the supernatural voices in the air that the remarks above give some illustration of.
As to the voices of trolls which are heard passim in the folk-tales, (cf. to quote one
more instance: sei henni Deld at Dild dat i eld = motiv: den store Pan er død;
Moltke Moe, Episke Grundlove, Edda '15, 3, p.p. 90, 91) I should like to remind the
student of two interpretations of it in later literature, one already century-old: cf.
Washington Irving's Rip van Winkle and one on the contrary quite recent: Selma
Lagerlöf who makes such a splendid use of it in one of the most wonderful products
of her pen: Gammal Fäbodsägn (Troll ock Människor, 1915, p. 72). —

ikke at have gjort det!" Henrik Jæger (1888, p. 203) [1] has explained the apparent contradiction by calling attention to the fact that Peer says this as the typical Norwegian, Peer Normand, — "nationens representant — da bliver der mening i anklagerne". But there is not really any s e l f-reproach. Peer Gynt is rather the accused and surely there is nothing extraordinary in it that the p o e t once more tells Peer Gynt and his public by these accusing voices what he thinks of Peer?

4009.　　Graad af Barnerøster. like children's weeping.

Compare a story by Blicher (Høstferierne) of the unborn children's souls punishing the married couple that might have been their parents.... When the old woman kneels at the altar twelve little children come flying to her and beat her: "this you get because you might have been our mother" etc., then fifty who might have been her grandchildren and quite a church full of her great-grandchildren i n p o s s e. Feilberg, Norden, 1902, p. 194. — Which somehow as a materialisation reminds one of Kong Haakon in the Pretenders who s e e s the unborn thoughts. (F, II, 408).

4016.　　　　　Pusselanker. feet to run on. —

One of the two words that Ibsen condescended to explain to Passarge (cf. Breve, II, 83): små trippende børneben eller børnefødder og udtrykket anvendes kun af mødre eller ammer når de pludrer med de små børn". The explanation is interesting for although it is quite common in Norwegian and Danish and not only in the mouth of mothers as Ibsen says (Saa skal jeg igjen see dine hvide Hænder og smaa Pusselanker, etc. a lover says to his lass in Bjerregaards Fjeldeventyr, Nordahl Rolfsen, No. digtere, p. 210; Feilberg, II, 900 in v. as well as in v. lanke; Ordbog over Gadesproget) the poet's express words about its function

---

[1] Compare Wörner, I¹ p. 261, who explains Peer's „sins of omission" in the same way, and by a reference to Paul Heyse's Martyrer der Phantasie, not as a possible source of course (its date is 1874) but as a parallel. —

show that such a word as tootsies (or, as we should have
said some years ago: trilbies!) comes nearer the original
in " rank" than the simple 'feet' by which the translators render it, — inclusive of......Passarge himself!

Jespersen in his recent book on the language of
children compares the formation of pusse — to what
he calls the "meaningless" (meningløse) substitution
of mavse for mave, and manse for mand-se, dreng.
(p. 257) ¹) From a private communication I add that as
to the word of which this pusse is likely to be an extension, he thinks of 'putterne' in "the language of nurses"
(ammesproget) and suggests a possible ultimate connection with pote. — Lanker is used by itself in this same
sense as the whole, — sometimes = hands. —

Dr. Western thinks of a possible connection with pus
= a kitten (this is also Falk og Torp's view), the baby
being compared to one and its feet to the kitten's paws.
The short vowel in pusselanker would be owing to
stresslessness, — I dare not say "less-stress-ness"!

4019. Fusk og skjæve Ben. a bungled crook-legged thing.

It will be remembered that the son of Peer and the
Green Lady is lame: Kan du ikke se, han er lam paa
Skanken? (l. 1513).

4035, 6. Faafængt var dog ej jer Fødsel; —
lægg jer stillt og tjen till Gjødsel.
Not in vain your birth, however; —
lie but still and serve as manure.

These two lines like some others in this scene are
afterthoughts in this sense that they were added by
Ibsen in the margin of U, the first draft. Under these
the word pent may be seen quite clearly in the facsimile
of this passage in Karl Larsen's ed. of the Episke
Brand (p. 34) and the Eft. Skrifter (I p. XLIV) and on
inspection of the M. S. I find it indeed to be there, but
not written either in ink or in lead-pencil, but scratched

¹) Johs. Brøndum-Nielsen (Politiken) thinks the extension is quite normal.

1, 222; 3, 226; F, 476; M, 284; 14, 205; J, 295; 16, 205.

in with a sharp instrument. It is not quite clear what it refers to nor by whom it is written. A burst of enthusiasm by a quondam proprietor? Hardly the only one we knew of, Pontoppidan; to go by the description Karl Larsen gives of him (Introd. p. p. 1. seqq.) he was not capable of any such appreciation. —

A little higher up on the same page of U (f°. 27, 3, recto) the word Viljer is found written twice in lead-pencil, — in what looks like Ibsen's handwriting. Possibly a reminder of a passing thought about 'the will' which he noted down for later use and which did find expression afterwards in the lines:

Tanker og Taarer og hele klatten
og Værker og Viljer —! Et Flor om Hatten!

found in U only but crossed out there after l. 4086:

jeg har mange Døde; jeg skal følge Lig. —

Observe that the Værker of Værker and Viljer had first been found in the line which now runs: Vi er et Løsen du skulde stillet os — for here Ibsen had written first in U: Vi er Værker du skulde villet os, — and later on the Værker find a place in what is now l. 4058:

Vi er Værker; du skulde øvet os.

4037. Susning i Luften. A sighing in the air.

The personification of the Sighing air reminds one of the still bolder one perhaps in the Classische Walpurgis-nacht of the Will-o'-the Wisp. — See also n. to l. 3995.

4040. kuget. cowed.

The Archers have hit upon the exact equivalent in meaning and in form. The form kuge for kue is archaic, — perhaps dialectal although it is neither in Aasen nor in Ross. See Fritzner in v. kúga.

4041. I din Hjertegrube. in thy heart's pit.

Or in thy heart's hollow as Mr. Ellis Roberts renders it. As Professor Julius Olsen has remarked in a note to his ed. of Brand (p. 328 = F, III, 243) the word (plainly based on German "Herzgrube") is not used

here by Ibsen in the current (dictionary-)meaning:
pit of the stomach, but = (inner) heart. —

4045.   dit dumme Stev! thou foolish stave!

Here too the literal dictionary-meaning of the word
would lead us astray. Stev cannot be here the refrain (as
little as in Paa Vidderne: nu bytted jeg bort mit sidste
Stev for et høiere syn paa Tingen, F, IV, 356) the burden of a song, but the refrain, the repetition of, much
more generally: what we have heard before, i. e. almost
= an echo. And surely the sighing in the air may be
called an echo, — that of Peer's conscience. —

This distich too was added later on in the margin
of U, first in the form: Fik jeg Tid till Digt og Væv?

This disclaimer of Peer's as to his poetry may be
compared to his reputation of being a vederstyggelig
Digter (l.l. 3867 seq.) but remember the play upon the
word there. Mr. Brons (p. 218) thinks Væv = gewebe
here! Fortunately he admits it is used figuratively. —

4048.   Vi er Taarer, der ej blev fældte. Isbrodd, etc.

We are tears unshed for ever. Ice-spears, etc.

Prof. Sturtevant (Publ. Soc. Adv. Sc. Study, I, p.
32 seq.) rightly compares this to a passage in the Pretenders: det er en stor Synd at dræbe en fager Tanke,
and to Brand's Ice-church. —

4056, 7.   Takk; — jeg græd i Rondesvalen, —
fik dog lige fuldt paa Halen!

Thanks; — I wept in Rondë-cloisters, —
none the less they tied the tail on!

Messrs. Archer seem to have taken the second line:
jeg fik paa, = I got (tied) on the tail — Halen, instead
of: I got something, i. e. a sound thrashing understood,
— on my tail! Or was it their innate bashfulness
which mede them shirk the odium of using "such" an
expression? For remembering the colloquial: sæt dig
paa din hale!, it should be said however blushingly
that hale (ɔ: nale, finale, = end) is that part of our

body which with a "decency forbids" we refuse to mention if we can help it. If the student wishes all possible doubt removed and can stand more of this, I refer him to the first reading of U:

Jeg har grædt i Rondesumpen,

lige fuldt jeg fik paa R......., where Ibsen himself did not venture to write that naughty word in full. And what is more: he evidently thought it altogether infra dig. and substituted Halen (written in full!) for R — and crossing — sumpen out in the first line, wrote not (Ronde)svalen as we should expect but: Rondesalen, which in view of the fact that the little imaginary ceremony referred-to took place in the Royal Hall — Dovrehallen (l. 1000) — gives a much better reading than Rondesvalen, which for want of a more suitable term we may translate with the Archers by the Rondë-c l o i s t e r s. But of these there is no further trace, and I know of one who thinks that the Rondesvalen of R and all the texts may be nothing but a slip. —

4060.   kværker. the throttler.

Compare S. I. S. p. 190: specifically Norwegian now; antiquated in Danish. —

4069.   Aases Stemme. Åse's voice.

Compare besides the n. to l. 3995, what J. Collin writes (l.l.p. p. 314, 315): Freilich, die "Humanen" werden den guten Sohn preisen, der dem leidenden Mütterlein das Sterben leicht gemacht hat". (Peer, says Collin, as a true romantic has consoled his mother by quoting, instead of the bible — the old popular tales!) "Der Dichter ist anderer Ansicht. Damit kein Zweifel darüber bestehe, lässt er am Ende seines Werkes Mutter Aase's Stimme den Sohn ob der durch seine Schuld verfehlten Himmelfahrt verklagen". See also the n. to l. 1618.

4075.   Fanden har forført dig med Kjæppen i Kottet!

1, 224; 3, 228; F, 477; M, 285; 14, 207; J, 296; 16, 207.

The Fiend has misled you with the switch from the cupboard.

Compare l. 1690: En Kjæpp, som vi fandt i Kottet, du brugte till Svøbeskaft, for the reference, which some do not seem to have understood. Our friend Passarge is evidently at sea: Bald wirst du den Teufel gewahren, mit dem Stocke hinter dir her!

4077.   Stakkar. poor fellow.

Cf. Prof. Storm, S. I. S. p. 187 on Danish stakkel and Norwegian stakkar. From 1870 on Ibsen seems to have used the form stakker, a cross between the two, pretty regularly; cf. the n. to l.l. 336 and 201.

4086.   Jeg har mange døde; jeg skal følge Lig!

my dead are many; I must follow their biers!

That Ibsen here refers to his thoughts and reminiscences the preceding events have awakened is clear enough as it stands; in U it was indicately even more clearly by the addition of the two lines, reproduced supra in the n. to. l. l. 4035: Tanker og Taarer, etc.

4095.   jeg er Knappestøber. Du skal i min Ske.

I'm a Button-moulder. You're to go into my ladle.

"Ibsen has scarcely ever shown so clearly elsewhere how familiar he was with the s p i r i t of our Folktales", Stavnem writes (Bugge Mindeskrift), "as when he created the figure of this Messenger of Death". (p. 110) And it is quite true that nothing like it is found there. The question out of which elements Ibsen has created it, has occupied scholars with two different results. According to Stavnem (l. l.) and Passarge (whom in this case I quote at second hand from Archer, p. VI) Ibsen must have worked up a hint taken from a Folktale: The Smith whom they dared not let into Hell. It is the well-known story of the Smith who sees the Lord cut off a horse's legs and shoe them, and later on he lays the smith's mother on to the anvil and forges her into a fine young girl. Now, this is all

1, 225; 3, 229; F, 478; M, 286; 14, 207; J, 296; 16, 207.

and it will be admitted that the resemblance is very vague indeed. The other supposed original is a passage from Oehlenschläger's Aladdin which J. Collin, the only one to my knowledge that has written about it quotes as follows:

> Bin schlecht gemacht. Ein misslungnes Werk.
> Ein Kannengiesser hat mir auch vertraut
> Dass man die Arbeit, die zum ersten Male
> Nicht recht gelingen wollte, in den Tiegel
> Zum zweiten Male wirft und giesst sie um.

The resemblance is certainly remarkable, only Collin has not observed that this occurs in the German translation only and that the Danish text, the one which we may expect Ibsen to have seen, reads:

> Du flux bevægelige Chaos, du!
> Hvoraf den størknede Natur sig reiser:
> Slug atter et mislykket slet Forsøg
> Her i din Smeltedigel! Støb mig om!

And, as will be remarked, there the very word that bears the supposed resemblance: Kannengiesser is not found and all that remains is the trite: Støb mig om; it is found passim in Holberg's works (not only in Den Politiske Kandestøber!) and elsewhere. Only, trite as the word is, it will prove of some importance; if instead of støbe om we substitute a synonym, we are lead in the direction of such well-known scriptural passages as Jeremiah VI, 29, IX, 7: Derfor saa siger den Herre Zebaoth: see, jeg vil smelte dem og prøve dem; Ezekiel, XXII, 20. etc. and Malachi III, 2, 3: thi han er som Smelterens Ild og som Tvetternes Lud. Og han skal sidde og smelte og rense Sølvet han skal rense Levi' Børn og luttre dem", etc. And in view of what Solveig's pietistic father says in U to Peer:

> Lad Livsens Alvor slaa dig sønder og sammen
> smelte dig, luttre dig till Due fra Ravn,

1, 225; 3, 229; F, 479; M, 286; 14, 209; J, 297; 16, 209.

it is difficult not to believe that Ibsen was familiar
with this biblical imagery and that moreover we have
in such a scriptural passage the very source both
of the lines in Aladdin ånd in Peer Gynt. If any one
should object that here we have smelte, not støbe
om, I reply that in U we read: skal du støbes om
where R has (l. 4147) Nej, følgelig, Ven, skal du
smeltes om. And not only did Ibsen make use later on
of imagery which creates a same sort of "atmosphere"
(so different from that in Aladdin!) when he makes e. g.
Hetman say that God every now and then could
"slumpe til at være uheldig" (Eft. Skr. III, 136) but
cf. Falk's words to Svanhilde in the first draft of
Kjærlighedens Komedie, (Eft. Skr. I, 459) where we
read about the world that 're-creates' her (skaber om)
in a way which clearly recalls our imagery. All these expressions: støbe om, smelte om, skabe om, etc. stand
of course for the very process of purification (luttre)
that the soul is to undergo and which Ibsen incarnated
in his Button-moulder. For that the Button-moulder
is really a Messenger of Death, a herald of that death
to the world only to reawaken, purified to that created
by Solveig's self-denial, is clear from his words (l. 4629)
'Beskik Dit Hus', for in Jesaiah we read: Beskik Dit
Huus, thi du skal døe (38, 1).

And as it is clear that this figure must have been
conceived together with the other Messenger of Death
we have met — the Strange Passenger — we conclude
that the Button-moulder w h o s e n a m e d o e s
n o t o c c u r i n t h e l i s t o f t h e C h a r a c t e r s
o f U e i t h e r, is an afterthought too. It is even
possible to fix with some amount of probability the
time when this took place. Here a conversation Ibsen
had at Ischia with Vilhelm Bergsøe gives us a very
clear hint. They were walking together, saying nothing,
when all of a sudden Ibsen burst out: Do you think one

could represent a man on the stage with a casting-ladle? Why not?, Bergsøe replied non-plussed as he had not the slightest idea what the poet was at. — This conversation must have taken place some time near the middle of July 1867.

This note, its length notwithstanding, is but a brief extract from a longer investigation of the point published in the Edda for 1917 (April) to which I must beg leave to refer for further particulars and further proofs. See also lower down the n. to the Lean One (l. 4429) for a further slight narrowing down of the dates of composition.

As to the casting-ladle itself, it should of course be remembered that this instrument has not the form of an ordinary s p o o n, but that it is like a little pannikin at the end of a handle, in which the metal is molten by holding it over the fire. —

4100.   men jeg har Ordre till, etc. but I have orders, etc.

Passarge here coolly adds a whole line: Auch glühen schon tüchtig des Meisters Kohlen". We shall no doubt some day find a learned scholar comment on them, as J. Collin does (n. to l. 4059) on the German Aladdin.

4103.   Saadan foruden Varsel —!
Det er gammel Vedtægt ved Gravøl og Barsel
i Stillhed at vælge Dagen till Festen,
uden ringeste Varsel for Hædersgjæsten.
                    withour any warning —!
It's an old tradition at burials and births
to appoint in secret the day of the feast,
with no warning at all to the guest of honour.

In the Danske Studier, 1914 p. 50, Mr. Anker Jensen compares Oehlenschläger's Sanct Hansaften-Spil:
den kan sige uden ringeste Varsel
hvem af mine Damer kan lave til Barsel,
commenting at the same time very minutely upon the delicate shades of difference between the two words; in

---

1, 226; 3, 230; F, 480; M, 286; 14, 209; J, 297; 16, 209.

Peer Gynt = respite, (frist), in Oehlenschläger, hint, intimation (vink, underretning). —

Compare Aasen, No. Ordsprog, p. 177: Dauden sender inkje alltid Fyrebod. —

4108. Kjært Barn har mange Navne.

A pet child has many nicknames.

Count Prozor evidently did not see the proverbial nature of the saying (Mau, II, 69) when he rendered it by: Votre Gentillesse a plusieurs noms. See l. 4122: Vig Satan, so Peer first thinks that Buttonmoulder is another name for the Devil.

4114. i værste Fald kan jeg kaldes en Flynder, —

at worst you may call me a sort of a bungler.

"First, the fish mentioned is commonly called flyn*dre*, not flyn*der*. This uncommon form must have been chosen for the sake of the rhyme. Secondly, why flyndre? What is there characteristic of this fish, to use it in this comparison? Can we believe that Ibsen was really in want of a rhyme, and so chose that which presented itself on the spur of the moment without any special meaning in it? I hardly think so. Of course, there may be other fishes that might have done as well — in so far that name was chosen to get a rhyme, but at the same time, Ibsen must have had something in view in choosing it. Now, as far as I know, a flyndre is a rather harmless fish, living at the bottom of the sea. It does not make any fuss in the fishworld. It is not a fish of prey, chasing and tearing other fishes (like the shark or even the cod). At the same time it does not soar very high, it seems to be "sig selv nok". It is a rather lazy fish, quite content to get something to eat without caring about others. So there is something *half* (noget halvt) about it, it is neither very good nor very bad, only "midt imellem og så som så". (Dr. W.)

4121. Mungaat og Bjor er beggeto Øl.

spruce ale and swipes, they are both of them beer.

1, 227; 3, 231; F, 480; M, 287; 14, 210; J, 297; 16, 210.

Mungaat originally a strong ale-sort brewn in Norway (Kalkar, and Ordbog over Gadesproget) is ncw on the contrary used for a very thin beer (Brynildsen). Of course, the idea is: you can c a l l yourself what you like, you are all the same the one I thought you to be. (beggeto in 1 — F.)

4122. Vig, Satan! Avaunt from me, Satan!

Compare S. Matthew, 4,10: Get thee hence, Satan! It must be a matter of mere chance that Peer uses the same "Vig fra mig", twice before to the Strange passenger (l.l. 3522 and 3635) for he had got no notion just then of the diabolic character of his interlocutor.

4136. storladen. grandiose.

Storladen is rare in Norwegian, almost Danish, "skjønt ikke i den grad som storslaaet (no. storslagen)", S. I. S. p. 179. —

4139. der kræves baade Kraft og Alvor till en Synd.
for both vigour and earnestness go to a sin.

As Mephisto had said to Faust (Trüber Tag, Feld) when the latter showed his remorse for Margaret's fate: "Warum machst du Gemeinschaft mit uns wenn du sie nicht durchführen kannst?" What characterises the sinner in the higher sense (du er ingen Synder i højere Forstand, l. 4117) is the thing Lady Macbeth finds wanting in het husband when he lets I dare not wait upon I would (Macbeth, I, 7, 44), — it is characteristic of so many personages in Ibsen, e.g. Rosmer and Kong Skule, who dares not break off all the bridges behind him and especially Solness whose conscience on the contrary is "unsettled" who has an utryg samvittighed (as it is called in the first draft of Rosmersholm; Eft. Skr. III, 136 [1]), who has not got a robust conscience 'robust samvittigheid' as Ibsen then put it, — a term that might serve for the Buttonmoulder's motto. If one

---

[1] Compare Henning Kehler, Edda 1915, p. 214 who quotes these very words (by Hetman-Brendel of course!): Utryg Samvittighed. Den er det som vi har faaet i Arv allesammen. Derfor er Menneskeheden ulægelig, uhjælpelig." under „Synd, Skyld, Samvittighed".

wants to sin, one should not do so in a foolish way, —
then you are wanting "dæmoniacal earnestness"; cf. the
n. to l. 4488,9: "gjorde det vaaset" and the commentators passim, e.g. Wörner I, p. 274 seq.; J. Collin, p. 313;
Eft. Skr. I, p. CXIII. From two of them, extracts will
be given — first a dissonant in the chorus of praise.

The Rev. A. Schack in his perfidious attack on Ibsen
(l.c. p. 69 seqq.) after expressing agreement with Georg
Brandes as to the latter's dictum that the poem as such
is "neither beautiful nor true", explains that Ibsen has
quite spoilt the leading idea of the drama by the introduction of the Buttonmoulder. The theory he is the
bearer of, as concisely expressed in this line, reminds
one of the æsthetic in Kierkegaard's Enten-Eller, whereas the problem 'to be oneself' is essentially ethic. For if
people on the whole are "too contemptible to be sinning" and "Peer therefore is threatened with annihil-
ation", it follows that this happens not because he
was a sinner, but because he was so contemptible that
he did not dare to sin, — there was no "dæmonisk
alvor" enough in him. And this æsthetic distinction
between the sinner in little and the other who has the
courage of his (wicked) opinion cannot stand the test
of ethics. If therefore Ibsen wishes to judge Peer ethic-
ally, he should not try to set up a distinction between
the two categories of sinners, if on the other hand he
should wish to do so, he may not condemn him as he
does from the ethic standpoint on account of his egoism,
—he should then condemn him because Peer was not con-
s i s t e n t in his evil-doing. But what Ibsen does do,
is to judge him from both standpoints. And it is the
mixing up of these two view-points that will prove the
cause of the absence of unity that Schack here tries to
point out and condemns. And Ibsen, although preaching
the ethic thesis of being oneself, clearly stands himself
on the side of the æsthetic precept of consistency in

---

evil and in the conflict, the ethic dogma is defeated by the personal æsthetic sympathy of the author. His idealism in "be yourself" is therefore not genuine. —

So far the Reverend Mr. Schack. It would be difficult to demonstrate the hollowness of the attack without discussing the whole of the book. Fortunately, so far as the point raised is concerned, I can quote an author who is not biassed against Ibsen by a religious standpoint like Mr. Schack is, and who consequently understands Ibsen better. —

Apropos of Hærmændene paa Helgeland, Prof. Gran writes in his sketch of Henrik Ibsen (in Nordmænd i det 19de Aarh., III, 234) that he makes the characters in that play truly Ibsenian ones, — Ibsen felt like a strange bird in the time he was put into; the present with all its conventions that make one feel like wearing a pair of corsets (vedtægter som snører et menneske ind), with all its compromises, which makes them give but half of themselves (som gjør dem delte og halve), all these considerations that detract from what was truly characteristic — alle dens hensyn som forkludrer præget — all this was for him little and ugly and disgusting. He loved a personality that gives itself as it is and that independently of society and social life (? community) — uafhængig af samfund og samhørighed — lived its own life without any compromise; he hated the present because it created "society-men" instead of individuals, fractions instead of unbroken numbers, compromisemakers instead of heroes or martyrs. In the old histories he found what was wanting in his own time, — individuals that were themselves in every instance, in cruelty and ruse, in heroism and stoic greatness, men-of-a-piece whom society had not split up and whom reflexion had not spoilt", — cf. the remarks supra on being oneself u r y g ge l i gt, n. to l. 3764.

Hence Ibsen could write: "Brand er mig selv i mine

bedste øieblikke" and Gran comments upon this by saying that there were moments "when there was not a luke-warm drop in his blood"

So what Ibsen means by saying that strength and earnestness are wanted for sinning is not to a p p r o ve of sin, but to express his admiration for a man that has the courage to be himself, e v e n t h o u g h, or rather: q u i t e a p a r t f r o m the fact that this courage should show itself in sin. Now that death comes and knocks at the door in the shape of the Buttonmoulder, we see that his good deeds do not suffice for heaven, nor his evil ones for hell, — and hence he must be "melted over", — here if anywhere we have a reminiscence of "the Smith whom they did not dare to let into Hell, and whose entrance into Heaven seems more than doubtful.

4141.   en skal buse paa, som de gamle Berserker.
            one has to lay on, like the old Berserkers.

Among the animals into which people could transform themselves, or if you like, whose souls could migrate into one's body (cf. n. to l. 692) was the bear [1] and he who was "possessed" in this way, would rage furiously as in the case of the Malayan Amok-making or running amuck, when in sheer frenzy the man sometimes kills as many people as possible. On the rumour that had reached Adam von Bremen of them, cf. n. to l. 3179. For older tales, I may refer to a German "Program": H. Güntert, Ueber Alt-isländische Berserker-Geschichten, esp. p. p. 19,24; Olrik, Nordisches Geistesleben p. 81 (139); Snorre, Ynglinga Saga, (ed. G. Storm, p. 11: hans egne mænd.... bed i sine skjolde og var sterke som bjørner.... de dræbte folk, *etc.*), Jantzen, Saxo's erste 9 Bücher, p.p. 312, 346, 347 (Haldanus' sieben Söhne.... in ihre Schilde beissen.... glühende Kohlen verschlucken, etc.); Dania, III, 340. Peer Gynt

---

[1] Bjørn; but an old norse form corresponding to Dutch and German beer, bär was bær —, now only found, besides in berserker, in a latinised form Bero (Saxo, cf. ed Jantzen, p. p. 184, 462; fem. bera, hunbjørn), — cf. n. to l. 724.

---

himself we find at one time in a mood, not essentially different from that of the Berserkers when (l. 1256) he bites in his own arm in the Boyg-scene and says: Claws and ravening teeth in my flesh! I must feel the drip of my own blood. See a description of the halling-dance in the n. to l. 551, where the dancer used to get into such a state of wild excitement that it was not unjustly compared to the Berserkergang.

Dr. Western suggests the connection with ber was established by the fact that the 'possessed' people wore a bear's hide instead of an ordinary dress, rather than that the spirit of the bear was supposed to take possession of them. —

4162.   ætle. designed.

Literally: to leave, to intend. The East Norwegian, more common form is esle; Ibsen's etle is West Norwegian. Compare, S. I. S. p. 191; Han glemte aldrig at esle (destine) lidt godt til den som holdt vintervagt; No. Sagn², 1902, p. 50, but Ibsen had written in Fru Inger til Østråt: han ætlede sig til Østråt, — he intended (to go).

4168.   min Sæl.

On the contraction in later editions into minsæl, cf. T. C. § 126 and the n. to l. 2636,7. —

4170.   Kongsberg.

A little town in (Buskerud Amt) Numedal, known for its silver-mines and the Royal Mint. Compare: dette er Stuven (stabben, a wood-block, but here of pure silver!) — Rødderne har de faaet fat i paa Kongsberg; Sølvkongen paa Medheiden, Norwegia, I, 152. —

4175.   hvad er d e t for en Mand i din Mesters Stilling? what is *that* to a man in your Master's position?

The Efterladte Skrifter give (III, 419) as the reading of U this remarkable collocation: i din Vorherres Stilling. No doubt these words are in the Manuscript, but it cannot have been Ibsen's first reading. Ibsen had written first: "hvad er det for en Mand i" evidently intending to write (as now in R): din Mesters Stilling, so he wrote down din but c r o s s e d it out and s u b s t i t u t e d Vorherre for din; this is quite clear from the fact that Vorherre does not stand on the same level as din. —

4176. Aa, saasom og eftersom Aanden er i en,
saa har en jo altid Metalværdien.
Oh, so long, and in as much as, the spirit's in one,
one always has value as so much metal.

As the words run, one is tempted to ask if on the contrary the metal value does not precisely come to the foreground when the spirit is nót in it any more. But this is clearly not what the poet can mean. The Buttonmoulder wants the spirit i.e. Peer's soul for his Master and says: as long as your own soul is only there, you are as valuable as metal is for a Button-moulder, — you are valuable enough.

4190. Det er en Overgang, ... og som Ræven sagde; — man venter.

It is... a mere transition, and as the fox said: One waits.

But the fox said nothing of the kind of what Messrs. Archer make him say! They have evidently not recognised the proverb that Peer quotes here: D'er ein Yvergang, sa' Reven daa dei snudde skinnet av honom (Aasen, p. 202) or as Mau gives it (II p. 113): Det er en Overgang sagde Ræven da de flaaede ham; cf. Hulda Garborg, Mot Solen p. 92: det er vel bare en overgang som ræven sa. The most typically Norwegian form of the proverb is however the one without the relative particle which Anders Krogvig quoted: Det er en overgang sa ræven, han blev flaadd.

4192. man træder tillbage. one lives in seclusion.

In view of the special bearing these words have on Peer's character (see the n. to l. 2027) Messrs Archers' rendering is far from felicitous if not an actual misunderstanding. —

4225.   Jeg er saare rædd. I am sadly afraid.

Both in U and in R, Ibsen had written very clearly: Jeg er svare rædd, but the first ed. changed svare into saare, which is consequently found in all the subsequent editions. Compare l. 4336: slig svare Magt and: Raabte da Jetten svare, and Det var sig Jetten svare, from Oehlenschläger's Nordens Guder.

4231.   næste Korsvej. The next cross-roads.

The cross-roads play a very important part in folk-lore and of a most varied nature in as much as the kors-vej both favours magic, which is by preference performed there, and seem to have the power of frightening spirits which cannot cross the place (Feilberg, II, p. 277). But as to the precise reason why the cross-roads must have been chosen here by the Button-moulder as a trysting-place, for once Feilberg's Dict. that veritable storehouse of folklore, leaves us in the lurch, although in his other publications what may be the reason is indicated clearly enough. (Jul I, 61; II, 25, 115, 117 seqq.) It is on the cross-way that the magician's soul, when his earthly view is unhindred on four sides, may be supposed to see further and hence deeper than other-wise. In other words: the cross-roads were the chosen place for divinatory purposes, where the old heathen sibyls (perhaps even the very Volve whose prophecy, the Voluspá, opens the Edda) were sitting to foretell the future (Hermann, Nord, Myth. p. p. 325, 559; Meyer, Myth. der Germanen, p.p. 31, 42, 151, 307 etc). Sometimes the precaution was taken not to say a single word, or at most: Gud ske Lov in the morning (Herr-mann, l.l. 559; Norwegia I, 198) but this is most likely a mixing up of motifs. Compare also the story of the King's son and the Peasant's son that Olsen tells of (p. 181) who had been playfellows all their young lives and when they were forced to part, the king's son put his knife into the earth and said that he who was the first

1, 232; 3, 236; F, 486; M, 290; 14, 215; J, 301; 16, 215.

to come back of the two must pull out the knife....
if it was bright, all was right, but if there were drops of
blood on the point, the other was in danger and wanted
help. The parting took place at cross-roads.

Hence, in the case of the Button-moulder it is very
possibly Peer's future the cross-roads are meant to
point to: he is made to understand his immediate fate
and as a matter of fact, the Button-moulder is a Messenger of Death, as in the last scene, the Voice of the
Button-moulder not unlike Mephisto's: ist gerichtet,
says that they will meet at the last cross-roads, where
Peer's doom is irrevocably sealed: "If then he can show
that he has found back something of his real self, he
is saved, if not, he is doomed", (Eitrem, Gads Danske
Magasin, 1913 p. 460).

A correspondent thinks on the other hand that there
is nothing in it except that it is "the place where their
roads cross each other". Dr. Western suggests that
korsvei here means simply the "skillevei" where one
has to choose between good and bad, or as Brand says
to Agnes when Einar tries to win her back: "Vælg, du
staar paa veiens skille". And it should be remarked in
this connection that (in the very words of our drama,
l. 4367) the Button-moulder stands "paa Vejskillet".

I add part of Dr. Western's note in his own words:

It takes a long time for him to get at a decision. He
tries to cheat himself twice and really succeeds in silen-
cing this inner voice the first and second time it is heard,
and it is only when at last he gets back to Solveig, that
he sees himself as he really is. When at this moment
the Button-moulder (his own better self) demands the
register, he does not refer him any more to his "good
works" or his "being himself", but begs Solveig "Skrig
ud min brøde", and when she does not mention any
crime at all, but calls him blessed, then he says: "Then
I am lost!" Now, a man cannot strip himself more

naked than that. Now he has chosen and chosen right, there is at present no more use for the Button-moulder, who leaves him without Peer asking him to go, and he will only come back at the last cross-roads, i.e. at the moment of death. —

4237.   Jorden brænder mig som gloende Jern.
The earth burns beneath me like red-hot iron.
Compare the n. to l. 896.

4240.   Verden er Fuskværk! The world is a bungle.
Or as a famous Aandsfrænde of Peer's would have put it: The world is out of joint, Oh, cursed spight that one must really p r o v e one's right!, although there is less of Hamlet here in Peer Gynt than elsewhere.

4243. Kjære, vakkre, — en Skilling till en husvild Kall!
Dear, kind Sir, — a trifle to a houseless soul!
That Ibsen made the Dovrë-king a beggar is not based on his sources. Kall, a popular word: old man, fellow; cf. n. to l. 1293 and T. C. §§ 117, 135. —

4244.   Skillemynt. small change.
Of course Peter the Great has his pocket full of banknotes! But later on he has forgotten his boast implying such a little promise — he is "somewhat hard pressed for cash, jeg er noget i Betrykk for Kontanter" (l. 4277) and is glad to get rid of the old Governor at the cost of — a character!

4247.   Faer! my boy!
The hypocoristic use of far = my dear man, my dear fellow — the Archers' translation is perhaps the best of all — has puzzled other translators.

4251.   sulten som en Skrubb. starved as a wolf.
Compare the well-known skrubsulten, very hungry; only it is not certain that the prefix is absolutely identical with the subst. skrub, = wolf. It is on the other hand, Prof. Jespersen nothwithsanding (Vilhelm Thomsen-Festskrift, 1894 and quite recently his Nutidssprog hos børn og voksne, p. 87: min i 1894

1, 233; 3, 237; F, 486; M, 290; 14, 216; J, 301; 16, 216.

givne forklaring af skrubsulten er blevet angrebet af flere men er visst dog rigtig) now generally supposed to be different; cf. Falk og Torp in voce and Dania, VIII, 83.

4262.   Hun gik nu for koldt Vand og Lud.
          She has led a deplorable life.

To this translation the Archers append a note: "literally: to live on cold water and lye — to live wretchedly and be badly treated". One shade of meaning the expression has is not taken into account, *viz.* not to be taken care of, to be left to one's own devices, "uden Omsorg og Tilsyn" as the Ordbog over Gadesproget renders it. And Messrs Archers' rendering is an inference from the fact of her having been neglected rather than a correct translation. In Lille Eyolf, Ibsen has the more usual form: Fordi du lod (Eyolf) gå for lud og koldt vand. —

4265.   i Valfjeldet. Of the Valfjeld.

Im Waldgebirge, Morgenstern (p. 574) translates!

4267.   ham jeg lokked Sæterjenterne fra.
          he I cut out with the sæter-girls.

This refers to the episode where with a "Jeg er tre Hoders Trold etc. (cf. n. to l. 867), Peer suddenly appears in the midst of the three girls who were calling upon the trolls. In the original tale (cf. ed. 1912, p. 157, Archer, p. 284) Peer shoots Trond, kills another with the butt-end of his gun whilst a third is overthrown by the dogs, — the fourth only escapes.

4283.   hverve mit Syn. to bias my sight.

On the misprint hverve in the first and second ed., cf. T. C. § 11, 30; on the operation, the n. to l. 1125 and l. 1132: aldrig vil Synet dit kverves.

4293.   han... smagte paa Mjøden. You...tasted the mead.
     See the n. to l. 1054 — hinc illæ lachrymæ!

4300.   Ordet, — det kløvende, stærke.
          The potent and sundering word.
     The reference is to l. 1048: "Nok", min Søn, det

kløvende, stærke Ord maa staa i dit Vaabenmærke. —
Later editions have Ordet? with a point of interrogation under the influence of the next line; cf. T. C. § 11. —
4314, 6. rødt paa Sort...Bloksbergs-Posten — Heklefjelds-
Tidende.

red and black... Bloksberg Post...Heklefjeld-Journal.

The delightful way in which Ibsen carries through the
imagery here — not black on white, which would smack
too much of the man-world — reminds us of the glorious
Sandt for Udyden! cf. n. to l. 1170. Thus Hingstehov,
Stallion-hoof, is of course the horse-shoe i. e. the Evil
one; cf. l. 4123: hestehov, 4451: Er den Hoven naturlig?

The idea of the newspapers in the Dovrëhall may
be owing to Heiberg's Sjæl efter Døden where there is
a skit on Danish journalists and the newspapers that
are kept in Hell. That this apocalyptic comedy has influenced Ibsen's Peer Gynt is generally accepted and
will be clear to the student who turns from it to Ibsen's
poem or vice-versa. And see our notes on the Furumo-
scene (l.3995), the Button-moulder and the Lean One,
both of which figures remind one of Heiberg's Mephistopheles. Mr. A. Leroy Andrews (Journal Engl. and
Germ. Philology, XIII, 241) thinks there is a general
influence of its third act on Ibsen's thrusts at Norway
as a troll-kingdom.

Bloksberg and Heklefjeld were of course the well-
known trysting-places of witches; the former the one
in the Harz-mountains of Faust-fame but quite common in Danish folklore too [1]), — the latter (cf. the
less original form Hekkenfeld, Feilberg in v. and the

---

[1]) Other names for such places are: Blaakulla in Sweden (cf. Steffen in the Feil-
berg-Festskrift, p. 536: derived from kulla = woman; cf. already Troels Lund,
Dagligt Liv i Norden, VII, 231 seq: = Blaakol in Norway, Huldreev. '12 p. 94: No.
Sagn², p. 11; Kleiven, Segner fraa Vaagaa, p. 45 and Publ. Soc. Advancement Sc.
Study 1916 p. 233) and Bovbjærg, Bredsten, Dovrefjeld, Lyderhorn, Nasafjäll,
Pommern (on account of alliteration with Pokker [i Vold]? Feilberg II, 860 in v.),
Troms Kirke, etc. etc. See Feilberg in v. Bloksbjærg, nordost, Hekkenfelt, helvede,
Troms Kirke; Tillæg p. p. 49, 61; Jul, II, 55, Troels Lund, l.l.

1, 238; 3, 242; F, 491; M, 293; 14, 220; J, 303; 16, 220.

form that Ibsen used in U: Hækkefeldts Tidende) is not called so after the Hekle-mountain in Iceland (Herrmann, Nord. Myth. p. 76) but conversely the Hekla called thus because the word means cape, mantle cf. Snehætte, snowmantle as a name for a mountain and the Mons Pil(e)atus in Switzerland. See Feilberg: "Vulcanoes were supposed in the Middle Ages to be the place of torture for damned souls". The extensive use of go to H — ekkenfeld in a sense practically identical with to go to H — ell, is no doubt owing precisely to the fact that the very word agreeably suggests the name of the — other place as Hamlet says, both words having the same initial sound, — just like Hälsike, Hälsingafyr, *etc.* in Swedish; see the notes to l. l. 1934, 2310. —

4323.   af Huden... en Rem. a strip of the hide.

The Norwegian expression is pròverbial: have a smack of something, as a rule something wrong, evil or disadvantageous; ikke være ganske fri for, have nogen del i en Fejl, as the Ordbog over Gadesproget explains and as clearly appears from its use in Adam Homo, (ed. 1879, II p. 456, 12e sang,:) Vel havde han (Adam Homo) en Rem af Huden med, Vel saaes han stunddom, Tidens Svaghed dele, Men o, hvor staaer han ædel i det Hele!

4335.   Dattersøns Afkom...har faaet...svare Magt.

my grandson's offspring have become overwhelmingly strong.

On the omission of the article, cf. the n. to l. 1001, on svare, that to l. 4425; on the sentiment that to l. 1515. Passarge's translation: Von den Töchterkindern ...nach dem alten Grossvater keins mehr fragt" is somewhat free of course but not so wrong as might appear at first sight. Peer's and the Dovrëking's grandchildren who have made their way in the world, "dette parveny-folkefærd har selvfølgelig ingen respekt for det gamle og ingen tro paa trold og slikt" as a corres-

1, 238; 3, 242; F, 491; M, 293; 14, 2?1; J, 304; 16, 221.

pondent writes. Wörner (I², p. 244) thinks the present passage is a skit upon Norway, "wo das Gyntische Geschlecht sich über das ganze Land verbreitet habe."

4338.   Det heder jo, værst er ens egne Frænder.

The saw says: One's kin are unkindest of all.

The allusion is to the proverb: Frænde er frænde værst, Mau, II, 305; variants: nabo er nabo værst (ib. II, 60) and to some extent: usel er usle værst, stakkarl er stodder værst (II, 362) and kvinde er kvinde værst (I, 577). It is this sentiment that inspired the Dutch proverbial: God beware mij voor mijn vrienden, voor mijn vijanden zal ik mij zelf wel bewaren. The English reader will observe that frænde, related to friend, is used in the Scandinavian languages in the general sense of relative, which is rare in English.

4341.   der er flere, det Uheld hænder.

there are others who share the same fate.

The "many" to whom this little accident happens, is of course Peer! cf. Peer's conversation with the Bailiff in the auction-scene.

4342.   vi selv har slet ingen Hjælpekasse,
          ingen Spareskillingsgris eller Fattigblok.
          we've no Mutual Aid Society,
          no alms-box or Penny Savings bank.

These institutions which the old man regretfully misses, with the necessary stress on: *We* have not got these, suggests of course, as a subaudition: such as the world of men does know. If so, it seems possible that Ibsen thought of Jaabæk's efforts to bring home to the Norwegian peasant a greater sense of parsimony. It was precisely in 1865 that this well-known politician (1814—1894) started his Folketidende and the Society of 'Bondevenner', the leading principle of which was the one enunciated above while in a general way he tried to reduce all state-expenses as much as possible. I must not forget to mention however that according to some

1, 239; 3, 243; F, 492; M, 293; 14, 222; J, 304; 16, 222.

Norwegian correspondents there is not likely to be such an allusion. —

4349   paa en nøgen Houg. fairly cleaned out.

Peer's apparently unusual expression — literally: on a bare hill — is as this very rendering suggests nothing but a fine polishing-up of "paa bar bakke"!

4356.   De søger i Bladet nationale Subjekter.

The papers are clamouring for national talents.

The word subjekter usually applied in a somewhat degrading sense (cf. daarlig subjekt and even simply: et subjekt) is here used in the somewhat technical sense of an actor. Mr. Anders Krogvig tells me that in the older theatrical language, it was the usual word in advertisements. And Mr. Brynildsen writes that Welhaven too uses Norske Subjekter in the sense of Norwegian actors. (Now also in his dict.) In the Publ. Soc. Adv. Sc. Study I, 214 (a paper unfortunately printed off uncorrected and hence full of the most puzzling misprints!) I have said that there could be "no reasonable doubt" that we have here one of Ibsen's skits on the craze for what is "Norsk-norsk" (cf. the notes to l. l. 1053, 3179 etc.) This may be so (although I should not now express it quite so cock-sure-ly!) if we only remember that, as explained above the subjekter refers to men not things. However this be, the rest of the note Mr. Krogvig favoured me with is worth reproducing. "It is not impossible, he writes, that the later meaning of subjekter (so: fellows) must also be thought of — at ogsaa den nyere betydning har spillet ind — at any rate it fits in very well. For what Ibsen may especially allude to is Ole Bull's affair with the Millboy — "Møllargutten" — and with his national dances, how real Norwegian peasants might be seen on the stage of the "Bergens Nationale scene" which he was at one time the leader of".

4360,1.   Jeg skriver en Farce, baade gal og grundig;
        den skal hede: "Sic transit gloria mundi."

1, 240; 3, 244; F, 493; M, 294; 14, 222; J, 304; 16, 222.

Professor Sturtevant (Publ. Soc. Adv. Sc. Studies, I, p. 31) thinks Ibsen was "irritated" at the want of taste of the "stupid public" that preferred the insipid productions of the present time to the higher type of literature which the Norwegian school of dramatists was advocating. A mad farce.... would exactly fill the bill".

Apart from the fact that the writer seems to base his explanation on the interpretation of subjekter as things (subjects) instead of (see the n. to l. 4356) actors, the fact which he overlooked that the joke about the farce was taken, rhyme and all, from Paludan-Müller's Adam Homo may make it necessary to reconsider the position. For there we find as the two last lines of the 9th Song: (ed. 1879, II, p. 343):

Mens op fra Hjertets Bund han sukked grundig:
Sic transit gloria mundi!

Ibsen seems to have been very fond of the proverb, for not only had he already adapted it in his Kjærlig-hedens Komedie, where Falk warns Svanhild that "sic transit gloria amoris" (F, II, 167) but he used it once more in his Ballonbrev (1870) where "Luxors hal....vidned stumt om stormens stund i et "sic transit gloria mundi."

The exquisite way in which the two German translators have turned their difficulty is worth recording: "Ich bringe in 'n Posse die ganze Historia, sic transit mundi gloria." (Passarge) and: "so tief wie heiter, Des titels: Sic transit, u. s. w., u. s. w,! (Morgenstern). (Add. 3343).

4368.   Det var fort bestillt! Well, that's short work!

The Archers' translation indicating as it does that the Button-moulder comes back too soon for Peer's taste, is of course correct. But Brons turns it all into nonsense by rendering it: 'k het 't straks be-steld: *I* have done it (if at least bestellen in Low-ger-man does mean to *do* as in Norwegian and not as in Dutch: to order!) at once!

1, 241; 3, 245; F, 494; M, 294; 14, 223; J, 305; 16, 223.

4381.   At være sig selv, er: sig selv at døde.
         To be oneself is: to slay oneself.

As Wörner says (I¹ 252,² 259): Brands weg gebaut aus Opfersteinen ist der einzige Weg zum Ziele. To be oneself, — at realisere sig selv, as Ibsen called it in a letter to Bjørnson (Breve II, 110: "det højeste et menneske kan nå til.... de fleste forfusker den (opgave) ib. 136: to Caspari; cf. Eft. Skr. I, p. LXXXI and which according to Eitrem (Maal og Minne, 1910, p.38) he may have found expressed in Wergeland "in almost the same terms" as well as in the latter's great master Herder (J. Collin, l. l. p. 28) — this 'at realisere sig selv' is of course a Leitmotiv of the play. Here the Button-moulder, Mr. Ellis Roberts writes (p. XII) is not altogether free from Peer's own fault, quoting old axioms without due thought. The Dominical injunction¹): "Whosoever will(s to) save his self (soul) shall lose it, and whosoever shall lose his self (life) for my shake shall save (find) it", cannot be taken apart from its complementary warning: "What shall it profit a man (is a man profited) if he gain the whole world and lose his own self (soul)?"

As to the apparent contradiction that to be oneself should mean to kill oneself, we may agree with Count Prozor (p. 27): Eh oui! être soi-même, ce n'est pas être Peer Gynt ou un autre, c'est être homme, c'est tuer en soi ce que Peer appelle orgueilleusement le moi Gyntien pour y faire vivre le moi humain". There is a duality in man, as remarked apropos of the Strange Passenger, who is Peer's better self, — to be oneself, i. e. one's better self, one's real self (med Mesters Mening til Udhængskilt, som man springer i Guds Tanke frem, l. 4660, med Guds Stempel paa ens Pande, 4665), — one

---

¹) I suppose his reference is to S. Matthew, 16, 25,26 which he seems to have quoted by heart — Mr. Ellis Roberts "is not altogether free from Peer's own fault quoting old saws without due thought" —; at least the divergencies from the A. V. (added in brackets) are important.

---

must kill oneself i. e. one's self-sufficiency — dette at være sig selv nok! — if Peer wishes to save his Dr. Jekyll he must kill his Mr. Hyde. Or: you can only get at the divine in man by killing in him what is of the earth, earthly.

We are reminded of this again in Emperor and Galilæan when, to the question of Julian (who, as has been remarked more than once, e. g. by Bernard Shaw, Quintessence of Ibsenism,[2] p. p. 36, 70, is a reincarnation of Peer Gynt), — when to Julian's question: What do you call the Most glorious (den herligste)? the mysterious voice replies: Life. And Julian again: And the reason of Life? (Livets grund) Death. And when to Julian's: And that of Death?, the voice (losing itself as in a sigh) answers: Aye, there is the rub (Ja, det er gåden!), the analogy becomes apparent for in Peer Gynt too the mystery is not cleared up by the words of the Button-moulder. —

Two more explanations shall be quoted of this central passage, one from the very first criticism of the drama (the one by Bjørnson in Norsk Folkeblad, for the 23[d] of Nov. 1867, nine days after it had appeared!) and another by one of the latest critics.

Bjørnson wrote: Meget fint gjøres opmærksom paa, hvorledes dette hos os saa yndede "at være sig selv", hvilket men saa gjerne bruger til Ros for sig selv og andre Cynikere, og hvori den misforstaaede Nationalitetsfølelse ogsaa gjerne vil have Landet forstenet — egentlig betyder "at døde sig selv" naar man dermed mener Uimodtagelighed for al Slags god Paavirkning eller mener en konsekventse som bare er konsekventse i det at være et Svin." It does not appear which alternative Bjørnson favours and his interpretation as so much else in his paper is of historical interest rather than that it brings any deep understanding to bear upon the questions touched on.

1, 242; 3, 246; F, 495; M, 295; 14, 224; J, 306; 16, 224.

The second criticism goes deeper and although it necessarily covers the same ground as the preceding remarks, a larger extract of it may be welcome: Ibsen taler i sine tidligere arbeider om noget som han snart kalder k a l d e t, snart at være sig selv, snart at møde med Mesters mening som udhængsskilt; det er hans mening at ethvert menneske har sin bestemmelse, at der inderst i hans sjæl bor noget, som er hans egentlige jeg, og som det er hans egen sag at ane; gjør han ikke det, er han hjemfalden til støbeskeen, men har han anet det, saa skal hans liv bestaa i at frigjøre dette egentlige, højere jeg; denne frigjørelse sker kun gjennem offer, offer af alt det ,som ogsaa findes i hans indre men som skygger for hans egentlige jeg, skal han blive et virkeligt menneske at opfylde sin bestemmelse, maa han samle al sin magt paa dette ene og give afkald paa sit lavere jegs mange tillokkelser. Dette er meningen med knappestøberens ord.

Eftersom Ibsen kom bort fra sin gamle religiøse overbevisning, forsvandt de mystiske, halvt teologiske betegnelser. — kaldet, bestemmelse, — han kalder det nu simpelthen at realisere sig selv; men det gjælder det samme, — spørgsmaalet om personlighedens frigjørelse er det som altid beskjæftiger ham". The question of the "liberation of personality", — it will be noticed that the critic enters fully if perhaps unconsciously into Ibsen's idealism of which the line under discussion is the clearest proof. For if to b e oneself means to kill one's troll-self in order to save one's better Solveig-self, it is clear that for Ibsen one's self is essentially one's better one!

Thus it is that Rebecca may be said to illustrate the Button-moulder's theory: she loves Rosmer, has killed Beate and is about to reach her goal when her erotic desires having hurt (stødt bort) Rosmer's feelings, she finds herself farther from him than ever. "Hun kjæmper

---

sig imidlertid op til ham, tilegner sig hans ædle aandige væsen, blir tilslut selv adelsmenneske; men under denne kamp har hun misted sin oprindelige kraft, hendes vilje til livet er borte, de to adelsmennesker magter ikke at leve sammen, kun i døden selv kan de blive forenet." And if the student does not find the last considerations particularly appropriate as an illustration of the parallel between Rebecca and the Button-moulder, — the parallelism is really there: it lies in the fact that Rebecca actually finds her (better) self in death only, i.e. by killing her earthly desires. —

4408.   et ældre Datum.

In this sense of date, datum is not now neuter. Datum = fact, item of information is neuter only. (Brynildsen).   .

4415, 6. Husk paa, hvad Justedals-Presten skrev: "det er skjeldent, at nogen dør her i Dalen."

Recollect what the Justedal parson wrote: "It's seldom that any one dies in this valley."

Matthias Foss, b. 1714, ob. 1792, became the parish-priest of Justedal in 1742 and wrote in 1750 a "short description of Justedal (a now unusual form of Jostedal). His description was printed in Thaarup's "Magasin for Danmarks og Norges beskrivelse, II, p.p. 1—42 and reproduced in Amund Helland's "Nordre Bergenshus Amt", I, p. 609 from which Anders Krogvig was good enough to send me (together with the substance of the rest of this note) the following extract as that which Ibsen may be supposed to be referring to here: "De (i.e. the inhabitants of Justedal) ere og meget langlevende, saa det er et rart eksempel nogen dør, hvilket tildeels maa komme deraf, at her er frisk og sund luft; tildeels forsyne de sig gierne med Angelicarod, som de kalde Quannerod, den de plukke eller grave op af jorden før St. Hansdag i fieldene, hvor den voxer, og for at præcavere sig for sygdomme gierne bide

derpaa; ligesom de og i slige tilfælde forsyne sig med
bævergæl og hvidløg, den de gierne have og bruge i
husene, naar sygdom skulde paakomme, saa man for-
nemmer ei her, som ved søekanten, til adskillige gras-
serende svagheder."

That Ibsen should have read Foss' description is of
course possible but far from certain. However, Mr.
Krogvig thinks it probable that Ibsen should have heard
about this "at his learned friend, Paul Botten Hansen's.
Such literary curiosities were precisely the sort of things
we may expect their conversation to have turned on". [1]

See on the meetings of the circle of friends in question: Gran, Nordmænd i det 19de Aarh. III, 226 and
his Norsk Aandsliv i det 19de Aarh. I, p. p. 165, seqq.
(especially p.p. 169, 175, 182): Ibsen og Morgenbladet.
The members of the circle were called "Hollændere"
or "Westphalerne". The former nickname was given
them "fordi en av dem en gang uttrykte sin beundring
for vertens evne til at opsnuse sjeldne bøker med den
bemærkning: "Pokker tage Hollænderen, han har sine
spioner ude alle vegne", (Gran, l. p. 169 n.) where the
allusion is to one of Holberg's plays: Jacob von Tyboe,
in which "the Dutchman" is thus said to get to know
everything about von Tyboe who boasts of his feats
when trailing a pike in the Netherlands. The exact
words are: Skam faae Hollænderen, han haver sine
spioner ude allevegne". Professor Gran seems even to
recognise a "Hollandsk tone" in some passages of the
play, e.g. in Vinje-Huhu's speech against the Maalstrævere (cf. n. to l. 3179). As to the "Westphalere", —
Botten Hansen used to call Ibsen Gert Westphaler
after the over-loquacious barber in Holberg's farçe of
that name: Gert Westphaler eller den meget talende

---

[1] Ibsen had also read about Justedal in Faye's Norske Sagn, whence he drew
the matter for his Rypen i Justedal, Eft. Skr. I, 344 but that is all about the Black
Death, so quite the opposite of the long life referred to here.

1, 244; 3, 248; F, 497; M, 296; 14, 226; J, 307; 16, 226.

Barber. So in those early days, he may not have been
very sphinx-like; cf. the n. to l. 3013. —

On the form skjeldent, see T. C. § 34, n. to l. 1817. —

4421, 2. Den tør være nyttig till mange Ting,
sa'e Esben, han tog opp en Skjæreving.

This may come in useful in many ways,
said Esben as he picked up a magpie's wing.

The allusion is to one of the most amusing little tales,
called "Questioning" (Spurningen) or "The princess
whom nobody could silence, Prindsessen som ingen
kunde maalbinde". There Esben Askeladd [1]) finds a
cringle, then a potsherd and finally a dead magpie
(in one version; in another, Eventyr for børn III, 97,
en død Skjæreunge) and it so happens that these things
apparently of no value at all, bring about his success
with her Royal Highness, so that he gets "the Princess
and half the Kingdom". The skjæreving was substituted by Ibsen for the magpie or the young one (skjæ-
reungen) of the story — one never knows what the most
insignificant little nothing may be good for! In H. and
E., Folkminnen, 1907, p. 519, there will be found an
amusing, if not very refined, variant of the story on
which see R. Köhler, Kleine Schriften, II, 465. —

4429. Den Magre. The Lean One.

This personage whose diabolical nature appears
with all the desired certainty from Peer's question
about the Horse-hoof: Er den Hoven naturlig? (l. 4451)
reminds one not only of Heiberg's En Sjæl efter Døden
(Paulsen; cf. Eft. Skr. I, p. LXIII) but he recalls also
a passage in Aladdin. In the fifth act we hear of a spectre
who in answer to Sinbad's question who he is, answers:
Kulsvieren, — the Charcoal-burner; remember what
the Famulus had said in Faust, II (Hochgewölbtes
Zimmer): Er sieht aus wie ein Kohlenbrenner, Ge-

---

[1])Askeladd is of course = Ashiepattle; see the n. to l. 255. By the side of Esben
(= Asbjørn!) we find Espen; cf. Asbjørnsen's No. Folkeev. 1914, passim, Moes breve,
p. 210, etc. —

---

schwärzt vom Ohre bis zur Nase. Compare also: Lige finder lige sa Fanden til Kulsvieren, Mau I, p. 610. And the spectre in Aladdin continues: Jeg tiener den rigeste Kulsvier.... Han brænder de bevægelige Skove, Hvor Løvet kaldes Haar og Grenen Arm".... I wish to add that the impression of resemblance is produced by the context rather than by any single word or expression such as can here be reproduced only. Compare also Mau, II, 330 : Kulsvierens Sæk er vel sort udenpaa, men endnu værre indentil.

As to the reason why this personage should be called the Lean One, — it is difficult to conceive the representative of Death as "fat and scant of breath"! Here however Faust may again have influenced Ibsen if it were only that Mephisto uses "seit vielen Jahren falsche Waden" and he appears continually as "der Abgemagerte".

His wonderfully quick voyage to the Cape is a "motif" which may h e r e be owing to Faust (cf. I, Studirzimmer,: Ein Bischen Feuerluft die ich bereiten werde Hebt uns behend von dieser Erde), — only, q u a motif, it may be due to the old tales where it reflects Odin's art (Herrmann, Nord. Myth. p. 257) and more distantly it reminds one of Mercury's. For other examples in the Norwegian folk-tales I refer in the first place to Jutulen og Johannes Blessom, Huldreev. ed. '12 p. 99, which Asbjørnsen connects with the Asgardsreien (No. Sagn², 1902, p. 13). Smaller distances were covered by the devil in Graverens Fortællinger who was but twenty miles to the north of Trondhjem when Peer's beloved called upon him in the Dovrë-mountains: I høst da jeg fødte, holdt Fanden om min Rygg. Compare Mephistofeles' feat in En Sjæl efter Døden who spreads out his black mantle and is in less than no time on earth, Huldreev. p.p. 93 and 326 (Tatere), and think especially of Askeladd who man-

---

1, 245; 3, 249; F, 498; M, 296; 14, 227; J, 307; 16, 227.

ages to fetch water from the end of the earth in ten
minutes (No. Folkeev. 1914, p. 20). In Faust II (IV,
Hochgebirge) Faust travels on a cloud! — Compare
moreover the corresponding tricks in Marlowe's Faust;
the Spirits in Aladdin (end of the first act, third act
and passim) a story in Dania, X, 9 from Vincentius
Bellovacensis, Feilberg, in v. luftrejse, II, 457 and
Tillæg, p. 261: på Luftrejsen støder hest imod Kirke-
tårn, — which reminds us of Baron Münchhausen. See
Hartland's Fairy and Folk-tales p.p. 10,108.

Now, if the student will remember the notes on the
Strange Passenger and the Button-moulder, it is clear
that these three personages in a way form a unity, a
unity of conception that is; they are all three messen-
gers from the Beyond, the first representing the voice
of Peer's better self, the second telling him that he is
to be entirely 'recast', 're-molten', — re-purified (smel-
ted om, støbt om, luttred om) if he is to come to any
good and the third showing clearly that he is not 'even'
good enough for hell — der kræves Alvor til en Synd!
And when then we observe that the Lean One's name
too is missing in that tell-tale list of characters in U, we
have no difficulty in concluding with a certain amount
of probalility that these three voices of warning so
humoristic in one way but so pathetic in an other, were
all afterthoughts of the poet, — or to express it more
exactly — formed o n e afterthought, one of Ibsen's
'Caprices', for more details of which see the paper quoted
before in the Edda, 1917 (probably April).

But we have not quite finished with the trio yet. For
although there is no extrinsic evidence properly
speaking to prove the hypothesis about this 'Caprice'
in the sense of afterthoughts, there is some very interesting matter that may be brought to bear upon it
and that may help us in the appreciation of the above
considerations.

When on the 8th of August, 1867, Ibsen sent the first three acts to the printers at Copenhagen, he added that the fourth and fifth act together would be of about the same length as the three first: "Det afsendte vil i tryk udgøre omkring 120 sider og det resterende lige saa meget." As a matter of fact the first three acts take up 113 pages of the first edition. The fourth and fifth acts on the other hand cover 145 pages and a half i.e.a difference of 32 à 33 pages. Now a simple calculation shows that in this very first ed. the scenes with the Strange Passenger, the Button-Moulder and the Lean One take up 8, $16^1/_2$ and $8^1/_2$ pages i.e. 33 in all. Truly a remarkable coincidence. — if the student does not prefer to look upon it as a sort of clincher that establishes the hypothesis beyond reasonable doubt.

And if the conclusion be admitted, some further light will be found thrown on the question of the date of the Buttonmoulder-scene. That was c o n c e i v e d as we saw on or about the fifteenth of July, but was it w r i t t e n o u t then too? The negative answer to the question is of course the only one that meets the circumstances of the case, — had it been written out — and then necessarily with the others — Ibsen would not have sent that certain computation to Copenhagen. This narrows down the working-out of the Button-moulder-conception to some day between the above 8th of August and the 19th of September when Ibsen began to write out the corresponding passage op the U-text in which the Buttonmoulder is found. Nearer it does not seem possible to get.

4434.   en, som skal himle?
          there's some one bound heavenwards?
     See the note on himle, l. 436. —

4438.   Heraus! Lægg an! *Heraus!* Go ahead!
     See the n. to l. 2601 on German words. This expression is also common in Jutlandish, it would seem; cf.

1, 245; 3, 249; F, 498; M, 296; 14, 227; J, 307; 16, 227.

Feilberg III, 911 where he explains: as a rule German was spoken to dogs! :"Heraus, willst du?", which is perhaps explicable in view of the feeling of antipathy which the "Herrer i Landet" continue to rouse there. The devil too is often made to speak German. Hr. Statsadvokat Haakon Løken quotes "om Holbergstidens snob": Med fruerne fransk, og tysk med sin hund... han talte. —

lægge an, a military expression: point arms; cf. fire away: speak out, which is about the meaning the expression has here. —

4445.   Synder en gros. sinning en g r o s.

It would be hypercritical to say that this French expression was w r o n g here (cf. the n. to l. 2208); it may be looked upon as a legitimate extension of the technical e n g r o s as opposed to retail, in great quantities, many, a semasiological development that the corresponding wholesale has also gone through.

4449. Et mærkelig udvikklet Neglesystem.

A nail-system somewhat extremely developed.

Here we see what might be called the classical description of His Satanic Majesty before our mind's eye (such as in Olsen p. 150: føtterne hadde store svarte stygge klør og der laa en hale snodd rundt bordfoten") and many such description might be quoted, notwithstanding Mephisto's dictum in the "Hexenküche": Das nordische Phantom ist nun nicht mehr zu schauen. Wo sieht man Hörner, Schweif und Klauen?

See for the necessary details Feilberg, Tillæg in v. djævel; add: in the form of a grey friar, cf. e. g. my Faustus-Notes p. 33. — Pictures in Troels Lund, Dagligt Liv i Norden, VII, 150, 189 and Asbjørnsen's Udv. Folkeev. I, p. 38 by T. Kittelsen: Skipperen og Gamle Erik. —

The nails and the horse-hoof (see n. to l. 4451) formed of course part of this traditional picture. Feilberg, II,

1, 246; 3, 250; F, 499; M, 297; 14, 228; J, 308; 16, 228.

p. 680 gives an interesting enumeration of the details relative to the folklore of human nails. —
On the adverb mærkelig, see T. C. § 123.—

4451. Er den Hoven naturlig? That's a natural hoof?

The horse-hoof too forms a necessary part of the devil when pictured with all the paraphernalia he has a right to; cf. n. to l. 4449. It was of course found in the Faust (not the Urfaust; Witkowski, II, 237).

4454,5. staar Salsdøren aaben, — sky Køkkenvejen,
kan du træffe Kongen, etc.

when the hall-door stands wide, — shun the kitchen-way, when the King is to be met with, etc.

When meeting with the Buttonmoulder, Peer had thought that he had got the Evil one before him, — Vig, Satan! — here his surprise is all the greater to meet, not an ambassador of his Satanic Majesty as he had first thought, but the "King" himself.

4474,5. Nogen Løn er egentlig ingen Nødvendighed;
kun en venlig Omgang efter Sted og Omstændighed. —
I shouldn't insist on a salary;
but treatment as friendly as things will permit.

The sly and dry humour of this passage becomes clear to him who remembers that the expression used reflects a standing phrase in advertisements, which Anders Krogvig tells me may even now be seen often enough in the papers. —
On the unfortunate misprint in the first edition which added the full stop at the end of the line, see T. C. § 18. —

4488,9. Der er dem, som drev Handel med Viljer og Sind,
men gjorde det vaaset, og slap altsaa ikke ind.
There are men that have trafficked in wills and souls,
but who bungled it so that they failed to get in.

This passage has been explained by Ibsen himself in a letter (of 10/5/80) to Passarge (Breve, II, 89): The signification of the two lines you ask about is as follows:

to make good his claim to come into hell, Peer Gynt recalls that he has been a slave-dealer. To which the Lean One replies that there are many who did worse things, e. g. who kept the spriritual, will and soul under subjection in their surroundings (underkuet det åndige, vilje og sind blandt sine omgivelser) but if one bungles over it, i. e. if one does this "without demoniac earnestness", even that does not qualify one for hell but only makes one fit for the casting-ladle". The interesting point here is the poet's interpretation of theword "vaaset" which literally means nothing but careless, slipshod. Truly, as we see now, "der kræves baade Kraft og Alvor till en Synd! (see the n. to l. 4139).

The adjective vaaset will be recognised in Aasen's vasutt: forviklet, knudet, skjødesløs i at tale, fuld af Fjas og Vrøvl. It is also used in Danish, cf. Ordb. f. Folket: vrøvlevorn, fjollet; Ordb. over Gadesproget, etc.

4491.   Atter Bedemandsstil! Mere fustian again!

No doubt, Bedemandsstil means: balderbash, fustian as when we read in En Sjæl efter Døden (p. 199) about a certain newspaper (adresseavisen) that "dens Indholds Flesk, behørigen tintet Med Asylprospecter og Vandprojecter I Bedemandsstil af Contorets Vægter" and when Ibsen himself writes of a critic's effusions: "Denne bedemandstirade kan jeg...forøge (F, X, 457). But this is hardly the meaning here! There is nothing highfalutin' in the communication that Peer had shipped Brahma-figures to China. That Bedemand does not exclusively suggest fustian is clear from such a saying as the one quoted by Mau (II, 160): Han sætter et Bedemands ansigt op! And this brings us to another shade of meaning, scarcely perceptible sometimes, in which we shall find that Ibsen used it here, — the meaning that is usually associated with bedemandstone, — the tone, half singing, half whining, of a "bidder" as the Dutch call the under-

---

1, 248; 3, 252; F, 501; M, 298; 14, 231; J, 309; 16, 231.

taker [1]) hence on the one hand something stupid and tedious [2]) the other lackadaisical, sentimental. When in the first draft of the Wild Duck, Werle has said: Ja, for jeg tænkte at det kanske af hensyn til din mors minde—", Gregers interrupts him and says: Nej, nej, nej, lad os ikke bruge bedemandsstil, far! (Eft. Skr. III, 25) i. e., I say, don 't let us grow sentimental [3]). And this is no doubt what we must think of here — do you really think, the Lean One says, to make an impression upon me by such sentiment?! That we laugh at! —

4496.   De flestes Seen ins Blaue slutter i Støbeskeen.

most people's Seen ins Blaue ends in a casting-ladle.

A correspondent asks what I make of this. I am a-fraid I must "late spørsmaalet gaa videre" as the editorial note runs to over-inquisitive questioners.

4503.   saa skillte jeg halvvejs en Kokk ved Livet.

so I half-way divested a cook of his life.

The half-measure is characteristic of Peer who never having learned the art of going the whole hog, always must see his way "at træde tilbage" (n. to l. 2027).

4504.   Jeg var tillfreds, De en Kokkepige

havde halvvejs skillt ved noget andet tillige.

It were all one to me if a kitchen-maid

you had half-way divested of something else.

Wörner has remarked about Ibsen that where the

---

[1]) Compare the description of a ridiculous person whom Ibsen met in the streets of Kristiania, in Paulsen's Samliv med Ibsen, I, p. 10: han så ud som en bedemand (undertaker) iført en hvid halsdug og nogle gamle sorte skindhandsker".

[2]) When the proper name Peder is now used (as in Vrøvle-Peder) to designate something stupid and tedious, Prof. Vilhelm Andersen, in his remarkable paper in the Thomsen-Festskrift (1894) ascribes this to the 'bi-tone' in that word of bede, bedemand. Of course this may or may nòt be so, — the fact that equivalents in other languages (cf. Dutch zeur-piet) miss that bytone certainly makes us pause! But to us it is interesting to hear what bytone the professor feels in Bedemand. —

[3]) There is some „smack" (bi-tone) of the (sentimentally-)pious in Jørgen Moe's: „Der er (Hør nu! atter Bedemandsstiil!) der er bestemt en Rand inderst i Sjelen, der fortoner sig, etc. When Ibsen in 1889 wrote to Halvorsen that he sees no objection to the printing of his letter to King Charlès (cf. Breve, II, 83) „skjønt jeg nu synes at det er holdt så temmelig i bedemandsstil", — we shall find, on looking it up (Breve, I, 113) that the word here may mean either, the tone is no doubt somewhat screwed-up, but the sentimentality is not wanting either. —

1, 249; 3, 253; F, 502; M, 298; 14, 231; J, 309; 16, 231.

"schlüpfrige element" came in his way, he touched it "not with the hand but with his stick" (l. l. I¹ 235, ²241) just as the Norwegian tales are on the whole not so refined in tone, Wörner reminds us, as the German ones, and this is no doubt true. We can only admire the delicate way of putting it. But as Ibsen substituted hale (cf. n. to l. 4056) for the word of which he only ventured to write the first letter R — and as he omitted a not overrefined if witty passage about a flag of peace to his hind-parts from U (cf. Eft. Skr. II, p. 85: ifald du render som en Pilt med Fredsflag fra dit Agterskilt), we may just wonder a very little that this was kept, — it cannot be said in any way to be essential. See the n. to l. 2977.

4509.   ødsle det dyre Brænsel, i Tider
som disse, paa saadant stemningsløst Rakk?
to throw away dearly-bought fuel in times
like these on such spiritless rubbish as this?

This delightful outburst is spoilt by the rendering of Rakk by rubbish. For rak is = mob, rabble. The Lean One says: do you think I should throw away my fuel on such fellows, — viz. on that body of sinners, — and then, seeing that Peer is hurt, he excuses himself by what follows: now, don't be cross, I was thinking of the s i n rather than the sinner, my sneer (Skosen) referred to your s i n s. Morgenstern who translates correctly: für solch Stimmungslos P a c k, spoils it again by continuing: ja, ja, S i e m e i n' ich! The Dutch translator is entirely at sea: uw zonden zijn boevenstreken, i. e. your sins are rogues' tricks!

4519.   hvad Svensken kalder "bra litet rolig."
What the Swedes call: "Mighty poor sport."

This excellent rendering of the Archers is spoilt by Mr. Ellis Roberts by the omission of Mighty. A comparison of the way by which the German translators have tried to get out of the difficulty is amusing. —

4524. det er ikke grejdt at forstaa, hvor Skoen trykker.
It's never so easy to know where the shoe is tight, etc.

Compare: det veit ingen kvar skoen klember, utan
den som gjeng i honom, eller: Det veit ingen kvar skoen
trykkjer utan den som hev honom paa seg, Aasen, p.
133. —

With regard to the form grejdt that Ibsen used both
in U and R, it may be nothing but a slip for grejt, the
Riksmaal adjective being grej and not grejd (cf. Dutch
gereed; Germ. dialect greit). Grejd is the Landsmaal
form which Ibsen is not likely to have used! On the other
hand, grejd may have been used under Danish influence.

4526. Det er sandt; jeg har — den og den være Lov. —
Very true; I have — praise be to so and so! —

By an aposiopesis evidently due to the desire not
actually to mention the evil one, by a sort of taboo we
we might say, not this time (cf. n. to l. 2310) out of
respect for the good but of fear for the evil, his Satanic
Majesty was called h i n in the Scandinavian languages,
standing for hin Onde, hin Karen[1]), hanselv[2]);
hence in the same way den og den is found used in the
very collection of tales that Ibsen drew upon for his
Peer Gynt story: Huldreev. (ed. '12 p. 61): "Pyt!
ikke værre, sa Kari... jeg har ikke noget at skaffe med
nissen og kommer'n til mig, saa skal jeg, den og den ta'
mig, nok føise'n paa dør (En gammeldags Juleaften).

---

[1]) cf. No. Sagn² 1902, p. 99: „Hin Karen....havde betinget at (baaden) ikke
maatte merkes. Paa den vis kunde den nemlig heller ikke tjærekorses i for- og
agterstavnen.''

[2]) Feilberg in v. Dennemand, which one might be tempted to look upon in the
same light, is supposed to be (by Feilberg in v.) a substitution for djævlen ta' mig.
'Den og den' may therefore perhaps be looked upon as a s t a n d i n g expression
for the devil (although its more usual sense is of course: so and so; cf. Du er saamen
ligesaa god Frøken du, som baade Den og Den hele gaden bortigjennem, Wergeland,
VI, p. 459) and in that case not, as the Archers' translation (and Ellis Roberts':
Thank you know who) suggests, made up by the Lean One as though he did not dare
to, or wish to utter the name, although it *may* of course be the Lean One's substitution for: Gudskelov. The good joke to put this expression in the mouth of this
gentleman himself, does not seem less witty in consequence. —

Compare: Naa ja! — det skulde daa vera som baade hin og den, om ein tjugeaars Bladmann ikkje skulde... Arne Garborg, Kolbotnbrev, p. 105.

The way the Lean one here speaks of himself reminds one of Mephisto's:

Ich möcht mich gleich dem Teufel übergeben
Wenn ich nicht selbst der Teufel wär! (Spaziergang), and his:

Denn wenn es keine Hexen gäbe
Wer Teufel möchte Teufel sein! (II; am oberen Peneios.)

4530. jeg skal hente en Steg, som jeg haaber blir fed.

I'm after a roast that I hope will prove fat.

See the n. to l. 3582. —

4539. være Vrangen eller Retten af Kjolen.

there's a right and a wrong side to the jacket.

Vetle Vislie in his biography of Aasmund Olavsson Vinje applies (p. 311) this theory to his hero: (Vinje) "var seg sjølv men paa Vrangsida" and continues: Difyr vart han den munnkaate, den slengekjeftade. "Du snur altid den skjemtefulle Sida fram av slikt, du", seggjer ein av Heltarne i "Elsk og Giftarmaal" (II, 381) og fær til Svar: That is my way of weeping!: Det er no m i n Maate aa graata paa, det, — kvar hev sine Taarer. And there are a good many people who delight in thus turning their wrong side out, who show themselves not only in their shirt-sleeves but in borrowed clothes that do not fit them at all.

4540. De ved, man har nylig fundet paa i Paris
at gjøre Portræter ved Hjælp af Solen.
Enten kan man direkte Billeder give,
eller ogsaa de saakaldt negative.

You know they have lately discovered in Paris a way to take portraits by help of the sun.

One can either produce a straightforward picture, etc.

An other reference to a 'Daguerreotypist' may be found in Sancthansnatten, Eft. Skr. I. 407. See on

this passage, Eitrem in Gads danske Magasin, 1913,
p. 462: Starting from what looks like reminiscences
of Paludan-Müller's and Heiberg's glorious playing with
popular motives (overlegent tumlende med folkeeven-
tyrlige motiver), Ibsen promises those who are themselves in a deeper sense, those who give positive or direct
reproductions of the creator's thoughts "en høi
himmel"; those who produce a sort of image, but negative
ones i. e. those who do not believe in ideals he re-
legates to hot hell, where by a fitting treatment they
will become 'positive' and hence worthy of heaven"
In Wörner (II p. 220) the reader may find a discussion
of some plays of Ibsen, containing the negative image,
opposed to the preceding ones where the poet had
given the positive one first: The Wild Duck and An
Enemy of the people; Hedda Gabler and Rosmersholm
and to a certain extent Peer Gynt and Brand. —

4560. komme som en Ravn, for at gaa som en Rype?
come.. black as a raven to turn out a white ptarmigan?

Cf. the imagery used by Ibsen in his first draft: Lad
Livsens Alvor...smelte dig, luttre dig till Due fra
Ravn, Eft. Skr. II, 91 and supra the n. to the Button-
moulder, p. 315

4564,5. Peter Gynt?... Er Herr Gynt sig selv? — Ja, det
bander han paa.
Is Herr Gynt himself? — Yes, he vows he is. —

Here Peer has practically the certificate he has been
longing to get — cf. the scene with the Button-moulder.
And it may be asked why he does not prevail upon the
Lean One to accompany him to the Button-moulder?

Dr. Western thus answers this question: To understand this we must remember that it was not enough
for Peer to prove that he had been himself, but
to have been himself in the sense which the Button-
moulder put into this phrase, i. e." sig selv at døde",
and Peer understands well enough that the testimony

1, 251; 3, 256; F, 504; M, 300; 14, 233; J, 311; 16, 233.

which the Lean one could give him, would not be taken
for good by the Button-moulder. — But we might ask:
why not use the Lean one as a witness of his being
"en stor synder" for in that case too he would be saved
from the casting-ladle. — I suppose this is another
example of Peer's propensity for going "udenom".
Of course, he might have seized this opportunity of
getting rid of the Button-moulder by catching this
witness or getting the "attest" that he had been himself on the wrong side, and so go to hell and be washed
clean there, but at the decisive moment he as usual
shrank back, he again tried a roundabout way instead
of going right through. — His behaviour now shows
him as he has always been — he is himself in his way. He
hopes to be able to cheat both the Lean one and the
Button-moulder. —

A correspondent does not see why Ibsen here uses
the form Peter whereas Peer would do just as well
from the point of the metre. It can only be that 'Peter'
is the natural 'beautified' form proper to an "official
document"!

4572.   paa staaende Fod. without delay.
See the n. to l. 4429 for the Lean One's swift voyages
through the air. —

4575.   nogle slemme Missionærer fra Stavanger.
ruined by missionaries from Stavanger.
Stavanger was and is the seat of the Norwegian
missionary society, to his sympathy for whose work
Mr. Brons testifies by saying that Stavanger is "der
Hauptsitz des Muckerthums (canting, snivelling hypo-
crites) in Norwegen". Here, as Dr. Western suggests,
Brons may have been thinking of the Stavanger society
as depicted by Alex. Kielland in St. Hans Fest.

4579.   Det var mig en Fryd at narre det Asen.
It delights me to humbug an ass like that.
We are reminded of this when we read (Feilberg,

I, 252; 3, 256; F, 505; M, 300; 14, 234; J, 311; 16, 234.

III, 699 in v. sygdom) that "sygdoms vætter kan narres f. eks. ved at skrive paa en dør: N. N. er ikke hjemme eller ved at give syg andet navn". On some other cases of illnesses looked upon and treated as living beings, see a note in my paper: Bøigens Oprindelse, Danske Studier, 1916 p. p. 180. —

Compare: Fanden er dum (l. 3913: det fik Fanden fordi han var dum.).

4587.   Broer Stjernerap! Brother Starry-Flash! —

Stjernerap = stjerneskud, — on the second element (=ráp) cf. the n. to l. 972. A shooting star, as Mr. Anders Krogvig writes, is popularly taken to mean that the star is lost. Peer thinks that this is to be his fate and that he too will 'glide out' into nothingness. So he ironically prays the shooting star to "give his kind regards" and announce his coming.

4599. Der sad ingen derinde. There was no one within it. —

Of course as Peer proceeds to say, the owner of the hut, Peer himself, was not at home, but to say that it was "folketom" is the clearest proof that even now he forgets Solvejg and has not an inkling of a notion of what she has been for him.

4601,2.   Dejlige Sol og dejlige Jord,

I var dumme, at I bar og lyste for min Moer.

Beautiful sun and beautiful earth,

you were foolish to bear and give light to my mother.

The meaning must be: my mother should not have been born, or at least should never have born me, for I have been quite useless. (W.)

4603.   Aanden er karrig og Naturen ødsel.

The spirit is niggard and nature lavish.

As in the later editions here, we find naturen e r ødsel in l. 2399. In our line the addition of er (cf. T. C. §63) must be owing to the influence of Aanden er karrig. —

4607.   Det lovede Land. the promised land.

Brynildsen is the only Dano-Norwegian dictionary at

my disposal that gives the expression, which he does without any note of warning but 'lovede' (land) seems to be Swedish rather than Norwegian. (A. Krogvig).

4608,9. se at faa Snedyngen over mig kavet;
    de kan skrive derover: "her en I n g e n begravet;"
    then try to get snowdrifts piled up over me.
    They can write above them: "Here *No One* lies buried".

Peer has just expressed the wish to see one more sunrise and his wish is to be fulfilled in reality and symbolically later on when he and Solveig are reunited. But here it seems as if it begins to dawn upon him — at last! we may well say when we remember that a whole life was to pass before he saw himself, found himself, before he truly w a s himself! — But his 'awakening' to the truth that his life was n o t h i n g, that he was nobody, comes too late. "Peer erkennt.... nachdem er, der Tote, zu spät erwacht ist, dass er lange vor seinem Tode gestorben ist", — "Hier liegt Niemand begraben". Truly the lesson of the "somebody" to whom the Dutch poet said: "be yourself" adding with a sigh: but he could not, he was nobody" (De Genestet: Wees U zelf zei ik tot iemand, maar hij kon niet, hij was niemand) might have been applied to Peer Gynt. "Für ihn, as J. Collin says, gilt das Mephistopheles' Wort: Es ist so gut als wär er nicht gewesen". The resemblance with Brand's end and at the same time the willed contradiction between the two figures is unmistakeable: Brand who i s buried under an avalanche but in whose case, that of a personality with a vengeance, surely no one would think of suggesting Peer's memorial inscription! And Collin is no doubt right (Prof. Christen Collin this time, the Kristiania professor in his Samtiden paper, Nov. 1913) when he reminds us of Professor Rubek in "Naar vi døde vågner", who "after having recognised that art for art's sake is bankrupt, wishes like Peer Gynt,

---

1, 254; 3, 258; F, 506; M, 301; 14, 235; J, 312; 16, 235.

to climb once more through mist and snow, to the
sun-lighted mountain-tops.... (he) ascends the glacier
and disappears in an avalanche"....And we can perhaps follow Collin in his comparison with Solness and
Borkmann, but he seems to go too far when he suggests
that Ibsen has chastised in Peer Gynt not only the
Norwegian people but also certainly himself. Collin
even asks if Ibsen in a moment of humility has not
possibly wished the inscription: "Here nobody is
buried" to be set over his own grave. Recalling Peer
Gynt's distress here, Collin, writes: I think this is
Henrik Ibsen himself who at one time in his life must
have lived through this moment of terror. It is himself
who in mortal agony has asked if he had perhaps lived
and worked in vain up till then, if he had not lost
something of his real self in the dream-life of poetry".
The problem is interesting and when introduced by
a man of Chr. Collin's stamp, it is worth taking up.
This is of course not the place to do so, — it raises the
question of the whole of Ibsen's work and life's views;
I can only say that he who at one time will tackle it,
must explain how Ibsen could be supposed to give
utterance to such despondency at the very moment
when, after the success of Brand he must have been in
a state of such elation that according to Collin himself, the whole of Peer Gynt is nothing but one cry of
Victory!, and when "efter gjennembrudet ved hjælp av
Brand" (Collin, l. l. p. 596) he enjoyed "a new summer-
happiness in Italy". No surely! this is not the Ibsen
of the time when life did nothing but smile upon him;
it is rather "the poor candidate for melting-honours"
(den stakkels Støbekandidat!) whom Jæger (1892, p.
80, 81) thus addresses:" Riot away, Peer Gynt — as
much as you like! Live your life, — that is no life!
Go about from Hægstad to the lunatic asylum at
Kairo, from the settler's hut on the heath to Anitra's

tent in the desert, — play at being a prince in the Rondë-mountains or a prophet in the Sahara, an antiquary among the pyramids or a Croesus at Charlestown, — it is all equally empty, just as much of a wretched bungler's work! You can peel yourself till nothing remains, just as you yourself peeled the onion, which like yourself consisted of swathings only without any kernel whatsoever! And the best inscription one can think of for you is "Here No One is buried!"

4615.   sjunger.

Compare S. I. S. p. 183: the obsolescent if not obsolete form sjunget was corrected by Ibsen in the second ed. of Catilina to sunget.

The whole of this song· by the Kirkefolk as well as Peer Gynt's frightened comment on it was added in R; it is not found in U. —

4620.   Synderegistret. list of sins.

A similar expression occurs in Adam Homo: Hans Dyder — her er Listen som dem melder. (II, 462).

4625.   lugter Lunten. The owl smells the daylight.

This expression, literally: to scent the slow-match, which seems to have slightly puzzled some of the translators, is quite clear to a Dutchman, in whose language too lont ruiken means to scent a danger, to smell a rat, as Mr. Ellis Roberts translates by divine inspiration. So the owl smells, feels that it is all up with Peer, — hence his doleful hoot. —

4626.   Ottesang. matin-bell.

The translation is of course perfectly correct, otte for ohte (cf. Dutch ochtend) meaning morning. Some of the translators have understood it as if = the eight hour bell! Just as on a famous occasion the lines from an old ballad: Hr. Oluf rider om Otte, was translated by: Sire Olaf chevauche à huit heures du matin! (Dania, VIII, 214).

4629.   Beskikk Dit Hus! Set your house in order!

From Jesaiah 38, 1, cf. ante n. to the Button-moulder, l. 4095.

4644.   Hun staar rank og mild.

           She stands there erect and mild.

Mr. Eitrem has given an interesting comparison between the last meeting of Peer and Solveig with the attitude of the latter's prototype in Paludan-Müller's Adam Homo; cf. Gads danske Magasin, 1913, p. 461: Ibsen har ikke git os et saa detaljert billede av Solveigs senere livshistorie som Paludan-Müller av Almas. Men av de faa linjer som er trukket op med en mesters faste haand, ser vi alligevel saa meget, at de to kvinders historie løper parallelt. De små Solveig-scener er likesom kvintessensen av "Almas Efterladenskab", — the heroine's lyrical outbursts supposed to have been left behind by her. One of these shall be quoted here too:

> Du har endnu en Debitor, du kjære!
> En fattig Sjæl mod hvem du gjorde vel!
>
> Hvad Skat af Fryd og Lykke her i Livet
> Har ikke gratis du mit Hjerte givet!
> Hvad Riigdom delte ei din Aand med mig!
>
> Hvis derfor een Gang Regnskab skal opgjøres,
> Lad frem med dig din Skyldner da kun føres,
> Med hvad du gav, hun klare vil for dig!

And Eitrem points even to a correspondence of words: Just as here Solveig stands there "rank og mild", so Alma, sitting as a sister of charity by the bed of her lover, is described as follows: Nakken er r a n k og Haanden fiin og lille.... med melankolske Øine, blaa og b l i d e".

4646.   (Solvejg) famler efter ham. groping for him.

        So she is nearly blind. —

4662.   de taagede Lande. the mist-shrouded regions.

Compare: det taagede graa, the grey of the mist (l. 4594.).

4666.   I min Tro, i mit Haab og i min Kjærlighed.
         In my faith, in my hope, and in my love.

The final salvation of Peer by Solveig like that of
Faust by Gretchen is a trait which has been judged
very differently by the commentators. The first critic
of the play, Bjørnson, having given what to us now
would seem the correct explanation that Peer has always been 'himself' in Solveig's Tro Haab og Kjærlighed, adds by way of afterthought that so at least it
'should' be understood, tor "the end is unfortunately
indistinct and far from properly worked out". Some,
and not of the least, such as Brandes and Wörner
condemn it, the former as "stødende doktrinært" that
she should save the "far too unworthy" soul of her
beloved (Henrik Ibsen, p. 110), the latter because he
feels the impossibility to understand Ibsen's "fatherly
feelings" when the author at the end of the play, as
Wörner expresses it, "presses the unworthy Peer to his
heart." And Kahle too (Henrik Ibsen, Bjørnstjerne
Bjørnson und ihre Zeitgenossen, p. 22) sounds the note
of Peer's unworthiness: "er hätte hinein müssen in den
Löffel des Knopfgiessers." Quite lately again, Mr. Arne
Bergsgaard has developed the same point with some
vigour in a paper: Kring Solveig og Peer Gynt (in Syn
og Segn, 1915, p. 49 seqq.) The final scene is illogical and
inconsistent, even Ibsen's belief in the "skirande og
renskande magt hjaa kvinna" does not make this "rime-
leg, ja, knapt nok synleg." [1]

---

[1] And Bergsgaard explains this in a remarkably ingenious way by turning Chr.
Collin's hypothesis (supra n. to l. 4608,9 and lower down) inside out: Peer is not
saved as Collin thinks because from the type he was (of the Norwegian people)
Ibsen has made him into an individual whom he, Ibsen to some extent identifies
himself with; on the contrary, Peer is saved because he is not only an individual but
also a representative of the Norwegian people and because it is Solveig, the type of,
or rather the incarnation of the Dagny-side of the Norwegian woman that waits for
him and gives him i. e. that gives it (viz. the Norwegian people) the new „termin"
(letter of 4, 3, '66 to Bjørnson) it wants so badly in order to be saved. And it is
woman, the Norwegian woman who is to save Norway, teste one of Ibsen's later plays
where woman is shown to be the t r u e „pillar of society".
Apropos of the "Dagny-type" that Bergsgaard mentions, cf. Henning Kehler

---

Of the opposite camp, it will suffice to quote Prof. Chr. Collin's view, who, not only in the various papers quoted but also in a German review has vigorously defended the end of the poem, showing that this end múst come because Ibsen was.... Ibsen and felt the need i n h i m s e l f to save Peer after having first thoroughly shown how unworthy he was!

"Henrik Ibsen selbst war wie Terje Vigen: "er musste Rache haben", hatte er aber einmal über altes Unrecht sein Strafgericht gehalten", Collin writes (Die Neue Rundschau, 1907, p. 1283), "dann war er weich und gut. Er gleicht jener Gottheit die er in Brand beschreibt, der Gottheit die alles oder nichts fordert und ohne Schonung straft, sich aber am Ende der Enden doch als "deus caritatis" offenbart. Diese Gottheit hat Ibsen nach seinem Ebenbilde geschaffen, aus dem Bedürfniss seines eigenen Herzens heraus. Der Schluss des "Brand" ist fast von allen Kritikern als unlogisch und schwach verurteilt worden. Aber die Erklärung liegt in des Dichters eigener zusammengesetzter Natur. Es gilt zu erfassen, dass nur dieser Ausgang den Dichter hat befriedigen können, und kein anderer.

Von dem gleichen Gesichtspunkt aus rückt auch der ebenso unlogische und ebenso häufig getadelte Schluss des Peer Gynt in neue Beleuchtung. Peer Gynt ist der Representant des Norwegischen Volkes, der, mit Märchen und Sagen aufgepäppelt davon träumt Kaiser zu werden und die alte Herrlichkeit des Geschlechtes wieder auf zu richten...... Fünf lange Akte wird dieser Norwegische Durchschnittsmensch kritisiert, um schliesslich für den Schmelzlöffel reif und dem Untergang geweiht zu werden. Aber, am letzten Schluss, schmilzt dennoch

(who distinguishes between Ibsen's fair and dark women; the former as a rule the good ones, the latter of an evil disposition; Edda, '16 p. 54): Det er et af Ibsens allermest anvendte Motiver at stille en Mand mellem to Kvinder der i de historiske Dramaer staar overfor hinanden som det gode mod det onde: Aurelia-Furia, Signe-Margit, Helena-Makrina. Hertil slutter sig Solveig-Hægstadjenten der er suppleret med Dovrekongens datter og Agnes-Gerd". —

1, 258; 3, 262; F, 510; M, 303; 14, 239; J, 314; 16, 239.

Ibsens Strenge gegen seinen Helden. Er kann trotz allem dem Gedanken einer Rettung nicht entsagen. Peer Gynt kann noch erlöst werden — mit Solveigs Hilfe. —

There is however one thing we should have considered first: Ibsen does not make it actually c e r t a i n that when the Button-moulder and Peer d o meet "at the next cross-roads" — or perhaps: not quite certain that i f they should meet, the soul of Peer will not after all find its way into the casting-ladle (which even Collin thinks he is only saved from because Ibsen turns a Deus Caritatis at the last moment) what the commentators generally [1]) agree about did not happen. Well, those whom nothing short of mathematical certainty can satisfy, may continue to doubt, — it would seem that Ibsen really intended to save Peer from the melting-process at the intercession of Solvejg, for otherwise we should be compelled to look upon the latter's final words as a "suggestio falsi". And we should certainly not go quite so far as Ellis Roberts who thinks the words mean: "n o t that Peer is rescued from his disastrous past by Solvejg's love, but that there never has been any other Peer than the one who fell in love with Solvejg" (p. XXIII) nor perhaps even as Dresdner who (Ibsen als Norweger und Europæer, 1907, p. 21) says that the life of love that Solveig has taught him to live "besteht und ist w i r k l i c h k e i t, während das andere in Scherben zerbricht", although it is prettily expressed when he adds that "aus der ganzen Phantasmagorie seines wilden Daseins bleibt nur ein einziges Erlebniss als dauerhaft und fruchtbar zurück: dass er einmal echte Liebe gefühlt, einmal echte Liebe

---

[1]) I noted one or two exceptions: Mr. A. Leroy Andrews, Journal of English and Germanic Phil., XIII, 240: As Margaret's spirit leads at the end Faust's soul to higher spheres, so Peer Gynt's soul „seems similarly to be saved through Solvejg's love; at least she herself is confident that such is the case, a confidence not necessarily shared by the reader nor actually confirmed by the author". And Arne Bergsgaard too in the paper mentioned lays stress on the fact that it is but hope of salvation (bergingsvon) that is held out to Peer.

---

erweckt hat." But what a difference between the two
"cases"! Peer's momentary outburst, only to sink back
into the depths of vilest egoism and Solveig's feelings
which make her appear like an incarnation of two
of the finest descriptions, if not: t h e sublimest interpretations of love that the world's literature knows:
Shakespeare's "love is not love which alters where it
alteration finds, or bends with the remover to remove" (Sonnet 116, so beautifully translated into
Norwegian quite recently by Professor Chr. Collin,
Det Geniale Menneske, p. 210) and the apostle's High
Song of love: "charity suffereth long and is kind,
charity envieth not, charity vaunteth not itself, is not
puffed up,.... seeketh not her own, is not easily pro-
voked, thinketh no evil.... beareth all things, be-
lieveth all things, hopeth all things, endureth all things,
Charity never faileth" (1. Cor. 13) to end in the words
that contain what may be the germ of our very passage [1]): "Saa bliver da Tro, Haab, Kjærlighed, disse tre;
men størst iblandt disse er Kjærligheden".

A more direct source is of course Paludan-Müller's
Adam Homo where the counsel for the prosecution
(actor; end of the twelfth song), the Advocatus Diaboli,
asserts that Adam does not come up to the Tro, Haab
og Kjærlighed of the Gospel, when a star comes (remember that Alma's maiden name is "Stjerne") and gives
him "Et Blik af evig Kjærlighed", whereupon he is
saved by Alma from spiritual death. The fullest and
clearest interpretation will be found in the easily accessible book of J. Collin, which those may read who share
Wörner's doubts or Brandes' scruples. —

Dr. A. Western writes: In my opinion Peer is saved
not by Solveig's love only; that would not be enough,

---

[1]) As remarked by Prof. Julius Olsen in his useful annotated edition of Brand, p.
339, the English: faith hope and charity do not fully correspond to our term.
Hence, the Archers, noting (p. 278) that Kjærlighed also means „charity in the bible
sense", for once sacrifice the metre of the line by rendering the word as l o v e . —

1, 258; 3, 262; F, 510; M, 303; 14, 239; J, 314; 16, 239.

but by his own repentance. From the moment when he has resolved to go t v e r s i g j e n n e m instead of u d e n o m, there is no more left of the Old Peer. He does not any more try to explain away his way of living. On the contrary: Har du dom for en synder saa tal den ud. He does not even ask for forgiveness. He asks for his sentence: Klag ud, hvor syndig jeg har mig forbrudt, and Skrig ud min brøde! And when Solveig answers that he has not sinned, that he has made her life into a beautiful song, and blessed him and this meeting, then he has only this answer: Så er jeg fortabt. — This repentance is deep and real, and this repentance saves him at last, — without his knowing it. And if we ask, how is that possible, I answer: because there is no longer any one to accuse him. The "counsel for the prosecution" has given it up. — "Has anybody condemned you?", Christ asks of the woman found in adultery, and when she answers: No, he says: "Then I do not condemn you either." — In the same way, since his accuser Solveig does not condemn him, but forgives and even blesses him, God will forgive him too. — He needn't be afraid of meeting the Button-moulder next time.

4668. Til Gutten derinde er selv du Moer!
Thou art mother thyself to the man that's there.

Mr. Ellis Roberts' 'to the lad' is perhaps preferable to the Archers' m a n — Peer surely feels more like a boy here than like a man — 'there' of course referring to Solveig's h e a r t or as she expresses it in the supreme words of the play that have just been commented upon: in my faith, in my hope and in my charity of love. So: you yourself are mother to, have created me thus, that image of me. And Solveig anwers: true! but who is its father (U had: who is y o u r father, d i n Fader); surely he who forgives at the prayer of the mother. And this reading of U: hvem er d i n Fader? will help those out of their doubt who might

---

hesitate as to whether "he who forgives" is God or Peer. For surely, this is a proof, if needed, that "gutten derinde" is Peer and 'din' Fader = God. —

Compare Philip Wicksteed's excellent booklet, p. 61: "Begotten of God in her virgin bosom at that first interview is an ideal Peer Gynt such as God would have him be. This child of her own pure heart will grow till it becomes her very life and, however sorely tried, she will never desert it, or cease to believe that it exists."

4671. Et Skjær af Lys gaar over ham.... Solen rinder.
a light shines in his face.... The sun rises.

There is of course at first sight nothing remarkable in the fact that Peer's face "lights up" with joy at the moment when he gauges the depth of Solvejg's love and that the sun just then should happen to rise — the very early morning hour has been indicated before. But it seems impossible in view of the folklore the drama is so full of, to overlook what may be a very clear allusion to one of its traits here. For who can forget that when in the folktales, the troll-monster can but be kept abroad until dawn, the troll, originally a mountain-spirit bursts and with a "stone thou wast, to stone returnest" is changed into its element again when the Light of the world sheds its first rays upon it. "Jeg er Verdens Lys", Christ had said (John, 8, 12) and that light had taken the place, when Christianity had triumphed, that fire had occupied in the pagan religious systems, — cf. e. g. such a fact as that tribes of the Malay Peninsula light fires near a mother at child-birth to scare away evil spirits. (Tylor, Primitive Culture, II, 194, seq.) The stories illustrating our point are legion, one of the prettiest is the one of a giant (Bugge-Berge, II, 45 and cf. Wigström, Sagor i Skåne, '84 p. 37) who is drinking up the pool in which Agnusmøy has hidden a little boy the giant is after. When

the giant is taking the last draught, the sun rises and
Agnusmøy, pointing to the east, exclaims: I say, look
at that bridal procession! The giant falls into the trap,
looks to the east and — bursts! What the light does
is symbolically also performed by the Cock: Hanen
slaar sin Vinge og Elfepigerne maa flygte (Elverhøj-
visen, Jæger, Ill. Lit. Hist., I, 119; R. Köhler, Kl.
Schriften, III, 581 and see further e. g. Feilberg, Jul,
I, 95 seqq., 232, II, 3: the dead live up again: "dagen
er din, natten er min!; "Nu galer Hanen den sorte, i
mørken Vraa, nu lukker op alle de Porte, og bort jeg
maa, (Aage og Else); Olav den Helliges Saga, p. 362 and
further: Feilberg, Ordbog III, 455 in v. sol; id. Bjærgtagen, p. 86; Paul's Grundriss I¹ 1032 = ²290, v. d.
Leyen, Herrig's Archiv, CXIII, 257, etc. etc. — But
the one that comes perhaps nearest to our case is the
story of the "lad that won the princess from the Troll"
that Olsen tells (p. 276): The boy has saved the princess out of the troll-monster's abode and is of course
overtaken by the latter who comes near them. Only: the
troll had forgotten that it must first gain the princess'
confidence before it could get her entirely in its power.
And the story itself will show you that the words: "Nu
var troldet som l a m m e t fordi gutten og prinsessen
holdt av hinanden" should not be taken figuratively
only, as the reader might be inclined to do. In Ibsen's
own work a perhaps still somewhat closer parallel may
be found: early in the second act of Gildet paa Solhoug
(F, I, 180) but especially at the end of the play (p. 214) at
the very moment that Margit has overcome her w o r s e r
s e l f, — "solen står op og kaster sit lys ind i stuen".
(Compare on the popular-tale element in this play,
Fred. Paasche's monograph). A clincher to the whole
of this will be seen in Ibsen's well-known lines to the
effect that "to live was óne battle with trolls in the
vaults of one's brain and one's breast": At leve er —

1, 258; 3, 262; F, 510; M, 303; 14, 239; J, 315; 16, 239.

krig med trolde i hjertets og hjærnens hvælv". And as Peer once before had overcome the Great Troll — Bøjgen — by the help of Solvejg (han var for stærk, der stod kvinder bag ham, 1. 1270), so again both Margit and Peer, when they have finally killed their vices, feel the first warm rays of the sun of their salvation. —

J. Collin (Henrik Ibsen, p. 346) recalls Christ's words: Except a man be born again he cannot see the kingdom of God (John, 3, 3) and Nicodemus' doubt "How can a man be born when he is old? can he enter the second time into his mother's womb and be born?" to add the remark that Ibsen here shows us h o w a man can be born again. —

4674.   Solvejg's song.

By the side of the English translations of Messrs. Archer and Mr. Ellis Roberts there is (a very pretty) one of the poems only and this song is of course among the number, by Mr. Garrett: Lyrics and Poems from Ibsen, London, Dent, 1912, p. 48. —

4687.   Sov og drøm du, Gutten min!
          Sleep and dream thou, dear my boy.

It may interest the student to know that Ibsen seems to have expressly said that here Peer actually dies this world (cf. n. to l. 4666) — it is Passarge who tells us so in the prefatory note to the second ed. of his translation: "Für meine Ansicht das Solvejgs Wiegelied symbolisch den Tod bedeute, habe ich ebenfalls die Bestätigung des Dichters". Here then, Peer who has been playing all the time at being himself, at last actualises it and, as J. Collin expresses it: indem sich Peer Gynt an sie schmiegt,.... vollzieht sich die mystische Vereinigung mit seinem selbst" (l.l,p. 290) — his worser self has died, — in order to become himself he must have killed it, for: at være sig selv er sig selv at døde (l. 4381) and so, just like Mefisto's: she is doomed does not weigh against the mysterious voice: she is saved, Peer becomes one of those Dead that can awaken.

Textual Criticism

of

Henrik Ibsen's Peer Gynt

PREFACE.

This critical study of the existing Peer Gynt texts, with the exception of §§ 140, 141 and a few notes added here and there in the text, was written in the spring of 1914 and even composed down to § 104. It was to have been published in the Recueil de la Faculté de Philosophie et Lettres de l'Université de Gand in the September of that year, contemporaneously with a short extract of this study in Prof. Gran's then new venture, the „Edda". The war broke out and only the latter paper, „Tilbake til Ibsen", did actually see the light (1914, no. 3), for every communication between author and printers of the longer study (at Bruges) ceased very soon after the catastrophe began and it was not until the spring of 1916, after many and various difficulties, that the manuscript and the sheets printed off could be got at and, as the continuation of the „Recueil" for the first was open to much doubt, that arrangements were made to transfer this study to Martinus Nijhoff of the Hague, who had kindly undertaken to publish it together with the preceding larger commentary on Ibsen's masterpiece.

Meanwhile, the Edda paper had not passed unnoticed; I think the general feeling among Ibsen-students must have been one if not of stupor, at least of great disappointment that so unreliable a text should continue to be served upon the unwary public. Chr. Brinckmann asked (Aftenposten, 1914, no. 606) if „Edda" had perhaps more of these „sensational papers in store like the revelation", the article in question „staggered" Ibsen-students with and it was therefore reasonable to suppose that subsequent editions would remedy the deplorable state of affairs pointed out and that the next edition would not see the light without a full collation of the oldest available text. Unfortunately, as § 141 infra will show, this has proved to be an illusion, — evidently a case of "over ævne" for the corrector. Or was it that Gyldendal did not think it worth while because they did not yet see how serious a state of affairs had gradually been brought about in the matter of Ibsen-texts?

The question and the doubt implied will appear justified by the reception that the Edda paper received at the hands of the said publishing house. Readers of my paper and of the present larger study too, will it is hoped see how purely objectively the matter had been treated, that it was not my aim to attack any person and certainly not either the firm in question nor of course in any the remotest way the competence of so esteemed a savant as Prof. Johan Storm, and that when the latter comes in for some share of the criticism it is as an editor and corrector of texts and not as a scholar. It is therefore much to be regretted that Gyldendal has thought it necessary to introduce the personal polemical element by flourishing such words as an „attack on the firm" the writer's „pedantry" and Professor Edward (sic!) Storm's „reputation",—since when is an honest pointing out of mistakes in a book an „attack" on the publishers? And is a man's scholarship at stake if he does not possess the art of the press-corrector to perfection and must stand convicted of some inaccuracies? And as to my own offence,—if a man had simply reprinted the old text as it stood, sticking very carefully to its punctuation, would he be a „pedant" and as such would he be to blame? Then why speak of pedantry when nothing but such accuracy is insisted upon?

In an interview to which the Berlingske Tidende (of Copenhagen) thought it desirable to submit Gyldendal's managing director, Hr. Peter Nansen, „for at spørge ham hvad man paa Forlaget har at sige til dette Angreb" (I have only seen a reproduction by the Bergens Aftenblad, 2/10/'14, which is the one I quote here), the director is reported „apparently not to attach any importance to the attack" and to have delivered himself as follows:

„Der kan naturligvis i alle Udgaver, saa stor Omhu der ogsaa anvendes, indløbe Trykfejl.... Vi lod Korrekturen besørge af

Folk, som — det tror jeg, jeg tør sige—gik til sit Arbeide med den størst mulige Alvor og Grundighed. Men naturligvis kan et eller andet Ord blive forvansket. Og netop for at komme bort fra dette, bad vi Professor Edvard Storm (sic) om at gjennemgaa alle Texterne, da vi udsendte Mindeudgaven. Hvad der nu er tilbage, kan vist ikke være saa slemt at det kan genere nogen almindelig Læser. Jeg mener og det mener vel alle, at Udgaver af Ibsen og andre Forfattere skal være saa gode, som det er muligt at fremstille dem. Men Kommafeil og den Slags har vist kun Betydning for Filologerne. Jeg hader Trykfejl, men jeg synes ogsaa at Pedanteri er en ubehagelig Ting."

In reply to my question whether he had really no other qualification than that of Pedantry for the criticism in question, Hr. Nansen replied:

„Jeg vil ikke negte at jeg kan have brugt Udtrykket „pedantisk" om *en Del* af Deres Korrektur-Kritik. Jeg er selv Skribent og jeg synes, at et komma mer eller mindre — naar det ikke forstyrrer Meningen — er hjærtens ligegyldigt. Hvorvidt Deres Kritik af Prof. Joh. Storm's Kompetence er berettiget, derom er jeg ikke i stand til at dømme. Prof. Storm nød (read: nyder) Ry som en af de fineste norske Sprogmænd og Ibsen-Kendere".

What shall we say to all this? The question of the Professor's scholarship was not at stake as I have explained before,— as to Mr. Nansen's theory about punctuation, — he seems precisely to forget those many cases where a wrong punctuation *does* spoil the meaning. And does it not seem rather cool to repeat calmly that his correctors have done their work „med størst mulig Alvor og Grundighed" and that the texts are as reliable *as possible ?* The proof of the contrary was to be found already in my Edda-paper, I wonder whether Gyldendal had read it carefully. And the admission in fact if not in theory that it was not done „as well as possible" lies in the 16th (cf. § 141) which corrected all the mistakes I had happened to point out. Will after this and now that my material has been laid more fully before the public, the firm maintain once more that what now remains „kan visst ikke være saa slemt at det kan genere nogen almindelig Læser"? This gentleman must be a

very easy-going one if he is content with Saa smukt (n° 183;
still in the 16 th. ed.) and the inversion of lines such as in n° 206,
(J.) but the utterance in question and what follows — such little
nothings are interesting *"kun* for filologer" — is of the greatest
interest because it brings us to the cardo questionis, viz. that
Ibsen now actually has become a „prey" to philologists whether the publishers like it or not, and that by the side of that
dear Almindelig Læser for whom a matter of 400 mistakes in
one text (and I repeat that my list is not exhaustive) does not
seem to count, quite a host of Ibsen-s t u d e n t s cry for a truly
reliable text for them to work on. As my Edda paper has evidently not convinced Gyldendal of the crimen læsæ scientiæ
they will commit if they refuse to issue a text as Ibsen actually wrote his work, and as it is to be feared that the personal
element its Director introduced into the controversy will prevent their recognising what the present monograph at least
cannot but convince the unbiassed reader of, it can do no harm
to quote the opinion of some others on the matter.

I begin with that of the identical scholar whose critical
acumen Prof. Storm had praised so much in nis Appendix
to the Memorial Edition, Hans Eitrem, now Rector at Haugesund. „De har ret — he writes — vi må få en samvittighets-
fuld, trainet og tålmodig filolog til at rense denne *Augias-
Stald"*. And Prof. Seip is no less categorical when he gives it as
his conviction that „forlaget pligter både å sørge for en slik utgave (a careful reprint of the manuscript) og for en *anstændig*
tekstutgave isteden for de *slemme* og *pietetsløse* folkeutgaver,
minne-utgaver og jubilæumsutgaver". Not to abuse of my
readers' patience I quote as the last if far from least of a series
of scholars, — others have expressed themselves to the same
effect, — Professor Gran who had seen both the Recueil-
treatise as it then stood and my Ibsen paper.

„De resultater De her uimotsigelig fremlægger er i sandhet
„bedrøvelige" (the word I had used in the Edda paper to
qualify them, truly less of a kraftuttryk than those used by
both Eitrem and Seip!), enhver Ibsen-forsker må være Dem
taknemmelig for det besværlige Arbeide De har pålagt Dem,
og nødvendigheten av en renset Ibsen-utgave fremgår med

evidens av Deres Dokumentation." And if any one would like
to hear the voice of the public too, as the above are „only"
philologists, he will have to be content with one, but a voice as
to whose weight there can be no doubt. The poet's son, Hr.
Statsminister Dr. Sigurd Ibsen, when acknowledging the receipt of a reprint of my Edda-paper, added that in his opinion
the Edda paper „turde komme til at vise sig som banebryden-
de. Nemlig for så vidt, som dens fremkomst rimeligvis vil give
stødet til at det Gyldendalske forlag i sin tid foranstalter en
udgave.... i overensstemmelse med Deres program: „et nøi-
agtigt aftryk, renset for alle de feil, som der virkelig i de
gjængse texter findes altfor mange af".

* * *

Since my study had been sent to press in June '14, two new
texts of Peer Gynt have appeared, a collation of which could
therefore be added only later on, in the summer of 1916. J,
having been printed and published before the battle cry Tilbake til Ibsen was sounded, could of course not have obeyed
the summons and profit by the lessons it was hoped the paper
would convey. As to the 16th edition, § 141 of this treatise will
tell the reader how mechanically the lesson was taken to heart,
the responsible man again drawing the line at the one thing
needful: a full collation of the oldest text. If, therefore, before
the publication of this study, any new Peer Gynt texts should
see the light, it is not proposed to investigate them. After the
experience from the 16th edition the case seems hopeless and
the result a foregone conclusion.

This preface added for the greater part only to meet the position taken up by the Copenhagen publishing house might
produce the impression that only polemics and controversy
would be found in the study itself. But even a cursory reading
of it will, I hope, convince the student that it is meant to serve

its own purpose too. It will be found useful for the possessors of all previous Peer Gynt texts (§ 4) and containing as it does, a good many explanations of various passages in the play, it was the almost necessary supplement of the Commentary itself.

INTRODUCTORY.

§ 1. "As is well known, Ibsen never read the proofs of his work himself; he left this to the printers and the publishers, who did this as well as they could. Real misprints are rare, but misunderstandings and Danish forms instead of Norwegian ones, it has not always been possible to avoid. That the punctuation is not quite what it should be, comes partly of Ibsen being somewhat whimsical in this respect. Most mistakes, both by the author and printers, occur in the older works with their somewhat difficult text. In the modern social dramas his meaning is as a rule quite clear and the mistakes are very few."

Thus Professor Johan Storm tells us in an appendix: Mindeudgavens Tekst, Retskrivning og Sprogform, printed at the end of vol. V. of the Memorial edition published shortly after the author's death (¹).

Several passages might be quoted to bear out Prof. Storm's statement. Compare first of all: "I send you (part of) my manuscript. So far as I am concerned you can begin printing at once. *I trust to your proof-reader*—and to my manuscript, in which I think there is not a single error. I should like to see the edition printed off at once for I cannot change or correct anything." (Breve I, 179: letter of March 14, 1869 to Mr. Frederik Hegel, the then chief of Gyldendal's publishing firm, about a new work, de Unges Forbund.) And in a letter to the same gentleman of Nov. 25, 1865, Ibsen gives us the ground for his trusting to the compositors, — he had tested their work and

---

(¹) The Mindeudgave will henceforth be found referred to as M.; Prof. Storm's appendix as S. M. See for further abbreviations, infra § 7; a full list will be given at the end of the present work.

"nogen yderligere forsendelse af korrekturark behøves ikke".
(Breve I, 101.) And in the Preface to Catilina we read (Saml.
V. I, 9) that proof-correcting was unnecessary „da man havde
et så smukt og tydeligt manuscript at trykke efter."

Anyone who has seen the splendid calligraphy of Ibsen's
MS. in the form in which he was in the habit of sending it off to
the printers, will be prepared to think that Ibsen was fully
justified in doing so, at least as far as the legibility of his work
was concerned. There was no excuse whatever for misreading
the author's manuscript. And Professor Storm is far too clem-
ent in his judgment when he says that it was not always
possible to avoid "misforståelser og danskheder". It would be
more true to the facts of the case if he had simply said that
they h a d n o t b e e n avoided. Ibsen seems to have detected misprints as by chance and then he wrote to correct them
to his publishers (Breve) or to theater-chef Schröder; see Edda,
1915, IV, p. 364 where he changes: Men du må jage på mig into:
Du må ikke jage på mig (Vildanden; cf S. M. p. 16) and:
Bolette, halvt f o r sig selv, into: halvt f r a sig selv.

§ 2.   A study of the text of Ibsen's Peer Gynt has led me to
a collation of Ibsen's own MS.—his "Renskrift", henceforth
referred to as R. (see § 6), which the Royal Library at Copenhagen was good enough to send down to our University Library at Ghent for the purpose. In his Commentary, Prof. Storm
has forty critical notes on Peer Gynt, of which about half
refer to mistakes that have crept into the editions preceding
Prof. Storm's, the other twenty refer to changes the Professor
himself either introduces into the text or regrets he for some
reason or other does not feel justified in taking up. The too
great leniency of Prof. Storm's words will at once appear
when my readers hear that the renewed investigation I have
gone in for, has yielded for the Peer Gynt-text alone of course,
about three hundred cases where the modern printed editions
deviate from Ibsen's Renskrift i. e. from that text which Ibsen
himself looked upon as final,—a minute comparison with
Ibsen's first draft, U. (=Utkast; also very obligingly put at my
disposal by the Royal Library at Copenhagen) has shown how
Ibsen had fully thought out some cases, — words or word-

forms. About three hundred cases surely justifies the much se-
verer judgment that, somehow, the "misunderstandings and
Danish substitutes" *should* have been avoided; and cf. § 4. Add
to this that the principles adopted by Prof. Storm for the con-
stitution of Ibsen's Mindeudgavetext, together with his own
mistakes yield another hundred cases at least where the text in
subsequent editions varies from Ibsen's own and the result of
this investigation will truly appear appalling. We shall have
occasion afterwards to prove that some cases at least of Prof.
Storm's deviations can hardly stand the test he himself has
chosen to adopt; and many of them cannot be assumed to
satisfy the wants of those students of Ibsen who wish to know,
not how he ought to have written according to modern critics
even if the critic in question should be the best equipped scholar of his time, nor even how Ibsen "would have written himself after a closer investigation" ([1]), but simply and solely how
and what Ibsen d i d write.

§ 3. These misunderstandings *should* have been avoided.
And after all, was it so very difficult for the printers of the
first edition to reproduce the text of the MS.,—can we really
excuse the fact that the first edition already deviates, and in not
so very few cases either, from the original, with a simple: "it
was done as well as possible"? And will this too cover the fact,
as our investigations show in detail, that every edition reprints
the former one, the immediately preceding one, with all its imperfections, and regularly, with few exceptions if any, adding
mistakes of its own, sometimes of no very great interest it is true,
as when a comma is changed into a colon (although even this
may influence the meaning, however slightly), but sometimes
of capital importance, as when Pungen is given for Pengene?
(cf. § 10, n°. 238). Why did not once in the course of the 18 reprints Peer Gynt has to undergo (the word is chosen on purpose), the responsible man go back to, say the first edition
which at least represents Ibsen's text approximately and
must be supposed to represent him quite? Why! Even Prof.
Storm, the only Editor our text as yet has had, did not even

([1]) "Jeg har kun rettet hvad jeg tror forf. selv efter nærmere undersøgelse vilde
have rettet," S.M., p. 3.

collate the older texts anything like systematically,—here and there quite at haphazard it would seem, when his own or Mr. Eitrem's critical sense seems to scent a mistake (see infra notes on bændende, Kuli, nos 81 and 174, etc.), the older editions are collated, but not regularly; and the MS. itself has not been looked into either, only twice a timid question seems to have gone the way of the Royal Library (cf. S. M., pp. 16, 40, once only with respect to the Peer Gynt-text).

§ 4. The present investigation, it is thought, may serve more than one purpose. First of all and generally speaking, it will show that, even in the case of an author but recently dead, it is never too early to be on one's guard against supposing that we have "of course" a reliable text; for it would seem at the first blush that these texts published again and again during the author's life-time might be supposed to be correct. And secondly, reasoning from a particular point of view, that of Scandinavian, or if you will Ibsen-philology, this textual collation will, it is hoped, be found useful for the possessors of the various Peer Gynt-texts, although it should be expressly stated that I have not in any way tried to be exhaustive in my treatment of the deviations. This would have swelled the list (infra § 10) to an enormous size, and to be practically useful, the exhaustive treatment should be reserved for a thorough collation with o n e text only, a work which I hope to publish later on (¹). And thirdly, as there is no reason whatever to suppose that the current editions of Ibsen's other works are more accurate than the Peer Gynt-text, a single look into Prof. Storm's brochure is indeed sufficient to show that they are not, this critical essay will be a continual and it is hoped effective plea for a "return to Ibsen" in this sense that subsequent editions should be based on Ibsen's own authorised text and carefully freed from misunderstandings of every nature, above all, from the remarkable misprints of which, as we shall see, each new edition has brought but too many. And it should

---

(¹) A proof that my list is not exhaustive will be found i n f r a in § 11 as well as in the notes to l.l. 614, 728, 799, 963, 1493, 1498, 1730, 2877 (Add.), etc. They were not added to my list in § 10 as the instances in question were discovered when the greater part of my collated texts had already been sent back to Kristiania or København so that the collation could not be given completely.

be borne in mind that to listen to this voice of warning that
will easily be recognized as coming from the philological camp,
is to cater not only for the present writer's brother-philologists
but also for the ever-increasing numbers of the General Reader
for whom accuracy of text is, if not a pressing need, at least
nothing to object to, nay more: something which they have a
right to expect.

The various texts referred to are here enumerated in order
of time.

§ 5. U. This is the earliest draft (Utkast) in existence
which Ibsen wrote in Italy, at Ischia and Sorrento in the year
1867. The first act is dated: 14/1, 67 at the beginning and 25/2,
67 at the end; the second 3/3, 67 (at end); the third 2/7, 67, and
at the end: Afsendt i Renskrift fra Ischia den 8e August 1867.
At the end of the fourth act we find: 15/9, 67 and: Afsendt i
Renskrift fra Sorrento 18e Septber 1867; at the beginning of
the fifth act we find: 19/9, 67, and at the end: 14/10, 67.

The manuscript consisted of 32 sheets of a varying number
of pages (but many pages are entirely crossed out and partly
replaced by other quarto and octavo pages inserted; a fuller
description may be found in Koht and Elias' edition of H.
Ibsen's Efterladte Skrifter, Kristiania og Kjöbenhavn, Gyldendalske Boghandel, Nordisk Forlag, vol. III, p. 413) and in
Karl Larsen's ed. of Ibsen's Episke Brand, pp. 31 and 198,
where it will also be found explained how the manuscript after
many vicissitudes reached the Royal Library of Copenhagen,
not, unfortunately, without having lost one whole sheet on the
way (containing part of the fourth act). The manuscript was
partly published—some (but not all, cf. Comm. n. to l. 2586) of
the more important passages and variant readings—by Messrs.
Koht and Elias as quoted above. As this fragmentary edition
(the text divided over two volumes and cut up really into 3
parts) does but whet the appetite, and the study of the whole
may prove of great advantage for Ibsen-philology, the present
writer hopes soon to be able to publish a full critical edition of
this manuscript. The introduction to that edition will be the
right place to discuss the question in detail whether U, as
Larsen thinks, is: "en stærkt rettet Renskrift efter en tidligere

Udarbejdelse"; or as there may be some reason to believe practically Ibsen's f i r s t draft. I say: practically, for some pages, such as the first sixteen or eighteen may well be a clean copy of an earlier text or rough draft, but this cannot be maintained (as I hope to show afterwards) of the greater part of our text. (Cf. Efterladte Skrifter, I, pp. xxxix, xliii.)

Pages from the manuscript have hitherto only been reproduced by Karl Larsen, in the work quoted, pp. 32, 33 and 34; 2/3 size and not very clear, and in the Efterladte Skrifter, vol. I, pp. xl, xliv; and one page in "Edda, 1914, p. 143 in my paper Tilbake til Ibsen, reproduced here opposite the n. to line 2586 of my Commentary.

§ 6. R. This is Ibsen's final copy (Renskrift) which he sent off to Copenhagen on the dates detailed in § 5, and where it was printed and published in the same year 1867; see § 7.

This manuscript has been described before, by Halvorsen, Samlede Værker, vol. III, p, viii, but very superficially; evidently only from an inspection of two pages at the Theaterudstilling of Copenhagen in 1898. A full description will be found in Karl Larsen's Episke Brand, p. 34. It consists of but 29 sheets, but here not a single page is crossed out entirely, all in all but six lines in the whole manuscript. All the sheets consist of four leaves, i.e. 8 pages, except sheets 21 and 29 that consist of six leaves, or twelve pages. The title and list of personages was added afterwards, for sheet 1 commences with the first act. As will appear from the present study, this manuscript has never been reprinted absolutely correctly. The present writer had hoped to be able to bring out a faithful reproduction, but the publishers, Gyldendalske Boghandel, Nordisk Forlag, Copenhagen, have as yet been applied to in vain to give up their copyright. A very excellent facsimile of one page, original size, of the manuscript (10, 1, r°) will be found in Jæger's Illustreret Norsk Literaturhistorie, vol. III (pp. 656, 657) and one in Karl Larsen (u. s. p. 35), in reduced (2/3) size, but very readable. This cannot be said of the facsimile reproduction, most likely at second or third hand, in the Dutch translation issued by Messrs. Meulenhoff and Co., at Amsterdam, in 1908, where the reproduction is rather unsatisfactory.

§ 7. 1. Peer Gynt, Et dramatisk digt af Henrik Ibsen,
Kjöbenhavn, Gyldendal (¹)   (Nov. 14) 1867.

2. Peer Gynt, Et dramatisk digt af Henrik Ibsen.
Andet oplag, Kjöbenhavn   (Nov. 28) 1867.

I. Refers to the copy of 2 used by Ibsen to introduce his corrections, almost without exception
of orthographical nature when preparing the
third ed. Ibsen's own copy of 2 here referred
to is the property of the University Library
at Kristiania and was most kindly sent down
to the University Library at Ghent for my
inspection and use. See infra, § 26.

3. Peer Gynt, Et dramatisk digt af Hendrik Ibsen,
Tredje   oplag 1874.

4.   do.   Fjerde   oplag 1876.
5.   do.   Femte   oplag 1881.
6.   do.   Sjette   oplag 1885.
7.   do.   Syvende   oplag 1886.
8.   do.   Ottende   oplag 1891.
9.   do.   Niende   oplag 1893.
10.   do.   Tiende   oplag 1896.

F. Samlede Værker, Folkeudgave, Tredje Bind 1898.

11. Peer Gynt, Et dramatisk digt, Ellevte oplag 1899.
12.   do.   Tolvte   oplag 1903.

13. Hendrik Ibsen, Peer Gynt, Et dramatisk digt,
Trettende oplag. Kjöbenhavn og Kristiania,
Gyldendalske Boghandel, Nordisk Forlag   1906.
(The publishing house of Gyldendal: new
style after the amalgamation with a Kristiania
firm.)

M. Henrik Ibsen, Samlede Værker, Mindeudgave, Andet Bind   1908.

14. Henrik Ibsen, Peer Gynt, Et dramatisk digt,
Fjortende oplag 1911.
15.   do.   Femtende oplag 1913.

(¹) The publishers are in each and all cases Messrs. Gyldendal, of Copenhagen;
the style of their publishing house is not always the same in the different editions;
the name of the printers added as a rule on the title page also changes.

When this investigation was practically finished, the vol. containing Peer Gynt of a new collected ed. of Ibsen's works was published; this edition I had not been able to see at the time of seeing this study through the press (June, 1914). But later, when recasting this critical study to some extent, as explained in the Preface, to form part of the larger Commentary which had been completed since then, the Jubilæumsudgave (J). and the sixteenth ed. (16) have also been collated:

    J. Henrik Ibsens Samlede Værker Tredje Udgave, Gyldendalske Boghandel Nordisk Forlag—Kristiania og København MDCCCCXIIII. Bind III.

   16. Henrik Ibsen, Peer Gynt, Et dramatisk Digt, Sekstende oplag, MDCCCCXV.

§ 8.   This investigation was begun in 1913 before the 15th ed. had reached me and it was therefore the 14th ed. that was first collated with some earlier editions, then with R, and later with all the other editions the present writer could collect or loan. A word of thanks should be addressed to the authorities of the libraries at Kristiania and Copenhagen for sending the various editions required on loan as well as and above all the two very valuable manuscripts to the University Library at Ghent; also to the Chief Librarian of the Ghent University Library, Professor Dr. De Vreese, more especially for the immense service he has rendered the writer by providing him with a photographic reproduction of the manuscripts U and R.

COLLATION OF THE R-TEXT
OF IBSEN'S PEER GYNT WITH THE PRINTED
EDITIONS AND WITH U.

§ 9. It should be noticed that the page-references to the first edition also show the way in the 2nd edition, the pagination there being the same, hence also to I. In the same way, the pagination for the third edition is identical with that of the following ones, inclusive of the 10th (being with one or two exceptions page for page reprints) so 3 refers to editions 3-10. F has a pagination of its own; so have 11 and 12; 13, and M. The reference to edition 15 is the same as that of 14 when not otherwise stated. J. has again a pagination of its own, whereas 16 is practically the same as 14 and 15. It is also most important to bear in mind that the text of R. (given before the square brackets) is compared with that of the printed editions *only so far as the point at issue is concerned* and does not e.g. take into consideration those changes that were introduced into I in consequence of the decisions of the Stockholm meeting (see infra, § 26 seq.). Likewise the words before the square brackets represent those of the f i r s t text mentioned behind them, beginning with R. The figures in the second column of the following list are the numbers of the lines in an ed. at one time contemplated; see the prefatory matter to the preceding Commentary. The references to the §§ in the last column show where the case in question may be found discussed; and the references *ib.* to the various texts show at a glance which of them is responsible for the variant in question or for its correction.

Where, as in the case of n° 13, (for U) two or more readings are recorded for U or for I, they represent in order of time the changes introduced by Ibsen in his first draft or I respectively.

§ 10.

1)   De handlende:] U. R-4.
    De handlende.] 5-10. Personerne:] F-16.   3,4; F,265; 11,1; 13,c; M,165; 14,4 J,171. 5,F. § 54,86

2) 18 Et [Hoftroldt]] U. R-4; M. J.16. En] 5-13; 14-15. 5, M. § 53,124
3) 25 Hougfolk] R-13; 14,15. Haugfolk] U. M. J. 16. M,14 § 113
4) 30 Master (Cotton)] R-13. M,14,15 § 108
    Mr.] M. J.16. Mister] 14,15. 1.
5) 32 v: (Eberkopf)] R. v.] 1-13; 14,15 J.16 v] M. 1. § 13
6) 34 To Tyve] R. En Tyv og en Hæler] 1-15. 1. § 15
7) 36 Beduinhøvdings] R-7, 16. 8. § 70
    beduinerhøvdings] 8-J. Beduinensdatter] U.
8) 42 Dr: phil:] R. Dr. phil] 1-16. 1. § 13,70
9) 46 Daarekistelemmer] R-10,16. F. § 86
    Daarekistemedlemmer] F-J. M,166;
10) Vogtere.] R-12; M,J. vogtere] 13,14; 15,16. J,172 13,M,15 § 96,128
11) 49 Passagér] R-I. passager] 3-16. 3. § 43
12) 52 En Rodemester] R. En Lensmand] 1-16. 3. § 15
13) 55 (af) dette (Aarh.)] R-11. det. 19.] 12-16. 12. § 94
    begynder i forrige og slutter i dette Aarh.;
    begynder i Förstningen af dette Aarhundrede
    og slutter henimod vore Dage] U.
14) (Förste) Handling] U. R-10 Akt] F-16. 1,1; 3,5; F,267; 11,3; 13,1; M,167; 14,5; J,173. F. § 86
15) 56 Lövtrær] U. R-13; M,15-16 løvtræer] 14. M,14,15 § 113
16) Kværnehus] R-13; 14. M,14 § 111
    kvernehus] M,15-16 kværn] U.
17) 57 standse] R-13; 14. stanse] M,15-16. 1,2; 3,6; F,268; 11,4; M. § 120
18) 62 Aannen] R-13. onnen] M-16. M. § 114

No.	Entry										
19)	82 (skulde du vel aldrig set!] U.R-13; 14. set!] M,15-16.	1,3;	3,7;	F,269;	11,5;	13,2;	M,168; 14,6;		J,174.	M,14	§111
20)	91 (stod med) et] U.R-13; 14. ét] M,15-16.			F,270;	11,6;	13,3;				M,14	§111
21)	112 (der vi) foer (fram)] U.R-2; 10-13. for] I-9. før] M-16.	1,4;	3,8;			13,4;	14,8;			I,10,M	§39,40,77,112
22)	176 engang] U. R-13; 14. én gang] M,15-16.	1,7;	3,11;	F,272;	11,8;	13,6;	M,170; 14,10;		J,176.	M,14	§111
23)	208 Faer(din)] U. R-13; 14. Far] M,15-16.	1,8;	3,12;	F,273;	11,9;	13,7;	M,171; 14,11;		J,177.	M,14	§112
24)	228 Storkarl] R-13; M². storkar] M-16.	1,9;	3,13;	F,274;	11,10;	13,8;	14,12;		J,178.	M.	§117
25)	231 Kjøbenhavn] R-2. København] I-16.						M,172;				§27
26)	288 Hvad? (Har du)] U. R-6; M,15-16 Hvad] 7-13,14	1,12;	3,16;	F,277;	11,13;	13,11;	M,173; 14,15;		J,179.	7,M,14	§65,128
27)	354 (det) taer (Tid)] U. R-13. tar] M-16.	1,16;	3,20;	F,280;	11,16;	13,14;	M,175; 14,18;		J,181.	M.	§112
28)	367 Fortred] R-13. fortræd] M-16.	1,17;	3,21;	F,281;	11,17;	13,15;	14,19;			M.	§111
29)	373 (jeg) ved (ej)] U. R-10. véd] F-16.			F,282;	11,18;	13,16;	14,20;		J,182.	F.	§85
30)	379 snaud] U. R-13. snau] M-16.	1,19;	3,23;	F,283;	11,19;	13,17;	M,176; 14,21;			M.	§120
31)	401 der over] R-13. derover] M-16.	1,20;	3,24;	F,284;	11,20;	13,18;	M,177; 14,22;			M.	§126
32)	408 (jeg) beer] U. R-13. ber] M-16.									M.	§111
33)	413 Benene,] (R-)3.benene] 4.benene,] U.5-16.			F,285;	11,21;		M,177;		J,183.	4,5.	§48,51
34)	416 Dit Bæst!] U. R-1; M,15-16. Dit bæst.] 2-13; 14.	1,21;	3,25;	F,285;	11,21;	13,19;	M,177; 14,23;			2,M,14	§21,128
35)	423 far vel] R-31. farvel] U. M-16.	1,24;	3,28;	F,288;	11,24;	13,22;	M,178; 14,26;			M.	§126
36)	473 kiger (efter dem.)] R-13. kikker] M-16. ser] U.								J,185.	M.	§44,130
37)	474 med et (tvungent Slæng] R-13; M,15-16. med] 14. med tvungent Omslag] U.			F,288;			M,179;			I4	§135
38)	488 (sidder saa) stout (paa Folen.) stout] R-14. staut] M,15-16. stout corr. into stout, or stout into staut?] U.			F,289;	11,25;					M,14	§113
39)	492 (Kvinderne) nejer (sig)] U. R,1; L-4; M-16. nejer] 2; 5-13.	123;	3,49;	F,289;		13,23;	M,179; 14,27;			2,I,5,M.	§22,39,51,130

40)	498	Engellands (Prins)] U. R-13; 14. Engelands] M, 15-16.	1,25;	3,29;	F,289;			M,179;	14,27;	M,14	§ 115
41)	503	(till nogle andre] thickly underlined in R. =spaced in 1-3. Printed as words preceding and following in 4-16; not thickly underlined in U.								J,186.	4. § 48
42)	508	(Men) Karl,] R-13 ;[Mᵃ kar] M-16. (Men,) Gut] U.	1,26;	3,30;	F,290;	11,26;	13,23;	M,179;	14,27;	M.	§ 117
43)	509	Sex] U. R-13. seks] M-16. sex changed into seks; ks crossed out again] I.								I,M.	§ 28,#,40,120
44)	517	Ung-Lam]R. Ung-lam]1-13; M,15-16; unglam] 14	1,27;	3,31;	F,291;	11,27;	13,24;	M,180;	14,28;	14.	§ 134
45)	519	(som vil) h a ' e (dir] R-13. ha] M-16.								M.	§ 112
46)	529	Ringagten] U. R-12 ringeagten] 13-16.					13,25;		14,29;	13	99
47)	532	mod (Bryllupsgaarden] R-13; M,15-16. ved] 14.								J,187. 14.	§ 135
48)	534	en (Mylder]] U. R-13; et] M-16.								M.	§ 125
49)	544	Kokkekoner] R-12; 16. K·okkekonen] 13-J. Kokkekonerne] U.	1,28;	3,32;	F,292;	11,28;		M,181;	14,29;	13.	§ 99
50)	547	ændse U. R-13; anse] M-16.	1,28;	3,32;	F,292;			M,181;	14,29;	M.	§ 120
51)	553	Faderen] U. R-10. FADEREN] F-13; 14+15,16. faderen] M.J.	1,29;	3,33; .	F,293;	11,29;	13,26;		14,30;	F,M,14	§ 84,128
52)	557	Brudgommen] R-10. BRUDGOMMEN] F-13;14,15,16. Brudgommen] M.J.								J,188. F,M,14	§ 84,128
53)	567	(fra Sans og) Samling]] M-16. samling.] U. 4+13. samling?] 14.	1,31;	3,35;	F,295;	11,31;	13,27;	M,182;	14,31;	4,M,14	§ 48,68,128
54)	570	(Hvor er de ledige), du?] U. R-I; M-16. du] 3-13; Mᵃ.							14,32;	3,M.	§ 43,128
55)	571	Peer Gynt] R-3. PEER GYNT Mᵃ J. Peer Gynt] 4-7. PEER GYNT] 8-15.				13,28;				J,189. 4,8.	§ 48
56)	576	Rigtig, ja] U. R-6: M,15-16 Rigtig! ja.] 7-13; 14; Mᵃ.	1,32;	3,36;	F,296;	11,32;				7,M,14	§ 65,128

#	Note	1	3	F	11	13	M	14	J		§
57)	580 stikke paa Kruset?] R-5; M-16. kruset!] 6-13; Mᵉ. Kruset.] U.	1,32;	3,36;	F,206;			M,182;	14,32;		6,M.	§ 61,128
58)	607 (værd at)bindes(i Baasen)] U.R-8;16, binde] 9-J.	1,35;	3,39;	F,298;	11,34;	13,31;	M,183;	14,35;	J,190.	9.	§ 75
59)	608 (han blir nok) bra'] U. R-13. bra] M-16.	1,36;	3,40;	F,299;	11,35;	13,32;	M,184;			M.	§ 112
60)	616 (smage paa mit.) Nej!] R-12; M,15-16. Nej.] U. 14.	1,37;	3,41;	F,300;	11,36;	13,33;	M,185;	14,36;		M,14	§ 129
61)	622 konster (du kunde)] U.R-13; 14. kunster] M,15-16.	1,38;	3,42;	F,301;	11,37;	13,34;		14,37;	J,191.	M,14	§ 114
62)	629 Nödd] U. R-13. nødd] I. nød] M-16.	1,40;	3,44;	F,302;	11,38;	13,36;	M,186;	14,38;		1,M.	§ 28,115
63)	641 (Det lovte) han;] R,1. han!] 2-16. han,] U.			F,304;	11,40;	13,38;	M,187;			2.	§ 20
64)	668 Kar'] R-13] U. M-16.	1,43;	3,47;	F,307;	11,43;	13,39;		14,40;	J,192.	M.	§ 117
65)	692 et (Troldt)] R-4; M,15-16. en] 5-13; 14.	1,44;	3,48;	F,308;	11,44;	13,40;		14,42;	J,193.	5,M.	§ 53,125
66)	704 fremst] R-3; 16. fremmest] 4-J.	1,45;	3,49;	F,309;	11,45;	13,41;	M,188;	14,43;	J,194.	4.	§ 49
67)	713 inderligt] U. R-13; 14. inderlig] M,15-16.	1,46;	3,50;	F,310;	11,46;		M,188;	14,44;		M,14	§ 123
68)	717 Klör!—] R-6. klør!] 7-16.							14,45;		7.	§ 65
69)	723 (paa) Gjetens (Vis)] U. R-2. t corr. into d] I. gedens] 3-13. getens] M-16.								J,195.	1,M.	§ 33,118
70)	724 (Han) bær'(hende, Moer)] U. R-13. bær] M-16.									M.	§ 112
71)	(som en) bærer (en Gris!)] U. R,1. bær] 2; M-16. bær'] I-13.									2,1,M.	§ 23,71
72)	736 (uden) e n] U. R,10. én] F-16.	1,49;	3,53;	F,312;	11,48;	13,42;	M,189;	14,46;	J,196.	F.	§ 85
73)	761 (brister i) Taarer] R-5; 16. Graad.] U. 6-J.	1,51;	3,55;	F,314;	11,50;	13,45;	M,190;	14,49;	J,197.	6.	§ 63
74)	781 utænkeligt, sligt] R-6. utænkeligt sligt] 7-16.	1,53;	3,57;	F,315;	11,51;	13,46;	M,191;	14,50;	J,198.	7.	§ 65
75)	796 E n (bruger) R-10. Én] F,12. En] 13-16.			F,316;	11,52;					F,13	§ 85,96
76)	828 (Der var ikke) e n] U. R,12. én] F-16.	1,56;	3,60;	F,318;	11,54;	13,48;	M,192;	14,52;	J,199.	F.	§ 85
77)	839 (Skyggerne) falder] U. R-3; 15-16. falde 4+14;M,J.	1,57;	3,61;	F,319;	11,55;	13,49;	M,193;	14,53;	J,200.	4,15	§ 49,138
78)	851 Trond (i Valfjeldet)] U. R-9; M-16. Trold]10-14.		3,62;	F,320;	11,56;	13,50;		14,54;		10,M.	§ 79
79)	855 Sælet] R-13. sælet M-16. selet, sælet] U. In R. æ corr.; fr. e?	1,58;								M.	§ 111
80)	871 spruter U. R-13. spruter] M-16.	1,59;	3,63;	F,322;	11,58;	13,52;		14,55;	J,201.	M.	§ 115

No.	Note	1	3	F	11	13	M	14	J	Ref	§
81)	896 (En) bandende (glohed Ring)] U. R-4; 16. brændende] 5-J. klemmer over Brynet; brændende] U.	1,61;	3,65;	F,323;	11,59;	13,53;	M,194;	14,56;	J,202.	5.	§ 57,58
82)	898 (der) bændte (mig)] R-9; M-16. brændte (mig)] 10-13;14. skrued; har bændet]U.									10,M,14	§ 58,77,130
83)	901 Digt og forbandet Løgn!] Løgn!] U. R-6; M-16 løgn?] 7-13.						M,195;			7,M.	§ 65,128
84)	916 dukke mig) ven (i)] U. R-10. vén] 14-16.	1,62;	3,66;	F,324;	11,59;	13,53;	M,195;	14,57;		F.	§ 85
85)	935 væk, (Gjærdet)] U. R-7. væk] 8-16.				11,60;	13,54;	M,196;	14,58;	J,203.	8.	§ 69
86)	951 klang:] U. R-11; M,15-16 klang:] 12, 13; 14.						M,196;			12,M,14	§ 91,128,133
87)	954 bliver] U. R-5. blive (?)] 6. bli er (?)] 7. blir] 8-16. (?) sic, end of line; r dropped? (?) sic; v dropped out?						M,196;			6,7,8	§ 63,65,68
88)	955 Løvtrær] R-1; M,15-16. løvtræer] 3-13; 14.	1,63;	3,67;	F,325;	11,61;	13,55;	M,196;	14,58;	J,204.	3,M,14	§ 42,113
89)	986 Boss:] R-1. Bos?] 2-13; 14. bos:] M,15-16. Boss,] U.	1,65;	3,69;	F,327;	11,63;	13,57;	M,197;	14,60;		2,M,14	§ 21
90)	1004 (Hu), hej;] R,1. hej,] U. 2-16.	1,66;	3,70;	F,328;	11,64;	13,58;	M,198;	14,62;	J,206.	2.	§ 20
91)	1012 stærkbygget] U. R-12; J. stærktbygget]13-15;16.	1,67;	3,71;	F,329;	11,65;	13,59;	M,198;	14,62; 14,63;		13.	§ 99
92)	1023 (stopp min) Gut; —] U. R-6. gut!—] 7-16. Gut,—] U.									7.	§ 65
93)	1025 (Brydes) et (af dem)] U. R-10. ét] F-16.	1,68;	3,72;	F,330;	11,66;	13,60;				F.	§ 85
94)	1030 kaldes for (Konge)] U. R-11. kaldes] 12-16.				11,67;	13,60;	M,199;			12.	§ 93
95)	1034 Gaadenöd] (n)add] d crossed out but added Gaadenød] (n)add] U. R-2; I-13. gådenød] M-16. again] I.									1,M.	§ 28,115
96)	1050 M a a] R-12. må] U. 13-16.	1,49;	3,73;	F,331;	11,67;	13,61;	M,199;	14,64;	J,207.	13.	§ 98
97)	1063 grundende] U. R-12; M,15,J,16. grædende]13;14.							14,65;		13,M.	§ 101,130

No. / Entry	Numeric references	ref.	§
98) 1067 Kristenmandsklæder] U. R-3. kristenmands-klæder] 4-16.	1,70; 3,74; F,332; 11,68; 13,61; M,200; 14,65;	4.	§ 48
99) 1087 et (Trold) U. R-12; M,15-16. en] 13, 14.	1,71; 3,75; F,333; 11,69; 13,63; M,200; 14,66;	13,M.	§ 99,125
100) 1091 Karl] U. R-M; 15-16. kar] 14.	1,72; 3,76; M,201; 14,67; J,208.	M,14.	§ 117
101) 1099 Tykkes? hm —] U. R-4. Tykkes? Hm!—] 5,6. Tykkes Hm!—] 7. Tykkes, hm!—] 8-16.	1,73; 3,77; F,334; 11,70; 13,64; M,201; 14,67;	5,7,8	§ 54,65,68
102) 1116 Kristenmandsbrogen] U. R-3. kristenmands-brogen] 4-16.	1,75; 3,79; F,336; 11,72; 13,66; M,202; 14,69;	4.	§ 48
103) 1148 (tvinge mig) voldeligt?] U. R-13; 14. voldelig!] M,15-16.	3,79; F,337; 11,73; 13,67; M,202; 14,70; J,209.	M,14	§ 123
104) 1157 (hvad det Hoftrold) bandt.] R-2. In R . corr. from; or vice versa. bandt:] U. 3-16.	J,210.	I.	§ 32
105) 1198 han :]] R. 13-15; 16. han)-] 1-12; M,J. han).]] U.	1,77; 3,81; F,339; 11,75; 13,69; M,203; 14,72; J,211. { 1,13.M.; 14,15; 13,M,14 }	—	§ 17,96,128
106) 1199 Hubro] U. R-12; M,15-16. bubro] 13, 14.	1,78; 3,82; F,340; 11,76; 13,70; M,204; 14,73;	5.	§ 100,130
107) 1211 han falder] R-4. falder om] 5-16.	1,79; 3,83; F,341; 11,77; 13,71; M,204; 14,74;	8.	§ 56
108) 1221 (Hvem er) d u?] R-7;16 du?] U. 8-J.	1,80; 3,84; F,342; 11,78; 13,71; M,205; 14,74; J,212.	5.	§ 53,68
109) 1226 (Hvem) er (du?)] R-4; 16. er] U. 5-J.	M,205; 14,74;	12.	§ 53,68
110) 1228 H v a d (er du?)] R-11; 16. Hvad] 12(1)-J. Hvem ; Hvad] U. (1) perhaps only H v spaced in 12.	F,342; M,205; 14,74;	—	§ 53,68,92
111) 1233 Böjgen] R-2; 3-16. Böjgen; bojgen; Böjgen:] I.	1,81; 3,85;	I.	§ 29
112) 1233 (Böjgen som er) saarlös] R-4; M-16. död] 5-13. uskadt; menfri; saarlös] U.	13,72; M,205; 14,75;	5.M.	§ 57,130
113) (Böjgen som fik] Men] U. R-2. mén] I-16.	J,213.	I.	§ 37
114) 1259 Ja; fod] R-7. Ja! fod] 8-16. Ja, fod] U.	1,83; 3,87; F,344; 11,80; 13,73; M,206; 14,76;	8.	§ 69
115) 1273 tungt (Öjekast)] U. R-4; 16, trægt] 5-15; J.	1,84; 3,88; F,345; 11,81; 13,74; 14,77; J,214.	5.	§ 56
116) 1275 Hvor er h u n?] R-11. hun] U. 12-16.	13,75; 14,78;	12.	§ 92
117) 1293 Kall] U. R-16. Kal ; kall] I.	1,87; 3,91; F,346; 11,84; 13,77; M,208; 14,80; J,215.	I.	§ 28

118) 1296 Staaltraadserk] U. R-I. ståltrådsserk] 3-16. 1,87; 3,91; F,348; 11,84; 13,77; M,208; 14,80; 3. § 44
119) 1317 Ren] U. R-2. rén] I-16. 1,88; 3,92; F,349; 11,85; 13,78; 14,81; I. § 37
120) 1331 Der (var den igjen)] U. R-12. Det] 13-16. 13. § 102
121) 1332 (En) barktaekt (Hytte)] R-12; M,16. J,216. M,209; 13,M,14 § 100,130
    barktæt] 13.14. barktækt] U.
122) 1336 (Der stuper han) skraas] U. R-12; M,15-16. 3,93; 13,M,14 § 101,130
    straks] 13.14.
123) 1337 Mylr] U. R-14. mylder] M-16. 1,89; M. § 121
124) 1341 kiger] R-I; M-16. kigger] 3-13. 3,M. § 44,130
125) 1351 (Det) var (Fanden)] U. R-3;16 er] 4-J. F,350; 11,86; 13,79; 14,82; 4. § 49
126) 1367 (Hvad er det, som] rumler?] U. R,1; 16. 1,90; 3,94; F,351; 11,87; 13,80; M,210; 14,83; 2. § 24
    ramler] 2-J. J,217.
127) 1375 Sengkanten] R. 16. Sengekanten] r-J. 1. § 16
128) 1382 han, Peer] R(?)-13; 14. 1,91; 3,95; M,14 § 129
    han Peer] M,15-16 den Gutten; han, Peer,] U.
    (?) comma added later on in R?
129) 1384 tillslut] U. R-13. til slut] M-16. 1,92; 3,96; F,352; 11,88; 13,80; M. § 126
130) 1405 ham, Jon] U. R-13; 14, ham Jon] M,15-16. F,353; 13,81; M,211; 14,84; M,14 § 129
131) 1425 De kommer med Mörket; etc. Under Sengen; etc.; 1,93; 3,97; F,354; 11,90; 13,82; M,211; 14,85; J,218. 13 § 97
    Hi-hi! etc. indented in] U. R-12. J,219.
    not indented in] 13-16.
132) 1429 Hi-hi! U. R-13; M,15-16. Hi-hi] 14. 13,83; M,212; 14,86; R,14 § 133
133) 1449 allene] R-2. alene] U. I-16. 1,94; 3,98; F,355; 11,91; 13,84; 14,87; I. § 27
134) 1473 strake Arme] U. R-I; M; J,16. strakte] 3-13; 14,15. 1,95; 3,99; F,356; 11,92; 13,85; M,213; 14,88; J,220. 3,M,15 § 44,130
135) 1479 (Ringt eller) gjildt] U. R-13; 16. godt] M-J. 1,96; 3,100; M. § 107
136) 1492 Kongsdatter] U. R-11. kongedatter] 12-16. 12. § 93
137) 1502 (jeg gjorde saa) dengang] U. R-11. 1,97; 3,101; F,357; 11,93; 13,86; M,214; 14,89; J,221. 12. § 91
    dengang,] 12-16.

138) 1511 Du kan da vel] U. R-8. Du kan vel] 9-16. 1,98; 3,102; F,358; 11,94; 13,87; M,214; 14,90; 9. § 75

139) 1528 (om du) tör] U. R-I; M,15-16 tør] 3-13; 14. 1,99; 3,103; F,359; 11,95; 13,88; M,214; 14,91; M,215; J,222. M,14 § 43,128 9. § 72

140) 1533 kælen,] U. R-8. kælen,—] 9-16. 14. § 134

141) 1537 s'gu] U. R-13; M,15-16. sgu] 14. 5. § 56

142) 1541 for et Hoved] U. R-4; 16. for hoved] 5-J. 1,100; 3,104; F,360; 11,96; M,14 § 126

143) 1542 af Dage] R-13; 14. ad dage] M,15-16. 13. § 97

144) 1561 Anger, etc. indented in] R-12. 1,101; 3,105; F,361; 11,97; 13,89; J,223.
not indented in] 13-16.

145) 1574 strake arme] U. R-5; M,15-16. strakte 6-13; 14. 13,90; M,216; 14,93; 6,M,14 § 44,62,130 I.M. § 28,115

146) 1576 Læg] U. R-13. læg] M-16. læg; læg] I. M. § III

147) 1578 menløs] U. R-13. ménløs] M-16.

148) 1603 braat] U. R-13; M,15-16. brat] 14. 1,103; 3,107; F,363; 11,99; 13,91; M,217; 14,94; J,224. 14. § 135

149) 1604 Aa(dersom) U. R-I; M-16. Ase] 3-13. 3. § 44,45

150) 1625 bli (gjild)] U. R-13; M,15-16 blive] 14. 1,104; 3,107; F,364; 11,100; 13,92; 14,95; J,225. 14. § 133

151) 1671 (som) gut] R-3. gut] 4-16. gut.] U. 1,106; 3,110; F,366; 11,102; 13,95; M,218; 14,98; J,226. 4. § 48

152) 1680 allerbedste] U. R-13. aller bedste] M-16. 1,107; 3,111; M,219; M. § 126

153) 1720 Grane] R-2; I-16. grane; Grane] I. (Grane] 13.) 1,109; 3,113; F,368; 11,104; 13,97; M,220; 14,100; J,227. 29 § 29

154) 1727 Det er Granene] U. R-13. F,369; 11,105; J,228. M,14 § 124
Det er granerne] M,15-16. Der] 14.

155) 1755 de myldrer] U. R-13; M,15-16. det myldrer] 14. 1,111; 3,115; F,371; 11,107; 13,99; M,221; 14,102; 14. § 135

156) 1759 mener] U. R-6. mener,] 7-16. 7. § 65

157) 1814 Stewart] U. R-13; 14. Steward] M,15-16. 1,114; 3,118; F,374; 11,110; 13,102; M,223; 14,105; J,231. M,14 § 108

158) Master Cotton] U. R-13. Mr. Cotton] M. M.
Mr. Cotton] 14,15-16. Mr: Cotton] U.

159) Werry] U. R-2. Very] I-16. I. § 34

160) 1817 skjelden] U. R-2. sjelden] I-13; M,15-16. 1,115; 3,119; F,375; 11,111; I,14 § 34,135
sjelden] 14.

161) 1820 v: Eberkopf] U. R. v. E—] 1-16. Eberkopf] U. 13,103; 14,106; 1. § 13

162) 1830 Ej wass!] U. R-2. Ej was!] I-16. — 1,115; 3,119; F,375; 11,111; 13,103; M,224; 14,106; J.232. I. § 29,38
163) 1842 (Aa ja) saamen] U. R-13. sámaen] M-16. — 1,116; 3,120; F,376; 11,112; 13,104; 14,107; M. § 111
164) 1849 henkastende] R-5. henkastet] 6-16. — 1,117; 3,121; F,377; 11,113; 13,105; M,224; 14,108; 6. § 63
165) 1855 De forstaar;] R-4. De forstår] 5-16. — 5. § 54
    De forstaar,] U.
166) 1884 gier] U. R-11. gir] M-16. — 1,118; 3,122; F,378; 11,114; 13,106; M,225; 14,109; J.233. M. § 112
167) 1893 De (alting maaler)] U. R-4; 6-11; M-16. de] 5; — 5,6,12,M. § 52,60,90,106
    12,13, M².
168) 1900 Methodisk] U. R-13. Metodisk] M-16. — 1,119; 3,123; F,379; 11,115; 13,107; M,226; 14,110; J.234. M. § 116
169) 1917 Vesten?] U. R,1; M-16. Vesten!] 2-13, M² — 2,M. § 21,128
170) 1918 Karl] U. R-13; M,15-16. kar] 14. — 14. § 135
171) 1928 Charlstowns Rhedre] U. R. — 1,M. § 16,108
    Charlestowns Rhedre] 1-13.
    Charlestons redre] M-16.
172) 1948 Konsekventserne] U. R-13. konsekvenserne] M-16. — 1,120; 3,124; F,380; 11,116; 13,108; M,227; 14,111; J.235. M. § 116
173) 1964 udklarerte] U. R-16, uklarerte] M² — 1,121; 3,125; F,381; 11,117; 13,109; 14,112; M. § 106.
174) 1970 Kulier] U. R-13. kulij M-16. — M. § 70,n;108
175) 1976 Der (sejred] U. R. Der] 1. Der] 2-16. — 1,122; 3,126; 11,117; J.236. 1,2. § 11,19,20
176) 2083 men selv dig tabte] R,1. — 1,126; 3,130; F,386; 11,122; 13,114; M,230; 14,117; J.239. 2. § 20
    men selv dig tabte] 2-16.
177) 2088 Mit (Pandehvælv)] R-1. min] 3-16. — 1,127; 3,131; 3. § 44,47
178) 2092 (Höj som) Digter!] R,1. digter] 2-16. — 1,128; 3,132; F,387; 11,123; 13,115; M,231; 14,118; 2. § 21
179) 2105 a (la Lippe-Detmold) R-2. å] 1-16. — 1. § 35
180) 2135 Exemplar] R-13. eksemplar] M-16. — 1,130; 3,134; F,389; 11,125; 13,117; M,232; 14,120; M. § 121
181) 2136 Yankee] R. Yankee] 1-16. — J.240. 1. § 14,15
182) 2142 Det (er at være) R-11. Det] 12-16. — 12. § 92
183) 2163 Slaa (smukt)] R-12. J. Så] 13-15; 16. — 1,131; 3,135; F,390; 11,126; 13,118; M,233; 14,121; J.241. 13. § 102,140
184) 2174 Sejervinder] R-12. 16. sejervinder!] 13-15; J. — 1,132; 3,136; F,391; 11,127; 13,119; M,233; 14,122; 13. § 96

No.	Lemma	1	3	F	11	13	M	14	J		§
185)	2181 God dam!] R-2. Goddam!] 1-16. -	1,133;	3,137;	F,392;	11,128;	13,120;	M,233;	14,123;	J,242.	I.	§ 35
186)	2190 Sverd] R-2. svard] 1-16.									I.	§ 27
187)	2191 Yanke] R. Yankee] 1-16.									1.	§ 14,15
188)	2254 Lade (Herren raade] U. R-11; 16. Lad] 12-J.	1,136;	3,140;	F,395;	11,131;	13,123;	M,235;	14,126;	J,244.	12.	§ 93
189)	2263 (Men alligevel) —. Jeg] U. R-5. — Jeg] 6,7 — jeg] 8-16.									6,8.	§ 61,68
190)	2264 Akazier] U. R-13. akacier] M-16.									M.	§ 120
191)	2265 klyve] U. R-1; M-16. flyve] 3-13, Mᵃ	1,137;	3,141;	F,395;	11,131;	13,123;	M,235;	14,126;		3,M.	§ 44,130,136
192)	2275 imod min Person;—] R-12. person —] U. 13-16.									13.	§ 96
193)	2288 forbandet!] R-5 J. forbandet;] 6-15, 16. forbandet.—] U.			F,396;	11,134;	13,124;	M,236;	14,127;		6.	§ 61
194)	2321 (Der er) Yngelen] R-7. ynglen] 8-16.	1,139;	3,143;	F,397;	11,133;	13,125;	M,237;	14,128;	J,245.	8.	§ 70
195)	2325 et Fjeldkløft] R,1. en] 2-16.		3,144;	F,398;	11,134;				J,246.	2.	§ 25
196)	2356 Firbenen] U. R-13. firbenet] M-16.	1,140;	3,144;	F,399;	11,135;	13,127;	M,238;	14,130;		M.	§ 125
197)	2371 Salomons] U. R-12. Salomons] 13-16.	1,141;	3,145;						J,247.	13.	§ 102,
198)	2405 Højden (er smal)] R-4. Højen] 5-16.	1,142;	3,146;	F,400;	11,136;	13,128;	M,239;	14,131;	J,248.	5.	§ 56
199)	2450 (flytte en) Hest—?] U. R-4. hest—!] 5-16.	1,143;	3,147;	F,402;	11,138;	13,130;	M,240;	14,133;	J,249.	5.	§ 54
200)	2461 Araberhövding] R-I. araberhövding] 3-16. Araberfyrste] U.	1,144;	3,148;							3.	§ 30,44
201)	2463 Profeten er kommen!] U. R-13; 16. Profeten er kommen! Profeten er kommen!] M-J.								J,250.	M.	§ 107
202)	2473 mælken] U. R-13. melken] M-16.	1,145;	3,149;	F,403;	11,139;	13,131;	M,240;	14,134;		M.	§ 111
203)	2506 Uhr] U. R-13. ur] M-16.	1,146;	3,150;	F,404;	11,140;	13,132;	M,241;	14,135;		M.	§ 116
204)	2512 (saa er det) en selv] U. R-4. en selv] 5-16.									5.	§ 53
205)	2513 Pundsterling] U. R-13. pund sterling] M-16.									M.	§ 126

#	Lemma	1,x	3,x	F,x	11,x	13,x	M,x	14,x	15,x	J,x	M.	§
206) 2531	Sig dem, de kan... opp; / sig dem, jeg hörer... Bönner] U. R-13; 16. / Sig dem, jeg hörer... bönner. / ...sig dem, de kan... op] M-J.	1,147;	3,151;	F,405;	11,141;	13,133;	M,242;	14,136;		J,251.	2,1,8	§ 107
207) 2539	(Dans for) mig,] U. R,1; 8-16. mig] 2-7.										14.	§ 20,39,68
208) 2544	Paradiset] U. R-13; M,15-16. paradiset] 14.										5.	§ 134
209) 2554	(yderlig) mager;] U. R-4. mager,] 5-16.								15,137;		M.	§ 54
210) 2564	Houri] U. R-13. Huri] M-16.	1,148;	3,152;	F,406;	11,142;	13,134;	M,243;	14,137;		J,252	5.	§ 108
211) 2576	(nogen) stor (Sjæl] U. R-4. stor] 5-16.	1,149;	3,153;	F,407;	11,143;	13,135;	M,243;	14,138;			I.	§ 53
212) 2586	ziehet] R-2. zieht] I-16. ziet, ziehet] U.	1,150;	3,154;	F,408;	11,144;	13,136;	M,244;	14,139;		J,253.	M.	§ 38
213) 2587	Luth] U. R-13. lut] M-16.										M.	§ 116
214)	betydeligt (yngre)] U. R-13. / betydelig] M-16.										1,4	§ 123
215) 2601	Hieb] U. R-3. hieb; Hieb] I. hieb] 4-16.										M.	§ 29,48
216) 2606	Angoragjedens] U. R-13 / Angoragetens] M-16.								15,140		M.	§ 118
217) 2613	udrappert] U. R-13. udrapert] M-16.	1,151;	3,155;	F,409;	11,145;	13,137;	M,245;	14,140;		J,254;	M.	§ 115
218) 2637	Bedst, (hun kom)] R-13] M,15-16. Bedst] U. 14.				11,147;	13,139;	M,246;	14,142;		J,255.	14.	§ 133
219) 2683	Rosenstrimer] R,1; I-16. osenstrimer] 2.	1,154;	3,158;	F,411;							F,M.	§ 128
220) 2684	gyldent:] U. R-10; M-16. gyldent:] F-13.				11,148;	13,140;	M,246;	14,143;		J,256.	2,I.	§ 19
221) 2703	(tungvindt) naaer] R-2. naar] I-16.	1,156;	3,160;	F,412;	11,149;	13,142;	M,248;	14,145;		J,257.	I.	§ 27
222) 2754	(just er ved) det;—] R-4. / det:] 5-16. det,—] U.			F,413;							5.	§ 54
223) 2793	er (du Profet?] U. R-12. er] 13-16.	1,158;	3,162;	F,415;	11,151;	13,144;	M,249;	14,147;		J,258.	13.	§ 98
224) 2806	Du (faar ikke] R,1; 3-16. Da] 2.	1,159;	3,163;							J,259.	2.	§ 19
225) 2825	Galfrands] U. R-F Galfrans] M-16. g—: G—] I.			F,417;	11,153;	13,145;	M,250;	14,148;			I.	§ 29
226) 2832	Livgjord] R-2; 3-16. livgjord; livjord] I.	1,160;	3,164;							J,260.	I.	§ 29
227) 2833	(en hæftig) Sorg;—] R-5. sorg:] U. 6-16.					13,146;		14,149;			6.	§ 61

No.	Line	Reading									J.		§
228)	2837	Forlangt!] U. R.-2. For langt!] 1-16.	1,161;	3,165;	F,418;	11,154;	13,147;		14,149;			I.	§ 35
229)	2844	Tyrkeklæderne] R-2; 3-8.	1,162;	3,166;	F,419;	11,155;	13,147;	M,251;	14,150;		J.260.	I.,3,9	§ 30,42,73
		tyrkeklæderne] I; 9-16. Tyrkedragten] U.							14,151;		J.261.	2,M.	§ 25,111
230)	2872	(man) ter (sig)] R,1; M,15-16. tér] 2-13; 14.										9.	§ 74
231)	2873	(For) s a a (vidt)] U. R-8. så] 9-16.					13,148;					2,3.	§ 20
232)	2881	(jeg er plukket) slemt!] R,1.											
233)		Naa;] R. 1,2. slemt-] U.											
234)	2884	(paa Fantestien) kommen.—] R-13; M,15-16.										M,14	§ 129
		kommen.] 14. kommen—] U.											
235)	2886	Kudsk] U. R-2. kusk] 1-16.			F,420;	11,156;						I.	§ 27
236)	2887	ingen (Besvar)] U. R-13. intet[M.16.										M.	§ 125
237)	2891	(et sluttet) Kapitel;] R-12.	1,163;	3,167;	F,420;			M,252;	14,151;			13,15	§ 96
		kapitel] 13,M,14. kapitel,] U,15-16.											
238)	2898	(Möjen og) Pengene] R-12;J.								15,152;		13.	§ 102,140
		pungen] 13-15; 16. Penge] U.											
239)	2900	Efterfölgelse?] R-6. efterfølgelse?—] 7-16.										7.	§ 65
240)	2917	(saa langt jeg) rakker.—] U. R-13.					13,149;		14,152;		J.262.	M.	§ 129
		rakker.] M.16.											
241)	2919	underfundig;—] R-5.										6.	§ 61
		underfundig;—] 6-16. underfundig;] U.											
242)	2934	Nu (bare holde ud)] U. R-3. N u] 4-16.	1,164;	3,168;	F,421;	11,157;	13,150;	M,253;	14,153;			4.	§ 48
243)	2936	(og föler mig) selv.] R-9. selv] 10-16.										10.	§ 78
244)	2946	(En Flok) Gjeder] U. R-13; 14.									J.263.	M,14	§ 33,118
		geter] M,15-16.											
245)	2947	synger.]] R.										1,13,M.	§ 17,96,128
		synger:] 1-12; M; J. synger:]] 13,14,15,16.											
246)	2953	(synger) igjen.] R-12; J. igen:] 13-15,16.	1,165;	3,169;	F,422;	11,158;						13.	§ 96

#	line	1,	3,	F,	11,	13,	M,	14,	15,	J,	ref	§
247)	2077	1,166;	3,170;	F,422;	11,158;	13,151;	M,254;	14,154;			10.	§ 78
248)	2095			F,443;	11,159;	13,152;		14,155;		J,264.	1,10,13,M.	§ 17,77,128
249)	3005	1,167;	3,171;	F,443;							M.	§ 129
250)	3008	1,167;	3,171;								M,15	§ 123
251)	3012	1,167;	3,171;	F,444;	11,160;	13,153;	M,255;	14,156;	15,156;		8.	§ 70
252)	3015										F.	§ 84
253)	3017										M.	§ 129
254)	3022										I.	§ 32
255)	3025	1,168;	3,172;	F,424;						J,265.	2.	§ 20
256)	3040	1,171;	3,175;	F,428;	11,164;	13,157;	M,257;	14,160;	15,157;	J,266.	M.	§ 120
257)	3092									J,267.	I,M.	§ 28,m; 122
258)	3096	1,172;	3,176;	F,429;	11,165;	13,158;		14,161;			14.	§ 133.
259)	3104										1.	§ 13
260)	3117	1,173;	3,177;	F,430;	11,166;	13,159	M,258;	14,162;		J,268.	12.	§ 91
261)	3127	1,174;	3,178;	F,431;	11,167;	13,160;	M,259;	14,163;			13.	§ 99
262)	3129	1,175;	3,179;	F,433;						J,269.	2.	§ 25
263)	3144										13.	§ 102
264)	3172	1,176;	3,180;		11,169;	13,161;		14,164;		J,270.	1,(13)	§ 17,96
265)	3193	1,177;	3,181;		11,169;	13,162;	M,260;	14,165;			13.	§ 98
266)	3195										14.	§ 133

247) 2077 [Haver og] Skjöger —] R-9. skøger,] 10-16. Skjöger—] U.

248) 2095 (synger)] R; 10-13,14,15,16. (synger):] 1-9.

249) 3005 Sænkning.—] R-13. sænkning.] M-16. Sænkning.] U.

250) 3008 tydeligt Klangen,] U. R-13. tydelig klangen,] M, 14. J. tydelig klangen,—] 15,16.

251) 3012 (gaar) vidre] U. R-7. vidre] 8-16.

252) 3015 Peer Gynt] U. R-10. omitted in] F-16.

253) 3017 [For truffet) ‹let,] U. R-13; M°. det] M-16.

254) 3022 Söjlestubber.] U. R-2. søjlestubber.—] 1-16.

255) 3025 [har jeg ogsaa) h a m] R-1. ham] 2-16.

256) 3040 Tydsk] U. R-13. Tysk] M-16.

257) 3092 flux] R-2. fluks] 1-13. flugs] M-16. flux—] U.

258) 3096 (store) Peer;—] R-13; M,15,J.Peer;] U. 14,16.

259) 3104 Kl: 11] U. R. Kl. 11] 1-16.

260) 3117 en Naal; —] R-11. en naï;] 12-16. en Naal—] U.

261) 3127 endvidre] U. R-12. endvidere] 13-16.

262) 3129 (de) saakaldt (kloge)] U. R.11;16. saakaldte] 2-15.

263) 3144 (mig selv i et) og i alt] U. R-12; 16. og alt] 13-J.

264) 3172 (bukker)] R.13. (bukker)] 1-12; 16. M-J.

265) 3193 s a a (lange Nætter] R-12, så] U. 13-16.

266) 3195 forstummet;] U. R.-13; M,15-16. forstummet;—] 14.

Nr.		1,	3,	F,	11,	13,	M,	14,	J,	M./I.	§
267)	3221 exemplarisk,—] R-13. eksemplarisk,] U.M-16.	1,178;	3,182;	F,434;	11,170;	13,163;	M,261;	14,166;	J,270.	M.	§ 129
268)	3238 E r (jeg Kong Apis?)] R-9;16.Er] U. 10-15.J.	1,179;	3,183;	F,435;	11,171;	13,164;		14,167.	J,271.	10.	§ 79
269)	3241 Deres Højhed] R-2; I-16. højhed; Højhed] I.									I.	§ 29
270)	3283 ryddig (for Rotter) U. R-4; 16. ryddelig] 5-15.J.	1,181;	3,185;	F,437;	11,173;	13,165;	M,262;	14,168;	J,272.	5.	§ 56
271)	3286 (aldeles) lig (med)] R-7. lige] (U.) 8-16.	1,182;	3,186;			13,166;		14,169;		8.	§ 70
272)	3303 (Ikke endnu)— Gal?] R-6. — Gal?] 7-16. ! Gal?] U.			F,438;	11,174;	13,166;	M,263;	14,169;	J,273.	7.	§ 65
273)	3308 besvares?] U. R-13. besvares!] M-16.	1,183;	3,187;	F,439;	11,175;	13,167;		14,170;		M.	§ 129
274)	3318 (Hvad jeg] duer (til)] U. R-13. duger] M-16.	1,184;	3,188;	F,440;	11,176;	13,167;	M,263;	14,170;		M.	§ 121
275)	3332 Der (er Ordet)] U. R-5. Det] 6-16.					13,168;	M,264;	14,171;	J,274.	6.	§ 63
276)	3337 (Havd skal)jeg—] R-12. jeg—?] 13-16. jeg!] U.					13,169;		14,172;		13.	§ 96
277)	3341 (i en) Hast:] R-8. hast! — —] 9-16.									9.	§ 72
278)	3344 knejser;] R-6. knejser! — —] 7-16.									7.	§ 65
279)	3355 Folgefonden; Folgefaannen] R. Folgefaannen] 1-13. Folgefonnen] M-16. Folgefonden] U. (R.)	1,186;	3,190;	F,442;	11,178;	13,170;	M,265;	14,173;	J,275.	M.	§ 114
280)	3365 S a a (omtrent)] R-6. Sä] U. 7.16.	1,187;	3,191;	F,443;	11,179;	13,171;	M,265;	14,174;		7.	§ 66
281)	3390 (saa slipper en] U. R-4; 16. jeg] 5-15.J.	1,189;	3,193;	F,445;	11,181;	13,172;	M,266;	14,175;	J,276.	5.	§ 56
282)	3415 (Tror) De, (jeg)] R. De] U. 1-16.	1,191;	3,195;	F,446;	11,182;	13,174;	M,267;	14,177;	J,277.	1.	§ 17
283)	3417 Mynt?] R-7; M-15. Mynt?] 8-13. Mynt] U.				11,183;	13,174;				8,M.	§ 128
284)	3424 (kan) De (slaa)] R-13; M,16. de] U. (corr.); 14.			F,447;						14	§ 134
285)	3428 ustyrtelig] U. R-5; M-16. ustyrlig] 6-13.									6,M.	§ 62,130
286)	3430 (paa) Vej—]! R-9. vej—] 10-16. Vej;] U.									10.	§ 78
287)	3436 De (skal bande]] R-8. de] U. 9-16.					13,175;	M,268;	14,178;	J,278.	9.	§ 74
288)	3447 kommanderer] R-1. kommanderer] 3-16.	1,192;	3,196;	F,448;	11,184;	13,175;	M,268;	14,178;		3.	§ 44,47

289) 3471 vogsomt] U. R-13. vågsomt] M-16.
290) 3477 duer] U. R-13. duger] M-16.
291) 3486 Stasen] U. R-13. stadsen] M-16.
292) 3494 Luven] U. R-13. luen] M-t.́
293) 3508 [Havet gaar) höjt,] R-12. höjt] 13-16.
294) 3513 (for galt—!] R-3. galt—] 4-15,16. galt!] U.J.
295) 3517 f: Ex:] U. R. f. ex.] 1-13. f eks.] M-16.
296) 3535 ustyrtelig] U. R-5; M,15-16. ustyrlig] 6-13; 14.
297) 3540 (hilser) venligt] U. R-4. venlig] 5-16.
298) 3541 (om ikke) för;] U. R-5. for!] 6-16.
299) 3585 (Giv os) idag—] U. R.-11. idag!] 12-16.
300) 3594 (hörte) Raab;—] R-11.
     raab!— 12-16 Raab:] U.
301) 3597 [Plads for] e n!] R-10. én!] F-16. en!] U.
302) 3614 (har De) e n (Gang)] U. R-10. én] F-16.
303) 3637 uforsagt:—] R-12.
     uforsagt!] 13-16. uforsagt:] U.
304) 3653 vegt] R-13. vekt] M-16.
305) 3670 (en) Morgen;] U. R-12. (morgen:] 13-16.
306) 3674 Sergeanter] U. R. Sergenter] 1-16.
307) 3704 Lomb] U. R-13. Lom] M-16.
308) 3708 fortalte] U. R-2. fortalte,] 1-16.
     kröget.] R-11.
309) 3719
     Han] R-F.
     kröget.] 12.
     han] U. 12-16.
     kröget,] 13,M²,14. kröget:] U. 12-16.
310) 3721 föged,] U. R-16. foged] M³.

J			F			M			§
J,*79.	1,194;	3,198;	F,449;	11,185;	13,177;	M,269;	14,179; 14,180;	M.	§ 114
								M.	§ 121
		3,198;	F,450;	11,186;	13,177; 13,178;			M	§ 122
J,280.	1,194;	3,198;		11,187;	13,179;	M,270;	14,181;	13.	§ 96
	1,196;	3,200;	F,451;					4.	§ 48
								1,M.	§ 13,121
J,281.	1,198;	3,202;	F,452;	11,188;	13,179;		14,182;	6,M,14	§ 62,130
			F,453;	11,189;	13,181;	M,271;	14,183;	5,M.	§ 55
								6.	§ 61
J,282.	1,201;	3,205;	F,457;	11,193;	13,184;	M,272;	14,186;	12.	§ 91
J,283.	1,202;	3,206;			13,185;	M,273;	14,187;	12.	§ 91
J,284.	1,204;	3,208;	F,458;	11,194;	13,185;		14,188;	F.	§ 85
	1,205;	3,209;	F,459;	11,195;	13,186;	M,273;	14,189;	F.	§ 85
J,285.			F,460;	11,196;	13,187;	M,274;	14,189;	13.	§ 96
	1,206;	3,210;	F,461;	11,197;	13,188;	M,274;	14,190;	M.	§ 121
	1,207;	3,211;		11,197;	13,189;	M,275;	14,191;	13.	§ 96
J,286.	1,208;		F,462;	11,198;				1.	§ 11
			F,463;	11,199;	13,190;	M,276;	14,192;	M.	§ 120
	1,208;	3,212;		11,199;	13,190;	M,276;	14,192;	I.	§ 32
								12,13,M,14,15 {	91,96,128, 133,137

M. § 106

311) 3726 Skaret] U. R-13. skardet] M-16.
312) 3728 og der, (hvor Stien)] U.R-M; 15-16. og dér,] 14.
313) 3736 (af dem), han] R-M; 15-16. han] 14. som] U.
314) 3772 mig (der sov)] U. R-12. mig] 13-16.
315) 3782 lifgemaade] U. R-13. i lige måde] M-16.
316) 3783 endvidre] R-I. endvidere] 3-16.
317) 3797 Elven.] R,1. Elven] 2. elven;] 1-16.
318) Megen Almue] R. Megen Almue] 1-7.
  Megen Almue] 8-13;15. Megen Almue] M,J.
319) 3814 Stas] U. R-13. stads] M-16.
320) 3817 (Kramkarl=Skræppen)] U. R-3; M-15,J.
  ?] 4-13, M². kramkarlskræppen] 16.
321) 3819 (Svoger till) Döden] R-I. døden] 3-16.
322) 3823 ved Næsen—] U. R-5. ved næsen—] 6-16.
323) 3833 Fellen] U. R-13. felden] M-16.
324) 3836 Egg] U. R-2; 3-16. Eg] I.
325) 3841 (kjender mig) gammel; —] R-5.
  gammel!—] 6-16. gammel!] U.
326) 3847 Flokken (stimler)] R-7; r6, Folk] 8-J.
327) 3870 (undskyld,) Ven,—] R-5.
  ven—] 6-16. Ven,] U.
328) 3885 San Franzisco] R-13. San Francisco] M-16.
  San Franzesko] U.
329) 3887 tærne...... knærne] U. R-13.
  tærne...... knærne] M-16.
330) 3889 Vers] R-12. vers.] 13-16.
331) 3898 drappieren] U. R-2.
  drappiren] I-13. drapiren] M-16.

Line	1	3	F	11	13	M	14	15	J	M.	§
311	1,209;	3,213;			13,191;		14,193;	15,193;		M.	§ 122
312									J,287.	14.	§ 134
313										14.	§ 135
314	1,210;	3,214;	F,464;	11,200;	13,192;	M,277;	14,194;		J,288.	13	§ 98
315			F,465;	11,201;						M.	§ 126
316										3.	§ 44
317	1,211;	3,215;	F,465;		13,193;	M,278;	14,175;			2,1.	§ 20,39
318										8,M.	§ 68
319	1,212;	5,216;	F,466;	11,202;	13,194;	M,278;	14,196;		J,289,	M.	§ 122
320										4,M.	§ 48,128
321	1,213;	3,217;	F,467;	11,203;	13,194;	M,279;	14,196;	15,197;		(I),3	§ 31,42
322					13,195;		14,197;			6.	§ 61
323	1,214;	3,218;	F,468;	11,204;	13,194;	M,279;	14,198;		J,290.	M.	§ 120
324										I.	§ 28
325										6.	§ 61
326	1,216;	3,220;	F,470;	11,206;	13,198;	M,280;	14,200;		J,291.	8.	§ 70
327										6.	§ 61
328	1,217;	3,221;	F,471;	11,207;	13,208;	M,281;	14,200;			M.	§ 120
329										M.	§ 113
330										13.	§ 96
331	1,218;	3,222;	F,471;	11,207;	13,199;	M,281;	14,201;		J,292.	I,M.	§ 39,115

No.	Entry								J.	M./I.	§
332)	Tyskeren] R; 3-16. Tydskeren] 1-I.	1,218;	3,222;	F,471;	11,207;	13,199;	M,281;	14,201;		1,3	§ 16,42,47
333)	3905 (till) Slutning] U. R-8. slut] 9-16.	1,218;	3,222;	F,472;	11,208;	13,199;	M,281;	14,201;		9.	§ 75
334)	3910 (studeret); —] R-13. !—] M-16. forceret; (altfor studeret —] U.									M.	§ 129
335)	3921 Nebukadnezar] U. R-13. Nebukadnesar] M-16.					13,200;	M,282;	14,202;		M.	§ 120
336)	3936 (Spaamands=) Gjög] U. R-13. gøk] M-16.	1,219;	3,223;	F,473;	11,209;	13,200;			J.293.	M.	§ 121
337)	3961 (for en) Dag?] U. R-6; M-16. dag!] 7-13.	1,220;	3,224;	F,474;	11,210;	13,201;	M,283;	14,203;		7,M.	§ 65,128
338)	3969 klōer] R-2. klør] U. I-16.	1,221;	3,225;	F,475;	11,211;	13,202;	M,284;	14,204;	J.294.	I.	§ 27
339)	3995 hærjet] R-13. harjet] U. M-16.									M.	§ 120
340)	3998 for inden] U. R-16. forinden, for inden] I.	1,222;	3,226;	F,475;		13,203;		14,205;	J.295.	I.	§ 32
341)	4007 Petrus Gyntus Cæsar fecit] U. R-3. Petrus Gyntus Cæsar fecit!] 4-16.			F,476;	11,212;					4.	§ 48
342)	4018 (skjænkt till) e n; —] R; 6-10. e n:—] 1-5. ēn; —] F-16.	1,223;	3,227;	F,477;		13,204;	M,285;	14,206;		1,6,F.	§ 17,60,83
343)	4030 ynkeligt] U. R-13. ynkelig] M-16.				11,213;	13,204;				M.	§ 123
344)	4038 (sunget) os!]) R. os! —] 1-16. os,] U.	1,224;	3,228;	F,478;	11,214;	13,205;	M,285;	14,207;		1.	§ 17
345)	4047 Duggdraaber] R-9; M-J. dugdråber] 10,14,16.								J.296.	1,10,M.	§ 28,77,115
346)	4066 Kjæltringstreger] R-4. kæltringestreger] 5-13. Keltringestreger] M-16.									5,M.	§ 56,111
347)	4091 heder] U. R-5; M-16. hedder] 6-13.	1,225;	3,229;	F,479;	11,215;	13,206;	M,286;	14,208;	J.297.	6,M.	§ 62,130
348)	4101 Mesters] U. R-2; 3-16. mesters, Mesters] I.	1,226;	3,230;	F,480;	11,216;	13,207;	M,287;	14,210;		I.	§ 29
349)	4109 d e r (, du skal havne] R-4. der] 5-16.	1,227;	3,231;	F,480;	11,218;	13,208;	M,288;	14,212;	J.298.	5.	§ 49
350)	4148 (for) Kneb I] U. R-12. kneb, I] 13-16.	1,229;	3,233;	F,482;		13,210;				13.	§ 96
351)	4162 D u (...ætlet)] R-12. Du] U. 13-16.			F,483;	11,219;					13.	§ 98
352)	4168 min Sæl] R-13. minsæl] U. M-16.	1,230;	3,234;						J.299.	M.	§ 125
353)	4201 tilgavns] U. R-13. tilgagns] M-16.	1,231;	3,235;	F,484;	11,220;	13,212;	M,289;	14,214;	J.300.	M.	§ 121

354) 4218 ivare] U. R-13. i vare] M-16.
355) 4228 engang] U. R-13. én gang] M-16.
356) 4260 skammen;] R-4; 15-16.
    skammen!] 5-13, M²; skammen] M,14.
357) 4261 rent (skejet ud)] R-6; M-16. ren] 7-13.
358) 4283 kverve] U. R; I-16. hverve] 1,2.
359) 4289 Thinge] U. R-13. tinge] M-16
360) 4330 et Trold? —] R-5. et troldt! —] 6-16.
    et Trold?] U.
361) 4335 Men Dattersöns] R-16. Cf. S.M. pp. 11, 40.
362) 4361 Sic] R. "Sic] 1-3. "Sic] 4-16.
363) 4364 (Dette dovriske) n o k] U. R-11. nok] 12-16.
364) 4382 spildt;] U. R-6; M-15; 16. spildt?] 7-13.
    spildt! (og)] J.
365) 4384 Udhængskilt] R. Udhængsskilt] U. 1-16.
366) 4432 (Stien er) fæl —] U. R-5. fæl —] 6-16.
367) 4440 redeligt] R-13. redelig] U. M-16.
368) 4449 mærkelig] U. R-4; M,15-16.
    mærkeligt] 5-13; 14, M².
369) 4475 Omstændighed —] U. R; I.
    Omstændighed. —] 1,2; 3-16.
370) 4490 Bramafigurer] U. R-13.
    Brahmafigurer] M-16.
371) 4493 Literaturer, —] R-5. literaturer —] U. 6-16.
372) 4495 (spillet) Profet!] U. R,1
    Profet;] 2,I. profet.] 3-16.
373) 4510 Ja, (bliv) U. R-12. ja,] 13,M,15-16. ja.] 14.
374) 4514 skaffed Dem] R,1; I-16. dem] U. 2.

1,232;	3,236;	F,485;	11,221;	13,213;	M,390;	14,215;	J,301.	M.	§ 126	
1,233;	3,237;	F,486;	11,222;	13,213;				M.	§ 126	
1,235;	3,239;	F,288;	11,224;	13,215;	M,291;	14,217;	J,302.	5,M.	§ 54,128	
1,236;	3,240;	F,489;	11,225;	13,216;	M,292;	14,218;		7,M.	§ 66,130	
				13,217;		14,219;		1,1.	§ 11,39	
							J,303.	M.	§ 116	
1,239;	3,243;	F,492;	11,228;	13,219;	M,293;	14,221;	J,304.	6.	§ 62	
							J,305.	M.	§ 130	
1,240;	3,244;	F,493;	11,229;	13,221;	M,294;	14,223;		1,4.	§ 14,48	
1,241;	3,245;	F,494;	11,230;		M,294;	14,223;		12.	§ 92	
1,242;	3,246,	F,495;	11,231;	13,222;	M,295;	14,224;	J,306.	7,M.	§ 65,128	
								1.	§ 16	
1,244;	3,248;	F,497;	11,233;	13,225;	M,296;	14,227;	J,307.	6.	§ 61	
1,245;	3,249;	F,498;	11,234;	13,225;	M,296;	14,227;		M.	§ 123	
1,246;	3,250;	F,499;	11,235;	13,226;	M,297;	14,228;	J,308.	5,M,14	§ 55,123	
1,247;	3,251;	F,500;	11,236;	13,228;	M,298;	14,230;		1,1,3	§ 18,39,42	
							J,309.	M.	§ 108	
1,248;	4,252;	F,501;	11,237;							
								6.	§ 61	
1,249;	3,253;	F,501;	11,237;	13,229;	M,298;	14,231;		2,1,3	§ 21,39,42	
		F,502;	11,238;	13,229;						
							J,310.	13,14	§ 97,133	
			M,299;					2.1.	§ 36	

No.	Line	Reading								J		§
375)	4547	(faa) den (frem.)] U. R-I. dem] 3-16.	1,251;	3,255;	F,503;	11,239;	13,231;	M,299;	14,233;	J,311.	3.	§ 46
376)	4542	Behandling;] R-6. behandling.] 7-8. behandling.] U. 9-16.	1,251;	3,255;	F,504;	11,240;	13,231;	M,300;	14,233;	J,311.	7.9.	§ 65,72
377)	4555	(med Svovl) og med] R-8. og] 9-16. og andre, og med lignende] U.									9.	§ 75
378)	4566	Naa;] R.1, Naa,] U. 2-16.	1,252;	3,256;			13,232;		14,234;		2.	§ 20
379)	4583	Stasen] U. R-13. stadsen] M-16.	1,253;	3,257;	F,505;	11,241;	13,233;	M,301;	14,235;	J,312.	M.	§ 122
380)	4603	(Naturen) ödsel.] U. R-5; 16. er ødsel] 6-J.			F,506;	11,242;	13,233;		14,236;		6.	§ 63
381)	4617	D e r (er örk]) R-12. Der] 13-16.	1,254;	3,258;	F,506;		13,234;			J,313.	13.	§ 98
382)	4629	griber i ham] R-13; M,15-16. griber ham] 14.	1,255;	3,259;	F,508;	11,244;	13,235;	M,302;	14,237;		14.	§ 135
383)	4631	(Der er) det]] R-10; M-16. det?] F-13. det —] U.									F,M,14	§ 83,128
384)	4634	(Til tredje) Korsvejen] R-I. korsvej]] 3-16. (den tredje) Korsveje] U.	1,256;	3,260;	F,508;						3.	§ 44
385)		(men s a a] R-I. så] 3-16.	1,257;	3,261;	F,509;	11,245;	13,236;	M,303;	14,238;	J,314.	3.	§ 44
386)	4657	Nævn dem?] U. R. Nævn dem]] 1-16.	1,258;	3,262;	F,510;	11,246;	13,237;	M,303;	14,239;		1.	§ 18
387)	4661	(Kan du sige mig) det?] U. R-11. det]] 12-16.									12.	§ 91
388)	4671	(Lys gaar over) ham;] U. R. ham,] 1-16.									1.	§ 17
389)	4674	(synger) sagte.]] U. R. sagte.]] 1-10. sagte]: F-12; M,J. sagte:]]] 13,14,15,16.									1,F,13,M,14	§ 17,83,89,128
390)		a line space between the 5 distichs in] R-12. not in] 13-16.								J,315.	13.	§ 97
391)	4685	(og) s a a (faar vi se]] U. R-4. så] 5-16.	1,259;	3,269;	F,511;			M,304;	14,240;		5.	§ 53

THE VARIOUS EDITIONS
OF PEER GYNT.

I.

§ 11. Our list contains a good many deviations from R already in this first edition, twenty-six in all, not counting all that I have noted; it will be remembered, as I have already hinted, that only typical cases have been given once, or at most twice; for other mistakes, see lower down and § 17. But these deviations do not all bear the same character.

To begin with a down-right misprint, see n° 358. "I vilde med Magt og Vold kverve mit Syn," Ibsen had written, but both 1 and 2 print hverve and Ibsen detected the mistake in I and corrected it there, both in the text and in the margin. In the same way, on p. 174 of this first ed., we read (l. 3135, not noticed in the preceding list): God mogen, for God morgen and thus 2 of course corrected it. A little more serious was the following misprint: "Der sejred ogsaa min Moral" (see n° 175), Peer Gynt says to "Master" Cotton, and neither in U nor in R did Ibsen underline Der. Yet all the later texts print D e r spaced, which of course is a tempting reading, but still! How is this to be accounted for? Simply because 1 printed De r, i.e. the r at a respectful distance from its predecessor and so of course 2 "improved" this into D e r. An other mistake of some importance is that on p. 232 the Button-moulder is made to say: jeg er s a a r e rædd, de blir vraget of Mester, instead of the s v a r e which is found (l. 4225) both in R and in U.

§ 12. I have my doubt as to whether n° 306 presents a misprint or not. In any case both in U and in R, Ibsen had written Sergeanter, but already 1 changes this into the usual Sergenter, followed by all the later texts.

§ 13. Both in U and in R, Ibsen writes v: Eberkopf, Dr: phil:, kl: 11 and f: Ex: with colons to indicate the abbreviations; see n°s 5, 8, 161, 259, 295; yet in all these cases 1 quietly prints a full-stop. By the way, it is interesting to note that in his earlier draft, U, Ibsen had called Peer's German travelling-companion first Eberkopf, in the course of his writing he adds the predicate von, thus ennobling the Boar's head with one stroke of the pen.

§ 14. These cases may be mere misprints,—they may also be conscious attempts to improve the text, such as undoubtedly was the case with n°s 362 as well as 181 and 187: Here R has (362) Sic transit gloria mundi",—the first of the quotation-marks omitted. Even the severest stickler for a text as the author wrote it will not hesitate to approve of 1 for writing "Sic etc. and if anyone should by any chance be so critically austere I may call attention to U where Ibsen had already written "Sic transit gloria mundi"; by the way, 4 wrongly prints these words in italics and is of course followed by 5-16.

§ 15. Our first edition is also responsible for the substitution (twice, see n°s 181 and 187) of Yankee for Yanke, no doubt a very unusual spelling if admissible at all. But of greater importance is the fact that whereas Ibsen had given To tyve and En Rodemester in the list of his Dramatis Personæ, in 1 we here find substituted (see n°s 6 and 12, respectively) En Tyv og en Hæler and En Lensmand. Here, I suspect, that if the proof-sheets of the time could speak, they could a tale unfold whose slightest word would end our puzzling. But a careful study of U seems (in the case of n° 6 at least) to hint in any case at the time when and the reason why the change was made. The list of personages given before U, does not contain either the Rodemester or the two thieves or the Bailiff, but there can be no doubt that Ibsen had copied out this list, however calligraphically written, (like the first pages of U themselves which were very possibly originally meant for a Renskrift; see supra the description of U) provisionally only. When, on the 18th of September 1867, he sent off his final copy of the fourth act to Copenhagen to be printed, he added a request not to print the list of personages yet, "da jeg muligens kunde ville opføre endnu et par bifigurer" (Koht og Elias, Efterladte Skrifter, III, p. 414). Hence in accordance with this request, in the first (and the second) edition, the text actually begins on p. 1, and the list of dramatis personæ together with the title do not enter into the pagination of the text. Now Ibsen's desire "at opføre endnu et par bifigurer", may of course mean that he reserved himself the right to add the n a m e s of a couple of minor personages, already figuring in the play, on to the list of the dramatis personæ. But whether he had this in his mind or not, he may also have used the opportunity thus given him of adding a personage or substituting one personage for an other. At any rate, in the text of U, there appear instead of the To Tyve, mentioned in the dramatis personæ, and in a stage direction, one Hestetyv and one Klædningstyv of which it is the latter that speaks the words: Min Fader var Hæler; hans Søn maa hæle, and hence it must have struck Ibsen when copying out U for the press, i.e. when writing out R, that in all consistency (as the hestetyv was called t h e thief because his father was one, so) the other thief, Klædningstyven, should be called t h e Receiver and he changed it accordingly. As to the Rodemester, this case is very puzzling and I cannot think of any explanation; for in U, the Lensmand occurs in each of the few cases where he is found in R and the printed texts. Consequently it would seem that the list of the Dramatis personæ of R dates from a period, or at any rate reflects a period b e f o r e the corresponding portion of U was written, i.e. before the fifth act, in which the Lensmand occurs, was composed. [1]) I hope that some one of my readers will be able to give the explanation which I have been unable to supply. Perhaps the Lensmand is not a s u b s t i t u t i o n for the Rodemester at all, but the former merely one of those personages whom he had reserved himself the right to add, and the Rodemester one for whom on reflection he had no further use. But here especially the proofsheets might bring light, for although Ibsen, as we know, did not correct any himself, they may bear traces at least of the

---

[1]) This will be found borne out by subsequent investigations on Ibsen's „Caprices" in the drama: see the notes to the Strange Passenger, the Lean One, the Button-moulder and even the Boyg.

time when the change was introduced and hence allow of a guess or even a hypothesis about its author and his reasons.

§ 16. The next batch is one of four that can conveniently be considered together; see notes n°s 127, 171, 332 and 365. Sengkanten is changed by 1 into Sengekanten and Udhæng-skilt into udhængsskilt, certainly more in accordance and in analogy with udhængsark, udhængsexemplar. The printer of 1, if not already in his grave, will be interested to hear that in the latter case his spelling is also that of U! The equivalent of Sengkanten is not found in U and the present writer would not venture to pronounce on the respective merits of the forms, — we have sengkammer and sengkamerat by the side of any amount of senge-compounds. So at any rate there was no reason for 1 to change. Rather dubious on the other hand seems the point raised by n° 171, where both U and R have Charlstown which 1 changes into Charlestown and which S.M. afterwards changed into Charleston on the plea that the name of that American town *is* (now) written so. I think we are here at the bottom of the fundamental difference between a text such as suits the purposes of your philologist on the one hand, your General Reader on the other. The only way to conciliate the two standpoints would be to give one reading in the text and another in the notes. However, this question will be taken up more in detail later on, cf. §§ 108 seqq.; considering that in a passage lower down (F, p. 403; S.M. p. 10) Ibsen himself writes Charlestown, no great blame can attach to 1 for bringing Ibsen in accordance with himself—if such was his purpose! In con-nection with this point, n° 332 is interesting where 1 changes the Tyskeren of R into Tydskeren, cf. n° 256 where both U and R have Tydsk; and note that here again (in n° 332) U too had Tydskeren. Professor Storm omits the d in all these cases and at present most Norwegians would do the same.

§ 17. The rest of the 1-cases are all concerned with the punctuation, and with regard to six of these it will suffice to refer the curious reader to n°s 105, 245, 248, 264, 388 and 389 of our list; they are of comparatively little importance. N° 282 is a doubtful case: Tror De, jeg er gal, Ibsen had written in R, but 1 followed by all the rest omits the comma. Rightly or wrongly? When we find that U has not got the comma either, this might at first blush seem to bear out the proofreader of 1 and his imitators, but is it not on the other hand apparent that as Ibsen a d d e d the comma, when copying U out for R, he did so with a purpose? N° 342 is rather interesting when we come to think of it; the difference between (Livet har jeg skjænkt til) e n;—and en: with a colon is a very delicate one, difficult to express in gross words, but we feel it; it is as though our expectation were raised a little more by the colon and as if the next line more clearly than by the semi-colon gives the result: det blev Fusk og skjæve Ben! With regard to n° 344 it should be noticed that the point of exclamation in R was corrected by Ibsen from a comma, which is in U and the dash behind it was very clearly crossed out by Ibsen; for all that 1 prints: os! — followed by all the rest. And the presence or absence of such a dash is a thing a p p a r e n t l y of little or no consequence, but certainly meant to convey a meaning as must be clear to anyone who has had the good fortune to study both Ibsen's first draft and his final copy and who has observed how often Ibsen adds it or omits it, clearly with some little different shade of meaning in view (¹).

(¹) The importance that Ibsen attached to punctuation, and its soul, if I may say so: the different pauses to be made in 'saying' the printed text, appears very clearly, and most interestingly, from one of his earlier criticisms: "Lord William Russell og dets udførelse på Christiania teater, 1857, to be found in the Samlede Værker, vol. X, p. 393, where, commenting upon the acting of a young actress, Miss Svendsen, he says: hun synes at have ladet det bero med den første og tarveligste regel, at man bør standse noget ved komma og lidt mere ved punktum; men dette "lidt mere" kan varieres i det uendelige. Har hun midt i sin replik et tankespring at gøre, en overgang fra en forestilling til en anden, så må man dog af pausens ejendommelighed, af ansigtets udtryk og den forandrede tone se, at denne nye tanke opstiger,".... etc. It is of course allowable to interpret this as if Ibsen intended to indicate these 'tankespring', these abrupt transitions in thought, by his punctuation, his dashes more especially. — In the preface to Catilina, we find an amusing passage about the use he sometimes put these dashes — tankestregene — to: they were often used where the correct expression did not at the moment of writing suggest itself. (Saml. V. F., 1, p. 8). The number of them was greatly increased in the printed ed., cf. Eft. Skr. III, 376. In a paper by Ibsen dated 11/9/1862 which Eitrem has recently unearthed from the "Morgenbladet" of that year, I find a similar passage which it may be interesting to reproduce. Speaking of the "gifted artist" he says that she "does not seem to have a good ear for the true value und meaning of punctuation; the commas which *should* be the "fence-sticks of diction" — Dictionens Gjærdestave — esh jumps over with a remarkable nimbleness!" (Morgenbladet, August, 1916).

Two more cases of punctuation, not mentioned in the preceding list, may be added here. On p. 29 (l. 559) a boy at Hægstad exclaims: Nu kommer der Liv i Tingen! Peer Gynt er paa Gaarden? ,where the point of interrogation after *Gaarden* is a mere misprint for a point of exclamation. This was so obvious that it was corrected very early into the proper reading. In the same way on p. 92, we find du er søn till Jon Gynt; whereas R had a point of exclamation after *Gynt* (l. 1404); this mistake has been perpetuated and may still be found in the very last edition, 16.

§ 18. A full-stop may make a great difference too,—case n° 369 proves it, if necessary, to the sceptic! To the Lean One, Peer Gynt says that all he wants is "kun en venlig Omgang efter Sted og Omstændighed—" and here the Lean One i n t e r r u p t s him with the witty question: Varmt Værelse? The whole point of this interruption is spoilt already by 1 (followed by 2) by printing: Omstændighed.—Ibsen notices this and crosses out the full stop in I. Notwithstanding this very clear hint, 3 again prints it and is of course followed by all the rest.

When Peer Gynt at the final meeting with Solvejg exclaims that he is surely lost unless Solvejg can guess riddles, the latter says: Nævn dem. And Ibsen makes Peer Gynt answer: Nævn dem? i.e. clearly *Shall* I mention them? a question. But 1, followed by all the rest, makes this into an exclamation: Nævn dem! (n° 386) The critically inclined among my readers may like to refer me to S. M. pp. 22-24, especially the last page, but I hope not to be accused of hyper-criticism if I should call this a vicious circle,—the fact is that Prof. Storm's account of Ibsen's punctuation is (like the rest of his grammar) too much based on those very texts so often reprinted of which it is my sad duty to show the untrustworthiness. The safest plan will be to print: Nævn dem? as both U and R read.

To sum up,—it would seem to me that for a first edition of the manuscript the number of deviations from it is rather considerable—some thirty at least—even if we cannot but approve of a couple of them from a certain point of view, it does not promise much for the result of Ibsen's explicit trusting in the printers! As to his faith in his manuscript, it is interesting to see that there is but one case that can be nothing but a slip of the pen, n° 362.

2.

§ 19. This second edition inherits one mistake or rather the germ of a mistake from the first (see supra the case of n° 175, § 11) and adds at least twenty-one other deviations of its own. I take two sheer misprints ([1]) first, n°s 220 and 224, where 2 had Da faar ikke instead of Du faar ikke and osenstrimer instead of Rosenstrimer. In the copy of 2 that Ibsen used for the preparation of his third edition he found the a of Da already corrected into u and the R added, both in violet ink; his own corrections and changes are recognisable not only, in many cases at least even when but one letter, by his characteristic handwriting, but also by the fact of his invariably using lead-pencil. See § 30.

§ 20. N° 175, as explained, exemplifies the case of a word not underlined by the author and yet spaced in the printed editions. Cases n°s 176 and 255 show the reverse process. This (especially n° 255) is of course somewhat more serious: har jeg ogsaa h a m fra et Eventyr? is much more powerful than the tame: har jeg ogsaa ham etc.? The *men* of n° 176 is not quite so important of course. The next six cases, n°s 63, 90, 207, 232, 317 and 378, are all concerned with punctuation and need no elucidation or further remark, except perhaps that in n° 232 Ibsen (in I) had overlooked the misprint Naa; instead of Naa! and that 3 did notice it but changed the wrong way, the next Naa into nå;, eliminating the capital N, and was followed by all in this.

§ 21. Cases n°s 34, 89 and 169 had already been noticed by Prof. Storm (S.M., pp. 9 and 40) who corrects his F by the aid of I, not by the m.s. Similar cases are n°s 178 and 372, where in either case it is a point of exclamation that has disap-

---

[1] I think I ought to add that mere misprints are mentioned only, quite exceptionally, when some peculiarity attaches to them or when they are repeated in subsequent editions. When (as in 3, p. 70) storfolk is printed storfok, corrected at once into storfolk in 4, such a mistake will not be taken cognizance of here, even when indicated in my m.s. notes.

peared, in favour of a full-stop and a semicolon respectively.

§ 22. "Kvinderne nejer sig" (n° 39) Ibsen had written both in U and in R. This quite modern, in fact the only common form, was changed by 2 into the old fashioned plural neje sig, a mistake that Ibsen corrected in I, properly followed by 3 and 4. But the spirit of the whole passage was evidently too much again for 5 who, followed by a 11 texts down to 13 inclusively, enhances the solemnity of the ladies' act of reverence by printing once more: kvinderne neje sig, which would seem to make it all the greater honour for our Jack-a-dreams. Professor Storm who often follows 13 through thick and thin, here corrects that text and it is pleasant to find that up till now all texts (16 inclusively) have followed this example of modernity. Neje sig seems unusual for neje; see n. to l. 492.

§ 23. Som en bærer en Gris!, Ibsen had written (n° 71) both in U and R; -er in U rather carelessly added, but it i s there! Our text changes this into b æ r, a form often enough used by Ibsen although not here [1]). Ibsen, not remembering that he had written bærer originally, adds an apostrophe behind: bær', a form consequently found in all texts down to 13 inclusively and then changed by M into bær.

§ 24. Very interesting is n° 126, where both U and R, followed, by 1, made Aase on her death-bed exclaim: Hvad er det som rumler? However correct the form in itself may seem to be that 2 substitutes: hvad er det som ramler (compare lower down: Der faldt Kongsgaarden min med Braak og Rammel! and of course: Det er ikke ramlet sammen endnu; Når vi døde vågner, F, X, 304), this change must be looked upon as a misprint. No one has doubted the reading, not even the Editors of the Efterladte Skrifter, III, 416, who quote rumler from U, but for all that did not only omit to inquire what R had, but did not even look up 1; the wrong reading is therefore found in all subsequent texts until 16 copied the correct rumler from my Edda-paper; cf. infra § 141 and n. to l. 1367.

---

[1]) Other cases of bær, bær' and bærer used promiscuously by Ibsen (at least if the reprint may be trusted in this respect!) I note from the Folkeudg., S. V., vol. X, pp. 80 and 554: bærer; ib., pp. 116, 117, 158: bær', and ib., pp. 484, 561 and 563: bær. — And cf. De selv bær' Dem ad. (F, IX, 116).

§ 25. "Vitterlige Sprogfejl, f. eks. urigtigt køn, er rettede", we read S.M., p. 3. Here the Professor "unbeknown to him" has found a predecessor in the proofreader of our text. See n° 195: R had i et Fjeldklöft, and so 1 had printed; but 2 corrects this into en, followed by 3-16. And that even the Shades of Ibsen cannot protest would seem to be clear from the fact that U here had i en Bjergkløft, and that in our very text, R, Ibsen himself writes a little lower down: i Fjeldklöften. So it was nothing but a slip of the pen. It will be sufficient to refer to n⁰ˢ 230 and 262 to complete the list of the sins of our second edition. We may differ as to the advisability of writing tér or ter, about which anon, but there can be no doubt whatever that the reading of U and R: de saakaldt kloge should be reinstated in the place of honour, as 16 did, cf. § 141, however much de saakaldte kloge may appeal to many a delicate ear.

I.

§ 26. Under the influence of the then reigning form of Scandinavism (¹), a meeting was held at Stockholm in 1869 (²) from July 25th to 30th, where an effort was made to approach the orthography of Swedish on the one hand and Dano-Norwegian on the other as it was then commonly called, although it would now seem a heresy to many to continue doing so.

The meeting did not wish more than to set a more or less official stamp upon some changes in the orthography of the "two" languages that had already been before the public for some considerable time, proposed by individuals of mark, such as Rask and N.M. Petersen, with a view "to facilitate for the

---

(¹) The word-form Scandinavism will, I hope, be pardoned me even though not found in the N. E. D., because it seems necessary to express like its Scandinavian counterpart Skandinavisme: a desire for Scandinavian Unity, political or otherwise, a sort of Pan-Scandinavism in fact. If Scandinavism is really un-English (although Brynildsen in his Norsk-Engelsk Ordbog uses it) the definition given above should at least have been added to that of "the characteristic ideas of the Scandinavian people" given under Scandinavianism in the N. E. D.

(²) Compare Jakob Løkke, Beretning om det Nordiske Retskrivingsmøde i Stockholm, Kristiania, 1870, from which I take the following details. I have not seen the similar accounts drawn up by the Dane Lyngby and the Swede Hazelius. On Ibsen's orthography just before that meeting, cf. a short note Eft. Skr. III, 359. He used until then Capital letters in the substantives.

Scandinavian peoples mutual understanding and acquaintance with each other's literatures" (p. 2); nor did the congress intend to do more than p r o p o s e these changes and i n v i t e authors and others to adopt them. The points about which a practical unanimity was reached are not all of direct importance for the subject in hand here: Ibsen's change of orthography from 1870 onwards; I wish therefore to restrict my extracts to this aspect of the case only. It was decided to recommend the abolition of capital letters in substantives [1]), except in proper names of course, one or two pronouns, I == you, for the same obvious reason for which Englishmen write I, not : i; De, etc., and at the beginning of sentences. Secondly, double vowels such as in fåer, leer, skeer, foer, broer. etc., it was proposed to simplify into: får, ler, sker, for, bror, etc. Then, å would be introduced more generally than hitherto for a a; the j should be abolished between k or g and the palatal vowels (so henceforth ged, købe, gøre, kære, give, etc. It was proposed to substitute ks for x at least in native words; to omit the mute d before s, such as kusk instead of kudsk; to write nn instead of nd as much as possible, especially (p. 24) in Norwegian dialect words, such as fonn ("formerly fond"); to leave off writing a double consonant where, as in loggre, it was up till then often found double, after short vowels. The very delicate question of e versus æ was regulated as well as the use of å versus o, and the question of writing some words together as one: iligemaade, or separately: i lige maade.

Henrik Ibsen was one of the Norwegian members ([2]) together with Professor Ludvig Daa, the well known Knudsen of orthographic fame, and (besides Løkke, the author of the pamphlet mentioned) Professor Sophus Bugge, who however was unable to be present. It is not known whether Ibsen took a very active part in the proceedings and whether, and if so where, he dissented from any of the propositions adopted. In

---

[1] In Sanct Hansnatten, "substantiver med smaat" are made fun of as being characteristic of „en Folkets Mand der gaar med Tollekniven"; cf. Eft. Skr. I, 405 (n. to l. 1053).

[2] Til S. rejste Ibsen med offentligt stipendium af den norske stat den 21de Juli 1869, deltog der i det nordiske retskrivningsmøde.... og studerede svensk kunst og undervisningsvæsen. (Breve I, p. 321; notes).

any case he found occasion very soon afterwards [1]) to show that so far as he was concerned the meeting had not been in vain. For, when in 1874 a new edition of Peer Gynt was called for, Ibsen conformed his orthography in the main at least, as will be seen, to that of the Stockholm meeting, and taking a copy of the second edition of 1867 he introduced into it the changes now deemed necessary in concordance with the results there obtained.

In how far Ibsen was actuated only by a desire to conform to the orthographic principles of the Stockholm conference, is a matter that remains to be considered. From his letters to Frederik Hegel, the then head of the Gyldendal-house, it would seem that there was here somewhat „more than meets the eye". See the letter to Mr. Hegel (Breve I, 100, 101) where he looks upon it as his duty to change his own orthography in accordance with his Danish publisher's desire,—of course to please the Danish readers, and compare Prof. D.A. Seip's interesting paper: Henrik Ibsen og K. Knudsen, Det sproglige gjennembrud hos Ibsen, in the new periodical Edda I, pp. 145 seqq., especially p. 155 and 163: Naar Ibsen ryddet norske ord av „Kjærlighedens Komedie," var det i k k e fordi de danske ord svarte mer til hans sprogfølelse. Forandringerne blev gjort av yttre grunner." See infra, § 115.

§ 27. However this may be, it is in accordance with the principles of the Stockholm meeting that we find Ibsen change (in „I") all, or practically all capitals of the substantives into small letters (by underlining the capital in question with lead-pencil; ink is not used by Ibsen in I; the few ink-notes in I are by another hand; cf. §§ 19 and 30), and omitting the j's between k or g and palatal vowels, as well as crossing out now superfluous letters such as d or e etc. (Cf. in our list notes 25, 133, 186, Løkke pp. 32 seq., 221, 235 and 338.)

§ 28. The practice of underlining capital and double letters and of crossing out the j and x seems at one time to have got

---

[1]) It is necessary to remind my readers that the purpose of the present study is one of the texts of Peer Gynt exclusively, so that I do not here take into account any earlier proof of this that may exist in connection with other plays; this side of the question I have not yet been able to investigate.

such a habit that it happened more than once that Ibsen underlined or crossed out some that should have been left alone (as conversely he once or twice omits to do so, which does not prevent 3 from conforming to Ibsen's evident desire) and then Ibsen not only crosses out the stroke or letter, as the case may be, but, to make „assurance double sure", once more writes the right form in the margin. This is interesting for, as in the case of notes 62, 95, 117, 146, 324 and 345, it results in an unusually strong proof that for a special reason (see the note) Ibsen wanted these double letters to stand, Stockholm conference or no, viz. Nødd, Kall, Lægg, Egg, Duggdraaber, which makes it a hard nut to crack for subsequent culprits such as (n⁰ 345) 10 and M (62, 95 and 146) if they should be called upon to defend their conduct of simplifying the double consonant all the same ([1]).

§ 29. It is interesting to note (n° 111) that Ibsen first changed Böjgen as well as lower down Böjg into böjgen and böjg and then changed his mind before he got to the third occurrence of the word. See also in this connection n° 215, where it is quite clear that Ibsen on reflection decided to keep the capital in the German word Hieb for he underlined the H first, then crossed out the stroke under H, and added a capital once more in the margin; so our fourth edition is very bold, at any rate certainly wrong in „correcting" it into hieb. Ibsen's reason? It may have been that he wished the word to be felt as German; although he does not always distinguish sufficiently between Norwegian and German, teste n° 162; cf. lower down.

Grane (153), Galfrands (225), Højhed (269) and Mester (348 and passim) were also first „decapitalised", but the sign of honour restored by Ibsen himself. Compare also n° 226

([1]) Compare nᵒˢ 43 and 257: Sex first changed into seks and then restored, and flux changed into fluks. M changes the former all the same into seks and the latter into flugs.

Flugs Ibsen also uses in Gildet paa Solhoug, — at least it is so found in F (II, p. 155).

Particular attention is directed to a letter by Ibsen to his Danish publisher, Mr. Hegel, of Nov. 25, 1865, where we find the reason indicated why he wanted these double consonants to stand: so as to distinguish egg (edge) from eg (the oak), dugg (dew) from dug (tablecloth), viss (a certain) from vis (wise), etc. See infra, § 115.

(Livgjord), where Ibsen had also mechanically crossed out the j, then restored it again.

§ 30. Case n° 229 seems to throw some light on the relation (of time) between the hand that added the rare notes in (violet) ink in I and Ibsen himself (see § 19). There the T of Tyrkeklæderne is underlined by Ibsen so Ibsen intended the word to be tyrkeklæderne. But the violet-ink-pen puts a stroke o v e r the T and a point of interrogation in the margin evidently hinting that the T should stand. The violet ink is therefore posterior to Ibsen's lead-pencil and can only be the proofreader's, it would seem. The third edition has Tyrkeklæderne. But it is curious that in a preceding passage (cf. n° 200) the Araberhövding of R-2 was left unchanged by Ibsen not only but that t h e r e the third edition actually changes it into araberhövding.

§ 31. Another case of non-„decapitalisation" should be noted more especially; see n° 321: han var Svoger til Døden R-2 had, where Ibsen did change the S but not the D into a small letter. Yet 3 prints døden. As at least once (however wrongly it seems to me) the Døden here has been explained not as death but as t h e d e a d o n e (cf. a review by Mr. B.A. Meuleman in De Beweging, May 1909, of the Dutch translation of Peer Gynt by Mrs. Clant van der Mijll) I must not in honour omit to mention this fact, out of which my honourable opponent might like to squeeze an argument in favour of his view. That döden cannot possibly be: the dead one is a fact that will be apparent on reflection to Mr. Meuleman himself,—it is not susceptible of proof, being a negative statement; the burden of proof for his contention would be on his shoulders. All that can be said is that the case of adjectives used substantively is restricted to a few such as Blakken, gamlen, styggen, etc. Moreover, as Ibsen wites passim den magre, det taagede graa, den graaklædte, den sørgeklædte, etc. without capitals but Døden with one, it is quite clear that he did not take Døden as the dead one, when it would be an adjective used as a subst. See Comm. n. to l. 3819.

§ 32. With regard to Ibsen's changes of the punctuation, I refer to cases n⁰ˢ 104, 254 and 308. N° 104 presents an interesting case of the author's unconscious return to the punctuation of U which he had abandoned in R; here the comma of the semicolon was crossed out by him and thus made into a full stop. In I the author again changes the comma into a full stop! The slight element of reflection added by Ibsen by means of the dash in case n° 254 was rightly kept by all subsequent texts, and the comma behind fortalte (308) is a decided improvement too on U, R-2. See n° 340 for another case where *I* introduced a change only to cross it out again.

§ 33. Some stray notes must follow here, each presenting some interesting point or problem. Ibsen had written (n° 69) both in U and in R: paa Gjetens Vis, with the specially Norwegian form G(j)e*t*en instead of the Dano-Norwegian G(j)e*d*en. In I the author changes the t into d so that, in connection with the other usual changes, the expression now runs: på gedens vis; Ibsen evidently thought that the special Norwegian form was little in its place here with its so-called „hard" consonant amidst all the other Dano-Norwegian forms. In the same way, lower down (cf. n° 244) Gjeter had already been changed into Gjeder in R. Well, even this leaves an opening, perhaps, for an o p i n i o n, founded on arguments about the merits of the form Gjeten, but Prof. Storm leaves us in the dark as to his reasons when he simply says: „den norske form maa restitueres (S.M., p. 9 and compare § 12, pp. 26-27). I venture to think that, especially in view of the above considerations many will disagree with him (cf. § 118).

§ 34. The impossible cockney Sam Weller-ian Werry well (159) was changed by Ibsen himself into Very well and the equally impossible skjelden (¹) (160) into sjelden; as well as „det er skjeldent" (I, p. 244) into sjeldent,—apparently, for the copy of I having been bound very carelessly, the sj is cut off by the binder! (the j had in the two cases been deleted by

---

(¹) This peculiarity — it can be nothing but a mere blunder (but a pretty common one as Dr. Chr. Lange tells me) — is too much even for the editors of the Efterladte Skrifter. They reprint all the texts very faithfully after the manuscript (vol. I, p. VIII), but they write: "Og en enkelt stående egenhed i Ibsens stavemåde, nemlig at han fra 1850 helt frem til 1870 ofte skriver "skjelden", istedenfor "sjelden", har vi ikke ment at burde udstille."

Ibsen and restored in the margin in the first case; presumably also in the second).

§ 35. Further improvements, not strictly orthographical in nature, are (179) à (la Lippe-Detmold) instead of a; Goddam! (G o cut off by the binder) instead of the impossible God dam of R-2 (185); For langt! in two words (228) instead of For-langt! which in the context was absurd; yet Ibsen had written it in U and R, and it had been printed so by both 1 and 2.

§ 36. „Hvad vandt De, om jeg skaffed Dem Kost og Bolig?" the Lean One asks (cf. 374), which 1 prints correctly but 2 misprints into „skaffed dem". It is amusing to find that this misprint, duly corrected in I by the author, is found as a slip of the pen in this very passage in U; dem, where Ibsen overlooked it! See lower down, § 52, § 134.

§ 37. (Vejde Ren (119) and (Bøjgen som fik) Men (113) of U and R are changed by Ibsen into rén and mén respectively, thus creating an interesting antecedent for the numerous cases where, as we shall subsequently find, other texts add the distinguishing accent on many an e.

§ 38. Two interesting cases of what I cannot but look upon as a mistake of Ibsen may be mentioned here together; cf. notes 162 and 212.

Ej wass! as spoken by von Eberkopf is either nothing but a half-Norwegianisation of Ach wass, or a partial Teutonification of ej hvad, or of a Danish Ih hvad; in any case, the spelling Ej for German ei is Danish. However this be, there can be no doubt that wass is a German word. So there was not the slight-est reason for crossing out one s of wass (as in U and R-2) and printing Ej was, as Ibsen himself indicated; I can only think that it came about by the process of mechanical crossing out of a n y double consonant after a short vowel that he met with! (§ 28). And hence the absurd Ej was figures in all texts not even changed by the „grand corrector of the realms of (Ibsenian) rhymes" in M. But n° 212 is perhaps even more interesting.

When Peer Gynt wittily quotes from an „esteemed author": das ewig weibliche zieht uns an! (the reading of all the texts subsequent to I), many a rhythmical Epicure will feel something of a shock, and as matter of fact as everybody knows, Goethe's words actually run: das Ewig weibliche zieht uns hinan, which could not of course shock the most delicate ear. Curiously enough the two German translators, Ludwig Passarge and Christian Morgenstern quote the words as given here but it was reserved for an English translator to change the an into hinan —Messrs. Archer append the following note: Ibsen writes „ziehet uns an" (¹). We have ventured to restore the exact wording of Goethe's lines." In a paper in „Samtiden" for 1906 Mr. Eitrem has tried to show that Messrs. Archer were wrong in doing so, that this was one of Ibsen's little mystifications of his public, and that Messrs. Archer have fallen into the trap. Just as according to Eitrem Ibsen mystifies the public by the words of the Memnonstøtte (cf. Comm. *n.* to l. 2995) Ibsen here too simply wished to 'do' (at lure) his readers and wrote 'Das ewig weibliche zieht uns an' on purpose, by way of a joke which Messrs. Archer spoil by their corrections and it is „moreover" rather characteristic of Peer's 'half-culture' (Peers halvdannelse) that he continually quotes wrong or misunderstands his quotations.

In itself it would of course be quite possible —a wrong quotation such as this would no doubt together with other little touches be an excellent means of showing that Peer's culture was at most superficial —but I think that if we should conclude at once to half-culture in case of a misquotation, the aggregate culture of the world will be found sadly reduced. Ibsen himself would be the first victim of the conclusion as we shall see lower down, so we had better be careful in the choice of our criterium. Moreover, in order to be really a proof of Peer's half-culture, it seems to me that in that case the wrong quotation—the same wrong quotation—must be either in Ibsen's original text or clearly introduced by him into it for this purpose. And what do we see? Ibsen's first draft, U, is particularly instructive here; see the facsimile, supra, p. 219. He had first written (U, 17, 4, v°): „Das evig weibliche ziet uns herann!", the v of evig, t of ziet (for zieht), herann, with its her and its

---

(¹) The reading of the first and second editions, see infra.

double n clearly shows that Ibsen had not got the Faust before
him, that he quoted from memory and that his memory was
not absolutely faithful,—only, and this is interesting, the
m e t r e was there! He then changes t of ziet into (zie)het, and
(crossing out her and one n of herann) changes herann into
an,—so the metre was again there,—or still so. And so this is
what we find in R, except that there Ibsen has corrected evig
to ewig, and from R the text: „Das ewig weibliche ziehet uns
an!" passes into 1 and 2; so Messrs. Archer quote this text, see
supra. In I, it is the author himself who changes ziehet into
zieht, leaving a n as it was. Must we really conclude that this
change was introduced by Ibsen to characterise Peer's half-
culture? Is it not sufficiently apparent from Ibsen's various
changes that he himself is the culprit and stands convicted of
(horresco referens) a slip of the memory? If he had really wished
to do as Eitrem thinks, the *her*an (instead of *hin*an) which had
escaped him would have served his purpose so splendidly that
I for one can see no reason for his then eliminating this; see
§ 39, infra § 102 and Comm. n. to l.l. 2583-6 (facsimile).

§ 39. Ibsen's part in the final form of cases 39 (neje), 71
(bær), 207 (Dans for mig), 317, 358, 369 and 372, has already
been touched upon ante in the section devoted to editions 1
and 2. Only notes 21 and 331 remain to be considered. „Man
muss sich drappieren som Tydskeren siger", Ibsen had written.
Curiously enough, Ibsen may again have confounded German
and Norwegian, as in the case Ej wass (§ 38), in so far as the
correction into drappiren may have been made ander the influence of the *ie* being considered less desirable i n N o r-
w e g i a n. Although, as usage was not quite settled in German either, neither with regard to the double or single p, nor
even with regard to the ie or i, it may be that he has here been
correcting the German, as Prof. Storm apparently does when
he crosses out the one p. (cf. Drapperier and drapperer sig with
two p's; F, VI, 475 and 290).

§ 40. Of greater importance is n° 21, for it brings us to
Ibsen's inconsistencies. In perfect accordance with the Stockholm meeting (see Løkke, p. 15), Ibsen changes foer into for
(changed by M into fór) just as he changes farbroer into far-

bror, on p. 130; but he had previously (on p. 120) left farbroer unchanged. And he leaves not only Faer, taer, beer (and always *Peer* Pynt), gier and tæerne, knæerne (n° 329) unchanged, but also Moer, passim. Most double consonants (after short vowels) are simplified, but readers of the preceding pages (§ 28, *n*) will remember that of some, such as egg, nödd, it is most emphatically indicated (by the „correction" being deleted) that the consonant has to remain doubled! And although the x is, as we have seen, replaced as a rule by ks, we have already seen that sex (n° 43) was kept; so in exempel p. 176. The third edition often changes all the same when Ibsen seemed to have merely overlooked the case; cf. pp. 3, 188 and 193, where uvilkaarligt, tykkner, voxer were left untouched in *I*, but changed all the same into uvilkårligt, tykner and vokser by 3.

§ 41. The conclusion should be that although Ibsen (who, it is of course quite evident, did but read through this copy of 2 currente calamo without collating either 1 or R),—although Ibsen did not correct all the mistakes that had crept into 1 or 2, he certainly eliminated some of them, as well as some oversights of his own, and that the text of 3 profited by it. At the same time, the very fact that Ibsen after various fluctuations fixed upon a certain word-form for the third edition should cause us to think twice before changing it, as in done but too often by M (see infra).

3.

§ 42. Some five changes introduced by 3 (n°ˢ 229, 321, 332, 369 and 372) have already been discussed supra and need not be touched upon any more. Our man is perhaps consistent with himself when he changes Ibsen's Lövtrær (n° 88) into løvtræer, although the irony of the case is rather amusing: he thus introduces a form which Ibsen should have eliminated if hé had been consistent with himself and the Stockholm meeting; M therefore reintroduces løvtrær.

§ 43. Ibsen had written Passagér (n° 11; see ante on Mén and rén, § 37) just as Ibsen sometimes, but not quite consistently, writes Rén, bét and also kammél, but 3 changes this into passager. Two cases of the interchange of a point of exclamation and a point of interrogation will be found noticed under nᵒˢ 54 and conversely 139. See Prof. Storm, S.M, pp. 39 and 10 respectively. In either case the change proposed by Storm is not only supported by 1 and 2, but also by R and U.

§ 44. Our text introduces flyve derop instead of klyve derop (n° 191; S.M., p. 40) and changes Araberhøvding (U: Araberfyrste) into araberhøvding (n° 200; cf. ante, § 30), komanderer into kommanderer (3-15; n° 288) and endvidre into endvidere (n° 316); is reponsible for an unspaced saa (n° 385) in a context that undoubtedly requires the added emphasis of the spacing; and changes Korsvejen into korsvej (n° 384) in Til tredje Korsvejen; it is true that U has korsvej too, but in a different context: Den tredje Korsvej faar du huske paa. Staaltraadsærk of U and R is given another s (n° 118), and mit (Pandehvælv) is changed, apparently wrongly, into min (n° 177) (¹). Case n° 134, strakte arme instead of strake arme, had already been noticed by Prof. Storm (S.M., p. 10); cf. also n° 145 where the Danish strakte was not introduced until in the 6th edition, noticed infra. For cases like n° 124, see Storm, S.M., pp. 10 and 27: Prof. Storm changes the Danish kigger of 3 to kiger, as in 1 and 2 (and in R; the passage is not found in U), and, taking it up into his own edition, adds: I senere stykker endnu mere norsk kikke. Case n° 36 w... show my readers that Prof. Storm has somewhat inconsistently introduced this „even more Norwegian form" into that passage, and not here. See Når vi Døde vågner (F, X, 215): kikker, which is later Ibsen's usual spelling; Prof. Storm (S. I. S. p. 195 compares the spelling of kikkert.

§ 45. The change by 3 (cf. S.M., p. 10) of Aa, dersom jeg bare vidste (where Ibsen, in I, had crossed out the second a and changed A into Å) into Åse, dersom jeg bare vidste (jeg ikke har holdt ham for strengt) is the most momentous of all and has misled many a commentator and especially many a

---

(¹) In Kongsemnerne we find (F, II, p. 378): til stjernehvælven blå. Brynildsen in his first edition quoting this very passage, gives hvælv as neuter and common gender; in the second edition the neuter gender only is recognised. In Danish too it is neuter only. The min may be nothing but an "attraction" (unconsciously of course) to pande.

translator into the wrong direction; cf Comm. n. to l. 1604.

§ 46. A rather important case entirely overlooked hitherto, is n° 375, where both U and R, followed by 1-I, had written about the photographic negatives: „men Ligheden hviler dog ogsaa i dem, og det gjælder ikke andet, and at faa *den* frem, where 3 changes den into dem; at faa dem frem, as if referring to the *negatives*! The reading is obviously wrong.

§ 47. Taken all in all, the third edition is responsible for twenty changes of which at most two (n° 288, kommanderer, and 332, Tyskeren) may seem improvements; at most, and only from the point of view of the general reader. The philologist has no reason whatever to be thankful to the printer of this edition.

4.

§ 48. We have already seen two changes (notes n°ˢ 215 and 362; see §§ 29 and 14) introduced by 4; neither of them of any great importance, so they should now only be mentioned here in passing for completeness' sake. In exactly the same way as with n° 362, the fourth edition again introduces italics wrongly in the case of n° 341, where neither U nor R had underlined the latin words. A somewhat similar case is n° 242, only of a little more importance, as the Nu italicised in Nu bare holde ud (under the influence of the *nu* italicised in the preceding line) takes away the stress on bare with which it should of course be read. Cases n° 41 and 55 are changes on the same lines; nogle andre being thickly underlined in R (not so in U) i.e. to be spaced. Conversely, in n° 55 Peer Gynt was nót thickly underlined in R, yet 4 spaces it and from 8 onwards the words are even printed in a different type altogether. In cases 33, 53, 151, 294 and 320, our fourth edition introduces a wrong punctuation; in spænd med benene the semicolon has evidently dropped out after having been printed, *teste* the fact that the final e is still printed below the line. When 5 corrects this, he introduces a comma instead of the semicolon. With regard to n° 53, see Prof. Storm, S.M., pp. 9 and 24; ib. p. 24 for n° 151; ib. p. 40 for n° 320, but Prof. Storm prints kramkarlskræppen without its hyphen. In the case of n°ˢ 98 and

102, such a hyphen is introduced into kristenmandsklæder and kristenmandsbrogen, wrongly of course, by our text.

§ 49. Three more cases, n⁰ˢ 66, 77 and 125 complete its list of sins,—they are of somewhat more importance. Why print fremmest instead of fremst? (66); skyggerne falde instead of falder (cf. the case of neje, n° 39, supra, § 22)? and Det er fanden til krop, instead of (det) var etc., much more idiomatic here =what a devil of a fellow he was : cf. Comm. n. to l. 1351. All three changes are kept down to the latest edition, I have seen, except that miraculously the fifteenth edition as if for once to assert its independence, changes falde to falder. Moreover, 16, having found fremst and det var fanden indicated in my Edda paper, restores these correct readings.

§ 50. Taken all in all, the fourth edition is responsible for 16 changes, three of which only have met with the approval of Prof. Storm, so that at least 13 new corruptions must be said to be the balance against this edition.

5.

§ 51. Two cases have already been treated of, n⁰ˢ 33 and 39; n° 33 contributing an attempt at a correction; see §§ 48 and 22.

§ 52 Med samme Norm De alting maaler (case n° 167), Ibsen had written in R, where 5 by a mistake such as we have already treated of (supra, § 36) prints de alting måler; 6 corrects this, 12 and 13 fall into the same error and (cf. S.M., p. 40) so does apparently Prof. Storm, or I should say: so did apparently Prof. Storm, for not only does he there apologise for this mistake, but, as Overlærer Stavnem of Stavanger, tells me, his copy of the Mindeudgave, actually prints: de alting måler, and indeed this is the only explanation of Professor Storm's words on the page in question. But what should we then think of the fact that my copy gives: D e alting måler, and that in this same edition, or I should say in this same copy, the correction of de into De is still to be found? Well, the only explanation possible is one that throws a curious light on the care, not to say carelessness, with which this Mindeudgave was printed. For we can only conclude that there exist certain copies where some mistakes were corrected and others where this is not so, and in the first case, the corresponding statement in the appendix was left unchanged. See lower down, § 106, the notes on cases 173 and 310. Observe that U too had here *de* corrected into De, just like U too has: de (spidser till), corrected into De; compare also § 134.

§ 53. Twice, 5 is responsible for the change of the Norwegian et trold into the Danish en trold, see n°s 2 and 65 and § 99; as well as for five cases of the non-spacing of a word, in more than one case of extreme importance, although in all the five cases the word remained un-spaced throughout all the editions I have seen! Compare cases 109, 204, 211, 349 and 391. Case n° 109, perhaps the most important of all: Hvem *er* du? should be compared to n°s 108, 110. The questions addressed by Peer to the Bøjgen have fared ill as we see at the printers' hands; for the two corresponding changes editions 8 and 12 are responsible.

§ 54. Cases 1, 101, 165, 199, 209, 222 and 356 are concerned with the punctuation and do not call for any special comment.

§ 55. Cases 297 and 368 may be considered together.

Han hilser venligt (of R and U) is changed by 5 into han hilser venlig, and conversely (et) mærkelig (udviklet neglesystem) is here changed into mærkeligt. See lower down § 123, where this question will be treated of at more length.

§ 56. The next seven cases deal with an of course entirely uncalled-for substitution of forms and even words such as falder om for falder (107), trægt for tungt (115), for hoved instead of for et hoved (142), højen for højden (198), ryddelig for ryddig (¹) (270), kæltringestreger for k(j)jæltringstreger (346), (²) and last not least: saa slipper en ogsaa for Krus paa Bryggen (281), where 5 introduces the more personal saa slipper *jeg* også for krus på bryggen; much more personal, but I must be greatly wrong if the impersonal *en* does not add a zest that was lost upon our man. And even if it did not, *en* is what Ibsen wrote and it should of course be restored (³). The 16th ed. has correct-

---

(¹) The form ryddig is found in Ibsens Kæmpehöjen (F, X, 11); Fru Inger (F, 1. 236), Gengangere, (F, VI, 365).

(²) Cf. Kæltringstreger (F, IV, 9)

(³) When Madame Rundholmen says (F, IV, 25) about Steensgaard: Kunde *en*

ed some of these cases,—of course only those (115, 142, 270, 281) that were mentioned in my Edda paper!

§ 57. The two last changes to be treated of shall each have the honour of a section to itself, nᵒˢ 112 and 81. N° 112 has already been noticed by Prof. Storm (S.M., p. 9) or rather it was Mr. H. Eitrem, now Rector at Haugesund who first, it would seem, called Prof. Storm's attention to the mistake in the then current text in this passage where, the eye of the printer (of 5) having been caught by the following line apparently, he substituted Det er Bøjgen som er død, for the correct reading: Det er Bøjgen som er saarløs, og Bøjgen som fik Men (¹). But it is U, Ibsen's first draft, that calls for a word of comment here. Ibsen had first written:

Bøjgen, Peer Gynt; en eneste en,
det er mig som er uskadt (²) og mig som fik Men,
det er mig som er død og mig som lever.

Then Ibsen crosses out mig four times, each time substituting Bøjgen for it, and changes uskadt first into menfri, and then into saarløs. So we must be doubly thankful that this "Smertensbarn" of Ibsen's, which it had cost him such pains to produce, is not now hid away any longer in the older editions which no one seems to consult any more—we shall presently find a very unexpected proof of this—but that it has been restored by Prof. Storm to all its pristine glory.

§ 58. When Peer Gynt after his nightly adventure with the three sæter-girls begins to feel the inevitable reaction, his head burns and he exclaims (to quote Mr. Ellis Robert's translation which is far the best I know of in any language):

---

ikke gerne kysse ham, she is also more impersonal, Daniel Hejre makes this quite clear in his remark: would y o u like to kiss him? Her "innate modesty" would not have allowed her to speak in the first person! But see Comm. n. to l. 3390.

(¹) And the wrong reading will be found echoed in several translations; that by Morgenstern (Passarge has properly gefeit = virtute magica imbutus), Brons and Count Prozor's le courbe frappé probably reflect død rather than saarløs. Archer's unwounded and Ellis Robert's untired are not very satisfactory in any case.

(²) The reading uskadt is tolerably certain, but not quite clear enough to speak with absolute certainty.

It beats on my brows as a bell, as
A red-hot ring of lead.
I cannot think who in hell has
Fastened it round my head!

These words render very satisfactorily the metre and very
excellently the sense of the original text as printed in most
modern editions:

Hu, hvor det værker i panden.
En brændende glohed ring—!
Jeg kan ikke mindes, hvem fanden
der bændte mig den omkring!

Until Prof. Storm brought out his memorial edition, the
immediately preceding texts had all presented a somewhat
different reading of the last line, where, under the influence no
doubt of the "brændende glohed ring", we find: "hvem fanden
der brændte mig den omkring!", hence such a rendering as
that of the German translation by Morgenstern: mit dem
Band, dem brennheissen um sich! Zum Satan! Wer hat mir
nur das u m g e b r a n n t! (p. 457). (¹)

Professor Storm has already told us, see the note on p. 9,
S. M. — that this "emendation (it would be better to speak of
a *restoration* as we shall see) is owing to a young learned philologist, Cand. mag. Hans Eitrem", (see § 57), and that the
mistake in question brændte for bændte did not come in until
the 10th edition as a "danish misunderstanding of Norwegian
bænde equalling English to bend;" (see S. I. S. p. 191: bændes
specifically Norwegian) and Prof. Storm compares a preceding
line in Peer Gynt: Peer Gynt eller jeg skal i bakken bændes.—

There is a good deal to be said here apropos of these remarks. First of all, it is a remarkable thing that neither Mr.
Eitrem nor Prof. Storm seems to have looked into any of the
earlier editions, at least closely looked into them, for as the
Professor tells us that the word *bændte* is properly found in

---

(¹) Much better is, as we shall presently find, Wörner's translation, given as in
passing (I¹, 224): Ein glühender Ring *presst* ihn um die Schläfe. —

1-9, it is to be presumed that either Storm or Eitrem, if not both, have really looked up these editions. But if so, it is incomprehensible that they have not seen that 1-4 print the second line as follows:

En bændende glohed ring—!

And it is our fifth edition that is responsible for the change of bændende into brændende. Hence my treating of the two questions, intimately connected as they are,— cf. n°s 81 and 82—here in this section, thus anticipating the one on the 10th ed.—

Considering that this fifth ed. came out in 1881, the reading En brændende glohed ring has now been before the public during thirty three years and we may therefore expect many a reader to feel this brændende glohed ring as something sacred, like the keepsake we inherit from a dear relative and it will perhaps for many a conservative mind require an effort to give it up and accustom itself to the bændende glohed ring. As a matter of fact, the first question many a student of Ibsen will ask himself, will be: is not bændende a misprint in 1? And I can even imagine that when hearing that bændende is found in R, he may ask: could it be a lapsus calami on the part of the author,—as to my personal knowledge some did actually ask themselves. And if not, we must explain first of all what bændende means here and secondly how it got corrupted into brændende. I will try to give a satisfactory answer to these several questions.

It is worth while to give in full the various elaborations that the expression of this thought has given rise to. Ibsen had first written:

Hu, det klemmer over Brynet;
værker, værker; hvem for Fanden,
skrued (1) mig denne Ring om Panden.—

---

(1) Skrued did not seem absolutely above suspicion in U, but as I afterwards found, Prof. Koht gives the same reading without any hesitation in the Efterladte Skrifter (II, 93), so there can be no doubt about it. Prof. Koht does not mention that the whole of this passage, as so many in U, is crossed over and scarcely legible without a great effort for the eye.

Ibsen crosses out the whole of the passage in which these lines occur and substitutes the following lines for them:

> Hu, hvor det værker i Panden.
> En bændende glohed Ring!—
> Jeg kan ikke mindes, hvem Fanden
> har bændet mig den omkring?

And let us now compare the passage in R, adding one line to those already quoted:

> Hvad Vægt paa mit Øjenbryn!
> Hu, hvor det værker i Panden.—
> En bændende glohed Ring—!
> Jeg kan ikke mindes hvem Fanden
> der bændte mig den omkring!

And one thing will then be beyond cavil at a glance, viz. that whatever the explanation of the world bændende, no rational doubt can exist as to its being the right reading.

As to the meaning of bænde, here too the comparison of the various passages gives us a very valuable hint and I am not quite sure that Prof. Storm's, (English) to bend and his comparison with the bændes i bakken will prove to have hit the mark. So far as the signification is concerned, if Prof. Storm intends to compare it to that of to bend and not the form only, I do not think that this line helps us much, although he is of course right (cf. *e.g.*: "nedunder fandt de ei stor svær steinhelle, og den var det ikke mer end saa de var karer til at *bænde av*", De tre Kongsdøtre i berg t det blaa, Asbjørnsen, No. Folkeev. 1914, p. 229). The bendes quoted would seem to be = that bendast, brydes med hinanden that Aasen and Ross give. The bænde of our passage may be Aasen's 2 binde, sætte Baand paa, which is there quoted from Smaalennene in v. benda [1]). But a better meaning, a better equivalent can be

---

[1]) I append in a note some suggestions from various correspondents that are sure to interest my readers.

Stavnem, on looking through this passage, gave it as his opinion that bendes might here be explained as klemmes, presses, trykkes, compares: lægge en i bakken

found. The Norwegian friend I consulted about this passage, Hr. Overlærer Stavnem of Stavanger, gave it at once as his first impression as well as as that of a colleague (to both the reading bændende was new) that the nearest approach to this use of bændende was Norwegian klemmende. After having first reminded me of bænde = stramme (s.m.l. substantivet bændestang, Huldreeventyr, p. 176 i Asbjørnsen's Plankekjørerne,=en stang hvormed surringsrepet strammes fastere om læsset), he suggested this klemmende, unaware at that moment how beautifully this suggestion would be borne out by the comparison of various texts. For it must now be apparent that bændende actually has taken the place of Klemmer[1]) over Brynet, just like bændte (for : har bændet) is the actual substitute of skrued. And if any doubt should remain, a line in Ibsen's first draft of Brand, (Episke Brand, 1. 252, ed. K. Larsen, p. 63 or Eft. Skrifter II, 14) will set it at rest. We read there:

Han kjendte som en Jernring klemt om Hodet. ([2])

= kaste en til jorden. If this is correct — and I would leave it to others to judge — bænde i bakken would contain the same verb as that in bændende glohed, but would not be = eng. to bend. He quotes "om kraftanstrengelser av forskjellig art", such expressions as: Spyt i Næven, hug Kløerne i, bænd og bryd, og lad mig se, hvad du duer til" and "Mumle bændte og brød med Øxen" (both from Asbjørnsen's Mumle Gaaseæg.).

Prof. W. B. Kristensen writes to say that he knows *bænde* = snore fast sammen" also from the Mandal-district.

But the most interesting suggestion regarding our passage and very characteristic for the mind of its author and his methods of interpretation, is that with which Prof. Chr. Collin (of Kristiania) favoured me and which I think it worth writing out in its entirety:

"Naar Ibsen skrev et for almindelige byfolk saa besynderlig ord som "bende" to gange i to linjer, maa det være fordi han fandt ordet særlig malende".... "Jeg har vanskelig ved at forklare mig Ibsens glæde ved dette ords uttryksfuldhet uten ved at anta, at han i sin barndom eller ungdom har hørt ordet brukt om at sætte baand paa (en tønde eller et kar), altsaa: baandsætte. Digteren maa, tror jeg, ha set for sig et anskuelig billede, av ringen (helst en jernring om et kar eller en fustage) som klemmer eller strammer om panden" after having been "av bødtker ophetet så den blir glohet." If we can imagine that he has *seen* this with his own eyes at Skien (I Skien var jo sagbruk) the expression would be "allerbedst fra kunstnerisk standpunkt."

([1]) Ibsen uses klemme in other places; cf. e.g. in Hærmændene paa Helgeland: der er noget som klemmer mig for bringen (F., II, 98) and : Ulivs-sår.... har min gamle bringe klemt (ib. II, 101).

([2]) Compare what Oswald says in Gengangere (F., VI, 431): Det var som om en trang jernring blev skruet om nakken og opover.

So bændende = klemmende, perhaps (see Collin in the note) with the notion of klemme, presse, trykke r o u n d a b a r r e l, baandsætte. And it is not very difficult to see either how it could get corrupted into brændende,—of course I do not say: how it must have got corrupted, for certainty is out of the question here, but what may have occasioned the change. The very word glohed that follows contains the notion of burning, which, added to the "nearness in form" of bændende to brændende, sufficiently accounts for the association of ideas and hence for the change; compare a little lower down in our drama: Jorden brænder mig som gloende Jern, says Peer Gynt when he wants a witness and an attest that he has always been himself. (F. p. 486; M. p. 290). And how near we are to this idea of burning here,—I may say, how near Ibsen himself was to using this very word, appears from a passage in the early Olaf Liljekrans where we read: Tre uger efter skulde vort bryllup stande—men det tykker mig at,— nej, det brænder i min pande! (F, vol. X, p. 97). In Catilina: Min pande brænder (F, 1, 58) and: det brænder og værker i mit hoved (Fru Inger til Østråt, F, 1, 372). But however close he came to it, he *did* not actually use it.

§ 59. To sum up, the fifth edition is responsible for 23 changes of which at most one may be looked upon as some sort of improvement and this fifth edition has moreover the (somewhat doubtful) honour of being that where the Gynt-hunter may run to earth the most elusive piece of quarry. N° 81 is one of the most interesting Gynt-puzzles the present writer has come across.

6.

§ 60. Two changes in 6 have been noticed before, viz. cases 167 and 342, the former a mistake, corrected later on by M; the latter, n° 342, one that to a certain extent may be looked upon as a correction, although we have no reason to suppose that in fact it was anything but chance that led to this return to R; see supra §§ 52 and 17.

§ 61. Cases 57, 189, 193, 227, 241, 298, 322, 325, 327, 366 and 371 have all reference to a change in punctuation, one of which (n° 57) having been noticed and corrected by Prof. Storm. How important these questions of punctuation sometimes are, appears clearly from a study of the translators here (n° 57). All that I have had occasion to consult seem to be under the influence of the point of interrogation here and take the Kitchen-Master's words as a hearty invitation to drink. But the point of interrogation makes Ibsen's meaning very clear in its delicate irony: the kitchenmaster who is far from pleased to see him, asks: Since you are here, I suppose you will take a drink too?, i.e. I suppose I h a v e to a s k you to take a drink,— "I hope you won't," would have expressed his meaning better. At any rate: the question is there and so should the point of interrogation be. All the other cases have found a definite place hitherto in all the later editions, except that in the case of n° 189, the full stop before Jeg having disappeared, the next edition but one, n° 8, almost inevitably changed Jeg into jeg,thereby spoiling the sense (however delicate the difference!) for good; the other cases do not call for any special comment.

§ 62. Nos 145, 285, 296, 347 and 360 are five Danicisms again, all introduced by 6 and corrected by Mr. Eitrem or Prof. Storm; cf. S.M. p. 11. With n° 145 cf. n° 134, ante, § 44; the difference between the two cases lies in the fact that in the latter case, the Danish form strakte was also too much for 15, although generally 15 follows M very closely. According to Prof. Storm, it is the Danish corrector who substituted ustyrlig for ustyrtelig. This would seem to suggest that ustyrtelig was misunderstood by him and t h e r e f o r e replaced by ustyrlig. It would however seem that the meaning ungovernable, unruly has had something to do with it, as it fits in very well at least with ungeflok (F, 447) and mængde (F, 474)—if one does not consider the context, as the compositors never do; cf. den ustyrlige kraft (F, VI, 463) but han tjente ustyrtelige penge (F, IV, 10) cf. n. to l. 3428.

§ 63. Nos 73, 87, 164, 275 and 380 are the most important mistakes: a substitution of gråd for tårer (73; cf. n. to l. 761, Comm.), blir for bliver (87, where the process of the change, or rather the progress of it, is interesting to follow), henkastet for

henkastende ([1]) (164), Det for der (275) and the addition of e r
in Naturen er ödsel (380); all of these unchanged in later editions, except that n°ˢ 73 and 380 having been noticed in my
Edda-paper, will be found corrected in 16.

§ 64. Summa summarum: 6 is responsible for one return
to R, and twenty-two mistakes.

7.

§ 65. Two mistakes of 7 (n°ˢ 87, 101) have been noticed
before, ante, §§ 63 and 54; the latter referring to the question
of punctuation. So do the bulk of the changes introduced by
this edition; cf. n°ˢ 26, 56, 83, 337 and 364, all five noticed and
corrected by Prof. Storm (cf. S.M. pp. 9 and 11) and further
n°ˢ 68, 74, 92, 156, 239, 272, 278 and 376, which he overlooked.
Mark especially n° 74 where the omission of the comma behind
utænkeligt is of some importance. In the case of n° 364, J. for
once introduces a new reading: spildt!

§ 66. Only two more cases remain, n°ˢ 280 and 357; on
which latter, see S.M. p. 11; Prof. Storm restores the form rent
(skejet ud) of R-6. The spacing of S a a in n° 280 will be
found to restore the necessary emphasis on the word.

§ 67. Seventeen changes, not one of which can by any
stretch of imagination be called an improvement, so all must
go to the debit-side.

8.

§ 68. Four cases of wrong punctuation (n°ˢ 87, 101, 189
and 207) have been noticed before; see supra §§ 65, 61, 39.
So has n° 55 (§ 48) where 8 introduces small capitals instead of
the spacing in Peer Gynt; on the same lines with the latter is
n° 318, and to a certain extent n° 108, a very important case
for the meaning, when the Bøjgen is asked: Hvem er du?
instead of Hvem er d u? cf. n°ˢ 109 and 110 and ante § 53
under 5; infra § 92.

§ 69. Three cases of wrong punctuation by 8 may be
grouped together here: n°ˢ 85, 114 and 283; the last noticed by

---

([1]) Cf. henkastende, used in Bygmester Solness (F, IX, 39); in J. G. Borkman
(F, IX, 336); in Dukkehjem (F, VI, 201) and in Når vi døde vågner (F, vol. X, p. 201).

Eitrem, cf. S.M. p. 11; n°s 85 and 114 unfortunately standing uncorrected to this day; especially the comma in n° 85 is important and should not have been omitted.

§ 70. N° 8 (Beduinerhøvding for Beduinhøvding), 194 (ynglen for yngelen), on the other hand videre for vidre (251), lige med instead of lig med (271) and Folk stimler om ham instead of flokken stimler ([1]) om ham (326) contain a comparatively moderate number of these downright mistakes ([2]) to which we have now gradually got accustomed. N° 326 was noticed in my Edda-paper und consequently corrected in 16.

§ 71. All in all: 8 has 15 changes to its debit, none to its credit.

9.

§ 72. Three cases of change in punctuation, n°s 140, 277 and 376, the last of which has been noticed before (§ 65).

§ 73. Case n° 229 (Tyrkeklæderne) has been noticed before, ante under 5; § 30, 42.

§ 74. N° 287 explains itself; I wish only to add that if U has de too, this is to be explained in connection with the fact that in the preceding line U has Unger—and not Unger!, which makes all the difference. For s a a vidt with spaced saa was changed by 9 into saa, unspaced (231).

§ 75. Cases 58, 138, 333 and 377, although of different degrees of importance, may conveniently be grouped together in one paragraph. In n[os] 138 and 377, 9 omits a word (da and med respectively), in n° 333 til slutning (quite usual in Ibsen, e.g. F, vol. X, pp. 13, 511) is unnecessarily changed into til slut (as in F, IX; 324, 355, 362, 429), and note in n° 58 the substitu-

---

([1]) Cf. de stimler sammen i store flokke (Kongsemnerne, F, II, 444). In itself, the expression Folk stimler is of course right enough, cf: Kan De se hvor folk stimler did, Sigurd Ibsen, Robert Frank, p. 79.

([2]) Of course here, as often in this investigation, mistake is used from the standpoint taken up of the desirability of faithful adherence to Ibsen's text. But they are not all to be placed on the same footing: with Ibsen's Beduiner by the side of Beduin which is the more common form we may perhaps compare his kulier by the side of the only usual kuli, cf. § 108, and the well known Rabbiner by the side of Rabbi?; cf. Comm. n. to l. 1970. The change ynglen is entirely uncalled for since even now yngelen is used. (Morgenbladet, 14 april 1914: Hvad torskeyngelen lever av.) Videre is now of course more common than vidre (cf. endvidre, n° 261, § 99). But the three others are downright mistakes from any point of view.

tion of the active inf. for the passive one; there is no note in
S.M. on the subject where we should expect it, p, 35, § 41;
cf. Comm. n. to l. 608.

§ 76. The ninth edition introduces 10 changes, all more or
less important mistakes.

10.

§ 77. Three changes by 10, one of punctuation (248) and
two of spelling (21 and 345) have already been commented
upon in §§ 17, 39, 40, 28; a fourth (n° 82): Jeg kan ikke mindes
hvem fanden der brændte mig den omkring, has been explained
anticipatorily in the section on 5, ante § 58.

§ 78. Our edition is further responsible for three lesser deviations from R in punctuation (n⁰ˢ 243, 247 and 286), —
possibly all three mistakes, though one may well doubt if the
comma in n° 243 (jeg) knejser og føler mig selv, som manden
Peer Gynt, ogsaa kaldt menneskelivets kejser,—if the comma
had not better be omitted as in 10, which would raise this
change to the dignity of a reading.

§ 79 But two more changes must be recorded,—n° 78,
where Trond i Valfjeldet will be found hidden away among the
more general Trold—by a very comprehensible association of
ideas—until Prof. Storm unearthed him again in M, and
another case of unspacing of some importance: E r jeg Kong
Apis (268) where the un-spaced er of 10-J, although apparently
supported by U, is of course to be rejected. The 16th ed. has
the right reading from my Edda-paper.

§ 80. Nine cases in all, of which but one, as we have seen,
is possibly a correction or rather a possible correction.

* * *

§ 81. The pagination of the various editions that have
been considered up till now was practically the same,—if we
but remember that in the first and second editions titles and
dramatis personæ, 4 pages in all, were counted apart and that
these were included in the pagination from the third edition
onwards; hence a constant difference of four pages in the
numbering of 1 and 2 as against 3-10. We were therefore

prepared for the conclusion that these considerations have have led up to: that of the editions considered hitherto, each is a more or less careless reprint of the preceding one. For F the case is not quite the same.

F.

§ 82. Here the pagination is n e c e s s a r i l y quite different, for F is the first collected edition of the poet's works and our drama begins neither at p. 1 nor at p. 5, but in the middle of a volume (III, p. 263). It is true that even here both editions (F as well as 10) containing as a rule the same number of lines on a page on the average, the Folkeudgave very often reprints the preceding one (10) page for page, but this is not quite so regular an occurrence as in 1-10. Yet here again we shall be unable to avoid the conclusion that F is mainly nothing but a not over careful reprint of its predecessor, 10. But we shall make the readers judge for themselves.

§ 83. Two cases (n°s 342 and 389) have already been mentioned; they both belong to the category of punctuation, as do also n°s 220 and 383, both observed and corrected by Prof. Storm, S. M. p. 11; only by an interesting mistake Prof. Storm attributes the incorrect reading to the 11th ed., whereas they are both found already in F. I call Prof. Storm's mistake "interesting" and the reason for this is worth pointing out. The fact is that Professor Storm says expressly (S. M. p. 3): Da det ærefulde hverv blev mig overdraget at gennemse og rette teksten i Hendrik Ibsens Samlede Værker (F o l k e u d g a - v e n, 1898 etc.) til t r y k n i n g a f d e n n y e "Minde- udgave", etc., where the spacing is of course mine. The mistake pointed out supra raises a first doubt as to whether Prof Storm has stuck to this plan of reprinting F. Our subsequent investigation will justify our doubt as to this statement and make it practically certain that an other text was used by the Professor, at any rate in the case of Peer Gynt.

§ 84. The fact that F was set up in a different type is the cause of the change in n°s 51 and 52 which speak for themselves. In n°s 252 F by mistake omits the words Peer Gynt (indicating that he is speaking the following lines) altogether; curiously enough not one of the subsequent editions has discovered this mistake, not even the editor of M.

§ 85. Cases nos 72, 75, 76, 93, 301 and 302 and nos 29 and 84 (chosen more or less at random; they might be multiplied almost ad infinitum) exemplify the love that F has for the accented é; it is here substituted for the spacing of the word in question in the former and for the ordinary e in an unstressed word in the latter batch.

§ 86. Of greater importance are three changes introduced by this text at the beginning of the drama. For De handlende (n° 1) F substitutes Personerne (¹), for (Første) Handling (n° 14) we get Akt (²) (of course also above each of the four subsequent acts) both apparently (although I cannot now investigate this) because in the Folkeudgave there should be uniformity in this as in other respects. And lastly, F by a sheer mistake substitutes daarekistemedlemmer (n° 9; a form that nearly provokes a smile; daarekistelem is certainly the more usual word as Ibsen himself elsewhere uses galehuslem) (³) for daarekistelemmer and is unfortunately followed by all subsequent texts, except 16—from my Edda-paper.

§ 87. If we do not count nos 1 and 14 as mistakes—which, whatever we may think of the change as such, it would be difficult to do—F's account stands as follows:

§ 88. 18 deviations, of which ten at least unnecessary if harmless; 6 downright mistakes, two that seem to be owing to the inclusion of our text in a collected edition.

II.

§ 89. The paragraph on this edition will be eloquently

(¹) Compare, de handlende personer, F, vol. X, p. 382, and: de optrædende personer, ib. p. 195 (Når vi døde vågner.)

(²) In a letter of March 8, 1867, Ibsen speaks of Handling (Breve, I, 149). In his earlier plays, Catilina, Rypen i Justedal, Sanct Hansnatten (E.S. I, 333, 339, 371) etc., Ibsen had himself used the word akt (spelled act in the cases quoted) but cf. Personerne, E.S. I, 340, 372.

(³) A galehuslem Peer Gynt calls den Fremmede (5th Act) and cf. familjelemmer (F, II, 252, Kjærlighedens Kom.); hospitalslem (F, VI, 218, Dukkehjem). If Welhaven had given Wergeland "rang blandt Parnassets daarekistemedlemmer" instead of daarekistelemmer (Nordahl Rolfsen, No. digtere, p. 226), he would no doubt have turned the tables unconsciously upon himself, causing his readers to ask if he were not ripe for the place too.

brief: it does not add a single mistake to those it unfortunately inherited from its predecessor F,—at least so far as those cases are concerned that I have been led to compare or investigate.

12.

§ 90. N° 167 has been touched on before in § 52 (de for De).

§ 91. Cases 86, 137, 260, 299, 300, 309 and 387 refer to punctuation and do not call for any special comment,—the omission of the dash in n° 299 is the most momentous of all. A similar misprint (F, p. 505, M, p. 300) is that, where instead of Min tid er knap;, den Magre is made to say Min tid er knap? which as it is only reprinted in 13 and did not go further was not noticed in our list.

§ 92. This text is particularly unfortunate with regard to the non-spacing of important words. See n°ˢ 110 (H v a d er du?), 116 (Hvor er h u n?), 182 (D e t er at være Gynt med ære), and 363 (Dette dovriske n o k) all of them rather serious cases; not one of them is corrected in any later edition; except 16, — my Edda-paper had pointed them out.

§ 93. Kongedatter (n° 136) for kongsdatter will be understood and by some condoned because of the many compounds with Konge ([1]) as analogues, whereas the form kongsdatter has but a few, such as Kongsemne and Kongsgaard to support it. Still, it should of course be restored. But there is no excuse whatever, it would seem, for cases 94 and 188: where kaldes for Konge and Lade Herren raade are made into kaldes Konge and Lad Herren raade; the context in the latter case will show clearly that lade is an infinitive: Og så *unde* ham frist. Lade herren råde; ikke *hænge* med ørene—. Ed. 16 has Lade again from my Edda-paper.

§ 94. The only change that will be very generally approved of, is n° 13.

The twelfth edition was the first to appear in the twentieth

---

[1] "Kongestormeren Nansen", Morgenbladet, 20 mai, 1914, is the latest addition I know of to those in the dictionaries.

century. Hence Ibsen's words "af dette Aarhundrede" might be misleading (¹) and were changed into: af det 19 Århundrede. But even here a change appears a ticklish thing. Why then keep all the time what follows: "and slutter henimod vore dage"? For if the student or reader of Peer Gynt may be trusted with so much discernment that "vore dage" means about 1867, surely "dette Aarhundrede" can cause no difficulty either? At any rate a note would have been desirable here and will be necessary in any critical edition.

§ 95. Summa summarum: 16 new deviations from Ibsen of which one only not quite uncalled-for and at least seven (§ 92 and 93) of importance.

13.

§ 96. To take, as usual, the punctuation-cases first, nᵒˢ 75, 105, 245, 264, 309 and 389, I have had occasion to mention

---

(¹) It will be noticed that the author had first written (in U): begynder i forrige og slutter i dette Aarh. which he there changes into: begynder i Förstningen af dette Aarhundrede og slutter henimod vore Dage, which he repeated in R. Ibsen seems to have thought that Peer Gynt actually lived at the end of the 18th and in the beginning of the 19th century; see his letter to Mr. Hegel of 8/8, 67 (Breve I, 151 "Hvis det kan interessere Dem at vide, så er Peer Gynt en virkelig Person, der har levet i Gudbrandsdalen, rimeligvis i Slutningen of forrige eller i Begyndelsen of dette årh." We know better now: he must have lived in the 17th century; see the paper by Per Aasmundstad in Syn og Segn for 1903. For although Aasmundstad's paper does not exactly make a very scholarly impression, the result would really seem to go far towards establishing his point. Peer is said to have lived at Kvam according to Asbjørnsen's version, but he appears to have been born at Søtorp quite close by. He may have been born, but of this we are not sure, at the very farm where he seems to have lived all his life: Nordre Haagaa as the dialect form runs, i. e. the riksmaal Hagen, the Garden. But there is reason to believe that it was formerly called Haugen, i. e. the Hill. After his father Ole (to add some further details about the "historical" Peer Gynt) he must have been called Peer Olsen, but after the farm: Peer Hagen, and indeed a huldre is reported to have actually adressed him thus. As to the name Gynt — see the n. to l. 3063 (Comm.). He seems to have been quite a big gun, for he possessed not only that farm at Søtorp but also various stuer, one of which is reported to have been used as late as 1858; it was the identical hut near the Atta-lake where tradition makes him meet the Boyg. The farm Hagen is now still in existence at least if report speaks true and known as the Peer Gynt-stue of the Sandvigske Samlinger at Lillehammer. Sandvig thinks it was built ab. 1660. (cf Sandvig p. 53). Readers of Dutch may be referred to a paper in the Tijdspiegel, 1915: Peer Gynt voor Ibsen. Count Prozor's opinion that Peer's dreams about his becoming an Emperor remind one of Napoleon, should be considered in connection with these dates. (Comte M. Prozor, Le Peer Gynt d'Ibsen, Paris, Mercure de France, 1897; pp. 16 and passim); cf. Comm. n. to l. 1981. And compare Jæger, 1892, p. 73: "Tidskolorit er Sekstiaarenes."

before; they are each and all of slight importance. Ed. 16 has for once the right punctuation, by mere chance it must be supposed,for the case is too insignificant to think of collation. The same must be said of at any rate the first four new cases, n°s 10, 246, 305 and 350. Cases n°s 192, 276, and 303 introduce a reading that really changes the meaning a little, however slightly. So does n° 330 where many would look upon the change as an improvement. Very unfortunate on the other hand was the introduction by 13 of a point of exclamation behind sejervinder, in n° 184, which makes perfect havoc of the distich:

> Jeg saa mig alt som sejervinder!
> i kreds af skönne Grækerinder!

Apart from the sense, or rather nonsense, the i (not: I) of the next line should have pointed to the mistake that, incredibly enough, is not even corrected by the editor of M; 16 corrects it from my Edda-paper.

§ 97. It will suffice to refer to n° 373 as well as n°s 131, 144 and 390; the last three constituting merely typographical errors, of arrangement of the text.

§ 98. Considering the care that Ibsen took, in R, to underline the words that he wished to be emphasised, 13 is singularly unfortunate in rendering the author's meaning in no less than 6 cases, n°s 96, 223, 265, 314, 351 and 381; some of these are very important, and not one of them is corrected by M, 14 or 15.

§ 99. Changes in the form of words by mere misprints are to be found in n°s 49 where Ibsen's kokkekoner (U: kokkekonerne) dwindle down to one single ‚kokkekone' (16 has the plural again from my Edda-paper); 91 (stærktbygget for stærkbygget, undoubtedly, as in U and R, and as in all texts, including 13-15!, in the first stage direction of the first act: en stærkbygget tyveaars Gut) (¹); 261, endvidere for endvidre,

---

(¹) Compare also en stærkbygget liden en, En Brudevielse, (F., vol. X, p. 410) and: Gallus, en smuk, stærkbygget ung mand (Kejser og Galilæer, first draft, Eft. Skr. II, 94) but in two words: stærkt bevæget samtale, (Fru Inger til Østråt F.. 1, 255 and in one, ib. 254: stærktbygget mand.

but cf. ante § 70; n° 99: the Danism en (¹) trold was too tempting here for 13; and I have little doubt that even n° 46: ringeagten for Ringagten is nothing but a misprint on the part of 13. For, whatever one may think of the form that Ibsen uses both in U and in R, Ringagten —many will no doubt look down upon Ringagten with something like the feeling expressed by the word itself—13 is not in the habit of correcting his text, so it is not likely that he should have done so here. Undoubtedly Ibsen's form represents the more colloquial slurring over of the e and might have been kept,—restored that is, by the editor of M. (²)

§ 100. Undoubted misprints are, on the contrary, nᵒˢ 121 and of course 106, bubro for hubro; the only remarkable thing about them is that they were kept by 14; see infra.

§ 101. Some very bad misprints must close this chapter of woes: 13 is responsible for the following substitutions of words: grædende for grundende (no 97) and straks for skraas (n°. 122) in which two cases Professor Storm, in M, fortunately gives us the correct words.

§ 102. This is unhappily not the case with the five following changes, some of which are rather important: Det for der in Der var den igjen (n° 120) which gives at least sense. So do cases nᵒˢ 197, 238 and 263, however amusing the result may be, as in 238: Møje og pengene værd which 13 changes into Möje og pungen værd. Here, J., for once has returned to the right reading, but 16, copying 15 and not finding it in my Edda-paper, prints pungen.

In n° 197 Peer Gynt wonders where he has read about: "Nok? Sig selv—?"—where was it?—i en saakaldt Storbog. Var det Huspostillen? Eller Salomons Ordbog? If we take these words about a dictionary literally it would almost seem as if 13 by using the form Salomo instead of Salomon, substituted by one bold stroke of the pen the celebrated Israelite King for that of the author of some sort of Encyclopædia

---

(¹) We find trolden also in Olaf Liljekrans (F., vol. X p. 103); but who guarantees that it is not a misprint there too? cf. § 53.

(²) In other plays Ibsen uses (at least the printed text, F, makes us think so!) the forms ringeagtende, ringeagtes, etc., F, VI, 145, 209, 230.

(such as Salmonsen's konversations-lexicon!!) where Peer
vaguely remembered to have read something about this "being-
self-sufficient". But of course no such dictionary is known—
Salmonsen was not published until much later, else we might
think of a good joke on the part of Peer to confound these
two!—and there can consequently be no doubt that Ibsen
thought of the wise king although the latter is usually called
Salomo in the Scandinavian countries, which will of course
turn out to be the very reason why 13 substituted that form.
That Ibsen used that form of the name which, if not exclusively used by Roman Catholics, is at least t h e common form
among them, is most likely owing to his having composed
Peer Gynt in that most Catholic of countries—Italy. In other
words, when Ibsen speaks of Salomons Ordbog, he can only
have been thinking of Salomos Ordsprog i.e. the Proverbs of
Solomon.—As to the reason *why* Ibsen did not actually use
ordsprog,—the rhyme would have been no objection—I confess to having been slightly puzzled at the outset. And when
I asked the opinion of a couple of Norwegian friends, one correspondent suggested a joke or ignorance, an other thought
that, as ord is often used more or less pregnantly for ordsprog,
so ordbog would be practically, and very pithily = ordsprog-
bog i. e. ordsprog. A third is apparently half inclined to look
upon this seemingly promiscuous use of the words ordsprog
and ordbog, or rather this use of ordbog instead of ordsprog as
one more proof (cf. ante § 38, *n* 1) given by Ibsen of Peer's
"half-culture".

So far I had come when I got the opportunity of comparing
the corresponding passage in Ibsen's first draft,—and here
once more U casts an unexpected and very welcome light on
our little problem. For we there see that Ibsen had first written

Nok? sig selv? Hvor er det, det staar,
Lad mig se; var det ikke i Salomons Ordsprog,
i Huspostillen eller slig en Storbog.

The words: var det ikke i Salomons Ordsprog are changed
first into det var en eller anden Storbog, then into det staar i en

saakaldt Storbog, whereas Ordsprog is corrected into Ordbog, and the words slig en Storbog are changed first into Salomons ordbog and later on again this Ordbog is corrected into Ordsprog. Moreover, in the same line i (Huspostillen) is changed first into enten i, later on into: var det Huspostillen). So one thing is quite certain viz. that it was not a m i s t a k e, i g-n o r a n c e, on the part of Ibsen. As to the other possibilities we can think of, although mathematical certainty is here as so often of course excluded, I incline to think that we have really as one of my correspondents guessed, a joke intended by the author to show that Peer had really a very superficial knowledge only. See ante § 38 on Peer's condescending attitude towards Goethe,—a splendid parallel to which is found in Kjærlighedens Komedie (F, ii, 241) where we find Styver clapping Goethe once more patronisingly on the shoulder as it were, when he says: Hvad siger ej etsteds geheimeraad (¹) Goethe," —for don't you see: Styver, if not quite a geheimrath, is at least very far advanced on the social ladder! And as to his poetic gifts,—when Falk says to him "Hvad vilde du paa den galej", namely of l o v e, he is quite puzzled and exclaims: Er elskov en galej? Comm. n. to l. 2500. So, Goethe and Styver, or I suppose, Styver and Goethe, are double colleagues. And Peer is thus delightfully characterised as another Styver.

To conclude: the change by 13 of Salomon into Salomo is absolutely uncalled for.

In n° 263, 13 omits i in: mig selv i et og (i) alt. It should of course be restored, although in other plays Ibsen uses i et og alt if his manuscripts have here been reproduced correctly; cf F, I, 263 (Inger); II, 174: (Kærlighedens kom.); and VI, 417: Gengangere.

But what shall we think of n° 183: Slaa smukt for Frihed og for Rett!, where our text introduces the perfectly absurd Saa instead of Slaa, reading: Jo mer De øger stridens brand, desbedre kan jeg buen spænde. Saa smukt for frihed og for ret! Löb storm! etc. This is left unchanged by M and the rest,

---

(¹) The German form geheimrath would fit so much better into the rhythm that one ventures to hope that it will prove to be in Ibsen's M.S. Or: geheimeraad von Goethe?!

16 inclusive. Only J. has somehow found out the mistake and corrected it.

Conclusion: 13 is a very careless reprint of 12. Of the 41 changes introduced two or three at the most will be either hailed with glee or at least passed, if not with great enthusi-asm, — the lowest estimate of the mistakes is thirty-eight.

M.

I.

§ 103. Whereas, as we have seen, each of the preceding editions was a mere reprint of the preceding one, at most sup-ervised very carelessly by a proofreader, we have now come to the first edition that boasts an Editor, and an editor with a highly respected name at that. Consequently the greatest number of changes will be found to be those introduced by Professor Storm in accordance with a system purposely adopt-ed and very consistently applied, and even if there should be found those that do not agree with the principles underlying the Editor's systematic changes, the objection can be formul-ated to the system only and no blame laid at the door of him who applies it. Still, as this investigation was undertaken to show how un-Ibsen-like a text the student of Ibsen has to work on, as the disagreement augments with every deviation from Ibsen's original text, a consideration and an appreciation of the systematic changes introduced into M falls within the scope of the present section of our commentary.

§ 104. The first question that will require an answer is whether M. like the other editions is a reprint of the immediately preceding one, in casu 13, or not. As we have seen in § 83, the Editor speaks about M. as if F. had throughout been the basis of his work of purification. But as that same paragraph also suggests in the case of Peer Gynt at least, it is difficult to ac-cept this statement without very important qualifications. Whatever M'.s source may have been for the other plays (and with those we have no concern) this investigation will make it abundantly clear that here too the immediately preceding edition, the 13th, was used as layer for the text of M. If any one wishes to maintain the contrary statement: that F. was really the source of M., he will have to explain how it is that nearly all the mistakes introduced by 11, 12, and 13, so by editions that are posterior to F, are also found in M. That would necessarily mean that M. had itself introduced as many as 3 other editions or at least that if, by the most remarkable of coincidences they were introduced independently by the printers of M., that the editor had overlooked them all when correcting his proofs. And let us remember that among these mistakes common to M on the one hand and 11, 12 or 13 on the other, are such glaring absurdities as: Saa smukt (n° 183; cf. § 102) apart from a good many others (n[os] 94, 136, 184, 188, 238 etc.) less important no doubt but still in their aggregate absolutely precluding chance or coincidence. And to mention orly those that are found in 13, n[os] 183 (Saa smukt), 197 (Salomo) and 238 (Pungen) are in themselves sufficient to show that the Editor of M., for which reason does not appear, did not stick to his plan of reprinting F. It is a great pity for with all its mistakes, F. is infinitely superior to 13, which it so happens is about the most slovenly reprint one can imagine.

§ 105. Now, if the Editor had only subjected his 13 to a searching examination, all would have been well. And this would have meant nothing more difficult than a collation with the first edition which the Editor had of course at his disposal and which he actually does quote in a comparatively large number of cases; see infra. A collation of R. would of course have been even more effectual but it is only fair to admit that in the case of this essentially popular edition, the need of such a collation with the M.S. may not have seemed so urgent and that at any rate it would have taken much, perhaps too much, time. Unfortunately 13 was reprinted without any attempt at a systematic collation, and the consequence is that all too many of the mistakes accumulated in the 14 preceding editions (1—13 and the Folkeudgave) were perpetuated in M. followed as we shall presently see, with very few exceptions by the rest. Of course Prof. Storm did eliminate very many mistakes — see infra §§ 127 seq. — but if his collations instead of being haphazard and few and far between, had been regular and thorough, his text might have a better chance of standing the wear and tear of time.

§ 106. If my reader will refer to n°. 167 and the discussion supra, § 52, he will see that in some cases misprints were found that the Editor detected in time to be corrected in a certain number of copies apparently struck off later; we have therefore practically two "sets" of M! Other cases are n°s 173 and 310; see S. M. p. 40, where in each of the three cases the copy of M. at my disposal at Ghent reads exactly as Prof. Storm tells us it should be corrected: De, udklarerte, føget, whereas other copies read: de, uklarerte, føged; in my notes this latter set is indicated as M^2 as chance threw it in my way in the second place. —

§ 107. Well, bad as it is, those mistakes were at least detected and corrected; it would have been better to print "corrected edition" or some such words on the title page of this second set of copies. But the Editor of M. or his printer is guilty of other mistakes, few in number may be, but rather grave in character. See n° 135, where M. is the first to introduce (Ringt eller) godt for gjildt, and especially n[os] 201 and 206. In the former case, M. prints the words Profeten er kommen! twice:

(p. 240) PIGERNES KOR. Profeten er kommen!

Profeten er kommen!

Profeten, herren, den alting vidende etc. whereas R.—13 have these words only once. In the second case M. inverts the order of two lines, printing (p. 242): Stop!

Sig dem, jeg hører i afstand deres bønner.

Sig dem, de kan i afstand troppe op;

where in R.—13 our third line ending in op precedes our second one ending in bønner. This is rather bad and I have in vain tried to think of an excuse, i. e. an explanation how such a mistake can be accounted for.

In either case, M. is here followed by the rest except that 16 corrects both after my Edda-paper.—

§ 108. N°s. 4, 158, 171, 174, 210 and 370 may conveniently be treated together. Here the Editor changes Ibsen's Master

Cotton, Stewart, Charlstown, Kulier, Houri and Brama into
Mr. Cotton, steward, Charleston, kuli, huri and Brahma; see
S. M. p. p. 10, 11; (on Brahma also p. 14) and no one will like
to contest that in each case Prof. Storm has substituted a correct form for an incorrect one used by Ibsen. But we may well
ask if the Editor was justified in so doing; the question at
issue is a large one, which dominates the whole body of changes
introduced by the Editor's system.

§ 109. From a philological point of view, few will deem it
going too far when I maintain that critical acumen, when e-
mending a text, must drawn the line at the correction of the
author. And the reason for this is clear. If we break through
this rule und correct not the text but the author, we introduce
the thin end of the wedge that will ultimately serve to cut
down the most solid tree of all sound philology. When in the
case of a seventh-rate author a mistake is corrected away by a
printer,—well, the mischief done, if any, is a negligible quantity. But as a matter of principle it should not even be tolerat-
ed there and certainly not in the case of a star of the first
magnitude such as the one we are dealing with. To correct
away his mistakes is the introduction of the vicious circle, the
Boyg of philology, that we have all met with in some form or
other, or shall we say: in some formlessness or other, and which
mutatis mutandis, consists in saying: Jones is a great writer.
A great writer could not commit such a stupid mistake. The
great writer did not commit such a stupid mistake. This stupid
mistake is not the great author's. Delete the stupid mistake,
— and when this is done and the text has been "emended"
Jones is of course great and the critic is his prophet.

Far from me the desire to suggest even, that Prof. Storm
should have been guilty of this or a similar reasoning. But
precisely because all who know him must think him incapable
of it, the pleasant possibility remains that the Editor of M.
and the present writer may agree about this question of principle: the process of correcting an author is unscientific. If we
change the author's words or forms, in any case those he has
deliberately adopted, we try to stop the very life of language,
for a living language is a changing language and what may

seem a mistake to day is quite common to-morrow and a possible current, nay, who knows?, the only "proper" form of the future. In a paper that Ibsen wrote in the autumn of 1862 and which Mr. Eitrem has recently reproduced in the Morgenblad (Aug. 1916, etc.), I find a passage that is worth reprinting. In connection with a representation of Øhlenschläger's „Axel og Valborg" he wrote: „Naar Theatret bringer Øhlenschlägers Stykker paa Scenen, saa bør det skee med kritisk Hensyn til de forskjellige Udgaver; Originaludgaverne bør vistnok lægges til Grund, men enkelte af Forfatteren senere foretagne Forandringer maa dog ansees som Forbedringer og bør da ogsaa paaagtes". It is interesting to find that Ibsen insists upon the value of the changes introduced by the author and here no one will presumably be inclined to contest his position. More problematic on the contrary is what follows, when, having laid down that absurdities (such as: that the Danish for Vilhelm is Vilhjalmur) should be omitted, he decrees that „before all, patent mistakes might be corrected — fremfor Alt aabenbare Feil (kunde uden Skade) rettes". This recalls almost in the very words used, Professor Storm's „Vitterlige Fejl" that had to be corrected.

„Dette er imidlertid ikke gjort; Axel taler saaledes om Druiden, som sidder i Træet og ryster sine grønne Lokker", uagtet Kritiken allerede for mange Aar siden har paatalt denne Urimelighed. Digteren har naturligvis ment „Dryaden". What Ibsen actually does say, is that such mistakes might be corrected without any risk, but it is more than probable that what he meant was that he approves of such a proceeding, which would seem grist to the mill of those who attack the position taken up here in this discussion. If further investigation should really prove Ibsen to be on their side, my position would be considerably weakened but I should still be in honesty bound to make them a present of the argument. I would however have them reflect before they count too much on the author's aid. For it must seem clear that there is something understood by the context, *viz.* that such things may be corrected as in the case of the first paragraph, when approved

by the author. But apart from this, what does away with any value Ibsen's words might have had for my opponents, is that the accuracy of the original text with a view to a representation is to be put on a level with the needs of the General Reader which are admittedly entirely different from those of the student of Ibsen-philology.

But I can imagine that some of my readers would have liked to stop this flow of eloquence to see if the whole question at issue is not precisely one of difference of "view-point", only. If Professor Storm can reconcile his duty as an editor for the masses (of the General Reader) to his conscience as a philologist i. e. a leader of classes, — of students of philology, why should he not do so? The answer to the imaginary question asked is of course affirmative and it gives me the welcome opportunity of once more giving expression to what I hope to have made clear even if I have not expressly said so before, *viz.* that my quarrel is not with a person, and certainly not with so highly esteemed a one as the Editor of M., but with a system, a system that may have, nay that *has* its value for those readers who are shocked at the inconsistencies that are no doubt frequent in Ibsen's manuscripts, and who require a text which they can enjoy for the sake of what he says, without having their attention called to peculiarities in the way by which that meaning is conveyed. But this discussion of a question of principle was necessary, the main purpose of this study being to show that, however great may be the merits of M. for the General Reader, the needs of the Ibsen-*philologist* have been sadly neglected and that it is high time to provide him with the pabulum he requires.

II.

§ 110. Some points in Professor Storm's Ibsen-canon (S. M. p. 3.: Inledning) must be reproduced here and discussed.

1. The text of the original editions should be re-introduced where mistakes have crept into the later ones.

We have already seen that this process of reproducing the original text has not been carried out at all consistently.

Nothing short of a full collation of the first ed. or the Ms. (§ 105) would have been required.

2. What must be acknowledged to be nothing but a mistake in the author (vitterlige fejl) are corrected, e. g. wrong genders. This standpoint has already been discussed. But it may be as well to ask if this process of changing the author does not also, apart from its being anti-scientific, bring the perpetrator into practical difficulties? For if once we begin, where should we stop? These vitterlige fejl are corrected Prof. Storm had said, "når dette kan ske på en lempelig måde." Many a reader will be inclined to object in Ibsen's own words: "Lempe er vold", — as some cases will show: e. g. where Ibsen had written Bramafigurer. Prof. Storm introduces the form Brahmafigurer, but hesitates at Buddhafigurer, which — we can see his fingers itch — "would have been" the correct thing. Oh! the misery of the would-have-been's unrealised ideal! — And Ibsen speaks (quite wrongly of course as Professor Storm points out) of Sir Gynt, and the Professor adds: This barbaric title cannot possibly be changed (lar sig ikke forandre); but this means, I suppose, that if the metre had allowed of the change, it would have been introduced? At any rate, it requires very little ear to hear the Editor's inaudible sigh at this impossibility to change. Considering that Ibsen allowed these mistakes (as some of them undoubtedly are) to stand in I, would it not have been better to leave them alone too? And it is interesting to consider this question in connection with the third point:

3. The forms of language are essentially Ibsen's own, carried through with greater consistency (Sprogformen er væsentlig Ibsens egen, gennemført med noget større konsekvens) and then comes an utterance that I cannot but look upon as in flagrant contradiction with all that precedes (i. e. that follows in S. M.): In cases where the author and language waver, that wavering is reproduced!

How can this be that the orthography and forms adopted should on the one hand carry out certain rules with full consistency and on the other, respect the wavering of the author between two (or more) forms?

If the Editor had acted up to this professed respect for Ibsen's dual forms, a great part of the following remarks need not have been written. Unfortunately these principles which we can but applaud, have in the great majority of cases given way for the process of levelling in the sacrosanct name of consistency. Hence:

4. "Obsolete and unusual forms have been corrected",— which a good many will find it difficult to approve, — and I wonder whether Ibsen himself would have done so? And yet this is what Professor Storm suggests when he says: "On the whole I have tried to set to my task with the greatest piety and discretion. I have but changed what I think the author himself would have changed on further investigation if he had lived."

It is owing to this wavering between theory and practice that the Editor of M. introduces the greater part of the changes that I shall now briefly have to discuss.

§ 111. Ibsen uses æ (in R) in Kværnehus (16), Sælet (79), mælken (202) and Kjæltringstreger (346) where M. introduces e (§ 56; in F. IV, 9 we also find Kæltringstreger). With regard to 79, it is interesting to note that in R., æ seems to have been corrected from e and that in U., Selet and Sælet are both used. On the other hand, in Fortred (28) and saamen (163) Ibsen's e is changed by M. into æ. Note that in saamen, en in R. is corrected from another letter and that U actually has Fortræd. For beer (32) M. substitutes ber. In his Norsk Sprog (1896, p. 12) Prof. Storm quotes beer, be'r, bér, ber as four forms all used by Ibsen. Ibsen's beer is certainly inconsistent: for ter (230) U has yet teer, but even M. keeps Peer which it seems Ibsen did not want to give up. This ter (230) was already changed by 2 into tér (§ 25). And as we have seen Ibsen himself often accented such an e; so it is not without authority that M. introduces this in nos. 19, 20, 22 and passim. See especially n°. 147 and ante § 37. Some hesitation may be observed in his older writings too. Thus in the Fjeldfuglen, Eft. Skr. I., we find vént (p. 445) by the side of vent (p. 440).

§ 112. M. changes faer, taer and gier (23, 27, 166, etc.) into far, tar, gir, although Ibsen himself had left these unchanged in I. And *for* as Ibsen had written in I (n° 21) instead of foer of U, R.-2, is changed by M. into fór. M. does not seem to like the apostrophe that Ibsen had written in such forms as ha'e and bra' (45, 49) and in bær' (70 in U as well as in R) and that Ibsen had introduced (in I) into that selfsame bær, the misprint (in 2) for bærer (cf. n°. 71, ante § 23).

§ 113. Ibsen had written tæerne and knæerne (329) both in U and in R and kept these forms when preparing I. On the other hand, we find løvtrær (15, 88, both in U and R.) As Professor Storm professes to respect the author's wavering, he might well have left these forms unchanged. The most recent practice, I think, would seem to go in favour of trær, tær, knær, etc. so that if any levelling is necessary, the latter form may with advantage be chosen, as Professor Storm has actually done. The same holds good of houg and stout (n°ˢ. 3, 38), where M. introduces the modern haug and staut, — there and passim. In Sct. Hansnatten Ibsen himself had wavered between Haug and Houg; cf. Eft. Skr. I, 394, 395 etc.

§ 114. Case 289, I think, is somewhat more dubious. Both in U. and R. Ibsen writes vogsomt. Ibsen often interchanges o and aa (cf. infra) and moreover Ross gives voga as a by-form of vaaga, "Tel. sjelden"; yet Prof. Storm rejects vogsomt for vågsom, S. M. pp. 11, 28, on the ground that vogsom is "hverken norsk eller dansk", and that although in his "Ibsen og det Norske Sprog" (S. I. S.) p. 147, he had quoted vogsom as a more "folkelig" form; whereas voga was there admitted to be elder Danish (Peder Syv's Kjæmpeviser). So it should surely have been kept as a peculiar Ibsen-form? [1]. Similarly Konster is rejected as gammeldansk (S.M. p. 9); it is however used as late as Ibsen's own time, Ingemann uses both konst and konstig in his Fire Rubiner (pp. 21, 30, 33.).

---

[1] In his first draft, Ibsen writes voghals, Eft. Skr. II, 94 (U. b. ad 9/4). But both in earlier and later works, I find (at least in the printed texts, even those before M.) the form vovsom(t), Hærmændene, F. II, 104; vovhalse, Kongsemnerne, F, II, 463 (Danish vovehals, Ordb. over gadesproget) and Dette er vovsomt, Samfundets Stötter, F. VI., 115. Landstad (Folkeviser, p. 380) has vágehals. — I find vaage sig in Riksmaalsbladet, July 4, '14 quoted from Den 17e Mai: "fordi vi har vaaget os til at staa paa bondesiden i denne sak". In Rypen i Justedal (Eft. Skr. I, 364) Ibsen wrote both voge and vaage (= to watch), here merely quoted to illustrate his wavering in spelling.

And it is the usual spelling in one of Ibsens's possible sources, viz. Paludan Müller's Adam Homo, I, 39 [1]). Moreover, apart from the fact that it might also have been used under Swedish influence and Ibsen's Swedish forms cannot be extirpated without more ado, it is actually found in the eastern Norwegian dialects, both as konst and kaanst; cf Ross, p. 418. M. also changes Ibsen's Aannen (18) into onnen, and his Folgefaannen into Folgefonnen (n° 279). With regard to the latter word it may be interesting to state that Ibsen had first written it Folgefonden in U. and in R. He then (in the m.s. of R.) changed it into Folgefaannen, (twice, in the text and in the margin, and in I., Ibsen writes Folgefånnen; yet this deliberately constituted reading is changed by M. It is true that in Till de Medskyldige, Ibsen had written first faan and faann (l. 3, cf. Karl Larsen, Episke Brand, p.p. 46 and 47, and later on, l. 394) fonnen, but this merely illustrates Ibsen's wavering. In Toget til Ulrikken, Eft. Skr. I, 124, I find Folgefonden, but the orthography of the Eft. Skr. has been tampered with; cf. ib. III, 338. It does not therefore seem safe to conclude that the master himself would have changed this if he had lived See the Comm., n. to l. 622.

§ 115. Turning from the vowels to the consonants, we find that in n°⁵ 62, 95, 146 and 345 Ibsen had not only not changed the double consonant (in I) of nödd, lægg and dugg but had clearly indicated that on reflection he wished them to stand. Compare ante § 28, n. And as a matter of fact, usage has always been wavering in this respect, so much so that even now (with the possible exception of dugg?) these words may be found written with a single or a double consonant. So why should M. „correct" Ibsen here? See also cases 217 and 331 udrapert and drapiren, for Ibsen's udrappert and drappi(e)ren; here M. is at least in accordance with modern usage, if not with Ibsen. Similarly, (han) sprutter (n° 80) is changed to spruter, because sprute is the Norwegian form and sprutte is Danish. (S.M. p. 9 refers to Ny Retskr. II, 64, but the reference must be wrong; for there is nothing to be

---

[1]) Even Lynner, Hærmændene paa Helgeland, p. 55 still writes: skaldekonsten.

found). If we were to eliminate all Ibsen's Danisms, a good deal more would in all consistency have to be changed; it would moreover amount to a suggestio falsi; or rather we should not only be suggesting but creating a falsum, for Ibsen was not averse to Danish words or forms; see supra § 26, end.—M. is also the first to change Engelland to Engeland; see n° 40; S.M. p. 9 and Comm. n. to l. 498.

§ 116. The changes in n°s 168, 172, 203, 213 and 359 (Metodisk, konsekvenserne, ur, lut and ting for methodisk, konsekventserne, uhr, luth and thing) are at least all in accordance with modern usage; and yet, although it is impossible to say that Ibsen might not have approved of them, it is a fact that he did not actually do so, at least in 1874, for he left the forms in I.

§ 117. Cases 24, 42, 64, 100 and 170 should be considered together, where Ibsen uses the form Karl three times in R., against once kar'; of the three times that the corresponding passage is found in U., Ibsen uses once Karl, once Kar, without the apostrophe and once G u t. Professor Storm, doubtless in perfect accordance with modern usage, evidently favours the more colloquial kar [1]), but in n°s 100 and 170, copying the 13th ed., he prints karl; 14 improves upon M. here, changing it into kar. As Ibsen actually once wrote Kar in U., and Kar' in R., I think we have a right to conclude that the author *heard* the word as kar, even when writing it traditionally with an l, so if anywhere, the levelling of the orthography is to be approved of here, but why leave karl in one case?

§ 118. As to the word for goat (in N°s 69, 216 and 244), Ibsen wavers between Gjet (69, U. and R.) and Gjed (U. and R. in 216 and 244), but it should be remembered that Ibsen unambiguously decided for the d; see supra, § 33. Where is Professor Storm's respect for the author's wavering when in each case he prints get? Note that it is not of course until the spelling reform of 1907 that the „hard consonants" have become general.

§ 119. The next, rather numerous, group of changes in-

---

[1]) Kar without the l is already found in Bjerregaard; cf. Seip, Wergeland p. 25.

troduced by M. in the matter of consonants, shall be considered here from the point of view in how far the changes are in accordance with later use.

§ 120. Thus in nᵒˢ 17 (stanse for standse), 30 (snau for snaud), 50 (ænse for ændse and so passim), 190 (akacier for akazier (¹), 256 (tysk for tydsk), 292 (luen for luven (²), 307 (Lom for Lomb), 323 (felden for fellen) 328 (San Francisco for San Franzisco), 335 (Nebukadnesar for Nebukadnezar) and 339 (hærje for hærge, (³) all the spellings introduced are those used largely if not exclusively at present, which consideration, if it does not entirely remove any objection we may feel to the change, certainly mitigates it to some extent.

§ 121. In the case of nᵒˢ 43 (M's seks for sex; cf § 28 *n*), 123 (mylder for mylr (⁴), 180 (eksemplar for exemplar), 274, 290 (duger for duer), 295 (eks. for ex.), 304 (vekt for vegt) (⁵), 336 (gök for gjög) and 353 (tilgagns for Ibsen's tillgavns) usage is even now hesitating, the two forms being found by the side of each other. Observe that in the case of sex (nᵒ 43) Ibsen had first changed the x into ks (in I) and then re-corrected it again both in the text and in the margin, so it would seem clearly enough that Ibsen did nót desire to change.

§ 122. In the case of nᵒˢ 257 (flugs for flux, changed into fluks), 311 (skardet for skaret) and 291, 319, 379 (stads for stas) modern usage goes largely if not entirely against the forms introduced by M., so it is difficult to see on which ground they can be defended. However in Ep. Brand (l. 586) Ibsen himself had actually changed skaret into skardet!—

§ 123. The next group is that of the adverbs. In each of these cases (nᵒˢ 67, 103, 214, 250, 297, 343, 367 and 368) Ibsen's t-forms (of R. and U; only once, in nᵒ 367, U favours the

---

(¹) Juels Tønnesen spells it with an s.

(²) Not only that Ibsen writes this word (= a cap) Luven in R., but he has actually changed what would seem to be the only "correct" spelling Luen (in U) into Luven by adding a *v*.

(³) In F. X p. 13, I find hærjed twice, but the spelling may have been modernised there too.

(⁴) In the Ballonbrev (F. IV, 386): i et mylr, som kaver, stunder, the rhythm precludes all change.

(⁵) Veke is found in Gildet paa Solhoug (F. II, 170) and Kongsemnerne (F. II, 472).

t-less form) such as inderligt, voldeligt etc. are changed into inderlig, voldelig etc. (¹) See S.M. p. 36, § 45 where Prof. Storm's reasons will be found indicated. While one notes there with satisfaction that under *a*, adverbs of manner, Ibsen's wavering is recognised and for once respected, curiously enough, under *b*, and *c*, Ibsen is found fault with and corrected because he sins against „uniform usage" (fast sprogbrug)! As to *a*, adv. of manner, although Ibsen's right to use the form he likes is expressly recognised there, nᵒˢ 67, 103, 250, 297, 343, 367 and 368 mentioned above, all adverbs of manner, are yet corrected by M.,—comprenne qui pourra. And as to the „fast sprogbrug", it is certainly surprising to find that the authority invoked there for Norwegian is not a Norwegian, e.g. the editor himself, which no one would have been shocked at, but Mikkelsen's—D a n s k sproglære! We need not go quite so far as Vinje who wept when his teacher held up Molbech's Danish dictionary as the authority for Norwegian usage (²), but the proceeding can hardly be admitted. Moreover what Prof. Storm quotes as u n i f o r m usage will be found qualified in Mikkelsen himself, by such expressions as: usually, commonly etc.

§ 124. As to recent usage here, even if Poestion (Lehrbuch der Norwegischen Sprache, § 212, p. 153) undoubtedly goes too far when he hints that there is never any difference between the adverbial and adj. forms in the case of *-ig* and *-lig*; in other words that t is never added there, certain it is that the present tendency lies in this direction and that ere long the t may possibly, with so much else that smacks of Danish or Riksmaal be a l w a y s omitted there. This may constitute an excellent e x c u s e for Prof. Storm's changes, I do not think it a r e a s-o n.—Here a place may be found for n° 154, where Ibsen's Granene will be found changed into granerne, although (S.M. p. 31, 32, § 33), the two forms are quoted as existing side by side.

§ 125. The mistakes in gender are corrected by M. Hence et (trold) for en, as the Danish printers made Ibsen say; cf.

(¹) The uvillig of U, R, and the earlier editions (l. 728; cf. ante, § 4) was changed later on (F, etc.) into uvilligt.

(²) "Vinje gret mang ein gong nær læraren tok fram Molbechs danske Ordbok og viste paa det som der var set upp till mynster." Koht, Gran's Nordmænd, III, p. 6.

n°s 2, 65, 99 and passim. So this is one of the many restitutions of the author's reading (cf. infra § 127). Such is not the case with n°s 48 and 236, where Ibsen's en (mylder) is changed into et, and ingen Besvær into intet besvær; both cases in accordance with modern usage. (Når vi døde vågner: midt i mylderet, F, X, p. 277). But considering that Brynildsen recognises both firbenen and firbenet (in his first and second editions) it would seem that even from Prof. Storm's own standpoint there is no reason for the change in n° 196; see Comm. n. to l. 2356.

§ 126. Cases 31, 35, and 352 exemplify S.M. p. 19, § 2, all three it would seem in accordance with later usage,—with regard to 352, minsæl for Ibsen's min Sæl of R., it is interesting to see what may seem grist on Professor Storm's mill, that U had minsæl in one word; we have in reality a case of Storm versus Ibsen, on which see lower down.

Conversely, Ibsen's compound or at least composite forms such as tillslut (129), allerbedste (152), Pundsterling (205), iligemaade (315), ivare (354), and engang (355) are cut up into their component parts. As Prof. Storm recognises himself at least in the case of allerbedste (S.M. § 2, f., p. 22) that it is „often" written aller bedst, he implies that this is not always so (^{1}); hence in accordance with his own principles of toleration, that form at least should not have been ruled out of court. And here I may insert a word on case n° 143, where we find Ibsen's af Dage in Du blir Faer din opp af Dage changed into op ad dage,—as a matter of course, many a reader will be inclined to add, for Ibsen's form is "wrong"! Well, yes, perhaps so,—from a certain point of view it is certainly wrong. But as King Canute could not stay the sea in its real motion, nor Marlowe's Faust like another Joshua the sun in its imaginary one,—so surely it is a hazardous undertaking to try and stay the usual trend of language,—after all, changes will take place and it is perhaps safer to recognise them when they find expression in an author like ours.

In S.M. p. 36, (§ 47) it is admitted that af is often used for ad,

---

(^{1}) cf. Eft. Skr. I, 225, 228, where we find both isaahenseende and i saa Henseende.

but af Dage is corrected as one of the more shocking cases. I wish to add that U. actually had ad Dage! This may at first seem to be a (much required) justification for the professor's standpoint. But I should like to ask: if Ibsen wrote ad Dage first and thén: af Dage, does not this look like a deliberate change that should make us pause all the more before we alter again? See above the discussion of min Sæl, n° 352. The substitution is of course owing to the fact that both af Dage (ta sig af Dage) and ad Dage were pronounced with an enclitic a'; by a precisely similar process English of and on were ground down into an equally stressless, enclitic, o', and hence a very frequent confusion of *on* and *of*; see e.g. N.E.D. in voce o, o' sub c. Similarly Dano-norwegian og and at have both dwindled down to o' and hence such „mistakes" as the following from Bjørnson: „hver gang han skulde til og tale", where og of course stands for o' =at, every time he should begin *to* speak (Jespersen, En sproglig værdiforskydning, Dania, III, 145, and compare Språk ock Stil, 1901 p. 82). Where would Jespersen's paper be—and philology altogether—if all such examples had been „edited away"? And it should be noted that „op *af* dage" is quite common and recognised e.g. by Brynildsen. See my Commentary, n. to l. 1542.

III.

§ 127. It feels like a relief to turn from these criticisms to the consideration of that long list of cases where Professor Storm has restored the reading of the original text. It is impossible not to admire (and perhaps even not to envy) the „flair" with which, precisely because he did not undertake a systematic collation of the older editions, he must be supposed to have scented and hunted out the right reading.

§ 128. The cases exemplifying this have nearly all been touched on already in the preceding paragraphs, but I enumerate them here for the sake of completeness: 10, 26, 34, 53, 54, 56, 57, 83, 86, 89, 139, 169, 219, 234, 283, 320, 337, 364 and 383, and refer to S M. p.p. 9—11, 24, 39—40 for Prof. Storm's notes on them. Only in n°ˢ 105, 245, 248, 309, 356 and 389 does the punctuation in M. differ from the original one; all these cases will be found to be of little or no interest. See also cases 51 and 52, and Comm. n. to l. 567.

§ 129. Coming to some cases of punctuation that have not yet been noticed, I refer to n° 60 where Prof. Storm has once more scented out the original punctuation, whereas in cases 640, 249, 253, 267, 273 and 334 this is not the case. Of course most of them are again of little interest; yet the presence or absence of a little dash behind a word (as in 249, 267, where M's reading is that of U!) may often be of some importance and should at least be noted. In n° 253, the proper punctuation was restored in M², but it appears to be the wrong text (M¹) that the subsequent editions follow. The points raised by nᵒˢ 128, 130 and 273 are interesting, see on the latter S.M. p. 11 and especially p. 22 seq. Her er Noter, som skal besvares?, Ibsen had written where M. has a point of exclamation after besvares instead of a point of interrogation. Does the case belong (S.M. p. 24) to category d or e? Let the reader try to give an answer to this question; I have not been able to do so, but precisely when this is so, and especially in connection with the fact that Ibsen's punctuation is somewhat whimsical (Storm l.l.),—„hands off" would here too seem to be the best policy. As to nᵒˢ 128 and 130, see S.M. p. 10, where it is remarked that instead of han, Peer, blev jer dyr (¹), it would be better and more idiomatic to write: han Peer blev jer dyr. Now, it is interesting to find that the comma in the Ms. is somewhat thinner and possibly in paler ink than otherwise, as if added later on and blotted at once. This, if so, will to some at least seem to speak rather strongly in favour of Ibsen's express desire not to have this interpreted as the popular Norwegian han Peer, although it might conceivably be construed differently. But when Professor Storm goes on to suggest that (in case 130) we must read: Gud forlade ham Jon, instead of ham, Jon, I wonder whether he does not go a little too far. Here again I note it is just possible that the comma was added later on, although the ink is certainly not paler, whatever deductions we may wish to make from this circumstance. But should it

---

(¹) cf. in J. G. Borkman: han blev sine venner en dyr ven, — han, John Gabriel (F. IX, 334); cf. Comm. n. to l. 1382.

not be Gud forlade han Jon, if we omit the comma? See the Comm. to l. 267.

§ 130. Cases 39 (nejer), 82 (bændte; cf. 81), 97 (grundende), 106 (hubro), 112 (saarløs), 121 (barktækt), 122 (skraas), 124 (kiger; cf. no. 36), 134, 145 (strake) 191 (klyve), 285, 296 (ustyrtelig), 347 (heder), 357 (rent) and 361 (Men dattersøn) all exemplify the Editor's desire to restore or keep (361) as much as possible Ibsen's own words instead of the Danisms and other changes that had actually crept into the text, or, as in the last mentioned case, threatened to creep in. This last case is interesting; it should have been mentioned in my list between n°s 357 and 358 in connection with a preceding passage: Men Dattersøn er bleven baade fed og stor, on which see S.M. p. 40 and also (on our case n° 361) p. 11. As Prof. Storm observes (on p. 40), the 9th ed. changed this Men into min and this was not changed again until in M. It appears from S.M. p. 11 that others have actually proposed to change the men in Men dattersøns afkom also into min,—Professor Storm argues that as men is necessary „for at betegne modsætningen" and „dattersøn er efter norsk sprogbrug at opfatte bestemt" there is no need for a change. Moreover that Ibsen did write Men in each case, is here corroborated by a reference to the manuscript,—one of the two cases where that was consulted by, or rather for, Prof. Storm (see S.M. p. 16). We may compare Kristenmands søn without any article or pronoun (F. p. 328 and M. p. 198) and Salig provstinden (F. p, 370 and M. p. 220) but see Comm., n. to l. 1001.

§ 131. If then, we must sum up, it should be said that the text of M. if judged from the standpoint of the Editor, i.e. from that of the General Reader has some advantages over its predecessors, and it introduces but three (uncorrected, grave) mistakes of its own. Only, as unfortunately without due systematic collation of the earlier texts, or the manuscript, it reprinted a very corrupt text (ed. 13) of which but very few mistakes were found out, it must be pronounced quite unreliable as not reproducing Ibsen's text at all faithfully. And the system adopted is one that certainly cannot stand the test of criticism from an other point of view — that of philology.

14.

§ 132. A single look into this edition will show that it is practically a reprint of 13, with almost the same pagination,—just as 15 will be found in nearly the same way to be a page for page reprint of 14, and 16 of 15,—with but very few deviations in this respect. Only, although 14 has copied 13, it must have instituted a sort of haphazard comparison — if it were more thorough we should call it a collation, of M.

§ 133. Cases 86, 132, 218, 258, 266, 309 and 373 (some of which mentioned before) have regard to punctuation and do not call for any further comment. If in n° 218, our reading proves to be the one of U., this is nothing but a mere coincidence; the comma should of course be there.

§ 134. Cases 44, 141, 208 and 284 are mere proofs of the printer's negligence,—the last case: de for De, very venial of course! Not only that we have had a similar case before (§§ 36, 52) but as any one will be able to testify that has ever written in Norwegian or received Norwegian letters, the substitution is a blunder one very easily falls into,—teste (if any testimony is needed) the fact that here too in U, Ibsen himself wrote de first, correcting it into De afterwards. Here n° 312 may be mentioned: dér for der.

§ 135. In n°ˢ 37, 47, 148, 150, 155, 160, 170 (see § 117), 313 and 382, we have some misprints, all fortunately corrected by 15 which in their aggregate value especially throw a very favourable light on it. Only one of these cases may require an additional word of comment, n° 313. Ibsen had written:

Han var en kortsynt Mand. Udover Ringen
af dem, ham nærmest stod, han intet saa,—

where the construction af dem, ham nærmest stod may well appear somewhat forced. Ibsen had first writen (in U:) af dem som nærmest stod, but changed som into ham in R. Here 14 is guilty of, or, if you like, responsible for the substitution of han for ham: af dem, han nærmest stod. Of course ham should be restored (as 15 prints apparently after M.) but the substitution is quite comprehensible and if it is not admissible, it gives at least good sense; see the Comm. ib. —

To sum up: 21 more deviations from R, of which at least 20 without any need and without any semblance of reason,— except negligence.

15.

§ 136.   As in the case of 14, this edition is a literal reprint of its predecessor, even the type and typographical disposition being generally speaking the same. But whereas 14 reprinted 13 and copied it out, going to another edition, apparently M., for a correct reading in a few cases only, we have here in the 15th edition the most remarkable case of a printer having gone in for what we may well do him the honour of calling a rather careful collation of M.,—with one very important qualification. For whereas the study of our list will show that 15 in the case of words and wordform agrees most closely with M,—in the case of the punctuation it follows 13 almost slavishly and hardly to its advantage. To quote but one instance: cf. n° 184, where 15 copies out the absolutely meaningless point of exclamation behind sejervinder which was introduced by 13 and on the other hand 15 has all the new forms that the Editor of M., in accordance with his system had introduced into Peer Gynt, — cf. n° 191 — as well as Prof. Storm's restorations of the earlier texts, such as klyve (n° 190) for flyve, the mistake of the third edition.

§ 137.   In cases 250 and 309 we shall find 15 exceptionally introducing a new punctuation, independently of 14, and curiously enough in the latter case the punctuation given is that of U. In either case 15 is here followed by 16.

§ 138.   In one single case, 15 (followed by 16) improves even upon M., viz. n° 77, where M. had copied the form falde inherited by 13 from 4 and the rest, and 15 (led by his modern sense of what was proper because usual, of course and not by the result of any comparison texts older than M.) restores the form falder, which was not only in R-3, but also in U.—

§ 139.   To sum up: 15 is a very careful reprint of its immediate predecessor, or rather predecessors, 14 and M. It does not so far as I can see, introduce any more important mistakes than the cases mentioned in § 137.

J.

§ 140. The Peer Gynt text of this third ed. of the Samlede Værker, the so called Jubilæum-edition because it appeared in the year of the national Jubilæum (1814—)1914, is undoubtedly reprinted from the last collected ed., M., and not from its immediate predecessor, 15.

This is proved by the fact that, with the very few exceptions to be mentioned presently, J. has always the reading of M. and not that of 15 where these differ from each other; cf. eg. n° 2. Particularly instructive is case n° 318 where J. is the only one besides M. to print *Megen Almue* in italics.

Cases nos 24, 42, 54, 56, 57, 167, 169, 173, 191, 253, 309, 310, 320, 368 show that J. follows a copy of the M¹-set (cf. § 106, ante) in other words that the changes Prof. Storm introduced into his second set and indicated in the appendix to vol. V. of the memorial ed. were taken into consideration. Once or twice, these changes constitute in reality mistakes i. e. deviations from the original texts; cf. n° 252. —

J. is guilty of at least two mistakes of its own, both very venial ones: cf. n° 294 where the omission of a dash happens to coincide with the reading of U; and n° 364 where an unnecessary point of exclamation is introduced. On the other hand it introduces four corrections, cf. n° 183 (where it has smelt out Slaa for Saa); nos 193 and 246 which may be due to mere chance; n° 238 where the original reading (Møjen og) *Pengene* was evidently remembered and given the place of the impossible Pungen (§ 102).

16.

§ 141. That 16 has copied its immediate predecessor 15 is what one expects on remarking that the typography and pagination of the two editions are absolutely the same.

It reads strake (with M?) in stead of strakte, n° 134, and agrees with the punctuation of edd. 14 and 12 respectively (but it may be mere chance) in cases 258 and 264. And cf. n° 320 for another mistake of as venial a character, the omission of a point of exclamation.

On the contrary it introduces so far as I can see the correction of *all* the mistakes the present writer indicated in his Edda-paper, Sept. '14; cf. n°s 7, 9, 49, 58, 66, 73, 81, 108, 109, 110, 115, 125, 126, 127, 135, 142, 184, 188, 201, 206, 262, 263, 268, 270, 281, 326, and 380. But the only conclusion wanted: that the whole of the text should have been collated, it does not draw and all the other mistakes are therefore left uncorrected. —

CONCLUSION.

§ 142. We have now seen what the existing editions of Peer Gynt are, — it can do no harm to say a word or two about what we may reasonably expect future editions to be.

Of course here especially it is of importance not to lose sight of the fact that there are two categories of readers to be expected for those future editions as there exist the same two for the existing ones: the simple r e a d e r who wishes to enjoy the poet's thoughts, and the s t u d e n t of Ibsen who wishes to study these thoughts too, but who would like if possible to be aided in getting at the process of genesis and development of -these thoughts. In one very important respect the needs of these two groups of future readers are the same, they both want a faithful text, to conform as much as possible to what Ibsen really wrote.

§ 143. But now comes a more delicate point, and it will be as well again to confine ourselves in what follows, here to the text of Peer Gynt, however clear it will be that mutatis mutandis (and not so very much either!) the same will apply to the other texts. In going "back to Ibsen" as the battle-cry (but a very peaceful battle!) now should run ¹), shall we go

---

(¹) cf. Edda I, part 3, "Tilbake til Ibsen".

back to his former or his later self? i. e. must we reprint his own final manuscript (R) or his texts in the later spelling, in our case, the second edition as "emended" by himself in 1874, our "I"? (see §§ 26—41).

If the present writer may gauge the opinion of his brother-students of Ibsen by his own, he would like to flourish the trumpet of a "consensus of opinion among philologists" and decide in favour of the former contingency. And it should at least be remembered what the objections are to the second course. Leaving small details out of consideration (see the §§ just referred to), the changes introduced by Ibsen into his text in consequence of the Stockholm meeting were three: 1° No more capitals in substantives, 2° å for aa, and 3° k and g before palatal vowels instead of kj and gj. — Of these three only the first is followed both generally if not yet quite without exception in Denmark and Norway. As to n° 2, in Norway, aa is used almost without exception, in Denmark most people use aa, only comparatively few stick to å; in regard to k and g, Ibsen and the Stockholm conference are not followed by the present generation, although of course Denmark now generally omits the j which is not pronounced as she has done for some time. The fact is therefore quite apparent that Ibsen's orthography which he admittedly adopted mainly if not merely to please his Danish publishers (cf. the letter to Mr. Hegel quoted ante § 26) is not that of the present and we may be sure of a future Norway, but for say about two-thirds only that of the present Denmark. But I quite understand that it will be no very easy matter to get the consent of those most concerned for the return to Ibsen's very first form. At least not for a future edition of the collected works.

On the other hand, for the purposes of scholarly work alone, an exact reprint of R, compared all-through with Ibsen's first draft, U, as well as an edition of that text in full, are each of them, a consummation devoutly to be wished, indeed absolutely indispensable to the scholar, for the fragments given in the Efterladte Skrifter cannot possibly satisfy his wants. They are badly arranged and not fully reliable. And the present writer will do his best to realise this deep-felt double want such an edition of R and U, if an arrangement with the publishers, the possessors of the copyright of Ibsen's works, can be arrived at.

§ 144. It must at any rate be apparent to the readers of the preceding pages that no one's purpose is served with a text such as the one we have now seen evolving itself gradually but slowly out of Ibsen's own.

I think I may speak in such a general way about the text of Ibsen, although I have proved my case (at most, but as I fondly hope to have done) about one of his plays only. For there is no reason to expect that the text of Peer Gynt should be the only one that has fared so ill at the printers' hands. Indeed it is Professor Storm's great merit to have shown conclusively in his critical apparatus to the Memorial edition that all the texts were corrupted more or less in the process or progress (if progress it can be called!) of time! The present investigation must show, — will show I venture to hope, that the evil was greater than even Professor Storm suspected and that in the case of Peer Gynt at least, the editor of M. had not eradicated that evil. It will be quite plain that it is high time to raise this cry that an accumulation of misprints causes to be sounded over the head of any author of mark, when his time comes, that we must have a fully reliable text to read the man's thoughts in. And Ibsen's time has come. There can be no doubt that at a not very distant hour Ibsen's works will knock at the door of philology, or perhaps better: that philology will knock at Ibsen's door. Indeed, the note of alarm sounded in my paper "Tilbake til Ibsen" was a very modest knock but not by any means the first, *teste* Seip's paper in the Edda, mentioned before, as some time ago Professor Storm's excellent study in the Ibsen Album, besides of course his critical remarks in the Memorial edition. And the knocking has already become louder and louder, — apart from Henning Kehler's study of Ibsen's language as the expression of his characters, (announced in "Edda", 1916, 51), there is the present writer's preceding commentary. It is quite clear then that the present and future student of Ibsen should be provided with an authentic text, — the author is great enough to bear the "opprobrium" of any mistakes or any inconsistencies he has allowed himself, or even, perhaps been "guilty of"! So when at these repeated knockings, the door shall open, there can be no objection whatever if a future edition gives us the text, not as subsequent misprints or even the best of editors have transformed it, but show us the great Master — as he was!

ADDENDA AND CORRIGENDA.

308. The name of Ibsen's early flame given as Clara E. on p. 25 is in full Clara Ebbell, as Hr. Statsadvokat Haakon Løken tells me and as I now also find in print, — in Bergwitz' book on Grimstad, p. 21.

363. Add that Det Ubæst at the end of the first act (l. 721) takes the place of Det Afskum of U.

572. The next line Det gnissler som Sagbladet under en Fil should have been quoted too as it contains the very word from Ibsen's reminiscences: sagblade.

584. On the model of Solveig — at least on a model — see the booklet by Bergwitz on Ibsen's Avstamning p. 13: „Det er visst nok ikke uten grund, for ikke at uttrykke det sterkere, at Hedvig Stousland" (Ibsen's sister) "ansees for et storslaaet Forbillede for Typen 'Solveig' i 'Peer Gynt', ... End dypere seet skal samme Solveig fremstille Gudsbegrepet, saaledes som Ibsen saa det i sin egen Mor." It is comfortable to find that this notion which the author gives on the express authority of Mr. Consul Stousland, Ibsen's brother-in-law, is much qualified by the fact that it is „at any rate" Ibsen's sister who thinks so: „Paa den Maate vil i al fald hans Søster ha det opfattet"

645. for som en Brand. tore off in a flame.
This rendering is not very satisfactory, — it is true that the pun is well-nigh untranslatable: en brand meaning not only a flame but also a daredevil, a devil of a fellow, so if here we read of the devil that he tore off through the roof "som en brand" we see that "fanden"

is said to do this "wie der Teufel", i. e. 'as quick as the devil', like the devilish firebrand he was, we may perhaps translate, — cf. like blazes for a similar imagery.

1000. My suggestion (p. 96) that the „Professor-trold" may contain „a pointed reference to a contemporary" would seem to be borne out by a communication from Hr. Statsadvokat Haakon Løken who writes: Professortroldet (Visdomstroldet) er sikkerlig Professor Monrad, prof. i filosofi. Han talte ustanselig samme tale om igjen og om igjen "om skjønhet og sandhet".

2199. A correspondent asks if the Kongstanke which was finally 'crowned' in 1905 by the separation from Sweden is perhaps a misprint for finally 'drowned'. It certainly is not but the question proves that I have not made my point clear. The Kongstanke here thought of is not the one of a n y Scandinavianism, but that "Samlingstanke" which created the new Norway of 1905. Compare what was written but yesterday of Christian Michelsen on his sixtieth birthday: "han, den eneste.... som har evnet at samle folket i én stor tanke, i én sterk vilje" and "stor var der gjerning han øvet, da han skapte vaarbrudd i folkesjælen og samlet riket i én sterk beslutning" etc. Morgenblad, March 15, 1917.

2310. Those who should be inclined to favour the suggestion as to 'han' being an aside, I would refer to a passage in the second ed. of Georg Brandes' book on Ibsen (p. 156) where we are reminded of the fact that in contradistinction to Dumas and Augier (on whose shoulders Ibsen stands) Ibsen's new art knew little or no 'afsides Replikker'. And although this very passage shows of course that Brandes is wrong when he says that Ibsen never uses monologues, as to the aside we must hold with him here. Why should, how could Peer go in for an aside here directly after the line when i n t h i s m o n o l o g u e he adresses the monkey with a: 'dear old fellow'!

2439. Asnet i Arken. like the ass in the ark.

Professor W. Brede Kristensen in reply to my question if he could explain the allusion suggests that what Ibsen

may have had in his mind here is the conundrum:
hvilket æsel har skrydt saa høit at alverdens mennesker
hørte det? And the answer is of course: æslet i Noae
Ark!

2609. Bergwitz, in his book on Grimstad, tells (p. 22) of a
conversation with Due, Ibsen's friend and contemporary in his Grimstad-days, who had criticised Ibsen's
tendency to use these „stereotype Utbrudd: ha!" —
too often in his Catilina, which Ibsen apparently took
ad notam.

2877. V e d at svinge og svanse, will be found changed in later editions (M. etc) into f o r at svinge.... (= to
cope with the current) i n o r d e r t o caper and
prance!!

3045. It has been suggested again and again that Ibsen being
of German extraction had inherited much from his
German ancestors, — cf. e. g. Jæger, '88 p. 3 according
to whom he had "Tyskerens Anlæg for det spekulative",
and "hans sans for den konsekvente og systema-
tiske Tænkning". In this connection a study of Bergwitz' book on Ibsen's descent is interesting cf. especially ib. p. 55: "hvad Ibsen har av fremmed ved sig, maa
han ha faat under Livet i fjerne Lande, i frivillig Land-
flygtighet."

3213. 14. tude med de Ulve, som er ude.

be howling with the wolves that are about you.
Compare Mau, II, 492: Man skal tude med de Ulve
man er iblandt (French: hurler avec les loups ou braire
avec les ânes, etc., Stoett, n° 844. On the prudent sentiment itself, see the n. tot l. 2520. —

3343. For the use of later investigators I add that crowns
of straw are also mentioned in U, in the passage corresponding to l.l. 4360, 1:.

God Lykke, Gubbe, og vel derned!
Kan jeg rive mig lös, saa kommer jeg med.
Vi skal spille sammen med Kroner af Straa
En Kejser og en Konge med Haler paa!
Jeg skriver en Farce," etc.

4391.   Dette her er en yderlig filtret Affære.
            This matter's excessively complicated.
        Filtret, a form owing to influence of filtre, to filtrate
    on the more original filtet, matted, entangled, intricate.
4504. On Ibsen's treatment of the 'Schlüpfrige element' see a
    remark by Brandes, H. Ibsen p. 162.
    § 140. (p. 460). Another mistake by J. is the omission
    (p. 309) of *i* in De flestes seen ins blaue ender i støbeskeen,
    which makes perfect havoc of the sense.

ABBREVIATIONS AND BIBLIOGRAPHY.

The author has to apologise for the fragmentary state of this bibliography. He had left his home on what was meant to be but a short visit to Holland and had expected to have the works themselves at hand by the aid of which to work out his notes. When the return to Ghent was refused him, he had to fill up the gaps largely from memory. That the bibliography is not quite so incomplete as would otherwise have been the case is owing to the kindness of a Norwegian friend who however at the last moment was unable to fulfil his promise quite. It was then too late to call in the aid of others in foreign countries at a time when correspondence is slow and the attention of the world turned to graver matters.

Aasen, Gr.: Norsk Grammatik. Omarbeidet Udgave af Det norske Folkesprogs Grammatik. Christiania, 1864, 1890.
Aasen, No. Ordspr.: Norske Ordsprog, samlede og ordnede af I. Aasen. Chria. 1856. 2. Udg. 1881.
Aasen, No. Ordb.: Norsk Ordbog med dansk Forklaring af Ivar Aasen, Tredie Oplag, Alb. Cammermeyers. Forlag. (Chria. 1900).
Aasen, Prøver.: Pröver af Landsmaalet i Norge. Af I. Aasen, Chria. 1853. Anden Udgave. Med et Tillæg af Amund B. Larsen, Kristiania, 1899.
Abbott, Sh. Gr.: A Shakespearean Grammar, London Mac Millan.
Adam Homo.: Paludan-Müller's Adam Homo, vol. 4 and 5 of the Complete Works, ed. 1879. København, Gyldendal.
Ahlstrøm.: Om Folksagorna. Svenska Landsmålen.
Andersen, Vilh.: Sammenfald og Berøring. Et bidrag til dansk betydningslære. Festskrift til Vilhelm Thomsen, København, 1894.
Archer(s).: Peer Gynt A dramatic Poem by Henrik Ibsen. Authorised translation by William and Charles Archer, London, Scott. n. d.
Asbjørnsen, No. Folk.: Norske Folkeeventyr, Christiania, 1914.
Asbjørnsen og Moe.: Norske Huldre-eventyr og Folkesagn, fortalt av P. Chr. Asbjørnsen, fjerde utgave bearbeidet av Moltke Moe o ; Anders Krogvig, Folke Utgave, Kristiania, 1914. Aschehoug.
　　Norske Folke-eventyr fortalt av P. Chr. Asbjørnsen og Jørgen Moe, ottende utgave revideret ved Moltke Moe. Folkeutgave, Kristiania. Aschehoug, 1914.
　　The first part of this collection appeared in 1912 and this is the date assigned to it in the body of the present work. See on the use of dialect in the Huldre-eventyr, Samtiden, 1912, pp. 315—325; see the Comm. n. to l. 1970.

Berge-Bugge.: cf. Bugge-Berge.
Bergsgaard.: Kring Solveig og Peer Gynt, Syn og Segn, 1915.

Bergström ock Nordlander.: Sagor, Sägner ock Visor, Svenska Landsmålen.
Bergsöe, Vilhelm. Henrik Ibsen paa Ischia, og "Fra Piazza del Popolo", Köbenhavn, Gyldendal, 1907.
Bjørnstjerne Bjørnsen.: "Anmeldelse" in Norsk Folkeblad. 1867, Dec. N⁰ 47, quoted from a copy by Anders Krogvig.
Bjørnson-Studier. Smaaskrifter fra det litteraturhistoriske seminar, Utgit av Gerhard Gran, VII—XIII. Kristiania, 1911.
Bergwitz. Henrik Ibsen i sin avstamning Norsk eller fremmed? av Joh. K. Bergwitz, Kristiania og København, Gyldendalske Boghandel, Nordisk Forlag, 1916.
    Grimstad 1800—1850. Som type paa en Norsk Smaaby. Med en indledning: Henrik Ibsens ophold i Grimstad. id. 1916. (Out of print).
Brand, ed. Olsen. Henrik Ibsen, Brand. Et dramatisk digt. Edited with introduction and notes by Julius E. Olson, Chicago (Andersen), 1908.
Brandes, Ibsen. Georg Brandes. Henrik Ibsen, København, 1898. The "Illustreret udgave, ib. MDCCCCXVI." contains an additional paper by Brandes, first published in 1906, in „Verdens Gang"
Breve. Henrik Ibsens Breve, udgivne med indledning og oplysninger af Halvdan Koht og Julius Elias, I—II. København, 1904.
Brons, Peer Gynt, En dramatisk Gedigt van Henrik Ibsen. In 't Plattdüts vertaald döör Bernhard Brons. Emden, Haynel, 1899.
Brynildsen, Norsk-Engelsk Ordbog, Kristiania, Malling, 1890. Norsk-Engelsk ordbog, av J. Brynildsen, anden omarbeidede utgave, Kristiania, Aschehoug, 1913—17.
Bugge-Berge. Norske eventyr og sagn. Optegnet av Sophus Bugge og Rikard Berge. I, Kristiania 1909, II, 1913. (The work was published in Riksmaal and in Landsmaal).

Chantepie de la Saussaye, The Religions of the Teutons, London.
Clant van der Myll. Henrik Ibsen, Dramatische Werken, vertaald naar de oorspronkelijke Noorsche uitgaven door J. Clant van der Mijll—Piepers. Met een inleiding door Dr. W. G. C. Byvanck. Amsterdam, Meulenhoff, 1906.
Collett, Camilla, I de lange Nætter. Af Forf. til Amtmandens Dötre Christiania, 1863. Camilla Collett. I de lange Nætter. Kristiania,. 1892, 3 Opl. 1906.
Collin, Chr. Bjørnstjerne Bjørnson, hans barndom og ungdom. Kristiania, Aschehoug, 1902—1907.
Collin Chr. Morgenblad. Memmon-Støttens Sang og Oprindelsen til Ibsens Peer Gynt. Morgenbladet, 13—16 Nov. 1913.
    (reprinted in Det Geniale Menneske, ch. 7. Ibsens „Peer Gynt") Samtiden, Nov. 1913, reprinted in Det Geniale Menneske, ch. 4.— Det Geniale Menneske, Kristiania, Aschehoug, 1914.
    (repeatedly reprinted).
Collin, Josef. Henrik Ibsen, Sein Werk, seine Weltanschauung, sein Leben, Heidelberg, 1910.
Comm. The present Commentary on Henrik Ibsen's Peer Gynt.
Craigie. Scandinavian Folklore, London. Alexander Gardner, 1896.

Dania. Tidskrift for folkemål og folkeminder. Bd. 1—10. København 1890—1903.
Dansk ordb. f. F. Dansk ordbog for Folket, udarbejdet af B. T. Dahl, H. Hammer, Hans Dahl. København, Kristiania. 1907—1914.

Danske Studier, the organ of the Dansk Folkemindesamling, København, Gyldendal.

Dietrichson. Lorenz, — Svundne Tider, I—III. Kristiania, 1896 f.f.

Dresdner, A. Albert Dresdener. Ibsen als Norweger und Europäer, Jena, 1907.

Due, Erindr. Erindringer fra Henrik Ibsens Ungdomsaar af Chr. Due, Toldkasserer, København, Grebes Bogtrykkeri, 1909.

Dølen. cf. Vinje.

E. D. D. The English Dialect Dictionary by Joseph Wright, Oxford, Clarendon Press.

Edda, Nordisk Tidskrift for Literaturforskning. Redaktør Gerhard Gran. Kristiania, Aschehoug, 1914 f.f.

E. S., Eft. Skr. Henrik Ibsen Efterladte Skrifter, Udgivne of Halvdan Koht og Julius Elias, I—III, Kristiania og København, 1909.

Eitrem. Nogen av de danske forutsætninger for Brand og Peer Gynt. Paludan-Müller og Henrik Ibsen. Af Cand. mag. H. Eitrem, Gads danske Magasin, 1913.

Ellis Roberts. Peer Gynt by Henrik Ibsen, A new translation by R. Ellis Roberts, London. Martin Secker, (1912).

E. B., Ep. Brand. Henrik Ibsens Episke Brand udgivet efter original-manuskripterne af Karl Larsen, København og Kristiania, Gyldendalske boghandel Nordisk Forlag, 1907.

Eriksen. Sammensatte Ord hos Ibsen. En sproglig undersøgelse af Alfred Eriksen. Nyt tidskrift redigeret af I. E. Sars og Olaf Skavlan. IV, 1885, pp. 371 seqq.

F., "Folkeudgave" of Ibsen's Works, cf. T. C. §§ 7, 83 seqq.

F. Ev. cf. Asbjørnsen og Moe Folkeeventyr.

Falk og Torp. Etymologisk Ordbog over det norske og det danske sprog af Hjalmar Falk og Alf Torp, I—II, Kristiania, Aschehoug, 1903—06.

Norwegisch-dänisches etymologisches Wörterbuch. Von H. S. Falk und Alf Torp. 1—2, Heidelberg, Winter, 1910—'11.

Falk og Torp, Hjalmar Falk og Alf Torp, Dansk-norskens syntax i historisk fremstilling. Kristiania, Aschehoug, 1900.

Torp og Falk, Dansk-norskens lydhistorie med særligt hensyn paa orddannelse og böining. Kristiania, 1898.

Fataburen, The organ of the Nordiska Musæet at Stockholm.

Fausbøll. cf. Ordbog over gadesproget.

Faye, Norske Folkesagn, samlede og udgivne af Andreas Faye, 2. Opl. Christiania, 1844.

Feilberg, ordb. Bidrag til en ordbog over jyske almuesmål. Af H. F. Feilberg, København, 1886—1914.

Feilberg, Festskr. Festskrift til H. F. Feilberg fra nordiske sprog-og folkemindeforskere, København, 1911.

Feilberg, Bjærgtagen. Studie over en gruppe træk fra nordisk alfetro. Köbenhavn, 1910.

Feilberg, Sjæletro. København, 1914.

Feilberg, Jul. Bd. 1. Allesjælestiden; Bd. 2. Julemörkets Löndom. København, 1904.

Folkeeventyr. cf. Asbjørnsen og Moe.

Folkeviser. Norske Folkeviser, samlede og udgivne af M. B. Landstad, Christiania, 1853.

Norske folkeviser fra middelalderen. Med indledninger og anmerkninger ved Knut Liestøl og Moltke Moe, Kristiania, 1912. (an edition in Landsmaal as well as in Riksmaal).

Fritzner, Ordbog over det gamle norske Sprog af Dr. Johan Fritzner. Omarbeidet, forøget og forbedret Udgave, Kristiania, Den norske Forlagsforening I—III. 1886—96.
Fædrelandet. 1867. N° 279 Lördag 30 Nov. contains Clemens Petersen's criticism of Peer Gynt, quoted from a copy by Mr. C. L. Christensen.

G. R. M. Germanisch-Romanische Monatschrift, Heidelberg, Winter. Gadesproget, cf. Ordbog.
Garrett. Lyrics and Poems from Ibsen, London, Dent, 1912.
Gosse. Edmund Gosse, Northern Studies, London, 1890.
Edmund Gosse, H. Ibsen. Hodder and Stoughton. London. 1907.
Gran. Gerhard Gran. Bjørnstjerne Bjørnson, København Schønbergske Forlag, 1916.
Gran. Nordmænd i det 19de Aarhundrede, Udg. ved Gerhard Gran. Kristiania, 1902—07.
Gerhard Gran. Norsk aandsliv i hundrede aar. Sprædte træk. Kristiania, 1915.
Güntert. H. Güntert, Uber Isländische Berserker-Geschichten, 1912. Beilage zum Jahresbericht des Heidelberger Gymnasiums.

H. Ev. cf. Asbjørnsen og Moe.
H. R. list of the Dramatis Personae (de Handlende) in Ms. R. ± Oct. '67.
H. U. list of the Dramatis Personae (de Handlende) in Ms. U. ± Jan. '67.
Harland, Science. E. S. Hartland, The Science of Fairy tales, London, 1891.
Hartland, F. F. T., E. S. Hartland, English Fairy and Folktales. London, 1890.
Herrmann, Paul Herrmann, Nordische Mythologie 1903.
Henning Kehler, Studier i det Ibsenske Drama, in the Edda, 1915, 1916. (is announced to be published separately with additional chapters).
Heiberg, J. L. En sjæl efter Døden, apocalyptisk komödie.
Hjelmström. A. Hjelmström, Från Delsbo, Svenska Landsmålen.
Huldreeventyr, cf. Asbjornsen og Moe.
Hægstad, Marius, Norsk maallæra elder grammatik i landsmaalet. Bergen 8th, (latest) ed. 1912.
Høst, Drøm og Daad. Sigurd Høst. Henrik Ibsen, Drøm og Daad, Edda, 1915, p.p. 328 f.f.

J. Jubilæumsutgave (cf. T. C. §§ 7, 140) of Ibsen's works: Samlede Værker, Tredje Udgave, 1914.
J. Germ. Teut., Phil. Journal of Germanic and Teutonic Philology, Urbana, Illinois, U. S. A. vol. 13 : A paper on Faust and Peer Gynt by A. Leroy Andrews.
Janson, Folke Ev. Kr. Janson. Folke-Eventyr fra Sandeherad, 1878. (contains an interesting introduction by Moltke Moe).
Jespersen, O. A Modern English Grammar. Heidelberg, Winter. (I) 1913.
Jespersen, O. Større Engelsk gramm. København, Gyldendal.
Jespersen, O. Nutidssprog hos børn og voksne, 1916. København.
Jespersen, O. A paper on Subtraction in the V. Thomsen Festkrift, 1894.
Jæger, Ill. No. Lit. hist. Henrik Jæger, Illustreret norsk Literaturhistorie, Bd. 1—2. Kristiania 1896.
Jæger, '88. Henrik Jæger, Henrik Ibsen, 1828—'88. København, 1888.
Jæger, '92. Henrik Jæger, Henrik Ibsen og hans værker. En fremstilling i grundrids, Kristiania, 1892.

Kahle, B. Kahle, Henrik Ibsen, Bjørnstjerne Bjørnson und ihre Zeitgenossen, Leipzig, 1908.
Kalkar, Ordbog. Ordbog til det ældre danske sprog (1300—1700) af Otto Kalkar, Bd. 1—4. København. 1881—1907.
Kleiven, Ivar. Segner fraa Vaagaa, Kristiania 1894.
Kleiven I. I gamle Daagaa. Forteljingo og byggda-Minne fraa Vaagaa. Kristiania, 1908.
Kristiansen, cf. Ordbog over Gadesproget.
Krogvig. Fra det nationale gjennembrudstid. Breve fra Jørgen Moe til P. Chr. Asbjørnsen og andre. Med en indledning utgit av Anders Krogvig, Kristiania, 1915.

Larsen. cf. E. B.
Leroy Andrews. cf. J. Germ. Teut. Phil.
Liestøl. Knut Liestøl, Norske Trollvisor og Norrøne Sagor, Olaf Norlis Forlag. Kristiania, 1915.
Liestøl og Moe. cf. Folkeviser.
Luftskipperen og Atheisten. Paludan-Müller. (København, Gyldendal, 1903).
Løland No. Ev. Norsk eventyrbok. Etter uppskrifter av A. E. Vang etc. ved Rasmus Løland. Oslo (1905).

M. Mindeudgaven: Henrik Ibsens Samlede Værker, Minde udgave, Kristiania og København, Gyldendalske Boghandel, Nordiske Forlag, 1908.
(cf. T. C. §§ 7 and 103 seqq.)
M.M. Maal og Minne, Norske Studier Utgit av Bymaals-Laget ved Magnus Olsen. Kristiania 1909 seqq.
Mannhardt. Baumkultus der Germanen, 2 Ausg. 1904.
Mau, Ordskat. (A collection of Danish proverbs in two volumes).
Meyer, Myth. E. H. Meyer, Mythologie der Germanen, 1903.
Mikkelsen. Dansk Sproglære med sproghistoriske tillæg.... af Kr. Mikkelsen. København, Lehmann & Stages Forlag, 1894.
Moe, Jørgen. cf. Krogvig.
Moe, Moltke. cf. Folkeviser.
Moe, Moltke, Ev Sagn. Topografisk-statistisk beskrivelse over Finmarkens ambt. Udg. ved Amund Helland. D. 2 Kristiania, 1906.
S. 565—665: Eventyrlige sagn i den ældre historie.
(Hr. Bibliotekar Hjalmar Pettersen of Christiania tells me that according to a communication from Mr. Helland, the stories were dictated to him by Prof. Moltke Moe late of a night — "i en sildig nattetime.")
Mont (de) en De Cock, Vlaamsche Vertelsels. Gent 1898.
Morgenstern. Henrik Ibsen, Sämtliche Werke, Zweiter Band, S. Fischer, Verlag, Berlin, 1911.
(The translation of Peer Gynt is by Morgenstern)
Munthe, Katt-Eder, Om användningen af ordet Katt i Svenska Eder och liknande uttryck. Strödda antekningar af Åke W: son Munthe. Nyfilologiska Sällskapets i Stockholm Publikation 1901.

N. E. D. A New English Dictionary on historical principles. Oxford, Clarendon Press, 1884—.
N. S. Henrik Ibsens Nachgelassene Schriften in vier Bänden Herausgegeben von Julius Elias und Halvdan Koht, Berlin, Fischer, 1909.
Neophilologus, Driemaandeliks Tijdschrift voor de wetenschappelike beoefening van levende talen en van haar letterkunde. Groningen J. B. Wolters, 1915, v. v.

No. Sagn. Norske Sagn. 2. opl. Kristiania, Cammermeyers Boghandel, 1902.

Nordahl Rolfsen, No. digt. Norske Digtere. En Anthologi med Biografier. Udg. af Nordahl Rolfsen, Bergen, 1886.

Nordmænd i det 19de Aarh. cf. Gran.

Norsk Folkeblad cf. Bjørnstjerne Bjørnson.

Norvegia, Tidskrift for det norske folks maal og minder. Bd. 1. 2. Kristiania, 1884—1908.

Olafsen, O. Olafsen. I gamle Dage. Fortællinger og Skildringer fra Hardanger. Bergen, 1908.

Olrik. Nordisches Geistesleben. Heidelberg, Winter.

Olsen, No. Ev. og sagn. O. T. Olsen. Norske folkeeventyr og sagn samlet i Nordland. Kristiania. (1909—) 1912. Med efterskrift af Moltke Moe.

Ordbog for folket. cf. Dansk Ordbog f. F.

Ording, Kj. Kom. Henrik Ibsens "Kærlighedens Komedie." Av Fr. Ording. Kristiania Kappelen 1914.

Paasche. Gildet paa Solhaug. Ibsens nationalromantiske digtning. av. Fredrik Paasche.

Smaaskrifter fra det literaturhistoriske seminar. Udg. af Gerhard Gran. V. Kristiania, Aschehoug, 1908.

Paludan-Müller, cf. Luftskipperen og Atheisten, Adam Homo.

Passarge. Henrik Ibsen. Ein Beitrag zur neuesten Geschichte der norwegischen Nationallitteratur von L. Passarge. Leipzig, 1883.

Passarge, Ein Dramatisches Gedicht von Henrik Ibsen. Ubersetzt von L. Passarge, Leipzig, Reclam, 1880, 1887.

Paul's Grundriss. Grundriss der Germanischen Philologie.... herausgegeben von Herman Paul. Strassburg, Trübner 1896, 1898.

Paulsen. John Paulsen. Mine Erindringer. København. 1900.

John Paulsen. Nye Erindringer. København, 1901.

John Paulsen. Samliv med Ibsen. Nye Erindringer og Skitser, København, 1906.

Petersen, Clemens. cf. Fædrelandet.

Poestion N. Gr. Lehrbuch der Norwegischen Sprache für den Selbstunterricht. Von J. C. Poestion, Wien und Leipzig, A. Hartleben's Verlag.

Zweite, dritte Auflage (1914).

Poestion D. Gr. Lehrbuch der Dänischen Sprache für den Selbstunterricht. Von J. C. Poestion. Dritte Auflage, Wien und Leipzig, A. Hartleben's Verlag (1912).

Prozor. (Comte) M. Prozor. Le Peer Gynt d'Ibsen. Paris, Mercure de France, 1897.

Henrik Ibsen. Peer Gynt. Poëme dramatique en cinq actes. Traduit du norvégien et précédé d'une préface par M. Prozor. Paris 1899, 1903, 1907, 1912.

cf. the Commentary, p.p. 166, 167.

Publications Soc. Adv. Adv. Sc. Study. Publications of the Society for the Advancement of Scandinavian Study. Managing Editor George T. Flom. University of Illinois, 1914 seqq. Urbana, Ill. U. S. A.

Qvigstad og Sandberg. Lappiske Eventyr og Folkesagn ved J. Qvigstad og G. Sandberg, Med en indledning af Moltke Moe, Kristiania, 1887.

R. "Renskrift" of Ibsen's Peer Gynt.
 cf. T. C. § 6.
Riegel, Quellen. Julius Riegel. Die Quellen von William Morris' Dichtung The earthly Paradise. Erlangen, 1890.
Rietz, Svenskt Dialekt-Lexicon af Johan Ernst Rietz. Ordbok öfver Svenska Allmoge-Språket I, II, Malmø, Cronholm, 1867.
Ross, Norsk Ordbog af Hans Ross. Tillæg til "Norsk Ordbog" af Ivar Aasen. Christiania Alb. Cammermeyers Forlag, 1895.
 id. Nyt Tillæg til "Norsk Ordbog" af Ivar Aasen. ib. 1902.

S. I. S. cf. Storm, I. S.
S. M. cf. Storm, M.
S. V. cf. F. (Samlede Værker, 1898).
Samtiden Tidskrift for Politik Litteratur og Samfundsspørgsmaal Redigeret af Gerhard Gran, Kristiania Aschehoug 1889 seqq.
Sämtl. Werke. Henrik Ibsen Sämtliche Werke Volksausgabe in fünf Bänden, herausgegeven von Julius Elias und Paul Schlenther, S. Fischer Verlag, Berlin 1911.
 Sämtliche Werke in Deutscher Sprache Durchgesehen und eingeleitet von Georg Brandes, Julius Elias und Paul Schlenther, Berlin, Fischer 1903.
Sandvig. De Sandvigske Samlinger i Tekst og Billeder, Lillehammer, Stribolt, 1907.
Saxo. Neun Bücher Saxo's.
 Jantzen
Schack. A. Schack. Om udviklingsgangen i Henrik Ibsens Digtning. København 1896.
Seip, Wergeland. Norskheten i Sproget hos Wergeland og hans Samtid, Kristiania, Aschehoug, 1914.
Shaw. Bernard Shaw, The Quintessence of Ibsenism. (first ed. 1891) Now completed to the Death of Ibsen. London, Constable and Company. 1913.
Skard. Nynorsk Ordbog for rettskrivning og Literaturlesnad av Matias Skard. Kristiania, Aschehoug, 1912.
Stavnem. Overnaturlige Væsener og symbolik i Ibsens Henrik "Peer Gynt" Av P. L. Stavnem, Mindeskrift over Prof. dr. Sophus Bugge, Kristiania 1908.
Steffen. Dr. Richard Steffen. Firstrofig norsk Folkelyrik.
Dr. Richard Steffen. Norske Stev.
 Published in the "Svenska Landsmålen".
Stoett. Nederlandsche Spreekwoorden. Spreekwijzen, Uitdrukkingen en Gezegden, naar hun oorsprong en beteekenis verklaard door Dr. F. A. Stoett. Zutphen Thieme en Co, Tweede druk 1905. Derde druk 1917.
Storckenfeldt, Västgötasägner, Svenska Landsmålen.
Storm. I. S. Ibsen og det Norske Sprog, Samtidens Ibsen Album, 1898. s.s. 147—205.
Storm, M. Mindeudgavens Tekst Retskrivning og Sprogform.
 Appendix to vol. V of M(indeudgaven).
Storm, N. S. Norske Sprog. Kraakemaal og Landsmaal, København, 1896.
Sturtevant. Journal of Germanic and English Philology, IX, p.p. 43—48, a paper on Paa Vidderne and the Peer Gynt.
Syn og Segn, Norsk tidskrift, Kristiania, 1894 f.f.

T. C. Textual Criticism of Henrik Ibsen's Peer Gynt, supra p.p. 367 seqq.

Thiele, Da. Folk. Danmarks Folkesagn. Samlede af J. M. Thiele. Kjøbenhavn, 1843—60.

Torp. Nynorsk Etymologisk Ordbog av Alf Torp, professor. Kristiania Aschehoug, 1915 seqq.

Torp. cf. Falk og Torp.

Troels Lund. Dagligt Liv i Norden. XIV vols. København.

Tylor. E. Tylor, Primitive Culture, London 1903. 2 vol⁸.

U. Utkast; Ibsen's first draft, published (extracts only) in the E(fterladte) Skr(ifter). cf. T. C. § 5.

Vang, Gamla reglo aa rispo fra Valdres, Oslo 18..

Weininger. Otto Weininger. Ueber die letzten Dinge, 2 Aufl. Wien, Leipzig, 1907.

Weis, Sägner på Aspelandsmål, Svenska Landsmålen.

Welhaven, Norges Dæmring.

Wergeland S. S. Henrik Wergelands Samlede Skrifter udgivne af Hartvig Lassen, Christiania, Tønsbergs Forlag, VI, 1855.

Western. August Western. Skriv norsk. Nogen punkter av riksmaalets sproglære, Kristiania 1915.

Wicksteed. Four lectures on Henrik Ibsen by Philip H. Wicksteed, London Swan Sonnenschein, 1892.

Witkowski. Goethes Faust Herausgegeben von Georg Witkowski. I—II. Leipzig, Hesse, 1906.

Vinje, Utv. A. O. Vinje. Skrifter i Utval. I—IV. Kristiania (1890?)

Vislie. A. O. Vinje ved Vetle Vislie, Bergen 1890.

Wörner. Roman Woerner. Henrik Ibsen. I—II München 1900. 2 Aufl. 1912.

Wright. E. L. Wright, Rustic Speech and Folklore, Oxford, Clarendon Press.

INDEX.

The numbers with § before them refer to the paragraphs of "Textual Criticism", the second part of this work. The other numbers refer to the notes in the first part, the Commentary proper. —

a, ae, § 112.
aa, o, § 114.
Aa, Aase, § 45.
aabne Øjne, 66.
aanden, 4176.
aandrigt, 2896.
aandsfrænde, 3771.
aannen, § 114.
aarhundrede, § 94, 1981.
Aase, Aa, § 45.
Aase, 727.
Aase og jeg, 717.
Aases stemme, 3995, 4069.
aatte, 1444.
ab esse ad posse, 2452.
abekat, 2285.
ad dage, cf. af dage.
Adam (den gamle —) 1120.
Adam Homo, cf. Paludan-Müller.
adelstrold, 1850.
adverbs, § 123.
af dage, 1542, § 126.
afterthoughts of Ibsen's in the drama, 1228, 3499, 4069, 4429.
agt, 3467.
agterskilt, 4504.
ak, 2609.
akacier, akazier, § 120.
Aladdin, 951, 2444, 2461, 3348.
alvor, 3992.
anger, 1557, 1561.
angst, 3615, 3637, 8.
Anitra-Ingrid, 2782.
Anker (Bernt —), 692.
Apis, 3237, 3267.
asen (narre), 4579.
Askeladden, 255, 4421, 2.
Asgardsreien, 4429.
asnet i arken, 2439.

atter og fram, 1239.
attraa og begjær, 1176.
au, ou, § 113.
baaden (losse), 1160.
bag, 709.
bank, 1792.
barktækt, § 100, 130.
barn (kjært —), 4108.
barnebys, 1792.
Baubo, 994.
Becker, 2916.
bedemandsstil, 4491.
Beduin(er)høvding, § 70, 1970.
beer, 408, § 111.
begjær, 1176.
Begriffenfeldt, 3045.
ben (skjæve) cf. fusk.
ben (venstre), 3598.
Bender, 2129.
bendes (i bakken) cf. bændes.
benene fat, 1283.
benet og brogen, 992.
ber (ler?), 3939.
bergtagen, 509, 1000.
Bero, 724, 4141.
berserker, 3179, 4141.
beskik dit hus, 4095, 4629.
bespottelig, 3533.
besvær, § 125.
bét, 2871.
betydelig(t), § 123.
bevares, 83, 3172, (3303, 4281).
bindes i baasen, 608, § 75.
bjart, 1489.
bjørn, 845, 4141.
Bjørnson, 845, 2319, 2833.
Bjørnson's Halte Hulda, 729.

blaa- (= sort), 4314—4136, n. p. 328.
Blaahø, 3350.
Blaakulle, 4314, 6.
blandingskræ (vokser fort) 1191, 1515.
Blasenfeldt, 3045.
Blessom, (Johannes), (4572), 4429.
bliv, sb., 2362.
Bloksbjerg, 1005, 4314, 6.
Blom, H. Ø, 1053, 3179.
bomuldsmagnaten, 1807.
Bornu, 2422.
Borough-English, 255.
bos, 986.
bra litet rolig, 4519.
Bra(h)ma, § 108.
Brand, 308, 3107, 3179, 4609.
brand, (for som en —), 645. A.—
Brand (Episke —), 1342, 3670.
brogen, cf. benet.
bror, 1812.
Brose, 969.
brot, 733.
brudehest, 994.
bruderov, 726, 799.
brummet (blir der—), (3196), 3179.
bryde (paa), 3040.
bræer, 102.
b(r)ændte, b(r)ændende, 896, (4237), § 58.
budsendt, 1433.
buk, 69, 3835.
(skille bukkene fra faarene) 1958.
bukkeskind, 1185.
Bull (Ole), 801, 2432.

bus, 2309.
buse paa, 4141.
Buttonmoulder, cf. Knap-
pestøber.
bygderne, 1772.
bytting, 418, 779, 3023.
bænde, bændende, § 58,
896.
bændes, 704, 896.
bær, 724, § 23, § 112. cf.
Bero.
bærmen, 3369.
Bøjgen, 801, 1217, 1228,
1232, 1234 (§ 109).

Caprices (Ibsen's —), cf.
afterthoughts.
Charlesto(w)n, § 16, § 108.
comparative (use of —),
2525.
contamination, 535, 1970,
3477.
Cotton, 1807, § 108.
cow-dung, 987, 1216.
crikey, 1934, 2310.
cross; cf. contamination.

d (in words as standse),
§ 120.
da (vel), § 75.
daad, 845, 1029, 1579,
2026.
daarekiste, 1135, 3107.
daarekistelem, § 86.
dagblak, 1172.
daguerreotyp, 4540.
dattersøns afkom, 1001,
(4267).
datum, 4408.
De, de, 1893.
de (tyve), 173.
dem, den, § 46.
den og den, 4526.
der, det, § 63, § 102.
derhos, 3247.
desert (scene in the —),
2114.
digt, digter, 57, (2086),
(2092), 3867, (4341).
Dovregubben, Dovrekon-
gen, 965, 1000, 1146.
drap(p)i(e)ren, § 39, § 115.
drappieren (man muss
sich —) 3898.
dratte ned, 416.
draugen, 801.
dreng, 3166.

drikke, 1054, 1509.
dryger, 1599.
drøm, (Peers —), 308, 1176.
due for, 3477.
du(g)er, § 121.
dugdraaber, 3995.
dunk, 547.
dyden, cf. sandt for —
dydig, 3796.
dænge, 421.
dævel f. djævel, cf. minsæl.
døde sig selv (være —),
4381.
døden, § 31, 3819.
Dølen, 1053, 1125.

e, é, § 37, § 85, § 111.
e, æ, § 111.
ed, 1163.
efterretteligt, 2359.
Eivind Bolt, 955.
Ej was, 1830, § 38.
en (ind. pron.), 842, 3390.
— ende (piskende død), 535.
enfin, 2208.
Engeland (criticism), 1807.
Engel(l)and, 498, § 115.
English (Ibsen's familiarity with —), 1807.
Enten-Eller, cf. Kierke-
gaard.
er (added), § 63.
er (var), § 49, 701, 1351.
Esben, 4421.
est, 952.
Eventyr-motif, 751, 962,
1020, 1054, 4425, etc.
evjen, 374.
evigt (hvert — ord), 59.
Ewig weibliche, § 38, 2585.

fadervor, 3591.
falde(r), § 49, § 138.
falder (om), § 56.
fanden (gutten og —) cf.
gutten.
fanden i nødden, 629.
fanden, (hvem —), 897.
(jeg ved —), 3608.
fanden — —, 1110, 2843.
fanden (med), 1059.
fanden (description), 4449,
4451.
fanden (det svier), 1547.
fanden (holder en om ryg-
gen), 1521.
fang (i—), 1278.

fange, 2680.
fant, 684.
fantasi, 57, 878.
far, 4247.
farbror, 1812, 1934.
fattigblok, 4342.
fatum, 1872.
Faust, cf. Goethe.
feber, 3029.
felden, fellen, § 120.
fellah'en med en Konge-
mumie, 3237.
femte akt (dør i—), 3637.
fik, 876.
filtret, 4391.
finger (hugge af—), 1339.
finger (skjære — over struben), 957.
firben, 2356, § 125.
flire, 463.
flokken, § 70.
fluks, § 28, § 122.
flynder, 4114.
fnug, 2299.
fodlet, 1538.
fole, 113.
Folgefonnen, 3350, 3355.
folk, § 70.
folkesangen, 3203.
forlad, 2137.
forlagt, 1850.
forliget, 1461.
forloren (hale), 2303.
forsvinder (alt —), 1216.
forsvinder (troll —), 4671,
cf. svinder.
fort (vokser—), 1191, 1515.
fortidsmusik, 3004.
fortolkeres kreds, 3088.
fram, 113, 1239.
Francisco (San —), 3884.
fransk, 216, 1829, 2208.
Frasenfeldt, 3045.
Fremmede, (den — Passa-
ger), 3499.
fremmest, § 49.
frygten, 3611, (3499).
fugle (sover mine —),
2995.
fugleskrig, 1258, 2995.
fun, Peer makes fun of
God, cf. gud.
Ibsen makes fun of him-
self, 2833, 2924.
Peer makes fun of him-
self, 2027, 2319, 2924,
3936.

Furumo-scene, 3995.
fusk og skjæve ben, 4019.
frænde, 4338.
fylgja, 692.
fæstekvinde, 3702.
fødder (gi —), 208.
førsled, 3720.

gaaden, 1229.
Galdhøpiggen, 3350.
galehuslem, § 86.
galej, 2500, § 102.
galfrands, 2825.
ganger, 996.
gantes, 1171.
garun, 2310.
ged, cf. gjed.
gemyt, 2040.
Gendin-eggen, 99.
German words, 2601, 4497.
Germans (Ibsen and the –),
3045.
Gert Westphaler, (3179)
4415.
gevalt, 2323.
g(j)ed, § 33, § 118.
Gjendin-eggen, 99.
gjenganger-motif, 208, 466,
796, 2333.
gjild, 1625.
gjøg, 3936, § 121.
gjøre det, 1359.
gjøre i, 1931.
glemselsdrik, 1054.
Glesne, 174, (652).
Glittertinden, cf. 3350.
gloende jern, 4237.
glohede jernet, 871.
glohed ring, 896.
glup, 538.
glytted, 80, (1344, 1531).
goddam, 2181, § 35.
Goethe, 584, 994, 2461,
2583—6, 2995, 3550,
3995, 4429.
golly, 1934.
good (for: god), 1934.
graad, 761, § 63.
graad af barnerøster, 4009.
graaklædte (den —), 3798.
graamus, 1200.
Grane, 57, 1720, 1753.
graveren, 3780.
grejdt, 630, 4524.
Grimstad, 2452, 2461, 3615.
grind, 1146.
gris, 994.

grisk, 2436.
gros (en —), 4445.
gruen, 255.
grundende, § 101, § 130.
grædende, § 101, § 130.
græstørv, 409, 956.
grønklædt kvinde, 956,
1494.
grøsser, 1337.
gubbe, 842, 965.
gud (Peer's attitude to
God), 2234.
Gud fader, 1773.
gud naade dig, 1289.
gudbevares, 3172.
Gudbrand Glesne, 174,
(652).
Gudrun, — Garun, 2310.
gutten derinde, 4668.
gutten og fanden, 169, 629.
Gynt (name), 3063.
Gynt, Jon, 208.
Gynt, Peer, (the histor-
ical —), § 94.
Gynt, Peer, (character),
151, 461, 781, 845, 1228,
1359, 1579, 1762, 1806,
1898.
Gynt, Peer, (attitude to
sailors), 3415, 3571.
Gynt, Peer, and Askelad-
den, 255.
Gynt, Peer and Brand,
4608,9.
Gynt, Peer —'s death,
3992, 4687.
Gyntiana, 2432.
gø — cf. gjø —.

haaret (i— trække), 962.
Haartejgen, 3350.
Habes, 2423.
hale, 1070, 4056.
halfculture, cf. halfdan-
nelsen.
halfdannelsen, 99, 2208,
2371, 2583—6.
hallingkast, cf. kast.
Hallingskarven, 3350.
halsløs (daad), 757.
halve riget, 313, 871, 1020,
2444.
Hamlet, 1228; cf. træde
tilbage.
hamrer, hamres, 286.
han, 2310 (as pron. sec.
person).

han, ham, § 135.
han Jon, § 129.
han Peer, § 129, 1382.
handlende, § 86.
handling, § 86.
Hardangerjøkel, 3350.
haugfolk, § 113.
Haugianer, cf. stille.
heads (number of —; trolls)
867.
Hedalen, 576.
hed(d)er, § 62, § 130.
Hegel, 2095.
Heibergs Sjæl efter Døden,
2027, 4316, 4429.
hej, 1493.
hejsan, 353.
Heklefjeld, 4314.
heks, 1005.
helligbrøde, 1587.
henkastende, henkastet,
§ 63.
heraus, 4438.
hersens, 1124.
hestehov, 4314—6.
hieb, 2601, § 29, § 48.
himle, 436.
himmelspring, 130.
hjemkommerøl, 3809, 10.
hjemlige, 1053, 4357.
hjertegrube, 4041.
hjælpekasse, 4342.
hode, 867.
Holberg, 4095.
Holland (Dødens —), 2406.
hollandsk tone, 4415.
Hollænder, 3179, 4415.
horn (usynlige), 3267.
houg (nøgen —), 4349.
hougfolk, § 113.
hoved (for et —), 1541.
hoven, 4451.
hovmod, 2380.
Huhu, 3166, 3179.
huldre, 962, 1070.
huldrin, adj. 1125, 1509.
hule haand, 3014.
hun Ingrid, cf. han —.
hund, 3550.
huspostillen, 1708.
Hussejn, 3308.
hvidbjørnen, 3833.
hvirvlens vætter, 120.
Hægstad (auction-scene),
3798.
hægtekrog, 3853.
hæld, 725.

hælde med øret, 689.
hængt, 362.
hærjet, § 120.
høj(d)en, § 56.
højt paa straa, 434.
høvelig, 1076.

I (pronoun), 439.
i, ie, § 112.
i (alt), § 102.
Ibsen and Wergeland, 1053.
Ibsen, cf. uryggelig.
Ibsen's Life-dream, 308.
Ibsen (Sigurd), 1110 n.
igjen, imod, 2021.
ihob, 651, 3869.
ihærdig, 2870.
ikke (with infinitive), 413.
indelicate (Ibsen's treatment of — matter), 709, 2977, 4056, 4504.
inderligt, § 123.
ingen begravet, 4609.
Ingrid, 729, 3798.
isbrod, 4048.
isflak, 113 (118).
itte (at —), 439.

Jaabæk, 4342.
jeg (repeated), 668.
jeg (en), § 56, 3390.
jente, 1653.
jers, 439.
Jomfru Maria, 1739.
jord (af —), 3924.
jordløg, 3917.
jüngste Recht, 255.
Justedalspræsten, 4415.

Kaare, 851.
Kaba, 2487.
kaldes (for), §.93.
kalket grav, 3995.
kall (= karl), 1293, 4243, § 28.
kall (a tree), 1293.
kanonmad, 2156.
kanske, 1829, 2645.
kant (paa en —), 686.
kapringsfarer, 1981.
kar, karl, (228), 508, § 117, § 135.
Karl (Kong —) 308.
Karl XII, 2111, 2129.
karmesprede, 1678.
kast, 551.

Kastale, 2186.
katten paa Dovre, 3833.
katten klore mig, 1110.
kaut, 229, 553.
kejser (at bli —), 308.
kejserdom 3615.
Kierkegaard, 3615, 3629, 4139.
kiger, § 44, § 130.
kikker, § 44, § 130.
kime cf. klokkerne.
kirkebrøde, 1587.
kjært barn, 4108.
kjætten paa Dovre cf. katten — —
kjødet (i — skaaret), 2848.
kjøgemester, 544.
kjøgemesterlader, 1776.
klokkerne, 1213, 1281.
klore, 1110.
klude, 987.
kludetræet, 1125.
klyve, § 44, § 130, § 136.
knap (= head), 2330.
knappestøber, 1400, 4095, 4139, 4231, 4429.
knark, 1293.
knas (i —), 1198.
know of a dog, 3550.
knøv, 230.
kokkekonen, § 99.
kokken, 3563, 3571.
kommer han, 1259.
kongedatter, § 93.
kongetanken, 2199.
Kongsberg, 4170.
kongsgaarden, 1187.
kongstanken cf. kongetanken.
konster, 622, § 114.
korp, 514.
kors, 602, 1741.
korsvej, 4231, § 44.
kothurner, 3629.
kristenmandsbrogen, § 48
kristenmandsklæder, § 48.
kristenmands søn, 1001.
Kristian (Kong —), 1403.
kronen, (3343), 3857.
kroning, 3345.
krus paa bryggen, 3390.
kry, 229.
krydsningsdyr, 3023.
kryr, 2301.
ks, x, § 28, § 121.
kugle, 2345.
kuli, 1970, § 70, § 108.

kulsvieren, 4429.
kverve, 1125, 4283, § 11, § 39.
kvinde (— værst), 4338.
kvinderne (skrøbelig slægt), 2945.
kvinder (bag ham), 3348.
kvitkufta, 1053.
kværke, 4060.
kære vb. 1837.

laak, 471.
lad(e) 2245, § 93.
lag (i, — et), 404.
lage (vb.), 1315.
Lagerlöf, 551, 878, 3995.
langele(i)k, cf. langspil.
langspil, 3754.
Latin, 2452.
lempe, 856.
lensmand, § 15.
ler (ber?), 3939.
leve, 2714.
lider, 102.
lifligt, 2798.
lig(e), § 70.
lig(t; var det—), 963.
ligene (ler), 3514.
lime, 479, 1005.
ljaa, 102.
lok, 1675.
Lom(b), § 120.
losse (baaden), 1160.
lovede land (det —), 4607.
lud og koldt vand, 4262.
lukt (i vandene), 102, 106.
Lunde, 264, 3670.
lunten (lugte —), 4625.
lus, 1211.
luttre, 4095, 4560.
luven, § 120.
lys (et skjær af —), 4671.
lysets bud, 3613.
lysningen (den —), 1730.
læser, 689.
løg, 3936.
løgn, 57, 708, 1302.
Lørdagsnat, 870.

M, M², § 106.
maade (paa en —), 151, (1579).
maalløs, 186.
maalstræv, 3179, 3203.
Macbeth, 57, 1228, 2444.
mad og drikke, 1054.
magre (den —), 4429.

— 481 —

majoriteten, 2520.
Manderström, 1806, 2211, 3308.
mandsstemme, 452.
mane fanden, 626.
mareridt, 2215.
materialism, 1807.
Memnons sang, 2971, 2995.
men (dattersøn), § 130.
Merchant of Venice, 3995.
Mester, 819, 4175.
mestermand, 819.
metalværdien, 4176.
middels, 2556.
Mikkelsen's Danish grammar, § 123.
minsæl, 2636, 4168, § 126.
missionærer, cf. Stavanger.
mjøden (smage paa —), 4293.
morgenen — kveld, 2268.
morgensang, 2971.
morgenstund, 2347.
Münchhausen, 4429; aal, — ræv, 3115.
muldet, 2099.
mungaat, 4121.
mylder, § 121, § 125.
mystifications, 2995, 3088.
mærkelig(t), § 55, 123.

name part of personality, 4579.
nar, cf. fun (make — of).
narre (det asen), 4579.
nationale, cf. hjemlige.
nationale subjekter, 4357.
natur (tvinge din —), 1063.
naut, 557.
Nebukadnezar, § 120.
negative, 4544.
neglesystem, 4449.
neje (sig), 492, § 22.
nemme, 233.
nerium, 2809.
nisse, 1203.
nissebuk(tanker), 1424, 1466, 3981.
nistebomme, 1274.
nok, 1044, 4300.
noksagt, 3172.
Norge, Kjæmpers Fødeland, 1000.
nybagt, 3462.
nød (i — skal kjendes næsten), 242.
(oplader pungen), 3524.

nøjd, 1023.
nøkke, 801.
nøre ild, 1315.
nøster, 1216, 4011.

o, aa, § 114.
o, oe, § 40, § 77.
odelsjente, 331.
odelsret, 3491.
Oehlenschläger, 952, 2461.
offerpynt, 3472.
Olympen, 2182.
onnen, § 114.
ordløse tanker, 463, 1424.
ormebøl, 3809.
ottesang, 4626.
overgang, (3301), 4190.
overmand, 2232, 2260.
overtvert, 1945.

Paa Vidderne, 584, 845, 925, 1424, 1611, 3014, 3415, 3499.
paaholden pen, 3336.
padde, 2364.
pakkamel, 2232, 3063.
Paludan Müller, Adam Homo, 914, 955, 2545, 3415, 3531, 3629, 4644, 4666.
Luftskipperen og Atheisten, 3629.
passager, cf. (den) Fremmede Passager.
Passarge, 1506, 1515, 1541, 1680, 3088, 4100, 4335, 4488.
Paulsen (Julian —; Sct. Hans Natten), (1070), 3179.
Peer, 1756.
pengene, § 102.
Petersen (Clemens —), 3019, 3336, 3499.
Pil(e)atus (Mons —), 669.
pilt, 1172.
piskende død, 535.
pladen (Lys i —), 3407.
plent, 635.
poltron-episoden, 1342, (3771).
portrætter (i Paris), 4540.
postillen, 1708.
prest, 1388.
prins, 313.
prinsessen og halve riget, cf. halve riget.

professortroldet, 1000, (Add.).
profet i sit eget land, 2493.
profit (mod —), 1807, 1966.
provstinden, 1739.
prøv om I tør, 716.
pugger, 2436.
pungen, § 102.
pusselanker, 4016.
pusten, 75.
pynt, 1935, (3472).
pytt, sa 'e Peer, 2827.
pøjt, 2797.
pølse i slagtetiden, 3484.

raadløs, 124.
raake, 1500.
rak, 4509.
rakt, 102.
Ramaskrig, 218.
ramle, rammel, 1367, § 24.
— rap, cf. Stjernerap.
rape, 972.
Rapfod, 1495.
ravn, 4560.
redelig(t), § 123.
registret, cf. synderegistret.
rem (af huden), 4323.
renbuk, 3835.
rensdyrshorn, 1420.
ren(t), § 66, § 130.
Richard III, 2444.
ridestellet, 996, 2455.
riget (halve —), cf. halve riget.
ringeagten, § 99.
rispe i øjet, cf. Øjet.
rivende gal, 535.
robust samvittighed, 4139.
Rodemester, § 15.
Ronden, 878, 3350.
Rondeporten, 994, 996.
Rondesumpen, 4056.
Rondes(v)alen, 4056.
rude, 1128.
rukken, 374.
rumle, 1367, § 24.
rumpe, 4056, 4504.
rusk, 986.
rydd(el)ig, 3283, § 56.
ryg (fanden), 1521.
rygge, 881.
rype, 4560.
rægle, 169.
ræglesmed, 169.
ræv bag øre, 3971.

ræven (sa —), 4190.
røre, 1506.
røsen, 80.
røst, 1219.

saa (slaa), § 102.
saakaldt(e), § 25.
saare, 4225.
saarløs, § 57, § 130.
sagblad, 572.
sagen, sagn (syn for —), 1182.
sakne, 234.
salmebog, 586.
Salomo(n)s ordbog, 2371, § 102.
saltstrød, 227.
samum, 2483.
samvittighed, cf. robust — samvittighedsfred, 3475.
San Franzisco, 3884, § 120.
sandt for udyden, 1170.
Sankt Peder, 1733, 1757, 1773.
satan (Vig —), 3635, 4122.
Satan, cf. fanden.
scirocco, 2483.
seen ins blaue, 4496.
selv, 2093.
døde sig —), 4381.
(tabe sig —), 2081.
(være sig —), 1044, 1221, 3148, 4539, 4564, 4687.
selv er bedste drengen, 3166.
selvgjort, 1053, 3328.
selvmant, 318.
send, 460.
sending, 460.
sendingsfolk, 460.
sendingskorv, 460.
sendingskost, 460.
sendpige, 460.
seng(e)kanten, § 16.
separat beskyttet, 2247.
septuagint, 3088.
sergeanter, § 12.
sfinks, 3014.
shipwreck, 3350.
Shakespeare, 2238, 2444, 2945, 3995.
sic transit gloria mundi, 4360.
sig selv at døde, 4381.
signe rejsen, 437.
silence, cf. taushet.
Sir Gynt, 2108.

sjelden, 1817, (4415), § 34.
sjunger, 4615.
sjæl, 2567.
sjølvmint, 318.
skabe om, 692.
skabilken, 3016.
skallen (i —), 3028.
skar(d)et, § 122.
skaresneen, 73.
skarv, 254.
skidt, 2577.
skier, 1431, 1463.
skigard, 220.
skikkelse (ingen —), 1228, 1245.
skillemynt, 4244.
skilling, 3816.
skilnad, 1035.
skipperløgner, 57.
skjelden, cf. sjelden.
skjæms, 684.
skjæmt, 1583.
skjære, cf. skære.
skjøger, 2977.
skoen (hvor — trykker), 4524.
skolt, 89.
skorstenpiben, 1202.
skosaale, 2940.
skosen, 4509.
skraas, § 101, § 130.
skred, 102.
skrub, 4251.
skrubsulten, 4251.
skruer (paa —), 3629, n.
skræppe, 245.
skuden (sejle — paa grund) 2069.
skudsmaal, 387.
skumme fløden, 2915.
skyds (tak for —), 377,1795.
skytterløgne, 57.
skær, skærer, 892.
skære (med fingren over struben), 957.
skæreving, 4421.
slaa (saa), 963, § 102.
slire, 93.
slottet vestenfor maane og østenfor sol, 1686.
slug, 115.
slut, 2861.
smage paa mjøden, 4293.
smeden som de ikke torde slippe ind i helvede, 629, 4095, 4139.
smeden (Aslak), 3830.

smidje, 639.
snau(d), § 120.
sneen fra ifjor, 216.
snus (for en —), 3477.
sodd, 1005.
solen rinder, 4671.
Solvejg, 584, 2984, 4599, 4644, 4646, 4666, 4668, 4674, 4687.
Solvejg's song, 4674.
sorg (heftig —), 2833.
Soria Moria Slot, 1686.
spaanens dæmper, 3754.
spareskillingsgris, 4342.
spe, 259.
spike, 1315.
spilopper, 2807.
spjeld, 1130.
spor (ikke —), 805.
sporespænder, 2129.
sprede, 584, (1678).
sprutter, § 115.
spytte i hænderne, 715.
spytte i øjet, 1125.
spædebarn, 3702.
spændebogen, 1263, 3853.
spøgefuld i grunden, 2657.
staaltraad(s)særk, § 44.
stabburdør, 3821.
stabejs, 2721.
sta(d)s, § 122.
stakkar(s), 201, 336, 4077.
Stavanger (missionærer fra —), 4575.
stavre, 328.
steg, 3582, 4530.
stelle, 1315.
stemme, 1219.
stenene, 409.
stev, 1675, 4045.
steward, § 108.
stikke op, 710.
stikke paa, 580.
stilke, 978.
stille, 689.
stind, 3021.
stjernerap, 4587.
storbog, 2370.
storladen, 4136.
straa (højt paa —), 434.
straa (kronen af —), 3857.
strake, (1473), § 44, § 62, § 130.
straks, § 101, § 130.
strakte, cf. strake.
struben (skære over —), cf. skære.

stry, 978.
stud (bløder som en —), 1348.
(grov som en —), 1517.
(olme —), 1130.
stulle, 1315.
stutt, 1669.
stutthoser, 1102.
styg, 701, 1583.
styggen, 90, 1696.
style (Ibsen's —), 911.
stærk(t)bygget, § 99.
støbeske, 3813, 4095.
støder, 2721.
stødt, 643.
subjekter, 4357.
sugg, 218.
suicide, 692.
sulten som en skrub, cf. skrub.
supinum, 1603.
susning i luften, 4037.
svanse, 1082.
svare, 4225, § 11.
svart, 872.
svarte, 3402.
svartekjolen, 1215.
Sveacisms, 733, 1807, cf. svensk.
svensk, 1807, 1934, 2129, 4607.
svinder ind til intet, 1269.
svoger, 3819.
sværm, 3629.
symbolism, (1070), 1498, 1515, 1523, (3857).
syn for sag(e)n, 1182.
synderegistret, 4620.
synsk, 1125.
sæl (lige —), 523.
sælet, 855, § 111.
sæter, 855.
sæterjenter, 851.
sø, 1005.
sølvspændt bog, 1263, 3320.
sølvtop, 484.
sømmene (gaa efter i —), 3531.

t, adv. § 123.
taagede graa, 4662.
taagede lande, 4662.
taarer (brister i —), 761, § 63.
taboo, 2310, 4314, 4526.
tak for skyds, 377.

tak som byder, 548.
taushet, 4231.
Tieck's Verkehrte Welt, 3637.
tilgagns, § 121.
tippe, 2817.
tiurleik, 227.
tolder (for — sømmeligt), 3629, 3632.
Tombuktu, 2421.
tomsing, 711.
tomtegubbe, 1203.
traakig, 3641.
traakken, 538.
tre(d)s, cf. tres.
trehoderstrold, 867.
tres, 3089.
troen gaar frit, 1186.
trold, 955, 1000, 1035, 1070, 1092, 1110, 2859, § 53, § 99, § 125.
troldeligt, 1151.
troldelig-nationale, 4320.
troldsmurt, 1235.
trommestikker, 2545.
Trond, 851, 4267, § 79.
Trumpeterstraale, 1807.
Trumshest, 1420.
Trumskar, 1420.
trykfejl, 3321.
træde tilbage, (1029), 1579, 2027, 4192.
træer, § 113.
trægt, § 56.
tudse, cf. padde.
tunge (fra det —), 1618.
tungt, 1273, § 56.
tungvindt, 1305.
tusen, 1934.
tusse (bit), 418, (855).
tydelig(t), § 123, § 137.
ty(d)sk, § 16, § 120.
ty(d)skeren, § 16, § 42, § 47, (cf. German).
tyndt (bede —), 659, 3866.
tyri, 1315.
Tyrken, 2846.
tænk det, 2900 n.
tørst, 581.

u —, 1100.
ubæst, 363, 1100.
udenom, 1220.
udhængs(s)kilt, § 16.
ufortolket, 3169.
ulvelegen, 1200.
unreliableness, (Peer's —),

cf. 99 and halfdannelsen.
urder, 102.
urskogssproget, 3190.
uryggeligt, 3764.
ustyggelig, 1100.
ustyrtelig, 3428, § 62, § 130.
usynlighedshatten, 669, 3839.
usynlighedskuften, 669, 3839.
yr, 762, 1638.
utryg samvittighed, 4139.
uvillig, 728.

vaaset, 4488.
Valfjeld, 4265.
var (er), 701, 1351, § 49.
var (om saa —), 2351.
varsel (foruden —), 4103.
varulf, 692.
vassen, 850.
vedtægt (gammel —), 4103.
veg, vek(t), 3653, § 121.
weibliche (das ewig —), 2583.
— veig, 584.
vejskillet (paa —), 4231.
velgjort, 3329.
Welhaven, 1053, 2362.
venlig(t), § 55, § 123.
venstre ben, cf. ben.
verdensborgerdomforpagtning, 1821.
Wergeland, 218, 245, 1053, 2362, 2567, 3343, 3345.
very, wery, § 34.
vesle, 697.
vestenfor maanen, cf. slottet.
Vidderne (paa —), cf. Paa Vidderne.
vig fra mig, cf. satan.
viljer, 4035.
vindlagt, 3857.
vingeslag, 1258.
Vinje, 1053, 2027, 2199, 2924, 3179, 4539.
vinløv, 2813.
vissne blade, 3995.
witchcraft, 1005.
vogsomt, 3470, § 114.
vold og lempe, 854, 856.
Vorherre og Co., 2232, 2247.
vrangen, 4539.
værget, 1235.

værst (—er egne frænder), 4338.

zie(h)t, § 38.

æg, cf. vindlagt.
ætle, 4162.

Yankee, § 14, 15.

yng(e)len, § 70.
ynkelig(t), § 123.
yr, 762, 1638.

æ, e, § 111.
æ, æe, § 113.
Ægypten, 2957.

ødsel, 4603.

øget, 710.
øjet (rispe i —), (978), (987), 1125, (4283).
øjet (forarger dig —), 1141.
øret (hælde med —), cf. stille.
ørken, 2842.
østenfor sol, cf. slottet.